The Political Guide to
Modern Scotland

To the Hassans of Dundee:
Rose, Rita, Nessie, Brian, David and Doreen . . .

. . . and the Hassans of Denver:
Art, Kathy and Vera . . .

. . . and the Frasers of Gifford . . .

. . . and the politicians of Scotland.

The Political Guide to
Modern Scotland

People, Places and Power

Gerry Hassan
and Douglas Fraser

POLITICO'S

First published in Great Britain 2004 by
Politico's Publishing, an imprint of
Methuen Publishing Limited
215 Vauxhall Bridge Road
London SW1V 1EJ

10 9 8 7 6 5 4 3 2 1

Copyright © 2004 Gerry Hassan and Douglas Fraser

The authors have asserted their moral rights

A CIP catalogue record for this book is available from the British Library.

ISBN 1 84275 048 8

Printed and bound in Great Britain by Bell and Bain, Glasgow

Contents

Index of Constituencies, MSPs, MP and MEPs

Johann Lamont	240	Eleanor Scott	405	Eric Joyce	191
Carolyn Leckie	389	John Scott	67	Charles Kennedy	348
Marilyn Livingstone	287	Tavish Scott	327	Archie Kirkwood	353
Richard Lochhead	423	Tommy Sheridan	396	Mark Lazarowicz	169
George Lyon	63	Elaine Smith	96	Helen Liddell	54
Kenny MacAskill	410	Iain Smith	199	Iain Luke	124
Frank McAveety	250	Margaret Smith	181	John Lyons	363
Tom McCabe	273	Nicol Stephen	43	Tom McAvoy	245
Jack McConnell	313	Stewart Stevenson	72	Calum Macdonald	385
Lewis Macdonald	35	Jamie Stone	78	John MacDougall	195
Margo MacDonald	411	Nicola Sturgeon	398	David Marshall	251
Bruce McFee	433	John Swinburne	391	Michael Martin	255
Jamie McGrigor	401	John Swinney	367	John McFall	114
Kenneth Macintosh	152	Murray Tosh	434	Anne McGuire	358
Kate Maclean	128	Jean Turner	362	Ann McKechin	237
David McLetchie	172	Jim Wallace	326	Rosemary McKenna	101
Michael McMahon	267	Mike Watson	220	Dr Lewis Moonie	288
Maureen Macmillan	402	Andrew Welsh	58	Michael Moore	375
Duncan McNeil	262	Sandra White	399	Jim Murphy	152
Pauline McNeill	231	Karen Whitefield	53	Martin O'Neill	321
Des McNulty	87	Allan Wilson	104	Sandra Osborne	68
Campbell Martin	433			Anne Picking	147
Paul Martin	254	**MPs**		Alan Reid	63
Tricia Marwick	416	Irene Adams	333	John Reid	267
Jim Mather	403	Douglas Alexander	337	Angus Robertson	308
Michael Matheson	389	John Barrett	182	John Robertson	210
Stewart Maxwell	434	Anne Begg	44	Ernie Ross	128
Christine May	194	Gordon Brown	133	Frank Roy	316
Nanette Milne	423	Russell Brown	119	Alex Salmond	73
Margaret Mitchell	390	Desmond Browne	284	Mohammad Sarwar	226
Brian Monteith	417	Malcolm Bruce	259	Malcolm Savidge	39
Alasdair Morgan	428	David Cairns	263	Jim Sheridan	380
Alasdair Morrison	384	Menzies Campbell	199	Robert Smith	48
Bristow Muldoon	296	Alistair Carmichael	328	Rachel Squire	138
Mary Mulligan	292	Lynda Clark	173	Gavin Strang	163
David Mundell	429	Tom Clarke	96	David Stewart	280
John Farquhar Munro	347	Michael Connarty	186	Bill Tynan	273
Elaine Murray	119	Robin Cook	296	Michael Weir	59
Alex Neil	390	Tam Dalyell	292	Brian Wilson	105
Irene Oldfather	109	Alistair Darling	258	Pete Wishart	370
Peter Peacock	403	Ian Davidson	241	Anthony Worthington	88
Cathy Peattie	185	Brian Donohoe	109	James Wray	215
Mike Pringle	177	Frank Doran	36		
Jeremy Purvis	374	Peter Duncan	204	**MEPs**	
Nora Radcliffe	258	Annabelle Ewing	343	Elspeth Attwooll	436
Keith Raffan	418	George Foulkes	84	Ian Hudghton	436
George Reid	320	George Galloway	232	Neil MacCormick	437
Shona Robison	123	Nigel Griffiths	178	David Martin	438
Euan Robson	352	David Hamilton	303	Bill Miller	438
Mike Rumbles	48	Tom Harris	221	John Purvis	439
Mark Ruskell	419	James Hood	92	Struan Stevenson	439
Mary Scanlon	404	Adam Ingram	142	Catherine Stihler	440

Acknowledgements

The production of a book such as this entails the help, advice and assistance of numerous people. We are enormously grateful and thankful for the time and expertise that has been given to us by everyone we have encountered from officials to politicians and experts in various fields. Firstly, our deepest gratitude to David Walsh and Bruce Whyte for Health Scotland, formerly the Public Health Institute of Scotland, compiling constituency data. Their understanding of the nature of health inequalities and statistics at a constituency level is truly staggering and anyone looking for more detail than we have listed in socio-economic areas should look at: www.phis.org.uk

Secondly, many thanks to Myles Fitt and Susan McPhee of Citizens Advice Scotland for access to CAB data. Dougie Wands of the Electoral Commission supplied the figures for the 2003 Scottish Parliament and 2001 Westminster elections, and listened patiently to our endless queries and rechecking of figures. David Denver at the Department of Politics at the University of Lancaster has positioned himself as the Rawlings and Thrasher of Scottish politics, and assisted in allowing us to make sense of the draft Westminster boundaries. So has Martin Baxter, as explained in Section 8.

Chris Eynon, of the opinion pollster System Three has provided an unparalleled public service compiling thirty years of consistent and comprehensive opinion polling of the Scottish public's voting intentions, and he has provided us with access to all of it. Stephen Low of BBC Scotland proved that he had as formidable or possibly anorakish a memory as the authors for the trivia of Scottish politics, while Paul Hutcheon, editor of *Holyrood*, assisted us with enthusiasm and support. Peter Lynch, Department of Politics at the University of Stirling, contributed to this book by his work on the previous publication, *The Almanac of Scottish Politics*. Elinor Kelly, research fellow, University of Glasgow, contributed her research expertise on socio-economic indicators. Thanks also to colleagues at the *Sunday Herald*.

Many thanks also go to John Curtice, Professor of Politics at Strathclyde University, and Peter Jones, Scotland and North of England correspondent of *The Economist* for contributing to this book, and for assisting in other ways. We would also like to offer our deepest gratitude to John Schwartz and the team at Politico's Publishing with whom it has been a joy and a privilege to work. Politico's Publishing has, in the last few years, produced an impressive range of books, and we are proud to be associated with them. Finally, and not least, our thanks and indebtedness are due to our long-suffering partners, Rosie Ilett and Isabel Fraser, who put up with us working on this book through late nights, weekends and over holidays.

This project is by its nature a work in progress, capturing a moment in Scottish politics at the level of local government, the Scottish Parliament, Westminster and the European Union, and we hope by doing so giving a deeper sense of the nation, its culture, history, values and opinions. It is also shaped by the ebbs and flows of public debate, discourse and discussion, and to that end, we would be delighted to hear from readers about what they like in the book, any key facts or figures we have omitted or which need to be corrected, and any suggestions for future editions.

Gerry Hassan
and Douglas Fraser

The Emerging Political Landscape of Scotland

The Scottish political landscape, created by the establishment of the Scottish Parliament in May 1999, is now five years old. Its contours, shape and future possibilities are beginning to become clearer, but much still remains ambiguous or open to new interpretation. The Scottish political system emerging north of the border at the Scottish Parliament is increasingly divergent from the one Scots have grown familiar with at Westminster, at least in terms of party representation, if not policy and values.

And yet, fundamental questions remain about a number of key areas. What is the ambition and aspiration in the body politic of the Scottish Parliament and Scottish Executive? Will the politics of the centre – of the British state – remain, as they seem today, untouched and unmoved by this unprecedented period of constitutional upheaval? Can the centre retain the mindset of a unitary state in the politics of a union state? The Blair Government's sudden announcement in 2003 of an UK Supreme Court without any UK consultation or consideration of possible Scottish implications was not an atypical one. Scotland may have gained a Parliament and a new voice, but it has fallen off the Westminster and Whitehall radar. And in the evolving politics of post-devolution Scotland, where Barnett, the Scottish Parliament electoral system, EU negotiations on fisheries policy and many other areas, are decided at Westminster, this matters.

This book attempts to offer a comprehensive guide to the emerging democratic dispensation north of the border. It offers detailed, in-depth portraits of the national politicians who represent Scotland in the Scottish Parliament, Westminster and the European Parliament. And it provides factual and impressionistic sketches of the constituencies – historically, socio-economically and culturally. In this we attempt to show the ebbs and flows, forward marches and retreats of parties across the 20th century from the decline of the Liberals to the emergence of the more pluralist and unpredictable multi-party politics of the Scottish Parliament. It shows the socio-economic characteristics of seats using a wide range of data from the 2001 census, as well as changing employment, jobs created and jobs lost, and public sector developments and changes such as hospital and school investment often by the controversial use of private finance. And finally, it offers a cultural perspective - charting the contribution of constituencies through a variety of areas of Scottish life such as film, fiction, football, and even music. We feel that this comprehensive picture allows readers to read a political history of Scotland within a wider setting, a cultural account with a political backdrop, or both.

This introduction aims to bring together some of the wider patterns and trends found in the book and identify some of the long-term developments which have shaped Scottish politics. Firstly, it looks at the changing patterns of party competition from the dominance and then decline of the Liberal Party, to the rise of Labour from the 1920s onwards, emergence of the Nationalists and decline of the Conservatives. We also acknowledge the existence of different political cultures rather than one homogeneous political culture in this small country. In particular, we examine the contours of the Labour-SNP battleground over the last thirty years, and the repeated failure of the Nationalists to challenge Labour successfully.

Secondly, we focus on the changing role of the political classes and politicians. The sort of person who becomes a politician has undergone a social revolution in the last century, as has the expectations and demands they face from constituents, party members, the media and organised lobbyists. Gone are the patrician politics of old, but so are the class based, hierarchies of the industrial age. Thirdly, we examine the socio-economic inequalities of Scotland over the last twenty years, and in particular, look at the quiet revolution which has occurred in housing with the rise of owner occupation and slow residualisation of council housing. We analyse the degree to which this unprecedented transformation has not yet led to political change and why this is. Finally, we explore public attitudes to the politics of post-devolution Scotland, and ask what kinds of future change may emerge – what faultlines, values and types of consensus.

A Work in Progress: The Parliament Building As Metaphor

An appropriate and revealing metaphor for the work in progress that is the new Scottish democracy is the debate around the Holyrood Building Project. One of the defining stories of the first five years has been the widespread corrosive sense of cynicism, aided by certain sections of the media. They have used the spiraling costs of Enric Miralles' Holyrood Parliament, from its original estimate of £40 million to over £430 million, to lambast the competencies and skills of the new parliamentarians. And the simplicity of this tale with its own litany of heroes (Margo MacDonald, Donald Gorrie) and villains (the Holyrood Progress Group, the Scottish Parliament Corporate Body, Romanian-speaking construction workers) has made it perfectly suited for tabloid serialisation.

Despite this, other explanations clearly abound about this episode. Another account puts the blame for the whole sorry tale on the pre-devolution Scottish Office and Whitehall's colonial manner of governing Scotland without debate and discussion. This puts the decision to adopt the Holyrood site and Miralles' design as part of New Labour's modernising mantra when it was elected in 1997. Holyrood was the Cool Caledonia version of the Cool Britannia excitement which briefly defined Blair's honeymoon in 1997-99 when anything seemed possible; instead and ironically, the Scots have ended up with their very own version of the Dome (Black, 2001).

A differing explanation, and one given added impetus by the Fraser Inquiry into the escalating costs of the building, is to see the whole process as tarnished and tainted by the closeted, secretive networks of cosy arrangements which have administered Scotland for decades. In this account, first, Scottish Office, then, Scottish Executive civil servants, did not see potential clashes of interest in the way they did business, for example, in the multiple roles of Kirsty Wark, broadcaster, or in the way parts of the project were handled.

All of these accounts have gained credence and profile in the last few years, damaging belief in the possibilities of Scottish democracy. The only account that has little chance of winning many adherents is one that acknowledges subtlety and shades of grey rather than black and white, and which accepts much of what happened was to quote Henry McLeish in a different context, 'a muddle, not a fiddle'. Scottish political debate, and the media's reporting of it, tends to more simplistic, snappier judgements. The Holyrood Building Project saga has provided to some journalists and public prejudice just too tempting a story and too easy a target. It offers the prospect of scapegoats and villains, and a public that is being fleeced out of value for money to the tune of millions.

The long view of this matters. It will take years for many Scots to see Miralles' creation as more than a vastly over budget construction and management fiasco. But how long will it take before we can see the Parliament building in a wider historical context in the way Sidney Opera House is divorced from the financial problems which plagued its construction? In this the story of the Parliament building may come to be seen as a defining metaphor for post-devolution Scotland, and the triumph of the soundbite and superficial account shaped by short timeframes, over a longer-term horizon which nurtures vision and imagination. This contest and dilemma goes to the heart of what kind of democracy and nation we want to live in. The test of Scottish democracy, as with the test of the Holyrood Parliament is whether the possibilities of the latter may be defeated by the former.

The Rise and Fall of Political Parties

In any political system, party fortunes wax and wane, small parties grow big and once mighty ones fall away to nothing. In the last two decades, ruling centre-right parties in Italy and Spain have disappeared off the electoral map and in Canada suffered electoral annihilation. Scotland has seen less dramatic change. Emerging from a political system which owed much to religious cleavages and strife, the 19th century was a battle between Conservative and Liberal, but was unable to shake off the influence of religious politics from Ireland. From those days, there remains, in name at least, the Scottish Conservative and Unionist Party, and while some in it would like to pretend the unionism is about the link across the Cheviots, the name came from its dedication to the cause of Irish unionism. The rise of Labour in the 1920s saw a brief period of three-party competition with the Liberals and Conservatives, before Labour's formation of a government in 1924, led to the decline of the Liberals, and the establishment of the main political divide between Labour and anti-Labour to the electoral benefit of the Conservatives for the rest of the 1920s and 1930s (Brown, 1981).

The period from 1945-1970 saw the battle between Conservative and Labour fought out as it was throughout England and Wales. Conservatives gained more than half the Scottish vote and seats in 1955 – the only post-war party to have done so. But with social change leading to a weakening of the link between voting and religious affiliation, the working class Orange vote which had been a bedrock support for the Conservative Party in Scotland died out or shifted allegiance. The Tories could have sought to shore up support through succeeding decades of electoral decline by appealing to that departing Protestant vote, risking the re-emergence of a sectarianism which had scarred urban politics in the inter-war years, but to their credit, they avoided doing so. Instead, they made two strategic errors. One was to lose touch with the working class roots which had served the party well for the century since the franchise had been extended – the Teddy Taylor populist vote which had departed by the time he lost Glasgow Cathcart in 1979. Unlike the appeal Margaret Thatcher successfully made for the skilled working class in England, Scottish Conservatives continued to lose ground. And second, they allowed their opponents to portray them as an anti-Scottish party from the mid-1960s onwards and particularly during the Thatcher-Major years, at a time when Scottish politics was being shaped by the rise of nationalism and national identity.

The Scottish National Party began to make small, but significant ripples in the early 1960s – polling respectably in the Glasgow Bridgeton and West Lothian by-elections in 1961 and 1962 – the latter against Tam Dalyell (Brand, 1978; Lynch, 2002). In 1967 in Hamilton, the Nationalists achieved the breakthrough that had long eluded them, when Winnie Ewing famously won one of the safest Labour seats in the UK and effectively began the modern era of Scottish politics. Subsequently, the SNP went through numerous peaks and troughs of success, and was at its most effective following its 1974 electoral success in pushing a resistant, unconvinced Scottish Labour establishment into what was at first, an unconvincing embrace of devolution. But it struggled after that to build out of the previously Conservative, rural seats it picked off. In urban Scotland, and particularly the West of Scotland, it found the Labour Party being most successful in picking up on Conservative decline, and while post-1974 Scottish politics have been dominated by a Labour-SNP tussle for the spoils of Tory decline, Nationalists have still not found a means to challenge Labour effectively in those heartlands. Labour was holding on to the working class heartlands it had built up from the start of the century while drawing in new supporters. It portrayed itself successfully as the main party of Scotland and therefore with Scotland's interests at heart – most notably through taking a difficult road to the embrace of devolution. It also ran far ahead of Tony Blair and New Labour in winning over the middle class – personified by Blair's predecessor as Labour leader, John Smith – at first public sector professionals but later surprising even itself with its success in wooing suburbia. As one London Labour activist was heard saying after the election loss in 1992: 'We need to do what Labour has done in Scotland, appealing to people in

Morningside with two cars in the driveway.' By the 1997 landslide, when Conservatives disappeared off the parliamentary map of Scotland, Labour had built up a formidable coalition of Scottish voices and interests. The question became – and remains – how to hang on to that broad coalition, and which bits would fragment most quickly and most damagingly for the party's electoral prospects.

One Scottish Political Culture Or Several?

Such a potted history of the party battles in Scotland should not ignore regional divisions. Religion and Ireland was supplanted through the 20th century by class and national identity as the dominant factors in political battle, but the map of Scotland reflected geographical differences which are perhaps unusually wide for such a small population. The Liberal hegemony of the 19th century was built on rolling together the interests of industrialists, farmers and, with the widening of the franchise, the working class. The Liberals dominance of Scottish politics before the advent of universal suffrage was almost total, with the party winning a majority of the popular vote in every one of the twenty general elections held between 1832 and the start of the First World War.

The radical heritage of Gladstonian Liberalism was incorporated into the ethos of Scottish Labour – emphasising land reform, temperance, home rule, and anger at injustice. Scottish Labour established itself as a national electoral force in 1922, and did so most effectively in Glasgow and the West of Scotland, while Edinburgh did not turn Labour at council level until 1984 or at parliamentary level until 1987, and significantly shifted away from the party in the 2003 Scottish Parliament elections. Part of Labour's electoral success was in identifying closely with the West of Scotland where a large population has delivered large numbers of MPs and councillors and where, unlike the other mainstream parties, its headquarters remain. At least until 1997, other parties exaggerated their importance on the political map of Scotland by representing large tracts of thinly-inhabited rural Scotland.

Led by Jo Grimond, who was first elected as the Orkney and Shetland MP in 1950, the Liberals made a gradual comeback into rural Scotland by giving a party label to a long-standing tradition of independently-minded Highland radicalism which tended to stop well short of socialism, and they were careful not to offend socially conservative sensibilities. It continues to be the case that Liberal Democrats stand under independent labels, and independents stand under the Lib Dem banner. This results, for instance, in John Farquhar Munro, MSP for Ross, Skye and Inverness West, taking liberties with party group discipline which leave Labour coalition partners either mystified or infuriated, with the collision of urban and rural, Labour and Liberal traditions. There are distinct political traditions also in the North East, where the SNP has been successful in putting down deep roots in fishing and farming communities which were once strongly Conservative, yet where Lib Dems have been equally successful at building constituency bases in next door seats. The South of Scotland had perhaps the least developed rural, regional identity before the first Scottish Parliament election in 1999, but within four years, it had emerged as the hardest-fought region of Scotland. It is in rural Scotland that genuinely pluralist, multi-party politics is at its most vibrant, with independents playing a significant role at council level.

It could be that the electoral system – with 56 MSPs elected to represent regions rather than facing constituency constraints – could contribute to growing regionalism in the Scottish Parliament. In the first Parliament, there was a much louder voice for, say, Glasgow, than before, while the North-West continued to have the special status which had won the area its own institutions such as Highlands and Islands Enterprise and, in previous years, the Hydro Board and its own Development Board. It was less evident that Central Scotland or Mid-Scotland and Fife took on a strong new political identity, but that is one of the areas to watch as devolution develops. And what has happened in addition to clearly emergent regional voices has been a sharper individual competition between MSPs at constituency level (mostly Labour) and at regional level (mostly SNP and Conservative), as incumbents have been frustrated to find their defeated rivals elected by new means and given the platform to take on their own constituency profile.

The shape of regional Scotland at the Scottish Parliament elections in 2003 displayed a much greater sense of pluralism and diversity than the overall figures suggest. Of Scotland's four main cities (see Table One), Glasgow is the only one where Labour's hegemony is unchallenged. Aberdeen is shaped by a three party politics with the Lib Dems in first place and Labour in second, Dundee has Labour closely challenged by the SNP, and Edinburgh has evolved into a genuinely competitive multi-party politics where all four main parties have significant support. If we look at the pattern across the rest of regional Scotland, Labour are dominant in six areas, while the SNP is the leading party in Perth and Angus, and the remaining five have differing patterns of party competition (see Table Two).

Table One: Party Share of Votes in Major Cities Constituency Vote 2003

	Lab	SNP	Con	Lib Dem	SSP
Aberdeen	27.0	24.0	13.3	32.0	3.6
Dundee	36.2	34.3	8.8	6.7	2.9
Edinburgh	31.5	17.0	21.6	23.5	6.2
Glasgow	45.9	19.9	8.5	8.1	15.2

Source: Denver (2003)

Table Two: Party Share of Votes in Regions by Constituency Vote 2003

	Lab	SNP	Con	Lib Dem	SSP
Highlands and Islands	23.3	23.6	15.3	30.9	5.5
North East Scotland	12.1	31.9	24.3	27.3	3.0
Perth and Angus	14.8	41.1	28.5	11.1	3.4
Fife	34.7	20.4	13.5	18.1	5.4
Central Scotland	35.8	25.9	13.2	7.3	3.5
Lothians	44.0	26.6	12.3	11.5	5.3
Lanarkshire	48.5	23.1	10.5	7.5	7.7
Renfrewshire	39.2	21.4	16.2	14.4	6.5
Dunbartonshire	37.0	18.1	12.1	13.9	4.8
Ayrshire	42.0	23.1	22.2	5.7	6.3
Borders	17.4	19.3	25.4	33.5	3.8
Dumfries and Galloway	27.7	24.6	37.4	6.9	3.1

Source: Denver (2003). For Tables One and Two cities and regions do not correspond to areas used for regional votes.

This tells us differing things about the parties. Labour's strength is significantly over-exaggerated by the electoral system. There is the exceptionalism of Glasgow, which along with Lanarkshire is the only place where Labour wins anything near to 50 per cent. The party won just over a quarter of the votes in Aberdeen, under a third in Edinburgh, and just over a third in Dundee. The SNP's support is relatively evenly distributed across the country and this means the party has a problem converting support into constituency seats. In 2003 it again won more votes than the Lib Dems, but won fewer first-past-the post seats.

The Lib Dems on the other hand, are a weak political force across large swathes of the Central Belt, polling derisory levels of support in Glasgow and Dundee. However, Lib Dem support is concentrated in Aberdeen, Highlands and Islands and the Borders, where the party is first in votes, and Edinburgh and North East Scotland, where it is in second place. All but one of the Lib Dems 13 constituency seats are in these five areas (the exception being North East Fife). The Conservatives are equally weak in Glasgow, Dundee and across the Central Belt, retaining a degree of strength in Edinburgh. The only region they are in first place is Dumfries and Galloway. And finally, the Scottish Socialists are still, on constituency figures, a regional based party, winning twice the portion of votes in Glasgow compared to their next best area (Lanarkshire). This points to the lack of a single party system and homogeneity across all of Scotland. The degree of pluralism and competition if it continues could lead to future problems for the party with the most to lose: Scottish Labour.

Shifting Political Terrains and Battlegrounds

The most significant political rivalry in recent decades has been between Labour and the SNP. With the foregoing historical background, it is worth looking at how that battle has been waged over time and across Scotland. In October 1974, the SNP's high point, the party won 11 seats at Westminster. Most were formerly Conservative, but what really worried Labour was that the SNP was in second place in 35 out of Labour's 41 seats. Labour was increasingly dominant at Westminster, but vulnerable. A further 5 per cent swing would have doubled the number of Nationalists seats to 22 (Steed, 1975, p. 356).

By the 1999 Scottish Parliament election, the SNP polled within 1 per cent of its peak 25 years before, but the electoral geography of the party's support had changed. The SNP's vote was more evenly dispersed across the country. It still had many second places to Labour, but fewer were marginal with only nine Labour-SNP seats where Labour's majority was under 10 per cent (see Table Three). The SNP had shifted to a strategy of targeting what marginals it could, but that only increased the party's frustration when it failed to make much headway in the seats in which it invested resources and hopes. The SNP's vote in 1999 showed signs of third party 'plateau effect', something well known to the Liberals across the UK, where the party does less well in areas of strength, and thus, can fail to win target seats. The party's vote rose by 6.6 per cent across Scotland on the first vote, but fell on average in the six seats it was defending, while it achieved huge swings in safe Labour seats such as Glasgow Baillieston and Shettleston it had no chance of winning.

The 2003 election saw the SNP take seats from Labour in Aberdeen North, Dundee East and Ochil – successes which were more than cancelled out by the loss of regional list seats. But significant to its prospects and momentum was the fact that there was then a lack of obviously winnable new marginals. The shift of votes from SNP across to the Scottish Socialist Party, particularly in urban areas such as Glasgow, effectively split the anti-Labour vote, and made the ruling party appear even more dominant in its heartlands. The SNP has historically a lamentable record challenging Labour in its West of Scotland heartlands outside of by-elections, and the emergence of the Scottish Socialists competing for the same working class, left-wing vote, has merely emphasised the long-term SNP weakness in this part of the country.

Table Three: Top Ten Labour-SNP Marginals 1974-1999

October 1974	SNP Vote	Margin	Winning Party	
1. Kinross and West Perthshire	41.5	0.2	Con	
2. Stirlingshire West	38.2	0.9	Lab	*cont'd*

3. Lanark	35.8	1.8	Lab
4. Inverness	29.6	2.8	Lib
5. Ross and Cromarty	35.7	3.2	Lab
6. Stirling and Falkirk Burghs	39.8	3.5	Lab
7. West Lothian	40.9	4.4	Lab
8. Dunbartonshire West	33.7	4.5	Lab
9. East Kilbride	36.7	5.2	Lab
10. Dundee West	35.1	5.9	Lab
1999			
1. Dundee West	37.2	0.4	Lab
2. Aberdeen North	35.7	1.4	Lab
3. Ochil	38.2	6.4	Lab
4. Argyll and Bute	28.5	6.4	Lib Dem
5. Glasgow Govan	36.7	6.7	Lab
6. Kilmarnock and Loudoun	37.1	7.0	Lab
7. West Renfrewshire	28.8	8.5	Lab
8. Linlithgow	36.5	8.7	Lab
9. Dundee East	34.3	9.0	Lab
10. Ross, Skye and Inverness West	28.6*	10.3	Lib Dem

* SNP Third

The Rise of the Career Politician

A central theme of this book is the individuals who make up the Scottish political classes – who they are, where they have come from, their skills, backgrounds and opinions – as well as the places and communities they represent. The role of being an MP, the demands and expectations faced, have changed dramatically in the 20th century with universal suffrage, the rise of political parties with mass memberships and the role of the media in creating a less deferential, more sceptical environment.

This book provides a backdrop which charts the changing contours of politics, politicians and representative democracy over the course of the 20th century. Would be MPs are routinely asked in selection meetings 'Will you live in the constituency?', whereas Scots Tory MP William Anstruther-Gray answered it by declaring, 'I will hunt over it' (Paxman, 2002, p. 72). If we take the examples of Winston Churchill and John Strachey – two UK national figures who both represented Dundee, described by Harry Pollitt as 'that most proletarian of cities' – we see a politics very different from today. Churchill was Liberal MP for the city from 1908-22 and Strachey Labour MP from 1945-63. As English born MPs in what Roy Jenkins observed is 'not a heartstring-clutching place for Sassenachs', both had busy and exciting Westminster lives and Dundee did not rank high on their priorities. Churchill as MP for the city for fourteen years seldom visited outside of elections, and according to Jenkins, 'did not much return except for a few days each autumn' (Jenkins 2001, p. 132). Strachey who sat for Dundee while he underwent his conversion from Marxist theorist to Gaitskillite revisionist commented that his most enjoyable time representing the city was 'when he settled into his seat over the Tay estuary – going south.' (Jenkins 2001, p. 132)

This strange world did allow independent minded characters and mavericks to be thrown up and sometimes survive and prosper. The 1920s and 1930s saw an influx of Labour men and the occasional woman, and while the 'Red Clydesiders' have been endlessly written about to the point of hagiography, the story of such Scottish Labour women as Jennie Lee, Jean Mann and Margaret 'Peggy' Herbison are less seldom commented on. These women usually came to prominence in the more left-wing ILP than mainstream Labour. Jennie Lee became the first Scottish Labour woman MP elected for North Lanarkshire in 1929 despite Catholic Church opposition because of her support for birth control. Although she lost the seat in 1931, she went on to marry Nye Bevan and become Minister of Arts in the 1964-70 Labour Government. Mann earned the nickname 'haud the wean' and the chauvinism of Labour male colleagues for daring to be a young mother with five children, a Glasgow councillor, and then MP for Coatbridge from 1945-59.

The Conservative tradition allowed men of independent means and minds to be elected. MPs such as Bob Boothby, MP for Aberdeenshire East from 1924-58, took courageous positions which defied party orthodoxy on Chamberlain's appeasement policy in the 1930s, Eden's Suez adventure in 1956, and supported homosexual law reform, which until very recently Labour and the SNP have been silent on. Perhaps one of the greatest Tory idiosyncratic personalities of the inter-war era was the Duchess of Atholl, commonly known as the 'Red Duchess', who served as MP for Kinross and West Perthshire from 1923-38, and was the first ever woman MP elected in Scotland. She fearlessly flaunted traditional Tory orthodoxy, championing causes home and abroad, from supporting measures to improve the condition and health of poorer children, to being responsible for bringing out an English translation of the unexpurgated version of Hitler's *Mein Kampf*. From Hitler's ascent to power in 1933 she campaigned against the anti-Semitic nature of the Nazi regime, opposed the British Government's non-intervention in the Spanish Civil War, and campaigned against the Chamberlain's abandonment of Czechoslovakia at Munich in 1938. This famously caused her to be deselected by her Conservative association, and she stood in a December 1938 by-election as an independent and despite Labour and Liberal support, was defeated by the official Conservative candidate by 1,313 votes.

These and many other tales are told in this book. This is an era, where if one examines *The 1955 Tory Year Book* – the high point of Scottish Unionism preceding its steady decline – one finds a very different world from today. This is a world of Conservative candidates such as Major Duncan McCallum, Commander Thomas Dunlop Galbraith and Mr. Derek Matthew Hutchison Smith (father of Nigel Smith, chair of 'Scotland Forward', the 1997 pro-devolution campaign). They had distinguished military backgrounds in the Great War in such battles as Ypres, or in the Second at Salerno and Anzio, and served in the Argyll and Sutherland Highlanders, the Royal Armoured Corps, and on the battlecruiser *Hood* to take a few random, but representative examples from the *Yearbook* (Scottish Unionist Association, 1955). The Labour candidates they faced often came from an equally defined social world – trade unions, school teachers, journalism, and if they had a military background, they made less of it, and would usually have served below officer class.

By contrast, the latter 20th century saw the rise of the career politician – dating from the introduction of salaries in 1912 to break the gentleman's private club ethos of the House of Commons. The role of the MP has changed dramatically from when Roy Jenkins could write of arriving in the Commons, 'I found being an MP in the late 1940s an easy life' (Jenkins 1991, p. 73). Constituency duties were few and far between, but the post-war extension of the state has increased the workload of MPs, often transforming their role to that of a glorified social worker. In the 1940s and 1950s MPs got two to three letters a day, whereas by 1997 many got 200 (Paxman, 2002, p. 134). The twin-pronged ascendancy of party and the decline of Parliament as a check on the executive along with the professionalisation of politics into a full-time job, have reduced the potential for individually-minded MPs. And a social revolution has broken down the distinctions between the kind of person who becomes a Labour and Conservative member, while both are now shaped by a managerial ethos. SNP politicians are increasingly cut from the same cloth, while the only major party which allows patrician local heroes and individually-minded people to still become national politicians is the Lib Dems.

The slow atrophying of political parties and politics has been apparent for a long time. The writer and social entrepreneur (who would have frowned at the term) Michael Young, author of Labour's 1945 manifesto in his classic, *The Rise of the Meritocratic Society*, looking forward to Britain in 2034 from the vantage point of the 1950s, saw a Labour Party that no longer stood for progress, had given up on the workers, repositioned itself as the party of the middle, and had abandoned, not only the claim of Labour, but the name, rebranding itself as the Technician's Party (Young, 1958).

The end of the Cold War and Communism as a viable alternative political system at the end of the 1980s has contributed to this narrowing of political possibilities. The post-Cold War shift from 'the politics of ideas' to 'the politics of presence' has even made its mark on Scottish politics which used to be – apart from the odd formidable Labour woman and SNP by-election victor – a man's world. The first Scottish Parliament's achievement in terms of women's representation was a cultural genderquake, and did have major ramifications for how the Parliament acted (Fraser, 2004). However, for much of the time, Labour and SNP women acted in many ways similar to their male colleagues.

An Increasingly Unequal Scotland

Devolution has coincided with economic circumstances which have been relatively good for Scotland. Unemployment on the official count stood at 3.1 per cent in May 2003, living standards are rising, and there is a growing sense of prosperity in the majority of the population, seen in rising house prices, increasing disposable incomes and consumer spending which drives so much of today's service economy. In this Scotland is not that different from the rest of the UK, and is the backdrop to which New Labour won re-election in 2001.

But there is another, compelling story of contemporary Scotland's economic position. The nation's economic growth has significantly lagged UK growth for the last thirty years – with average Scottish growth over this period of 1.5 per cent versus an UK average of 2.1 per cent. Scottish public spending as a percentage of GDP has risen over the period since New Labour was elected to just under 50 per cent of GDP – a level that raises questions about the Treasury's Barnett funding formula and long-term sustainability. And worrying for the future, Scotland's population faces increasing ageing, stagnation and decline, as the fertility rate ranks along the lowest in Europe alongside Italy, Spain and Germany, and migration is not rising to fill the gap (Joshi and Wright, 2004).

These are serious problems, but other issues diminish and disfigure contemporary Scotland such as the embedded and widening nature of inequality and poverty where large parts of Scotland face exclusion from a mainstream society four times wealthier than 1950. Seven years of Labour government, with eight Gordon Brown redistribution-by-stealth budgets – along with numerous Scottish Executive initiatives – has seen a society which has grown more unequal between those who see themselves as winners and those who are left behind.

If we examine the communities most excluded and disconnected from the mainstream, a grim picture emerges. Despite this being a period when according to official counts of unemployment we are near the post-war definition of full employment (3 per cent or under), large parts of Scottish society are increasingly disconnected from the formal labour market. It is also widely recognised that the official and even International Labour Organisation levels of unemployment do not show the real levels of economic inactivity (Beatty et al, 2002). Glasgow Shettleston with a claimant count of 5.3 per cent has a 'real' unemployment level of 33 per cent of the working age population, combining unemployment benefit with incapacity benefit and severe disability allowance, while neighbouring Glasgow Springburn with an official level of 5.0 per cent has a 'real' unemployment rate of 26 per cent. These two disadvantaged communities are two of the hardest pressed areas in Scotland and the UK, and were rated several years ago in an academic survey the most unhealthy places in the UK (Shaw et al, 1999). The constituency they rated the most healthy in Scotland – Aberdeenshire West and Kincardine, which only came in at the 123rd most healthy in the UK, had the lowest 'real' unemployment in Scotland, with an official count of 1 per cent and 'real' of 4.9 per cent, one seventh of the level of Shettleston. Not surprisingly there is a direct relationship between economic exclusion and political engagement. Those constituencies with the highest exclusion from the labour market experience the lowest turnouts in the Scottish Parliament elections (see Table Four). This also confirms research undertaken by the Scottish Social Attitudes Survey published in 2002, which showed that the socio-economic groups most dissatisfied with devolution were those which felt excluded and disconnected, while those who felt most satisfaction and inclusion comprised professional Scotland (Paterson, 2002).

Table Four: Real Level of Unemployment 2003

Top Ten	JSA/IB/SDA	JSA	2003 Turnout
1. Glasgow Shettleston	33.1	5.3	35.8
2. Glasgow Springburn	26.3	5.0	38.0
3. Glasgow Maryhill	26.0	5.9	37.5
4. Glasgow Baillieston	25.1	4.5	39.8
5. Glasgow Pollok	21.8	4.6	46.0
6. Glasgow Govan	20.7	4.8	44.0
7. Glasgow Anniesland	20.4	4.6	44.1
8. Paisley North	19.9	4.2	49.7
9. Motherwell and Wishaw	19.9	4.1	49.3
10. Cunninghame South	19.6	5.4	46.0

Lowest Ten	JSA/IB/SDA	JSA	2003 Turnout
1. Aberdeenshire West and Kincardine	4.9	1.0	50.9
2. Gordon	6.1	1.2	47.7
3. North East Fife	6.7	1.7	50.4
4. Orkney	7.0	1.9*	52.1
5. Edinburgh South	7.3	1.7	52.1
6. Shetland	7.4	1.9*	52.3
7. Edinburgh West	7.6	2.0	55.7
8. Moray	8.5	2.0	46.7
9. Tweeddale, Ettrick and Lauderdale	8.5	1.6	53.0
10. Eastwood	8.6	1.7	58.3

* Orkney and Shetland figure

Sources: IB/SDA figures are from IAD Information Centre 5% sample; NOMIS JSA figures on their own from May 2003

In terms of life expectancy, Glasgow Shettleston has the lowest male life expectancy in the country, at 63.9 years. Female life expectancy is 11.3 years longer – the largest such gender gap in the country, which ought to tell us something about male and female roles in Shettleston. Life expectancy is of course a long time 'lag' and will take more than seven years of UK Labour Government to begin to shift, but other figures show a similarly worrying set of trends. A low weight at birth is one of the best indicators of future life chances and outcomes. The latest overall Scottish figures show these are increasing, particularly in the most deprived urban areas such as Glasgow and Dundee.

During the past 20 years in Scotland, prosperity has risen but inequalities have deepened. A sense of fatalism and silence has crept into public debate on these subjects despite all the government and public agency action, and professed sense of egalitarianism. Many subjects remain taboo or too sensitive even to raise in policy or government circles such as the widening 'Scottish effect' in terms of health and life expectancy. Since 1981 the gap between Scotland and the rest of the UK has expanded. Part of this is due to socio-economic differences, but twenty years ago 95 per cent of the difference between Scotland and the rest of the UK could be explained by deprivation, whereas today less than half can. The largest contribution is now due to other factors such as culture, behaviour and values. The UK Government and Scottish Executive are committed to the abolition of child poverty in a generation, but ever since Johnston's 'Great Society' vision for the USA was shipwrecked by the costs and divisions of the Vietnam war, few politicians anywhere have been prepared to commit publicly and with passion to challenging and ending exclusion. Without political commitment and imagination, poverty and inequality are subjects that are seldom raised in mainstream discourse, except indirectly via concerns over pension insecurity or consumer debt.

The Housing Revolution

Scotland has undergone a revolution in relation to housing tenure in the last twenty years. In 1981 52 per cent of Scotland's housing was council housing and 36 per cent owner-occupied, whereas by 2001 this had dramatically reversed with owner occupation making up 63 per cent and council housing a mere 22 per cent (Wilcox, 2002). This has dramatically changed the geography and culture of Scotland's cities and communities in a way unimaginable twenty years ago. In 1981 large swathes of the West of Scotland had massive, monolithic concentrations of council housing approaching Stalinist Eastern European proportions. In 1981, 40 out of Scotland's 72 constituencies had over 50 per cent council housing, and Glasgow Provan had the highest proportion with 96 per cent council housing, followed by Glasgow Garscadden with 90 per cent (see Table Five). Ten years later, in 1991, after a decade of Thatcherism, council house sales and a freeze on new building, change had begun to happen with only 14 out of 72 constituencies having over 50 per cent, and the top ten more concentrated in Glasgow. The top two, Airdrie and Shotts and Motherwell and Wishaw, had 62.5 per cent council housing each, while Glasgow Provan's successor seat, Baillieston, had fallen back to third place and 61.4 per cent.

Table Five: Council Housing 1981-2001

1981	*%*
1. Glasgow Provan	95.5
2. Glasgow Garscadden	89.7
3. Motherwell North	82.4
4. Motherwell South	80.8
5. Aberdeen North	80.2
6. Monklands East	79.7
7. Cunninghame South	77.2
8. Greenock and Port Glasgow	76.3
9. Glasgow Springburn	75.9
10. Dunfermline East	74.7
1991	*%*
1. Airdrie and Shotts	62.5

cont'd

2. Motherwell and Wishaw	62.5
3. Glasgow Baillieston	61.4
4. Glasgow Springburn	59.3
5. Glasgow Maryhill	58.9
6. Glasgow Pollok	57.1
7. Coatbridge and Chryston	56.0
8. Glasgow Shettleston	55.4
9. Cunninghame South	55.3
10. Glasgow Anniesland	54.9

2001	%
1. Motherwell and Wishaw	37.2
2. Airdrie and Shotts	36.2
3. Glasgow Springburn	34.9
4. Coatbridge and Chryston	32.4
5. Hamilton North and Bellshill	31.4
6. Glasgow Baillieston	31.1
7. Falkirk West	30.7
8. Linlithgow	30.7
9. Hamilton South	30.2
10. Glasgow Anniesland	30.2

Sources: 1981, 1991, 2001 Censuses

By 2001, not one of Scotland's 72 constituencies had over 50 per cent council housing and the highest two were the same as ten years previously, Motherwell and Wishaw and Airdrie and Shotts, where that sector had fallen to 37.2 per cent and 36.2 per cent. Despite this having been a Thatcherite transformation of how Scots live, their attitudes, how they see themselves and others, whether by choice or default, this housing revolution has barely registered with the political classes. It has fundamental consequences for the kind of society we live in, the balance between individualism and collectivism, social mobility, inheritance, and social space and layout of cities.

How much has this fundamental shift altered politics? Margaret Thatcher commented in her memoirs that, 'The balance sheet of Thatcherism in Scotland is a lopsided one: economically positive, but politically negative' (Thatcher 1993, p. 623). Thatcher believed that the Scots had embraced the benefits of Thatcherism – council house sales, tax cuts, share options – but refused to embrace the Conservatives. The reasons for this are complex, but one of the most influential factors was many Scots perceived Thatcherism, Thatcher and the Conservatives as quintessentially English. Thus, the Scottish Tories were seen as 'alien' and in opposition to majority Scottish social democratic opinion. As we have argued, this contributed to how Scottish Labour saw and positioned itself increasingly effectively post-1979 as the national party of Scotland, as a host of economic and social issues became enmeshed in the national dimension. Despite losing council housing as one of the central pillars of its political strength in post-1945 Scotland, Scottish Labour not only survived in the period 1979-97 but increased its dominance of Scottish representation at Westminster.

Change has occurred at other levels and under a Labour-led government. The sharp decline in the extent of council housing, along with such developments as Glasgow City Council's Housing Stock Transfer, have weakened the clientism that was at the heart of old Labour's extended state of patronage and preferment. And when combined with the impending introduction of PR for councils for 2007, this signals the death knell of a certain kind of Labour politics – one that was monopolistic, seeking to govern on its own, driven by producer interests, shaped by internal rather than external pressures, and scornful of alliances, partnership and dialogue. These changes will eventually produce a different Labour politics. Labour will have to become a more normal political party, rather than one reliant on clientism and the patronage of the local state, and operate within a more challenging pluralist politics than it has been used to, both locally and nationally (Hassan, 2004).

Holyrood Awakening

Scottish politics is still adjusting to the arrival of devolution. The first Scottish Parliament was elected against the backdrop of disillusionment with adversarial politics, but expectation it could deliver 'a new politics'. It has been more female, younger and somewhat more varied. This was a very different voice from public Scotland before in age and gender, if not views. The first Parliament passed an impressive 62 acts – making the home rulers' case that most of these bills would have never seen the light of day under Westminster. But most of these acts were administrative or technical measures with little profile or contentiousness, and the degree of change of those that were contested (such as warrant sales or land reform) was open to question. It also passed 48 Sewel motions which allowed Westminster to legislate in devolved areas, causing some to worry it was setting a bad precedent for voting away its rights and powers too easily. The degree of instability in the Scottish Executive in the first four years with three First Ministers and a total of 39 ministers meant that the main drivers within the new institutional arrangements remained the senior civil service who provided the policy and institutional continuity and expertise in the face of such unprecedented personal turnover.

The first four years led from high expectation to low disappointment. The Scottish Social Survey at the time of the 1999 devolution referendum reflected this when it asked who would have most influence in Scotland, and found the Scottish Parliament marginally ahead of the UK Government by 41-39 per cent. By the following year, when asked who had most influence, Scottish opinion had moved decisively in favour of the UK Government giving it 66 per cent to a mere 13 per cent for the Scottish Parliament. The latest figures for 2003 give the UK Government 64 per cent, while the Scottish Parliament has risen slightly to 17 per cent (Curtice, 2004, p. 220). However, from 1999 onwards when Scots have been asked who should have the most influence they have consistently given 72-74 per cent to the Scottish Parliament and 13-14 per cent to the UK Government. Bromley and Curtice conclude from this that 'a large gap has opened up between whom the public thinks should have most say in how Scotland is run and who actually does' (Bromley and Curtice, 2003, p. 17).

Conventional wisdom on how this new and subtler 'democratic deficit' should be resolved is to suggest that the Scottish Parliament should be given more powers, along with fiscal autonomy. This does seem a very institutional definition of the problem and its solution, rather than thinking about how the political classes and public debate can show more imagination and do things differently. The verdict of the Scottish public about the Scottish Parliament and devolution seems to be one of 'not proven' – while still having an optimistic view of the future. Thus, while most people do not think the Scottish Parliament has made a difference, only a small minority of the electorate think it has had a negative impact or would want to see it abolished. In the longer term there is still a sense of optimism – with well over two in five thinking the NHS will improve under devolution and only one in ten the opposite. There are similar figures for the Scottish economy. At the point of the 1997 referendum, 79 per cent believed the Scottish Parliament would give ordinary people more say in how Scotland is governed, but this had declined to 39 per cent by 2003 (Curtice, 2004, p. 223). However, there is some evidence of the much vaunted 'new politics' with 51 per cent saying they believe MSPs of different parties work together for the good of Scotland versus 29 per cent saying the same of MPs of different parties in the House of Commons (Bromley and Curtice, 2003, p. 18). Public opinion has not turned against the Parliament or devolution, but remains well disposed towards it, waiting for it to prove itself. People are still optimistic about it in the long-term and the impact it can make to Scotland, the economy, health and education.

The Scottish Parliament's 2003 elections pointed to a changing political culture: a six-party pluralist and increasingly fragmented party system in which coalition is a pre-requisite to majority government. Viable majority alliances may become more difficult in the future, and two national parties now sit firmly to the left of Labour and SNP – the Scottish Greens and Scottish Socialists. There are now five substantial party groups positioned to the left of centre, and the Conservatives not all that far to the right, at least in terms of their support for the role of the state in public service provision.

Contrast this with Westminster, where a system based on Labour's dominance particularly of West of Scotland constituencies gives the party 78 per cent of Scotland's seats on 43 per cent of the vote. These different political cultures now shape the two institutions' views of national politics (Mitchell, 2004). Westminster is still driven by a narrow, monopolistic sense of party chauvinism where Labour can claim to speak for most of Scotland, and dismisses other political parties as irrelevant or minuscule. This is the mindset which allows David Marshall, Labour MP for Glasgow Shettleston, elected with 26 per cent of the electorate in 2001, to dismiss the Scottish Parliament electoral system after the 2003 election as 'bizarre', while Brian Donohoe (Cunninghame South) and George Foulkes (Carrick, Cumnock and Doon Valley), have proposed changing the electoral system to reassert Labour's dominance. This arrogance fails to acknowledge that all political parties in Scotland are minorities, and that governing Scotland requires different parties to come together. It also belittles the smaller parties such as the Greens and Socialists which each won 6-7 per cent of the regional list vote, sizeable enough national support in most European countries to make parties a permanent feature of the political landscape. Many Labour MPs, and some MSPs, still have the old-fashioned view that the regional list vote is somehow a lesser vote, or believe that voters still do not understand how it works, and the new 'rainbow alliance' Parliament of 2003 is some horrible mistake.

These views increasingly misunderstand the dynamics of Scottish politics where the trend is clearly towards greater pluralism and competition, hence the Scottish Parliament 2003 election, proportional representation for the European Parliament, and forthcoming PR for local government. Westminster is the anomaly here – the political institution which least accurately reflects the voting booth choices of the Scottish people.

Shifting Consensus

The Scottish Parliament's electoral politics increasingly resemble those of continental Europe more than the rest of the UK. In particular, there is a similarity with party systems in Scandinavia, whereby within a social democratic consensus, there is a dominant centre-left party which has shaped much of the politics, policy and institutions of the post-war era, but now increasingly has to operate in alliances and negotiation with other partners. The vote for such dominant parties has slowly declined as politics have become more pluralist. In Norway and Sweden, for example, Labour and Social Democratic parties have lost power to centre-right coalitions, while still shaping the political environment.

It may be that this pattern has much to teach Scotland, and Labour in particular. Scottish politics have shifted in the last decade or so through two distinct phases (Hassan, 2003), and seem to be entering a third, with which Scandinavians are familiar:

An anti-Tory coalition of the pre-devolution years

During the Thatcher-Major era, the Scottish opposition parties (Labour, SNP, Lib Dems) united behind a social democratic consensus which included the demand for a Parliament, and increasingly portrayed the Conservatives as 'alien' and a pariah party. The primary faultline in this period was between the majority democratic demand for a Parliament and the minority Tory unionist defence of the status quo.

An anti-Nationalist consensus

With the establishment of the Parliament, the old home rule consensus in favour of constitutional change broke down. A political environment began to emerge around a new unionist politics, with which Labour identified and was more assertive. This laid stress on the majority wishes of most Scots to remain in the United Kingdom, and brought to the fore the unionist values of the Labour and Lib Dem parties. The party excluded by this new consensus was, much to its surprise, the SNP, the party of independence, emphasising the minority support for its position. It found itself in the run-up to the 1999 Scottish Parliament elections facing increasing challenge from the other parties who all accepted the new unionist settlement, and who focused an unprecedented degree of scrutiny and criticism on the Nationalists.

An anti-Labour consensus

The 2003 Scottish Parliament election showed the first major sign of a new political paradigm by which Labour as the political establishment of most of Scotland and incumbent party at most levels of government, began to be challenged and held to account by voters. Part of this was the length of time Labour had been the leading party of Scotland, while another contributory factor was the emergence from 1997 onwards of a number of Labour scandals in town halls with the unifying thread of Labour cronyism, corruption and a blurring between party and state boundaries. In the 2003 Scottish Parliament election, despite retaining its position as Scotland's leading party in votes and seats, Labour faced a challenge from across the political spectrum from a 'rainbow alliance' of SNP, Lib Dems, Conservatives and Independents. This recognisable shift is unlikely to begin and end at the 2003 elections given that Labour is still the lead party in Edinburgh, rules from London and controls so many council chambers.

It may be that Scottish politics is living with the overlap of such phases. Anti-Toryism may be weakening, but it has not departed from the political lexicon. For the foreseeable future it will remain one of the mobilising stories of progressive Scotland. The poll tax has become part of Scottish political folklore, and become for one generation what the Jarrow March and appeasement were for another – totems with which to bash your political opponents. In the same way, the Iraq war and the elusive hunt for Weapons of Mass Destruction (WMD) may become a defining and mobilising story about Blair and New Labour.

Similarly, anti-Nationalism (stressing the capital 'N') will continue to be a major factor in limiting the SNP's appeal. There have been numerous surveys and voter vox pops which have shown that while a majority of Scots think benignly of the Nationalists' ability to stand up for Scotland's interests, there is something in their appeal which prevents a majority of Scots voting for them. This includes seeing the SNP as too narrow in its appeal, too Nationalist, worrying about separatism, its costs and potential instability, and seeing the SNP as a one issue party which does not speak to a wider agenda of economic and social issues. Survey evidence suggests the SNP has a consistent core vote of a mere 10 per cent of the electorate versus 35 per cent for Labour (Paterson, 2003).

Despite this, it seems that we may be moving more towards an era of an anti-Labour consensus, whereby the problems and pitfalls of labourism, and the inability of Labour to renew itself and embrace a different, more democratic politics while remaining in power, will increasingly pose difficulties for the party. Labour has shaped Scotland for several generations – in the realm of ideas from its emergence as a national party in the 1922 election, at an administrative and governing level, from the emergence of the Tom Johnston 'negotiated state' of the 1940s, and increasingly as the dominant leading party of Scotland from 1964 onward as the Scottish Conservatives electorally declined.

These three political phases are all within the context of a Scottish social democratic consensus that some see as increasingly problematic and the cause of Scotland's problems. This is a caricature drawn by those outside the consensus, which fails to distinguish between the problem being the kind of social democracy, as opposed to social democracy per se. Scotland's social democracy has become institutionally fossilised around a Labour Party politics of patronage and risk aversion, but this does not mean Scotland in a global age should abandon the values of social democracy for the embrace of unfettered market forces and possessive individualism.

What's the story?

Amid this shifting consensus, and with the background of continuing popular support for devolution despite sharply reduced expectations of it, what has been missing in the first years of Scottish devolution has been a positive narrative or storyline about what kind of society this constitutional change is meant to bring about. The dominant narratives of these crucial, early years have been negative, for want of obvious positive alternatives. Thus, we have had explanations of this period such as the Parliament dismissed as a 'souped up' Labour council of well-remunerated 'numpties', of the political classes as a self-serving, incompetent group defined in the public eye by the escalating costs of the Holyrood Building Project, of a 'toy-town' Parliament without real power to fundamentalist Nationalists, and of a politically-correct orthodoxy imposing restrictions whenever it can (Section 28, fox hunting, etc.).

Howard Gardner, in his penetrating analysis of political leadership, defines one of its main characteristics as the ability to tell stories which shape a vital historic and political moment, and do so in competition, debate and dialogue with other counter-stories (Gardner, 1996). If we use this to examine contemporary Scotland, we find that the negative narratives which all have an underlying theme of dismissing the degree and potential of change, have become dominant almost by default, in that there has been a silence where there could have been a multiplicity of more positive narratives offered by politicians, civil Scotland and the social forces which fought for and achieved devolution.

Scotland pre-devolution had a sense of this mission and purpose, situated as it was around the centrality of the anti-Tory consensus and the prospect of constitutional change releasing the nation's potential. Now that we have a real Parliament filled with real politicians at a point where faith and hope in party politics is at a low ebb, and the 'fantasy Parliament' of the pre-devolution era has disappeared, that certainty has dissipated and any sense of vision has clouded.

Labour has come to dominate Scottish politics while voters have also chosen to back Nationalism in sufficient numbers for the constitution to spend a generation as the key dividing line within politics. At a transitionary phase, we are bound to ask what comes next? Whatever it is, it will be within the context of a Scotland with at least an element of home rule. Devolution, the offspring of that Labour dominance with a Nationalist opposition, has become deeply embedded, and while Nationalists may wish for home rule to go further, there is little sign of it being rolled back. And while devolution's early years have been accompanied by disappointment and some disillusion, the impact of setting up a new Parliament in Edinburgh for the first time in 300 years has not only had a seismic effect on Scottish politics, but also a dynamic one.

The directions it takes next will depend on the choices, or timid lack of choices, made by the political classes, and how that is reflected in the electorate's choices. These choices will partly depend on outside forces and influences; rapidly shifting patterns within the global economy, presenting Scotland at least as much as the rest of the developed world with unprecedented challenges: demographic shifts which present Scotland with the rare challenge of not only an ageing population but a falling one as well; the lifestyle decisions made by individual Scots which will define how healthy or unhealthy the nation becomes: the centralising political forces at work in Brussels: and what becomes of Tony Blair, 'the project' that used to be called New Labour, the future for Gordon Brown, and the weak Conservative Party throughout the UK. Of these, the Scottish Tories are the most reliant on factors out of their control. For all their attempts to clamber back into the political mainstream, their fortunes seem closely tied to those of their southern cousins. The SNP must also look to external influences to determine their future. However much they preach a positive case for Scotland taking control of its own affairs, electoral revival looks likely only on one of two conditions; first, that Labour is seen to fail or lose touch and that the Nationalists are the party best able to exploit that: second, that they can exploit revived anti-Westminster or anti-English sentiment. Either way, the SNP's future prospects depend on Labour and/or Westminster politicians.

A paradox of the current position is that the constitutional future of Scotland remains one of the dominant political faultlines in a Parliament that gives the debate more profile, yet the very existence of that Parliament has taken the wind out of the Nationalist sails. Nationalists would like to keep that faultline, and some in Labour are equally comfortable with it, in the belief that portraying their opponents as 'separatists' intent on 'divorce' will keep Labour winning elections. But in the absence of an English nationalism against which to react, and in the absence (for now) of a threat to Scotland's share of UK spending, the prospects for independence in the short-to-medium do not look rosy. If that status quo and lack of salience for the big dividing line is to remain, it raises a tricky challenge to mainstream party politicians: how does Scotland handle a prolonged period of consensus across other major issues; provoking public interest and even excitement in politics: testing policies against adversarial scrutiny: and avoiding the limited areas of disagreement from gaining disproportionate attention?

And if the constitutional question is to diminish in importance over time, where will the new Scottish political faultlines develop? If not religious denomination, as in the past, will class or at least socio-economic interest groups come to play a more prominent role in creating political cleavages? Could a new public-private sector dichotomy open up, driven by conflict over resources? Will regionalism become more of a force, or more of an urban/rural divide? Will the ageing population create growing political fractures between young and old? There is a lack of well-founded analysis evident within politics with which to address these questions. There is also a shortage of independent policy-making capacity as well as a lack of willingness to listen to what little there is.

This then is a view of the first years of 21st century Scotland – one filled with contradictions, paradoxes, messy compromise, but ultimately, still a degree of hope that new politics and devolved government can make a difference. The early days of Scottish devolution have occurred in what are relatively good economic times. The politics of Labour in power in London and Labour and the Lib Dems in Edinburgh have ensured stability, but also restricted the opportunities for differentiation north and south of the border. Post-Iraq, as the Blair Government increasingly runs into political difficulties, the votes of Scottish Labour MPs have become increasingly crucial in winning votes on foundation hospitals and tuition fees – in both cases a majority of English MPs voted against. If Labour win a historic third term in 2005-6 it will likely be with a smaller UK majority where Scots Labour votes are even more crucial and controversial, and Labour's overall majority is possibly reliant on them. And further down the line there is the spectre of the return of the Tories at Westminster in the context of a British state which has set up new devolved institutions, but not reformed itself.

What will happen when we enter such turbulent times will do a lot to determine the strength of the devolution settlement and the public's faith in it. When either an economic downturn occurs or there is a move from Labour's control or dominance in Westminster or Holyrood, the shapes of emerging Scottish politics will become clearer and more fluid.

References

Bauman, Z. (2001), *The Individualised Society*, Polity Press, Cambridge.

Beatty, C., Fothergill, S., Gore, T. and Green, A. (2002), *The Real Level of Unemployment 2002*, Centre for Regional Economic and Social Research, Sheffield Hallam University, Sheffield.

Black, D. (2001), *All the First Minister's Men: The Truth Behind Holyrood*, Birlinn, Edinburgh.

Brand, J. (1978), *The Nationalist Movement in Scotland*, Routledge, Kegan and Paul, London.

Brown, G. (1981), *The Labour Party and Political Change in Scotland 1918-29: The Politics of Five Elections*, Edinburgh University unpublished PhD, Edinburgh.

Bromley, C. and Curtice, J. (2003), 'Devolution: Scorecard and Prospects', in C. Bromley, J. Curtice, K. Hinds and A. Park (eds), *Devolution: Scottish Answers to Scottish Questions?*, Edinburgh University Press, Edinburgh, pp. 7-29.

Curtice, J. (2004), 'Restoring Confidence and Legitimacy? Devolution and Public Opinion', in A. Trench (ed.), *Has Devolution Made A Difference? The State of the Nations 2004*, Imprint Academic, Essex, pp. 217-36.

Denver, D. (2003), 'A 'Wake Up!' Call to the Parties? The Results of the Scottish Parliament Elections 2003', *Scottish Affairs*, No. 44, Summer 2003, pp. 31-53.

Fraser, D. (2004), 'New Labour, New Parliament', in G. Hassan (ed.), *The Scottish Labour Party: Histories, Institutions and Ideas*, Edinburgh University Press, Edinburgh, pp. 127-45.

Gardner, H. (1996), *Leading Minds: An Anatomy of Leadership*, Harper Collins, London.

Hassan, G. (2003), 'Paradise Postponed or Regained? The Strange Case of Scotland', *Soundings*, No. 25, Winter 2003, pp. 72-82.

Hassan, G. (2004), 'The People's Party Still? The Sociology of Scotland's Leading Party, in G. Hassan (ed.), *The Scottish Labour Party: Histories, Institutions and Ideas,* Edinburgh University Press, Edinburgh, pp. 1-18.

Jenkins, R. (1991), *A Life at the Centre*, Macmillan, Basingstoke.

Jenkins, R. (2001), *Churchill: A Biography*, Macmillan, Basingstoke.

Joshi, H. and Wright, R. (2004), *Life in Scotland in the New Millennium*, Fraser of Allander Institute, Glasgow.

Lynch, P. (2002), *The SNP: The Scottish National Party*, Welsh Academic Press, Cardiff.

Mitchell, J. (2004), 'Scotland: Expectations, Policy Types and Devolution', in A. Trench (ed.), *Has Devolution Made A Difference? The State of the Nations 2004*, Imprint Academic, Essex, pp. 11-42.

Paterson, L. (2002), 'Social Capital and Constitutional Reform', in J. Curtice, D. McCrone, A. Park and L. Paterson (eds), *New Scotland, New Society?*, Edinburgh University Press, Edinburgh, pp. 5-32.

Paterson, L. (2003), *Attitudes to Scottish Independence and to the SNP*, paper to seminar to the SNP, August 22 2003, Dunblane.

Paxman, J. (2002), *The Political Animal*, Michael Joseph, London.

Scottish Unionist Association (1955), *The Year Book for Scotland and Scottish Parliamentary Election Manual*, Scottish Unionist Association, Edinburgh and Glasgow.

Shaw, M., Dorling, D., Gordon, D. and Davey Smith, G. (1999), *The Widening Gap: Health Inequalities and Policy in Britain*, Policy Press, Bristol.

Steed, M. (1975), 'The Results Analysed', in D. Butler and D. Kavanagh, *The British General Election of October 1974*, Macmillan, Basingstoke, pp. 330-56.

Thatcher, M. (1993), *The Downing Street Years*, Harper Collins, London.

Wilcox, S. (2002), *UK Housing Review 2002-2003*, Chartered Institute of Housing, Council of Mortgage Lenders and Joseph Rowntree Foundation, Coventry, London and York.

Young, M. (1958), *The Rise of the Meritocratic Society*, Penguin, London.

The First Term of the Scottish Parliament: Big Change and Big Sameness

Peter Jones

What is the most striking aspect of this year's election campaign? One is the almost total consensus between the main parties with all four contesting a congested centre ground. They are all pledged to raising educational standards, improving health care and tackling crime by the far from revolutionary strategy of recruiting extra teachers, additional doctors and nurses and more police officers. The only slight difference is in the precise numbers they propose to employ.

John McTernan, *Scotland on Sunday*, 27 April 2003.

Archie: 'Davie, can ye tell me the difference between Whig and Tory noo-a-days?' Davie: 'Yes, if ye'll tell me the difference between twice five-an'-twenty an' twice twenty-five; for I'm blest if I can see ony. I'm thinkin' it'll puzzle a transcendental hair-splitter to discover ony difference.'

Archie and Bess, *Glasgow Weekly Mail*, 22 January 1876 (quoted in Donaldson 1989, p.116).

Politics goes in many cycles. One is the opening and closing of ideological differences between the main political contestants. Sometimes the gulf between them seems huge, as it was between neo-Conservatism and democratic socialism in the 1980s. Sometimes the gap seems to disappear, as was noted by John McTernan and practically every other Scottish political commentator writing over the 2003 Scottish Parliamentary election campaign.

This political sameness is nothing new. Yet the 1876 comment was written just four years before a general election which was perhaps the most rancorous of the Victorian era. Oddly enough, the divisive factor in the 1880 election, which famously featured William Gladstone's Midlothian campaign rhetoric, was agitation over British imperial policy in the Middle East, of which there was more than an echo in 2003. Thus history teaches that the present centrifugal quagmire in which Scottish politics is seemingly glued cannot endure. No one can know what the catalyst might be. But certainly, something will come along to unravel the hegemony of centre-left social democracy.

Lessons in Survival and Novelty

While we are waiting, it is well to learn the lessons of the first four years of the devolution experiment. The first is that it survived at all. Right wing politicians and commentators, and a few from the left, feared that the Parliament would be a big stage on which the Scottish National Party could perform and flourish. It was variously the slippery slope, the fast track or the motorway to independence. They also warned that there would be endless fighting between the Scottish and Westminster Parliaments and governments. There was indeed debate about the nature of the constitutional settlement, particularly about the financing of the Scottish Executive budget and the alleged lack of Scottish influence in the European Union, but these discussions struck no chord with the voters. On the evidence of the first four years, the devolved Scottish Parliament was more than the settled will of the people, it was the settled constitutional will.

The second is that it introduced some democratic novelties. Proportional representation, without which a major party (the Conservatives) and two minor parties (the Scottish Socialists, the Greens) would have gone unrepresented. A new pluralism replaced the old majoritarian Westminster system, instituted through the committees for managing the Parliament's business and in the legislative process. Backbenchers obtained a firm place in law-making – of the 62 bills passed in the first session, nine were private member's bills. These included a bill to abolish debt recovery by warrant sales and poindings which was promoted by Tommy Sheridan MSP, surely the first example in Britain of a law advocated by a revolutionary socialist to reach the statute book.

The Parliament's committee system, combining the scrutiny and legislative functions which are separated at Westminster, was another, generally successful, innovation. It enabled MSPs to accumulate real expertise in specialist areas, as the designers had intended. There were some criticisms. The biggest was that the legislative function was spread unevenly, resulting in the Justice committee being so burdened with proposed laws to examine that it had little time to spend examining the Executive's justice department. Eventually, the complaint was dealt with to some extent by setting up a second Justice committee.

Other complaints were more subjective. Often, the quality of a committee's output seemed to depend on the ability of the specialist topic advisers recruited rather than the ability of the MSPs. Sometimes, a committee looked less than thorough in its examination of all the pros and cons or a particular proposal and seemed predisposed to arrive at a particular conclusion. But the political partisanship routinely displayed in plenary session seemed to be more absent than present. They also had power to initiate legislation, which was used successfully on three occasions for laws setting up a children's commissioner, a parliamentary standards commissioner, and on domestic violence. While the committees and their operation could be improved, no one is suggesting a radical overhaul is needed.

The public gained access to law-making too, through the petitions committee. Unlike Westminster, where petitions from the public are dumped in a bag behind the Speaker's chair and then forgotten, Scottish public petitions are considered by a committee. If they make a point which seems worth considering, they are sent on to the appropriate subject committee. In the first session, 615 petitions were submitted and about a fifth were judged worthy of further consideration. Some, indeed, eventually led to action. The most remarkable example was that submitted by residents of Blairingone, a village near Dollar, who complained that their lives were being made miserable and their health endangered by the legal spreading of raw blood and offal from abattoirs on adjacent fields. The practice was eventually outlawed. Such a response is inconceivable under Westminster rules.

The Parliament also tried to move closer to the public. Its committees journeyed the length and breadth of the land, taking evidence on legislative proposals and pursuing inquiries into issues of concern. The Parliament also sat in plenary session in Glasgow and Aberdeen, though this decampment was more to do with the need to vacate its usual Edinburgh home to allow its landlords, the Church of Scotland, back into the Assembly Hall for its annual week-long General Assembly.

The expected additional scrutiny and transparency of government in Scotland also arrived. Pre-devolution, about 1,700 Parliamentary questions a year were asked of the Scottish Office. In the first term of the Parliament, just under 9,000 questions a year were asked, a five-fold increase. Additionally, a 60 per cent increase in ministerial correspondence and the need to make some 40 ministerial statements a year, clogged up the bureaucratic machine to the extent that simple questions went unanswered for 2-3 weeks (Scottish Executive, 2000).

Some of the innovations managed to impress Westminster. In a report on how Westminster might be improved, the Hansard Society recommended that the House of Commons should follow the Scottish example and set up a Public Petitions Committee (Hansard Society Commission on Parliamentary Scrutiny 2001, p. 87). Indeed, Robin Cook, leader of the House of Commons 2001–03, indicated he thought this was a good idea (Winetrobe 2001, p. 114). Tony Blair, several years after the Scottish Executive reorganised the agriculture and fisheries department into a rural affairs department, did the same with the Ministry of Agriculture, Fisheries and Food. In a different vein, the decision of the House of Commons to allow TV broadcasters to use Westminster's Central Lobby for live interviews was also apparently attributable to Scottish broadcasters' use of the Assembly Halls' black and white corridor.

Holyrood Headlines

Such a long list of successful innovations, yet the media coverage of the Parliament, virtually from the day it began work in September 1999 was almost unremittingly negative. This is odd, given that the Scottish press, with the exception of the *Scottish Daily Mail*, had all urged their readers to vote for devolution in the September 1997 referendum. There are several reasons for this u-turn by the opinion formers.

First, the default position of the media is to be critical of the political establishment. The media's job is to expose wrongdoing, malpractice, shoddiness and incompetence. They have been doing it for years with the pre-devolution Scottish Office, so nobody should have been surprised that the same criteria should have been applied to the Parliament and the executive. What was surprising was the sheer hostility of the coverage. When it was decided that the Parliament should sit in formal plenary and committee sessions for three days a week, this was interpreted as MSPs voting themselves a three-day week. When it was decided that these formal sessions would be held for 35 weeks of the year, this was portrayed as MSPs voting themselves 17 weeks holiday a year. The fact that MSPs do constituency work on Mondays, Fridays and often on Saturdays too, or that they do constituency work when the Parliament is not sitting, was ignored.

This hostility stemmed mainly from the second reason for media attitudes: changes in media ownership and editors which put people with anti-devolution and anti-politician views in charge of previously pro-devolution newspapers such as the *Scotsman* and the *Daily Record*. Behind these changes lay commercial rivalry which turned into a classic newspaper war. Pre-devolution, newspaper management thinking was that a parliament would generate lots of Scottish news which they, rather than London-based competitors were better placed to exploit through increased sales. But in fact, sales of all Scottish newspapers dropped in the first year of the Parliament. The *Scotsman* lost 10,000 daily sales, the *Herald*, the *Courier and Advertiser*, the *Press and Journal* lost another 10,000 between them and the *Daily Record* slid from 685,000 sales to 611,000 (*The Economist*, 7 September 2000). This is why, 'in repatriating Scottish politics, devolution has repatriated contempt for politics, politicians, and Parliament.' (Mitchell et al, 2003, pp. 136-7) The winners were the *Scottish Sun* and the *Scottish Daily Mail* which led the way with attacks on the Parliament, pushing editors into frantic searches for ever blacker headlines.

Fairly typical was a *Daily Record* leader which attacked Donald Dewar as the 'dithering first minister'. It concluded: 'And although we have always defended Donald through disaster after disaster during his 10 short months in government, even we finally have to ask ourselves: is he really the best man for the job?' (*Daily Record*, 25 February 2000) After Dewar's death on 11 October, 2000, things changed. 'Dithering Donald' suddenly became 'Saint Donald'. The *Daily Record* sonorously intoned: 'It goes without saying that there must be a lasting memorial to such a Great Scot. Donald's place in history is assured, but future generations should know that his own generation held him in such high esteem.'

Post-Devolution Leadership

The press hostility threw a harsh light on questions of leadership. Pre-devolution, Scottish political leaders led a double life – high profile in Scotland, but bit players in Westminster, their main political arena. Devolution raised their profile even higher, and also transformed them into lead players. Nobody coped well.

Dewar had all the political weight that came with a career spanning nearly four decades which won him a huge amount of trust from voters and the Labour establishment in London. Yet he seemed curiously ill-prepared for the demands of the new institution which he had fought for and helped to design. In large part, that was because he, almost alone amongst the Labour establishment that came to power in 1997, refused to engage in the game of continual announcement and media management spin that characterised New Labour. He was also cautious, believed in step-by-step deliberative progress, and abhorred the politics of gestures and visionary leaps. None of this suited the mood of 1999–2000. The public had overly high expectations of what the Parliament would deliver, as did the media, and Dewar's style did not fit.

Alex Salmond did not easily fit into the new Parliament either. He had won the SNP leadership when the party was at a low ebb in 1990. He had successfully built it into a significant force and the second biggest party in the 1999 elections. Leading the opposition in the new Parliament looked a tailor-made job for him, especially as he had always espoused the gradualist route via devolution to independence. But many of his party still saw devolution as a snare and Salmond struggled to maintain the cohesion of the 35-strong group of MSPs. Had he not decided in 2000 to go back to Westminster he would have faced a leadership challenge. John Swinney comfortably defeated fellow MSP Alex Neil to become SNP leader in September 2000, but similarly struggled to win the loyalty of his group to the extent that two of them – Margo MacDonald and Dorothy Grace Elder – left the SNP in 2003.

The junior partner in the Labour-Liberal Democrat coalition, Jim Wallace, should also have found the new politics to his liking. Indeed, as deputy first minister, he stepped ably, albeit temporarily, three times into the top job - during Dewar's heart surgery, after Dewar died and after Henry McLeish was forced to resign. In this role, and by remaining with his justice job during the first term's two re-shuffles, he provided continuity and much-needed stability, an unexpected by-product of coalition politics which some suppose to be inherently unstable. But repeated rebellions by a minority of his 17-strong Lib Dem group against the executive they were supposed to support told a story of weak leadership, undermining the executive's certainty of purpose.

That purpose came even more under question during Henry McLeish's year as first minister. McLeish got off to a bad start when he won the Labour leadership against Jack McConnell by the surprisingly narrow margin of 44-36. Things got worse when Wendy Alexander, the enterprise minister, refused to accept the water industry as part of her brief. Even McLeish's flagship policy – introducing free personal care for the elderly – wobbled about uncertainly as his own health minister, Susan Deacon, appeared to reject it and the executive was then forced by the Parliament to accept it before costs and implications had been properly worked out. That allowed everybody but McLeish to claim credit for the policy.

McLeish's weakness was glaringly exposed as the media, led by the *Mail on Sunday*, got its teeth into the story of expenses claimed for his constituency office in Glenrothes. This had nothing to do with the Scottish Parliament; it related to McLeish's time as a Westminster MP and to the rent from sub-lets of the Glenrothes office. This was not declared to the Commons authorities, but should have been so that they could reduce his office allowance accordingly. McLeish received no benefit from this money (about £36,000); it was all spent, he said, on the office. A more confident politician could have taken charge of the story and sorted it out quickly, but McLeish had to have it dragged out of him bit by bit, and that dragged him down. He resigned on 8 November 2001.

The episode said a number of things about politics in the new Scottish Parliament. First, the lax old Westminster ways will not do. MSPs have to have not just clean hands, but scrupulously clean hands. Second, the greater scrutiny and accountability that the Parliament was supposed to bring, has actually arrived. It is working in the way that the designers (McLeish in his chairmanship of the consultative steering group which wrote the rules was, ironically enough, one of them) intended. Third, that the rather cosy, comfortable Labour party network of power – linking trade unions, councils, national politics, and associated hangers-on – has found the new environment rather chilly. That was also the message from the Lobbygate affair of 1999. The Parliament's standards committee investigated a newspaper story that Beattie Media, a lobbying firm, had undue influence with the Executive, through its employment of Kevin Reid, son of John Reid, then Scottish Secretary, and its previous employment of Jack McConnell, then finance minister (*Observer*, 26 September 1999). The committee found no wrong-doing, but it was a salutary reminder of the need for scrupulousness.

McConnell's election as the third first minister of the first term marked, a lot sooner than anyone had expected, the handover of the executive from the Westminster old guard to a new breed of Scottish politicians. With the exception of Wendy Alexander, who was one of Dewar's special advisors when he was Scottish Secretary, McConnell cleared out the Dewar and McLeish appointees from his Cabinet. The replacements were his supporters from the backbenches, suggesting that he valued dependency on him rather than talent for his ministerial team. His choice betrayed an insecurity which was remarkable given that there was no obvious rival, especially after Alexander resigned as enterprise and lifelong learning minister a few months later. The principal opposition leaders, Swinney and McLetchie, also had no Westminster background, though McLetchie's relentless pursuit of McLeish's expense accounts showed that was no handicap to successful opposition politics.

Scottish Solutions for Scottish Problems

The weakening, if not severing, of the Westminster umbilical cord might have been expected to increase the divergence of the Executive's policy programme from that of the UK Labour Government. The language for such a divergence – Scottish solutions for Scottish problems – had even been clearly set out by Dewar in his speech announcing the Executive's first legislative programme. And indeed there was quite a lot of early policy divergence. The most notable included the replacement of up-front student tuition fees by a form of graduate tax, the implementation of free personal care for the elderly, and a more liberal freedom of information regime.

Two of these could claim to be born of Scottish values – a belief in the availability of education to all rather than the wealthy and the universal provision of welfare support. The third is harder to square with the traditional Scottish belief in state paternalism and provision. Perhaps it is easier to regard them as happenstance outcomes, the product of chance rather than evolving principle. Tuition fee abolition was the product of coalition negotiations, free personal care because McLeish used it to make his mark, and freedom of information because a Liberal Democrat had that ministerial responsibility. There also happened to be the money available to pay for them from the unexpectedly large additions to public spending stemming from Gordon Brown's budgets. The Scottish Executive's budget rose from £16.5bn in 1999-2000 to £22.8bn in 2003-04, a real terms increase of 2.6 per cent a year.

This largesse was all too easily consumed. Health spending went from £5.1bn in 1999-2000 to £7.3bn in 2003-04, local government spending rose from £5.1bn to £6.5bn, and the McCrone inquiry into teachers' pay resulted in a 23 per cent pay rise over three years and additional spending of some £800m. Again, this could be portrayed as a reassertion of the Scots' traditional esteem for public services, partic-ularly education. A more plausible explanation is that it was appeasement of powerful interest groups – councillors, the teaching unions, the medical professions – as these rewards resulted in only modest improvements in public services. Governments usually use cash hand-outs to such interest groups as a sweetener for reform, but that opportunity was largely spurned by the Executive.

To the public, the failure to improve services was the major disappointment of the first term. Surveys have shown that, for example, where 56 per cent thought in 1999 that having a Parliament would improve education, by 2001, only 27 per cent thought that devolution had done so (Bromley et al 2003, p. 16). Thus, the political parties' concentration on better services in the 2003 election was entirely correct, but the lack of differentiation between the alleged policy solutions on offer and the emphasis on more money as a cure was also disappointing and may help explain the relatively poor voter turn-out. Health policy was largely driven by target-setting and only in the last year did a Scottish health policy – the formation of health partnerships to help drive local delivery of health care accompanied by the rejection of foundation hospitals proposed in England – begin to emerge from the Executive.

Radicalism seemed notable as the exception rather than the rule. Two such exceptions were breath-taking in scale. Even five years before the Parliament arrived, who would have forecast that Glasgow Council would get rid of all its houses, or use private finance to rebuild all its schools? Yet in 2000, the council agreed to a £220m plan to rebuild and modernise all the city's 29 secondary schools using private finance. And in 2003, it handed its 84,500 council houses to a housing association. In reality, the council was backed into a corner from which private money was the only way out for its schools. A stock transfer for its houses – worth minus £200m but needing £2bn worth for repairs – was the only way improvement could feasibly occur and a Treasury bribe – taking over the council's £900m housing debt – silenced the doubters.

Land policy stands out as more truly radical. The Land Reform Act, passed in January 2003, was much assailed as more motivated by anti-landlord class prejudice than by beneficial principle. True, landlords, especially those with thousands of Highland acres, are unloved by Scottish politicians. The Act gave community groups rights of purchase when land they live on is put on the market, gave crofters absolute rights to buy croft land and fishery rights, and gave the public rights of 'responsible' access to walk on land. The move was entirely in tune with Scottish values concerning community and public (as opposed to individual) rights.

The idea of prejudice, however, gained credibility from Lord Watson's bill to ban foxhunting, introduced in March 2000 and passed two years later. Despite their being very little foxhunting in Scotland and pretty solid public opposition to the cruelty entailed, this backbench measure prompted considerable criticism and some turbulent demonstrations. The most notable fact about this bill, which went unnoticed, was that it was passed, unlike similar backbench bills at Westminster. The key difference between the two legislatures is that devolution has banished the House of Lords from Scottish law-making. Whereas Commons foxhunting bans perish in the Lords, there is no such second hurdle (which would have also blocked land reform) for Scottish laws to leap. Thus has the creation of the Scottish Parliament, in abolishing the role of privileged landed interest in law-making, completed, in Scotland ahead of the rest of Britain, reforms that began with the 1832 Reform Act.

This achievement, however, was lost in a cacophony of criticism that the Parliament was obsessed with political correctness, especially when Dewar's executive proposed to abolish the law which forbade local authorities from promoting homosexuality. This law, known as Section 28 or more correctly as Section 2A (of the 1986 Local Government Act), had been passed by a previous Conservative government apparently fearful that children were being corrupted by sinister homosexual teachers. In fact, it was not much more than a piece of senseless discrimination. That did not deter the *Daily Record* from savaging the move. Cardinal Winning, then leader of the Scottish Catholic Church, weighed in ferociously. Even more unexpectedly, Brian Souter, the wealthy owner of Stagecoach, a bus company, and also a fundamentalist Christian, spent a fortune on running a private postal referendum against the plan. The Dewar executive squirmed, but stuck to its guns and Section 2A was abolished.

ciously. Even more unexpectedly, Brian Souter, the wealthy owner of Stagecoach, a bus company, and also a fundamentalist Christian, spent a fortune on running a private postal referendum against the plan. The Dewar executive squirmed, but stuck to its guns and Section 2A was abolished.

This bruising episode, perhaps more than any other, seemed to convince McLeish and McConnell that it was better to avoid controversy. It is noticeable that the radical measures listed above – the Glasgow housing handover, the use of private finance in public construction, land reform – all stemmed from Dewar's administration. His successors – quite understandably given the ferocity of the media battering which threatened to fatally undermine the brand new Parliament – retreated into a cautious conservatism. That timidity, which created an impression that the executive was prone to caving in when under pressure, served them ill as it laid paths trodden by all manner of protestors – from fishermen demanding hand-outs for doing nothing to community groups demanding the preservation of inadequate hospitals. Quite remarkably, the executive so mishandled a scheme to spend £700m on modernising Glasgow's hospitals that Labour lost a seat, Strathkelvin and Bearsden, to a hospital campaigner in the 2003 election.

Another single issue campaign group – pensioners – also won a Central Scotland regional seat in those elections, quite incongruously as pensioners had benefited more than most from devolution. Pensioners gained the gradual extension of free bus travel, free personal care and free installation of central heating where it was lacking. But Falkirk and Motherwell pensioners evidently felt there should have been more.

The broad conclusion which emerges is that the Parliament's institutions have been a success, but the people occupying them have failed to live up to public expectations. Those expectations were, admittedly, unreasonably high but politicians, many of whom went into the Parliament, were also responsible for that. A charitable view would be that no one should have expected great things from 129 people mostly new to full-time politics. But voters are never charitable and the politicians will have to raise their game.

That might be not too bad a verdict on the first term of a new institution, but for one thing – the scandalously escalating costs of the Parliament's new home at Holyrood. From a ridiculously low figure of £40m estimated in the white paper on which the 1999 referendum was held, the bill has risen ten-fold to perhaps £400m and maybe even more. Even at the more realistic figure of £109m estimate given when the site and design became known, there has been a four-fold increase, and the delay on completion stretched to more than a year. What has been catastrophic for the reputation of the Parliament is that nobody has seemed able to control the costs. No sooner did the public get used to one new estimate, than another higher prediction came along. The public were quite entitled to ask, as they frequently did in the election, if the politicians were so incapable of managing the building of their own home, why should they be trusted to build a better Scotland? And that, in many ways, helps to sum up the first term: some brave gestures but much incompetence, much expectation but little fulfilment, and much trust invested but with little return. Like the Holyrood building, the foundations and structure of an impressively modern democracy were laid in the first term, but its fitting out with equally impressive people and policies has yet to be completed.

Peter Jones is the Scotland and North of England Correspondent of The Economist *and the author (with Christopher Harvie) of* The Road to Home Rule, *Polygon, Edinburgh, 2000.*

References

Bromley, C., Curtice, J., Hinds, K., and Park, A. (2003), *Devolution: Scottish Answers to Scottish Questions?*, Edinburgh University Press, Edinburgh.

Donaldson, W. (1989), *The Language of the People: Scots Prose from the Victorian Revival*, Aberdeen University Press, Aberdeen.

Hansard Society Commission on Parliamentary Scrutiny (2001), *The Challenge for Parliament: Making Government Accountable*, Vacher Dod Publishing, London.

Mitchell, J. et al. (2003), 'Third Year, Third First Minister' in R. Hazell (ed.) *The State of the Nations 2003: The Third Year of Devolution in the UK*, Imprint Academic, Essex, pp. 119-42.

The 2003 Election: Lessons for Devolution

John Curtice

The outcome off the 2003 Scottish Parliament election had three notable characteristics. The first was the turnout. Not only was it nearly nine percentage points lower than four years earlier, at 49.4 per cent it failed to reach the 50 per cent target that the First Minister himself had suggested needed to be met. The second feature was the distribution of party support. Support for both of Scotland's main political parties, Labour and the SNP, dropped substantially while both the Greens and the Scottish Socialist Party did well enough to secure significant representation. Meanwhile, the third feature was the re-election of the Labour-Liberal Democrat coalition. Yet this happened even though the two parties secured far less than 50 per cent of the vote.

In this chapter we consider what these features tell us about the health and character of Scotland's devolved institutions. What have we learnt about the public's attitudes towards devolution and the Scottish Parliament? How far does the advent of a rainbow Parliament signal a change in the character of Scottish politics? And what have we learnt about how the Parliament's additional member electoral system operates?

Turnout

There had been concern about the likely turnout in the election long before polling day dawned. After all, survey evidence had long suggested that the public felt the Parliament was not living up to the high expectations that they had had of it prior to its creation, and that Westminster still had more influence than Holyrood over what actually happens in Scotland (Bromley and Curtice, 2003). The level of turnout recorded in local elections has regularly registered the relative reluctance of voters to turn out and vote for institutions they do not consider to be very important.

But of course, a low turnout might not necessarily be a reflection of attitudes towards devolution. Other electoral contests, including not least the 2001 UK general election, have also experienced record low turnouts in recent years. How far this reflects a general disengagement amongst voters with politics, and how far it has been occasioned by the recent character of party competition in Britain is the subject of some debate (Bromley and Curtice, 2002). But whatever they are, those forces could still be acting to depress turnout in the 2003 Scottish election. And of course how the parties fought the 2003 election itself could also make a difference.

In fact, survey research commissioned by the Electoral Commission immediately after the election and undertaken by ICM confirms that the public remained doubtful about the importance of the Parliament at the time of the 2003 election (ICM, 2003). Just 24 per cent said that the believed that the Scottish Parliament has most influence over the way that Scotland is run, while as many as 50 per cent said the UK Government did. True, this represented a nine point increase in the proportion believing that the Scottish Parliament had most influence as compared with the figure obtained by the Scottish Social Attitudes survey two years previously, but it still compared starkly with the position at the time of the 1999 Scottish election, when no less than 41 per cent thought the Scottish Parliament would have most influence and only 39 per cent, the UK Government.

This attitude also fed into people's perceptions of how much difference the outcome of the election would make. In 1999, as many as 56 per cent said that it made 'a great deal' or 'quite a lot' of difference who won a Scottish Parliament election. By 2003 just 42 per cent felt that way. Of course, someone might believe that the outcome of an election does not make much difference because whoever won would pursue largely the same policy rather than because they thought the institution itself could not do very much. And indeed at 37 per cent the proportion thinking there was a great difference between Labour and the SNP was four points down on the proportion taking that view four years previously. But if that were the only reason why perceptions of the importance of the Scottish Parliament elections had declined we would expect to see a parallel fall in the perceived importance of the outcome of elections to the House of Commons. Yet the proportion thinking the outcome of these make a great deal or quite a lot of difference was, at 52 per cent, not only well above the proportion taking that view of Scottish Parliament elections, but was just three points down on the equivalent figure in 1999.

Unsurprisingly, this perception that the outcome of the election would not make much difference certainly made a difference to whether people voted or not. According to ICM's survey, no less than 73 per cent of those who said that the outcome of a Scottish Parliament election made a great deal or quite a lot of difference made it to the polls on 1 May 2003, whereas only 40 per cent of those who said it did not make very much or any difference at all did so. In short, at least one important reason why turnout was so low in 2003 was because the Scottish Parliament is not regarded as sufficiently important to bother (albeit perhaps not as unimportant as the National Assembly for Wales for which only 38 per cent turned out to vote in 2003). Such an outcome can only be regarded as a disappointment for those who hoped that devolution would help reconnect the Scottish public with their political system.

Not however that all the blame should be laid – directly at least – at the Parliament's door. One of the striking findings of the ICM survey was that 37 per cent said they had received too little information about the party leaders whereas less than a quarter of voters across Britain as a whole said the same thing after the 2001 UK general election. Moreover one of the persistent findings of the campaign opinion polls was that many people lacked strong impressions of the party leaders, Tommy Sheridan perhaps excepted. Thus, for example, System Three found that 38 per cent were unable to say who the most trustworthy party leader was, while two surveys conducted towards the end of the campaign by YouGov found 35 per cent and 29 per cent unable to say which leader impressed them most (Curtice, 2003). And this failure of the leaders to make an impression seems to have discouraged voters from going to the polls. As many as 67 per cent of those who said they received the right amount of information went to the polls, compared with only 46 per cent of those who said they had received too little.

So Scots stayed away from the polls not only because they were none too sure that the Parliament mattered, but also because the choice of leaders laid out before them appeared none too impressive. Of course we can speculate about whether a relatively unimportant legislature necessarily engenders relatively uninspiring leaders. But the Parliament would certainly benefit from a larger dose of charisma amongst its senior membership.

Party Support

For the most part the disappointing performance of the SNP secured more attention than the decline in Labour's support. Yet Labour's performance was hardly much better than the Nationalists. On the first vote, the decline in Labour's share of the vote compared with 1999 was, at 4.2 per cent, only slightly less than the 4.9 per cent drop suffered by the SNP. And even on the second vote Labour's share fell by 4.3 per cent to less than 30 per cent, while the SNP's dropped by 6.4 per cent.

Moreover, Labour's share of the vote in 1999 had already been well below what the party expected to achieve in UK general elections in Scotland. Some people who were willing to vote Labour in a UK general election demonstrated a reluctance to do so in a Scottish Parliament contest, a result, it seemed, of a belief that the party would not use the Parliament to stand up for the interests of Scotland (Paterson et al, 2001). That reluctance was still evident four years later. In the three months prior to polling day, six opinion polls, conducted by System Three, YouGov and Populus, all asked people how they intended to vote in a Westminster contest as well as how they would vote in a Scottish Parliament election. On average the proportion saying they would vote Labour in a UK general election was six points higher than the proportion who said they would do so on the first vote of a Scottish Parliament election.

So it appears that people are still voting differently in a Scottish Parliament election from the way that they would have done in a UK general election. That must be considered largely good news for the health of devolution. It suggests that the Parliament's mandate is not simply a clone of that received by Westminster. Some voters at least do provide a distinctively Scottish answer when asked a distinctively Scottish question in a distinctively Scottish election. But what of course also matters is whether the drop in Labour's support since 1999 also reflects a judgement on its performance in Holyrood over the last four years rather than reflecting disenchantment with the regime at Westminster. Certainly it is striking that the drop of just over four points in Labour's support is almost identical to the average drop of 4.7 per cent in the party's support in a BBC/*Economist* sample of the results of English local elections held on the same day. Perhaps Scotland was simply sending the same message to Downing Street as England, rather than casting a judgement on the work of the Executive.

In fact the public's evaluations of the work of the Executive were far from rosy. According to YouGov, 61 per cent believed that its record on the NHS was 'poor' or 'very poor', while only 34 per cent rated it 'excellent' or 'good'. There were similar negative evaluations of its record on public transport, law and order and agriculture. On the other hand its record on two of the Executive's most distinctive policies, care for the elderly (56 per cent excellent or good) and university tuition fees (49 per cent) were more favourable, though of course it is possible that the Liberal Democrats were given more credit for these than Labour. So it is possible at least that Labour lost ground because of its perceived record at Holyrood and not just because of a decline in the popularity of the Labour Government in London, but to demonstrate this conclusively will require further survey evidence than is currently available.

The SNP's decline, meanwhile, lead to speculation that perhaps devolution is finally helping to put the nationalist genie back into the bottle, and that the party would need to move away from its policy of independence for Scotland (even if only after a referendum) to a more Catalan strategy of seeking to enhance Scotland's relative autonomy within the United Kingdom. But this is probably a misreading of the election result. First, the ICM survey for the Electoral Commission found that support for independence is, at 24 per cent, much the same as it had been four years previously. Second, disappointing as it might have been, opinion poll evidence still suggests that, just as fewer people vote Labour in a Scottish Parliament election, the opposite continues to be true so far as the SNP is concerned. The Nationalists' share of the first vote in 2003 was, after all, still four points higher than it had been in the 2001 UK general election. And third, much of the damage to the SNP appears to have been done by the Scottish Socialist Party (SSP). In constituencies where the SSP share of the first vote was up by more than seven points on four years ago, the SNP's vote fell on average by no less than 6.4 per cent, whereas the constituencies where the SSP increase was less than 3.5 per cent, the SNP was down just 2.4 per cent. Labour's performance in contrast was not evidently affected by that of the SSP. It appears the SNP's difficulty was that those who in the past might have used a vote for the SNP as a means of expressing dissatisfaction with Labour now felt that a vote for the SSP was a more effective vehicle for articulating their views – rather than any new found reluctance to embrace its policy of independence.

Of course that is not to deny that continued success for the SSP might pose difficulties for the political ambitions of the SNP. Nor would it be correct to suggest that support for the SSP or the Greens was simply a means of expressing protest. Certainly the SSP and the Greens did best in precisely the kind of constituencies that one would expect them to, if their support was based on the policies that they promulgated – the Greens in places where a relatively large proportion of those with a university education, the SSP in constituencies with a relatively high proportion with characteristics commonly associated with social exclusion, such as being a lone parent or not being in good health.

But still, voters' willingness to vote for other than the big four parties was probably facilitated in part by the more effective opportunities to do so afforded by the Additional Member electoral system. Certainly by putting up no less than 75 lists, those who wished to challenge Scotland's political establishment demonstrated an apparent recognition that a party only needed to secure between 5 per cent and 6 per cent of the list vote in a region to secure a seat. The Greens concentrated their efforts entirely on securing list votes, and won no less than 6.9 per cent. Whereas on the first vote just 3.4 per cent voted for a smaller party other than the SSP or the Greens (albeit including victories for Independent candidates in Falkirk West and Strathkelvin & Bearsden) no less than 9 per cent did so on the party list vote. Even so, the SSP's share of the first vote was, at 6.2 per cent, almost the same as its share on the second, 6.7 per cent, even though the party did not contest three of the constituency contests. So not all of the defection from Scotland's four main parties can apparently be simply put down to the electoral system.

Meanwhile, one other possibility should also probably be discounted. This is that people were happy to experiment with voting for a small party because they thought the Scottish Parliament or the outcome of the Scottish Parliament election did not matter very much. At 23 per cent the proportion of those who felt that the outcome of a Scottish election made a great deal or quite a lot of difference who voted for someone other than the four main parties on the second vote was only a little lower than the 27 per cent who did so amongst those who felt the outcome made not very much or no difference at all. Whatever else it was, the rise in support for Scotland's smaller parties was not an exercise in frivolity.

Seats

The outcome of the 1999 election had already indicated that there were some significant constraints to the proportionality of the version of the Additional Member electoral system used to elect the Scottish Parliament. In particular, Labour won as many as 43 per cent of the seats despite winning just 34 per cent of the party list vote, which is the vote to which the system attempts to make the overall allocation of seats as proportional as possible. Not least of the reasons for this was that Labour won as many as seven more constituency seats than it would have secured if all the seats in each region had been allocated in accordance with the D'Hondt formula rather than just the seven top-up seats in each region (Curtice and Steed, 2000). In other words, the election result demonstrated that the typical ratio of seven top-up seats to nine constituency seats was often too small to produce a proportional outcome within a region.

This Labour 'over-representation' was also a feature of this election. And this time it also had significant consequences for the balance of power. Labour again won seven more seats than it should have done, and although it also lost a seat due to a similar overrepresentation of the Liberal Democrats in the Highlands and Islands, the party still obtained a net advantage of six seats in the constituency contests. This advantage accounted for half of the discrepancy between the 39 per cent of the seats that Labour captured and the 29 per cent of the list vote that it won. Most importantly, together with a one seat net advantage to the Liberal Democrats, this overrepresentation accounts entirely for the overall majority secured by the Labour-Liberal Democrat coalition. Without the seven extra seats this overrepresentation gave them, the coalition would have been five seats short of a majority rather than enjoying an overall majority of five.

Democrat coalition. Without the seven extra seats this overrepresentation gave them, the coalition would have been five seats short of a majority rather than enjoying an overall majority of five.

Thus two parties who between them secured just 41 per cent of the party list vote were able to secure an overall majority even though the Scottish Parliament is often described as a proportional one. It would seem that semi-proportional would be a better description of the system. There is certainly an irony about Liberal Democrat ministers helping to form part of a majority government on the basis of so small a share of the vote after many years of their party criticising the Westminster electoral system for giving Labour and the Conservatives overall majorities on the basis of not dissimilar shares of the vote.

Conclusion

The outcome of the 2003 election has further helped puncture some of the rhetoric and high expectations that surrounded the creation of the Scottish Parliament. Fewer people voted for it than did four years previously because the institution is perceived as being less powerful than they expected, a process further encouraged by the electorate being faced with what many regarded as largely an uninspiring set of political leaders. Meanwhile the electoral system proved not to be a barrier to Scotland being ruled by a majority government that had failed to secure half the vote.

But at the same time the election demonstrated that devolved elections do make a difference. Although we cannot as yet be sure how far voters voted on the basis of the record of the Executive over the previous four years, it does appears that, as in 1999, voters did not simply vote in the same way as they would in a UK general election. And in part, at least, the different electoral system used in elections to the Scottish Parliament has helped generate a greater diversity of political expression and representation than has yet been seen at Westminster. As to whether the more diverse character of the Parliament will help raise the stature of the Parliament in the eyes of voters or, in contrast, do it harm, we will, however, have to wait and see.

John Curtice is Professor of Politics at Strathclyde University.

References

Bromley, C. and Curtice, J. (2002), 'Where have all the voters gone?', in A. Park, J. Curtice, K. Thomson, L. Jarvis and C. Bromley (eds), *British Social Attitudes: the 19th Report*, Sage, London, pp.141-67.

Bromley, C. and Curtice, J. (2003), 'Devolution: Scorecard and Prospects', in C. Bromley, J. Curtice, K. Hinds and A. Park (eds), *Devolution: Scottish Answers to Scottish Questions?*, Edinburgh University Press. Edinburgh, pp. 7-29.

Curtice, J. and Steed, M. (2000), 'And now for the Commons? Lessons from Britain's First Experience with Proportional Representation', *British Elections and Parties Review*, 10, pp. 192-215.

Curtice, J. (2003), 'Elections and Attitudes towards Parties', in *Scotland Devolution Monitoring Report*, May 2003. Available from http://www.ucl.ac.uk/constitution-unit/leverh/monitoring.htm

ICM (2003), *Scottish Elections Research May-June 2003* Edinburgh: The Electoral Commission. Available at http://www.electoralcommission.gov.uk/

Paterson, L., Curtice, J., Hinds, K., McCrone, D., Sproston, K., Surridge, P,. and Park, A., (2001), *New Scotland, New Politics?* Polygon, Edinburgh.

A Guide to Scotland's Parliamentary Constituencies, MSPs and MPs

The following section contains an in-depth guide to Scotland's 72 Westminster first past the past constituencies and 73 Scottish Parliament constituencies. It also contains comprehensive profiles of all the first past the post MPs and MSPs for these seats, with profiles of regional list MSP profiles contained in the following section. Each constituency contains a set of socio-economic indicators, tables and statistics, and the following guide, explains the definitions used and sources.

Sources

- *Constituency Population aged 16-64 years 2001:* From 2001 Census.
- *Claimant Count as a Percentage of Working Age Population May 2003:* From NOMIS (Population Denominator from 2001 census).
- *Incapacity Benefit/Severe Disablement Allowance Claimants as a Percentage of Working Age Population February 2003:* From Department of Work and Pensions.
- *Life Expectancy at Birth 1999-2001:* From Health Scotland (using 2001 census populations) (including persons living in communal establishments) and GRO (S) Death Registrations 1999-2001 and applying Chiang II Methodology as devised by ONS 2003).
- *Housing Tenure Definitions 2001:* Owner occupied includes either owned outright, owned with a mortgage or loan, or paying part rent and part mortgage.
- *Socially rented excluded privately rented:* From 2001 Census (SCROL).
- *Average Property Prices 2001:* From Communities Scotland (original data supplied to Communities Scotland by Land Valuation Information Unit, Paisley University).
- *Average Gross Household Income 2001:* From Communities Scotland (original data supplied to Communities Scotland by CACI).
- *Low Birthweight Babies 1999-2001:* Definition of low birthweight babies is 1,500 to 2,500 grammes. From Scottish Neighbourhood Statistics website: www.sns.gov.uk. Crown copyright material is reproduced with the permission of the Controller of HMSO.
- *Teenage Pregnancy Rates for 13-19 year olds 1999-2001:* From Scottish Neighbourhood Statistics website: www.sns.gov.uk Crown copyright material is reproduced with the permission of the Controller of HMSO.
- *No of Lone Parent Households 2001:* From 2001 Census (SCROL).

CAB Enquiries

There are 52 Citizens Advice Bureux across Scotland. The following CAB categories are used to record the work of local bureaux throughout Scotland and contain the following issues:

- *Benefits:* Income Support, Housing, Sickness, Council Tax, Social Fund, Unemployment/Job Seekers Allowance, Family Credit/Working Families Tax Credit, Child Support, Retirement Pension, Debts, Community Charge, National Insurance Contributions, Discrimination, Other.
- *Consumer:* Debt, Good and Services, Credit and Finance, Insurance, Discrimination, Other.
- *Employment:* Terms and Conditions, Dismissal, Redundancy, Self-employment, Debts, Unemployment Schemes, Discrimination, Others.
- *Housing:* Debts, Environment/Neighbour, Conditions, Threatened Homelessness, Actual Homelessness, Costs (Non-arrears), Security of Tenure, Discrimination.
- *Legal:* Access to Justice, Injury Compensation, Legal Aid, Debts, Discrimination.
- *Relationships:* Separation, Children, Death and Bereavement, Debts, Discrimination
- *Tax:* Council Tax, Income Tax, Community Charge, Discrimination.
- *Other:* Issues relating to Community Care, Education, Health, Immigration, Nationality, Miscellaneous, or Signposting.

Debt is not a category itself, but is recorded across each category (e.g. consumer debt, employment debt, housing debt) and separately tallied. It is only listed in constituency profiles where this figure is seen as unusual.

Electoral Profiles

- *2003 Scottish Parliament Election:*
  Comparison of vote share is with the 1999 Scottish Parliament election.
- *2001 Westminster Election:*
  Comparison of vote share is with the 1997 Westminster election.

All 2003 and 2001 figures are taken from the Electoral Commission.

Electoral Contests 1945 Onwards

- *Abbreviations:*
  B – By-election
  1974 F – February 1974
  1974 0 – October 1974

Aberdeen Central

Predecessor Constituencies: created anew for the 1997 general election.

Socio-economic Indicators:

Constituency Pop. (16-64)	48,573
Claimant Count (May 2003)	2.2% (28.7% below average)
IBA/SDA Claimants	9.1%
Life Expectancy – Male	72.0 (1.4 yrs below average)
Life Expectancy – Female	78.2 (0.5 yrs below average)
Owner Occupied	48.7%
Social Rented	32.7%
Average Property Prices	£63,555 (31st)
Average Gross Income	£27,290 (21st)
Low Birthweight Babies	124 (6.6%)
Teenage Pregnancy Rates	516 (5.5%)
No. of Lone Parent Households	2,539 (7.4%)

CAB Enquiries

Issue	No. of cases	Percentage of total cases (%)
1. Consumer	4156	22.9
2. Employment	3468	19.1
3. Benefits	3444	19.0
4. Legal	1847	10.2
5. Housing	1771	9.8

2003 Scottish Parliament Election

Electorate: 49,501   *Turnout*: 20,964 (42.4%)   *1999 Turnout*: 50.3%

Candidate	Party	Votes	Votes%	99 %	Change%
Lewis Macdonald	Labour	6,835	32.6	38.9	– 6.3
Richard Lochhead	SNP	5,593	26.7	28.7	– 2.0
Eleanor Anderson	Lib Dem	4,744	22.6	16.6	+ 6.0
Alan Butler	Con	2,616	12.5	13.8	– 1.3
Andy Cumbers	SSP	1,176	5.6	2.0	+ 3.6

Labour majority: 1,242 (5.9%)   *Swing*: 2.1% Labour to SNP

2001 General Election

Electorate: 50,190   Turnout: 26,429 (52.7%)   1997 Turnout: 65.6%

Candidate	Party	Votes	Votes%	'97 Votes%	Change%
Frank Doran	Labour	12,025	45.5	49.8	- 4.3
Wayne Gault	SNP	5,379	20.4	16.2	+ 4.2
Eleanor Anderson	Lib Dem	4,547	17.2	13.2	+ 4.0
Stewart Whyte	Con	3,761	14.2	19.5	- 5.3
Andy Cumbers	SSP	717	2.8	–	–

Labour majority: 6,646 (25.1%)   *Swing*: 4.2% Labour to SNP

Aberdeen – the Granite City – is Scotland's third city in status and size after Glasgow and Edinburgh and the economic and social hub of Grampian and the North-East. Its politics have, since the mid-1970s and the discovery of North Sea Oil, been shaped by the resulting economic boom in jobs, house prices and growth in population. This has, of course, meant good times and bad times for the city dependent on the fluctuating level of oil prices, but what is interesting is that for all the potency of the 'It's Scotland's Oil' message, the SNP has not made headway in the city until recently.

Aberdeen Central is the least prosperous of the city's three seats. Average property prices are 5.8 per cent below the national average having risen 50.2 per cent during the 1990s. However, it has witnessed major property development in recent years. Central sites being developed include the King Street bus depot and part of the Cornhill hospital site. The level of growth has raised local concerns about pressures on local public services, in particular schools, hospitals and roads. Traffic congestion remains a major local issue, and it did not help when large parts of Union Street were closed for most of 2002 due to a building collapsing.

Grampian Health Board has faced problems with hospital beds being taken up by elderly people waiting for places in nursing homes in the city, and with the Health Board over-stretching its budget, there have been recent fears Aberdeen Royal Infirmary may have to make some of its workforce redundant.

Aberdeen CAB is situated in Central and covers enquiries from all three Aberdeen seats, and shows that consumer and employment issues are the top issues, while the lower level of benefit issues reflects the lower reliance on benefits in the area.

Aberdeen Football Club is based in the constituency at Pitoddrie Stadium and was famously successful under the tutelage of Alex Ferguson in the 1980s. They applied as part of Scotland's Euro 2008 bid to move from Pitoddrie to a £30 million stadium at the out-of-town site of Kingswell. This met significant local opposition from local residents worried about traffic congestion.

Aberdeen City Council has major concerns about over-dependence on the oil industry, and has hosted a series of initiatives to attempt to aid the diversification of the local economy. Aberdeen Network, an alliance of the city council, employers and the city's two universities, has taken the lead in developing a diversification strategy. The decision of the Scottish Executive to place a Scottish Energy Initiative in the city was widely welcomed with the potential to bring civil service jobs and win research and development monies. Local politicians believe Aberdeen as a city region loses out to the Highlands and Islands with European funds and to the Central Belt in relation to the Scottish Parliament and Westminster, and believe that they have less influence and clout than these other areas.

The Aberdeen Central seat contains such working class areas as Seaton, Linksfield, Balgownie and Tillydrone, as well as the more affluent areas of Rosemount, Queen's Cross, Harlaw and Rubislaw. Apart from the city centre, the seat also contains the University of Aberdeen – one of Scotland's oldest and grandest universities.

In 1995, when the boundary changes for the new Central seat were announced, Labour's Frank Doran, (previously MP for Aberdeen South from 1987-92) stood for the Labour nomination against Bob Hughes who had been MP for Aberdeen North since 1970. In a bitter and acrimonious selection, Doran emerged the victor by one vote and then went on to win the seat easily. In the 1997 election Doran gained an impressive majority of 10,810 over the Conservatives. In 2001 Doran easily held the seat for Labour at Westminster although Labour's vote fell by 5,500 and 4 per cent, while the SNP moved from third to a distant second – losing 400 votes on a lower turnout.

At the 1999 Scottish Parliament election, support for the SNP increased dramatically with a rise in Richard Lochhead's vote by 1,842 and nearly 13 per cent. Labour's vote declined by over 7,000 votes, giving Lewis Macdonald a majority of 2,696. This was enough to give both parties the hope that they could build on this at the next election. The May 2003 Scottish Parliament elections witnessed Labour hold this seat by an uncomfortably narrow margin. Lewis Macdonald saw his vote fall by 3,500 and 6 per cent, while Richard Lochhead was unable to make any major headway, losing 2,000 votes and 2 per cent. Labour's majority was cut in half to 1,242. The Nationalists managed a 2.1 per cent swing from Labour, but had required 5.1 per cent to win. The real winners in the election were the Lib Dems, who put 6 per cent on their vote. In the regional vote Labour won 26.6 per cent to the SNP's 22.6 per cent, while the Greens polled 7.4 per cent and the SSP 6.1 per cent.

At the next election, Boundary Commission proposals for Westminster would see this seat merged with Aberdeen North into a new North seat with Labour favourites to hold. Here, the aspect of most interest may be the internal machinations of Labour selection procedures as Frank Doran and Malcolm Savidge compete for one seat. At the Scottish Parliament's future elections, this seat does not look a safe prospect for Labour. The city is turning significantly to the SNP and Lib Dems and the former have established themselves as the main challengers to Labour for the Scottish Parliament seat.

MSP

LEWIS MacDONALD was born in Stornoway in 1957, but grew up in the North East of Scotland as a son of the manse. He attended Inverurie Academy and gained a history degree from Aberdeen University, followed by a doctorate in African studies from Lagos University, Nigeria. He joined the Labour Party in 1980 and has been a member of the party's Scottish Executive. He was employed as a researcher for MP Frank Doran from 1987-92 and 1997-99. He was a lecturer in history at Aberdeen University from 1992-93 and worked as a shadow cabinet adviser for Tom Clarke from 1993-97, when the Lanarkshire MP was covering Scotland, international development and disability. Macdonald contested the Moray constituency at the 1997 Westminster election.

In winning the Labour candidacy for Aberdeen Central, he saw off Lord Sewel, a former Aberdeen Council leader and, at that time, a Scottish Office minister. Securing the marginal seat, Macdonald played a vocal role on both the audit and education committees of the Scottish Parliament until October 2000. That year, when the Holyrood building project hit one of its earlier crisis points, it was continued only on condition that a progress group of MSPs and building experts was set up to monitor it. Macdonald was made convener, but only after the SNP refused to let George Reid take the post for fear of its unpopularity rebounding on his party. However, that appointment was also a sign that Macdonald was on the fast-track to ministerial office. In a March 2002 reshuffle, Henry McLeish made him transport and planning minister, as deputy to Sarah Boyack. Under Jack McConnell, he continued in the transport brief, as deputy first to Wendy Alexander and then Iain Gray at enterprise, transport and lifelong learning. It put him in a strong position to ensure a pre-2003 election promise of Executive support for a western peripheral road for Aberdeen. Following the election, he continued in that department, but without the transport role, having special responsibility for energy instead. This may prove sensitive with pressure for a new nuclear power plant in Scotland. Macdonald once admitted on STV's *Seven Days* that his favourite song of all time was 'Imagine' by the Beatles (even though it was a John Lennon solo recording).

MP

FRANK DORAN was born in Edinburgh in 1949, and educated at Ainslie Park Secondary and Leith Academy, Edinburgh. He then studied law at Dundee University. There, he became active in local Labour politics alongside George Galloway, with whom he was drawn into a financial row involving Dundee Labour Club after the 1987 election. The issue was the subject of a Channel Four programme and Tayside Police investigations.

Doran was a solicitor from 1977-87, standing unsuccessfully as Labour's North East Scotland candidate in the 1984 European election. He was elected to the Commons in 1987, representing Aberdeen South, and was Opposition spokesperson on energy from 1988-92, urging better oil rig safety in the aftermath of the Piper Alpha disaster. He also became part of the left-wing dissenters 'Supper Club' which had John Prescott and Margaret Beckett as its most prominent members. After the Conservatives regained his seat in 1992 – the party's only Scottish loss that year – he worked as a researcher for his partner, Joan Ruddock, MP for Lewisham Deptford and previously CND chair, while he co-ordinated the campaign for trade unionists to vote for political funds, as required under new Tory legislation. With boundary changes, he ousted Aberdeen North's MP, Bob Hughes, in a 1995 selection battle for Aberdeen Central, regaining a seat in the Commons in 1997. He was Parliamentary Private Secretary to Ian McCartney at the Department of Trade and Industry in 1997-98, then moving with him to work at the Cabinet Office until 2001. Since that year's election, he has been a member of the culture, media and sport select committee, while active in all-party groups on fisheries and oil and gas. On the knife-edge issue of top-up fees for students in England, he signed an early-day motion criticising the policy but voted for it in January 2004.

Aberdeen North

Predecessor Constituencies: none.

Socio-economic Indicators:

Constituency Pop. (16-64)	45,964
Claimant Count (May 2003)	1.4% (53.9% below average)
IBA/SDA Claimants	7.5%
Life Expectancy – Male	73.8 (0.4 yrs above average)
Life Expectancy – Female	79.4 (0.7 yrs above average)
Owner Occupied	65.1%
Social Rented	28.9%
Average Property Prices	£61,755(32nd)
Average Gross Income	£27,551 (20th)
Low Birthweight Babies	156 (7.0%)
Teenage Pregnancy Rates	466(4.7%)
No. of Lone Parent Households	2,917 (10.5%)

2003 Scottish Parliament Election

Electorate: 52,919   *Turnout*: 25,027 (47.3%)

Candidate	Party	Votes	Votes%	99 %	Change%
Brian Adam	SNP	8,381	33.5	35.7	– 2.2
Elaine Thomson	Labour	7,924	31.7	37.2	– 5.5
John Reynolds	Lib Dem	5,767	23.0	17.1	+ 5.9
James Gifford	Con	2,311	9.2	10.0	– 0.7
Katrine Trolle	SSP	644	2.6	–	–

SNP majority: 457 (1.8%)   *Swing*: 1.6% Labour to SNP

2001 General Election

Electorate: 52,876   *Turnout*: 30,357 (57.4%)   *Turnout 1999*: 51.0%

Candidate	Party	Votes	Votes%	Change%
Malcolm Savidge	Labour	13,157	43.3	– 4.5
Alisdair Allan	SNP	8,708	28.7	+ 6.9
Jim Donaldson	Lib Dem	4,991	16.4	+ 2.3
Richard Cowling	Con	3,047	10.0	– 5.0
Shona Foreman	SSP	454	1.5	–

Labour majority: 4,449 (14.7%)   *Swing*: 5.7% Labour to SNP

1945–97 Westminter

	Lab%	Con%	SNP%	Lib%	Other%	Turnout%
1997	47.9	15.0	21.8	14.1	1.2	70.7
1992	47.0	17.1	24.0	11.9	—	66.5
1987	54.7	14.3	13.2	17.8	–	70.0
1983	47.0	18.1	9.3	24.7	0.9	65.0
1979	59.3	17.0	12.9	10.8	–	69.7
1974(O)	50.9	11.3	29.7	8.1	–	69.7
1974(F)	47.7	16.7	23.3	12.3	–	75.5
1970	62.0	22.0	8.4	6.4	1.2	69.9
1966	67.5	20.6	–	10.2	1.7	72.1
1964	68.9	31.1	–	–	–	74.8
1959	64.5	29.7	5.8	–	–	76.7
1955	67.0	33.0	–	–	–	74.6
1951	64.7	35.3	–	–	–	82.9
1950	60.5	30.0	–	6.8	2.7	82.9
1945	69.6	25.1	5.3	–	–	67.2

Despite its name, most of Aberdeen North lies outside the boundaries of the city, comprising such working class estates as Mastrick and Northfield, and areas such as Daneston, Persley and Bucksburn. Aberdeen's international airport, Dyce is also in the constituency and has grown impressively as a result of the oil boom.

There are significant pressures on local services due to the growth in the area and average property prices have risen 40.8 per cent in the last ten years. Traffic congestion is one of the high profile issues in Aberdeen, and after years of lobbying and campaigning, the Scottish Executive agreed to plans for an Aberdeen ring road – something long advocated by the local business community and Aberdeen Chamber of Commerce in particular. In early 2002 the closure of Granholm Bridge in Persley caused chaos and gridlock with thousands of commuters suffering delays in travel to work times.

Despite the low unemployment levels, there have been several sizeable job losses in the constituency. Granholm Mills, a paper mill, shut in 2001 with all 260 employees losing their jobs and the site will be developed into a housing estate. McIntosh of Dyce, a meat processing company, had to call in the receivers threatening 300 jobs, with a management buy-out eventually safeguarding 50 jobs in ready meals, while the bakeries' sale saved another 75. The oil industry has not been immune to such announcements, and in 2002 BP shed 200 staff at its North Sea offices based at Dyce.

Aberdeen North was, until recent years, a rock-solid Labour seat. The boundary changes which occurred before the 1997 election substantially changed its political complexion. Bringing in 20,000 voters from the Lib Dem seat of Gordon produced a constituency with a lot more competition and potential for upset. In particular Bridge of Don and Dyce – two of the added areas – had significant areas of Lib Dem support.

Labour first won Aberdeen North in 1918 and William Wedgwood Benn, Tony Benn's father, won the seat in a 1928 by-election for Labour, holding it until 1931. Hector Hughes secured the seat for Labour in 1945 until retiring at the 1970 election. Bob Hughes followed in his footsteps, gaining a reputation as an old-fashioned Tribunite left-winger and a committed anti-apartheid campaigner. He represented the seat from 1970 until 1997. After Bob Hughes attempted and failed to secure the Labour nomination of the safer Aberdeen Central, the newly selected Labour candidate was Malcolm Savidge, who held the seat comfortably in 1997 in spite of the boundary changes. In the 2001 Westminster election Savidge was again safely returned. However, even at this election his majority over the SNP was slashed by over half. Boundary Commission proposals at Westminster see the merger of Aberdeen Central and North in a new North seat which will probably assist Labour's electoral hold.

At the Scottish Parliament, Labour has come under renewed and successful challenge from the SNP and the Lib Dems in a much more competitive party politics than the kind it is used to for Westminster. An indication of Scottish Labour's changing fortunes in Aberdeen North is that between 1945-70 Labour averaged a polling of 65 per cent. It took until the February 1974 election for Labour to poll under 50 per cent in this seat. The Nationalists ran Labour desperately close in the 1999 election, in what should have been a safe Labour seat. Elaine Thomson held on by a mere 398 votes – far removed from the 10,010 majority of 1997. Brian Adam, a well-known local councillor increased the SNP vote by more than 1,500 votes and 14 per cent. In 2003 the SNP needed a 0.7 per cent swing to win what was their second target seat after Dundee West, and just managed to do it. The question in Aberdeen North will be whether the SNP and Brian Adam can convert their recent narrow victory into a permanent SNP hold.

MSP

BRIAN ADAM was born in 1948 in Newmill and educated at Keith Grammar School and Aberdeen University, with a BSc in biochemistry in 1970 and another BSc, this one 21 years later, in clinical pharmacology. From 1970-73, he was a section leader with QA Laboratory, Glaxo, and from 1973-88 a biochemist then senior biochemist with Aberdeen City Hospital. He moved to Aberdeen Royal Infirmary from 1988-99 as senior and then principal biochemist. He was a councillor on Aberdeen City Council from 1988-96 and on its unitary successor from 1995-99, as his party's group leader throughout that time. Adam first stood for Westminster in Gordon in 1992, finishing a distant third. He first contested the Aberdeen North constituency, which included his council ward at the Westminster election of 1997, finishing a far off second to Malcolm Savidge. However, in 1999, Adam achieved a 12 per cent swing against Labour and went on narrowly to secure the seat in 2003.

Adam is the only representative of the Mormon faith in the Scottish Parliament, which helps to explain a conservative positioning on some social issues. He identified his most important achievement in the first Parliament as successfully lobbying for the Western Peripheral Route for Aberdeen – though there are many laying claim to getting that on the political map. The amiable new constituency MSP is a relatively low profile figure in the SNP group, who has never been identified as a high-flyer or part of the party leadership clique. However, as one of the few SNP politicians to be able to win a Labour urban seat, he must be doing something which the SNP needs to appreciate if it is to succeed. In the 1999-2003 Parliament Adam sat on the Parliament's audit committee and social inclusion committee from 1999-2000 and on the finance committee from 2001-2003. He was SNP deputy whip from 1999-2001 and deputy spokesperson on finance from 2001-2003, and convener of the all-party group on tobacco. Following the 2003 election, he was put on the enterprise and culture committee, and made his party's deputy spokesman on education and lifelong learning. Then, in October 2003, he replaced Tricia Marwick as convenor of the standards committee, after she had lost other members' confidence. Adam has five children.

MP

MALCOLM SAVIDGE was born in Redhill, Surrey in 1946, and educated at Wallingham Grammar School, Aberdeen University and Aberdeen College of Education. He was a maths teacher in Peterhead and Aberdeen from 1971-97, and was an activist in the Educational Institute of Scotland. He joined the Labour Party in 1972 and was a district councillor in Aberdeen from 1980-96. He was finance convenor, policy vice-convenor and deputy leader of Aberdeen District Council from 1994-96. He contested the Kincardine and Deeside by-election in 1991, where he faced gentle ridicule for his charisma-free approach, finishing fourth while the Lib Dem Nicol Stephen won. Savidge stood in 1992, and came fourth again, before being selected for Aberdeen North in 1995. In his maiden speech to the Commons in 1997, he made a plea for all Scotland's political parties to back a Scottish Parliament given that all Scotland's MPs did, while also making a special plea for an Aberdeen ring road.

Having lived down to his reputation as a faceless, characterless and slightly eccentric Blairite loyalist in the first Parliament (his interests include real ale and heraldry), he was transformed by his 2001 re-election and found his voice. It seems the Labour Government's fudging of Lords reform in 2000 was a turning point for him. He took on a much higher profile: while he backed the UK intervention in Sierra Leone in 2000, and was willing to support UN action and policing of the no-fly zone over Iraq, Savidge was a more vocal opponent of war in Iraq than most Labour rebels. His repeated TV appearances also gained him an audience outside Scotland. He continued his rebelliousness into votes against foundation hospitals in England in May and July 2003. He abstained on the vital vote on the issue in December 2003, and after signing a rebellious early-day motion on top-up tuition fees for students in England, he also abstained on that knife-edge vote in January 2004.

Aberdeen South

Predecessor Constituencies: none.

Socio-economic Indicators:

Constituency Pop. (16–64)	50,384
Claimant Count (May 2003)	1.8% (43.0% below average)
IBA/SDA Claimants	6.8%
Life Expectancy – Male	75.7 (2.3 yrs above average)
Life Expectancy – Female	80.2 (1.5 yrs above average)
Owner Occupied	69.9%
Social Rented	19.4%
Average Property Prices	£80,012 (13th)
Average Gross Income	£31,971 (3rd)
Low Birthweight Babies	136 (5.8%)
Teenage Pregnancy Rates	364 (4.2%)
No. of Lone Parent Households	2,498 (7.2%)

2003 Scottish Parliament Election

Electorate: 59,025 *Turnout*: 30,124 (51.7%) *Turnout 1999*: 57.3%

Candidate	Party	Votes	Votes%	99 %	Change%
Nicol Stephen	Lib Dem	13,821	45.9	32.6	+13.3
Richard Baker	Labour	5,805	19.3	27.5	– 8.2
Ian Duncan	Con	5,230	17.4	20.2	– 2.8
Maureen Watt	SNP	4,315	14.3	19.2	– 4.8
Keith Farnsworth	SSP	953	3.2	–	–

Lib Dem majority: 8,016 (26.6%) *Swing*: 10.7% Labour to Lib Dem

2001 General Election

Electorate: 59,025 *Turnout*: 36,890 (62.5%)

Candidate	Party	Votes	Votes%	Change%
Anne Begg	Labour	14,696	39.8	+ 4.6
Ian Yuitt	Lib Dem	10,308	27.9	+ 0.3
Moray Macdonald	Con	7,098	19.2	– 7.1
Ian Angus	SNP	4,293	11.6	+ 1.9
David Watt	SSP	495	1.3	–

Labour majority: 4,388 (11.9%) *Swing*: 2.1% Lib Dem to Labour

1945–97 Westminster

	Lab%	Con%	SNP%	Lib%	Other%	Turnout%
1997	35.3	26.4	9.8	27.6	1.0	72.8
1992	34.8	48.5	15.1	11.6	–	69.8
1987	37.7	34.8	6.6	20.9	–	67.2
1983	29.9	38.9	5.0	26.2	–	68.7
1979	39.2	40.7	8.5	11.6	–	78.6
1974(O)	34.8	35.3	20.6	9.6	–	76.3
1974(F)	33.2	39.6	13.5	13.7	–	82.1
1970	45.3	45.4	5.3	6.0	–	77.2
1966	46.0	42.5	–	11.5	–	81.3
1964	43.9	51.7	4.4	–	–	81.0
1959	36.6	53.8	–	9.6	–	81.6
1955	42.3	57.7	–	–	–	80.2
1951	41.3	58.7	–	–	–	82.7
1950	35.5	53.7	–	10.8	–	84.9
1946B	45.2	54.8	–	–	–	65.6
1945	42.3	46.8	–	10.9	–	71.9

Aberdeen South's socio-economic profile shows this to be the most affluent of the three Aberdeen seats. The claimant count is the lowest proportion of working age population on benefits in the city and average property prices have risen 55.2 per cent in the 1990s. Aberdeen South contains Aberdeen harbour which has been transformed over the last two decades into a major international oil industry facility. At the same time, the traditional industry of fishing has been in steep decline, crippled by decades of over-fishing and European Union restrictions, which have meant that the industry is shaped by the growing number of boats being decommissioned and debates over support schemes.

There was recent controversy over proposals to shut Tor-na-Dee hospital at Milltimber, which is the only convalescent hospital in Scotland. Grampian Health Board has said that it wishes to relocate the services provided by the current hospital to a new facility, and this led to a local campaign to save the hospital. A particularly popular visitor attraction is Duthie Park, which has won numerous awards for its rose displays and winter gardens. Indeed, the city of Aberdeen prides itself on its skills in public floral displays, and has won the Britain in Bloom flower competition several times.

Aberdeen South constituency was substantially altered by the boundary changes prior to the 1997 general election. The seat lost Conservative wards to Aberdeen Central – Queen's Cross, Rosemount and Rubislaw – while gaining wards from the Conservative-Lib Dem marginal Kincardine and Deeside. Working class areas from this Lib Dem-held seat such as Kincorth and Nigg have reverted back to Labour, while the Lib Dems have strong support in the Bridge of Dee area and affluent communities such as Cults and Peterculter.

Historically, Aberdeen South was Conservative, with comfortable majorities from 1918 to 1966. The delightful sounding old Tory Lady Tweedsmuir was Conservative MP from her victory at a by-election in 1946 until 1966 when Donald Dewar defeated her at Harold Wilson's high tide. This was a brief interlude, as Dewar experienced his first and only election defeat when he was thrown out by the Conservative Iain Sproat in 1970. Sproat then abandoned Aberdeen South in 1983 due to boundary changes making it more vulnerable and headed south to fight what he thought was the more favourable Conservative territory of Roxburgh and Berwickshire in the Borders. This proved to be a remarkable misjudgement on every level. Not only did Gerry Malone, the new Conservative candidate in Aberdeen South, successfully hold the seat with a 3,581 majority over Labour, but Sproat lost Roxburgh and Berwickshire to Archy Kirkwood. Sproat became MP for Harwick in 1992 and lost one of the safest Tory seats in the UK partly due to a large Referendum Party vote.

The Aberdeen seat changed hands at a succession of four elections through the 1980s and 1990s. It was won in 1987 by Frank Doran for Labour over the Conservatives' Gerry Malone – one of several affluent, middle class Conservative seats Scottish Labour gained that year. Malone was also known for addressing the 1987 UK Conservative conference and pleading with Prime Minister Margaret Thatcher in typical Tory sycophantic style to implement the poll tax in England and Wales in one go, rather than in stages. She and the Tory leadership listened – to their own cost.

Doran only held Aberdeen South for Labour for five years, losing to the Conservative Raymond Robertson in 1992 by 1,517 votes. This was the only seat in the whole of the UK which the Conservatives gained from Labour that year – although they also won back the neighbouring Kincardine and Deeside which they had lost in a 1991 by-election to the Lib Dems. On the back of these two victories, the Scottish Conservatives – having been faced with dire predictions of a wipeout – spun the result as the turning point of their long-term decline. Their two seats increase and gain of 1.7 per cent turned out instead to be a mere blip before the momentous events of 1997. Aberdeen South was re-won by Anne Begg for Labour in the 1997 landslide with Raymond Robertson, the sitting MP, relegated to third place. In June 2001 Begg was again comfortably returned.

In the first Scottish Parliament elections of May 1999, the seat was won by Nicol Stephen for the Lib Dems. This was only one of three FPTP seats to change party hands in the 1999 elections – the other two being Inverness East, Nairn and Lochaber and Falkirk West. In the 2003 Scottish Parliament election, Aberdeen South seemed to move into the category of a safe Lib Dem seat with Nicol Stephen putting 13 per cent on the Lib Dem support as Labour's vote fell by 8 per cent – one of the party's worst showings in the country. In the regional list vote, the Lib Dems won 31.4 per cent to 19.8 per cent for Labour, while the Greens won 5.6 per cent and SSP 3.8 per cent.

Boundary Commission changes for Westminster see relatively little change to Aberdeen South – with it taking a few wards from Aberdeen Central to become a larger seat – but this will have no political consequences and not affect Labour's majority. At the Scottish Parliament, Aberdeen South has shifted relatively quickly from a three-way marginal between Lib Dems, Labour and Conservatives to a Lib Dem safe seat, reflecting the ability of the Lib Dems to win and retain seats in this part of the country.

MSP

NICOL STEPHEN was born in Aberdeen in 1963. He was educated at Robert Gordon's College, Aberdeen, studied law at Aberdeen University and did his diploma at Edinburgh University. He practised as a solicitor for Milne and Mackinnon from 1983-99, was senior manager at Touche Ross corporate finance from 1988-91, and was director of Glassbox Ltd from 1992 until the 1999 Scottish election. He was a regional councillor in Grampian from 1986-92 and a founding director of Grampian Enterprise.

Stephen was Lib Dem MP for Kincardine and Deeside from 1991-92. Having contested it in the 1987 general election, he won the by-election caused by the death of Conservative MP Alick Buchanan-Smith. Then a safe Conservative seat, Stephen's breakthrough contributed considerably to the growing sense in the run-up to the 1992 election that the Tory Government's unpopularity would see disastrous Conservative results. As it turned out, when Stephen stood in the 1992 election, he lost it to Tory businessman George Kynoch, giving them enough momentum to be able to claim some legitimate grasp on power in Scotland for the next Westminster Parliament. Stephen stood in Aberdeen South in 1997, coming second to Labour's Anne Begg, before winning in 1999.

His looks are youthful and demeanour can be nervous. He is always canny about what he says, but is perhaps the most trusted lieutenant to Lib Dem leader Jim Wallace, being appointed to the ministerial team in 1999, and staying there as Wallace and Ross Finnie have also done. He was deputy minister for enterprise and lifelong learning in the Scottish Executive from 1999, handling the reform of student finance which had been the greatest source of disagreement between Labour and Lib Dems and which saw up-front tuition fees abolished, to be replaced with both a student endowment and grants for poorer students.

In the October 2000 reshuffle, Stephen became deputy minister for school education, plus Europe and external affairs, the two latter elements being the result of his cabinet boss, Jack McConnell, demanding to keep them in his portfolio. Stephen became involved in the latter stages of negotiations which led to a teachers' pay and conditions settlement. In 2001 Cathy Jamieson replaced McConnell when he became First Minister, the ministry changed to education and young people (without Europe and external affairs), and there was some astonishment that one of her first moves was to hand the schools brief to Stephen, while she got on with her first interest of policy for young people in care. He contributed to the Executive's national debate on education, which tended to conclude that the system was working fine, though Stephen took from it some ideas for the 2003 Lib Dem manifesto, such as a later start to primary school.

After the 2003 election, Stephen was part of the coalition negotiating team for the Lib Dems, alongside Tavish Scott – the two likely contenders to replace Wallace when the time comes. The Aberdeen MSP got half a promotion, when he became minister for transport, sitting in the cabinet while on junior ministers' pay, a similar position to Frank McAveety. It upset some in Labour, that the two key economic portfolios were under Lib Dems. The transport brief gave Stephen the opportunity to drive through the promised western peripheral road for his home city, as well as returning to pursue the aims of a previous lobbying role he had as chair of the Campaign for Rail Electrification Aberdeen to Edinburgh (CREATE).

MP

ANNE BEGG was born in Forfar in 1955, and educated at Brechin High School, Aberdeen University, where she studied history and politics, and Aberdeen College of Education. She was an English teacher before her election in 1997, having to fight for three years for registration from the General Teaching Council which had blocked a wheelchair-using teacher from working. She taught at Webster's High, Kirriemuir and at Arbroath Academy from 1998-97, as principal English teacher for six of those years. She was also an activist in the Educational Institute of Scotland, serving on its national council from 1990-95 and on the board of the GTC from 1994-97. She is patron of the Scottish Motor Neuron Society and of the National Federation of Shopmobility, and was named Disabled Scot of the Year in 1998.

Begg joined the Labour Party in 1983, its lowest point, and was selected from an all-woman shortlist for Aberdeen South in 1995. Having been elected, she was an enthusiastic devolution supporter, including backing for proportional representation, which she said, presciently for Labour, would be 'of supreme importance to people in the North East of Scotland'. She became a member of the Scottish affairs select committee in the Commons from 1997-2001, in addition to serving on Labour's National Executive Committee in 1998-99. After the 2001 election, she had a place on the work and pensions select committee. Having backed a motion against war in Iraq during 2002, she voted against the Government position in two pre-war votes.

Aberdeenshire West
and Kincardine

Predecessor Constituencies: Aberdeen and Kincardineshire (1945), Angus North and Mearns (1950–70) and Kincardine and Deeside (1983–92).

Socio-economic Indicators:

Constituency Pop. (16-64)	52,666
Claimant Count (May 2003)	1.0% (68.9% below average)
IBA/SDA Claimants	3.7%
Life Expectancy – Male	76.7 (3.3 yrs above average)
Life Expectancy – Female	81.2 (2.5 yrs above average)
Owner Occupied	73.9%
Social Rented	14.0%
Average Property Prices	£91,636 (9th)
Average Gross Income	£31,621 (4th)
Low Birthweight Babies	145 (5.9%)
Teenage Pregnancy Rates	237 (2.2%)
No. of Lone Parent Households	1,995 (6.3%)

2003 Scottish Parliament Election

Electorate: 62,545   *Turnout*: 31,636 (50.6%)   *Turnout 1999*: 58.9%

Candidate	Party	Votes	Votes%	99 %	Change%
Mike Rumbles	Lib Dem	14,553	46.0	35.9	+10.1
David Davidson	Con	9,154	28.9	29.5	– 0.6
Ian Angus	SNP	4,489	14.2	21.5	– 7.4
Keith Hutchens	Labour	2,727	8.6	13.0	– 4.4
Alan Manley	SSP	713	2.3	–	–

Liberal Democrat majority: 5,399 (17.1%)   *Swing*: 5.3% Conservative to Liberal Democrat

2001 General Election

Electorate: 61,391   *Turnout*: 37,914 (61.8%)

Candidate	Party	Votes	Votes%	Change%
Robert Smith	Lib Dem	16,507	43.5	+ 2.5
Tom Kerr	Con	11,686	30.8	– 4.1
Keith Hutchens	Labour	4,669	12.3	+ 3.2

cont'd

Candidate	Party	Votes	Votes%	Change%
John Green	SNP	4,634	12.2	– 0.8
Alan Manley	SSP	418	1.1	–

Liberal Democrat majority: 4,821 (12.7%)   *Swing*: 3.3% Conservative to Liberal Democrat

1945–97 Westminster

	Lab%	Con%	SNP%	Lib%	Other%	Turnout%
1997	9.1	34.9	13.1	41.1	1.9	73.1
1992	9.1	43.7	11.3	35.1	0.7	78.7
1991B	7.7	30.6	11.1	49.0	1.6	67.0
1987	15.9	40.6	6.4	36.3	0.6	75.3
1983	15.2	47.7	7.7	29.4	–	71.5
1979	19.3	57.5	23.2	–	–	73.8
1974(O)	12.3	43.6	34.2	9.9	–	72.3
1974(F)	12.8	48.8	23.3	15.1	–	78.6
1970	18.4	53.1	16.9	11.6	–	74.7
1966	20.2	50.4	–	29.4	–	76.2
1964	16.6	49.3	–	34.1	–	77.0
1959	32.6	67.4	–	–	–	71.3
1955	31.0	69.0	–	–	–	72.3
1951	35.9	64.1	–	–	–	76.3
1950	27.7	51.5	–	20.8	–	81.4
1945	–	51.5	–	48.5	–	68.7

Montrose District of Burghs (1945)

	Lab%	Con%	SNP%	Lib%	Other%	Turnout%
1945	41.8	58.2	–	–	–	72.3

Aberdeenshire West and Kincardine contains the towns of Portlethen and Stonehaven, which are largely commuter towns for Aberdeen, as well as the Royal Deeside rural towns of Aboyne, Ballater, Banchory and Braemar. This seat contains the Royal Family's Scottish residence, Balmoral, as well as the Mearns, an area of fishing and farming communities immortalised in Lewis Grassic Gibbon's legendary trilogy 'A Scots Quair'.

Aberdeenshire West and Kincardine's profile reflects the affluence and prosperity of most people in this seat. The claimant count is the lowest in the country, while incapacity and disability benefits are also the lowest. The proportion of the working age population on benefits in Aberdeenshire West is 4.7 per cent – one-seventh the level of the rate in Glasgow Shettleston. Average property prices are 35.9 per cent above the national average and rose 44.6 per cent between 1991 and 2001. Low birthweight babies are the third lowest in Scotland. It was also rated across a basket of indicators the most healthy constituency in all of Scotland – although given 'the Scottish effect' in relation to ill-health this still only makes it the 123rd most healthy place to live in Britain.

Aberdeenshire West and Kincardine's agricultural communities have faced increasing difficulties in recent years such as the BSE issue and then the foot and mouth crisis in 2001 which saw major restrictions on livestock movements. Tourism has also been affected by the unstable international environment after the 2001 attacks on the World Trade Centre and the Pentagon. Land reform is also an important issue given the number of large estates in the area, and issues of access, rambling and conservation are hotly debated. In 2002, after decades of debate, the Scottish Executive passed a Land Reform Act which gave ramblers the right to roam and communities the right to buy land from landowners and landlords.

This is also prosperous commuter belt territory and transport links and investment are crucial to the success of the local economy. There is a longstanding campaign advocating the electrification of the Aberdeen-Edinburgh rail line, while reopening of the Inverurie-Stonehaven rail link is being considered by the Scottish Executive. Aberdeenshire Council has proposed a PPP package for increasing investment into the constituency's schools and this will see Portlethen Academy enlarged and extended in facilities and size. However, other proposals involve merging existing schools and replacing them with a new school in Banchory and merging three schools in Kincardine. These have encountered widespread local opposition.

Politically, this constituency had a long Liberal tradition which was submerged when the National Liberal and Unionists (Conservatives) contested the seat in the absence of the Liberals themselves. The seat saw a long series of Liberal-Conservative two-way contests from 1923 to 1945, before Labour began contesting the seat from 1950 onwards and the Liberals faded away. Colin Thorton-Kemsley was first elected Conservative MP for what was Kincardine and Western from 1939, through boundary changes making it Angus North and the Mearns in 1950, finally retiring in 1964.

When the Liberals began contesting the seat again in the 1960s, the depth of their support showed and they polled 34.1 per cent in 1964 after failing to stand in the three previous elections. Although they slipped back after 1964, coinciding with the rise of the SNP in the 1970s, the Liberal-SDP Alliance re-emerged in 1983 as a serious challenger to the Conservatives, having failed to put a candidate up in 1979.

The seat was held by the moderate and popular Conservative, Alick Buchanan-Smith, from 1964 until his death in 1991. The Lib Dems had cut Alick Buchanan Smith's majority in 1987 to 2,063 and Nicol Stephen won the by-election in November 1991 with a majority of 7,824 over the Conservatives. This Lib Dem victory allowed them to leapfrog the Conservatives in the number of Scottish MPs each had, reduced the Conservatives to third party status, and provided fuel to the constitutional question and 'democratic deficit' in the run-up to the 1992 election. However, this was to prove another false dawn for home rulers, as the Conservatives were re-elected at a UK level in June 1992 and George Kynoch won back the seat with a 4,495 majority over the Lib Dems' Nicol Stephen.

The Liberal Democrats regained the seat in May 1997 when Sir Robert Smith defeated Kynoch by the relatively narrow majority of 2,662 on an 8 per cent swing from the Conservatives to the Lib Dems. In June 2001 Smith nearly doubled his majority at Westminster to 4,821 over the Conservatives.

In the Scottish Parliament election of May 1999 the Lib Dems' Mike Rumbles won the seat with a similar and smallish majority of 2,289. On a reduced turnout, the Lib Dems saw their vote fall by 5,000, while the Conservatives lost 4,500 – in both cases amounting to drops of 5 per cent, while the SNP gained 2,000 votes in third place. In 2003 Mike Rumbles had an even better result, more than doubling his majority over the Conservatives to 5,399, putting 500 votes and 10 per cent on his support.

The Boundary Commission proposals for Westminster see Aberdeenshire West and Kincardine relatively unchanged with a small part of the seat going to Gordon, making little difference to the Lib Dems' prospects in the area. At the Scottish Parliament, the Lib Dems have been entrenching their support in the area which will auger well for future elections, but the Conservative vote – unlike other ex-Tory seats – has not melted away. Considering the wealth, affluence and culture of this part of Scotland – of Royal Deeside, the Mearns and the commuter towns in Aberdeenshire West and Kincardineshire – the Tories must still harbour hopes that they can make a comeback here.

MSP

MIKE RUMBLES was born in South Shields in 1956. He was educated at St James' School, County Durham, and went on to university in Durham and Wales, where he did a masters in economics, before going to Sandhurst army college. He was an army officer for 15 years, reaching the rank of major, before becoming a team leader in business management at Aberdeen College from 1995-1999. He is a fellow of the Institute for Personnel Development.

In the Parliament's first term, he was convenor of the standards committee, which gave him an early high profile in October 1999 at the time of the 'Lobbygate' affair, the first test of how well the Parliament would police itself. Though cautious as a convener, the committee passed the test, as did those being investigated. The committee oversaw a new code of conduct for MSPs and was developing rules on lobbying through the first term, including a harsh spotlight being put on the Parliament's business partnership organisation. It also saw through legislation creating an independent post of standards commissioner, an early sign of how different the Scottish Parliament would be from Westminster.

Rumbles had a strange double role during the first term: when not the gamekeeper of standards, he was the poacher causing all sorts of difficulties for ministers. He would question almost any Executive measure he was required to vote through, without it having been in the partnership agreement or given prior approval by the party group. This was true even when the issue had limited impact on his constituency, which he fought as if the most marginal in Scotland. The fisheries decommissioning scheme in March 2001 was one he opposed, resulting in one of only three defeats for the Executive, and after which he resigned his post as party spokesman on rural affairs. He also used several opportunities to raise pressure on Labour ministers to approve council voting reform, talking up the possibility of a coalition split if they did not. This style sometimes antagonised his own party MSPs as well as Labour's, but Rumbles is not one to be cowed by such concerns and appears to relish the ruffling of political feathers. Indeed, it sometimes suited Jim Wallace to be the ministerial team player, while Rumbles and a few others fought the public battle for a distinct Lib Dem profile. While spending the whole of the first four years on the rural development committee, the Aberdeenshire MSP campaigned vigorously against fox hunting legislation.

After the 2003 election, Jim Wallace sought to bring Rumbles into the leadership tent, with a place on the coalition negotiating team. This was a test of whether the agreement itself would work with backbenchers, but also tied Rumbles into what was being agreed, and ensured that there were more robust methods written into the document requiring ministers to consult early and often with backbenchers from both coalition parties. If Rumbles thought a ministerial post might be the reward, he got that wrong, becoming instead his party's spokesperson on health, with a place on the health committee. In March 2004, he angered colleagues by arguing for a radical position in favour of full fiscal powers for the Scottish Parliament. His speech was crucial to swinging a vote passed only by 52 to 48 votes at the Lib Dem conference in Dundee, and was seen as an embarrassing snub to Wallace, who had wanted a more moderate, cautious approach.

MP

SIR ROBERT SMITH was born in 1958, and inherited his title through a political dynasty. He was educated at Merchant Taylors' School in London and Aberdeen University, and was manager of the family estate near Inverurie from 1983-97, spending his leisure time on sailing. The first baronet, his grandfather, was Sir William Smith, MP for Central Aberdeenshire and Kincardine from 1924-45, while he is also distantly related to Alick Buchanan-Smith, Conservative MP for Kincardine and Deeside from 1964–91.

Sir Robert, better known as Bob to his friends, joined the Social Democrat Party at its creation in 1981. In 1992, in the wake of a fourth Tory victory, he contributed to a conference debate on Lib Dem links with Labour, rubbishing its claims of commitment to constitutional reform, saying Labour was only committed to getting its hands on power for its own sake. He had stood for the Liberal-SDP Alliance in Aberdeen North in 1987, and served on Aberdeenshire Council from 1995–97 as councillor for Upper Donside. He was education spokesperson during that time, as well as being vice-chair of Grampian Police Board. On his 1997 election to Westminster, he returned to that hostility to Labour, saying there was a need for a Scottish Parliament not dominated by 'Strathclyde Labour'. He was made part of the Lib Dem transport team in the Commons and sat on the Scottish affairs and catering committees. Following his re-election in 2003, he became deputy whip, with committee places scrutinising trade and industry and procedure.

Airdrie and Shotts

Predecessor Constituencies: Coatbridge (1945), Coatbridge and Airdrie (1950–82) and Monklands East (1983–92).

Socio-economic Indicators:

Constituency Pop. (16-64)	50,237
Claimant Count (May 2003)	3.8% (21.1% above average)
IBA/SDA Claimants	15.2% (10th Highest)
Life Expectancy – Male	71.7 (1.7 yrs below average)
Life Expectancy – Female	77.2 (1.5 yrs below average)
Owner Occupied	55.4%
Social Rented	38.9%
Average Property Prices	£44,165 (67th)
Average Gross Income	£24,162 (47th)
Low Birthweight Babies (av. 1996-98)	185 (7.3%)
Teenage Pregnancy Rates (av. 1996-98)	474 (4.5%)
No. of Lone Parent Households	4,211 (13.7%)

CAB Enquiries

Issue	No. of cases	Percentage of total cases (%)
1. Benefits	3428	43.9
2. Consumer	1008	12.9
3. Employment	836	10.7
4. Other	754	9.6
5. Housing	689	8.8

2003 Scottish Parliament Election

Electorate: 56,680   *Turnout*: 25,086 (44.3%)   *Turnout* 1999: 56.8%

Candidate	Party	Votes	Votes%	99 %	Change%
Karen Whitefield	Labour	14,209	56.6	55.2	+ 1.4
Gil Paterson	SNP	5,232	20.9	28.2	– 7.3
Alan Melville	Con	2,203	8.8	9.6	– 0.8
Fraser Coats	SSP	2,096	8.4	–	–
Kevin Lang	Lib Dem	1,346	5.4	7.1	– 1.7

Labour majority: 8,977 (35.8%)   *Swing*: 4.4% SNP to Labour

2001 General Election

Electorate: 58,349   *Turnout*: 31,736 (54.4%)

Candidate	Party	Votes	Votes%	Change%
Helen Liddell	Labour	18,478	58.2	– 3.6
Alison Lindsay	SNP	6,138	19.3	– 5.1
John Love	Lib Dem	2,376	7.5	+ 3.3
Gordon McIntosh	Con	1,960	6.2	– 2.7
Mary Dempsey	Scot Un	1,439	4.5	–
Kenny McGuigan	SSP	1,171	3.7	–
Chris Herriot	Soc Lab	174	0.5	–

Labour majority: 12,340 (38.9%)   *Swing*: 0.7% SNP to Labour

1945–97 Westminster

	Lab%	Con%	SNP%	Lib%	Other%	Turnout%
1997	61.8	8.9	24.4	4.2	0.7	71.4
1994B	49.8	2.3	44.9	2.6	0.4	70.0
1992	61.3	16.0	18.0	4.6	–	75.0
1987	61.0	16.9	12.9	9.3	–	74.8
1983	51.2	23.9	8.9	16.0	–	73.0
1982B	55.1	26.2	10.5	8.2	–	56.3
1979	60.9	27.5	11.6	–	–	75.3
1974O	51.6	17.2	27.9	3.3	–	77.8
1974F	54.1	28.6	17.3	–	–	77.8
1970	58.9	35.1	6.0	–	–	76.5
1966	64.2	35.8	–	–	–	77.2
1964	62.1	37.9	–	–	–	81.2
1959	50.9	49.1	–	–	–	84.0
1955	55.8	44.2	–	–	–	79.4
1951	57.4	42.6	–	–	–	85.5
1950	56.6	40.2	–	–	3.2	86.1
1945	61.1	38.9	–	–	–	76.0

Airdrie and Shotts was previously known as Monklands East. The Monklands name – helpfully for Labour – vanished in the local government reorganisation in 1995 and the subsequent parliamentary boundary changes. The new seat contains over two-thirds of the old seat centred on the main population centre of Airdrie, as well as a group of smaller towns and villages from the old Motherwell North seat including Bonkle, Cleland, Dykehead, Greengairs, Newmains, Shotts and Stane.

Airdrie and Shotts' socio-economic profile reflects the poverty of many of its constituents. The seat has 38.9 per cent social housing including 36.2 per cent council housing – down from 62.5 per cent ten years ago. Average property prices are 34.5 per cent below the average.

The constituency contains several communities with high levels of unemployment and creating new employment opportunities is one of the top issues in the area. In 2000 the Dutch pharmaceutical company Organon – the inventors of the male contraceptive pill – announced they would be expanding their research site at Newhouse in nearby Airdrie, creating 100 new jobs. However, recently announced job losses, including the closure of Cummins engineering plant at Shotts, plus a Boots manufacturing plant have harmed employment prospects.

Health is another important issue given the ill-health of many of Airdrie's constituents – with the seat ranked the 23rd most unhealthy constituency in Britain, and the third most unhealthy in Scotland outside Glasgow. Lanarkshire Acute Hospitals NHS Trust recently found itself the centre of a major national controversy on the lack of Accident and Emergency consultants. The Trust had to resort to the short-term solution of using 'flying doctors' across the three major Lanarkshire hospitals. At the end of 2001, Monklands Hospital children's ward was temporarily closed as part of a cost-saving exercise, forcing children and families to travel to nearby Wishaw for care.

Airdrie Football Club has faced a very shaky last few years with the original club – founder members of the first Scottish League – going into receivership and finally bankruptcy. Airdrie thus went out of existence, but were quickly replaced by a new club – Airdrie United – which applied for membership of the Scottish Football League and, due to Clydebank going bankrupt, re-entered the top flight of Scottish football. The town of Airdrie is not known for its architectural charms and splendour and this was highlighted in 2000 when the architectural journal *Unlimited* voted Airdrie the most unattractive Scottish town centre. Its unappealing aspects are visible also around Greengairs village, where open-cast mining and landfill sites have become a messy political battleground.

Labour's support in this seat goes back well into the inter-war years with the party first winning what was Coatbridge in the 1922 election, losing it narrowly in the 1931 debacle, before winning again in 1935. Jean 'haud the wean' Mann, a Glasgow city councillor held the seat in 1945 with a 6,777 majority over the Unionists. She was unusual for a woman MP of the time in that she had five young children, and provoked the wrath and male chauvinism of some of her supposed Labour colleagues, including James Maxton. In 1950 the seat became Coatbridge and Airdrie and Mann remained MP until retiring before the 1959 election when she was succeeded by James Dempsey. Coatbridge and Airdrie was seen then as providing a Labour seat for life and Dempsey was elected seven times by the constituency. The nearest challenge emerged from the Nationalist high-tide of October 1974 when his majority fell to 10,568.

Dempsey stood for the last time in 1979 and died in 1982, forcing a by-election on the Labour Party at the height of the Falklands war. Its candidate, Tom Clarke, won 55 per cent of the vote, with the Conservatives a distant second. In 1983, most of the Coatbridge and Airdrie seat became Monklands East, centred around the town of Airdrie, and John Smith, the MP for neighbouring Lanarkshire North stood as Labour candidate, while Clarke moved to Monklands West, which also contained part of his old seat.

Smith was elected with impressive majorities of 9,799 in 1983, rising to 16,389 in 1987 – on both occasions over the Conservatives. In the 1992 election, Smith played a prominent part in Labour's election campaign, as Shadow Chancellor unveiling his Shadow Budget which was seen by many as a major factor in the party's historic fourth election defeat. He was returned with a 10,334 majority over the SNP. Smith then became party leader, easily beating a challenge from Bryan Gould, and set about taking Labour back to power. During his two years as leader, Labour established an impressive lead over the Conservatives in the polls, but many in the party saw his approach as a 'safety first' one filled with complacency and a lack of urgency. Smith died of a heart attack on May 12th 1994 and what kind of Prime Minister he would have made is a question for future historians, but for many in the party he will always be seen as one of Labour's great lost leaders.

Smith's death gave Labour a number of challenges: a leadership contest the party was not expecting and a difficult by-election. There had been serious allegations of corruption involving Monklands

District Council whereby the council's Labour leadership, known as the 'Coatbridge Mafia', was accused of cronyism and favouritism. The allegations centred on Labour councillors (mostly Catholic) favouring relatives in job applications and distorting expenditure and services towards the Coatbridge part of the constituency with its large Catholic population, and against the Airdrie part with its large Protestant population. Labour rejected the need for an independent inquiry into these issues before and during the by-election campaign, until the candidate, Helen Liddell, was forced to do so during the campaign – a considerable u-turn even though the neighbouring MP, Labour's Tom Clarke, opposed any inquiry. In a highly charged election campaign both Labour and the SNP fought a campaign which was ugly, bitter and acrimonious at points, and which had echoes of a sectarian Scotland many people had thought long gone. Kay Ullrich, the SNP candidate seemed sometimes out of her depth – and while Labour was constantly on the defensive over its local record, Liddell held on by a majority of 1,640 votes over the SNP. An opinion poll conducted just before polling day showed the religious divide in terms of voting with 80 per cent of Catholics voting Labour and 65 per cent of Protestants SNP. While Ullrich had achieved an impressive 19 per cent swing in John Smith's former seat, the party had missed a historic opportunity to strike a blow against Labour cronyism and corruption.

This result was as close as the SNP got. At the following 1997 general election in the new seat of Airdrie and Shotts, the Nationalists managed to reduce Labour's lead compared to the notional result five years ago, but this still left Labour with a 15,412 majority. In 2001, Liddell saw her vote fall by 7,000, but her percentage majority increased while the SNP declined even faster.

The SNP's Gil Paterson managed to cut Labour's lead in the May 1999 Scottish Parliament elections by 8 per cent, as Labour's vote declined by 8,000, while the Nationalists fell by 695 votes on a lower turnout. This was a far cry from the excitement and real challenge to Labour's citadels the party had been able to mount in the Monklands East by-election. In the May 2003 elections for the Scottish Parliament, Labour's hold on the constituency remained impregnable with Karen Whitefield's majority showing a fall of seven votes on 1999 on a lower turnout, and thus an increase in share of 7 per cent. In the regional list vote Labour won 45.0 per cent to the SNP's 17.5 per cent, while the SSP won 7.7 per cent, the Scottish Senior Citizens 6.9 per cent and the Greens 3.5 per cent.

Boundary Commission recommendations at Westminster alter the political geography of Airdrie and Shotts but do not change its political character in the slightest. At the Scottish Parliament, Labour are impressively dug in against a variety of opponents, and its biggest enemy in future years will be a sense of complacency on its part, a slowly, declining party machine, and the increasing apathy of parts of the electorate in Labour's heartlands. 'Lanarkshire Labour' may have become a pseudonym for the unacceptable face of Scottish Labour in the early years of devolution, but Labour is still a successful brand in this part of the country.

MSP

KAREN WHITEFIELD was born in Bellshill in 1970, a niece of Peggy Herbison, the late great North Lanarkshire MP and social security minister. She was educated at Calderhead High School, Shotts, and graduated from Glasgow Caledonian University with a degree in public administration and management. She then worked briefly as a civil servant with the Benefits Agency. She had a Congressional scholarship in Washington DC in 1990. From 1992-99, she was personal assistant to Rachel Squire, the Dunfermline West MP. She held a number of offices in her local Labour Party and became a CLP representative on the National Policy Forum in 1998. Her seat was placed in the Labour gender twinning arrangements alongside Motherwell and Wishaw, meaning her votes helped deliver the tiny majority by which Jack McConnell won his candidacy. In the Parliament, she has been an enthusiastic member of his backbench fan club. At first on the social inclusion and audit committees, she switched from January 2001 to serve on both social justice and education, culture and sport. McConnell made her a Parliamentary aide to the law officers until the 2003 election, and she was convener of the cross-party group on carers. After that election, she became deputy convener of the justice 2 committee and a member of the standards committee. She has been criticised for the calibre of her contribution to Parliamentary debate, though she occasionally turns in a telling attack on the Scottish Socialists, and she is teased even by her own side for her loyal devotion not only to Airdrie and Shotts but also to 'the surrounding villages'. Her leisure interests include the Girls' Brigade and cake decorating.

MP

HELEN LIDDELL was born in Coatbridge in 1950 and educated at St Patrick's High School, Coatbridge and Strathclyde University. She said of her background: 'where I come from, they don't put you down for Eton, they put you down for the Labour Party'. She was a researcher with the STUC from 1971-76, worked briefly as economics correspondent for BBC Scotland from 1976-77, and served as Scottish Labour general secretary from 1977-88. In that position, she was responsible for the infamous 1978 Liddell memorandum which discouraged Labour co-operation with other parties in the 1979 devolution referendum. It stated 'the Labour Party is the only party which believes in devolution for its own sake'. As secretary of the Labour Movement Yes campaign, she said at a press conference: 'We will not be soiling our hands by joining any umbrella Yes group'. She was beaten by Larry Whitty in her application to become Labour's UK general secretary in 1985. She then worked for, and was repeatedly humiliated by Robert Maxwell as director of personnel and public affairs at Mirror Group Newspapers in Glasgow from 1988-92. He famously required her to follow him into the gents lavatory to take notes. She was subsequently chief executive of a business venture programme.

At this time she also published a steamy novel, *Elite*, a rip-roaring read about Ann Clarke, who wanted 'power – in politics and in bed'. Clarke, Deputy Prime Minister, was according to the publisher's blurb 'a ruthless, politically ambitious, beautiful and brilliant woman . . . a modern Joan of Arc wrapped in the tartan flag of the Scottish Labour Party'. Obviously this was a purely fictional character. In a recent study of political fiction written by politicians the journalist Johann Hari claimed the book stood out in the last 20 years as head and shoulders above the rest. He claimed it was a work characterised by 'psychosis' which was 'better than any Cuban surrealism'. Liddell's qualities as a futurologist should also not be over-looked. The book has a young-looking Labour leader who challenges the party to change, runs a 'court' of hangers-on, and who, when elected Prime Minister, ages horribly. Even more spookily this dream Labour leader is called Tony, and has a wife who is significantly more intelligent than he is.

Liddell was elected to the Commons in 1994, having previously stood once as a candidate, in Fife East in October 1974. The Monklands East by-election, following John Smith's death, was a particularly unpleasant one for Labour, as sectarian politics reared its head with claims of council employment bias. She denounced any such bias and demanded an investigation, which infuriated some fellow Lanarkshire Labour politicians. She was an enthusiastic backer of Tony Blair's campaign to ditch Clause Four, helping secure a Scottish Labour conference vote on the subject which turned the tide of the debate. Once in Government, and with the early backing of Gordon Brown, she had a variety of ministerial posts, starting with Economic Secretary to the Treasury from 1997-98, being responsible for sorting out the pension mis-selling mess. She was made minister of state at the Scottish Office from 1998-99, with responsibility for education, and Tony Blair also installed her as Donald Dewar's deputy to quell bickering about status among other junior ministers. She was minister for transport briefly in 1999 and then moved to become minister for energy and competitiveness at the Department of Trade and

Industry, a post held from 1999-2001. A confirmed Nat-basher in her time as general secretary and as Scottish Office minister, she was passed over for the post of Scotland Secretary after the devolved elections of 1999 – much to the disappointment of the SNP.

However, Liddell finally became Secretary of State for Scotland in January 2001, when Peter Mandelson resigned for the second time and John Reid was moved from the Scotland Office to the Northern Ireland Office. She was the first woman to occupy the post, though she was dogged throughout her tenure by claims that she did not have enough to do. This was not helped by a leaked diary, showing she had a lot of spare time in which to take mid-afternoon French classes – perhaps not unrelated to the role she adopted of being the Cabinet's most ardent Europhile. It was evident that she was seeking work to do, being beaten to the additional European brief by Peter Hain at the Welsh Office. But to her credit, she calmed down the unpleasant turf wars which had damaged relations between John Reid and Donald Dewar.

She played her part in the 2001 election in which Labour held all its Scottish seats, and led a consultation which angered some of her backbenchers by concluding that the number of MSP seats should be kept at 129, requiring a change in the law. Although going to some lengths to show her loyalty to Tony Blair through the build-up to the war in Iraq, making difficult TV appearances and a defiant speech at a fractious Scottish Labour conference in Dundee, her reward was to be bundled out of the Cabinet in Blair's botched reshuffle of June 2003 – the Scotland Secretary's job being ditched and then reinstated in the office of Alistair Darling. On her departure, she warned the new Constitutional Affairs Secretary, Lord Falconer, of the 'sheer nastiness and viciousness of politics in Scotland'. Liddell faced a battle with John Reid among others to win the Labour nomination in one of the reduced number of Lanarkshire seats, and there was a report she might get a posting instead as High Commissioner to Australia. Her name was also connected with the British appointment to the European Commission due in late 2004. She was confirmed in April 2004 as High Commissioner to Australia.

Angus

Predecessor Constituencies: Forfarshire (1945), Angus South (1950–79) and Angus East (1983–92).

Socio-economic Indicators:

Constituency Pop. (16-64)	48,764
Claimant Count (May 2003)	3.0% (3.2% below average)
IBA/SDA Claimants	7.3%
Life Expectancy – Male	74.4 (1.0 yrs above average)
Life Expectancy – Female	78.5 (0.8 yrs above average)
Owner Occupied	68.3%
Social Rented	20.7%
Average Property Prices	£64,691 (28th)
Average Gross Income	£26,508 (29th)
Low Birthweight Babies	99 (4.4%)
Teenage Pregnancy Rates	450 (4.8%)
No. of Lone Parent Households	2,807 (8.6%)

CAB Enquiries

Issue	No. of cases	Percentage of total cases (%)
1. Benefits	1563	21.8
2. Consumer	1377	19.2
3. Employment	1371	19.1
4. Other	933	13.0
5. Housing	670	9.3

2003 Scottish Parliament Election

Electorate: 60,608 *Turnout*: 29,789 (49.2%) *Turnout* 1999: 57.7%

Candidate	Party	Votes	Votes%	99 %	Change%
Andrew Welsh	SNP	13,251	44.5	46.5	– 2.0
Alexander Johnstone	Con	6,564	22.0	20.7	+ 1.3
John Denning	Labour	4,871	16.4	20.0	– 3.7
Richard Spiers	Lib Dem	3,802	12.8	12.8	=
Bruce Wallace	SSP	1,301	4.4	–	–

SNP majority: 6,687 (22.4%) *Swing*: 1.7% SNP to Conservative

2001 General Election

Electorate: 59,004   *Turnout*: 35,013 (59.3%)

Candidate	Party	Votes	Votes%	Change%
Michael Weir	SNP	12,347	35.3	–13.0
Marcus Booth	Con	8,736	25.0	+ 0.3
Ian McFatridge	Labour	8,183	23.4	+ 7.7
Richard Speirs	Lib Dem	5,015	14.3	+ 4.9
Bruce Wallace	SSP	732	2.1	–

SNP majority: 3,611 (10.3%)   *Swing*: 6.7% SNP to Conservative

1945–1997 Westminster

	Lab%	Con%	SNP%	Lib%	Other%	Turnout
1997	15.6	24.6	48.3	9.4	2.1	72.1
1992	12.6	38.1	40.1	8.2	0.9	75.0
1987	10.8	39.0	42.4	7.8	–	75.5
1983	8.0	44.1	36.0	11.4	0.5	73.5
1979	10.1	43.6	41.5	4.8	–	79.9
1974o	10.5	39.2	43.8	6.5	–	74.5
1974F	13.8	49.5	36.7	–	–	79.8
1970	20.8	56.1	23.1	–	–	73.9
1966	29.6	70.4	–	–	–	71.2
1964	22.6	58.2	–	19.2	–	75.6
1959	19.0	57.1	–	23.9	–	75.9
1955	27.3	72.7	–	–	–	73.6
1951	29.1	70.9	–	–	–	76.6
1950	25.6	53.9	–	20.5	–	82.0
1945	31.1	51.6	–	17.3	–	68.9

Angus takes in the coastal towns of Arbroath and Montrose, its main population centres, and also includes Carnoustie and Monifieth, which are effectively suburbs of Dundee. The socio-economic profile of Angus reflects its 'middle Scotland' position – neither hugely wealthy nor significantly impoverished. Average property prices are 4.1 per cent below the average, having risen 73.7 per cent between 1991 and 2001.

The farming and fishing communities of Angus have faced a difficult period in recent years with BSE, foot and mouth disease and fishing boat decommissioning. Farm incomes in the area have fallen dramatically over the last few years, with numerous farms going into receivership and bankruptcy. A related industry – food processing – also encountered problems: in 2001 Esk Frozen Foods, a Montrose based business went into receivership. Recent decommissioning schemes backed by the European Union met widespread opposition and Angus Council took the Government to the Court of Session to challenge the exclusion of Arbroath from areas seen as needing government assistance and support, but lost the case.

Job growth in the last few years has been seen in the oil industry, particularly around the Montrose basin area. Commuter towns such as Monifieth, Carnoustie and Longforgan have grown, servicing the expansion of biomedical and bioscience jobs in the Dundee region. Invergowrie has become home to the Scottish Crop Research Institute. Tourism remains a crucial boost to the local economy supporting thousands of jobs and a variety of services. Carnoustie gained a big boost in 1999 by hosting the Open Golf Championship - one of the most prestigious tournaments in the world – and the first time it had hosted it for 24 years.

From 1924 until 1974, this constituency was safely Conservative, represented by Captain James Duncan from 1950-64, when the seat was known as Angus South. His successor was Jock Bruce-Gardyne, a respected *Financial Times* journalist and supporter of Margaret Thatcher, who held the seat until October 1974. The SNP first contested the seat in 1970, coming second, before winning it at the third attempt in October 1974 with a majority of 1,824. In the Conservative victory of 1979 Peter Fraser narrowly won back the seat with a majority of 963, as both main parties increased their support – the Conservatives by nearly 5,000 and the Nationalists by 2,000 on an increased turnout. Fraser won the seat as Angus East over Andrew Welsh in 1983 with a 3,527 majority, but in 1987 in their third contest Welsh finally emerged triumphant. He had a 1,544 majority over the Conservatives on a 5.7 per cent swing – clearly benefiting from a degree of anti-Tory tactical voting. In 1992 the small Conservative recovery north of the border nearly won Angus East back for them as Welsh's majority fell to a precarious 954.

In the 1997 general election Welsh achieved a 10,189 majority over the Conservatives, putting 9 per cent on the notional 1992 result, while the Conservative vote collapsed by more than 13 per cent, making Angus the second safest SNP seat in the country after Banff and Buchan. In June 2001, Angus suddenly came back into play. The transfer from Andrew Welsh to Michael Weir as SNP Westminster candidate saw a collapse in the SNP vote of 8,000 and 13 per cent with Weir only saved by the inability of the Conservatives to advance at all – falling back by 2,000 votes and seeing their percentage share stagnate. The main gainers were Labour, who increased their vote by 1,500 and 8 per cent.

The SNP are hugely assisted in Angus by their strength on the ground and local government base, having controlled Angus Council since 1984. In the most recent 2003 local elections, the SNP won 17 out of 29 council seats with 40.4 per cent of the vote, while Labour is the biggest opposition with six seats and the Conservatives have been reduced to a rump of two seats.

In the 1999 Scottish Parliament election, Welsh won easily with an 8,901 majority – representing a 2 per cent increase on his Westminster majority. At the 2003 Scottish Parliament election Welsh saw his majority cut from 8,901 to 6,687. In the regional vote, the SNP won 34.4 per cent to the Conservatives 20.3 per cent, while the Greens won 6.1 per cent and the Scottish Socialists 4 per cent.

New boundaries for Westminster see a radically changed Angus with parts going to Dundee East and West, and a link up with Perth reducing the number of potential SNP constituencies in this part of the country from three to two. Analysis of ward votes suggest it will be a key Tory target.

MSP

ANDREW WELSH was born in 1944 in Glasgow, and educated at Govan High School and as a mature student at Glasgow University, where he took an MA in modern history and politics, followed by a teacher training qualification. He worked as a clerk in the National Commercial Bank of Scotland from 1962-66, before going to university, then worked as a history teacher from 1972-74. From 1979-84, he was senior lecturer in business studies and public administration at Dundee College. Having briefly been a councillor on Stirling District Council, he was first elected to Westminster for Angus South in October 1974, as one of the 11 SNP MPs whose presence there did so much to shape the politics of the 1970s. Welsh has never been one to take a particularly high profile, being chief whip through that period and whipping the famous 'turkeys voting for an early Christmas' division which saw the SNP help bring down the Callaghan Government. He lost his seat in 1979, and contested it unsuccessfully in 1983.

He was a leading part of the most consistent SNP campaign to put down roots in any part of Scotland, returning to elected politics in 1984 when he became a councillor and provost of Angus District Council, at the time the SNP took control of it. This gave him a public profile that assisted him in winning the Angus East seat in 1987 from the Conservatives' Peter Fraser (who would later return to Scottish politics as Lord Fraser of Carmyllie and independent inquirer into the Holyrood building project). An MP from 1987-2001 when he stood down (the seat was called Angus from 1997), Welsh was mainly notable for his conservatism on social issues, including support for the death penalty in June 1988. He was a member of the select committee on members' interests from 1990-92 and of the Scottish affairs select committee from 1992-2001.

Elected an MSP in 1999, as with the rest of the then Westminster group, Welsh again took the lowest national profile of the six, nursing his seat effectively, serving on the Corporate Body, and acting for four years as chair of the important but little-noticed audit committee. Working with Robert Black, the auditor general, Welsh was able to claim credit at the 2003 election for the fruits of Black's influential reports, including implementation of major reforms of the health service and further education systems, reorganising the ambulance service, and improving accountability throughout the public sector. Re-elected in 2003, he was not given any of the party's four convenerships or a front bench role, but he was made a member of the Corporate Body, with special responsibility for communication and public information. His leisure interests include Chinese and being a Church elder, while he is also a member of the Prayer Breakfast in Scotland. He is an old-fashioned Nationalist in style, appearance and his approach to social issues, so it was no surprise he was absent from the Section 28 vote on homosexuality in the school curriculum.

MP

MICHAEL WEIR was born in Arbroath in 1957 and educated at Arbroath High School and Aberdeen University. He was a solicitor with Charles Wood & Son from 1981-83 and with Myers & Wills from 1983-84, becoming a partner in the firm J & DG Shiell from 1984-2001. Having joined the SNP in 1976, he was a councillor on Angus District Council from 1984-88, as convener of general purposes throughout. He stood in Aberdeen South in 1987, coming fourth. His election as MP for Angus was in 2001, replacing Andrew Welsh after the MSP had opted to stand down from Westminster to focus on the Scottish Parliament. Weir became a member of the Scottish affairs select committee, and spoke in his maiden speech about pressures on the National Health Service in his constituency, particularly with the controversial closure of three small hospitals. He was one of three SNP MPs to vote against war in Afghanistan in 2001. He was given responsibility as party spokesperson covering three Whitehall departmental areas; rural affairs with environment, trade and industry and health.

Argyll and Bute

Predecessor Constituencies: Argyll (1945–79).

Socio-economic Indicators:

Constituency Pop. (16-64)	38,991
Claimant Count (May 2003)	2.8% (10.4% below average)
IBA/SDA Claimants	9.0%
Life Expectancy – Male	74.0 (0.6 yrs above average)
Life Expectancy – Female	78.7 (national average)
Owner Occupied	61.6%
Social Rented	23.6%
Average Property Prices	£53,801 (49th)
Average Gross Income	£22,681 (65th)
Low Birthweight Babies	92 (5.9%)
Teenage Pregnancy Rates	229 (3.2%)
No. of Lone Parent Households	2,397 (8.4%)

2003 Scottish Parliament Election

Electorate: 48,330   *Turnout*: 27,948 (57.8%)   *Turnout* 1999: 64.9%

Candidate	Party	Votes	Votes%	99 %	Change%
George Lyon	Lib Dem	9,817	35.1	34.9	+ 0.2
David Petrie	Con	5,621	20.1	16.5	+ 3.6
James Mather	SNP	5,485	19.6	28.5	− 8.9
Hugh Raven	Labour	5,107	18.3	20.1	− 1.8
Desmond Divers	SSP	1,667	6.0	–	–
David Walker	SPA	251	0.9	–	–

Liberal Democrat majority: 4,196 (15.0%)   *Swing*: 1.7% Liberal Democrat to Conservative

2001 General Election

Electorate: 49,175   *Turnout*: 30,957 (63.0%)

Candidate	Party	Votes	Votes%	Change%
Alan Reid	Lib Dem	9,245	29.9	-10.3
Hugh Raven	Labour	7,592	24.5	+ 8.9
David Petrie	Con	6,436	20.8	+ 1.8
Agnes Samuel	SNP	6,433	20.8	− 2.4
Desmond Divers	SSP	1,251	4.0	–

Liberal Democrat majority: 1,653 (5.3%)   *Swing*: 9.6% Liberal Democrat to Labour

1945–97 Westminster

	Lab%	Con%	SNP%	Lib%	Other%	Turnout%
1997	15.7	19.0	23.2	40.2	2.0	72.2
1992	13.6	27.7	23.8	34.9	–	76.2
1987	12.1	33.5	17.1	37.3	–	75.4
1983	9.3	38.6	24.6	27.5	–	72.8
1979	16.0	36.8	31.8	15.4	–	76.1
1974O	13.6	36.7	49.7	–	–	72.0
1974F	12.6	38.4	49.0	–	–	77.0
1970	25.3	44.8	29.9	–	–	74.0
1966	30.1	43.2	–	26.7	–	72.3
1964	28.9	47.2	–	23.9	–	70.3
1959	25.9	58.4	–	15.7	–	71.0
1958B	25.7	46.8	–	27.5	–	67.1
1955	32.4	67.6	–	–	–	66.6
1951	31.9	68.1	–	–	–	67.1
1950	31.8	66.5	–	–	1.7	75.1
1945	31.9	56.5	–	11.6	–	63.7

Argyll and Bute is big with an immense coastline and hard to get around, running from Oban to Campbeltown to Dunoon, including the islands of Islay and Jura, Mull, Tiree, Coll and Bute. Its socio-economic profile paints a mixed picture. Average property prices are 20.2 per cent below the average, having risen 60.3 per cent through the nineties. Transport is a lively subject in this far-flung, diverse constituency. The cost of petrol, ferry fares and freight charges are controversial, with the price of petrol sometimes 20p per litre more in remote areas than in the Central Belt. Ferry services are a crucial lifeblood for many parts of the seat, and in 2001 the Scottish Executive announced two new Caledonian MacBrayne ferries for the area, along with plans to redevelop Dunoon Pier after years of local campaigning. However this last decision was put in question by CalMac announcing a review of its activities. In an unprecedented move in 2001, the UK Government agreed to transfer to the Scottish Executive the power to pay a subsidy to re-start the ferry service from Campbeltown to Ballycastle in Northern Ireland. Services did not get under way for over a year due to delays whilst the Scottish Office put out tenders. Another initiative which helped transport links was Gordon Brown's decision as Chancellor in 2000 to abolish Air Passenger Duty on flights from Highlands and Islands airports.

Local agriculture has had a difficult time in recent years with Argyll badly hit by the European Union ban on lamb exports, while dairy farmers have also had problems due to low prices, and in particular, supermarkets driving down prices. Rural services are stretched by high costs, with problems in communities such as Campbeltown and Dalmally recruiting GPs. The scale of the problem was illustrated in 2001 when Oban and Inverclyde Hospital were placed at the bottom of a Scottish league table of medical staffing levels. In 2001 the Scottish Executive introduced a 'Golden Hello' policy to aid the relocation costs of GPs. In March 2002, in a positive move, the islanders of Gigha situated three miles to the west of Kintyre succeeded in collectively buying their island in another blow against absetee landlordism. This allowed them to begin to reverse the long-term population decline of their community, and two years later they repaid a £1 million loan to the Scottish Land Fund, which had allowed them to buy it.

The American base at Holy Loch – site of nuclear submarines – closed in 1992, taking over 700 US armed forces service jobs out of the area, as well as hundreds of indirect local jobs. The base – known as

Argyll Site One, in a spoof of George Orwell's reference to the UK as Airstrip One – was always seen as a temporary guest in the local community, but its closure showed the difficulties communities can face post-Cold War. In this case, a high tech company – Telecom Services Centres – took over some of the base and created as many jobs as those lost.

This seat was known as Argyll until 1979 and has had a long and varied history. In April 1940 as Britain sat in the grip of an uneasy 'phoney war' awaiting the unleashing of Hitler's Blitzkrieg on the West, Major Duncan McCallum came home from General Wavell's Middle East staff to win the seat at a by-election. The most noteworthy point about the contest was the decision of the SNP to stand and win 37 per cent. McCallum represented the seat until his death in 1958 and the subsequent by-election in June 1958 saw the election of Michael Noble despite the Liberals coming from nowhere to achieve second place one month after they had won Torrington – part of the first post-war third party wave. Noble was Secretary of State for Scotland from 1962-64 and retired in February 1974 at which point Iain MacCormick came from a distant second to seize the seat for the SNP.

McCormick held the seat with a majority of 3,913 in October 1974, but in the Conservative victory of 1979 John MacKay won the seat from McCormick with a majority of 1,646 as the SNP vote fell by 18 per cent. MacKay, who emerged briefly as one of Margaret Thatcher's hopes for the Scottish Conservatives, held what was now known as Argyll and Bute in 1983 with a 3,844 majority over the Liberal-SDP Alliance's Ray Michie, while the SNP fell to third place. In the 1987 'Doomsday Scenario' which saw the number of Scottish Conservatives cut in half while Thatcher was returned on the strength of English votes, Ray Michie won the seat with a 1,394 majority over MacKay. Anti-Tory tactical voting does seem to have aided her challenge with the SNP vote falling back further, and Labour's vote going up by a fraction of its pan-Scottish rise.

In 1992 Michie was re-elected with a lead of 2,622 over the Conservatives as the SNP with Neil MacCormick – brother of the former MP Iain – put on 7 per cent in third place. Five years later, Michie was safely returned with a 6,081 majority over MacCormick – the SNP's re-emergence in second place due to the 9 per cent collapse in the Conservative vote. In the June 2001 Westminster contest, Argyll and Bute was that rare exception in Scotland – a genuine four party marginal where each of the main parties had a serious prospect of victory. Although his vote declined, new candidate Alan Reid held on for the Lib Dems, while Labour's Hugh Raven moved impressively from fourth to second. The real losers were the SNP as they fell back from second to fourth. Reid's 29.9 per cent was the second lowest vote ever recorded for a winning candidate at a Westminster election – beaten only by Russell Johnston's winning 26 per cent in Inverness, Nairn and Lochaber in 1992.

At the May 1999 Scottish Parliament election, the Lib Dems' George Lyon was returned with a much narrower majority of 2,057 over the SNP's Duncan Hamilton, two-thirds of the Lib Dems' Westminster lead having disappeared. Labour moved into third place, while the Conservatives – holders of this seat until 1987 – slipped into fourth place.

At the 2003 election, Lyon was returned with less difficulty, seeing his majority double. This time it was the Conservatives who moved from fourth to second, and the SNP – despite an energetic campaign by Jim Mather, fell back. He was at least consoled with being elected a list MSP for the Highlands and Islands Region. In the regional vote, the SNP were marginally ahead with 21.9 per cent to 20.5 per cent for Labour, 19.9 per cent for the Conservatives and 18.9 per cent for the Lib Dems. All of the four main parties came within 1,000 votes of each other. The Greens polled 7.3 per cent and the SSP 6.1 per cent.

Boundary Commission recommendations for Westminster for Argyll and Bute could dramatically change the political balance of this close-fought seat by adding 20,000 voters from the towns of Helensburgh and Dumbarton, and broadly assisting Labour's aspirations in the seat. At the Scottish Parliament, the Lib Dems seem to be in an impressive pole position – aided by the political dynamic which Labour gains from across Scotland – a fragmented political opposition. The SNP has had its chance in this seat, particularly in 1999, and it could not come close to winning. Since then, despite high profile candidates, it has fallen back at subsequent Westminster and Scottish Parliament elections, and must feel this seat has now slipped out of its grasp.

MSP

GEORGE LYON was born in Rothesay in 1956, and was educated at Rothesay Academy. He is a farmer with a 1350-acre family farm and became president of the National Farmers Union of Scotland in 1997 until his election to the Scottish Parliament in 1999, covering some of the worst periods of mad cow disease and beef-on-the-bone controversies. He was the recipient of a Nuffield Scholarship to New Zealand in 1987, and was a director of Argyll and the Islands Enterprise.

In Parliament, at first he served as the Lib Dem spokesperson on enterprise and lifelong learning and sat on the Parliament's enterprise and lifelong learning and public petitions committees. From 2001-03, he was on the justice 2 committee. He was the party's backbench spokesman on agriculture, home affairs and land reform in 2001-03, putting him in an awkward position when it came to legislation proposing a right of tenant farmers to buy their farms. He backed the move, and Conservatives attacked him for standing to gain substantially if he used the legislation to buy land on Bute at low cost, then being able to sell it on at a much higher price.

He was convener of the Parliamentary group through the first term, meaning he was an important link between front and back bench colleagues, and chairing some of the most important private debates through the first term, on which the Executive's majority depended. In summer 1999, he was one of those to visit other Liberal parties in continental Europe, including Holland, to learn from their experience of coalition. At constituency level, he took a leading role in securing the community buy-out of the Isle of Gigha, while pushing Executive ministers to accept an Argyll Council alternative to the established system of private finance of schools.

He developed a high media profile, as an able defender of the performance of the coalition administration across a range of issues, though he is seen by sometimes envious Lib Dem colleagues as a bit over keen to secure promotion to a ministerial post, having a strong record of backing difficult Executive voting requirements. If they are right, the 2003 team will have disappointed him. The second Parliament saw him on the audit committee, while his party's chief whip (previously a ministerial task) and party spokesman on agriculture, home affairs and land reform.

MP

ALAN REID was born in Ayr in 1954 and educated at Prestwick Academy and Ayr Academy, then at Strathclyde University, where he studied maths. He trained as a teacher at Jordanhill College and was employed as a maths teacher by Strathclyde Regional Council from 1976-77, becoming a computer programmer between 1977 and 2001 – the period from 1985 as computer project programmer at Glasgow University, while also applying his methodical mind to being an excellent chess player. He was on Renfrew District Council from 1988-96 as group secretary, contesting the Paisley South by-election in November 1990, coming fourth with 9.8 per cent, fighting it again in the 1992 general election when he ended fourth again with 9.1 per cent. He fought Dumbarton in 1997 and was election agent to George Lyon in Argyll and Bute in the 1999 Scottish Parliament elections. He was second choice to stand in the Argyll seat in the 2001 election, when Lib Dem Ray Michie retired. The party had selected Paisley University academic Paul Coleshill, who falsely claimed on his CV that he had a PhD. Coleshill had to stand down, and Reid took his place as candidate, meaning less time to prepare to defend a hard-fought four-way marginal. He used his maiden speech to praise Europe and trumpet the gains for his new constituency of having had Objective One status, claiming the decision not to join the euro at its outset was 'a financial disaster for many businesses in Argyll and Bute'. He also indicated his intention to campaign for the Gaelic language and culture. He is whip of the Scottish Lib Dem MP group.

Ayr

Predecessor Constituencies: Ayr District of Burghs (1945).

Socio-economic Indicators:

Constituency Pop. (16-64)	43,457
Claimant Count (May 2003)	3.6% (16% above average)
IBA/SDA Claimants	10.1%
Life Expectancy – Male	73.8 (0.4 yrs above average)
Life Expectancy – Female	78.3 (0.4 yrs below average)
Owner Occupied	71.1%
Social Rented	20.1%
Average Property Prices	£65,883 (27th)
Average Gross Income	£26,835 (25th)
Low Birthweight Babies	117 (6.0%)
Teenage Pregnancy Rates	362 (4.3%)
No. of Lone Parent Households	2,842 (9.2%)

2003 Scottish Parliament Election

Electorate: 55,523   *Turnout*: 31,591 (56.9%)   *Turnout 1999*: 66.5%

Candidate	Party	Votes	Votes%	99 %	Change%
John Scott	Con	12,865	40.7	38.0	+ 2.7
Rita Miller	Labour	10,975	34.7	38.1	– 3.3
James Dornan	SNP	4,334	13.7	19.5	– 5.7
Stuart Ritchie	Lib Dem	1,769	5.6	4.4	+ 1.2
James Stewart	SSP	1,648	5.2	–	–

Conservative majority: 1,890 (6.0%)   *Swing*: 3.0% Conservative to Labour

2001 General Election

Electorate: 55,630   *Turnout*: 38,560 (69.3%)

Candidate	Party	Votes	Votes%	Change%
Sandra Osborne	Labour	16,801	43.6	– 4.9
Phil Gallie	Conservative	14,256	37.0	+ 3.2
James Mather	SNP	4,621	12.0	– 0.6
Stuart Ritchie	Lib Dem	2,089	5.4	+ 0.7
James Stewart	SSP	692	1.8	–
Joseph Smith	UK Ind	101	0.3	–

Labour majority: 2,545 (6.6%)   *Swing*: 4.0% Labour to Conservative

1945–2000

Scottish Parliament

	Lab%	Con%	SNP%	Lib%	Other%	Turnout%
2000B	22.1	39.4	29.0	2.5	7.0	56.3
1999	38.1	38.0	19.5	4.4	–	66.5

Westminster

	Lab%	Con%	SNP%	Lib%	Other%	Turnout%
1997	48.4	33.8	12.6	4.7	0.5	80.2
1992	40.6	40.8	10.9	7.5	0.2	83.1
1987	39.1	39.4	6.7	14.8	–	80.0
1983	26.8	42.8	4.9	25.6	–	76.6
1979	36.9	43.3	9.2	10.6	–	79.8
1974O	34.6	42.4	16.9	6.3	–	79.4
1974F	38.6	50.4	11.0	–	–	83.1
1970	42.1	52.7	5.2	–	–	81.6
1966	49.4	50.6	–	–	–	85.3
1964	47.8	52.2	–	–	–	83.0
1959	45.3	54.7	–	–	–	79.1
1955	40.9	59.1	–	–	–	77.1
1951	41.7	58.3	–	–	–	86.5
1950	41.4	58.6	–	–	–	84.7
1945	49.2	50.8	–	–	–	71.5

Ayr constituency encompasses some of the most exclusive residential areas to be found in Scotland, including Troon and Prestwick – golfing country with a 'Costa Geriatrica' reputation. Ayr itself is a Labour town with expensive neighbourhoods sitting beside run-down, high unemployment council estates. The socio-economic profile illustrates the affluence and wealth of part of this seat alongside hardship and disadvantage. Average property prices are 2.3 per cent below average, having risen 38.5 per cent in the 1990s.

The Ayr economy has a sizeable defence procurement sector with thousands of jobs reliant on its maintenance. BAE Systems has a large presence at Prestwick, and has recently been supported by a £500 million assistance package by the UK Government to develop a new jumbo jet called the A3XX which will be designed by a European consortium. In 2000, HMS Gannet, a naval air base near Prestwick, shut after a government defence review removed its anti-submarine capability.

Prestwick Airport used to have Scotland's transatlantic monopoly but has now been overtaken by Glasgow and Edinburgh Airports. It went into decline in the early 1990s but bounced back defiantly with the dawn of low budget travel, and Ryanair in particular. The UK Government is committed to building a £60 million National Air Traffic Control Centre at Prestwick, but this has encountered delays following the privatisation of National Air Traffic Services, an issue which has caused Labour candidates discomfort among its employees.

Tourism is a major income generator in this part of Scotland aided by the towns of Prestwick and Troon. Troon has hosted the Open Golf Championship, while Ayr is well known for its racing course and hosts the Scottish Grand National, the main race of the Scottish racing calendar and a big day out for Scotland's social glitterati.

Ayr had a long, proud Conservative lineage until recently. In 1918, it was won for the Conservatives by Sir George Younger with a majority over the Liberals of 4,155. The only threats to Conservative hegemony came at the high mark of Labour's appeal: their majority fell to 728 in 1945 and 484 in 1966. Ayr's second George Younger (grandson of the first) represented the seat from 1964, holding it with a majority of 3,219 in October 1974 over Labour and 2,768 in 1979. One would not have given Younger much chance of holding out during the Thatcher-Major years with such a wafer-thin majority. However, in 1983 Younger increased the Conservative majority to 7,987 over Labour, before seeing it fall to 182 in 1987.

Younger was Scottish Secretary and Defence Secretary through the Thatcher years, retiring from the Commons in 1992, becoming chairman of the Royal Bank of Scotland and dying in 2003. His seat was contested for the Tories by Phil Gallie, who held on with a majority of only 85. The 1997 boundary redistribution removed some of the most Tory wards and gave Labour a notional majority of 1,895. In the May 1997 contest, in a notional Labour seat, Sandra Osborne increased Labour's vote by 3,000, while the Conservative vote fell by over 2,000 resulting in a Labour majority of 6,543. Turnout of 80.2 per cent was the second highest in Scotland, only bettered by Stirling. In 2001 the Conservative Phil Gallie needed a 7.3 per cent swing from four years previously and achieved just over half that – 4 per cent – cutting Labour's Sandra Osborne's majority to 2,545.

In the 1999 Scottish Parliament elections, Ayr was even more keenly fought with a 69.3 per cent turnout – again the second highest in the country. Labour's Ian Welsh just managed to hold on with a majority of 25 votes – making Ayr the most marginal seat in Scotland, as Labour's vote fell by over 7,000 and the Conservatives' by under 1,000. Six months into the Parliament, Welsh resigned, disenchanted with the life of a Labour backbencher. The March 2000 contest was the first by-election of the new Parliament and the Conservatives' John Scott was elected with a majority of 3,344, as the SNP's Jim Mather finished second, pushing Labour into third. This was a watershed result: the first Scottish by-election victory by the Conservatives since Edinburgh North in 1973 and their first gain since Glasgow Pollok in 1967. Ayr was a significant result, ending the Conservatives' pariah status and giving them their first constituency MSP in the new Parliament. In the Scottish Parliament election of May 2003 John Scott held his by-election vote and marginally increased his share of the vote as Labour came back from its disastrously distant third place to secure second place, but were still 1,890 behind. The SNP, who had polled well in the March 2000 by-election, fell back significantly even on their 1999 support. Troon still managed in 2003 to elect three out of four Conservative councillors with a 71 per cent vote in Troon South. In the regional list vote, the Conservatives won 35.5 per cent to Labour's 30.8 per cent – a 1,476 Tory lead over Labour – while the SSP secured 5.7 per cent and the Greens 4.6 per cent.

Boundary Commission proposals at Westminster may end the era of exciting, cliffhanging contests at Ayr by removing the Conservative areas of Prestwick and Troon and replacing them with the Labour Carrick and Cumnock from the Carrick, Cumnock and Doon Valley seat. Ayr's marginal status at the Scottish Parliament means that both the Conservatives and Labour will spend the next few years putting resources and effort into developing their party machines in the seat, the Tories hoping to build a council base there. Whether the Conservatives' recent victories in Ayr at the Scottish Parliament open a new epoch of Ayr politics remains to be seen, but this seat has contributed a disproportionate amount of suspense and theatre to Scottish political life in recent years.

MSP

JOHN SCOTT was born in 1951 in Irvine, and educated at George Watson's College in Edinburgh, followed by civil engineering at Edinburgh University. After leaving university, Scott went west again, to become part of the family farming business, W. Scott and Son, and then set up a fertiliser sales agency. He was a founding director of Ayrshire Country Lamb, and in 1999, set up Ayrshire Farmers' Market, going on as an MSP to champion the cause as chairman of the Scottish Association of Farmers' Markets. From 1994-96, he was Ayrshire president of the National Farmers' Union-Scotland, and convenor of the NFU hill farming committee from 1993-99.

In the Scottish election of 1999, Scott stood in Carrick, Cumnock and Doon Valley, where he polled respectably, increasing the Conservative vote by 3 per cent. The following March, after Ian Welsh had resigned as Labour's Ayr MP, complaining his talents were not being properly used as a backbencher, Scott stood in the first by-election of the Scottish Parliament. The candidate might have been Ayr's former Tory MP, Phil Gallie, but he would have had to have stood down as a South of Scotland list MSP, risking the seat he already had.

Scott, a quietly-spoken, shy but determined operator, became a member of the petitions committee, and his party's spokesman on transport and the environment 2000-2001, then the environment, including the water industry from 2001-03, shadowing the Executive's reform of the water boards, and building up the business case that Scottish Water was over-charging corporate Scotland. He also took up the cause of reforming one of the first laws passed by the Scottish Parliament, the Adults with Incapacity Act, saying parts of it were unworkable for GPs. Following the 2003 election, he became the Tory representative on the Scottish Parliament Corporate Body, with special responsibility for IT, facilities management and constituency offices. Widowed soon after his by-election success, Scott is a Kirk elder, with leisure interests in geology, curling and bridge.

MP

SANDRA OSBORNE was born in 1956 in Paisley and educated at Camphill High School, Paisley, Anniesland College, Jordanhill College and Strathclyde University, where she did a masters degree in equality and discrimination. She was a community worker in Glasgow from 1976-80 and a women's aid worker in Kilmarnock from 1983-97. She was a councillor on Kyle and Carrick District Council from 1990-95 and on the successor unitary South Ayrshire Council from 1994-97, where she was convener of housing and social work. She was elected MP for Ayr in 1997, the first time Labour has ever held the seat, after her husband, Alistair Osborne, had come within 85 votes of winning it in 1992. He was only prevented from standing again by a women-only shortlist.

At Westminster, she was considered a possible troublemaker on a leaked list drawn up by Peter Mandelson, having opposed New Labour on tuition fees and welfare cuts. She was noted for her low public profile, becoming a member of the Scottish affairs select committee from 1998-9, as well as that on information from 1997-2000. With the reshuffle of Scottish ministers after the establishment of the Scottish Parliament, Osborne became Parliamentary Private Secretary at the Scotland Office, working with Brian Wilson, George Foulkes and Helen Liddell until losing that role in 2003. Despite that position, she spoke in May 2000 against the part privatisation of air traffic control, but did not join the 46 MPs voting against the Government. She was more rebellious in February 2003, voting against the Government on the moves to war in Iraq, though swinging behind it the next month. She was on the Kerley Committee, looking into reform of local government, and in June 2000 wrote a minority report with Marilyn Livingstone, MSP for Kirkcaldy, arguing for retention of first-past-the-post voting. She was one of those to sign a motion critical of the government's policy on top-up tuition fees for students in England, but she supported it in the vital January 2004 division.

Banff and Buchan

Predecessor Constituencies: Aberdeen and Kincardineshire Eastern (1945) and Aberdeenshire East (1950–79).

Socio-economic Indicators:

Constituency Pop. (16-64)	48,179
Claimant Count (May 2003)	1.9% (40.5% below average)
IBA/SDA Claimants	10.0%
Life Expectancy – Male	74.1 (0.7 yrs above average)
Life Expectancy – Female	78.9 (0.2yrs above average)
Owner Occupied	66.2%
Social Rented	25.5%
Average Property Prices	£46,216(62nd)
Average Gross Income	£26,386 (30th)
Low Birthweight Babies (av. 1996-98)	122 (5.2%)
Teenage Pregnancy Rates (av. 1996-98)	373 (3.9%)
No. of Lone Parent Households	2,553 (8.3%)

CAB Enquiries

Issue	No. of cases	Percentage of total cases (%)
1. Benefits	2577	26.5
2. Employment	1991	20.5
3. Consumer	1952	20.1
4. Other	855	8.8
5. Housing	734	7.6

2003 Scottish Parliament Election

Electorate: 55,402   *Turnout*: 26,149 (47.2%)

Candidate	Party	Votes	Votes%	Change%
Stewart Stevenson	SNP	13,827	52.9	+ 0.3
Stewart Whyte	Con	5,463	20.9	+ 3.9
Iain Brotchie	Labour	2,885	11.0	– 2.6
Debra Storr	Lib Dem	2,227	8.5	– 8.2
Alan Buchan	SPA	907	3.5	–
Alice Rowan	SSP	840	3.2	–

SNP majority: 8,364 (32.0%)   *Swing*: 1.8% SNP to Conservative

2001 General Election

Electorate: 56,669   *Turnout*: 30,806 (54.4%)

Candidate	Party	Votes	Votes%	Change%
Alex Salmond	SNP	16,710	54.2	- 1.5
Alexander Wallace	Con	6,207	20.1	- 3.7
Edward Harris	Labour	4,363	14.2	+ 2.4
Douglas Herbison	Lib Dem	2,769	9.0	+ 3.0
Alice Rowan	SSP	447	1.5	–
Eric Davidson	UK Ind	310	1.0	–

SNP majority: 10,503 (34.1%)   *Swing*: 1.1% Conservative to SNP

1945–2001

Scottish Parliament

	Lab%	Con%	SNP%	Lib%	Other%	Turnout%
2001B	15.8	22.0	49.6	10.4	2.2	54.8
1999	13.6	17.0	52.6	16.8	–	55.1

Westminster

	Lab%	Con%	SNP%	Lib%	Other%	Turnout%
1997	11.8	23.8	55.8	6.0	2.6	68.7
1992	8.2	38.6	47.5	5.6	–	71.2
1987	7.5	38.7	44.2	9.6	–	70.8
1983	7.8	39.7	37.4	15.0	–	67.0
1979	15.8	42.8	41.4	–	–	72.4
1974O	9.4	35.5	48.5	6.6	–	70.5
1974F	6.7	35.0	50.8	7.5	–	76.5
1970	18.0	40.9	29.8	11.3	–	68.8
1966	22.1	41.4	8.9	27.6	–	68.2
1964	22.4	48.0	6.3	23.3	–	70.1
1959	36.6	63.4	–	–	–	67.1
1958B	27.1	48.6	–	24.3	–	65.9
1955	31.5	68.5	–	–	–	59.8
1951	31.9	68.1	–	–	–	70.0
1950	34.0	66.0	–	–	–	75.6
1945	45.1	54.9	–	–	–	65.7

Banff and Buchan contains the fishing towns of Fraserburgh (the Broch) and Peterhead (the Blue Toun), along with the coastal towns of Banff and Macduff and a number of inland towns and villages. The constituency is highly rural with a strong farming community and a substantial interest in fishing, containing the biggest fishing port in Britain, as well as a sizeable oil industry. Local employers also include RAF Buchan and Peterhead high security prison.

Banff and Buchan's socio-economic profile shows an area without some of the extreme poverty of the urban centres of Scotland, but is not hugely affluent either. Average property prices are 31.5 per cent below the average, having risen only 38.6 per cent in 1991-2001.

Banff and Buchan's economy was dealt a severe blow in 2000 when the Ministry of Defence announced the shrinking of facilities at the RAF base at Buchan taking £10 million out of the local economy and leaving a skeleton presence. A major public controversy arose in 2002 when the Scottish Executive decided that Peterhead Prison would close within the next three years. This would have entailed huge consequences for the local community as well as national debate over where to house most of the country's sex offenders housed at a specialised unit there. In 2003 after a local and national campaign, the Scottish Executive reversed its decision on closing the prison.

The local fishing and farming communities have been hard pressed in recent years. The Fraserburgh and Peterhead fishing fleets decided to make a high profile stand against European Union reduced fishing quotas – in March 2001 they sailed a small flotilla of boats up the Firth of Forth, and in June 2001 the Scottish Executive lost a parliamentary vote on its £27 million decommissioning scheme. The North East fishing communities fear that further European Union fishing cuts proposed in 2002 and 2003 mean that the fishing fleet will soon no longer be viable, and that will have a knock-on effect in the region. Peterhead was not helped when in 2003 the *Idler* magazine in a guide to 'crap towns' voted the town the 30th most awful place in the United Kingdom. This outraged the local paper, the *Buchan Observer* which condemned the decision as insensitive and wrong. Bill Russell, Chairman of Peterhead Tourism Initiative said that neighbouring Fraserburgh was an example of how media misinformation could degrade a town, 'We just have to look at Fraserburgh being called the drug capital to see the harm it does.'

Over the years, this constituency – first as Aberdeen and Kincardineshire Eastern, and then from 1950, Aberdeenshire East – has progressed from being safely Conservative to a safe SNP seat in which the Conservatives appear a spent force. From 1924 until his peerage in 1958, the seat was held by the iconoclastic and independent minded MP Robert Boothby. Boothby was one of a group known as 'the Glamour Boys' – anti-appeasement Conservative MPs who supported Winston Churchill's criticism of Neville Chamberlain. In the aftermath of the Suez crisis in 1956, he was one of only eight Conservative MPs who could not support the Eden Government. Patrick Wolrige-Gordon held the seat with little difficulty in the November 1958 by-election, aided by a split opposition vote between Labour and the Liberals. Conservative hegemony continued uninterrupted until February 1974 when the SNP's Douglas Henderson defeated Wolridge-Gordon, winning over half the vote; he won again in October 1974 when the Conservative candidate was Keith Raffan, later to become a Lib Dem MSP for Mid-Scotland and Fife.

The Conservatives retook the seat in 1979 when Albert McQuarrie defeated Henderson by the narrowest of margins – winning the seat with a majority of 558. In 1983 the seat was renamed Banff and Buchan and McQuarrie emerged victorious over Henderson in a rematch – increasing his majority to 937. The SNP had experienced its wilderness years in 1979 and 1983 and had still managed to remain fierce competitors in the seat, so it was no surprise that when the 1980s upswing in the Nationalists fortune began, Alex Salmond recaptured the constituency in 1987, defeating McQuarrie with a 2,441 majority.

Post-1987 Banff and Buchan was on its way to becoming that rare thing – a safe SNP seat. Salmond bucked the national trend towards the Conservatives in 1992 winning with an increased majority of 4,108. In 1997 Salmond increased his majority three-fold to 12,845 over the Conservatives in a distant second place, making Banff and Buchan the safest SNP seat in the country.

In the first Scottish Parliament election of May 1999 Salmond's majority fell slightly to 11,292, but increased in percentage terms by 3 per cent, as Conservative fortunes continued to slump, with their vote falling back to 17 per cent.

Alex Salmond was originally meant to be retiring from Westminster to concentrate on the Scottish Parliament, and in 2000 the party selected a new candidate, Stewart Stevenson, a close confidant of Salmond. However, after Salmond's surprising resignation as SNP leader in July 2000, he reconsidered his position and with the agreement of the local party, became the party's candidate for the forthcoming Westminster elections, while Stevenson became the candidate for the 2001 Scottish Parliament by-election.

At the 2001 Westminster election Alex Salmond saw his majority fall slightly from 12,845 to 10,503 – increasing by 2 per cent of vote share on a lower turnout – as the SNP vote declined by 6,000 votes, while the Conservatives lost 3,000 votes. On the same day Stewart Stevenson was elected MSP for the seat in the by-election polling just under 50 per cent support, achieving a 8,567 majority over the Conservatives. The SNP vote declined by 1,000 and the Conservatives increased by nearly 1,500 and 5 per cent. The Lib Dem candidate was Canon Kenyon Wright who was previously convenor of the cross-party Scottish Constitutional Convention from 1989-95, standing for the first ever time for the Lib Dems and finishing fourth with 10.4 per cent.

Stevenson was comfortably re-elected in 2003 with over half the vote and a majority of 8,364 – 3 per cent down on 1999, but marginally up on the by-election – as the Conservatives made a small advance. In the regional list vote, the SNP won 38.2 per cent to the Conservatives 18.3 per cent. The Fishing Party standing only in the North East Scotland regional seat, polled 7.7 per cent in Banff and Buchan – their highest vote in the region which accounted for 40 per cent of their regional vote – while the SSP and Greens both won 3.1 per cent.

Boundary Commission changes at Westminster mean a new Banff and Buchan seat, which will include the towns of Huntly, Turriff and Fyvie-Methlick from Gordon. That should not change the seat enough to threaten the SNP's hold here, leaving it as the party's only safe seat in the Commons. At the Scottish Parliament, Banff and Buchan is a safe SNP seat, with the largest SNP majority in the country, and one which has effortlessly made the transition from the party leader to a lower-profile MSP without affecting the party's majority. The decline of the Conservatives has been recent and spectacular in this seat, as they won 39 per cent as recently as 1992, but are now consistently winning 20 per cent in a succession of contests. This is proof of the changing face of rural Scotland, and the problems the Conservatives face if they are ever to become a viable national force across the country.

MSP

STEWART STEVENSON was born in Edinburgh in 1946, and educated at Bell Baxter High School, Cupar in Fife, and at Aberdeen University, where he studied maths. He worked first as a psychiatric nurse, and then, from 1969-98, for the Bank of Scotland, first as a trainee computer programmer and rising to become director of technology innovation, in a bank well-known for precisely that. He also lectured in business studies at Heriot-Watt University. From 1998-2001, he was a director of Business for Scotland, set up by the SNP as a semi-independent vehicle for business supporters and fund-raising, while also running the merchandising end of the SNP. With his banking interest, he was involved in the campaign against de-mutualisation of Edinburgh-based Standard Life, leading the Standard Life Independent Members' Organisation.

Stevenson came late to electoral politics while pursuing his successful business career. He was unfairly ridiculed in the media as merely Alex Salmond's chauffeur, though the relationship did sometimes appear to be akin to master and servant. Stevenson contested Salmond's home turf of Linlithgow in the 1999 election. As with the other parties, the SNP had a self-imposed rule against continuing dual mandates beyond the 2001 Westminster election. With Salmond's opting to focus on Westminster, he backed Stevenson as the candidate to replace him in the Scottish Parliament.

He slotted into the SNP team of MSPs with committee posts on justice 2 and rural development. He is sometimes ridiculed, and sometimes parodies himself with his anorak tendency, using his grasp of detail to outwit ministerial opponents. But he is not to be under-estimated as a political operator, having learned a lot from his chum Alex. He could lay claim, after only two years, to more than many others had done in four, having led the campaign to save Peterhead Prison from closure, successfully amending the Land Reform Bill to allow free access for those, such as mountain guides and photographers, who make their living on the hills, and posing a wide range of questions to ministers, some of which contributed to a sharp cut in the Executive's pre-election advertising budget. After the 2003 election, he got a place on the communities committee, and became deputy to Shona Robison as a front bencher on health and social justice. That should still leave time for his hobby of flying, having previously been a Scottish champion dinghy sailor.

MP

ALEX SALMOND was born in Linlithgow in 1954. He was educated at Linlithgow Academy and graduated in economics and history at St Andrews University, which he attended at the time it was a hothouse of radical right-wing politics. He sympathised with Labour, but joined the Scottish National Party when challenged to do so during a political argument with his then girlfriend. He worked as an agricultural economist for the Scottish Office from 1978-80, then joining the Royal Bank of Scotland as an economist specialising in the oil and gas sector, until his election in 1987. Having won the Banff and Buchan nomination for his party by only one vote in 1985, he won the seat at the first time of asking in 1987 and was already recognised as a high flier within the SNP. His elevation to SNP leader in 1990 was not unexpected, though his resignation in 2000 was.

Salmond was first elected to the SNP national executive in 1981, was vice-chair for publicity from 1985-87. His rise within the SNP was nothing short of phenomenal, at a time when many of the old guard had deserted it, leaving a vacuum in which Salmond had few competitors within his own generation. He was a leading figure in the left-wing '79 Group formed after the 1979 electoral disaster to develop a more radical agenda appealing to Central Belt Labour voters. When the party leadership proscribed the group in 1982, seven of its leading members were expelled, including Salmond, but their sentence was later reduced to suspension. Having courted political oblivion, he was elected an MP five years later, elected deputy leader that same year, and after only three years at Westminster, he beat Margaret Ewing, by the wider-than-expected margin of 486 votes to 186, to succeed Gordon Wilson as the party's national convener in 1990.

In the Commons, he made an early impression with a protest during the 1998 Budget speech which had him expelled for five days. He was the one who ended the poll tax non-payment campaign in 1991, when it was announced the tax would be abolished. His tactical and media skills were a boon to the SNP throughout his tenure as SNP leader, and provided the party with a strong political profile across Scotland and in the UK media too. A high point was the *Scotsman* Debate in Edinburgh's Usher Hall in 1992, in which Salmond ran rings round his opponents, particularly Donald Dewar. With such attributes, alongside a drive to professionalise the organisation with his friend and contemporary Mike Russell as chief executive, he turned Banff and Buchan into a safe seat with a solid membership base, particularly in the fishing communities. He also brought about a long-term gradualist ascendancy within the SNP during his leadership, which did much to infuriate fundamentalist critics such as Jim Sillars and Margo MacDonald, and is one reason behind the part-political, part-personal feud between Salmond and Sillars.

That feud became critical in 1988-89, with Sillars newly elected as Govan MP, outmanoeuvring Salmond and the gradualists in blocking SNP participation in the Scottish Constitutional Convention.

Their feud returned with a vengeance in the *Scotsman* letters page during the 2003 SNP leadership election campaign. Salmond nudged his party into support for the Yes-Yes side of the 1997 referendum campaign. In the subsequent run into the first Scottish Parliament elections, Salmond initially outmanoeuvred the Labour Party and by the summer of 1998 had stolen the initiative with the SNP nine points ahead of Labour in polls. They then faced concerted Labour retaliation, followed by significant SNP mistakes, such as Salmond's comments on the war in Kosovo being 'an unpardonable folly' and the rushed 'Penny for Scotland' campaign. Both were attempts to win back ground from Labour, but served to create an impression of inconsistency and opportunism for which the SNP came under ruthless pressure from Labour and its supporters in the press, most notably the *Daily Record*. The 1999 election results were disappointing compared to the expectations raised in 1998, but it was the highest SNP vote for twenty-five years, with 35 MSP posts and their staff transforming the party.

Salmond led his party for a year in the Scottish Parliament, with a rich vein of issues on which to hammer the Executive, but found more than his debating match in Donald Dewar. His resignation in July 2000, which surprised even some of those closest to him, encouraged much speculation, ranging across chronic back pain to his desire to spend more time with his beloved horse-racing. He said he had done his stint and the time had come, after 10 years, to move on. It also looked like a calculation that he could (accurately) foresee a run of difficult elections for the SNP, and little prospect of government office before 2007.

Having stood down from any front bench role, he responded to a request from his successor, John Swinney, to reverse his plans to leave Westminster, as Swinney and the other four MPs were planning to do, so that they could focus on the Scottish Parliament. It was argued that Salmond would provide expertise and continuity to the new batch of MPs they hoped to get elected in 2001, so he resigned as an MSP causing a by-election on the same day as the 2001 general election, and stood once more for the Banff and Buchan seat in the Commons. Although the party returned with one fewer MP, having lost Galloway and Upper Nithsdale, this put Salmond far from the heart of Scottish politics, leading to reported frustration.

He has said he intends to stand again as a Westminster MP at the election expected around 2005, he then hopes to return to the Scottish Parliament in 2007, and serve out another dual mandate until the following Westminster election, when he will stand down from the Commons. This encourages some speculation that, with Swinney struggling to keep the SNP together in the face of bad election results, Salmond would quite like to answer the call from his party to return to the leadership at a time when things might look more auspicious for it electorally. Meanwhile, as a visiting professor at Strathclyde University, he is focussing more attention on his economic expertise to make the case for independence, publishing a pamphlet on the subject in 2003. He remains a formidable figure in Scottish politics, feared by opponents and with a range of political skills to compete with the best at Westminster. The *Spectator* made him Tactician of the Year in 1998, while Matthew Parris wrote in *The Times* of his combination of 'an open countenance with an instinct for the low blow'. Former colleague Isobel Lindsay said of Salmond: 'If he has any flaw, then perhaps he enjoys the sport of political manoeuvring, the manipulation of people, rather more than he should'.

Caithness, Sutherland and Easter Ross

Predecessor Constituencies: Caithness and Sutherland (1945–92).

Socio-economic Indicators:

Constituency Pop. (16-64)	32,520
Claimant Count (May 2003)	3.7% (19.8% above average)
IBA/SDA Claimants	7.8%
Life Expectancy – Male	73.8 (0.4 yrs above average)
Life Expectancy – Female	79.1 (0.4 yrs above average)
Owner Occupied	62.5%
Social Rented	25.8%
Average Property Prices	£56,012 (44th)
Average Gross Income	£23,499 (56th)
Low Birthweight Babies	113 (7.9%)
Teenage Pregnancy Rates	270 (4.3%)
No. of Lone Parent Households	3,045 (8.4%)

CAB Enquiries

Issue	No. of cases	Percentage of total cases (%)
1. Benefits	3941	37.8
2. Employment	1384	13.3
3. Consumer	1291	12.4
4. Other	1007	9.7
5. Housing	923	8.9

2003 Scottish Parliament Election

Electorate: 40,462   Turnout: 21,127 (52.2%)   Turnout 1999: 62.6%

Candidate	Party	Votes	Votes%	99 %	Change%
Jamie Stone	Lib Dem	7,742	36.6	41.1	– 4.4
Deirdre Steven	Labour	5,650	26.7	24.2	+ 2.5
Robert Gibson	SNP	3,692	17.5	23.2	– 5.7
Alan MacLeod	Con	2,262	10.7	8.3	+ 2.4
James Campbell	Ind	953	4.5	2.1	+ 2.4
Frank Ward	SSP	828	3.9	(other 1.1)	–

Liberal Democrat majority: 2,092 (9.9%)   Swing: 3.5% Labour to Liberal Democrat

2001 General Election

Electorate: 41,315   Turnout: 24,867 (60.2%)

Candidate	Party	Votes	Votes%	Change%
Viscount John Thurso	Lib Dem	9,041	36.4	+ 0.8
Michael Meighan	Labour	6,297	25.3	− 2.5
John Macadam	SNP	5,273	21.2	− 1.8
Robert Rowantree	Con	3,513	14.1	+ 3.3
Karn Mabon	SSP	544	2.2	−
Gordon Campbell	Ind	199	0.8	−

Liberal Democrat majority: 2,744 (11.0%)   *Swing*: 1.6% Labour to Liberal Democrat

1945–97 Westminster

	Lab%	Con%	SNP%	Lib%	Other%	Turnout%
1997	27.8	10.8	23.0	35.6	2.8	70.2
1992	15.7	21.0	18.2	45.1	−	71.9
1987	14.9	16.7	10.3	53.6	4.4	73.6
1983	14.3	22.7	11.0	52.0	−	75.5
1979	41.5	30.5	28.0	−	−	78.4
1974O	35.3	18.8	23.9	22.0	−	78.1
1974F	36.2	21.5	16.1	26.2	−	83.0
1970	36.7	22.4	15.5	25.4	−	83.1
1966	39.1	22.0	−	38.9	−	79.2
1964	30.3	20.8	−	36.1	12.8	80.1
1959	34.6	65.4	−	−	−	69.6
1955	29.0	56.5	−	14.5	−	69.5
1951	34.1	49.3	−	16.6	−	73.5
1950	29.7	35.8	−	34.5	−	76.5
1945	33.4	33.5	−	33.1	−	64.0

Caithness, Sutherland and Easter Ross is a vast seat geographically and one that has dramatically changed political colours at Westminster several times. Its main towns are Wick, Thurso, Invergordon and Tain and the seat enjoys a large, sparsely populated interior and north-western coast of sea lochs and mountains. Average property prices are 17 per cent below the national average, and rose 86.6 per cent from 1991-2001.

A major issue has been the abolition of Caithness Council in 1996 and its replacement by a single tier Highland Council whose headquarters are in Inverness. This is seen as a centralisation of decision making to people living in Caithness with consequences for education and other services. Caithness and Sutherland NHS Trust was also recently abolished in a recent health reorganisation and loss of maternity services have become a major constituency issue.

Agriculture has been hit severely in the constituency in recent years through BSE and foot and mouth, while the Scottish Executive's Land Reform Act gives communities the right to buy their estates when they come on the market – a campaign issue for more than a century in an area where landlordism has a particularly unhappy history. Transport issues are vitally important in a vast constituency such as this and there are local demands to improve the East Coast rail line north of Inverness and upgrade Wick Airport. The state of the local roads was recently revealed by a survey that showed the A99 from Wick to Latherton as the second most dangerous road in Scotland.

Employment growth has been seen recently with BT Scotland opening a call centre in Thurso employing 600 people, and an Openworld internet centre at Alness. The Invergordon aluminium smelter – a controversial closure of the Thatcher Government – is long gone while the Nigg oilrig construction yard goes through employment peaks and troughs. The nuclear processing plant at Dounreay is in the process of being decommissioned and while this pleases many, it also has consequences for local jobs and has made the SNP's non-nuclear policy locally unpopular. Skibo Castle, situated near the town of Dornoch is a 7,000-acre internationally renowned resort used by celebrities. It was the site of popular icon Madonna's marriage to Guy Ritchie in December 2000, which saw the global A-list of celebrities descend on the area with hundreds of paparazzi and consequently fabulous publicity.

This seat has had a rich and varied political history. It was held as Caithness and Sutherland by Sir Archibald Sinclair from 1922-45, leader of the Liberals from 1935-45 and briefly Secretary of State for Scotland from 1931-32 as well as a member of Churchill's wartime coalition. In one of the most sensational results in 1945, the Conservative Eric Gandar-Dower won the seat by six votes over Labour, with Sinclair 55 votes behind in third place. David Robertson won it for the Conservatives in 1950 by the wider margin of 269 votes over Sinclair and held the seat in 1951 and 1955, before being returned as an Independent Conservative in 1959. In 1964, the seat was won by the Liberal George Mackie, who was then defeated in 1966 by Robert Maclennan, winning the seat in Wilson's Labour landslide with a majority of only 64 votes over the Liberals. Unlike many of Labour's gains in that year, he held the seat in 1970 and retained it in the two 1974 elections, winning in October that year with a 2,560 majority over the SNP.

In 1979, Maclennan as a Labour candidate had a majority of 2,539 over the Conservatives. In 1983, under the Social Democratic banner he transformed this into a 6,843 Liberal-SDP Alliance majority over the Conservatives. This was a result of epic proportions, both locally and nationally. There had been no Liberal candidate in 1979, and Labour's vote was cut by over 6,000 and nearly 27 per cent; it was also achieved against a backdrop of Social Democratic failure at a parliamentary level with only five defectors from Labour retaining their seats, including David Owen and Roy Jenkins. The SDP, with Charles Kennedy gaining neighbouring Ross, Cromarty and Skye, had half of their parliamentary representation based in Scotland. Maclennan subsequently held the seat through the various transformations of the centre parties in the 1980s.

In the May 1997 election, Robert Maclennan was returned with a much reduced majority of 2,259 over Labour who increased their vote by 12 per cent. In June 2001 following Maclennan's retirement, Viscount John Thurso continued the long family tradition of representing the area, slightly increasing his majority to 2,744 over Labour.

In the first Scottish Parliament election of May 1999, Labour could not build on their momentum and Jamie Stone was elected Lib Dem MSP for the seat with a 4,391 lead over Labour. In the May 2003 Scottish Parliament election, Stone was successfully re-elected with his majority over Labour cut in half from 4,391 to 2,092. In the regional list vote, Labour finished ahead of the Lib Dems by 410 votes winning 24.8 per cent to the Lib Dems 22.9 per cent, while the Nationalists secured 21.5 per cent. The Greens finished on 7 per cent and the SSP 4.5 per cent.

Boundary Commission recommendations for Westminster will see Caithness, Sutherland and Easter Ross extend southwards into the Lib Dem seat of Ross, Skye and Inverness West currently held by Charles Kennedy. It is not expected to threaten the Lib Dems and Labour is well established in second place.

MSP

JAMIE STONE was born in Edinburgh in 1954. He was educated at Tain Royal Academy and Gordonstoun, studied history and geology at St Andrews University and had a varied career in the oil industry, cheese-making, freelance journalism and even a brief time as a lavatory attendant. He was an English teacher in Sicily from 1977-78, a fish gutter in the Faroes in 1978, a stores clerk for Wimpey from 1979-81, site administrator for Bechtel Great Britain 1981-84 and administrative manager for Odfjell Drilling (UK) Ltd 1984-86. From 1986-94, he was a director of the Stone family firm, Highland Fine Cheeses Ltd, and can usually raise a cheer whenever he has to declare his cheese interest in Parliamentary debate.

Stone was a councillor on Ross and Cromarty District from 1986-96, and also vice-chair of policy and resources. For the first term of the unitary Highland Council, he was vice-chair of finance. While a councillor, he was also director of the Highland Festival at the time it was set up, plus a governor of Eden Court Theatre, Inverness and various cultural organisations in Tain. In the Scottish Parliament, he served on the education and local government committees at first, before joining the rural development committee, and he became the Lib Dem spokesperson for finance, equal opportunities and fisheries. Normally loyal to the Executive line, he resigned from the fisheries brief (later to return) after voting against the Executive on its March 2001 vessel decommissioning scheme. It is a constituency issue for him in Lochinver and Kinlochbervie. He was absent from the Section 28 vote on homosexuality and the curriculum. At a constituency level, he claimed to have worked to preserve casualty and maternity services in Caithness, while helping upgrade the A9 and Wick airport, and he congratulated Madonna in Parliament for getting married in his constituency's Skibo Castle in December 2001.

When Tavish Scott became a minister in October 2000, Stone took his place as the Lib Dem representative on the Holyrood Progress Committee, facing ferocious flak with cheerful optimism that things will work out in the end, and a jolly fine building it will be too. He took more criticism than most, in trying to justify an £88,000 reception desk as good value, though the attacks seemed to do little to dent his spirits. Looking like Harry Potter, the only MSP to volunteer his membership of the crusty, establishment New Club in Edinburgh, and by rapid turns both serious and then up to some Woosterish wheeze, his ambition is to write a comic novel based on contemporary Scotland. He would not make a bad leading character.

MP

JOHN THURSO was born in 1953 in Thurso, from an aristocratic lineage which has seen three of his forebears represent the area in Parliament. His great great great grandfather, Sir George Sinclair, first represented the seat during the Napoleonic Wars from 1811-1818 and again from 1831-41. His great great grandfather, Sir John Sinclair, represented the seat from 1869-85, and his grandfather, Sir Archibald Sinclair, first Viscount and fourth Baronet, represented the seat from 1922-45, as leader of the Liberal Party for the latter ten years and also as a member of Churchill's wartime administration.

The third viscount and sixth baronet was educated at Eton College and Westminster College, and rebelled against the expectations of a blue blood upbringing by going into the hotel trade and learning the trade from the bottom up. The start of his career, from 1971-85, was in the Savoy Group of hotels, learning the range of skills in kitchen, but increasingly specialising in customer relations in the Savoy, Claridges and then as general manager of the Savoy. In 1981, he was sent to manage the group's Hotel Lancaster in Paris, before he branched out into business under his own steam, pioneering a new type of exclusive country house hotel with the refurbishment of Cliveden House which he ran from 1985-92. He became chief executive of Granfel Holdings Ltd from 1992-95, and with a growing reputation for turning around failing and dowdy enterprises which were sliding from the top rank of the hospitality industry, he took on the challenge of turning around Champneys, a spa and health resort in Hertfordshire. This was recorded in a TV documentary about company doctors, and showed something of his friendly but ruthless effectiveness as a manager. It also featured him stripping naked to sample the pleasures of the spa treatment – something his opponents used against him in the 2001 election campaign to no obvious effect. He was rolling the Champneys brand out to city centre locations in London and across Europe, and also became chairman of a troubled wallpaper manufacturer, which gained some notoriety as the maker of the wallpaper expensively bought by Lord Irvine to refurbish the Lord Chancellor's apartment in the Palace of Westminster.

From 1995-2000, Thurso was also active on the Liberal Democrat cause in the House of Lords as a hereditary peer, where he was spokespeer on tourism from 1996-99 and food in 1998-99, while bringing some of his professional expertise to bear as a member of the Lords Refreshment Committee in 1997-99. He claims to have been happy to leave in 2000 when most hereditary peers were ejected from the upper house, meaning that he became eligible to stand for the Commons. He had criticised the Lords reforms as 'a giant step for complacency'. Having been elected, he quickly became his party's spokesman on Scottish affairs, and a member of the culture, media and sport select committee.

Carrick, Cumnock and Doon Valley

Predecessor Constituencies: Ayrshire South (1945–79).

Socio-economic Indicators:

Constituency Pop. (16-64)	52,610
Claimant Count (May 2003)	4.0% (29.6% above average)
IBA/SDA Claimants	11.6%
Life Expectancy – Male	73.7 (0.3 yrs above average)
Life Expectancy – Female	77.9(0.8 yrs below average)
Owner Occupied	61.4%
Social Rented	29.9%
Average Property Prices	£55,334 (47th)
Average Gross Income	£24,101 (49th)
Low Birthweight Babies (av. 1996–98)	147 (6.2%)
Teenage Pregnancy Rates (av. 1996-98)	515 (4.8%)
No. of Lone Parent Households	3,537 (10.2%)

CAB Enquiries

Issue	No. of cases	Percentage of total cases (%)
1. Benefits	2489	28.7
2. Consumer	2176	25.1
3. Employment	1335	15.4
4. Housing	823	9.5
5. Other	538	6.2

2003 Scottish Parliament Election

Electorate: 65,102   *Turnout:* 34,366 (52.8%)   *Turnout 1999:* 62.7%

Candidate	Party	Votes	Votes%	99 %	Change%
Cathy Jamieson	Labour	16,484	48.0	47.9	+ 0.1
Phil Gallie	Con	9,030	26.3	19.8	+ 6.5
Adam Ingram	SNP	5,822	16.9	26.4	– 9.5
Murray Steele	SSP	1,715	5.0	–	–
Caron Howden	Lib Dem	1,315	3.8	5.9	– 2.1

Labour majority: 7,454 (21.7%)   *Swing:* 3.2% Labour to Conservative

2001 General Election

Electorate: 64,919

Turnout: 40,107 (61.8%)

Candidate	Party	Votes	Votes%	Change%
George Foulkes	Labour	22,174	55.3	− 4.5
Gordon Miller	Con	7,318	18.2	+ 1.3
Tom Wilson	SNP	6,258	15.6	− 1.1
Amy Rodger	Lib Dem	2,932	7.3	+ 2.0
Amanda McFarlane	SSP	1,058	2.6	-
James McDaid	Soc Lab	367	0.9	-

Labour majority: 14,856 (37.0%)

Swing: 2.9% Labour to Conservative

1945–97 Westminster

	Lab%	Con%	SNP%	Lib%	Other%	Turnout%
1997	59.8	17.0	16.7	5.3	1.3	75.0
1992	59.1	20.0	16.2	4.7	–	77.0
1987	60.1	20.7	9.6	9.6	–	75.8
1983	51.5	24.1	6.5	17.9	–	74.2
1979	35.2	25.4	8.0	–	31.4	78.9
1974O	56.2	18.6	19.8	5.4	–	77.4
1974F	57.2	26.4	16.4	–	–	79.4
1970	61.8	30.2	8.0	–	–	76.9
1970B	54.0	25.6	20.4	–	–	76.3
1966	67.2	32.8	–	–	–	75.1
1964	66.7	33.3	–	–	–	77.6
1959	63.7	36.3	–	–	–	80.9
1955	61.6	38.4	–	–	–	76.8
1951	60.5	39.5	–	–	–	82.9
1950	60.2	39.8	–	–	–	85.4
1946B	63.6	36.4	–	–	–	69.0
1945	61.3	38.7	–	–	–	75.0

Carrick sits south of Ayr and ranges from towns on the outskirts of Ayr like Alloway, to coastal resorts like Girvan – both Conservative voting areas – to the more populous Labour areas of Cumnock and Doon Valley which are old South Ayrshire mining areas. The socio-economic profile of the constituency reflects the mix of prosperity with areas just making do. Average property prices are 18 cent below the national average, and rose 41.9 per cent in the nineties.

Attracting new jobs and employers to the area is one of the most pressing local issues. In the last two years in the aftermath of the 9/11 terrorist attacks there have been anxieties over aerospace job cuts at the nearby Prestwick Airport, while Falmer Jeans were put into receivership in 1998, but purchased by the company Matalan. In 2002 it was announced that the Child Support Agency were creating a data processing facility in Cumnock, bringing 170 new jobs. This is also Robert Burns country – with Alloway, his home town, a major tourist designation, although recently hit by the downturn in US visitors.

Hunterston nuclear power station is situated in the seat, and George Foulkes has pursued the issue of health and safety concerns relating to it, and in particular, the existence of leukaemia clusters around the plant. Other major concerns include health and education with Ayrshire and Arran Health Board announcing a £2.5 million investment in primary care services, and the possible closure of some of the Catholic primary schools as rolls fall.

Labour has a long tradition here, winning the seat in 1918 and holding it continuously through the inter-war years and since, with the exception of the aberration of 1931. Emrys Hughes was Labour MP from 1946 until his death in 1969, driving his vote up to 67.2 per cent in 1966. In March 1970 a by-election was called in which the Labour candidate was a young Jim Sillars, previously Hughes' agent in 1964 and 1966, who fought the campaign on a hard anti-Nationalist platform. Along with the Gorbals by-election the previous year, Sillars victory with 54 per cent to the SNP's 20.4 per cent was seen as the end of the SNP post-Hamilton surge of the Sixties.

Great things were expected from Sillars in the Labour Party, where his energy and intelligence were widely recognised and Sillars clearly expected great things to come to him. In October 1974, his majority over the SNP was 14,478, the safest Labour seat in Scotland. By this point, he had become a passionate devolutionist and he left Labour over its foot-dragging on devolution and set up his own Scottish Labour Party with one other MP in 1976. This was briefly, in the heady days of the 1970s, a shooting star in Scottish politics, mesmerising both the media and politicians, but quickly burning out.

By 1979, Sillars faced the task of holding Ayrshire South against Labour's George Foulkes. Sillars polled a respectable 31.4 per cent, attracting nearly two-thirds of his previous Labour vote, and saw the Labour vote fall by a massive 21 per cent, but he lost by the small margin of 1,521 votes. Sillars' political trajectory into and out of the SNP is well-documented, and as Carrick, Cumnock and Doon Valley from 1983 onwards the seat quietly returned to the Labour fold giving Foulkes majorities over the Conservatives of 11,370 in 1983 and 16,802 in 1987.

Labour's majority fell slightly in 1992 to 16,666 with boundary changes notionally cutting this by 2,000. In 1997, Foulkes put nearly 1,500 on Labour's vote, the Conservatives lost 5,000 and the SNP remained static and finished in third place just over 100 votes behind; Labour's majority was 21,062. In June 2001, Foulkes was returned for the sixth time although his majority was slashed by one-third from 21,062 to 14,856, as Labour's vote declined by 7,000.

The Scottish Parliament elections showed Labour's strength as it lost 10,000 votes without facing any threat, while the SNP increased their support by 2,500, securing a decent but distant second place 8,803 behind Labour. In May 2003 after Labour's shaky result four years previously the SNP had hopes of being able to further erode Labour's hold on the seat, but this was not to be. Cathy Jamieson was returned with a slightly reduced majority of 7,454, but this was due to Phil Gallie for the Conservatives replacing the SNP in second place – as he put nearly 1,000 votes on his support, while the Nationalists Adam Ingram fell to third, losing 5,000 votes. In the regional vote, Labour won 41.8 per cent, the Conservatives 21.9 per cent and the SNP 17.0 per cent, while the SSP won 5.8 per cent and the Greens 4.1 per cent.

Carrick, Cumnock and Doon Valley is to disappear under new boundaries for Westminster, much of it is to be replaced by the new Ayr, Cumnock and Carrick constituency, which looks safe for Labour. At the Scottish Parliament this is the kind of seat Labour can count on winning in good times and bad. Cathy Jamieson should be secure here as long as she wishes to stand as a Labour candidate.

MSP

CATHY JAMIESON was born in 1956 in Kilmarnock and educated at James Hamilton Academy, Kilmarnock, then Glasgow Art School where she obtained a degree in fine art, and also at Goldsmiths

College, London, where she gained a Higher Diploma in Art. She later attended Glasgow University and Glasgow Caledonian University where she qualified as a social worker. Jamieson is a qualified art therapist and was a social worker with Strathclyde Regional Council from 1980-86, a community intermediate treatment worker from 1986-92 and principal officer of Who Cares? Scotland from 1992 until 1999, an advocacy organisation for young people in care. While in that role, she was a member of the inquiry team into abuse in Edinburgh residential care homes.

In the Scottish Parliament, she began as deputy convener of the European committee and a member of the transport and environment committee until December 2000, before joining the rural development committee. Jamieson, a vegan, has an interest in animal welfare, and was deputy convener of that cross-party group.

Jamieson is on the left of the party and was, until ministerial office required some compromises of her, an active member of the left-wing Campaign for Socialism group, which grew out of grass roots opposition to Blair's rewriting of Clause Four in 1994. That year, she was election agent to hard left MEP Alex Smith in South of Scotland. From 1998-99, she was elected to Labour's UK national executive committee on the slate of the left-wing Grassroots Alliance, voicing opposition to the Blairite push for Third Way politics.

With Henry McLeish's elevation to the Labour leadership and First Minister, a dormant role of deputy leader was activated, with the assumption it would go to a woman MSP. Although a backbencher, Cathy Jamieson put herself forward as a candidate, and found herself unopposed. Other likely contenders were wary of standing for a post which could look too much like a bid for succession to McLeish, which was not then a problem for Jamieson. That has changed, since Jack McConnell brought her straight into his first cabinet in November 2001, as minister for education and young people. She astonished some by saying she was leaving the schools part of the brief to Lib Dem deputy Nicol Stephen, following the settlement of long-running pay and conditions negotiations. This allowed her to focus on her main interest of children's services, particularly cared-for children, for whom she would bring forward a number of initiatives in the subsequent months. In the shadow of McConnell, who had held the education post immediately before and was a maths teacher, Jamieson launched a national debate on education in March 2002, which the First Minister had himself intended to launch before become premier. That put the brakes on innovation while the forces of consensus gathered around the consultation, and Jamieson seemed too timid to lead the debate herself. She appeared on such occasions, including the statement which launched it, to be something of a creature of her officials. When, in spring 2002, McConnell set out to make anti-social behaviour by youth a strong Labour issue, he by-passed justice minister Jim Wallace and handed the role of co-ordinating this to Jamieson. She was less timid as one of those fronting the Labour campaign for 2003, and was then asked by McConnell to take the lead role in the negotiating team for the subsequent coalition. She was then given the cabinet's hottest seat as justice minister – though McConnell oddly took the anti-social behaviour legislation away from her and handed it to communities minister Margaret Curran.

Her left-wing credentials are not quite what they were, having to argue for private finance to build new and upgraded schools, and even attacking the SNP for opposing the policy on the same basis she had done. She backed the Labour leadership line on both Scottish Parliament Iraq war votes, making the case in the Parliament chamber with acknowledgement of the difficulty it caused her. She took some latitude in refusing to condemn striking firefighters, but nor did she publicly support them. She joins fellow leftists Patricia Ferguson and Malcolm Chisholm in protecting McConnell against attacks from the left. Seen by some observers to be capable in interviews and ministerial statements of spouting clichés with an air of self-righteousness, she was implausibly awarded in 2004 the title of Scottish Woman of Influence, defeating multi-millionaire author J. K. Rowling.

A big enthusiast for co-operatives and mutuals, she has been active in the Woodcraft Folk and CND. She is married with one son, and admits to being fanatical about Kilmarnock Football Club.

MP

GEORGE FOULKES was born in 1942 in Oswestry, and was elected for South Ayrshire in 1979, narrowly beating Jim Sillars. He has held Carrick, Cumnock and Doon Valley since 1983. He previously stood unsuccessfully in Edinburgh West in 1970 and Edinburgh Pentlands in October 1974. Foulkes was educated at Keith Grammar School, Haberdashers Aske's School, Hampstead, and Edinburgh University, from where he went on to be President of the National Union of Students Scotland from 1964-66. Foulkes was Director of the European League for Economic Co-operation from 1967-68, Scottish organiser of the European Movement from 1968-69 and director of Age Concern Scotland from 1973-79. Elected to Edinburgh Corporation from 1970-74 and Lothian Region from 1974-79, he was chair of the Lothian Region education committee from 1974-79, controversially seeking to take over private schools, and was also a member of COSLA's education committee from 1975-79.

Once in the Commons, he was transformed over the years from multi-cause dial-a-quote to a more congenial Commons character, noted for his abnormally high number of international fact-finding trips. This was at least partly explained by his front bench career, as spokesman on European Community affairs from 1983-85, on foreign affairs from 1985-92, on defence from 1992-93 and on overseas development from 1994-97.

He was also a critic of Britain's role in the Falklands War. His career took a dent and two years on the backbenches after 1993, when he received considerable publicity and a hefty fine for getting drunk at a Scotch Whisky Association reception, injuring a woman pedestrian while attempting to imitate Batman, and then assaulting the Metropolitan Police officer who arrested him for being drunk and disorderly. In Government, Foulkes became junior minister at the Department of International Development from 1997 to January 2001, and minister of state at the Scotland Office, as deputy to Helen Liddell, from 2001-02, when Tony Blair moved him aside in favour of new blood.

Foulkes was a consistent devolutionist post-1979 and was chair of the Labour Campaign for a Scottish Assembly from 1982-97 and author after Labour's defeat in 1983 of the 'Foulkes Memorandum'. It argued that the Tories had no mandate and it was 'no longer enough to put the head down and wait for the return of a Labour Government'. Instead, he said, Labour had to consider the heresy of working with the SNP and Liberal-SDP Alliance to get a Parliament, with non-Conservative MPs ceding authority to a broad-ranging convention representing the civic 'estates' of Scottish society. Donald Dewar at first dismissed such ideas, but after the 1987 election defeat, the idea was transformed into the cross-party Scottish Constitutional Convention.

Foulkes has been a passionate supporter of the first-past-the-post electoral system and became chair of the Labour Campaign for Electoral Success which was set up in early 1991, including Labour local government leaders Pat Lally and Eric Milligan. Their aim was to reverse the 1990 Scottish party conference decision to support an alternative to FPTP for the Scottish Parliament, but they were heavily defeated at the 1991 conference. He eventually accepted the additional member system as a compromise, while continuing to oppose electoral reform at Westminster. Since his return to the backbenches, his more mischief-making side returned to the fore, in voicing Scottish Labour backbench unhappiness at having their constituency numbers cut. In January 2004, ahead of the new constituency candidate selections, he announced he was standing down from the Commons at the next election. A subsequent elevation to the Lords would surprise no one. In April 2004 he began building his post-election portfolio when he became chair of Hearts Football Club.

Clydebank and Milngavie

Predecessor Constituencies: Dunbartonshire Central (1974–9).

Socio-economic Indicators:

Constituency Pop. (16-64)	42,346
Claimant Count (May 2003)	3.8% (21.3% above average)
IBA/SDA Claimants	9.4%
Life Expectancy – Male	73.5 (0.1yrs above average)
Life Expectancy – Female	78.6 (0.1yrs below average)
Owner Occupied	58.8%
Social Rented	35.7%
Average Property Prices	£68,868 (22nd)
Average Gross Income	£26,760 (26th)
Low Birthweight Babies	136 (6.4%)
Teenage Pregnancy Rates	356 (3.8%)
No. of Lone Parent Households	3,814 (13.2%)

CAB Enquiries

Issue	No. of cases	Percentage of total cases (%)
1. Benefits	1285	23.4
2. Consumer	1261	23.0
3. Employment	781	14.2
4. Housing	601	11.0
5. Other	435	7.9

2003 Scotish Parliament Election

Electorate: 51,327   *Turnout*: 26,514 (51.7%)   *Turnout 1999*: 63.6

Candidate	Party	Votes	Votes%	99 %	Change%
Desmond McNulty	Labour	10,585	39.9	45.3	– 5.4
James Yuill	SNP	6,051	22.8	31.2	– 8.4
Rodney Ackland	Lib Dem	3,224	12.2	12.5	– 0.3
Mary Leishman	Con	2,885	10.9	11.1	– 0.2
Dawn Brennan	SSP	1,902	7.2	–	–
Daniel McCafferty	Ind	1,867	7.0	–	–

Labour majority: 4,534 (17.1%)   *Swing*: 1.5% SNP to Labour

2001 General Election

Electorate: 51,979   *Turnout*: 32,491 (62.5%)

Candidate	Party	Votes	Votes%	Change%
Tony Worthington	Labour	17,249	53.1	- 2.1
James Yuill	SNP	6,525	20.1	- 1.1
Rodney Ackland	Con	3,909	12.0	+ 1.6
Catherine Pickering	Lib Dem	3,514	10.8	- 1.7
Dawn Brennan	SSP	1,294	4.0	-

Labour majority: 10,724 (33.0%)   *Swing*: 0.5% Labour to SNP

1974–97 Westminster

	Lab%	Con%	SNP%	Lib%	Other%	Turnout%
1997	55.2	12.5	21.1	10.5	0.7	75.0
1992	53.3	18.1	19.6	8.7	0.3	78.0
1987	56.9	15.7	12.5	14.9	–	78.9
1983	44.8	20.3	9.2	24.8	0.8	75.9
1979	51.9	21.6	15.3	7.8	3.4	80.0
1974O	40.2	17.2	29.1	4.8	8.7	79.8
1974F	40.4	24.0	14.5	6.4	14.7	83.1

Clydebank and Milngavie represents 'two nations' – two distinct communities with little in common but geographical proximity. The former is working class, with a high concentration of council houses and above average unemployment; the latter is middle class, leafy and suburban, with a high degree of owner occupation, spiralling property prices and low unemployment. The socio–economic profile reflects the split personality of the constituency. Average property prices are 2.1 per cent above the national average, and rose 51.4 per cent in the 1990s.

Economic development and tackling social inequalities are key issues in this seat, and in particular in working class Clydebank. In 2002 Clydebank received over £3 million from the European Union's Structural Fund to aid the redevelopment of the River Clyde waterfront. West Dunbartonshire Council is developing an innovative approach to council services, embracing a one-stop shop approach to education from pre-school through school and community facilities. This would be a significant departure in an area where Clydebank College has been hit by financial crisis having to lay off staff and in 2001 close its engineering department. West Dunbartonshire Council has also gained unwelcome publicity as the worst council in Scotland in terms of council tax collection, and also finished in 2000-1 the worst council in terms of staff absenteeism – with an astonishing average of 67 days per year.

With substantial financial support from the Conservative Government, Health Care's International (HCI) opened a massive state of the art private sector hospital in Clydebank, but despite trying to attract international trade, it was never viable. The Scottish Executive purchased HCI in 2002 for £37.5 million, naming it the National Golden Jubilee Hospital and using it as a national resource to reduce waiting times.

Clydebank Football Club has been one of the most recent additions to the Scottish Football League joining in 1965, but in recent years experienced major financial troubles, having sold their old ground at

Kilbowie Park and not obtained anywhere else. In 2002 they went out of business and thus left the town of Clydebank without a major football team – becoming the first Scottish team to depart from the league since the legendary Third Lanark in 1967.

The predecessor constituency Dunbartonshire Central was created in 1974 and enjoyed celebrity status as Jimmy Reid, popular tribune of the Upper Clyde Shipworkers' work-in, stood for the Communists in February 1974 winning an impressive 5,928 votes (14.6 per cent) – the highest Communist vote in a UK election since 1959. Hugh McCartney was returned for Labour as the seat's first MP. Reid's star faded in the October 1974 election, while the SNP cut Labour's majority to 4,385.

Tony Worthington became Labour MP for the seat in 1987, increasing his majority over the Conservatives to 16,304. In the following election, the SNP re-established themselves in second place – 12,435 votes behind Labour. In 1997, boundary changes reduced Labour's notional majority to 11,420 over the Conservatives, with the SNP in third place. Worthington increased Labour's vote by 1,500, while the SNP moved back into second place adding 1,000 votes to their support. As the Conservatives fell back into third place losing 3,500 votes, Worthington was returned with a 13,220 majority over the SNP. At the June 2001 Westminster election Tony Worthington was easily re-elected with his majority slightly reduced to 10,724 over the SNP with the Lib Dems moving into third place.

The SNP polled respectably in the 1999 Scottish Parliament elections reducing Labour's majority to 4,710. Des McNulty, Labour candidate, was elected, but saw the Labour vote fall by 6,000 on a lower turnout, while the SNP increased their support by 2,132. The Conservatives, a notional second in 1992, fell to a humiliating fourth, losing another 1,000 votes. In the 2003 Scottish Parliament election, McNulty was returned with a majority similar to four years previous. In the regional list vote, Labour won 35.1 per cent and the SNP 20.1 per cent, while the SSP secured 8.3 per cent, the Greens 6.3 per cent, and the Conservatives a lamentable 3.8 per cent.

Boundary Commission recommendations for Westminster see the abolition of Clydebank and Milngavie with its constituent parts split between the three new neighbouring seats of West Dunbartonshire, East Dunbartonshire and Cumbernauld, Kilsyth and Kirkintilloch East. At the Scottish Parliament, Clydebank and Milngavie has shown that it is not a rock solid safe Labour seat and is the sort of place where the Nationalists need to mount a serious challenge if they are ever to shake Labour's dominance of Scottish politics.

MSP

DES McNULTY was born in Stockport in 1952 and educated at St Bede's College, Manchester, followed by the University of York, where he did a degree in social sciences. He did post-graduate studies in politics at Glasgow University. McNulty worked for 21 years at what would become Glasgow Caledonian University from 1978-99; as a sociology lecturer from 1978-90, senior lecturer from 1990-91, assistant head of social sciences from 1991-97, and as strategic planning officer from 1997-99. McNulty was elected to Strathclyde Regional Council from 1990-96 and Glasgow City Council from 1995-99, where he was secretary of the Labour group and vice-chair of the policy and resources committee, at a time of maximum turmoil within the city chambers and the city's Labour Party.

He has taken a leading role in a range of organisations, as chair of Glasgow Healthy City Partnership from 1995-99 and chair of Glasgow 1999 Festival of Architecture and Design. McNulty was one of those not to win ministerial office in 1999. Instead, he has had to make do with being a member of the Scottish Parliamentary Corporate Body, the standards committee and rural affairs committee for the first 18 months, then shifting to transport and environment and enterprise and lifelong learning. Having been an enthusiastic supporter of Jack McConnell – or as enthusiastic as the calm and dry McNulty lets himself get – his reward on McConnell's rise to the premiership was the finance committee convener-ship. With the indiscretions of Richard Simpson, another reshuffle saw him at last brought into the ministerial team as deputy to Margaret Curran in the social justice brief, though this only lasted from November 2002 to April 2003. McNulty won the wooden spoon for being the shortest serving of any Scottish Executive minister in the first Parliament, and the 28th out of the 56 Labour MSPs elected in May 1999 to hold office. With the reshuffle that followed the 2003 election, McNulty was out of the ministerial team, getting the compensation of a return to the finance committee convenership – a job which ought to suit his grasp of detail, even if he does not communicate it that compellingly.

Constituency issues have included a tricky planning row while he was planning minister, over improvements to Mugdock reservoir near Milngavie, and with Labour badly split in West Dunbartonshire Council, he faced a challenge in 2003 from former council leader-turned-independent Danny McCafferty. With his planning interest, he is convener of the cross-party group on architecture and the built environment.

MP

TONY WORTHINGTON was born in 1941 in Hertfordshire and was elected for Clydebank and Milngavie in 1987. He was educated at City School, Lincoln, London School of Economics, York University and Glasgow University. He worked at HM Borstal, Dover, from 1962-66 and Monkwearmouth College of Further Education, Sutherland from 1967-71, then moving to Scotland to become a lecturer in sociology at Jordanhill College from 1971-87. He was elected to Strathclyde Regional Council from 1974-87, where he was convenor of the finance committee from 1986-87.

He was selected for the Clydebank and Milngavie seat by a margin of only 25 to 22 votes. Once in the Commons, Worthington became chair of the Labour Campaign for Criminal Justice from 1987-89. At this time, in spite of his high placing on the private member's bill ballot, his attempt to provide for a statutory right to reply to media accusations failed to make it to the statute book. He was front-bench spokesman on Scotland from 1989-92, covering education, then overseas development from 1992-93 and foreign affairs from 1993-94. In February 1994, he was held by Somali rebels for 17 hours, along with Conservative MP Mark Robinson, and was later sacked from his front bench post for going on the trip without permission, although he was then reinstated. His reputation as one of Westminster's most assiduous globetrotters was curtailed when he became a front bench spokesman on Northern Ireland from 1995-97. Upon Labour's election in 1997, he became Under-Secretary at the Northern Ireland Office where he lasted just over one year, being sacked in Blair's first government reshuffle in 1998.

Since then, he has associated himself at Westminster with international development issues, as a member of the international development select committee, chair of the all-party group on overseas development, chair of Parliamentarians for Global Action and treasurer of the MP group on population and development. He also voted against the Government in the Iraq war motions of early 2003. That year, he was one of the first Scottish Labour MPs to announce he would not stand for the Commons again.

Clydesdale

Predecessor Constituencies: Lanark (1945–79).

Socio-economic Indicators:

Constituency Pop. (16-64)	53,261
Claimant Count (May 2003)	2.7% (14.0 % below average)
IBA/SDA Claimants	12.3%
Life Expectancy – Male	74.1 (0.7 yrs above average)
Life Expectancy – Female	78.0 (0.7 yrs below average)
Owner Occupied	64.4%
Social Rented	28.5%
Average Property Prices	£55,530 (46th)
Average Gross Income	£25,995 (32nd)
Low Birthweight Babies	155 (6.1%)
Teenage Pregnancy Rates	359 (3.4%)
No. of Lone Parent Households	3,391 (10.1%)

CAB Enquiries

Issue	No. of cases	Percentage of total cases (%)
1. Consumer	4053	36.7
2. Benefits	3541	32.0
3. Employment	930	8.4
4. Housing	833	7.5
5. Tax	521	4.7

2003 Scottish Parliament Election

Electorate: 63,675   Turnout: 32,442 (50.9%)   Turnout 1999: 60.6%

Candidate	Party	Votes	Votes%	99 %	Change%
Karen Gillon	Labour	14,800	45.6	43.0	+ 2.6
John Brady	SNP	8,129	25.1	33.1	– 8.0
Alastair Campbell	Con	5,174	15.9	14.9	+ 1.0
Fraser Grieve	Lib Dem	2,338	7.2	9.0	– 1.8
Owen Meharry	SSP	1,422	4.4	–	–
David Morrison	SPA	579	1.8	–	–

Labour majority: 6,671 (20.6%)   Swing: 5.3% SNP to Labour

2001 General Election

Electorate: 64,423   *Turnout*: 38,222 (59.3%)

Candidate	Party	Votes	Votes%	Change%
Jimmy Hood	Labour	17,822	46.6	- 5.9
Jim Wright	SNP	10,028	26.2	+ 4.1
Kevin Newton	Con	5,034	13.2	- 3.1
Moira Craig	Lib Dem	4,111	10.8	+ 2.4
Paul Cockshott	SSP	974	2.5	-
Donald Mackay	UK Ind	253	0.7	-

Labour majority: 7,794 (20.4%)   *Swing*: 5.0% Labour to SNP

1945–97 Westminster

	Lab%	Con%	SNP%	Lib%	Other%	Turnout%
1997	52.5	16.3	22.1	8.4	0.7	71.6
1992	44.6	23.4	23.1	8.2	0.7	77.6
1987	45.3	23.5	14.8	16.4	–	78.1
1983	38.8	28.2	11.4	21.5	–	76.4
1979	43.2	30.9	18.8	7.1	–	81.8
1974O	37.6	23.2	35.8	3.4	–	82.2
1974F	41.7	36.5	21.8	–	–	84.1
1970	45.0	41.4	11.7	–	1.9	78.9
1966	51.7	38.2	10.1	–	–	83.7
1964	54.8	45.2	–	–	–	86.0
1959	50.5	49.5	–	–	–	87.2
1955	48.9	51.1	–	–	–	85.9
1951	47.8	52.2	–	–	–	87.0
1950	49.1	50.9	–	–	–	84.7
1945	52.8	47.2	–	–	–	74.8

Clydesdale's socio-economic profile reveals that while the area has significant economic and social problems, it is not among the poorest parts of the West of Scotland: average property prices are 17.7 per cent below the national average, and rose 44.8 per cent in the 1990s. CAB enquiries show the mix of the area with consumer issues ahead of benefits issues: however, 28.4 per cent of all work undertaken by the CAB has a debt element to it.

Clydesdale sits in Southern Lanarkshire, much of its area rural, but with its northern end more drawn into the Greater Glasgow economy. It contains small towns which used to be part of Lanarkshire's mining industry such as Coalburn, Douglas and Lesmahagow in the west, while further to the east is Biggar.

Clydesdale contains some communities which act as commuter towns for the Central Belt, and others which thrive on their own. A major employer in the area is still the mining industry with the Dalquhandy opencast site the largest opencast facility in Europe, employing 250 workers. Public sector investment is another high profile local issue with Lanarkshire Primary Care NHS Trust committed to building a new hospital at Stonehouse via private finance while Lesmahagow Primary School is also being rebuilt via a £10 million public–private funded scheme.

New Lanark is situated in this constituency and picturesquely located in the Clyde Valley. This was the site for Robert Owen's brave and innovative experiment at the turn of the 18th century whereby he developed and successfully ran a model town, with its cotton mills, care and support for workers and education for children. Owen's co-operative and socialist ideas became influential the world over, and today New Lanark is an international tourist destination.

Previously known as Lanark, the seat was held by the Conservatives for most of the inter-war era – Labour winning it in 1923 and 1929. Walter Elliot held the seat from 1919 until 1923 and went on to be Secretary of State for Scotland from 1936-38; Lord Dunglass, better known as Alec Douglas-Home was MP from 1931-45 during which time he was Parliamentary Private Secretary to Neville Chamberlain from 1937-40. Labour's Tom Steele defeated Dunglass in 1945, who won it back for the Conservatives in 1950 by 685 votes.

Dunglass's successor, Patrick Maitland was elected in 1951 with a bigger majority of 1,793 and he had the whip withdrawn from him from May to December 1957 due to his opposition to Anthony Eden's Suez adventure. In the subsequent general election in 1959 Labour's Judith Hart took the seat from him by the narrow margin of 50.5 per cent to 49.5 per cent. In October 1974, she held on against the SNP's Tom McAlpine by 698 votes before increasing her majority to 5,139 over the Conservatives in 1979, driving the SNP into a distant third place. In 1983 the seat was renamed Clydesdale, and Judith Hart won it with a majority of 4,866 over the Conservatives. Jimmy Hood was then elected for the seat for the first time in 1987, doubling Labour's majority over the Conservatives to 10,502. This fell slightly to 10,187 in 1992, but increased significantly in 1997 to 13,809, with Hood increasing Labour's vote to 52.5 per cent – its highest level since 1964 – while the SNP re-established themselves in a far-off second place. In the June 2001 Westminster election, Labour's majority was nearly halved, while the Nationalists managed to buck the national trend and increase their vote by 4 per cent.

The 1999 elections saw Clydesdale become less safe for Labour. Karen Gillon saw Labour's vote falling by 7,000 on a turnout 11 per cent down, while the SNP in their new role as challengers put on over 2,500 votes and 11 per cent, reducing Labour's majority to 3,880. In the 2003 Scottish Parliament election, the SNP had slender hopes that an upset might be possible in Clydesdale, with Labour defending a majority of under 10 per cent, but this was nothing but wish fulfilment. Labour's Karen Gillon was returned with an increased majority, while the Nationalists lost some 8 per cent. In the regional list vote, Labour won 37.4 per cent to the SNP's 22.4 per cent, while the SSP won 6.2 per cent and the Greens 5.4 per cent.

Not all of Clydesdale is rock-solid Labour. The SNP traditionally secure support in parts of the constituency in local elections to South Lanarkshire where in 2003 they won 27.3 per cent - a signifi- cant fall in both votes and seats - to Labour's 48.8 per cent. Tom McAlpine, a long-standing Nationalist councillor, also won their stronghold of Biggar with a commanding 64.6 per cent of the vote.

Boundary changes for Westminster see the brand name Clydesdale and much of its farmland taken into the hybrid Dumfriesshire, Clydesdale and Tweeddale, which will be close fought by the Conservatives. Other parts join Lanark and Hamilton East, which looks safer for Labour.

MSP

KAREN GILLON was born in Edinburgh in 1967, though she is more of a Borderer. She was educated at Jedburgh Grammar School and Birmingham University. She worked as a youth worker at the Terminal

One Youth Centre, Blantyre, from 1991-94 and as a community education worker for North Lanarkshire Council from 1994-97, before becoming constituency-based personal assistant to Helen Liddell, MP for Airdrie and Shotts, from 1997-99 – a useful place to be if you wanted to secure a safe candidacy.

She first caught the public eye as the photographic image of referendum night in 1997, wearing a 'yes-yes' T-shirt and celebrating euphorically. In Clydesdale on election night, she was the first woman elected an MSP, then with her maiden name of Turnbull, also being the first MSP to give birth, and going on to have another son in the first Parliament. She quickly made her mark with a valuable contribution as a member of the standards committee which investigated the 'Lobbygate' accusation against Jack McConnell. At first deputy convenor of the education, culture and sport committee from 1999 until 2000, she became convenor in January 2001 to replace Mary Mulligan when the Linlithgow Labour MSP became a deputy health minister.

While the blunt, amiable approach of this Rangers Football Club fanatic (and season ticket-holder) is well known, she has another side, seen in her enthusiasm for flower arranging. She can lack polish, but has proved herself to be a smart operator and thoughtful politician as committee convener, taking particular pride in the committee's role in establishing a children's commissioner. She has also, given her constituency interest, pushed for funding a rail extension from Larkhall to Milngavie. Following the 2003 election, she had a lower profile role as deputy convener of procedures, and showed her independence of mind with an abstention on voting reform for councils in March 2004.

MP

JIMMY HOOD was born in 1948 in Lesmahagow and elected MP for Clydesdale in 1987. Educated at Lesmahagow Higher Grade School, Coatbridge, Motherwell College and Nottingham University, he was a mining engineer in Lanarkshire and Nottingham from 1964-87, and a National Union of Mineworkers official from 1973-87. He led the Nottingham striking miners, a minority in that county, during the 1984-85 strike, and was regarded as a Scargillite loyalist fighting a difficult corner. He was elected a Labour councillor on Newark and Sherwood District Council from 1979-87. Once in the Commons, he warned that the wrath of the Scottish people if Ravenscraig closed would 'make the miners strike look like a picnic'. He said he would not pay the poll tax, but declined to join the cross-party and non-party Committee of 100 in campaigning for non-payment. In 1990, he co-sponsored a motion describing the Gulf War that year as 'the new imperialism', and voted against the defence budget in 1993. Ten years later, he also opposed the Blair Government's approach to war in Iraq. He was a chair and vice-chair of the Scottish group of Labour MPs and was chair of the miners group of MPs from 1990-92. He has been chair of the European scrutiny committee since 1992. Characterised by some as one of Scottish Labour's 'Jimmy' types, Hood showed such perceptions are unfair when he crucially intervened at Tony Blair's appearance at the Chairman's liaison committee the week after the Hutton Inquiry reported. After John Denham questioned the Prime Minister's lack of consultation on the Iraq war, foundation hospitals and tuition fees, and Blair replied that 'the process could be better', Hood had his moment. He asked the Prime Minister that if this was the case, how could he explain David Blunkett's sudden announcement that week of yet more restrictions to civil liberties to aid the conviction of suspected terorists. For once Blair was lost for words. A fierce opponent of proportional representation, he commented after Labour's deal with the Lib Dems after the 2003 elections that: 'It is no secret a number of us are looking at ways to prevent these changes going ahead. Given the choice of PR or no deal with the Lib Dems I would have chosen no deal and gone ahead with a minority administration.'

Coatbridge and Chryston

Predecessor Constituencies: Lanarkshire North (1945–79) and Monklands West (1983–92).

Socio-economic Indicators:

Constituency Pop. (16-64)	44,436
Claimant Count (May 2003)	3.3% (7.3% above average)
IBA/SDA Claimants	14.3%
Life Expectancy – Male	71.6 (1.8 yrs below average)
Life Expectancy – Female	77.7 (1.0 yrs below average)
Owner Occupied	59.8%
Social Rented	35.0%
Average Property Prices	£52,025 (53rd)
Average Gross Income	£23,442 (59th)
Low Birthweight Babies	143 (6.7%)
Teenage Pregnancy Rates	372 (3.9%)
No. of Lone Parent Households	3,799 (13.6%)

CAB Enquiries

Issue	No. of cases	Percentage of total cases (%)
1. Benefits	2889	33.4
2. Consumer	1655	19.2
3. Other	1498	17.3
4. Employment	662	7.7
5. Housing	572	6.6

2003 Scottish Parliament Election

Electorate: 51,521   *Turnout*: 23,862 (46.3%)   *Turnout 1999*: 57.9

Candidate	Party	Votes	Votes%	99 %	Change%
Elaine Smith	Labour	13,442	56.2	59.4	– 3.1
James Gribben	SNP	4,851	20.3	24.9	– 4.6
Donald Reece	Con	2,041	8.6	9.5	– 0.9
Gordon Martin	SSP	1,911	8.0	–	–
Doreen Nisbet	Lib Dem	1,637	6.9	6.3	+ 0.6

Labour majority: 8,571 (35.9%)   *Swing*: 0.7% SNP to Labour

2001 General Election

Electorate: 52,178   *Turnout*: 30,311 (58.1%)

Candidate	Party	Votes	Votes%	Change%
Tom Clarke	Labour	19,807	65.3	- 3.0
Peter Kearney	SNP	4,493	14.8	- 2.2
Alistair Tough	Lib Dem	2,293	7.6	+ 2.1
Patrick Ross-Taylor	Con	2,171	7.2	- 1.4
Lynne Sheridan	SSP	1,547	5.1	–

Labour majority: 15,314 (50.5%)   *Swing*: 0.4% Labour to SNP

1945–97 Westminster

	Lab%	Con%	SNP%	Lib%	Other%	Turnout%
1997	68.3	8.6	17.0	5.5	0.7	72.0
1992	61.3	15.9	16.6	6.2	–	77.5
1987	62.3	15.7	10.8	11.2	–	77.2
1983	54.2	22.0	6.5	17.3	–	75.6
1979	55.5	31.5	13.0	–	–	79.7
1974O	46.2	22.5	26.9	4.4	–	79.5
1974F	48.4	33.1	18.5	–	–	82.7
1970	51.8	40.0	8.2	–	–	77.9
1966	60.9	30.1	–	–	–	79.2
1964	60.6	39.4	–	–	–	82.0
1959	58.7	41.3	–	–	–	82.8
1955	57.9	42.1	–	–	–	81.5
1951	58.2	41.8	–	–	–	85.4
1950	58.3	39.0	–	2.7	–	84.7
1945	59.6	40.4	–	–	–	73.3

Coatbridge and Chryston is the old Monklands West seat which has shown its loyalty to Labour through good times and bad. The name was one which many in the Labour Party must have been happy to see removed from the political map prior to the 1997 election due to the controversies surrounding Monklands District Council.

Coatbridge's public profile in the last decade has been shaped by fallout from the Monklands scandal whereby Coatbridge with its predominantly Catholic population was seen as getting preferential treatment and expenditure in comparison to its neighbour, the mostly Protestant town of Airdrie. This came to a head in the 1994 by-election in neighbouring Airdrie and Shotts, when Labour candidate Helen Liddell conceded the Labour-run Monklands council had a problem with nepotism worthy of investigation. But Coatbridge MP Tom Clarke rejected the charges of wrong-doing, describing them as a 'McCarthyite smear'.

In 2001 after a House of Commons debate initiated by Tom Clarke, the UK Government announced that it would speed up compensation for ex-miners who were suffering from respiratory related illnesses.

The claims procedures had been deliberately delayed by the company dealing with claims, and the government gave a commitment that widows making claims on behalf of their deceased partners would be prioritised. Job losses have been frequent in the constituency with closures including the Cardowan mine, Buchanan's whisky distillery and the nearby Gartcosh steel plant – one of the emotional totems of those who held out against de-industrialisation. Opencast mining remains in the seat, and North Lanarkshire Council recently gave permission for a new opencast site at Badallan Farm, close to Fauldhouse. The area has also begun to make a visitor attraction out of its rich industrial heritage, with Coatbridge home to Scotland's only electric tramway in Summerlee Heritage Park using working exhibits from the industrial revolution.

This seat, one of Scotland's poorer, has gone through numerous changes, but one constant has been its attachment to the Labour Party and its election of women MPs. Labour first won this seat as Lanarkshire North in 1922, and seven years later, this was where Jennie Lee, a young, energetic left-winger, became the first ever Scottish Labour woman MP. She won a March 1929 by-election with an impressive 6,578 majority over the Conservatives, but lost it in the 1931 debacle and stood again unsuccessfully in 1935 under the Independent Labour Party banner as Mrs Aneurin Bevan, splitting the Labour vote. Lee went on with her husband Nye to establish the left-wing paper *Tribune* in 1937, which still exists. She served as minister of arts in the 1964–70 Wilson Government.

Margaret 'Peggy' Herbison won the seat back for Labour in 1945 by a margin of 9,762 votes, defeating the Conservative MP William Anstruther-Gray, who had held it since 1931. Herbison was widely seen as a Labour woman pioneer in a Scottish party renowned for its chauvinism. She became Minister of Pensions in the 1964 Wilson Government, and then Minister for Social Security, resigning in 1967 over the issue of means-testing.

Herbison's retirement saw a young advocate John Smith become Labour candidate who was easily elected in 1970 winning over half the votes with the Conservatives coming a credible second on 40 per cent. Even in October 1974 the SNP could make no serious challenge here and Smith was re-elected with a 8,341 majority. Smith became Secretary of State for Trade in the Callaghan Government, and held Lanarkshire North for the last time in 1979 with a 10,820 majority.

Lanarkshire North was divided between four seats with Coatbridge and Airdrie forming the largest parts of both the successor seats, Monklands East and West, but with the latter also containing a significant part of Smith's old seat. Smith decided to stand in Monklands East, while Tom Clarke, MP for Coatbridge and Airdrie from 1982, stood in Monklands West. The new Monklands West seat had Coatbridge at its centre and Clarke held the seat in the 1983 election with a 12,264 majority over the Conservatives. Four years later he improved on this, winning a massive 18,333 majority over the Conservatives. In 1992 Labour's lead fell back slightly to 17,065 with the SNP supplanting the Conservatives in second place.

Labour still had room to improve its position in this seat when it became Coatbridge and Chryston in 1997. The party's performance in 1997 was its best in the post-war period, obtaining a whopping 68.3 per cent of the vote and 19,295 over the SNP on only 17 per cent. In June 2001, Labour's Tom Clarke was returned with a 15,314 majority – 4,000 down on the previous election – with the SNP in a distant second place losing nearly 2,000 votes, and finishing on 15 per cent. The biggest talking point of the election was the electoral appeal of the Sheridan family with Tommy's sister, Lynne, winning 5.1 per cent and retaining the party's deposit – the only one saved outside Glasgow.

In the first Scottish Parliament election of May 1999, Elaine Smith won the seat for Labour with 59 per cent of the vote and a 10,404 lead over the Nationalists. In 2003 Smith predictably returned with a majority slightly down on 1999 and 4,500 fewer votes. The Scottish Socialists without the Sheridan name improved their standing and were on course to replace the Conservatives in third place. In the regional list vote Labour won 46.2 per cent to the SNP's 17.1 per cent while the SSP finished in third on 8.1 per cent, the Scottish Senior Citizens 6.7 per cent, and the Greens on 4.7 per cent.

Boundary changes for Westminster will see Coatbridge and Chryston become part of a new Coatbridge, Chryston and Bellshill seat, but that will not change the Labour representation in the area. Labour remains impressively strong here at local level, and can expect to continue to elect a Labour MSP to the Scottish Parliament for many years to come.

MSP

ELAINE SMITH was born in Coatbridge in 1963. She was educated at St Patrick's School, Coatbridge, Glasgow College where she obtained a degree in social sciences, and St Andrew's College where she trained as a teacher of modern studies and economics. She worked for two years as a teacher from 1986-88. Then, with a diploma in public sector management from Aberdeen College, she became a local government officer in Monklands District and Highland Region, before working as a manager on a pilot project in primary health care as part of Volunteer Development Scotland from 1997-98.

Elected to the Scottish Parliament in 1999, she tended to take one of the less compromising Campaign for Socialism positions, often under the cover of Dundee East's John McAllion, and with her rebellious confidence growing over time. Having first campaigned for better planning restrictions on mobile phone masts, she spoke out against the Glasgow housing stock transfer in March 2002, helped vote down the Executive on procedures to close fire stations in January 2003, backed the Labour line on the first Iraq war vote that month, but signed Susan Deacon's motion on the subject in February 2003, and voted against Labour's Iraq motion the following month, saying she was against war 'even with a second resolution'.

With her politics strongly feminist, she was a member of the equal opportunities committee in the first Parliament and notable for leading a debate on the importance of breast-feeding, introducing the Breastfeeding (Scotland) Bill in May 2001, which sought to make it more acceptable in public places, but did not become law. In the second Parliament, Smith re-introduced that bill, sitting again on the equal opportunities committee. She found the tactics of the SSP tended to draw her and other left-wingers into further rebellions against the Executive, but she lacked the support of McAllion, after his defeat at the hands of the SNP in Dundee East. Although she stood out from Labour in being willing to criticise the Westminster government for the detention of asylum seekers at Dungavel, she was not the first to do so, and her rebellion was treated by colleagues as predictable. She was one of two Labour MSPs to vote against council voting reform in March 2004, having been the only one to vote against the coalition deal in the Labour group in May 2003.

MP

TOM CLARKE was born in 1941 in Coatbridge. He was educated at Columba High School, Coatbridge and the Scottish College of Commerce. He began his working life as an office boy in 1956, and continued in clerical work for ten years. He then specialised in film at the Scottish Council for Educational Technology from 1966-82, and was assistant director of the Scottish Film Council over the same period. He also became a governor of the British Film Institute in 1987. He joined Labour aged 16, and two years later, at the 1959 election, he was the youngest election agent in the UK, working for James Dempsey. He was a councillor for many years, on Coatbridge Town Council from 1964-74 and then on Monklands District Council from 1974-82, where he was provost and also president of COSLA from 1978-80.

Clarke was first elected to Parliament at the Coatbridge and Airdrie by-election in 1982. Having been active in the expulsion of Militant and having assiduously cultivated backbench support, he secured strong support in shadow cabinet elections, resulting in him becoming shadow Scottish Secretary from 1992-93, following Donald Dewar, where he was given the difficult task of holding the Scottish Labour Party together after the unexpected election defeat in 1992. In the post-election environment, some felt Labour had been too enthusiastically involved in the Scottish Constitutional Convention, while those in 'Scotland United' pushed for Labour to go further. Clarke, holding the middle position, had criticism directed at him from both sides, failing to come close to matching the political skills of his Government opposite number, Michael Forsyth. His party leadership in Scotland was one over which Labour colleagues would prefer to draw a veil. He was shadow minister for international development from 1993-94 and then dropped by Blair in his first shadow cabinet, before becoming shadow minister for disabled people from 1995-97. This was after gaining strong credibility in that area as a backbench MP, for steering through, as a private member's bill, the Disabled Persons (Services Consultation and Representation) Act 1986 – widely seen as a significant advance in disability rights. To do this, he withstood pressure from the anti-abortion lobby which he supports to use the private members' bill opportunity to legislate for their cause.

With Labour in power, he became minister of state in the Department of Culture, Media and Sport from 1997-98, with responsibility for tourism and film, where his enthusiasm (as a sometime award-winning amateur filmmaker) shone through. However, he failed to impress Tony Blair and was one of the first to be sacked, with no subsequent signs of his career recovering. Although defining himself as a moderate, he opposed the Government on war in Iraq twice in early 2003.

Cumbernauld and Kilsyth

Predecessor Constituencies: created for the 1983 election.

Socio-economic Indicators:

Constituency Pop. (16-64)	43,536
Claimant Count (May 2003)	2.5% (18.6% below average)
IBA/SDA Claimants	10.8%
Life Expectancy – Male	74.3 (0.9 yrs above average)
Life Expectancy – Female	78.1 (0.6 yrs below average)
Owner Occupied	71.3%
Social Rented	22.7%
Average Property Prices	£57,226 (42nd)
Average Gross Income	£27,580 (18th)
Low Birthweight Babies	119 (5.7%)
Teenage Pregnancy Rates (av. 1996-98)	318 (3.7%)
No. of Lone Parent Households	3,246 (12.5%)

CAB Enquiries

Issue	No. of cases	Percentage of total cases (%)
1. Benefits	2889	33.4
2. Consumer	1655	19.2
3. Other	1498	17.3
4. Employment	662	7.7
5. Housing	572	6.6

2003 Scottish Parliament Election

Electorate: 48,667   *Turnout*: 24,404 (50.1%)   *Turnout 1999*: 62.0%

Candidate	Party	Votes	Votes%	99 %	Change%
Catherine Craigie	Labour	10,146	41.6	49.6	– 8.0
Andrew Wilson	SNP	9,626	39.4	35.7	+ 3.8
Kenneth McEwan	SSP	1,823	7.5	3.7	+ 3.8
Hugh O'Donnell	Lib Dem	1,264	5.2	6.6	– 1.4
Margaret McCulloch	Con	978	4.0	4.5	– 0.4
Christopher Donohue	Ind	567	2.3	–	–

Labour majority: 520 (2.1%)   *Swing*: 5.9% Labour to SNP

2001 General Election

Electorate: 49,739   Turnout: 29,699 (59.7%)

Candidate	Party	Votes	Votes%	Change%
Rosemary McKenna	Labour	16,144	54.4	– 4.3
David McGlashan	SNP	8,624	29.0	+ 1.2
John O'Donnell	Lib Dem	1,934	6.5	+ 2.7
Alison Ross	Con	1,460	4.9	– 1.9
Kenny McEwan	SSP	1,287	4.3	+ 3.3
Thomas Taylor	Scot Ref	250	0.8	–

Labour majority: 7,520 (25.3%)   *Swing*: 2.8% Labour to SNP

1983–97 Westminster

	Lab%	Con%	SNP%	Lib%	Other%	Turnout%
1997	58.7	6.8	27.8	3.8	3.0	75.0
1992	54.0	11.3	28.9	5.8	–	79.1
1987	60.0	9.1	19.6	11.4	–	78.5
1983	49.2	13.6	17.4	19.8	–	76.5

Cumbernauld and Kilsyth lies on the outskirts of Glasgow – fifteen miles away from the north-east corner of the city – and contains the new town of Cumbernauld as well as smaller towns such as Croy and Kilsyth. The name Cumbernauld comes from the Gaelic word Cumar-nan-Alt which means 'the meeting of the waters' with the River Kelvin running through the constituency.

Cumbernauld achieved world wide fame in 1981 with Bill Forsyth's film *Gregory's Girl* about young romance in a new town setting, starring John Gordon Sinclair in his screen breakthrough. The constituency underwent a revolution in housing tenure during the Thatcher years. When this seat was drawn up ahead of the 1983 election it had 70 per cent council housing, and by the 1991 census it had fallen to 39 per cent, as people exercised their right to buy their house from the new town's public sector development corporation. There was little gratitude show to Thatcher's party at election time.

The Conservative local government reorganisation of 1995 could have been seen as revenge for this, with Cumbernauld put in North Lanarkshire rather than East Dunbartonshire. This did not have any political implications for Cumbernauld, but was seen as part of a Conservative plan to create a 'safe Tory enclave' in East Dunbartonshire. However, such was the extent of Conservative unpopularity in 1995 that their objective failed and it won control of no councils at all. North Lanarkshire Council has not been particularly popular and in 1999 it announced it was closing four primary schools in the area including Cumbernauld Primary. More recently it attempted to amalgamate Cumbernauld High with Abronhill School, but this was success-fully resisted by a local campaign.

Clyde Football Club moved from the Southside of Glasgow to the area in the mid-1990s and a purpose-built new stadium where their fortunes have picked up. However, Cumbernauld town centre – long seen as one of the least attractive places in modern Scotland – picked up unwanted attention when in 2001 it won an award from the architectural journal *Unlimited* for 'the most dismal place in Scotland'.

The panel of experts who made the decision, expressed a high degree of ill-feeling towards the town centre calling it 'soulless and inaccessible' and 'something like Eastern Europe before the wall came down'. This was reinforced in 2003 when the *Idler* magazine in a guide to 'crap towns' rated Cumbernauld the second most awful place to live in the United Kingdom – only beaten by Hull.

The SNP has traditionally enjoyed significant levels of support in this part of the country. The Nationalists controlled Cumbernauld and Kilsyth District Council from 1974 until 1980. Prior to the existence of Cumbernauld and Kilsyth, most of this seat was within Dunbartonshire East, won by Margaret Bain for the SNP in October 1974. In those days, this seat was classic SNP territory, with young, confident, upwardly mobile voters in skilled occupations, who were SNP supporters in the mid-1970s. These voters were seen in the 1960s and 1970s as the harbingers of a new, classless politics in which the Nationalists would thrive.

However, when the current seat was first established in 1983, Labour's Norman Hogg was easily elected with a 9,928 majority over the Liberal-SDP Alliance, rising to 14,403 over the SNP in 1987, before falling back to 9,215 in 1992 over the Nationalists. It took a long time after the 1980s and early 1990s dip for this seat to rediscover its Nationalist side. In 1997, Norman Hogg announced his retirement close to the May general election, allowing Rosemary McKenna to be chosen at the last minute and she was safely re-elected with an increased majority over the SNP in a distant second place. At the 2001 UK election McKenna's majority fell to 7,520 – a decline of 5 per cent in her majority over the Nationalists.

However, in the first Scottish Parliament elections, Andrew Wilson, one of the talented young 'Nat pack', recorded an excellent result for the Nationalists with an 8.5 per cent swing from Labour. On a falling turnout he increased his vote by 910 votes while Labour's fell by 6,000. This still left Cathie Craigie with a comfortable majority of 4,259, but at least Wilson had brought Cumbernauld and Klisyth back into the category of marginal seats.

In 2003, Craigie and Wilson had a rematch given added excitement by the low ranking given to Wilson by SNP activists in the Central Scotland regional list, effectively meaning he had to win here to be returned as an MSP. Requiring a 7 per cent swing to win, Wilson achieved a 5.9 per cent swing, cutting Labour's majority back to a mere 520 votes. Wilson's campaign was modern, efficient and professional and showed that the SNP can have the capacity to challenge Labour in Central Scotland. But it meant he was out of the Parliament and returned to a job at the Royal Bank of Scotland. In the regional vote, Labour won 35.7 per cent to the SNP's 34.2 per cent – a Labour lead of 366 votes – while the SSP won 8.3 per cent, Scottish Senior Citizens 4.6 per cent and Greens 4.3 per cent.

Boundary changes for Westminster involve the addition of 18,000 voters and a new name – Cumbernauld, Kilsyth and Kirkintilloch East – reckoned to give Labour a notional majority above 12,000 and 30 per cent, though McKenna is tipped to stand down before the next election. At the Scottish Parliament, whether the SNP's 2003 support is a high water mark or a building block for future success is probably predicated on whether Wilson decides to run again in 2007.

MSP

CATHIE CRAIGIE was born in Stirling in 1954 and was educated at Kilsyth Academy. Work outside politics included being part of an audit team for chartered accountants. She was a councillor in Cumbernauld from 1984-96 and became leader of the council from 1994-96, as well as chairing several of its key committees. Craigie subsequently served on North Lanarkshire Council from 1995-99, becoming chair of environmental services and acting as one of the council's representatives on COSLA.

In the Scottish Parliament, she sat on the audit and social inclusion committees until December 2000, before becoming a member of the social justice committee. Much of her time in the first Parliament was taken up in fending off Andrew Wilson's determined bid to win Cumbernauld and Kilsyth for the SNP. She was foremost among Labour MSPs complaining about list MSPs passing themselves off as 'your local member'. She introduced a member's bill on mortgage rights, intended to reduce the extent of repossessions, which became law in 2001.

She was seen as one of those closest to Jack McConnell, embarrassing herself when it was found out she had made multiple calls to a newspaper phone poll in support of his leadership ambition. She had more problems with technology, in her equally embarrassing problem with using the Parliament's electronic voting system. Since McConnell became leader, she has not seen much return for such loyalty, which may explain her increasing rebelliousness. In March 2002, she voted against the group line on accepting the highly controversial 13.5 per cent MSP pay rise, and was one of four Labour MSPs to vote against the Executive in January 2003, on procedures for closing fire stations. Having previously voted with the revolt in 2000 which saw Tommy Sheridan's poindings and warrant sales bill enacted, she was therefore a key rebel in two of the three votes lost by ministers. Her rebelliousness did not extend to the Iraq war, however. In the second Parliament, she secured places on both the procedures and communities committees.

MP

ROSEMARY McKENNA was born in 1941 in Kilmacolm. She was educated at St Augustine's Secondary School, Glasgow and St Andrew's College, Bearsden and worked as a primary school teacher before her election in 1997. She was a councillor in the constituency from 1984-96, and also leader from 1984-88, provost from 1988-92 and COSLA President from 1994-96. She was also a board member of Scottish Enterprise from 1993-96, chair of Scotland Europa from 1994-96 and a representative on the European Union's Committee of the Regions from 1993-97. At Westminster, she was a member of a variety of committees including Scottish affairs from 1997-98, European scrutiny from 1998-99, and statutory instruments from 1997-99. She was made Parliamentary Private Secretary to the Ministers of State at the Foreign Office until 2001, losing that post after the 2001 election and taking places on the select committees on culture, media and sport as well as procedures.

She was also a founding member of 'The Network', later known as Scottish Labour Forum, the Blairite organisation which was responsible for defeating leading left-wingers on Scottish Labour's Executive in 1997. She was chair of Labour's selection panel process for the Scottish Parliament, which ran into a wall of criticism for excluding left-wingers and elements of the more nationalist wing of Labour, including several of her fellow MPs. McKenna faced criticism for the inclusion of her own daughter on the list, even though she had not taken part in that particular selection.

Cunninghame North

Predecessor Constituencies: Ayrshire North and Bute (1945–79).

Socio-economic Indicators:

Constituency Pop. (16-64)	43,628
Claimant Count (May 2003)	4.4% (41.3% above average)
IBA/SDA Claimants	9.9%
Life Expectancy – Male	73.6 (0.2 yrs above average)
Life Expectancy – Female	78.3 (0.4 yrs below average)
Owner Occupied	65.3%
Social Rented	25.9%
Average Property Prices	£52,114 (52nd)
Average Gross Income	£25,080 (41st)
Low Birthweight Babies (av. 1996-98)	125 (6.2%)
Teenage Pregnancy Rates (av. 1996-98)	405 (4.5%)
No. of Lone Parent Households	3,437 (11.1%)

CAB Enquiries

Issue	No. of cases	Percentage of total cases (%)
1. Benefits	4535	32.1
2. Consumer	3251	23.0
3. Employment	1783	12.6
4. Housing	1278	9.0
5. Other	1077	7.6

2003 Scottish Parliament Election

Electorate: 55,322   *Turnout*: 28,631 (51.8%)   *Turnout 1999*: 60.0%

Candidate	Party	Votes	Votes%	99 %	Change%
Allan Wilson	Labour	11,145	38.9	42.9	– 4.0
Campbell Martin	SNP	7,755	27.1	28.6	– 1.5
Peter Ramsay	Con	5,542	19.4	19.9	– 0.5
John Boyd	Lib Dem	2,333	8.1	8.7	– 0.5
Sean Scott	SSP	1,859	6.5	–	–

Labour majority: 3,390 (11.8%)   *Swing*: 1.3% Labour to SNP

2001 General Election

Electorate: 54,993   *Turnout*: 33,816 (61.5%)

Candidate	Party	Votes	Votes%	Change%
Brian Wilson	Labour	15,571	46.1	– 4.3
Campbell Martin	SNP	7,173	21.2	+ 2.8
Richard Wilkinson	Con	6,666	19.7	– 3.8
Ross Chmiel	Lib Dem	3,060	9.0	+ 3.5
Sean Scott	SSP	964	2.9	–
Louise McDaid	Soc Lab	382	1.1	–

Labour majority: 8,398 (24.8%)   *Swing*: 3.5% Labour to Conservative

1945–97 Westminster

	Lab%	Con%	SNP%	Lib%	Other%	Turnout%
1997	50.3	23.5	18.4	5.5	2.3	74.1
1992	41.0	34.1	18.2	6.7	–	78.2
1987	44.4	34.0	9.5	12.1	–	78.2
1983	34.6	38.7	8.6	18.1	–	75.7
1979	34.4	45.7	13.9	6.0	–	75.9
1974O	28.9	38.9	25.9	6.3	–	71.3
1974F	27.8	45.7	16.3	10.2	–	77.0
1970	35.4	53.6	11.0	–	–	73.6
1966	40.7	48.6	–	10.7	–	76.0
1964	36.1	49.8	–	14.1	–	74.6
1959	37.6	62.4	–	–	–	73.4
1955	35.5	64.5	–	–	–	71.5
1951	35.8	64.2	–	–	–	77.3
1950	35.7	64.3	–	–	–	79.1
1945	47.0	53.0	–	–	–	68.5

Cunninghame North combines a mixture of seaside resorts and islands in the Firth of Clyde, one of the most picturesque parts of Scotland. The seaside towns, including Largs, Ardrossan and Saltcoats, were once some of the primary destinations of the Glasgow working class on holiday. Largs has managed to reinvent itself enough to prosper; others, such as Ardrossan and Saltcoats, are in economic decline and face uncertain futures. The islands of Arran, Great Cumbrae and Little Cumbrae are in the seat, the former, with its main town Brodick, a prosperous tourist location. Further inland, old mining towns such as Beith, Dalry and Kilbirnie are to be found in the Garnock valley.

Given the old mining towns of Beith, Dalry and Kibirnie, a major issue in these communities is attracting new employment and investment. The more middle class parts of the constituency such as Largs – home of the famous Nardini's art deco restaurant on the seafront – thrive on visitors, while also having a large number of retired professionals who have opted for a relaxing life by the sea. Average property prices are 22.7 per cent below the national average and increased by 39.9 per cent in the 1990s. CAB work covers both the Cunninghame seats and benefits are the most prevalent issue, a common picture across Scottish CABs.

Transport issues are a key concern for this seat, and in 2001 Clydeport cancelled its plan for a new ferry link between Port Glasgow and Derry, but the following year announced a feasibility study to examine a new link between Ardrossan and Northern Ireland. There has already been a sizeable amount of investment by Clydeport in a new passenger terminal at Ardrossan which will operate the Cal-Mac ferry service to Brodick, the main town on the isle of Arran. This forms part of a £50 million regeneration of Ardrossan waterfront, which will include housing, retail and leisure developments and which it sorely needs given the 'ghost town' feel of its town centre. Not entirely unexpectedly, the town centre recently won the infamous wooden spoon from the architectural magazine, *Unlimited*, for the most dismal townscape in Scotland.

Cunninghame North was not changed in the 1997 boundary redistribution, having been created in the previous 1983 round from Ayrshire North and Bute. To this day, Cunninghame North still has deep pockets of Conservative voting. As Ayrshire North and Bute it was a safe Tory seat, electing Conservatives for the whole inter-war period from 1918 onwards. Charles MacAndrew held the seat from 1935 to 1959, and in 1945 his majority over Labour was cut to 2,443, but thereafter expanded dramatically. The legendary Fitzroy Maclean, SAS veteran, wartime adviser to Tito's Communist partisans and best-selling author, was an unlikely figure for an MP, let alone a Conservative, but he represented the area from 1959 until February 1974.

John Corrie became MP from February 1974 onward and won the seat in its first incarnation as Cunninghame North in 1983 with a majority of 1,639 over Labour. His main claim to fame in British politics was as the author of the Corrie anti-abortion bill in 1980 which failed to secure parliamentary passage. The year of 1987 was Scottish Labour's year of advance as it won several middle-class Conservative seats such as Glasgow Hillhead, Edinburgh South and Strathkelvin and Bearsden. Brian Wilson, Labour's candidate, seized the seat with a majority of 4,422 over John Corrie, increasing Labour's vote by 5,000, as the Conservatives fell by 1,000. The 1992 election was a year of relative Tory success in Scotland and Wilson saw his majority fall to 2,939 and Labour's vote by 1,500. Wilson was re-elected in 1997 with a sizeable 11,039 lead over the Conservatives, increasing his vote by 3,000, while the Conservatives' declined by 4,000. In June 2001 Brian Wilson's majority fell slightly to 8,398 on a reduced turnout as the SNP moved from third to second place.

In the 1999 Scottish Parliament elections, Labour's vote fell by 6,000 as the SNP's Kay Ullrich increased the 1997 vote by 2,000 and by 10 per cent to establish the SNP in second place. The Conservatives continued their decline, losing another 3,000 votes, and slipped into third place. In May 2003, Allan Wilson saw Labour's majority cut back to 3,390 as his vote fell back by 3,000. This result, while not of earth-shattering proportions, nearly brings Cunninghame North into the category of a Labour-SNP marginal, and in a good year, the SNP should be able to mount a challenge and shake Labour's hold. In the regional list vote, Labour won 32 per cent to 22.8 per cent for the SNP, with the SSP on 6 per cent and Greens on 5.6 per cent.

Boundary Commission proposals for Westminster see Cunninghame North abolished and replaced by a Ayrshire and Arran seat which will help Conservative fortunes, but not by enough to revive their prospects in this once Tory seat. Cunninghame North is a product of Labour's ability to win middle class and working class support in the 1980s, long before UK Labour learnt how to do it.

MSP

ALLAN WILSON was born in 1954 in Glasgow and educated at Spiers School, Beith. He was a trainee officer for the National Union of Public Employees from 1972 until 1975, an area officer from 1975 until

1993, during which time he edited NUPE News. He became a senior regional officer with UNISON from 1993-94, and then the officer in charge of UNISON's higher education section in Scotland from 1994-99. That gave him a role as a member of the independent review of pay and conditions in higher education institutions in Scotland. His role as Brian Wilson's election agent in Cunninghame North put him close to the heart of one of Scottish politics' more formidable political networks.

Elected to the Scottish Parliament in 1999, he became a member of the European committee and the enterprise and lifelong learning committee from 1999-2000. Then, in Henry McLeish's first ministerial reshuffle, Wilson was given the post of deputy minister for education, sport and culture, but without any responsibility on the schools side. When his cabinet boss, Sam Galbraith, left the cabinet in March 2001, the subsequent re-shuffle saw Wilson given a unique role, as a junior minister outside the cabinet reporting directly to the First Minister on sport and culture. This reflected McLeish's desire to be personally involved in sports promotion, winning the Ryder Cup and European football championships for Scotland as part of his 'Scottish confidence' agenda. Wilson's stumbling approach to public speaking has provided a rich source for Parliamentary sketch writers, but his appointment was seen as McLeish bringing an MSP into the ministerial team with a strong knowledge of Labour's trade union links, and he is credited with a willingness to listen to ideas beyond the civil service machine. Jack McConnell continued to see his value, moving him in November 2001 to the deputy rural development and environment brief under the Lib Dems' Ross Finnie, and retaining the duo there after the 2003 coalition agreement was struck, with Wilson's role being focussed on fisheries and the environment part of the job. With Finnie out of operation in early 2004 due to a cardiac operation, Wilson stepped up to the Cabinet temporarily, handling a tricky set of fisheries negotiations with Brussels. He also had to lead for the Scottish Executive in the Scottish Parliament debate in March 2004 which decided by one vote to support Westminster's plans for growing GM crops in Scotland.

MP

BRIAN WILSON (no relation to Allan) was born in 1948 in Dunoon and elected Labour MP for Cunninghame North from 1987. Educated at Dunoon Grammar School – also the old school for John Smith and George Robertson – followed by Dundee University and University College, Cardiff, where he trained in journalism. In 1972, Wilson became founding editor and publisher of the *West Highland Free Press*, a commercially successful local newspaper based in Skye which has campaigned from a socialist perspective on land reform and Gaelic, while reflecting the proprietor's strong antipathy to devolution and all things nationalist. Wilson has family connections to Lewis, which have given him a powerful presence in the Labour politics of the Highlands and Islands, and he has gathered around him a group of Wilsonite loyalists. He was briefly a member of the SNP, joining aged 13 in sympathy with its campaign against nuclear weapons. He was persuaded to join by fellow Dunoon pupil, and then Nationalist George Robertson (who went on to be Labour Defence Secretary in 1997), but left three years later. He joined Labour aged 24, becoming the protégé of Norman and Janey Buchan.

A notable theme running through his politics has been Wilson's passionately anti-devolution views and his loathing for the SNP and Scottish nationalism. He was chair of 'Labour Votes No' in 1979, as well as the 'Scotland Is British' campaign committee. By the time his party had swung fully behind devolution in the 1990s, he preferred not to talk about the issue publicly rather than even give it grudging accept-ance. His near-hatred of the SNP has, if anything, increased. With his acid, journalistic turn of phrase, his unattributed briefings are believed by friend and foe to fuel Westminster discontent with the direction of devolution. A typical diatribe came in the *New Statesman* in 1992, describing the SNP as having a philosophy based on 'scapegoating at best, racism at worst', with a 'crude appeal to selfishness and

Anglophobia'. Always bravely willing to pitch into difficult, controversial issues, he was an effective voice in steering Labour away from a poll tax non-payment campaign in 1987, backing Donald Dewar by telling a special Labour conference that year: 'The aim of this party should not be to advise people what to do when the poll tax bills come through the door – our aim should be to stop the bills coming through the door'. He then headed the 'Stop It' campaign, intended to destabilise the poll tax through disrupting registration for it by asking people to send back their registration forms uncompleted.

He stood for the party unsuccessfully in three Highlands seats; in Ross and Cromarty in October 1974, Inverness in 1979 and the Western Isles in 1983. Once in the Commons, Wilson was frontbench spokesman on Scottish affairs from 1988-92, and then on transport from 1992-94, where he pledged Labour to removing tolls from the Skye Bridge and effectively harried the Tory government over rail privatisation. He moved to trade and industry from 1994-95 and returned to transport between 1995-96. He was then moved into a full-time campaign role ahead of the 1997 election, alongside Peter Mandelson, his instinct for the political jugular coming in handy with the setting up of the fabled Excalibur instant rebuttal system. At the time of Tony Blair's campaign to rid Labour of Clause Four, Wilson the wordsmith sat in his sleeper train compartment one night and composed an alternative, which opened out the debate even though that was not the one eventually adopted. At the 1995 conference which saw the clause scrapped, he argued 'the change is not about opting-out of public ownership, it is about opting in to objective reality'.

In government, he was Minister of State for Scotland from 1997-98, with responsibility for education and industry, and was the minister for trade at the Department of Trade and Industry from 1998-99, then returned to being Minister of State for Scotland from 1999 to the beginning of 2001. When John Reid shifted from the Scotland Office to Northern Ireland in January 2001 after Mandelson's second resignation, Brian Wilson was Downing Street's first choice for the post of Secretary of State for Scotland. However, Wilson's move northwards was reportedly blocked by Henry McLeish and he was instead appointed Minister of State at the Foreign Office, only staying there briefly before moving to the Department of Trade and Industry, where he was responsible for energy and construction. Post-devolution, in both his Scotland Office and trade jobs, he made a point of stressing the value of Whitehall government in Scottish trade links. On the energy front, he was also notable for pushing the cause of renewables and a National Grid link into the west coast of Scotland, while edging forward the tricky political issue of whether the Government should approve more nuclear power stations.

When Tony Blair attempted to move him to another ministerial post in 2003, he resisted, preferring to return to the backbenches. There, free to speak his mind, he attacked the Scottish Executive electoral reform plans for councils, foisting four electoral systems on Scotland, while saying the different constituency boundaries at Westminster and the Scottish Parliament would be 'a dog's breakfast'. But he stayed in favour with Downing Street, taking on an unprecedented unsalaried role with the grandiose title of the Prime Minister's Special Representative on Trade Opportunities for Afghanistan, Iraq and Russia. In November 2003, appearing before Lord Fraser's inquiry into the Holyrood building project, he denied having called the previous intended home for the Parliament, the Royal High School, a 'nationalist shibboleth' – a phrase often attributed to his off-the-record briefing. If it was any symbol, he said, it was a 'shibboleth of devolution.' He has at various times been connected with jobs outside politics, such as a return to full-time journalism or at Celtic football club, about which he wrote the official centenary history.

Cunninghame South

Predecessor Constituencies: Ayrshire Central (1950–79).

Socio-economic Indicators:

Constituency Pop. (16-64)	43,114
Claimant Count (May 2003)	5.4% (74.6% above average)
IBA/SDA Claimants	13.5 %
Life Expectancy – Male	71.5 (1.9 yrs below average)
Life Expectancy – Female	77.2 (1.5 yrs below average)
Owner Occupied	56.5%
Social Rented	36.6%
Average Property Prices	£43,592 (69th)
Average Gross Income	£22,788 (63rd)
Low Birthweight Babies	132 (6.2%)
Teenage Pregnancy Rates	482 (5.1%)
No. of Lone Parent Households	3,779 (13.6%)

2003 Scottish Parliament Election

Electorate: 49,887   *Turnout*: 22,772 (45.7%)   *Turnout 1999*: 56.1%

Candidate	Party	Votes	Votes%	99 %	Change%
Irene Oldfather	Labour	11,165	49.0	52.8	– 3.8
Michael Russell	SNP	5,089	22.3	29.7	– 7.3
Rosemary Byrne	SSP	2,677	11.8	–	–
Andrew Brocklehurst	Con	2,336	10.3	11.4	– 1.2
Iain Dale	Lib Dem	1,505	6.6	6.1	+ 0.5

Labour majority: 6,076 (27.6%)   *Swing*: 1.8% SNP to Labour

2001 General Election

Electorate: 49,982   *Turnout*: 28,109 (56.2%)

Candidate	Party	Votes	Votes%	Change%
Brian Donohoe	Labour	16,424	58.6	– 4.1
Bill Kidd	SNP	5,194	18.5	– 2.2
Pamela Paterson	Con	2,782	9.9	– 0.2
John Boyd	Lib Dem	2,094	7.4	+ 2.9
Rosemary Byrne	SSP	1,233	4.4	–
Bobby Cochrane	Soc Lab	382	1.4	–

Labour majority: 11,230 (40.1%)   *Swing*: 0.9% Labour to SNP

1950–97 Westminster

	Lab%	Con%	SNP%	Lib%	Other%	Turnout%
1997	62.7	10.1	20.8	4.5	1.9	71.5
1992	52.9	16.3	24.2	6.2	0.3	75.9
1987	60.8	16.3	11.0	11.8	–	74.9
1983	54.1	21.2	6.9	17.8	–	73.3
1979	51.2	29.3	10.4	9.1	–	79.8
1974O	45.1	24.8	24.5	5.6	–	79.3
1974F	49.0	35.9	15.1	–	–	82.0
1970	52.4	41.8	5.1	–	0.7	80.7
1966	57.7	42.3	–	–	–	82.1
1964	56.4	43.6	–	–	–	84.2
1959	52.0	48.0	–	–	–	86.7
1955	49.8	50.2	–	–	–	83.3
1951	52.1	47.9	–	–	–	86.3
1950	49.0	43.8	–	7.2	–	85.6

Cunninghame South is situated on the Firth of Clyde. Its principal town is Irvine – one of Scotland's five post-war New Towns and the only coastal one in the UK. The other main centres, Kilwinning and Stevenson, are working-class towns, which, like Irvine, have a solid Labour vote and little support for the other main parties, whether the SNP, Lib Dems or Conservatives.

This is the poorer of the two Cunninghame seats with a higher level of unemployment. It is indeed one of the least prosperous parts of Scotland. The claimant total is the second highest rate in the country only beaten by Glasgow Maryhill. Average property prices are the fifth lowest in Scotland, 35.4 per cent below the average and up 42.5 per cent in 1991-2001. But in recent years the constituency has had a decent record attracting new jobs. Fullarton Computer Industries opened a new facility in Irvine in 2000, creating 700 new jobs, while the following year, Irvine-based Omne Communications announced major plans for connecting the south-west of Scotland to broadband, digital television and other internet services. However, the area has also seen job losses with Volvo closing its truck plant in Irvine with the loss of 250 jobs, having previously ceased production of buses at the same plant a year before. BT announced in 2002 that its international directory inquiry centre based on Bourtreehill would close with the loss of more than 100 jobs. Another blow came in 2003 when the award winning science centre The Big Idea, based in Irvine, announced its closure due to disappointing visitor numbers and competition from Glasgow Science Centre.

As Ayrshire Central, the seat was a wafer-thin marginal. Archie Manuel won it for Labour in 1950 when it was first created, by 1,962 votes, and in 1951 by 1,693 votes over the Conservatives. The Tories took the seat at their Scottish high point of 1955 with Douglas Spencer-Nairn winning 50.2 per cent of the vote. Manuel re-won it for Labour in 1959 and held it until 1970 when David Lambie took over. Even at the SNP's zenith of October 1974, Lambie enjoyed a 9,555 majority over the Conservatives with the SNP just behind in third place; by 1987, the last time Lambie stood, his majority had rocketed to 16,633 over the Conservatives.

In 1992, Brian Donohoe was returned as the Labour MP with his majority cut to 10,680. The SNP's Ricky Bell more than doubled the SNP vote putting on 5,000 votes and rising from fourth to second. There was no such excitement in 1997 as Donohoe increased Labour's vote by 2,500, while the SNP's vote fell by the same amount, resulting in a Labour majority of 14,869. In the 2001 Westminster election, Donohoe was returned again this time with a slightly reduced 11,230 majority. The Scottish Socialists polled what was for them, at a Westminster election, a respectable 4.4 per cent.

In 1999, Irene Oldfather saw Labour's support decline from 1997, while Mike Russell for the SNP increased his support by 1,000 to leave Labour with a 6,541 majority. In the 2003 Scottish Parliament election Oldfather had a rematch with Russell, made all the more fascinating by Russell's demotion down the SNP rankings in South Scotland. Russell was unable to make any headway into Labour's dominance which saw Oldfather re-elected, and he lost his regional list seat. In that regional vote, Labour won 41.4 per cent and the SNP 21.4 per cent – while the SSP achieved 11.2 per cent and the Greens 4.1 per cent.

Boundary changes for Westminster see the abolition of Cunninghame South but will do little to shake the foundations of Labour's strength in this area with two-thirds of the seat going to Central Ayrshire and the rest to the new Ayr, Carrick and Cummock seat. At future Scottish Parliament elections, Cunninghame South will remain the sort of seat Scottish Labour can depend on in good times and bad, as part of its West of Scotland bedrock.

MSP

IRENE OLDFATHER was born in Glasgow in 1954 and educated at Irvine Royal Academy. She studied politics at the University of Strathclyde and did a masters in political science. She worked as a researcher on alcohol for Dumbarton District Council from 1976-77, followed by a year as a lecturer at the University of Arizona in 1977-78. She was a researcher and policy analyst for Glasgow City Council from 1979-90 and researcher for Alex Smith, the South of Scotland MEP, from 1990-97. This overlapped with time as a freelance journalist on European issues from 1994-98, for *Scotland on Sunday* among others, and lecturing on the politics of health at Paisley University from 1996-98.

Elected to North Ayrshire Council from 1995-99, this ballet enthusiast was vice-chair of the education, culture and sport committee and chair of the COSLA task group on European economic and monetary union, vice-chair of the West of Scotland European Consortium and an alternate member of the European Committee of the Regions. With her enthusiasm for European affairs, it was unsurprising that Oldfather became a member of the Scottish Parliament's European Committee, moving into the convener's post in 2001 when Hugh Henry vacated it on his elevation to ministerial office. With the share-out of convenerships moving that post to the SNP, she had to settle for the deputy convener post on the European and external relations committee after the 2003 election.

MP

BRIAN DONOHOE was born in 1948 in Kilmarnock and first elected MP for Cunninghame South in 1992. Educated at Irvine Royal Academy and Kilmarnock Technical College, he worked at Ailsa Shipbuilding in Troon as an apprenticeship fitter-turner from 1965-70 and at Hunterston nuclear power station from 1970-77. He was a contract draughtsman at ICI from 1977-81 and a NALGO full-time union official from 1981-92. He was convenor of the Scottish political and education committee of TASS from 1973-79, secretary of Irvine and District Trades Council from 1973-78 and chair of North Ayrshire and Arran Local Health Council in 1977.

Donohoe was defeated in seeking the Labour nomination for the marginal Ayr seat in 1985. Once elected in Cunninghame South in 1992, he became a member of the select committees on transport from

1993-97, environment, transport and regional affairs in 1997-2001, and transport, local government and the regions after the 2001 election. He was convener of the Scottish Labour group of MPs from 1996-98. He voted against the Maastricht Treaty in 1993, publicly urged Gordon Brown to stand against Tony Blair for the leadership in 1994, and at first opposed the Government on Iraq in February 2003, switching the following month to abstaining on the anti-war amendment and supporting the government on the main motion. He has, until recently, been a party loyalist and seen as a hard-working constituency MP. He has ensured a high profile in the local press, though occasionally sounding off on television about the workings of the Scottish Parliament without thinking through the implications carefully. One such contribution was the idea of reforming the voting system so that two MPs – mainly Labour, of course – would be elected for each constituency. He is chairman of the Commons Scotch Whisky group, and founder of an MP group of *Coronation Street* enthusiasts.

Dumbarton

Predecessor Constituencies: Dunbartonshire (1945) and Dunbartonshire West (1950–79).

Socio-economic Indicators:

Constituency Pop. (16-64)	49,787
Claimant Count (May 2003)	3.5% (13.1% above average)
IBA/SDA Claimants	9.2%
Life Expectancy – Male	72.2 (1.2 yrs below average)
Life Expectancy – Female	78.7 (national average)
Owner Occupied	63.8%
Social Rented	28.0%
Average Property Prices	£64,210 (29th)
Average Gross Income	£27,561 (19th)
Low Birthweight Babies	145 (6.7%)
Teenage Pregnancy Rates	381 (3.7%)
No. of Lone Parent Households	3,463 (11.2%)

CAB Enquiries

Issue	No. of cases	Percentage of total cases (%)
1. Benefits	2298	28.0
2. Consumer	1188	14.5
3. Other	1155	14.1
4. Employment	1047	12.7
5. Housing	916	11.1

2003 Scottish Parliament Election

Electorate: 55,575   *Turnout*: 28,823 (51.9%)   *Turnout 1999*: 61.9

Candidate	Party	Votes	Votes%	99 %	Change%
Jackie Baillie	Labour	12,154	42.2	43.8	– 1.6
Iain Docherty	SNP	5,542	19.2	30.0	–10.8
Frederic Thompson	Lib Dem	4,455	15.5	11.6	+ 3.8
Murray Tosh	Con	4,178	14.5	14.6	– 0.1
Les Robertson	SSP	2,494	8.7	–	–

Labour majority: 6,612 (22.9%)   *Swing*: 4.6% SNP to Labour

2001 General Election

Electorate: 55,643   *Turnout*: 33,994 (61.1%)

Candidate	Party	Votes	Votes%	Change%
John McFall	Labour	16,151	47.5	− 2.1
Iain Robertson	SNP	6,576	19.3	− 3.9
Eric Thompson	Lib Dem	5,265	15.5	+ 7.9
Peter Ramsay	Con	4,648	13.7	− 4.0
Les Robertson	SSP	1,354	4.0	+ 3.3

Labour majority: 9,575 (28.2%)   *Swing*: 0.9% SNP to Labour

1945–97 Westminster

	Lab%	Con%	SNP%	Lib%	Other%	Turnout%
1997	49.6	17.7	23.2	7.6	1.9	73.4
1992	43.6	29.7	18.4	7.8	0.4	77.1
1987	43.0	31.7	12.1	13.2	–	78.2
1983	36.7	31.8	8.7	22.8	–	75.0
1979	48.4	33.7	17.9	–	–	80.2
1974O	38.1	23.2	33.7	5.0	–	78.3
1974F	39.6	33.2	27.2	–	–	79.6
1970	50.9	37.1	12.0	–	–	78.0
1966	52.3	33.1	14.6	–	–	81.9
1964	50.8	37.2	12.0	–	–	82.1
1959	52.5	47.5	–	–	–	83.7
1955	52.3	47.7	–	–	–	84.8
1951	51.3	45.4	–	3.3	–	86.6
1950B	50.4	49.6	–	–	–	83.4
1950	49.3	47.8	–	–	2.9	85.5
1945	50.7	49.3	–	–	–	71.7

Dumbarton constituency is situated on the north side of the Clyde positioned between the rural land-scapes of Argyll and Bute and the urban and suburban mix of Clydebank and Milngavie. Dumbarton itself is the largest town in the constituency; other communities include Helensburgh, one of the most prosperous towns in Scotland, and the Vale of Leven, which includes the small towns of Alexandria and Renton. It also includes the controversial Trident nuclear submarine base at Faslane and armaments base at Coulport which still employ around 6,000 people in the area. The end of the Cold War and demise of communism was always only going to spell bad news for this area in terms of defence related employment, and in 2002, the MOD announced 500 job losses at the two bases, as well as the privatisation of a range of services, with 1,700 workers transferred to Babcock Naval Services including work ranging across cleaning, catering and maintenance. This has met significant opposition from the trade unions and local MP John McFall. Regular protests and a constant vigil have taken place outside Faslane base and in October 2001, 168 anti-nuclear protestors were arrested including two MSPs – Tommy Sheridan of the Scottish Socialists and Lloyd Quinan of the SNP.

West Dunbartonshire Council is currently looking at revolutionising the provision of education in the area via a one-stop shop approach through Community Learning Centres which will offer a joined-up approach to education from pre- to post-school. Many residents are sceptical of these proposals when they are not confident that the council can do the basic things properly; in the year 2000-1 the council had the worst council tax collection rate in the UK, managing to collect just over 75 per cent of local tax revenue. Job losses in the area have included Polaroid announcing 235 redundancies at its Vale of Leven plant and J & J Bond, the distillers announcing 500 job losses. Average property prices are 4.8 per cent below the national average and rose 40.2 per cent in the 1990s.

Dumbarton is also the setting for BBC Scotland's ambitious soap *River City* which was launched in September 2002. Filmed in a purpose-built set at an old whisky bond and costing £14 million, the show has been hit by poor ratings and reviews. The town is also the unlikely setting for the birthplace of arty, cerebral David Byrne, lead singer of the 1980s US band Talking Heads.

Dumbarton was first won by Labour in 1923 and has leaned to Labour ever since, but not always by convincing margins. In 1941 the Labour candidate Adam Storey McKinlay became the MP for Dunbartonshire West in a wartime by-election, and in 1945 he defeated the Conservatives by a slender 747 votes and then by the even narrower margin of 613 votes in 1950. McKinlay died in March 1950, one month after his election, and in the April by-election Thomas Steele was elected by a mere 293 vote majority, remaining MP until 1970. Iain Campbell succeeded Steele as Labour MP in 1970 and in October 1974 his majority fell to 1,814 over the SNP, before increasing to 6,457 over the Conservatives in 1979.

In 1983 the seat was renamed Dumbarton and a strong challenge from the Conservative Iain Lawson (later a prominent Nationalist) cut Labour's majority to 2,115. Even in 1987, Scottish Labour's moment of glory, while John McFall increased his majority over the Conservatives to 5,222, the swing to Labour was well below the national average. However, McFall marginally increased his majority over the Conservatives in 1992 to 6,129.

Up until 1997, the Conservatives had polled respectably in Dumbarton, unusual for a Labour seat they had not won in post-war times. All through the Tory years post-1979 they polled at least 30 per cent with only a slight decline. This all changed in 1997, as McFall increased Labour's majority to 10,883 and the SNP moved into second place for the first time since 1974. The Conservative vote dropped to third place. In June 2001 John McFall saw Labour's majority increase, as the SNP failed to make any inroads to Labour's vote and the Scottish Socialists polled 4 per cent. The 1999 Scottish Parliament election produced a Labour majority over the SNP of 4,758. In the second Scottish Parliament elections, Jackie Baillie won with a 6,612 majority over the Nationalists. In the regional list vote, Labour won 33.1 per cent and the SNP 18.6 per cent, while the SSP secured 8.5 per cent and Greens 5.4 per cent.

Alexandria and Renton were known in the 1920s and 1930s as 'Little Moscows' due to their radical politics and propensity for the Communists to work in co-operation with Labour in local politics and on the council. There were a small group of distinctive 'Little Moscows' across the UK including West Fife and the Rhondda Valley, usually characterised by the dominance of mining (although this was not the case with Alexandria and Renton which were textile towns). The radical, left-wing culture of these communities has not entirely disappeared in the early days of the 21st century, and in the 2003 local elections, the Scottish Socialists won 10.1 per cent of the vote across West Dunbartonshire – their highest vote outside Glasgow. The SSP won the Renton/Alexandria South ward with 66 per cent of the vote – their only council seat outside Glasgow.

Boundary Commission changes at Westminster will see most of the seat included in a new West Dunbartonshire seat which has a similar Labour look to it. Dumbarton has never been an entirely safe or typical Labour seat and will continue to provide an intriguing contest at Scottish Parliament elections. The shift of opposition politics from Conservative to SNP has greatly assisted Labour in Dumbarton, just as it has helped the party across Scotland.

MSP

JACKIE BAILLIE was born in 1964 in Hong Kong where her father was a policeman, and was educated at St Anne's School, Windermere, Cumbernauld College and Strathclyde University, with ongoing studies at Glasgow University towards an MSc in local economic development. She worked in Ruchill Unemployed Workers' Centre from 1986-87, before becoming co-ordinator of Gorbals Unemployed Workers' Centre from 1987-90. She then became resource centre manager with Strathkelvin District Council from 1990-96 and community development manager at East Dunbartonshire Council from 1996-99, with a nationwide role through the Convention of Scottish Local Authorities officer working groups. Before being elected an MSP, she worked on the cross-party 'Yes-Yes' referendum campaign of 1997 and was a director of Volunteer Development Scotland 1997-99.

Baillie was chair of the Scottish Labour Party from 1997-98 – a pivotal and difficult time for Scottish Parliament selections and with disciplinary and legal problems within the party. Working with then general secretary Jack McConnell seems to have left a legacy of antagonism between the two MSPs. In the 1999 elections, she was campaign spokesperson on social inclusion, and after the elections was appointed as deputy minister for social inclusion, equality and the voluntary sector. As Wendy Alexander's deputy in the post, her people skills helped make up for those of her boss. It was no surprise that Henry McLeish promoted her to the renamed cabinet post of social justice minister in his reshuffle upon becoming First Minister in October 2000. This included responsibility for saving the flagship Glasgow Housing Stock Transfer from near collapse and changes to Scottish Homes, but it lost the portfolio's previous responsibility for local government, which moved to the finance minister's in-tray. She records her achievements from the first Parliament as having shaped and steering through the Housing Act 2001, bringing new rights for tenants and the homeless, helping with delivery of central heating for pensioners, and supporting the retention of Vale of Leven Hospital's maternity unit.

As Baillie supported Wendy Alexander's brief leadership bid against Jack McConnell in 2002, the new First Minister sacked her. She took a Labour seat on the education committee until the 2003 election, and after that on Justice 1 and petitions committees. Having remained publicly loyal to the McConnell leadership, the cheerful and amiable Baillie was first among backbench Labour MSPs to cause it real trouble in the wake of the 2003 election. When Margaret Curran, previously Baillie's deputy at social justice, announced plans for charity reform in the wake of a fund-raising scandal, Baillie proposed her own bill, in a successful bid to force Curran and her reluctant officials into an abrupt speeding up of plans. She went on to be one of six abstainers in the March 2004 vote on voting reform for councils. Baillie, in her 2003 election address, listed one of her main achievements in the previous four years as being the siting of the BBC Scotland soap *River City* in the constituency.

MP

JOHN McFALL was born in 1944 in Glasgow and has been Labour MP for Dumbarton since 1987. Educated at St Patrick's Secondary, Dumbarton, Paisley College of Technology, Strathclyde University, where he did a BSc and MBA, and the Open University where he did a BA. From 1974-87, he was a chemistry teacher and assistant head at Belarmine Secondary, Glasgow. After his arrival at the House of Commons, McFall became a member of the defence select committee from 1990-92, where he raised issues of the inflating costs of building the Trident nuclear base at Faslane, while also on the Commons information committee from 1990-97. He was made a Labour whip in 1989, resigning in 1991, and then made Labour spokesperson on education in 1992, rising to become deputy to George Robertson as shadow Scottish Secretary in the months before the 1997 move to government.

After the 1997 election, he was disappointed not to become a Scottish Office minister, instead getting a place in the whips office in 1997-98, and then he was appointed a minister in the Northern Ireland Office from 1998-2001, where he covered education, training and employment, health and community relations for the first year and then economy and education. Following the election in 2001, he lost his ministerial job and won the powerful position of chairing the Treasury select committee, taking a prominent role in pressuring finance companies which were responding to the stock market crash with sharply reduced pay-outs to customers. A pragmatic centre-left politician, McFall has shown the ability to combine Old Labour sensibilities with an awareness of New Labour priorities; he has in his past, like most of the party, been much more left-wing than he is now, including support for unilateral disarmament, even though many of his constituents work at Faslane.

Dumfries

Predecessor Constituencies: Dumfriesshire (1945–70).

Socio-economic Indicators:

Constituency Pop. (16-64)	50,855
Claimant Count (May 2003)	2.6% (16.1% below average)
IBA/SDA Claimants	7.4%
Life Expectancy – Male	75.3 (1.9 yrs above average)
Life Expectancy – Female	80.5 (1.8 yrs above average)
Owner Occupied	65.2%
Social Rented	22.0%
Average Property Prices	£54,757 (48th)
Average Gross Income	£23,461 (58th)
Low Birthweight Babies	136 (6.0%)
Teenage Pregnancy Rates	440 (4.5%)
No. of Lone Parent Households	3,045 (8.8%)

CAB Enquiries

Issue	No. of cases	Percentage of total cases (%)
1. Benefits	7829	44.5
2. Consumer	2255	12.8
3. Employment	2081	11.8
4. Housing	1914	10.9
5. Other	1159	6.6

2003 Scottish Parliament Election

Electorate: 61,517 *Turnout*: 32,110 (52.2%) *Turnout 1999*: 60.9

Candidate	Party	Votes	Votes%	99 %	Change%
Elaine Murray	Labour	12,834	40.0	36.6	+ 3.2
David Mundell	Con	11,738	36.6	27.2	+ 9.3
Andrew Wood	SNP	3,931	12.2	19.8	– 7.6
Clare Hamblen	Lib Dem	2,394	7.5	16.4	– 8.7
John Dennis	SSP	1,213	3.8	–	–

Labour majority: 1,096 (3.4%) *Swing*: 3.1% Labour to Conservative

2001 General Election

Electorate: 63,571   *Turnout*: 42,586 (67.0%)

Candidate	Party	Votes	Votes%	Change%
Russell Brown	Labour	20,830	48.9	+ 1.4
John Charteris	Con	11,996	28.2	+ 0.1
John Ross Scott	Lib Dem	4,955	11.6	+ 0.6
Gerry Fisher	SNP	4,103	9.6	– 2.4
John Dennis	SSP	702	1.6	–

Labour majority: 8,834 (20.7%)   *Swing*: 0.6% Conservative to Labour

1945–97 Westminster

	Lab%	Con%	SNP%	Lib%	Other%	Turnout%
1997	47.5	28.0	12.1	11.1	1.3	78.9
1992	30.0	43.1	14.3	11.8	0.9	80.0
1987	25.2	41.8	14.2	18.0	0.8	75.6
1983	20.8	44.5	10.8	23.9	–	73.0
1979	27.3	45.2	13.2	14.3	–	78.1
1974O	26.5	38.8	26.4	8.3	–	76.7
1974F	25.9	44.1	18.6	11.4	–	80.4
1970	33.5	53.1	13.4	–	–	76.2
1966	35.9	45.6	12.6	5.9	–	80.2
1964	39.1	48.7	12.2	–	–	81.6
1963B	38.5	40.9	9.7	10.9	–	71.6
1959	41.6	58.4	–	–	–	77.4
1955	38.7	61.3	–	–	–	73.7
1951	38.7	61.3	–	–	–	80.2
1950	40.7	59.3	–	–	–	78.6
1945	16.9	47.4	–	16.9	–	72.2

Dumfries is situated between Galloway and Upper Nithsdale to the west, the two Borders seats to its east and Carlisle and England to the south. The largest town in the seat is Dumfries itself but there are also smaller towns such as Annan and Annandale and many noteworthy towns such as Ecclefechan, birthplace of historian Thomas Carlyle and Gretna Green, site of many runaway marriages. It also includes Lockerbie, known worldwide for Pan Am flight 103 which was blown up above the town in December 1988, killing local residents as well as those on board.

    Education and health services have been involved in a series of controversial decisions in recent years. Dumfries and Galloway Council has developed PPP schemes to modernise the area's schools which involve the amalgamation of a number of small rural schools. The main hospital, Dumfries and Galloway Royal Infirmary recently opened its new Maternity and Day Surgery Unit, while four new community hospitals are planned, but local communities have concerns about the closure of traditional small rural hospitals.

Another major local issue has been the decision of the council's 13,500 tenants to vote for the Housing Stock Transfer of their homes from council control to being run by D&G Housing Partnership. With a mix of wealth and deprivation which is typical of rural Scotland, average property prices are 18.8 per cent below the average and increased by 34.9 per cent in the 1990s. Upland sheep farming is widespread in the constituency, and it was this area which suffered the worst consequences in Scotland of the outbreak of foot and mouth disease in 2001. With an inflow of compensation to farmers who had their flocks destroyed, the sector has bounced back reasonably well and special efforts have been made to help the area's tourist industry back on to its feet.

The area received a boost in 2002 when at the third attempt one of the local football teams, Gretna, was finally allowed membership to the Scottish Football League. Known as the 'Kings of the Borders' their 2,200 capacity ground Raydale Park, has seen attendances rise dramatically due to the appeal of the Scottish Third Division.

The seat has had a long and proud Conservative history. Major Murray won it comfortably in 1918, when it was Dumfriesshire, and Niall Macpherson easily held it for the National Liberals in 1945 with a 4,077 majority over Labour. He remained MP until 1963 when David Anderson held the seat for the Conservatives in a December by-election with 40.9 per cent to Labour's 38.5 per cent but he did not remain MP for the area for long. In the subsequent general election in October 1964, Hector Munro was elected and remained MP until 1997. In February 1974 the seat became Dumfries and even in October 1974, Munro held it with a 5,828 majority over Labour, with the SNP just behind. In 1979 Munro increased his majority to 9,004 over Labour and held the seat with slightly reduced majorities in 1983 and 1987. In 1992, the last time Munro stood, he retained the seat with a 6,415 lead, while Labour's Peter Rennie increased Labour's vote by 4.8 per cent, achieving a swing to Labour against the Scottish trend.

At the 1997 election Munro made way for Struan Stevenson, defending the second safest Conservative seat in Scotland (Eastwood being the safest), with a notional majority now of 6,766 over Labour. Stevenson saw a collapse in the Conservative vote of over 7,000 votes (a decline of 15 per cent) as Labour's Russell Brown increased his vote by an impressive 9,000 and 18 per cent. This was a swing to Labour of 16.5 per cent – over twice the Scottish average – and resulted in Labour achieving a majority of 9,643 over the Conservatives.

The 1997 result was an exceptional one for Labour – Russell Brown's majority was the largest Labour won in any of the Conservative seats it gained in Scotland. In the 2001 UK election Brown was easily re-elected, while the Conservative vote remained stubbornly static, unlike neighbouring Galloway and Upper Nithsdale.

Labour held the seat in 1999 with its vote falling 9,000 back to its 1992 levels and the Tory vote falling back a further 3,000. This represented a significant 5 per cent swing from Labour to Conservatives and a Labour majority of 3,654. At the May 2003 Scottish Parliament elections, Labour's vote fell back by nearly 1,300 as the Conservative David Mundell, a regional list MSP, increased his party's support by the same number of votes, cutting Labour's majority from 3,654 to 1,096. In the regional vote, the Conservatives won 31.8 per cent to 30.5 per cent for Labour – a Conservative lead of 414 – with the SSP on 3.9 per cent and Greens on 3.5 per cent.

Boundary changes for Westminster will see the expansion of the seat to include Kirkcudbrightshire and Wigtownshire, currently within Conservative held Galloway and Upper Nithsdale, to form a Dumfries and Galloway seat. This will be very close fought between Labour and Conservative, while the SNP also has hopes. However, it is Labour which is reckoned to start out with a narrow notional lead, based on past voting. In Scottish Parliament elections, the Conservatives have had a mini-renaissance in this part of Scotland – with their victory in the neighbouring Galloway seat, and they must fancy their chances of retaking Dumfries in the near-future and making the seat's affiliation to Labour a short one.

MSP

ELAINE MURRAY was born in 1954 in Hitchin, Hertfordshire, and educated at Mary Erskine School, Edinburgh, and the universities of Edinburgh and Cambridge, qualifying with a PhD in physical chemistry. She worked as a research fellow at the Cavendish Laboratory from 1979-81, before becoming a research fellow at the Royal Free Hospital, London, from 1981-4, then senior research officer at the Institute of Food Research in Reading from 1984-7. She was assistant to Alex Smith, the South of Scotland MEP, from 1990-3 and an assistant lecturer with the Open University from 1992-9.

Murray was elected to Strathclyde Regional Council from 1994-6 and South Ayrshire Council from 1995-9, where she was convenor of the educational services committee and chair of the women's advisory committee. She was also COSLA cultural issues spokesperson from 1996-9. She was a member of the enterprise and lifelong learning committee and rural affairs committee in the Parliament's first 18 months, then becoming a member of the rural development committee, while joining a wide range of cross-party groups.

As a nominee of Jack McConnell in the 2001 leadership election, her reward was a ministerial post as deputy to Mike Watson on tourism, culture and sport, with special responsibility for arts and culture. On the hottest issue affecting 'sport' at the time, they took opposing views, with Watson having sponsored the bill to ban fox-hunting with dogs, while Murray represented a rural seat which required her to oppose it as a litmus test of her commitment to rural Scotland. Murray failed to support the Labour line in the second Iraq war debate in March 2003, abstaining instead. She offered her resignation, but McConnell refused it, saying he was 'not a dictator', and that there was no reason to resign as it was not a matter covered by collective ministerial responsibility. While Murray's fate may indeed have been marginal in the scheme of international war and peace, this was an adroit move by McConnell, conceding to a deeply divided and uneasy party. Losing ground to the Tories' David Mundell in 2003, and possibly sensing she was out of favour with McConnell, Murray told him in advance of his post-election reshuffle that she wanted to return to the backbenches, to spend more time on her constituency. She was rewarded with seats on both the finance and education committees.

MP

RUSSELL BROWN was born in Annan in 1951, and educated at Annan Academy. He worked as a production supervisor in ICI Explosives, Dumfries, from 1974-92 and as a plant operative in ICI Films from 1992-97. He was elected to Dumfries and Galloway Regional Council from 1986-96 and was chair of Dumfries and Galloway public protection committee from 1990-94. The council was notable at that time for imaginative approaches to delivering local services, including free transport for senior citizens, working in partnership with local firms. He also served on Annandale and Eskdale District Council from 1988-96. In 1995, he was elected to Dumfries and Galloway Council, serving on it until 1999. Elected to the House of Commons in 1997, he was one of the few among that year's intake in Tony Blair's Parliamentary grouping to come from a genuine working-class background.

He was a Parliamentary private secretary to Lord Williams of Mostyn from 2002, but resigned in a bizarre turn of events over a vote on the Iraq war, when he voted with the government but then resigned in protest at the position he had just supported. Although named in press reporting of MP office expenses irregularities in 2001, he emerged unscathed after an investigation, and retained his position on the standards and privileges committee. Positions at the Commons have included posts on the European legislation select committee from 1997-98, European scrutiny 1998-99, Scottish affairs 1999-2001 and deregulation and regulatory reform from 2001.

Dundee East

Predecessor Constituencies: none.

Socio-economic Indicators:

Constituency Pop. (16–64)	45,924
Claimant Count (May 2003)	5.4% (72.8% above average)
IBA/SDA Claimants	11.2%
Life Expectancy – Male	71.9 (1.5 yrs below average)
Life Expectancy – Female	78.3 (0.4 yrs below average)
Owner Occupied	56.8%
Social Rented	30.3%
Average Property Prices	£51,042 (56th)
Average Gross Income	£24,107 (48th)
Low Birthweight Babies (av. 1996–98)	166 (7.0%)
Teenage Pregnancy Rates (av. 1996–98)	701 (7.4%)
No. of Lone Parent Households	4,212 (12.5%)

CAB Enquiries

Issue	No. of cases	Percentage of total cases (%)
1. Benefits	3963	25.6
2. Consumer	2877	18.6
3. Employment	2740	17.7
4. Other	1646	10.6
5. Housing	1505	9.7

2003 Scottish Parliament Election

Electorate: 53,876   Turnout: 26,348 (48.9%)   Turnout 1999: 55.3%

Candidate	Party	Votes	Votes%	99 %	Change%
Shona Robison	SNP	10,428	39.6	34.3	+ 5.3
John McAllion	Labour	10,338	39.2	43.3	– 4.0
Edward Prince	Con	3,133	11.9	14.0	– 2.1
Clive Sneddon	Lib Dem	1,584	6.0	6.8	– 0.8
James Gourlay	Ind	865	3.3	(other 1.7)	–

SNP majority: 90 (0.3%)   Swing: 4.7% Labour to SNP

2001 General Election

Electorate: 56,535   *Turnout*: 32,367 (57.3%)

Candidate	Party	Votes	Votes%	Change%
Iain Luke	Labour	14,635	45.2	− 5.9
Stewart Hosie	SNP	10,169	31.4	+ 4.9
Alan Donnelly	Con	3,900	12.1	− 3.7
Raymond Lawrie	Lib Dem	2,784	8.6	+ 4.5
Harvey Duke	SSP	879	2.7	+ 2.1

Labour majority: 4,466 (13.8%)   *Swing*: 5.4% Labour to SNP

1950–97 Westminster

	Lab%	Con%	SNP%	Lib%	Other%	Turnout%
1997	51.1	15.8	26.5	4.1	2.5	69.4
1992	44.1	17.8	33.4	4.1	0.7	72.1
1987	42.3	12.9	40.2	4.6	–	75.9
1983	33.0	15.5	43.8	7.7	–	73.7
1979	36.0	18.2	41.0	4.6	–	77.7
1974O	32.7	16.8	47.7	2.8	–	73.4
1974F	33.7	26.4	39.5	–	0.4	81.1
1973B	32.7	25.2	30.2	8.3	3.6	70.0
1970	48.3	42.4	8.9	–	0.4	76.1
1966	56.3	43.7	–	–	–	78.8
1964	54.8	45.2	–	–	–	80.0
1959	54.3	45.7	–	–	–	82.6
1955	54.3	45.7	–	–	–	82.3
1952B	56.3	35.6	7.4	–	0.7	71.5
1951	53.8	46.2	–	–	–	87.2
1950	53.4	44.4	–	–	2.2	88.6

Dundee has gained a reputation as a dour, lifeless place of monotony and little excitement, which it has had trouble losing. Charles Jennings, in his hilarious travelogue across Scotland, *Faintheart*, commented that in Dundee 'people were walking around in that tut-tutting way that middle-aged Scots have'. And yet, Dundee has dramatically changed in the last ten years. There has been the cultural renaissance of the Dundee literary scene with writers such as W. N. Herbert, author of *Dundee Doldrums*, Kate Atkinson and Bill Duncan. The city has also become a vibrant international centre of computer software games companies such as Viz Interactive, home of the Scottish Games Alliance and the Interactive Tayside initiative. Dundee University, situated in the West End of the city has become a major centre for bioscience and biochemistry.

The city's harbour facilities are found in Dundee East and these provide support and services to the offshore oil and gas industries, although not to the same extent as Aberdeen. A noteworthy attraction in one of the harbour docks is the presence of HMS Unicorn, the last floating wooden warship in the UK, and last put into service to host reserve Wrens in the Korean War.

Old industries remain in the city and of the areas represented by the three J's – jute, jam and journalism – which were once seen as Dundee's hallmarks, journalism remains as a vibrant industry. This is D. C. Thomson land whose printing works are located by the Kingsway East - the home of the Dundee based *Courier and Advertiser* and the world-famous *Sunday Post*, which used to hold the world record for market penetration, and remains a byword for parochialism and small-town couthiness.

Dundee contains the two closest professional football teams in the whole of the UK. Dundee Football Club and Dundee United Football Club, both Scottish Premier League Clubs are situated in the same street – Tannadice Street. In a strange quirk of fate when the great Dundee United team of Jim McLean won all their trophies in the 1980s they did so at their opponents' ground, Dens Park. Most famously they won the League Championship on the last day of the season, beating Dundee at Dens in 1983. United had many glorious European nights in the 1980s reaching and losing a UEFA Cup Final in 1987. Both clubs seem far removed from such experiences today. Dundee went into administration at the end of 2003, and in a cost-cutting move are considering moving from Dens Park into a ground-sharing arrangement with Dundee United across the road at Tannadice

Dundee has a long tradition of radicalism and causing upsets which challenge political orthodoxies. Dundee was one of the first places in Scotland to elect a Labour representative when Alexander Wilkie won in 1906 and sat for the city until 1922 – this being one of the first two seats Labour won in Scotland – the other being Glasgow Blackfriars. At this point, Dundee, a two-member seat was known as 'Juteopolis' due to the dominance of the jute and textile industries in the city's employment. The city was called 'a woman's town' because of the high rate of women working in the industries, while men were known as 'kettle boilers': a dynamic which has influenced gender relations, if not politics, in the city since.

The character of Edwin Scrymgeour contributed much to the city's politics in the early 20th century. He set up the Scottish Prohibition Party in 1904 and his mixture of ILP-style socialism, temperance and independence allowed him to attract Labour, Liberal and Conservative votes. In 1922, Scrymgeour was, at his sixth attempt, elected to Parliament, along with Edmund Dene Morel, the anti-war campaigner. This was a decisive defeat of Winston Churchill, who had been Liberal MP for the city since 1908 and served in the Asquith and Lloyd George Governments. T. E. Lawrence commented to Churchill on his defeat, 'What bloody shits the Dundeans (sic) must be', to which he replied, given the life 'the Dundee folk have to live', they have 'many excuses'. Scrymgeour was MP from 1922-31, falling in the National Government landslide of that year; Thomas Johnston, later to be Secretary of State for Scotland from 1941-45, was also briefly a Dundee MP from winning a by-election in 1924 until 1929.

Dundee remained a two-member seat until 1950. Dundee East returned Thomas Cook as its first Labour MP from 1950-52, who had previously been an MP for Dundee from 1945-50. He was followed by George Thomson from 1952-73, who became a European Commissioner, was anointed Lord Thomson and defected to the SDP.

The city's eastern seat is marginally poorer than the neighbouring west one. The claimant count is the third highest in Scotland and of its 30.3 per cent social housing, 21.3 per cent is council housing, down from 42 per cent ten years previously. Average property prices are 24.3 per cent below the national average and rose 74.2 per cent in the1990s. Teenage pregnancies are the highest in the country.

Since the 1970s this seat has been a Labour-SNP marginal and the SNP has done well in the city ever since. Former SNP leader Gordon Wilson nearly unseated Labour at a by-election in March 1973, reducing Labour's majority to 1,141. Wilson then went on to win the seat in February 1974 with a majority of 2,966 over Labour and 6,983 in October 1974, and then succeeded in holding it against the anti-SNP swing in 1979 with a majority of 2,519. This latter result was partly a product of the controversy caused by the Labour candidate, Jimmy Reid, who had in the previous year defected from the

Communists, and whose selection as Labour candidate had resulted in opposition on the NEC from Shirley Williams and other Labour right-wingers.

Wilson's 1983 majority of 5,016 was overturned in 1987 to provide John McAllion with a narrow 1,015 lead, which Labour built on in subsequent elections to turn a marginal into a safe Labour seat at the 1992 and 1997 elections. The party held the seat first by 4,564 votes over the SNP, and then, 9,961 votes in 1997 with the Nationalists now in a distant second. In the June 2001 Westminster election, Iain Luke took over as Labour candidate from John McAllion who had decided to concentrate on the Scottish Parliament. Labour's support declined by 6,000, while the Nationalist vote fell by 600 on a lower turnout, cutting Labour's majority in more than half from 9,961 to 4,466 and providing a harbinger of the 2003 election.

Although Dundee East looked as though it had become a safe Labour seat, the May 1999 Scottish Parliament election produced a good, but not sensational result for the Nationalists. The SNP were back within a shout in the East, but the headlines were taken by developments in the West seat. Dundee was one of the most hotly contested Labour-SNP territories in the second Scottish Parliament election, as well as at council level, and while West was the more marginal seat, East provided the more fertile ground: although Shona Robison's vote fell 400, John McAllion's Labour vote declined by 3,400, and the SNP won by 90 votes. Thus, McAllion's decision to concentrate on the Scottish Parliament proved brief and ill-fated, and lost one of the new legislature's most accomplished debators and committee convenors to a job in Oxfam. The Scottish Socialists had decided to stand down in the constituency contest to support McAllion's left-wing politics, but after his defeat, commentators wondered whether the SSP not standing had inadvertently hurt the Labour left-wing MSP. This thesis seems to be unfounded by the regional list voting in Dundee East where the SSP did stand and the SNP still came out top: the SNP winning 34.7 per cent to Labour's 30 per cent – an even larger majority of 1,228 – while the SSP won 5.1 per cent and the Greens 4.6 per cent.

Boundary changes at Westminster see Dundee East expanded into Angus to include Monifieth, Carnoustie and Sidlaw East. Analysis of voting histories in the new wards make this the most marginal seat in Scotland, giving Labour a tiny edge over the Nationalists. At the Scottish Parliament, the SNP's victory in the 2003 elections – their first in this seat since 1983 – offers the party the opportunity of putting down stronger urban roots and challenging further Labour's weakening hold over the city.

MSP

SHONA ROBISON was born in Redcar in 1966 and educated at Alva Academy, Glasgow University (social sciences), and Jordanhill College, where she gained a postgraduate certificate in community education. She worked for Glasgow City Council as a community worker and home care organiser, and was studying for a law degree at Strathclyde University when first elected an MSP. She contested the Dundee East constituency at the 1997 and 1999 elections, losing to Labour's John McAllion, who she then unseated in 2003 as one of the SNP's three constituency gains. Robison was deputy convener of the equal opportunities committee in the first Scottish Parliament and served on the health and community care committee, where she made good use of her experience of working within Glasgow care services at a time of major cutbacks. As secretary to the SNP's Parliamentary Group 1999-2002, she became something of an enforcer for the leadership with the group's various wayward elements.

Under John Swinney's leadership, from September 2000, Robison became the party's lead spokeswoman on health and community care, forming the third member, with Nicola Sturgeon and Fiona Hyslop, of the triumvirate of female MSP contemporaries working as his inner team. With Sturgeon, she took some credit for pushing the Executive into funding free long-term care for the elderly. Having international interests, she was convenor in the first Parliament of the cross party group on refugees and asylum seekers, and pushed for further controls on firework sales. She is married to Stewart Hosie, the SNP's national secretary until 2003 and a Dundee West candidate in the 2001 Westminster election. As the 2003 summer recess began, Robison gave birth to their first child, though she was soon stridently back in the front line and TV studios, arguing the Swinney cause against his challenger in the September leadership contest.

MP

IAIN LUKE was born in 1951 in Dundee, and became an MP in 2001. He was educated at Dundee University as a mature student, where he studied modern history and political science. He did a diploma in business administration at Edinburgh University and trained as an FE lecturer at Jordanhill College. From 1969-74, he was an assistant collector of taxes and from 1983-2001 he lectured at Dundee College. He was a councillor on Dundee City Council from 1984-96, where he was convener of cultural services from 1988-90, council leader from 1990-92, and convener of economic development from 1991-96. He was also a councillor on the unitary Dundee City Council authority from 1996-2001, and convener of housing.

Luke set out in the early 1980s as a Bennite member of the Labour Co-ordinating Committee, which was dominant in Dundee at the time. However, he quickly gained a reputation, reinforced over his years as a councillor, as a pragmatic moderniser. Luke's selection to replace John McAllion was not without controversies: Marlyn Glen, another councillor, was blocked from standing despite several branch nominations, and the contest had to be run twice. Glen went on to become a list MSP for North East Scotland in 2003. Although coming from the same radical tradition as McAllion, Luke is more mainstream and loyal – even though he voted against the Government on the Iraq war motions in early 2003 and was one of only five Scottish Labour MPs to vote against top-up student fees in January 2004. He also signed a Commons motion in June 2003 opposing Scottish Executive plans to introduce proportional representation into local government – an unsurprising position for a former Labour council leader. He became a member of the broadcasting select committee in 2001, while also sitting on the administration and procedures committee.

Dundee West

Predecessor Constituencies: none.

Socio-economic Indicators:

Constituency Pop. (16-64)	47,524
Claimant Count (May 2003)	4.3% (38.2% above average)
IBA/SDA Claimants	10.5%
Life Expectancy – Male	71.7 (1.7 yrs below average)
Life Expectancy – Female	78.1 (0.2 yrs below average)
Owner Occupied	50.1%
Social Rented	33.5%
Average Property Prices	£50,012 (57th)
Average Gross Income	£22,190 (66th)
Low Birthweight Babies	136 (6.7%)
Teenage Pregnancy Rates	581 (5.3%)
No. of Lone Parent Households	3,882 (11.8%)

2003 Scottish Parliament Election

Electorate: 51,387   *Turnout*: 25,003 (48.7%)   *Turnout 1999*: 52.2

Candidate	Party	Votes	Votes%	99 %	Change%
Kate MacLean	Labour	8,234	32.9	37.6	– 4.6
Irene McGugan	SNP	7,168	28.7	37.2	– 8.5
Ian Borthwick	Ind	4,715	18.9	–	–
Shona Ferrier	Lib Dem	1,878	7.5	10.3	– 2.8
James McFarlane	SSP	1,501	6.0	3.5	+ 2.5
Victoria Roberts	Con	1,376	5.5	11.5	– 6.0
Morag MacLachlan	SPA	131	0.5	–	–

Labour majority: 1,066 (4.3%)   *Swing*: 1.9% SNP to Labour

2001 General Election

Electorate: 53,760   *Turnout*: 29,242 (54.4%)

Candidate	Party	Votes	Votes%	Change%
Ernie Ross	Labour	14,787	50.6	– 3.2
Gordon Archer	SNP	7,987	27.3	+ 4.1
Ian Hall	Con	2,656	9.1	– 4.1

cont'd

Candidate	Party	Votes	Votes%	Change%
Elizabeth Dick	Lib Dem	2,620	9.0	+ 1.3
James McFarlane	SSP	1,192	4.1	+ 3.0

Labour majority: 6,800 (23.3%)   *Swing*: 3.7% Labour to SNP

1950–97 Westminster

	Lab%	Con%	SNP%	Lib%	Other%	Turnout%
1997	53.8	13.2	23.2	7.7	2.2	67.7
1992	49.0	18.5	23.6	7.5	1.4	69.8
1987	53.3	18.0	15.3	12.7	0.7	75.5
1983	43.5	21.7	17.1	17.1	0.6	74.4
1979	47.2	25.8	26.4	–	0.6	78.4
1974O	41.0	18.5	35.1	4.6	0.8	74.3
1974F	43.1	30.5	25.1	–	1.3	81.2
1970	51.5	38.2	8.7	–	1.6	76.3
1966	53.8	36.9	–	6.9	2.4	79.9
1964	53.4	44.2	–	–	2.4	81.5
1963B	50.6	39.4	7.4	–	2.6	71.6
1959	49.6	48.3	–	–	2.1	82.9
1955	50.5	46.9	–	–	2.6	82.7
1951	51.6	–	–	45.7	2.7	86.8
1950	53.5	44.6	–	1.9	–	88.1

Dundee West includes middle-class areas of the city such as Riverside, Roseangle, Gowrie Park and the West End around the University of Dundee and Duncan of Jordanstone College campus, as well as working-class areas such as Ardler, Charleston, Lochee, St Mary's and Menzieshill. When Dundee was known as 'Juteopolis' at the turn of the century, it was the centre of the global economy in the jute and textile industries. One of the main concentrations of industry and employment was in the close-knit community of Lochee, and a whole infrastructure of houses, social facilities and networks grew up around it which still shapes it to this day.

When the jute industries declined in the immediate post-war period, Dundee was at the forefront of attracting American multi-nationals such as Timex and NCR. The Dundee Timex plant saw several bitter conflicts, including a 1988 dispute between trade unions after the AEEU had agreed a no-strike agreement which fell through and cost the city thousands of potential car manufacturing jobs. Eventually Timex pulled out, but NCR remains with an enhanced research and development presence and Dundee has rein-vented itself, not only as a 'City of Discovery', but an international city of bioscience and biochemistry.

New jobs have come to the city including Tesco's, the supermarket chain bringing 160 new jobs, the Commission for the Regulation of Care locating its headquarters bringing 150 jobs, a new Pensions Office as part of UK government dispersal involving 550 jobs, and the Inland Revenue taking a lease on the building that was originally intended for One2One, creating 500 new posts. Job losses have also happened over the same period with Levi-Strauss announcing 460 job cuts due to labour costs.

Several other developments have improved Dundee's image. A Centre for Inter-disciplinary Research was announced in 2002 which will support medical research and life sciences at Dundee and St Andrews Universities, involve £15 million investment studying cancer, diabetes and nutrition, and creates 180 new jobs. Award-winning initiatives have included the opening of the Dundee Contemporary Arts (DCA) centre which has acted as a hub for the arts, design and creative industries in the area, and the unveiling in September 2003 of the Maggie Centre, a facility to support people living with cancer, designed by the internationally-acclaimed US architect Frank Gehry.

Slightly more affluent than its eastern neighbour, Dundee West has traditionally been a solidly Labour seat, but is less solid now. It was represented by John Strachey, the ex-Marxist thinker who by the 1950s was one of the leading Gaitskellite social democratic revisionists in the Labour Party and represented Dundee from 1945-50 and Dundee West from 1950-63, followed by Peter Doig from 1963-79, a loyal and faceless Labour right-winger. Labour seldom faced an electoral challenge until the SNP won 35 per cent in October 1974 – 2,802 votes behind Labour. Ernie Ross was first elected in Dundee West in 1979 when he was a determined hard leftist in sharp contrast to the politics of his predecessors, winning a 10,457 majority over the Nationalists. Ross maintained his majority in 1983, achieving a 10,150 lead over the Conservatives, with the SNP relegated to fourth place. He increased this in 1987 to an impressive 16,526 over the Conservatives, winning over half the vote. In 1992, Labour's majority was cut back to 10,604 with the SNP returning to second place.

In the May 1997 Labour landslide Ernie Ross won by a margin of 11,859 over the SNP and again won over 50 per cent of the vote. In the June 2001 UK election, Ross saw Labour's vote fall by 6,000, while the SNP declined by more than 1,000 on a reduced turnout. Given the scale of Labour's dominance in this seat at Westminster, this still left Labour on over half the vote and a 6,800 majority.

Before 1999, Dundee West seemed to be rock solid Labour territory, and then, unexpectedly, a political earthquake occurred. In the first Scottish Parliament elections, Kate MacLean, then leader of the ruling Labour group on Dundee City Council, stood against the SNP's Calum Cashley. Labour's vote collapsed by nearly 10,000 votes and 16 per cent, as the SNP increased their vote by 1,800 and 14 per cent. Labour's majority was slashed to a mere 121 votes – the most marginal Labour–SNP seat in Scotland. One reason put forward at the time was that MacLean was extremely unpopular as leader of the council, and most did not give her much hope of surviving four years later. In May 2003, Dundee West was the number one SNP target, and while Labour's vote fell by 2,700, the Nationalists could not make any headway and their vote fell by 3,600, increasing Labour's majority by nearly ten-fold. The SNP's inability to win Dundee West was a shock result, but it underlined that perhaps the 1999 result was an exception – an impressive SNP challenge in a seat in which they had no previous track record. The other major shock of 2003 was the powerful campaign and support by independent candidate and ex-Labour councillor, Ian Borthwick, who polled 19 per cent. Borthwick has been a local councillor for over twenty years, first for St Mary's, then for Brackens, where he won 64 per cent in 2003.

In the regional list vote, Labour won 33.5 per cent to the SNP's 29.6 per cent – a Labour lead of 980 votes – while the SSP won 7.9 per cent and Greens 4.9 per cent. The decline of the Scottish Conservatives in this seat speaks volumes for the changing contours of Scottish politics. In 1959 the Conservatives – in what has never been natural Tory territory – won 48.3 per cent; this had halved by 1979 to 25.8 per cent, but by 2003 they polled the minuscule level of 5.5 per cent and finished sixth – an example of urban Scotland's turn against Scottish Toryism.

Boundary changes for Westminster see the expansion of Dundee's two seats, with voting analysis suggesting a notional Labout majority in the West constituency of around 7,800 over the Nationalists. Dundee West has proven its commitment to Labour at Westminster and this looks set to continue in any new seat, but the future is less certain at the Scottish Parliament. The 2003 election does offer succour to Labour supporters who believe the 1999 Dundee West result was an aberration and that normal service will slowly be restored, but the counter-case has supporting evidence as well: the Nationalists are still within shouting distance of Labour, and are well dug in locally and impressively represented on the local council. Dundee – a city many in Scotland like to patronise and poke fun at – has proven many fascinating moments in Scottish politics, and it looks like this is set to continue for many years to come.

MSP

KATE MacLEAN was born in Dundee in 1958 and educated at Craigie High School, Dundee, spending 1976-88 as a mother and nurse. She was elected to Dundee District Council in 1988 and became whip of the Labour group in 1990. She was then leader of Dundee Council from 1992 onwards, before and after the district council became a single tier authority. Her public profile in that position was credited with Labour coming close to losing the Dundee West seat to the SNP in 1999. She also served as vice-president of COSLA from 1996-99.

In the election campaign for the Scottish Parliament, MacLean was appointed spokesperson on equality, and was one of only two Labour spokespeople not given ministerial responsibilities, the other being her fellow Dundee left-winger John McAllion. Instead, she became convener of the equal opportunities committee and was also a member of the justice and home affairs committee until December 2000. Her reputation was on the left and radical wing of the party, though that seemed to be muted by the experience of being an MSP. She allied herself with the team around Jack McConnell from early on, though again, there was no reward of patronage after he became First Minister. By 2003, she was in more rebellious mode, as one of those to back Susan Deacon's motion opposing war in Iraq. After the election, she lost her convenership, with places instead on the finance and health committees. With a fine line in self-deprecating, morose humour, MacLean's greatest claim to fame in the early months of the Parliament was when she admitted to *The Big Issue* that she had smoked cannabis: something which in those days caused a brief sensation in the press.

MP

ERNIE ROSS was born in 1942 in Dundee and educated at St John's Junior Secondary School, Dundee. He worked as an apprentice marine fitter at Caledonian shipyard, then as a quality control engineer with Timex before being first elected as an MP in 1979. His maiden speech in 1979 savaged the new Conservative Government plans to repeal the Scotland Act 1978. He was uncompromising in his hard left politics in the early 1980s, as a supporter of the Soviet-sponsored World Assembly for Peace. He was an advocate of the militant kind of class politics associated with Tony Benn and Arthur Scargill, was pro-Stalinist in the internal battles of the Communist Party, aligning himself with the *Morning Star* hard-liners against the Eurocommunists, and supported Dundee's Labour administration for flying the Palestinian flag. He was a supporter of the Bennite campaign for greater internal party democracy in the early 1980s. He was dubbed the MP for Nablus West or Moscow Central, with the *Morning Star* calling him 'a left MP of the kind Labour has needed in Parliament for a long time'.

In 1981, with Willie McKelvey, then MP for Kilmarnock, he drew up proposals to get Labour MPs to support the party manifesto and party policy, along with a loyalty oath binding MPs to conference decisions. He suggested Tribune Group MPs should show their ballot papers to the group secretary so their loyalty to the cause could be checked in the Benn–Healey 1981 deputy leadership contest. In the hothouse atmosphere of the early 1980s, such proposals were seen as an attack on Parliamentary democracy. He was affectionately known as 'Afghan Ernie' in Dundee Labour circles, following a photo of him posing in front of a Soviet tank in Afghanistan, at a time when he was defending the Soviet invasion as the defeat of feudalism and the spreading of progressive ideas around the world. It was somewhat less surprising for him to be an opponent of the Falklands conflict in 1982 and the 1991 Gulf War.

Coming in from the Cold War and into the mainstream Labour fold, he ran a creditable though unsuccessful race to be chairman of the Parliamentary Labour Party in 1992. Six years later, he was a senior member of Scottish Labour's selection panel for approving prospective candidates for the Scottish Parliament. As a once rebellious left-winger, his role brought dismay and criticism from the left-wing MPs who were excluded, including Dennis Canavan, Michael Connarty and Ian Davidson. His loyalty to New Labour was demonstrated with support for tuition fees. He has never gained any ministerial position, sitting through many long years of opposition, but has been a member of the standards, education and employment and foreign affairs committees in the Commons. He was suspended from the latter committee, and barred from the Commons for ten days in July 1999, following the leaking to Robin Cook at the Foreign Office of a sensitive report on arms sales to Africa, earning his description by Canavan as 'a Government nark'. Perhaps as a reward for that, he was made chair of the Westminster Foundation for Democracy that same month, having travelled a long way from his pro-Soviet days. Following the 2001 election, he sat on the standing orders committee and the court of referees, and was chair of the all-party group on poverty.

Dunfermline East

Socio-economic Indicators:

Constituency Pop. (16-64)	43,072
Claimant Count (May 2003)	4.0% (28.8% above average)
IBA/SDA Claimants	12.3%
Life Expectancy – Male	74.1 (0.7 yrs above average)
Life Expectancy – Female	79.8 (1.1 years above average)
Owner Occupied	61.3%
Social Rented	32.3%
Average Property Prices	£52,491 (51st)
Average Gross Income	£24,571 (45th)
Low Birthweight Babies	123 (5.7%)
Teenage Pregnancy Rates	454 (5.2%)
No. of Lone Parent Households	3,031 (10.5%)

2003 Scottish Parliament Election

Electorate: 51,220   *Turnout*: 23,154 (45.2%)   *Turnout 1999*: 56.9%

Candidate	Party	Votes	Votes%	99 %	Change%
Helen Eadie	Labour	11,552	49.9	55.9	– 6.0
Janet Law	SNP	4,262	18.4	26.6	– 8.2
Stuart Randall	Con	2,485	10.7	9.9	+ 0.9
Brian Stewart	LHC	1,890	8.2	–	–
Linda Graham	SSP	1,537	6.6	–	–
Rodger Spillane	Lib Dem	1,428	6.2	7.7	– 1.5

Labour majority: 7,290 (31.5%)   *Swing*: 1.1% SNP to Labour

2001 General Election

Electorate: 52,811   *Turnout*: 30,086 (57.0%)

Candidate	Party	Votes	Votes%	Change%
Gordon Brown	Labour	19,487	64.8	– 2.0
John Mellon	SNP	4,424	14.7	– 0.9
Stuart Randall	Con	2,838	9.4	– 0.6
John Mainland	Lib Dem	2,281	7.6	+ 1.7
Andy Jackson	SSP	770	2.6	–
Tom Dunsmore	UK Ind	286	1.0	–

Labour majority: 15,063 (50.1%)   *Swing*: 0.6% Labour to SNP

	Lab%	Con%	SNP%	Lib%	Other%	Turnout%
1997	66.8	10.0	15.6	5.9	1.7	70.3
1992	62.4	16.5	15.1	6.0	–	75.6
1987	64.8	14.8	10.0	10.5	–	76.5
1983	51.5	18.8	7.2	20.1	2.4	72.0

Dunfermline East's socio-economic profile illustrates that this is the least affluent of the two seats bearing the name of Dunfermline. This large, working-class constituency was dominated until the last decade by council housing and has been, not surprisingly, one of the safest Labour seats in the UK. Many of the towns in the constituency are former mining communities, with a legacy of high unemployment, such as Cowdenbeath, Ballingry, Lochore and Kelty. It also includes more middle-class commuter towns on the Fife coast such as Aberdour, Dalgety Bay and Inverkeithing which have little in common with the rest of the constituency. The constituency also stretches westwards to Rosyth, including the dockyard and naval base, and northwards to Cardenden, home village of author Ian Rankin. Average property prices are 22.2 per cent below the national average and rose 43.4 per cent in the 1990s.

The old mines of West Fife are long gone, replaced by new jobs and industries, particularly in electronics and computing. There has been significant investment in petrochemicals and in visitor attractions such as Deep Sea World aquarium in North Queensferry. Intelligent Finance, the banking and insurance firm announced a new call centre in Rosyth in 2002 which would create 600 new jobs. The Rosyth naval dockyard and naval base are major employers, but less so than in the past. Both have scaled down after the Conservative Government decided in 1993 to award the £5 billion contract to refit Britain's nuclear submarine fleet entirely to Devonport. Instead, Rosyth was given the much less lucrative contract to decommission old Polaris submarines.

New investment in the area has seen the development of a £12 million European ferry terminal at Rosyth which will provide a direct link with continental Europe at Zeebrugge. This, it is hoped, will create 1,500 new jobs in the local economy, the powers to regulate the new facility having been transferred to the Scottish Executive from the UK government. Transport congestion is a major issue with the high number of Fife commuters who travel over the Forth Road Bridge each day to work in the Edinburgh and Lothian area. The bus company Stagecoach helped to fund a park and ride scheme in Inverkeithing with the intention of reducing rush hour times, but it has got off the ground slowly, and not been aided by the high number of road works on the Forth Road Bridge.

The constituency's name – Dunfermline East – is slightly misleading – neither containing the town of Dunfermline (which is in West), nor being the successor seat to the old post-war seat of the town. Instead, the predecessors of this 1983 created seat can be found in the Fife West and Fife Central seats which were dominated until their latter days by the economics and politics of coal mining, and that meant a certain kind of left-wing politics (see Fife Central for results). Known for its 'little Moscows' such as Lumphinnans, with street names such as Gagarin Way (which in 2001 became the title for an award-winning play based on Fife politics) and a long Communist tradition, through electing Willie Gallacher as its MP from 1935-50, this seat has been a Labour heartland ever since.

The Communist legacy made its presence felt long after the fall of the Berlin Wall – with a Scottish Communist councillor elected even in 1999 in Ballingry and Lochore with an incredible 81 per cent of the vote and a Democratic Left (the successor organisation to the Communist Party of Great Britain) councillor elected the same year in Cowdenbeath Central with 69 per cent – both against Labour opponents. In the 2003 election both of these rare examples of left-wing electoral success, William Clarke and Alex Maxwell were easily elected on similar sized votes as independents. Despite such popularity, the Scottish Socialist Party has never found a receptive audience for its brand of left politics, only managing in the 2003 elections to secure 6.6 per cent of the vote.

In 1983 in the first election to the new seat, Gordon Brown won a majority of 11,301 over the Liberal-SDP Alliance, with over half the votes – the lowest vote he would ever get in the seat. Four years later, he won a 19,589 majority with the Conservatives in second, and in 1992, a 17,444 lead over the Conservatives.

In May 1997 Gordon Brown, masterminding Labour's victorious UK election campaign, was returned with his highest ever percentage vote – 66.8 per cent – and a majority of 18,751 over the SNP. After four years of Labour government, and what many commentators saw as a Blair-Brown Government, Brown was returned in June 2001 with a slightly reduced majority, and the SNP in a distant second place.

The first Scottish Parliament election, in May 1999, saw Helen Eadie elected for Labour with a significantly lower, but comfortable 56.9 per cent and 8,699 majority over the SNP. In the May 2003 Scottish Parliament election, Eadie was re-elected easily. The Local Hospital Closure campaign candidate, Brian Stewart, secured a respectable 8.2 per cent – half the support a similar candidate gained in Dunfermline West. In the regional list vote, Labour won 40.4 per cent to the SNP's 17.9 per cent, while the SSP won 5.9 per cent and Greens 4.8 per cent; the Fighting Scottish Hospital Closures won 5.1 per cent, and the Save Hospital Closures 3.9 per cent.

Boundary changes for Westminster see Dunfermline East divided between two new seats with most of the current constituency becoming part of the Dunfermline and West Fife seat, while the remainder of the seat becomes part of Kirkcaldy and Cowdenbeath. This would create problems for Gordon Brown except that Lewis Moonie, MP for Kirkcaldy, said in 2003 he would leave the Commons and make way for the Chancellor. In future Scottish Parliament elections, Labour will not have to worry too much, as the SNP nor anyone else has been capable of mounting a serious challenge.

MSP

HELEN EADIE was born in Stenhousemuir in 1947 and educated at Larbert High School, Falkirk Technical College and London School of Economics. She held a number of jobs including administrator for the GMB union in Glasgow, equal opportunities officer for the same union in London, and political researcher at Westminster for both Harry Ewing (MP for Falkirk East until 1992) and her father-in-law, Alex Eadie, long-time MP for Midlothian and one-time energy minister. She joined the Labour Party in the 1960s and held a number of local party posts in London and Fife, including a place on the executive of Greater London Labour Party. She also had a local government background as a councillor in Fife from 1986 until 1999, including holding the post of chair of the equal opportunities committee, while representing COSLA on lesser European affairs. She contested the Roxburgh and Berwickshire constituency at the 1997 Westminster election.

Once elected to the Scottish Parliament, she became at first a member of the public petitions and transport and environment committees, and then the European Committee. Being convenor of the cross-party group on strategic rail services in Scotland allows her to indulge a long-standing passion for improving the lot of her commuting constituents, taking pride in the new Rosyth-Zeebrugge ferry as well as improvements to stations and park and ride. Among various eyebrow-raising moments, she denies reports that she was in favour of replacing the Forth Bridge because of the cost of maintenance, but she does favour radical action to improve services between Fife and Edinburgh, including at least one sub-firth tunnel.

Eadie was one of those responsible, being absent without leave, for the Executive's loss of the fishing vote in March 2001 – one of only three votes lost in the first term. In the second term, she showed signs of causing more deliberate trouble for the party whip, as the Labour group's most vehement opponent of council voting reform, making no secret of her opposition to the coalition deal which forced it on Labour. Having been one of two Labour MSPs to vote against it in March 2004, she began a campaign for a referendum on the issue.

MP

GORDON BROWN was born in 1951 in Govan, Glasgow. A son of the manse, his first political memory was being taken by his father, a major influence in his life, to see the distress and hardship inflicted on Kirkcaldy people by the breaking of their sea wall in 1958. He was educated at Kirkcaldy High School and Edinburgh University, with an MA in 1972 and a PhD, awarded in 1982, on Labour in the inter-war years. Much of his thesis fed into his later published biography of James Maxton.

Quickly established as a campus radical and challenger of the establishment, he was elected rector of Edinburgh University from 1972-75 and was subsequently a lecturer at Edinburgh and Glasgow College from 1975-80. In 1975, he was editor and contributor to *The Red Paper on Scotland* – a book shaped by the politics of the Upper Clyde Shipworkers' work-in and Allende's Chile, which tried to understand the appeal and rationale of nationalism from a socialist perspective. Now its message seems more in keeping with the 'longest suicide note in history' manifesto of the 1983 general election than with the New Labour gospel of the post-1997 government. However, it showed Brown to be leader of a new generation of devolution enthusiasts, which would him see him take a prominent role in the 1979 referendum campaign. From 1980-83, Brown was a journalist with Scottish Television.

Elected an MP in 1983, he quickly established himself and was on the front bench within four years, as shadow Chief Secretary to the Treasury from 1987-89 and shadow spokesperson on trade and industry from 1989-92. With John Smith's elevation to the leadership, he replaced his fellow Scot as shadow Chancellor from 1992-97 and became Chancellor of the Exchequer in 1997. In opposition, Brown was highly popular within the Labour Party, winning the most votes at the Shadow Cabinet elections on four occasions, in 1988, 1989, 1991 and 1992. However, as Shadow Chancellor, he was vigorous in vetting all his colleagues spending commitments, contributing to nose-diving popularity with colleagues in the latter years of opposition; he fell to 14th in the 1996 Shadow Cabinet elections. Peter Hain, later to be Leader of the House of Commons and a possible future contender for the Labour Leadership against Brown, was one of those in a *Tribune* pamphlet to accuse him of 'unilaterally disarming on the question of macro-economic policy'. In Government, Brown has nurtured a reputation as the Iron Chancellor, taking much political flak from his own side in the first two years of government for sticking with Tory spending plans, and using large surpluses to reduce the national debt. Once that phase was over, he undertook spending reviews which unleashed an unprecedented increase in spending on public services, particularly on health and transport. He has proven central to the workings of the Labour Government across all domestic policy, using his Treasury power base to build in contracts with spending departments which allow him and his team to chase progress and hold ministers to account. Brown sees himself as the self-appointed conscience of the Labour movement. He is someone who knows the history of the party and movement, and understands its sense of itself, its idealism and romanticised view of its past. Indeed, he personifies the compromises Labour has to make to win power between a socialist idealism and a sense of realism and economic orthodoxy. His rhetoric appeals to the party's trade union roots, radical Christian socialism and Red Clydeside mythology, while he has been one of the key modernisers in arguing for labour market flexibility and gaining the trust of business and the markets. Analysis of his complex tax and benefit changes suggests he has been a stealthy redistributionist, almost obsessional about the centrality and virtue of employment to his economic and social policy, while he has taken an international lead in tackling the developing world's debt burden.

Brown has a close, problematic, grudge-fuelled and sometimes tempestuous relationship with Tony Blair. When both were rising stars under Neil Kinnock and John Smith, their relationship was a harmonious one, with Brown the senior of the two. However, Smith's unexpected death, and the manoeuvring in the days after that, led to Tony Blair emerging as the moderniser's candidate in place of Brown, primarily because Blair stood more chance of appealing to swing voters in England. A deal was famously done between the two in London's Granita restaurant, the details of which have been the subject of much speculation, centring around whether or not Brown was given the promise that Blair would stand down in his favour at a given time. While Blair has benefited from Brown's reputation on managing the economy, Brown has been notable for his silences when Blair has been in trouble during political squalls, most conspicuously with Blair on the defensive over his Iraq war strategy during 2003. The Prime Minister's preoccupation with foreign affairs left the Chancellor ever more dominant on domestic matters, and the growing talk of Blair's departure has left Brown ever more obvious as the likely successor. Blair has also been forced to kow-tow to Brown's reluctance to commit to membership of the euro currency, putting at risk a key part of the historic legacy Blair hoped to leave on his departure from Downing Street. The tensions within the Blair-Brown relationship burst into public in November 2003 when Tony Blair blocked Brown becoming a member of Labour's NEC. It became potentially damaging for the government when Brown toured the TV studios making his anger and hurt very obvious and marking a new stage in their 'political marriage'. Out of eight Labour Chancellors, Brown has been longest-serving, and he hopes to be only the second of them, after Jim Callaghan, to move next door to 10 Downing Street. That said, Blair is aware of Brown's extraordinary political talent. Recognising the Chancellor's nose for electoral campaign strategy, developed through close links to United States Democrat Party politics, Blair made him joint co-ordinator of Labour's election campaign for the 2001 UK election, alongside the Chancellor's protégé Douglas Alexander (see Paisley South).

Brown had a key behind-the-scenes role at the Scottish election in 1999, while also ensuring a team of his loyalists were put into the Glasgow headquarters to turn around the campaign. He was also a powerful figure, at a distance, in the early years of the Scottish Executive, having influence over Donald Dewar, Wendy Alexander and Henry McLeish. The Chancellor tried ineptly to have the latter anointed leader without a contest when Dewar died, in a bid to stop Jack McConnell becoming First Minister. When McLeish fell, Brown misjudged again in a further attempt to stop McConnell. The bid to coalesce forces round Wendy Alexander came unstuck when she pulled out the contest. With McConnell installed, Brown had to accept that an important part of his power base was in the hands of someone with whom he has had a chilly political relationship. With losses sustained in the 2003 election, Alexander is one of very few fully paid-up Brownites still sitting as MSPs.

Brown was famously asked on Sue Lawley's *Desert Island Discs* in 1996 about his sexuality, as she stated 'people think you are gay or have a personality flaw'. This line of questioning and Brown's evasive, but dignified rebuttal took the headlines rather than his choice of music which included Runrig's 'Loch Lomond' and a Gaelic rendition of the twenty-third psalm, which had been sung at John Smith's funeral. Although famously obsessional about politics, in 2001, he married Sarah Macaulay, a public relations executive. He was devastated by the death of Jennifer, a prematurely-born baby early in 2002 and in October 2003 he became the clearly delighted and proud father of a baby boy, John, named after his father.

Brown is author of numerous books and publications including *The Politics of Devolution and Nationalism* (1980), *Scotland: The Real Divide* (with Robin Cook), *Where There is Greed* (1989) and *John Smith: Life and Soul of the Party* (1994) and *Values, Visions and Voices: An Anthology of Socialism* (1995). He is already the subject of two biographies, and his relationship with Blair is a central theme in a number of other books.

Dunfermline West

Predecessor Constituencies: Dunfermline District of Burghs (1945–70) and Dunfermline (1974–9).

Socio-economic Indicators:

Constituency Pop. (16-64)	45,550
Claimant Count (May 2003)	3.2% (1.1% above average)
IBA/SDA Claimants	7.5%
Life Expectancy – Male	73.8 (0.4 yrs above average)
Life Expectancy – Female	78.7 (national average)
Owner Occupied	71.0%
Social Rented	22.1%
Average Property Prices	£68,428 (23rd)
Average Gross Income	£27,824 (15th)
Low Birthweight Babies	144 (6.5%)
Teenage Pregnancy Rates	398 (4.6%)
No. of Lone Parent Households	2,839 (9.8%)

2003 Scottish Parliament Election

Electorate: 53,915   *Turnout*: 25,240 (46.8%)   *Turnout 1999*: 57.8%

Candidate	Party	Votes	Votes%	99 %	Change%
Scott Barrie	Labour	8,664	34.3	44.2	– 9.9
David Wishart	LHC	4,584	18.2	–	–
Brian Goodall	SNP	4,392	17.4	27.8	–10.4
James Tolson	Lib Dem	3,636	14.4	18.2	– 3.8
James Mackie	Con	1,868	7.4	9.7	– 2.3
Andrew Jackson	SSP	923	3.7	–	–
Alastair Harper	Ind	714	2.8	–	–
Damien Quigg	Ind	459	1.8	–	–

Labour Majority: 4,080 (16.2%)   *Swing*: n/a

2001 General Election

Electorate: 54,293   *Turnout*: 30,975 (57.1%)

Candidate	Party	Votes	Votes%	Change%
Rachel Squire	Labour	16,370	52.8	– 0.2
Brian Goodall	SNP	5,390	17.4	– 1.8
Russell McPhate	Lib Dem	4,832	15.6	+ 2.0

cont'd

Candidate	Party	Votes	Votes%	Change%
James Mackie	Cone	3,166	10.2	- 2.4
Kate Stewart	SSP	746	2.4	–
Alastair Harper	UK Ind	471	1.5	–

Labour majority: 10,980 (35.4%)   *Swing*: 0.8% SNP to Labour

1945–97 Westminster

	Lab%	Con%	SNP%	Lib%	Other%	Turnout%
1997	53.1	12.6	19.2	13.6	1.5	69.4
1992	42.0	22.8	19.4	15.7	–	76.4
1987	47.1	23.1	8.7	21.1	–	76.9
1983	36.0	29.2	7.8	26.2	0.9	73.5
1979	44.3	30.1	14.3	11.3	–	79.3
1974O	40.1	23.0	28.6	8.3	–	75.9
1974F	39.3	30.3	17.8	12.6	–	81.1
1970	57.1	32.0	9.7	–	1.2	74.1
1966	58.4	26.6	15.0	–	–	76.3
1964	61.6	38.4	–	–	–	77.2
1959	61.4	38.6	–	–	–	80.1
1955	61.0	39.0	–	–	–	77.6
1951	61.1	38.9	–	–	–	85.5
1950	61.2	38.8	–	–	–	83.9
1945	64.7	35.3	–	–	–	73.0

Dunfermline West's profile shows that it is significantly more affluent than its neighbouring East seat. This seat is centred around the ancient burgh of Dunfermline itself and the towns and villages of West Fife, including Kincardine, Saline and Torryburn. On the Firth of Forth coast, it includes the National Trust for Scotland preserved village of Culross, recognised as 'a museum of social history' and a 'living exemplar of a sixteenth century Scottish burgh'.

For over 500 years, Dunfermline was Scotland's capital and its abbey was the burial place of Scottish kings and queens including the legendary Robert the Bruce. It was also the birthplace of one of Scotland's most famous emigrants – and hero of Dunfermline East MP Gordon Brown – Andrew Carnegie, industrialist and philanthropist. His generosity to his home town can be seen in several of its public buildings.

In March 2002 the future of Longannet, the last underground mine in Scotland, was put into question when it was flooded by seawater from the Forth. The mine had already seen staff laid off to cut costs, and the influx of millions of gallons of water meant the final closure of the pit with the loss of 599 jobs.

Public services have been a sensitive issue in the seat. Fife Health Board decided in 2002 to locate all emergency services in one hospital – the Victoria Hospital based in Kirkcaldy. This will change the status of the Queen Margaret Hospital in Dunfermline to day surgery, day care and out-patient services, in the face of widespread local opposition, including petitions signed by 60,000 people during Fife Health Board's recent review of services.

Despite Labour's historic electoral strength in the area, Dunfermline itself is politically mixed at local elections, with all the other main parties capable of winning council seats. Labour first won this seat as

Dunfermline in 1922 through William Watson, but then lost it in the debacle of 1931, retaining it in 1935 before Watson retired in 1950. James Clunie held the seat for Labour from 1950-59, followed by Alan Thompson in 1959 and Adam Hunter, a coal miner, who was first elected in 1964. He faced serious challenges from the Conservatives in February 1974 and then the SNP in October 1974 – who cut Labour's majority to 5,291. Hunter stood down in 1979 and was replaced by Dick Douglas who won by 7,313 votes over the Conservatives.

Douglas won in 1983 in the new Dunfermline West seat with a narrow majority of 2,474 over the Conservatives with the Liberal-SDP Alliance coming from nowhere to win 26.2 per cent of the vote. In Scottish Labour's triumphant year of 1987 Douglas increased Labour's majority three-fold to 9,402 over the Conservative Phil Gallie. Douglas, until then a faceless, characterless Labour backbencher and right-winger, against all predictions became incensed with the issue of the poll tax and Labour's lack of fight on the subject and defected to the SNP in 1990. However, he decided in 1992 to stand as SNP candidate not in this seat, but against Donald Dewar in Garscadden, where his impact was minimal. Rachel Squire was comfortably elected Labour MP in 1992 with only a slightly reduced majority of 7,484 over the Conservatives, with the SNP moving from fourth to third.

In May 1997 Rachel Squire was returned with a 12,354 majority over the SNP who replaced the Conservatives in second place. Labour's support of 53.1 per cent was 11.6 per cent on the notional 1992 result, and was the first time since 1970 Labour won over half the votes in the seat. In the June 2001 UK election, Squire was elected for the third time with her majority reduced to 10,980 – an increase of 2 per cent on a lower turnout – as Labour's vote fell 3,000 and the Nationalists by 1,500.

In the first Scottish Parliament election of May 1999 Scott Barrie was elected Labour MSP with his majority halved to 5,021 as the SNP established themselves in a credible second place. In the subsequent Scottish Parliament elections, Barrie was safely re-elected, but saw his majority cut to 4,080 – unchanged in percentage terms – as Labour's vote fell by nearly 5,000 and 10 per cent. A new challenger emerged in the form of the Local Hospital Closure campaign candidate, David Wishart. Labour's support was the lowest vote the party had ever received in the seat, but because of the fragmentation of their opponents, was not enough to threaten the party's grip.

In the regional list vote, Labour won only 28.8 per cent to the SNP's 16.7 per cent, while the Greens won 5.8 per cent and the SSP 4.2 per cent; the two hospital closure candidates polled substantially more than in East – the Fighting Scottish Hospital Closures winning 9.4 per cent and the Save Local Hospitals campaign 6.2 per cent.

Boundary changes for Westminster see the creation of a new Dunfermline and West Fife seat which will include part of the neighbouring Dunfermline East seat, and where Rachel Squire will be the favourite to win the Labour nomination and thus the seat. In the Scottish Parliament, Dunfermline West will probably remain a Labour seat, helped by the lack of a clear challenger. The Conservatives once posed a serious threat in this seat, for example, in 1979 polling 30.1 per cent of the vote, but in 2003 they polled 7.4 per cent. The SNP emerged as a possible challenger in the 1999 Scottish Parliament elections when they won 27.8 per cent, but slipped back dramatically in the 2003 election. Thus, Dunfermline West should remain safely Labour unless there is a further significant erosion of the party's support to the benefit of one clear opponent.

MSP

SCOTT BARRIE was born in St Andrews in 1962, and educated at Auchmuty High School, Glenrothes and Edinburgh University. He trained as a social worker at Stirling University, which he practised in Fife from 1986-99, rising to the rank of team leader in the children and families division. Barrie was a councillor on Dunfermline District Council from 1988-92, focusing on leisure and recreation, and was chair of his constituency Labour Party for six years, positioning him well to win the Parliamentary candidacy for 1999. In the first Parliament, he was a member of both the audit and justice 2 committee, as well as deputy convener of the Labour group. His interest in children's social work led to him taking a leading role in the controversy over Executive plans, ditched in 2002, to ban smacking of young children. Barrie had supported the ban, but then moved away from that position. He also took an active part in the Standards in Schools Act, pushing to ensure young people must be consulted on school decisions that affect them, and ensuring age-appropriate services were required in the Mental Health Act. Constituency interests, where he has Unison backing, highlight transport, while personal ones include Dunfermline Athletic, a John Peel-like love of the Undertones' 'Teenage Kicks', and membership of the Campaign for Real Ale.

MP

RACHEL SQUIRE was born in Carshalton in 1954. She was educated at Godolphin and Latymer Girls School, London, and studied anthropology at Durham University followed by social work at Birmingham University. She was a social worker in Birmingham from 1975-81, and then worked as an officer for the trade union NUPE from 1981-92, joining the Labour Party a year after starting work with the union. She was assistant agent to Tam Dalyell in the 1987 election, and agent to David Martin in the Lothian seat for the 1989 Euro elections. In 1991, she was the only woman elected to the trade union seats on the Scottish Labour executive, and was then elected to Parliament the following year. This saw her regain the seat for Labour following the departure of Dick Douglas who had held the seat for Labour since 1979. To get the Labour candidacy, Squire beat off competition from Pat Callaghan, leader of Dunfermline District council, and from Mark Lazarowicz, leader of Edinburgh District Council. She acknowledged the support of NUPE as 'absolutely vital' to her selection, conceding her lack of qualifications as a non-Fifer and non-Scot, but pointing out she had been working all over Scotland for the union for ten years.

Once an MP, she worked closely with neighbouring MP Gordon Brown to support Rosyth Naval Dockyard, though lost a vital campaign to have nuclear submarines refitted there. She was a member of the procedure committee in the Commons from 1992-97, as well as European legislation from 1994-97 and modernisation of the House of Commons from 1997-99. Squire was a Parliamentary Private Secretary to Stephen Byers at Education and Employment from 1997-98, and then to schools standards minister Estelle Morris from 1998-2001. She played a prominent role in Labour's reformed policy-making forums, chairing the Scottish one which sifted policies ahead of the 2003 Scottish Parliament election. This reflects her post-1997 role as a quiet, uncontroversial Labour loyalist, taking every opportunity to support the Government, particularly on defence and foreign policy where it is backed up by her constituency interest, along with Europhile positioning and a cross-party group interest in Scandinavia. She supported the Government in its Iraq votes in 2003 and on foundation hospitals.

East Kilbride

Predecessor Constituencies: created anew in 1974.

Socio-economic Indicators:

Constituency Pop. (16-64)	55,479
Claimant Count (May 2003)	2.6% (17.9% below average)
IBA/SDA Claimants	7.9%
Life Expectancy – Male	74.4 (1.0 yrs above average)
Life Expectancy – Female	80.3 (1.6 yrs above average)
Owner Occupied	75.5%
Social Rented	19.4%
Average Property Prices	£59,801 (36th)
Average Gross Income	£28,235 (12th)
Low Birthweight Babies (av. 1996-98)	115 (4.4%)
Teenage Pregnancy Rates (av. 1996-98)	352 (3.1%)
No. of Lone Parent Households	3,598 (10.2%)

CAB Enquiries

Issue	No. of cases	Percentage of total cases (%)
1. Consumer	1912	32.5
2. Benefits	1327	22.6
3. Employment	769	13.1
4. Housing	505	8.6
5. Legal	340	5.8

2003 Scottish Parliament Election

Electorate: 65,472   *Turnout*: 34,087 (52.1%)   *Turnout 1999*: 62.5

Candidate	Party	Votes	Votes%	99 %	Change%
Andy Kerr	Labour	13,825	40.6	48.4	– 7.6
Linda Fabiani	SNP	8,544	25.1	32.7	– 7.4
Grace Campbell	Con	3,785	10.6	10.8	– 0.1
Carolyn Leckie	SSP	2,736	8.0	–	–
Colin McCartney	Ind	2,597	7.6	–	–
Alex Mackie	Lib Dem	2,181	6.4	8.2	– 1.7
John Houston	Ind	419	1.2	–	–

Labour majority: 5,281 (15.5%)   *Swing*: 0.1% Labour to SNP

2001 General Election

Electorate: 66,572   *Turnout*: 41,690 (62.6%)

Candidate	Party	Votes	Votes%	Change%
Adam Ingram	Labour	22,205	53.3	– 3.3
Archie Buchanan	SNP	9,450	22.7	+ 1.8
Ewan Hawthorn	Lib Dem	4,278	10.3	+ 3.0
Margaret McCulloch	Con	4,238	10.2	– 1.9
David Stevenson	SSP	1,519	3.6	–

Labour majority: 12,755 (30.6%)   *Swing*: 2.5% Labour to SNP

1974–97 Westminster

	Lab%	Con%	SNP%	Lib%	Other%	Turnout%
1997	56.5	12.0	20.9	7.2	3.3	74.8
1992	46.9	19.1	23.5	10.5	–	80.0
1987	49.0	14.7	12.6	23.7	–	79.2
1983	37.1	24.3	10.1	27.9	0.5	76.9
1979	53.9	29.4	15.6	–	1.1	79.7
1974O	41.9	16.3	36.7	5.1	–	79.1
1974F	43.9	28.9	25.9	–	1.3	82.0

East Kibride is a New Town established in 1947 as an over-spill location for dispersing part of Glasgow's industrial population from over-crowded, sub-standard slums. Situated to the south of the city, the constituency includes the smaller market town of Strathaven and numerous rural settlements which contribute another 10,000 voters to the seat.

This is one of Scotland's most prosperous New Towns with low unemployment, numerous new businesses and existing ones expanding. Centre One – the main tax office in Scotland is based in the area. It came as a shock in June 2001 when Motorola announced that 200 jobs would go from their semi-conductor plant, coming as it did months after the closure of their Bathgate factory. Hospital and education services are being changed in ways which raise local worries. There have been major concerns over the scarcity of Accident and Emergency consultants at the main hospitals in the area, and the Health Board's proposals for dealing with this – which involved 'flying doctors' being shared by the main hospitals, has not gone down well. South Lanarkshire Council has decided to build three new schools in East Kilbride using private finance, which will see existing schools close or merge. New housing developments planned have also met local opposition with the council in 2001 giving planning permission to a new estate at Calderwood, while plans to build 200 new homes in Stewartfield Way and expand Kingsgate Retail Park have not been well received by local residents concerned about the pressures on local services. Average property prices of £59,801 are 11.3 per cent below the national average and rose by 57.6 per cent during the Nineties.

The biggest local issue in recent years has Scottish, UK and international consequences. Dungavel Detention Centre is close to the town of Strathaven, where illegal asylum seekers are housed while waiting to be deported. This is a Home Office run unit – and thus the responsibility of the UK Government – run by a private firm, Premier Detention Services Ltd. A major controversy exploded in 2003 over families and their children being detained in the high-security facility. Twenty-two children aged under 16 years were being held and educated there. This was brought to media attention by the case of Yurdugal Ay, from Kurdistan and her four children, who after spending over one year in Dungavel were deported to Germany. The Scottish Parliament debated Dungavel in September 2003 and asked the UK Government to rethink its position on education provision for children.

The SNP believed in the 1960s and 1970s that the New Towns provided the ideal kind of environment where they could make a breakthrough – representing a kind of classless society and new kind of voter who would be free from Conservative and Labour loyalties. In particular, the party had hopes of challenging Labour in Cumbernauld and Livingston, but in East Kilbride the party's electoral threat to Labour has been restricted at a parliamentary level to the 1974 elections. It had an electoral base through the council which they controlled from 1977-80 and briefly won 45 per cent of the vote.

East Kilbride was created as a parliamentary seat in February 1974 and Maurice Miller was elected its first ever Labour MP. In October 1974, the SNP seriously threatened Labour's hold on the seat, reducing Miller's majority to a mere 2,704 votes. In 1979's disaster for the Nationalists, Miller saw his majority rise to 14,273 over the Conservatives, while the SNP slumped to third place and saw their vote more than halved – falling 21 per cent. In 1983 Labour faced a new threat from 'the third force' of the Liberal-SDP Alliance, which cut Miller's majority back to 4,346. Miller retired in the run-up to the 1987 election, and was succeeded as Labour candidate and MP by Adam Ingram who won the seat with a majority of 12,624 over the Liberal-SDP Alliance in 1987, and then 11,992 over the SNP in 1992.

In May 1997 Ingram was elected with a 17,384 majority over the SNP with Labour winning 56.5 per cent – an increase of 9 per cent – only the second time in the seat's history that Labour had won a majority of the votes in the seat. At the June 2001 UK election, Ingram was elected with a 12,755 majority.

In the first Scottish Parliament election of 1999, Andy Kerr was returned for Labour over the SNP's Linda Fabiani with a 6,499 majority. In the May 2003 Scottish Parliament election, in the second Kerr–Fabiani contest, the SNP must have thought that they had an outside chance of winning or seriously challenging Labour. Instead, both the main parties saw their votes fall back – Labour losing 6,000 votes while the Nationalists fell back by nearly 5,000 – producing a Labour majority of 5,281 unchanged in percentage terms. In the regional vote, Labour won 34.8 per cent to the SNP's 22.2 per cent, while the SSP won a respectable 9.2 per cent and the Greens 6.2 per cent.

The Boundary changes for Westminster see East Kilbride – one of the bigger seats in terms of the electorate's size in Scotland – left relatively unchanged with small additions which do not affect its basic composition or political character. East Kilbride is not a monolithic Labour seat of the type which dominate the West of Scotland. It could in future be a weathervane seat: as long as Labour wins it, the party will remain the leading force of Scottish politics while Nationalists must win it if they are ever to become a party of government.

MSP

ANDY KERR was born in East Kilbride in 1962, the son of a Rolls-Royce worker. He was schooled at Claremont High, and is a graduate in social sciences of Glasgow College (later to become Glasgow Caledonian University). A student sabbatical officer at the college, where he ran a sizeable entertainments business, he was a full-time officer with the National Union of Students before beginning a career in local government. He was a research and development officer with Strathkelvin District Council from 1987-90, managing director of a consultancy, Achieving Quality, from 1990-93, and strategy and development manager within the land services department of Glasgow City Council from 1993. From 1998 until the 1999 election, he was special adviser to the council leader, Frank

McAveety (later to become MSP for Glasgow Shettleston), and helped to turn around the troubled fortunes of the council.

Kerr was secretary of East Kilbride Constituency Labour Party from 1989 until his election as an MSP, and acted as Adam Ingram's Westminster election agent and campaign co-ordinator. He was interviewed for the post of Scottish Labour general secretary after Jack McConnell left in 1998, and was seen as the favoured choice of the Blairites against the Brownite, Alex Rowley. Brown's influence is credited with winning it for Rowley, though he had an unhappy time in the post, and was sacked immediately after the 1999 election.

Kerr's fortunes were rosier. Donald Dewar was close to appointing him chief whip in 1999, favouring Tom McCabe instead. Instead, he was made convener of the Scottish Parliament committee on transport and the environment. Having been closely involved in council's direct labour organisations and with expertise in contracting out, he clashed with the Executive and transport minister Sarah Boyack when she handed two large contracts for trunk roads maintenance to private sector firms – contracts which Kerr would later oversee. While a backbencher, he was also co-ordinator of the Labour campaign in the 2000 Ayr by-election – though with a loss to the Conservatives, it was not one of his finer moments.

Always loyal to Jack McConnell and with strength as a political organiser, Kerr was campaign manager in his bid for the Labour leadership following Donald Dewar's death in October 2000. McConnell's campaign, which the party hierarchy tried to stop, was well organised, took Henry McLeish by surprise and defined the agenda, with McConnell losing to Henry McLeish by only 44 votes to 36. When McConnell's time came a year later, Kerr was again his campaign manager in what became an uncontested election, chairing the press conference at which McConnell admitted to having had an affair. Kerr was made finance minister, while having 'public services' added to his portfolio, stressing the new First Minister's desire to 'do less, better', and focus on jobs, transport, health, education and crime. He was also responsible for civil service reform and local government. Given the political proximity of McConnell and Kerr, this made the finance post an unofficial deputy within Labour ranks.

Kerr continued in that role after 2003, having been one of those to face the TV cameras during campaign debates with his slick though over-jargonised presentation. The Lib Dems had let it be known they wanted the finance post, but Jim Wallace moved to enterprise and lifelong learning instead, Tavish Scott moving in as Kerr's deputy where Labour's Peter Peacock had been. Local government became a much more difficult issue after the election, with opposition to voting reform plans and a series of policies which would see the Executive intervening in council powers. So Kerr was sent out with Margaret Curran to councils - Labour ones in particular - to sell the new message. Having been a forthright opponent of council voting reform, he was better equipped than others to empathise with angry Labour councillors, and was trying to placate them with a new package of better pay and pensions. He was charged with finding the finances for the 2003 coalition agreement, and drove a new spending review round in early 2004, with the Executive facing expectations of a tightening budget allocation from the Treasury.

MP

ADAM INGRAM was born in Glasgow in 1947 and has represented East Kilbride in the Commons since 1987. He was educated at Cranhill Senior Secondary School and is a graduate of the Open University. He worked in computers with the South of Scotland Electricity Board from 1965-77, and then as an official for the NALGO trade union from 1977-87. Joining the Labour Party in 1970, he was a leading anti-devolutionist in the 1979 referendum, and a district councillor in East Kilbride from 1980-97, falling out with the party group over his opposition to Trident in 1982, he then became council leader from 1984-87.

Ingram fought the Tory-held seat of Strathkelvin and Bearsden in 1983, coming third, then beating Michael Connarty to the East Kilbride nomination for the next general election. He was very active in the purge of Militant entryism in the 1980s, and once in the Commons, he became Parliamentary Private Secretary to Neil Kinnock from 1988-92, being credited with helping the Labour leader become more friendly, accessible and consultative in his dealings with Labour MPs. He was opposition spokesperson on social security from 1993-95 and on science and technology from 1995-97, being party minder to Helen Liddell during the Monklands East by-election in 1984, where he had to deal with its difficult sectarian undertow. Within the post-1997 Labour Government, he was admired for his ability as minister of state with responsibility for security issues at the Northern Ireland Office until the 2001 election, putting to rest claims that his youthful involvement in the Orange movement would be a hindrance to him. He then moved to the Ministry of Defence as minister of state for the armed forces, his profile raised by the 2003 Iraq war, while somehow avoiding the flak from opposition to it, the Hutton Inquiry into the intelligence and media strategies used to justify the invasion, or the inadequate supply of kit to the troops on the front line.

East Lothian

Predecessor Constituencies: Berwickshire and Haddington (1945) and Berwickshire and East Lothian (1950–79).

Socio-economic Indicators:

Constituency Pop. (16-64)	46,497
Claimant Count (May 2003)	1.6% (50.1% below average)
IBA/SDA Claimants	9.2%
Life Expectancy – Male	75.9 (2.5 yrs above average)
Life Expectancy – Female	80.0 (1.3 yrs above average)
Owner Occupied	62.3%
Social Rented	28.7%
Average Property Prices	£91,908 (8th)
Average Gross Income	£26,961 (24th)
Low Birthweight Babies	130 (5.7%)
Teenage Pregnancy Rates	390 (4.3%)
No. of Lone Parent Households	2,941 (9.4%)

CAB Enquiries

Issue	No. of cases	Percentage of total cases (%)
1. Benefits	942	30.1
2. Consumer	539	17.2
3. Employment	458	14.6
4. Other	282	9.0
5. Housing	271	8.7

2003 Scottish Parliament Election

Electorate: 59,227   *Turnout*: 31,204 (52.7%)   *Turnout 1999*: 60.7%

Candidate	Party	Votes	Votes%	99 %	Change%
John Home Robertson	Labour	13,683	43.9	54.0	– 10.1
Judith Hayman	Lib Dem	5,508	17.7	6.0	+ 11.7
Stuart Thomson	Con	5,459	17.5	16.7	+ 0.8
Thomas Roberts	SNP	5,174	16.6	23.3	– 6.7
Hugh Kerr	SSP	1,380	4.4	–	–

Labour majority: 8,175 (26.2%)   *Swing*: 10.9% Labour to Lib Dem

2001 General Election

Electorate: 58,987   *Turnout*: 36,871 (62.5%)

Candidate	Party	Votes	Votes%	Change%
Anne Picking	Labour	17,407	47.2	– 5.5
Hamish Mair	Con	6,577	17.8	– 2.1
Judith Hayman	Lib Dem	6,506	17.6	+ 7.1
Hilary Brown	SNP	5,381	14.6	– 1.1
Derrick White	SSP	624	1.7	–
Jake Herriot	Soc Lab	376	1.0	–

Labour majority: 10,830 (29.4%)   *Swing*: 1.7% Labour to Conservative

1945–97 Westminster

	Lab%	Con%	SNP%	Lib%	Other%	Turnout%
1997	52.7	19.9	15.7	10.5	1.1	75.6
1992	46.5	28.2	14.2	11.2	–	82.4
1987	48.0	28.3	7.3	15.5	0.9	78.7
1983	43.9	30.8	4.4	20.9	–	76.2
1979	43.5	40.2	6.5	9.8	–	82.9
1978B	47.4	40.2	8.8	3.6	–	71.2
1974O	43.3	37.6	13.2	5.9	–	83.0
1974F	42.3	43.5	14.2	–	–	85.8
1970	45.6	44.2	10.2	–	–	83.8
1966	51.9	48.1	–	–	–	86.1
1964	49.3	50.7	–	–	–	85.0
1959	46.6	53.4	–	–	–	83.2
1955	46.7	53.3	–	–	–	80.3
1951	47.2	52.8	–	–	–	83.8
1950	40.8	36.8	–	22.4	–	82.8
1945	54.5	45.5	–	–	–	70.3

East Lothian's socio-economic profile shows that this is a constituency which contains significantly more affluence than disadvantage – although it indisputably contains both. The consituency sits to the east of Edinburgh with a beautiful forty mile coastline along the Firth of Forth. It combines within its boundaries two very different worlds – one working class and shaped by former mining communities, the other, prosperous and commuter-driven. The west side of the seat is the less affluent – the towns of Tranent, Prestonpans and Ormiston, while the east is more prosperous - Haddington, North Berwick and Dunbar, reflected in the political contours of the seat, with the west more Labour and east more Conservative.

East Lothian contains some of the most beautiful and historic scenery of Scotland – places associated with Mary Queen of Scots, Cromwell and Charles I's numerous exploits – and most famously Bonnie Prince Charlie's Jacobite triumph at Prestonpans in 1745. Coal-mining has long gone from the area and even the opencast site at Blindwells has closed. Major employers include the Torness nuclear power station, Cockenzie coal fired power station and the Belhaven Brewery in Dunbar. Tourism and leisure are important income earners, most prominently the prestigious golf course, Muirfield, the world's oldest established golf club and site of Open Championships.

A big issue locally is the improvement of transport links with road, rail and bus links being stretched to breaking point because of the growing popularity of East Lothian as a commuter area where average property prices are 36.3 per cent above the national average and have increased by 72.6 per cent in the 1990s. The A1 road between Haddington and Dunbar is being upgraded to dual-carriage, while there are tensions over housing developments with the Lothian Structure Plan calling for 5,000 new homes to be built in East Lothian by 2015. Aberlady, for instance – a small town of 400 homes is set to expand by ninety-three homes – or one quarter – and this has led to massive protests with a petition signed by 500 of its inhabitants and the Aberlady Preservation Society arguing that the entire character of the town will be transformed.

There are also new pressures on education and health services. East Lothian Council got into trouble in 2002 when it took a decision to transfer the money given to it by the Scottish Executive to fund the McCrone pay deal for teachers from education to social work. The main teachers' union, the Educational Institute for Scotland, was shocked by this and agreed that if this became widespread such monies should be ring-fenced. The council's use of private finance to upgrade schools also ran into trouble in November 2003, when the consortium the council were working with went bankrupt.

As Berwickshire and Haddington, and Berwickshire and East Lothian, this was a real maverick seat. It elected Conservatives and National Liberals for most of the inter-war period, but went Labour with a majority of 68 in 1923. John James Robertson won it back for Labour with a majority of 3,157 over the Conservatives in 1945, but lost to Conservative William Anstruther-Gray in 1951 who had a majority of 2,358. He held it until Labour's landslide year of 1966 when a bright and able young Labour candidate, John P. Mackintosh, regained it for Labour.

In February 1974, while the UK swung to Labour and returned a Labour Government, Mackintosh lost his seat to the Conservative Michael Ancram, but won it back in October 1974 with a majority of 2,740. John Mackintosh's premature death in 1978 was a major shock and loss to Scottish Labour and the unexpected by-election could have caused major problems. However, John Home Robertson held the seat easily with a small but significant swing from the Conservatives to Labour, with the SNP in a distant third place seeing their vote reduced. In the 1979 election Home Robertson's majority narrowed to an uncomfortable 1,673 over the Conservatives.

Boundary changes in 1983 saw the creation of East Lothian, including Musselburgh with Berwickshire given a separate Borders seat. In that year's general election, Home Robertson increased his majority to 6,241, rising to 10,105 in 1987 over the Conservatives. The movement of Musselburgh back to Edinburgh East reduced Labour's notional 1992 majority to 7,099, but this was no problem in Labour's year of triumph as Home Robertson romped home with a 14,221 majority, while the Conservative vote fell by over 5,000. In 2001 Anne Picking, standing for the first time to replace Home Robertson, saw her majority fall back to 10,830 over the Conservatives with Labour's vote down 5,000.

In the 1999 Scottish Parliament elections, Home Robertson was one of the few candidates who saw Labour's share of the vote rise, while the SNP added nearly 1,500 to finish in a distant second place, 10,946 behind Labour. In the 2003 Scottish Parliament election, Home Robertson secured his seat with a slightly reduced majority of 8,175, while the Lib Dems trebled their vote in percentage terms and moved from fourth to second. In the regional vote, Labour won 34.4 per cent to the Conservatives 17.9 per cent, 15.4 per cent for the SNP and 13.5 per cent for the Lib Dems, while the Greens won 8.1 per cent and SSP 4.4 per cent.

Boundary changes at Westminster will see the creation of an enlarged East Lothian which looks a secure Labour seat. East Lothian has been a highly marginal seat capable of throwing up shocks, setbacks and making political headlines. Those days look long in the past, and in future Scottish Parliament elections, Labour look very safe here.

MSP

JOHN HOME ROBERTSON was born in 1948 in Edinburgh, elected MP for Berwick and East Lothian from 1978 until 1983 and for East Lothian when it was redrawn from 1983. He was one of six Labour MPs who chose to head north and stand for election as an MSP in 1999, being assured of selection as he could call for support on East Lothian's large membership – at its strongest in the Prestonpans Labour Club. Although popular in such former mining communities, he is far from having a traditional Labour background. He was educated at Ampleforth College and West of Scotland Agriculture College, and ran the 1,340 acre family farms in Berwickshire which he still owns, while a member of Berwickshire District Council from 1974-78. The family's Georgian mansion, Paxton House, was transferred to a public trust in 1988, with him as a trustee.

Robertson had worked for the Liberals on David Steel's successful 1965 by-election campaign in Roxburgh, Selkirk and Peebles, before joining the Labour Party in 1970. He has long been identified in Scottish Labour as a home rule advocate, and was one of only four Labour MPs who supported SNP leader Gordon Wilson's idea of a cross-party convention in 1980. In 1986, he anonymously wrote 'Strategies for Scotland from 1987' examining what options were available if the Conservatives won again based on English votes. This argued for a plan similar to the Scottish Constitutional Convention which ensued. He was then taking a radical stance, advocating guerrilla tactics at Westminster and not paying his poll tax. He was a member of the Scottish affairs select committee from 1979-83, and chair of the Scottish Labour Group of MPs 1982-83. Robertson was appointed an Opposition Scottish whip from 1983-84, Opposition front bench spokesman on agriculture from 1984-87 and 1988-90, and on housing from 1987-88. From 1990-97, he was a member of the defence select committee.

After Labour took power in 1997, he became Parliamentary Private Secretary to Jack Cunningham, the Secretary of State for Agriculture, Fisheries and Food, and in 1998 shifted with Cunningham when he moved to the Cabinet Office from 1998-99. In the 1999 Scottish elections, he was campaign spokesperson on agriculture, fisheries and rural affairs, and after the elections, his Westminster experience ensured he was appointed deputy minister for rural affairs, including responsibility for fisheries.

Whatever his talents, they were not immediately apparent as a minister, and he was one of only two ministers to face the sack when Henry McLeish became First Minister in 2000. Home Robertson became deputy convener of the European committee in January 2001, his international interests including Palestine and as a three-time volunteer truck driver to Bosnia with Edinburgh Direct Aid. But he also faced a poisoned chalice as a sort of compensation for being downgraded; he was asked to replace Lewis Macdonald as convener of the Holyrood Progress Group, at the time Macdonald became a minister. This has put him at the heart of the project, reporting to the corporate body, and taking some of the considerable public flak for the huge overspend. It is a task he has taken to with a sometimes masochistic relish, arguing that the cost will be viewed in a different context once Holyrood is completed.

MP

ANNE PICKING was born Anne Moffat in 1958 in Dunfermline and educated at Woodmilll High School in the Fife town. She was a relative of the legendary Scottish miners' leader Abe Moffat, a connection she was not slow to impress on the Labour activists of Tranent and Prestonpans. Her first election as MP for East Lothian was in 2001 to replace John Home Robertson when he chose to shift his career to the Scottish Parliament. She trained as a nurse from 1975, becoming an enrolled nurse in 1980, a student nurse in Northern Ireland from 1982-83, rising to become nursing sister at East Kent Community Health Care Trust, where she continued to work until 2001. From that professional interest, she became an activist in COHSE and its later merged incarnation as Unison, rising to the presidency of the union in 1999-2000. This was another useful position from which to launch her bid for a vacant parliamentary seat.   There was no other explanation anyone in Scottish Labour could find for her selection, after nearly two decades out of the country and no track record of involvement in Scotland.

She was a councillor on Ashford Borough Council from 1990-2000, as chair of the health committee and vice-chair of the finance committee, then as chair of the Labour group and of the Ashford Labour Party from 1994-98. At the TUC conference in 2000, Picking called for the NHS to be modernised rather than privatised, following with a maiden speech in the Commons which spoke of the privilege of working in the NHS, while raising doubts about the value for money of privately-financed hospitals. In 2003, she went on to vote against foundation hospitals for England. At the Labour conference which immediately followed the 9/11 terrorist attacks, she moved the party executive statement against international terrorism. In the Commons, she become a member of a Commons services committee while serving on the modernisation of the Commons committee and European standing committee B, also working on the committee stage of the Communications Bill. She burnished her feminist credentials by taking a swipe at honours for the England rugby team while backing the campaign for a statue of suffragette Sylvia Pankhurst on Westminster's College Green, saying, 'When we're honouring men who run about a field kicking balls, can we not commemorate someone who had some?'

Eastwood

Predecessor Constituencies: Renfrewshire East (1945–79).

Socio-economic Indicators:

Constituency Pop. (16-64)	56,104
Claimant Count (May 2003)	1.7% (44.2% below average)
IBA/SDA Claimants	6.7%
Life Expectancy – Male	76.3 (2.9 yrs above average)
Life Expectancy – Female	81.3 (2.6 yrs above average)
Owner Occupied	83.4%
Social Rented	12.3%
Average Property Prices	£100,262 (5th)
Average Gross Income	£32,862 (1st)
Low Birthweight Babies	163 (6.0%)
Teenage Pregnancy Rates	272 (2.3%)
No. of Lone Parent Households	2,934 (8.4%)

CAB Enquiries

Issue	No. of cases	Percentage of total cases (%)
1. Consumer	1008	29.4
2. Benefits	582	17.0
3. Employment	578	16.9
4. Other	333	9.7
5. Housing	328	9.6

2003 Scottish Parliament Election

Electorate: 67,051   *Turnout*: 38,889 (58.0%)   *Turnout 1999*: 67.5

Candidate	Party	Votes	Votes%	99 %	Change%
Kenneth Macintosh	Labour	13,946	35.9	37.4	– 1.5
Jackson Carlaw	Con	10,244	26.3	32.7	– 6.4
Allan Steele	Lib Dem	5,056	13.0	9.9	+ 3.2
William Maxwell	SNP	4,736	12.2	19.3	– 7.1
Margaret Hinds	LHC	3,163	8.1	–	–
Steven Oram	SSP	1,504	3.9	–	–
Martyn Greene	SPA	240	0.6	(other 0.8)	–

Labour majority: 3,702 (9.5%)   *Swing*: 2.4% Labour to Conservative

2001 General Election

Electorate: 68,297   *Turnout*: 48,368 (70.8%)

Candidate	Party	Votes	Votes%	Change%
Jim Murphy	Labour	23,036	47.6	+ 7.9
Raymond Robertson	Con	13,895	28.7	- 4.8
Allan Steele	Lib Dem	6,239	12.9	+ 1.2
Stewart Maxwell	SNP	4,137	8.6	- 4.5
Peter Murray	SSP	814	1.7	-
Manar Tayan	Ind	247	0.5	-

Labour majority: 9,141 (18.9%)   *Swing*: 6.4% Conservative to Labour

1945–97 Westminster

	Lab%	Con%	SNP%	Lib%	Other%	Turnout%
1997	39.7	33.6	13.1	11.7	2.0	78.3
1992	24.1	46.8	12.4	16.5	0.3	81.0
1987	25.1	39.5	8.2	27.2	–	79.6
1983	20.1	46.6	5.8	27.6	–	76.2
1979	24.4	49.9	7.7	18.0	–	80.6
1974O	20.8	41.4	23.2	14.6	–	77.7
1974F	20.1	50.6	10.4	18.9	–	82.9
1970	28.1	52.0	6.7	12.6	–	76.2
1966	33.1	53.1	–	13.8	–	79.9
1964	31.1	52.6	–	16.3	–	82.6
1959	28.8	58.7	–	12.5	–	82.9
1955	31.7	68.3	–	–	–	78.1
1951	34.2	65.8	–	–	–	81.7
1950	34.6	65.4	–	–	–	78.9
1945	46.4	53.6	–	–	–	67.2

Eastwood is one of the most prosperous and middle class parts of Scotland. The seat has the highest owner occupation in Scotland, average property prices are 48.6 per cent above the national average and increased by 58.7 per cent in the 1990s. Average gross income is the highest in the country. Both male and female life expectancy rates are the joint fourth highest in the country and teenage pregnancy rates the fourth lowest. This is the second most healthy constituency in the whole of Scotland, with only Aberdeenshire West and Kincardine ranked above it.

Eastwood sits to the south of Glasgow as part of the Greater Glasgow conurbation. Its main communities – Newton Mearns, Clarkston, Giffnock and Busby, are middle-class areas with high degrees of Conservative support. The ex-mining town of Barrhead is the most working-class area in the seat, which is predominantly Labour voting. A large Jewish community, 80 per cent of the Scottish total and some 14,000 strong live in the seat.

Eastwood is an area whose problems and issues are those of affluent Scotland. East Renfrewshire's schools perform well in the Scottish Executive's performance tables, with Newton Mearns finishing first in relation to Highers and in the top three for Standard Grades. St Ninian's was rated the best performing Catholic school in the country, while even Barrhead High was rated the most improved secondary school.

One of the most hotly debated subjects is the quality of commuter transport links between the constituency and Glasgow. Many of Glasgow's middle class commuters choose to live outside the city council boundaries – often for council tax or education reasons.

As Eastwood and previously Renfrewshire East, this was once safe Conservative territory, but is now New Labour. In the intense competition between Labour, Conservatives and Liberals in the inter-war era, Labour's Robert Nichol briefly held the seat in 1922 and 1923, with waver-thin majorities of 550 and 508 respectively. Ernest Guy Richard Lloyd won the seat for the Conservatives in 1945 with comparative ease, holding Labour off with a 5,676 majority. Lloyd remained Conservative MP until 1959 and was succeeded by Betty Harvie Anderson, MP from 1959-79; even in the SNP election of October 1974 she held on with a majority of 8,710 over the Nationalists.

Allan Stewart first won the seat in 1979 with a majority of 13,238 over Labour; in the 1983 and 1987 elections, the Liberal-SDP Alliance established itself as the main challenger to the Conservatives, cutting Stewart's majority to first 8,595, then to 6,014. However, this challenge dissipated in 1992, as Labour re-established its claim to second place and Stewart doubled his majority to 11,688, presiding over a 7.3 per cent rise in the Conservative vote, four times the Scottish average.

Eastwood would possibly have remained Conservative in 1997, but for a series of unprecedented events. First, Allan Stewart announced his sudden retirement weeks before the election; the reasons included a damaging criminal trial, in which he was found guilty of assaulting anti-motorway protestors and fined £200 for breach of the peace, revelations of a long-standing affair and health problems. Second, the favoured successor, Sir Michael Hirst, no sooner emerged than he had to withdraw amid allegations about his personal life. The Conservatives' third choice candidate, Paul Cullen, Solicitor-General for Scotland, suffered a collapse in the Tory vote, polling 7,000 fewer votes and seeing the party share decline by 13 per cent. Labour's Jim Murphy could not believe his luck as he became the constituency's first Labour MP for 74 years, increasing his vote by a staggering 8,000 and 16 per cent, to give him a 3,236 majority over the Conservatives.

The loss of Eastwood, previously the Conservatives' safest seat in Scotland, meant that no Conservative MPs were returned in Scotland for the first time in political history. At the June 2001 UK election, Jim Murphy not only held the seat, but also significantly strengthened Labour's hold and weakened the Conservative base. Labour's majority tripled to 9,141, as Murphy achieved the feat of increasing the number of Labour voters on a lower turnout of 70.8 per cent – the highest of any Scottish constituency. Labour's 47.6 per cent vote meant that it had nearly doubled its support in two elections from a mere 24.1 per cent in 1992.

In 1999 Labour held on to Eastwood – proof, if it were needed, of the party's ability to stretch its appeal to win seats and then hold them. Ken Macintosh, Labour candidate, saw the 1997 Labour vote fall by 4,000, while a strong challenge from John Young, a long-time Glasgow Conservative councillor, saw a small swing back to the Conservatives, cutting Labour's lead back to 2,125. In the 2003 Scottish Parliament contest, Ken Macintosh was safely re-elected for Labour – increasing his majority to 3,702 and nearly doubling Labour's lead in percentage terms on a turnout of 58.0 per cent, the second highest in the country and only beaten by the Western Isles. The Local Hospital Closure candidate, Margaret Hinds, seemed to damage the Conservative and SNP levels of support. In the regional list vote, Labour won 28.2 per cent to the

Conservatives 27.2 per cent – a Labour lead of 378 – while the Greens won 6.6 per cent and the SSP 5.8 per cent.

Labour never expected to win Eastwood in 1997, but it has proved that it was not entirely a product of the strange coalescing of factors which combined prior to that election to undermine the Conservative campaign. Jim Murphy has proven his ability as a conscientious, hard-working local MP with a superb professional organisation behind him. Boundary changes for Westminster see no major changes other than a name change to East Renfrewshire. At the Scottish Parliament, Eastwood is the kind of territory the Scottish Conservatives have to target if they are to challenge Labour's new found strength. Eastwood is natural Tory territory and the party still has significant strength at a local government level where it won 30.9 per cent of the vote in the 2003 elections to Labour's 31.8 per cent. The Conservatives must pray that their retention of a local base will mean that when UK Labour and Scottish Labour become unpopular, they will be able to reap the benefits.

MSP

KEN MACINTOSH was born in 1962 in Inverness and educated at the Royal High School, Edinburgh, and Edinburgh University where he gained an MA in History. He began work at the BBC in 1987 and for the next 12 years worked in current affairs and news covering Breakfast News, *Breakfast with Frost* and the *Nine O'Clock News*. When he left the BBC in 1999, he was the producer responsible for Scottish input into UK network news.

In the first Parliament, he began on the education, culture and sport committee, as well as subordinate legislation. On the finance committee from May 1999 to the end of 2000, he was appointed in April 2000 as its reporter to establish the extent of the burgeoning costs of the Holyrood building project. He escaped before the issue came back to bite him. From the start of 2001, he was on the standards and procedures committees, and after the 2003 election he became deputy convener of standards, while also having a place on the education committee. Bright and able, and although his polite, quietly reserved style no doubt works well with Eastwood voters, he is not entirely in keeping with West of Scotland Labour, which helps explain his failure to move from the backbenches amid the many ministerial shuffles. He has been a loyal Labour backbencher, often a poser of planted questions, but the closest he has come to ministerial office was in an aide's post in 2002, to support Cathy Jamieson as education minister. He resigned from that post in September 2002, over constituency pressure which required him to vote against the Executive over Glasgow hospital reorganisation.

MP

JIM MURPHY was born in 1967 in Glasgow and has represented the Eastwood seat from 1997. Educated at Bellarmine Secondary School, Glasgow, Milnerton High School, Cape Town and Strathclyde University, Murphy was president of the National Union of Students Scotland from 1992-94 and the National Union of Students at UK level from 1994-96. During that period, he led the union towards an acceptance of changes to student tuition funding, with a preference for post-graduate re-payment of fees. In the run-up to the 1997 election, he became projects manager of the Scottish Labour Party with special responsibility for the 'Partnership into Power' modernisation of the party. As perhaps Scotland's most ardent Blairite at the time, many left-wingers felt that Murphy's work within 'The Network' grouping and at party headquarters gave him the resources to run the Scottish Labour Forum pre-election plans to remove several left-wingers from the party executive.

He was as amazed as anyone to win Eastwood at the age of 29, and was notable for subsequently working the seat very hard for himself and for Ken McIntosh to be elected MSP. One feature of this was in cultivating Eastwood's Jewish vote with annual visits to Israel, rising to become chair of the Labour Friends of Israel in 2001, supported with denunciation of the pro-Palestinian positions taken by George Galloway in nearby Glasgow Kelvin. His constituency campaigning was treated as textbook material for Labour hopefuls, with its strategic media plan and the aim of getting to know key opinion-formers in community organisations.

His loyalty to Blair has seen him likened to an affable Peter Mandelson, a cheerful practitioner of the political dark arts, while the *Guardian* commented he is 'so on message that the message occasionally has to be surgically removed from his backside'. It was noted by the Speaker also, who reprimanded him in July 1998 for asking sycophantic questions, commenting 'it will be some time before I call him again'. While a member of the public accounts select committee, Murphy became a regular backbench exponent or apologist for the Blair Government in broadcast media, and in February 2001, he became Parliamentary Private Secretary to the new Scotland Secretary, Helen Liddell. In 2002, he was promoted to assistant whip.

Edinburgh Central

Predecessor constituencies: created in 1983 from Edinburgh Central (1945-79) and Edinburgh North (1945-79).

Socio-economic Indicators:

Constituency Pop. (16–64)	58,717
Claimant Count (May 2003)	2.5% (20.4% below average)
IBA/SDA Claimants	6.1%
Life Expectancy – Male	71.8 (1.6 yrs below average)
Life Expectancy – Female	78.5 (0.2% below average)
Owner Occupied	59.8%
Social Rented	15.9%
Average Property Prices	£104,379 (4th)
Average Gross Income	£27,970 (14th)
Low Birthweight Babies	114 (5.9%)
Teenage Pregnancy Rates (av. 1996–98)	348 (3.9%)
No. of Lone Parent Households	2,492 (6.3%)

CAB Enquiries

Issue	No. of cases	Percentage of total cases (%)
1. Consumer	744	18.6
2. Employment	734	18.4
3. Benefits	629	15.8
4. Housing	523	13.1
5. Other	429	10.7

2003 Scottish Parliament Election

Electorate: 60,824   *Turnout*: 28,014 (46.1%)   *Turnout* 1999: 56.7%

Candidate	Party	Votes	Votes%	99 %	Change%
Sarah Boyack	Labour	9,066	32.4	38.0	– 5.7
Andrew Lyons	Lib Dem	6,400	22.8	16.5	+ 6.3
Kevin Pringle	SNP	4,965	17.7	25.7	– 7.9
Peter Finnie	Con	4,802	17.1	16.1	+ 1.1
Catriona Grant	SSP	2,552	9.1	2.2	+ 6.9
James O'Neill	SPA	229	0.8	(other 1.5)	–

Labour majority: 2,666 (9.5%)   *Swing*: 6.0% Labour to Lib Dem

2001 General Election

Electorate: 66,089   *Turnout*: 34,390 (52.0%)

Candidate	Party	Votes	Votes%	Change%
Alistair Darling	Labour	14,495	42.1	- 4.9
Andrew Myles	Lib Dem	6,353	18.5	+ 5.4
Alistair Orr	Con	5,643	16.4	- 4.8
Ian McKee	SNP	4,832	14.1	- 1.8
Graeme Farmer	Green	1,809	5.3	+ 3.8
Kevin Williamson	SSP	1,258	3.7	–

Labour majority: 8,142 (23.7%)   *Swing*: 5.2% Labour to Lib Dem

1945–97 Westminster

	Lab%	Con%	SNP%	Lib%	Other%	Turnout%
1997	47.1	21.2	15.8	13.1	1.8	67.1
1992	38.8	33.4	14.1	11.5	2.2	69.3
1987	40.2	34.7	6.2	17.9	1.0	68.9
1983	31.1	38.0	4.9	25.6	0.3	64.9
1979	47.8	29.5	9.8	12.2	0.7	67.5
1974O	40.3	26.0	24.8	8.9	–	67.5
1974F	37.9	34.6	13.6	13.9	–	73.6
1970	46.2	38.6	8.0	7.2	–	66.0
1966	58.9	41.1	–	–	–	69.4
1964	54.0	46.0	–	–	–	71.8
1959	51.0	49.0	–	–	–	72.7
1955	51.4	48.6	–	–	–	68.8
1951	52.2	47.8	–	–	–	76.7
1950	47.9	39.4	–	10.0	2.7	74.3
1945	54.3	33.3	–	11.2	1.2	59.5

Edinburgh North (1945–79)

	Lab%	Con%	SNP%	Lib%	Other%	Turnout%
1979	30.1	43.6	10.8	15.5	–	71.8
1974O	25.9	39.3	23.5	11.3	–	69.2
1974F	26.2	45.8	12.7	15.3	–	76.4
1973B	24.0	38.7	18.9	18.4	–	54.4
1970	37.1	52.8	–	10.1	–	70.1
1966	39.2	50.3	–	10.5	–	73.9
1964	41.8	58.2	–	–	–	73.6
1960B	30.3	54.2	–	15.5	–	53.8

cont'd

	Lab%	Con%	SNP%	Lib%	Other%	Turnout%
1959	36.0	64.0	–	–	–	73.9
1955	38.3	61.7	–	–	–	72.0
1955B	40.6	59.4	–	–	–	46.4
1951	41.2	58.8	–	–	–	80.0
1950	39.3	51.2	–	9.5	–	78.7
1945	45.1	43.1	–	11.8	–	64.6

Edinburgh Central's socio-economic profile reflects its affluence as do current property prices, 54.7% above the national average, having risen 132.6% in 1991-2001 (the highest increase in the country). Central has the highest proportion of inhabitants born in England – over 20 per cent – of any Scottish seat.

This seat contains some of the most famous landmarks and attractions in Edinburgh which are synonymous with Scotland's international image. These include the Castle, Royal Mile and High Street, Murrayfield Stadium, the home of Scottish rugby, the present site of the Scottish Parliament at the Mound and the new, controversial Parliament building at Holyrood. Boundary changes in 1983 cut Edinburgh representation from seven to six and brought together in one seat the stunning lay-out and architecture of the Old and New Towns. The 1997 boundary changes deprived Edinburgh Central of this claim to fame, with the New Town, along with Stockbridge, being placed in Edinburgh North and Leith.

Major issues in Edinburgh Central include transport and housing. In 2002, the Scottish Executive announced plans for the major redevelopment of Waverley Station, Edinburgh's major railway terminal, involving £400 million of investment, and doubling the capacity of the station. At the same time, plans were unveiled for an Edinburgh airport rail link. However, since these announcements, doubts have arisen about their financial viability.

Edinburgh has undergone a major property boom from the end of the 1990s, both in prices and construction. Recent developments have seen a sizeable number of homes built in Haymarket next to the railway station, while future plans include 700 homes in the Dumbiedykes area. Heart of Midlothian Football Club have their stadium – Tynecastle – just off Gorgie Road in a built-up area, and have to move by 2010 due to UEFA regulations. This has motivated them to look at a number of options including ground-sharing in a new stadium with their neighbours and rivals Hibernian, playing at nearby Murrayfield, or building a new out-of-town stadium for their sole use. Murrayfield, too, may be demolished to cash in on development opportunities, while rugby would move elsewhere.

One of the most controversial public sector developments in recent years has been in Central – the new Scottish Parliament building situated at Holyrood at the bottom of the High Street. When first suggested by Donald Dewar in 1997 this was going to cost £40 million, but has risen to £430 million and rising, and is at least two years behind schedule, has seen three First Ministers, the death of the project architect Enric Miralles, and numerous political controversies. There has been real voter anger at its cost, though its supporters claim it will be a world class iconic building on a par with Sydney Opera House.

Central was first won by Labour in 1918 and lost in 1931 and 1935. It was won again by Labour's Andrew Gilzean in 1945 and 1950 and then by Thomas Oswald from 1951 until 1974. It has throughout its post-war history had a reputation as a marginal seat. Labour won it in 1959 by 51 per cent to the Conservatives' 49 per cent. Robin Cook won it as a young, eager left-winger on his 28th birthday on February 28th 1974 with a majority of 961 over the Conservatives. This was the first of three Labour victories in the 1970s as the seat slowly became more Labour. However, the boundary changes of 1983 brought in Tory areas making it more marginal, with the result that Cook fled to the safety of nearby New Town Livingston. He was right in his calculations, as Alex Fletcher won it for the Tories with a majority of 2,566 over Labour.

His hold was but a brief interlude and in 1987 Alistair Darling retook the seat for Labour with 40.2 per cent, putting 5,000 votes on to Labour's support and resulting in a majority of 2,262. This fell in 1992 to 2,126, before rising dramatically to 11,070 in 1997. Darling put 4,000 votes on Labour's notional 1992 result, while the Conservative vote fell to 21.2 per cent in one of the most prosperous seats in the UK, an indication of how unpopular the Conservatives had become in Scotland. In June 2001, Darling saw his majority slip from 11,070 to 8,142 – a fall of a mere 2 per cent on a reduced poll with Labour's vote down by 5,500, while the Lib Dems moved from fourth to a distant second increasing their vote by 750.

In 1999. Labour's Sarah Boyack lost nearly 6,000 votes on a reduced turnout, while the SNP gained nearly 3,000, establishing themselves in a respectable but distant second. The biggest shock was the Tory performance, finishing fourth in a seat where they had in1992, albeit on different boundaries, finished a mere 5.4 per cent behind Labour. In the May 2003 Scottish Parliament election, Sarah Boyack's Labour majority declined from 4,626 to a slightly uncomfortable 2,666 as Labour vote's slumped by 5,000. The Lib Dem Andy Myles, standing for the third consecutive election in the seat, put 213 votes on his support on a reduced turnout.

In the regional list vote, the Greens finished ahead of Labour in this seat, winning 19.7 per cent of the vote to Labour's 18.8 per cent – a lead of 260 votes. The Conservatives won 15.4 per cent to 12.2 per cent for the SNP, 10 per cent for independent candidate Margo MacDonald, with the SSP on 7.2 per cent.

Boundary changes at Westminster see the abolition of the current Edinburgh Central seat with Alistair Darling made homeless as a result. Edinburgh Central's fate in relation to the Scottish Parliament is a little less clear cut than its Westminster political preferences have been. For a seat that was Conservative as recently as 1983 they are now also-rans. However, the Lib Dems have polled well in this seat in recent years and had a good 2003 across Edinburgh. They are now sitting comfortably behind Sarah Boyack to pose a real challenge in future years.

MSP

SARAH BOYACK was born in 1961 and educated at Edinburgh's Royal High School, and Glasgow University, studying modern history and politics. Heriot-Watt University followed, for a diploma in town and country planning. Her link to devolution was already established before the 1999 election, through her father, the late Jim Boyack, and she shares two of his central passions, town planning and Scottish home rule. She worked in planning for the London Borough of Brent from 1986-88 and Central Regional Council from 1988-92, before becoming a lecturer in planning at Edinburgh College of Art and Heriot-Watt University from 1992-99.

Although appearing shy of the limelight, Boyack was active in student politics, as chair of the National Organisation of Labour Students, a founder member of Scottish Labour Action, the pro-home rule Labour pressure group, and a prominent mover against Militant entryism in the group Clause Four. At university, she flat-shared with Wendy Alexander, later to become Paisley North MSP. She was involved in environmental issues, was Scottish co-ordinator of the Socialist Environmental Resource Association (SERA) and convenor of the Royal Town Planning Institute Scotland. After her election as an MSP in May 1999, Boyack was part of Donald Dewar's five-member negotiating team, forging the first coalition with the Lib Dems. She was subsequently appointed minister for transport and environment, which may have been a promotion which came too early for her. She could often appear to be something of a rabbit in the headlights, with some evidence that her civil servants were particularly unhelpful to her attempts to drive an environmentally-sustainable transport policy. She lacked a deputy, faced intense pressure for localised trunk roads campaigns in the trunk roads review, and neither Donald Dewar nor Henry McLeish were particularly committed to the green agenda. A u-turn over plans for trunk road tolls was the first the Executive undertook. The Transport Act failed to tie together free bus travel for pensioners, requiring completion of that policy to be a major plank of the 2003 partnership agreement.

McLeish was understood to be ready to sack her when he became First Minister, but overplayed his hand through a strong attack by one of his closest advisers writing in the *Daily Record*. This meant she was kept in the cabinet, with her portfolio reduced to transport, while Sam Galbraith took responsibility for environment for the few months remaining before ill-health forced his departure. McLeish's government in its first weeks instigated a review of unpopular policies with the unofficial slogan 'dump the crap' which aimed to get rid of politically correct policies and return to bread and butter issues. Boyack in her new truncated role had to play a central part in this, abandoning the administration's proposals for workplace parking charges, which had met opposition from business groups. She also faced intense pressure from her own backbenchers, most prominently Andy Kerr, in pushing through the private contracting of trunk roads maintenance in 2001. Boyack was an unsurprising departure from the cabinet when Jack McConnell took over, while the portfolio shift of transport to join the enterprise portfolio after her departure from 2001-03 shifted the emphasis towards business-friendly road building, with backing for the M74 extension through South East Glasgow. Out of ministerial office, Boyack joined the European committee from 2001-03, and after the 2003 election, she became convener of the environment and rural affairs committee, writing early on that she thought the Executive should do more to raise its green profile with a dedicated minister. By that time, of course, seven Green Party MSPs had moved Scottish Parliamentary politics in her direction on that count.

MP

ALISTAIR DARLING was born in 1953 in London and has been MP for Edinburgh Central since 1987. With his mother's family from Lewis, he is the great-nephew of William Darling, Conservative MP for Edinburgh South from 1945-57. He was educated at Loretto School, Musselburgh, a public school, and Aberdeen University, where he studied law. He then worked in Edinburgh as a solicitor from 1978-83, and an advocate from 1984. In politics, positioned on Labour's left wing, Darling served on Lothian Regional Council from 1982-87, becoming convener of transport and blocking a Tory plan to build a motorway into the centre of Edinburgh. He was also on Lothian and Borders Police Board from 1982-86.

In the 1970s, he was a sceptic about devolution, arguing it was implausible that a Scottish Assembly could build a different kind of society when dependent on Westminster for its funding. By 1991, then as a supporter of devolution and proportional representation for a Scottish Parliament, he was on the Labour appointed Plant Commission looking at proportional representation for Westminster elections.

After his election to the Commons in 1987, Darling rapidly rose up the Labour hierarchy and became spokesman on home affairs from 1988-92, and from 1992-96, he was part of Labour's Treasury and economic affairs team, with particular responsibility for the City of London. He was Shadow Chief Secretary to the Treasury from 1996-97, and a key part of Gordon Brown's pre-election charm offensive in corporate board-rooms.

In Government, Darling continued to work closely with the Chancellor, Gordon Brown, being Chief Secretary to the Treasury for Labour's first year, and in July 1998, in the first major reshuffle, he was shifted to the post of Secretary of State for Social Security, replacing Harriet Harman, and tasked to bring peace in the civil war between Harman, Frank Field and the Treasury which had marred the first year under Labour. Symbolic of the New Labour approach is that his trademark black beard was shaven off. Facial hair was not New Labour.

In 2001, his department became Work and Pensions, and while stakeholder pensions were among the Labour Government's less impressive achievements, he somehow managed to avoid the flak and growing pensions crisis by moving on. With a growing reputation as a safe pair of hands, Blair asked him to calm down another department in turmoil when he replaced Stephen Byers at the deeply troubled transport ministry in 2002. The 'hopelessly optimistic' forecasts which his predecessors had pumped out were given a bracing reality check, as he completed the transition of privately-owned Railtrack into Network Rail. He voiced a renewed scepticism about road building as the panacea for congestion, moving Government policy towards radical thinking on road charging, and he undertook a long term review of aviation, courting controversy with new runways and terminals in South East England and the doubted future for Glasgow as against Edinburgh airport.

In June 2003, with Blair's botched reshuffle in which the post of Scottish Secretary at first disappeared and then had to be created again, it was Darling who was given that job in place of Helen Liddell, doing it alongside transport and promising to downsize the officialdom while eschewing continuation of turf wars with the Scottish Executive. That said, when in charge of the welfare system, he had blocked a budget transfer to St Andrews House of around £21 million per year, as Whitehall's punishment for introducing free long-term care of the elderly. In the post of Scottish Secretary, he was due to push through the amendment to the Scotland Act retaining the number of MSPs at 129, and was the one with the job of signing off constituency boundary changes which meant the disappearance of his own Edinburgh Central. He remained typically relaxed about getting a new seat in Edinburgh, particularly after Lynda Clark said she was standing down in Edinburgh Pentlands, leaving a south-west vacancy in the capital.

Edinburgh East
and Musselburgh

Predecessor Constituencies: Edinburgh East (1945–92).

Socio-economic Indicators:

Constituency Pop. (16-64)	47,994
Claimant Count (May 2003)	2.5% (19.5% below average)
IBA/SDA Claimants	11.3%
Life Expectancy – Male	72.0 (1.4 yrs below average)
Life Expectancy – Female	77.9 (0.8 years below average)
Owner Occupied	69.4%
Social Rented	21.3%
Average Property Prices	£77,513 (15th)
Average Gross Income	£25,882 (34th)
Low Birthweight Babies	175 (6.8%)
Teenage Pregnancy Rates	449 (5.4%)
No. of Lone Parent Households	3,518 (10.1%)

CAB Enquiries

Issue	No. of cases	Percentage of total cases (%)
1. Benefits	3034	26.4
2. Consumer	1980	17.2
3. Employment	1784	15.5
4. Other	1350	11.7
5. Housing	1140	9.9

2003 Scottish Parliament Election

Electorate: 57,704   *Turnout*: 29,044 (50.3%)   *Turnout 1999*: 61.5%

Candidate	Party	Votes	Votes%	99 %	Change%
Susan Deacon	Labour	12,654	43.6	46.2	– 2.6
Kenneth MacAskill	SNP	6,497	22.4	28.0	– 5.7
John Smart	Con	3,863	13.3	12.4	+ 0.9
Gary Peacock	Lib Dem	3,582	12.3	11.1	+ 1.2
Derek Durkin	SSP	2,447	8.4	(other 2.3)	+ 6.5

Labour majority: 6,157 (21.2%)   *Swing*: 1.5% SNP to Labour

2001 General Election

Electorate: 59,241   *Turnout*: 34,454 (58.2%)

Candidate	Party	Votes	Votes%	Change%
Gavin Strang	Labour	18,124	52.6	– 1.0
Rob Munn	SNP	5,956	17.3	– 1.8
Gary Peacock	Lib Dem	4,981	14.5	– 4.1
Peter Finnie	Con	3,906	11.3	– 4.1
Derek Durkin	SSP	1,487	4.3	–

Labour majority: 12,168 (35.3%)   *Swing*: 0.4% SNP to Labour

1945–97 Westminster

	Lab%	Con%	SNP%	Lib%	Other%	Turnout%
1997	53.6	15.4	19.1	10.7	1.3	70.6
1992	45.7	24.4	18.4	10.2	1.3	73.9
1987	50.4	24.7	9.5	15.4	–	74.1
1983	44.9	28.6	5.5	21.0	–	70.4
1979	53.7	33.5	12.1	–	0.7	76.1
1974O	44.9	23.1	25.6	5.9	0.5	76.2
1974F	43.7	31.6	15.4	8.7	0.6	81.1
1970	51.8	39.0	8.2	–	1.0	74.5
1966	60.5	39.5	–	–	–	77.4
1964	56.1	43.9	–	–	–	81.0
1959	50.4	49.6	–	–	–	80.7
1955	52.5	47.5	–	–	–	75.4
1954B	57.6	42.4	–	–	–	61.8
1951	54.1	45.9	–	–	–	83.8
1950	53.2	38.8	–	8.0	–	83.2
1947B	50.6	34.3	5.0	10.1	–	63.0
1945B	61.6	38.4	–	–	–	51.0
1945	56.4	37.3	6.3	–	–	69.4

Edinburgh East and Musselburgh is located to the east and south of the visually striking Arthur's Seat. It includes a diverse range of communities, from the middle-class, alternative atmosphere of Portobello and Joppa to the proudly distinctive 'honest toun' Musselburgh, to the deprivation and poverty of peripheral housing estates Craigmillar and Niddrie. Its socio-economic profile reflects the diversity of this Edinburgh constituency, where average property prices are the lowest in the city – 14.9 per cent above the national average – and rose 94.5 per cent in the 1990s. Local Citizens Advice Bureau enquiries show the highest number of benefit cases for any of the Edinburgh CABs.

Edinburgh City Council has declared its intention to build a new local school after Portobello High School, one of Scotland's largest, suffered water damage. The council's plans involve a £200 million public–private partnership which will modernise fifteen Edinburgh schools. The council has also put forward ambitious proposals for revitalising Craigmillar estate which include a Housing Stock Transfer to release extra resources from the Scottish Executive. Railway services are a key issue in this commuter area. A city crossrail now links to a new Brunstane station, and building a new Musselburgh Parkway station is seen as crucial for economic development, with potential delays in this and other investment viewed ominously.

Defence related jobs are a significant part of the local economy with Ferranti Defence Systems one of the biggest employers. The Alenia Marconi Systems plant recently won a Ministry of Defence contract to build the Meteor Missile for the European fighter aircraft, which guaranteed over 200 local jobs.

Hibernian Football Club's ground is located in the constituency at Easter Road. In June 2003 Hearts and Hibernian revealed that they were looking at the possibility of ground-sharing by moving to an out-of-town site off the City by-pass at Straiton on a site owned by Sir Tom Farmer, Hibernian's proprietor and Kwik-Fit millionaire. This met vocal opposition from large sections of both teams' supporters, and in October 2003 the Hibernian Board announced it had decided to remain at Easter Road.

Labour first won Edinburgh East in 1918 and has held it continuously since 1935. Labour's majority under Gavin Strang, MP since 1970, has never really been threatened, falling to 8,456 with the SNP high tide of October 1974. In 1983, when Labour were worried over the loss of Musselburgh, its lead fell to 5,866 over the Conservatives. Since then Labour has increased its majority, which rose from a notional 9,101 in 1992 to 14,530 in 1997, Strang putting on nearly 3,000 votes from the previous election. The SNP vote remained static, but moved into second place as the Conservatives lost 4,000 votes. In June 2001 Strang held on comfortably, seeing his majority fall slightly to 12,168 with the Nationalists in a distant second.

Labour's vote dropped in the first Scottish Parliament elections while the SNP's Kenny MacAskill made a strong showing in second place and cut Susan Deacon's Labour majority to 6,714. Four years later Deacon saw her majority decline slightly to 6,157 although she achieved an increase of 3 per cent on a lower turnout. In the regional list vote, Labour won 28 per cent to the SNP's 16.4 per cent, 11.6 per cent for Margo McDonald, the independent candidate who finished third, while the Greens and SSP won 11.6 per cent and 7.5 per cent respectively.

Boundary Commission proposals for Westminster propose a radical reshaping of this part of the city with Gilmerton and Newington from Edinburgh South being combined with Craigmillar and Portobello to form a new Edinburgh South East seat whose Labour affiliations would not be in doubt. At a Scottish Parliament level Edinburgh East and Musselburgh looks likely to continue in the tradition it has established of providing a secure Labour seat in Edinburgh through good times and bad.

MSP

SUSAN DEACON was born in 1964 in Musselburgh and educated at Musselburgh Grammar School, where she was head girl. At Edinburgh University, she studied social policy and politics, and went on to gain a Masters in Business Administration. She worked for West Lothian Council as a research officer from 1987 to 1989, East Lothian Council as a senior administrative officer from 1990-92, and as a services manager from 1992-94. Deacon became director of MBA programmes at Heriot-Watt University from 1994-98 and worked in freelance business and marketing from 1998 until the 1999 election.

The daughter of a railwayman and housekeeper, she has been a Labour Party activist from student days. Deacon played a leading part in developing the home rule and neo-nationalist Scottish Labour Action, in which others who would become MSPs were student contemporaries; Jack McConnell,

Wendy Alexander, Sarah Boyack, Frank McAveety. Deacon also met John Boothman through the movement, who would become her partner and father of her two children, as well as BBC Scotland's senior political producer. Neither of the leading lights in that organisation, Ian Smart and Bob McLean, were elected to the Scottish Parliament, their hopes falling foul of the gender twinning arrangements. Deacon herself nearly failed to make it: excluded from the first round of Labour's panel selection, she was the only person to appeal successfully. In the 1999 elections, she was Labour's spokesperson on education, and after the election was given the biggest catapult into an Executive hot seat, being appointed minister for health and community care.

In that post, Deacon advanced a progressive public health agenda, tackling resistance over sex education from conservative pro-life campaigners and the Catholic Church. She was in this period seen as a potential candidate in a Labour leadership contest whenever Donald Dewar chose to retire, but his death in October 2000 came too soon for her to consider standing, and she backed Henry McLeish for Scottish Labour leader over Jack McConnell. She retained her post unchanged in the resulting ministerial reshuffle, and there followed speculation that either she or Wendy Alexander would put themselves forward for the post of deputy Labour group leader, but neither did, leaving the post to the backbencher Cathy Jamieson. Deacon distanced herself from McLeish early on in his premiership, by making it clear she did not favour free long-term care for all elderly, believing it to be badly targeted and unaffordable in the long term. Although many other ministers backed her, McLeish won the battle with the backing of other parties.

Pregnant with her second child, the second leadership contest came at a bad time for Deacon as well. Any claim on the top job had been damaged by running into heavy weather with the health service, which was not responding to injections of new money as intended: there were crises in the Beatson cancer centre in Glasgow and in Tayside Health Board; a lack of care home places continued to cause hospital bed blocking trouble; she had come under pressure for the beds crisis during a 2000-01 flu outbreak; and her plan for the NHS was not delivering the necessary results.

She joined cabinet colleagues in backing Wendy Alexander as the alternative to a McConnell leadership, but was let down when Alexander swiftly pulled out. McConnell offered her the social justice cabinet post in his first cabinet, but she declined, leaving ministerial office instead, apparently throwing the new First Minister's plans into disarray and leaving Wendy Alexander as an isolated figure in the cabinet.

As a backbencher, Deacon joined the education committee, avoiding disloyalty to McConnell. She caused him big problems, however, in March 2003, when she rallied Labour MSP opposition to the Iraq war, publicly attending the huge anti-war march in Glasgow during February 2003 (held the same day as a UK Labour spring conference in the city), and tabling a motion on the subject when the First Minister thought he had kept the party group together. Six other Labour colleagues signed it, and she was one of five Labour MSPs to vote against the party line on the war in March 2003, just before Parliament rose for the election. Post-election, she became a member of the audit and enterprise and culture committees. She showed she was ready to take her own line, independent of the Executive, with carefully-worded scepticism about the new powers planned to allow the takeover of failing schools and criticism of the decision to move Scottish National Heritage headquarters from the capital to Inverness. She also criticised McConnell's administration for being too tough on crime, while being insufficiently tough on its causes.

MP

GAVIN STRANG was born in 1943 in Dundee and has been MP for Edinburgh East from 1970-97 and Edinburgh East and Musselburgh since 1997. He was educated at Morrison's Academy, Crieff and Edinburgh University, gaining both an honours degree and scientific PhD; and Churchill College,

Cambridge, where he attained a diploma in agricultural science. Strang worked for Tayside Economic Planning Consultative Group from 1966-68 and was a research scientist from 1968-70. After entering Parliament, his maiden speech was an attack on apartheid in South Africa and on British arms sales to the Pretoria regime. In 1971, he was one of 33 Scottish Labour MPs who voted against entry into the Common Market while only 11 voted for entry, and is the only one of those voting against still to be an MP. He was a spokesman on trade and industry from 1973-74, served in the 1974-9 Labour Government as a junior minister in the Department of Energy in 1974 and in Agriculture, Fisheries and Food from 1974-79. In Labour's long years of opposition, Strang was a spokesman on agriculture, fisheries and food from 1979-82, resigning from the front bench over Labour's support of the Falklands War. He became a member of the hard left Campaign Group in 1982, which usually precluded frontbench prospects. This stance involved an attack on former Labour Prime Minister Jim Callaghan for his intervention during the 1983 election campaign, which questioned the party's then policy of unilateral nuclear disarmament. Strang claimed Callaghan had sabotaged Labour's chances, even though Labour was doing plenty to sabotage its chances by other means. The Edinburgh MP became chair of the PLP defence committee from 1985-87 on a committed unilateralist platform, and was chair of the Scottish group of Labour MPs from 1986-87. In 1986, he came a distant second to Sam McCluskie in running for the Labour Treasurer's post, at least beating Ken Livingstone. And in 1987, he piloted a private member's bill onto the statute book, dealing with public health aspects of HIV/AIDS control. Although positioned to the left, he became spokesman on employment from 1987-89 and shadow minister for agriculture from 1992-97, with the support of good showings in shadow cabinet elections, rising to fourth place in 1996.

Upon Labour coming to power, Strang was given the post of Minister for Transport in John Prescott's super-ministry, which included a position at the Cabinet table, but his time there was blighted by unhappy relations with the Deputy Prime Minister. His support for more road building was vetoed by Prescott and the 1998 transport white paper had little of Strang's work included in it. Indeed, his ministerial career was never destined for great things or longevity, as his face and politics did not fit the Blairite New Labour agenda of the times and he was sacked in the first ministerial reshuffle in July 1998, only a month after the white paper was published. As a backbencher, Strang's clashes with Prescott became more public, as the Edinburgh MP became leader of the revolt against the government's attempts to privatise air traffic control – a policy which did not have much support amongst Labour MPs, and where his transport department experience gave his critique added weight, with warnings that the policy 'jeopardised safety standards'. After he led three sizeable revolts, the government eventually got its way on the issue in late 2000, when the House of Lords relented in its opposition to the programme.

As a backbench Privy Councillor, he had the seniority to become a member of the intelligence and security committee, which took on vastly increased significance in light of the post-Iraq war events of 2003. He signed the motion against war in Iraq in 2002 and voted against the impending war in February and March of the following year. Strang's career has in many ways mirrored his era for the Labour left: a split over Europe, long-time Tribune Group loyalty, he was associated with the hard-left Bennite Campaign Group, before becoming loyal to the New Labour cause and winning in 1997. Then, when he did not fit with the New Labour ministerial caste, he reverted to rebel mode on areas where the Blair Government was seen to transgress Labour principles, including public-private partnerships, the Iraq war and student top-up tuition fees.

Edinburgh North and Leith

Predecessor Constituencies: Edinburgh Leith (1945–97).

Socio-economic Indicators:

Constituency Pop. (16-64)	53,845
Claimant Count (May 2003)	3.2% (3.8% above average)
IBA/SDA Claimants	8.2%
Life Expectancy – Male	72.6 (0.8 yrs below average)
Life Expectancy – Female	77.9 (0.8 yrs below average)
Owner Occupied	64.1%
Social Rented	16.1%
Average Property Prices	£106,628 (3rd)
Average Gross Income	£28,884 (10th)
Low Birthweight Babies	135 (5.5%)
Teenage Pregnancy Rates	449 (6.5%)
No. of Lone Parent Households	2,896 (7.7%)

CAB Enquiries

Issue	No. of cases	Percentage of total cases (%)
1. Consumer	4172	17.6
2. Benefits	4082	17.3
3. Housing	3422	14.5
4. Employment	3401	14.4
5. Legal	3134	13.3

2003 Scottish Parliament Election

Electorate: 60,501   Turnout: 28,734 (47.5%)   Turnout 1999: 58.2%

Candidate	Party	Votes	Votes%	99 %	Change%
Malcolm Chisholm	Labour	10,979	38.2	46.9	– 8.7
Anne Dana	SNP	5,565	19.4	25.8	– 6.5
Ian Mowat	Con	4,821	16.8	13.7	+ 3.1
Sebastian Tombs	Lib Dem	4,785	16.7	11.0	+ 5.6
William Scott	SSP	2,584	9.0	2.5	+ 6.5

Labour majority: 5,414 (18.8%)   Swing: 1.1% Labour to SNP

2001 General Election

Electorate: 62,731   *Turnout*: 33,234 (53.0%)

Candidate	Party	Votes	Votes%	Change%
Mark Lazarowicz	Labour	15,271	45.9	- 1.0
Sebastian Tombs	Lib Dem	6,454	19.4	+ 6.4
Kaukab Stewart	SNP	5,290	15.9	− 4.2
Iain Mitchell	Con	4,626	13.9	- 3.9
Catriona Grant	SSP	1,334	4.0	–
Don Jacobsen	Soc Lab	259	0.8	–

Labour majority: 8,817 (26.5%)   *Swing*: 3.7% Labour to Lib Dem

1945–97 Westminster

	Lab%	Con%	SNP%	Lib%	Other%	Turnout%
1997	46.9	17.9	20.1	13.0	2.1	66.5
1992	34.3	21.1	21.8	12.3	10.5	71.3
1987	49.3	22.9	9.5	18.3	–	70.8
1983	39.7	26.3	6.5	27.5	–	67.2
1979	46.3	31.9	9.7	12.1	–	75.2
1974O	39.7	28.0	26.1	6.2	–	74.8
1974F	40.6	38.3	21.1	–	–	79.3
1970	46.3	41.0	7.0	5.7	–	73.2
1966	56.8	42.2	–	–	1.0	76.1
1964	55.5	45.5	–	–	–	77.9
1959	47.8	38.0	–	14.2	–	79.5
1955	49.4	32.3	–	–	18.3	77.8
1951	50.1	49.9	–	–	–	84.0
1950	49.3	43.0	–	7.7	–	80.7
1945	60.9	–	–	31.4	7.7	69.1

Edinburgh North and Leith's profile underlines the prosperity and hardship that sit cheek by jowl in this seat. The claimant total is the only Edinburgh seat above the national average. However, average property prices are the third highest in the country, 58.1 per cent above the national average, and rose 122.6 per cent in 1991-2001 – the second biggest increase in Scotland. Edinburgh North and Leith has been ranked the most unhealthy constituency in the capital – placed as the 33rd most unhealthy seat in Britain, and 17th in Scotland – a relative clean bill of health compared to Glasgow's bleaker health record.

In the last boundary changes Edinburgh North and Leith gained the middle-class, affluent areas of New Town and Stockbridge from Central, as well as Calton and Lochend from East; out went the council estate of Muirhouse to the West. These changes had very little political impact, cancelling each other out without threatening or strengthening Labour's hold. Leith includes the old port area which has been partially transformed through urban regeneration and gentrification in recent years so old harbour warehouses now contain fashionable, expensive restaurants and shops. The seat ranges socially from this booming waterfront, to the prosperous New Town and Stockbridge and the council estate of Pilton with major drug and crime problems.

Leith was eulogised in song by the Scottish group the Proclaimers led by the Auchtermuchty twins, Craig and Charlie Reid – 'Sunshine on Leith'. It is undergoing massive transformation symbolised by the presence of the Royal Yacht Britannia permanently moored in the harbour, and a whole host of property developments as well as numerous local controversies between different communities. One of the most high profile was the campaign by local residents to move Edinburgh's unofficial 'tolerance zone' for prostitutes away from nearby homes. This zone was championed by Edinburgh City Council and MSP Margo MacDonald, and had been trying to minimise the risks to women working the streets, but Leith's new inhabitants seemed more concerned about their property prices.

Edinburgh City Council's decision in 2002 to allow Wimpey Homes to develop a 300 home urban village off Leith Walk was taken in the face of major opposition: with both the local MP and MSP opposed as well as 61 letters of objection and a local petition. Another development at Granton called Edinburgh Park will include over one million square feet of office space, there are plans for 3,000 homes at the Western Harbour in Newhaven, and Edinburgh Academy has sold sports grounds to Applecross housing developers who intend to build two five-storey towers. Some local groups and communities feel the change is damaging the area, and excluding local people from affordable housing.

Leith has for long celebrated its radical credentials. The khaki election of 1918 saw the election of an Independent Liberal against Lloyd George's Tory dominated-coalition: Captain William Wedgwood Benn, who represented the seat until 1927, then switched to Labour and served in the 1929-31 and 1945 Labour Governments. Captain Benn was Tony Benn's father.

Leith went Labour for the first time in 1945, like the rest of the city resisting Labour's charms longer than Glasgow and the West of Scotland. This was James Hoy's first victory, and in 1951 he won the seat for Labour with 50.1 per cent against the Conservatives' 49.9 per cent and a majority of 72 on an 84 per cent poll. He held the seat until his retirement in 1970. Ron Brown was first elected in 1979 with a Labour vote of 46.3 per cent and a majority of 4,017 over the Conservatives; this rose to 4,973 in 1983 over the Liberal–SDP Alliance and a Labour vote of 49.3 per cent and majority of 11,327 in 1987.

Ron Brown was an idiosyncratic hard left-winger who combined uncompromising principles with the reputation of a loner. More controversially, he visited Afghanistan post-Soviet invasion and visited Libya in 1984 and 1985, meeting Colonel Gaddafi. His left-wing beliefs were not out of tune with his constituency party, but his personal antics were. There were allegations of an affair with a female assistant and then disruption and misbehaviour at his mistress's London flat culminating in Brown throwing female underwear out of the window. He was consequently de-selected by his local party in 1990 and replaced by Malcolm Chisholm.

Brown stood as independent Labour candidate in 1992 and polled 4,142 votes (10.3 per cent) finishing fifth; Chisholm polled 34.3 per cent, seeing Labour's vote drop 15 per cent and its majority reduced to 4,985. In 1997 Chisholm put 4,000 votes back on Labour's support and its majority climb back to 10,978. In the June 2001 Westminster election, with Chisholm having moved to the Scottish Parliament, Mark Lazarowicz was safely returned Labour MP with his majority of 8,817 unaffected in percentage terms.

The 1999 devolution elections saw Chisholm stand for Labour. Labour's vote fell by a mere 2,000 votes on a reduced turnout, while it actually rose in percentage terms – one of the few constituencies where this occurred leaving a majority of 7,736 over the SNP. Also standing in these elections was Ron Brown, who polled 907 votes (2.5 per cent) and finished fifth again. In May 2003 at the Scottish Parliament election, Malcolm Chisholm's majority fell 3 per cent to 5,414.

In the regional vote, Labour won 21 per cent to the Greens impressive 19 per cent – a Labour lead of only 579 – while the Conservatives won 14.3 per cent to 13.4 per cent for the SNP, with independent ex-Nationalist Margo MacDonald on 9.5 per cent and the SSP on 8 per cent.

Boundary changes for Westminster see Edinburgh North and Leith reconfigured into a new Edinburgh North East seat made up of Leith and parts of Edinburgh Central such as Holyrood, which will be a safe Labour seat. At the Scottish Parliament, North and Leith's Labour affections do not look in doubt for the foreseeable future, particularly given the inability of one clear challenger to emerge from the other parties.

MSP

MALCOLM CHISHOLM was born in 1949 in Edinburgh and was elected MP for Edinburgh Leith in 1992 and Edinburgh North and Leith as MP in 1997 and MSP in 1999. Educated at George Watson's College and Edinburgh University, where he studied English literature and Greek, he trained as a teacher, working in the capital's secondary schools for sixteen years. As chairman of Leith Constituency Labour Party, he was ideally placed to succeed Ron Brown after the notorious rebel was deselected in 1990.

Elected in the 1992 general election, Chisholm comes from the same political traditions as Ron Brown – while lacking the flamboyance and bringing rather more sophistication. He joined the hard left Campaign Group at Westminster, and was chairman of the Scottish housing group from 1994-96. In 1996, he became opposition spokesman on Scottish constitutional affairs, replacing his fellow left-winger John McAllion when the latter resigned over Tony Blair's announcement of a devolution referendum without even informing his own party's front benchers. In 1997, Chisholm became housing and local government minister at the Scottish Office, but a mere six months into office, in December 1997, he was the most senior resignation when 47 Labour MPs rebelled over single-parent benefit cuts.

Donald Dewar, a former Westminster whip, was not given to rewarding such behaviour with devolved ministerial office, particularly after it gave Chisholm a particular caché with the party's left. In the Scottish Parliament, the Edinburgh MSP took Labour's place as deputy convenor of the health and community care committee. But after Dewar's death, the left began a new lease of life on the Mound, and Chisholm's fortunes with it. He backed Henry McLeish for the Labour leadership, and, with the new First Minister's reshuffle, Chisholm was made deputy to Susan Deacon, then minister for health and community care. This was seen as a reward for constructive behaviour since the 1999 election, and just reward for a man with many talents and a passion about public health in Scotland. However, it began with one of the toughest tasks in that first term – making sense and reality of the promise of free long term care for the elderly.

With the fall of McLeish, Chisholm ran a very brief campaign for the leadership, beginning on morning radio but petering out within hours, when it seemed he could not muster the necessary seven MSP nominations. This was not something Jack McConnell held against him, when he became First Minister instead, promoting Chisholm again, along with others from Labour's left. After Deacon was offered the social justice post and refused, leaving the cabinet instead, Chisholm took over from her at health. The job had, by that time, become something of a poisoned chalice, with the National Health Service in Scotland failing to respond to injections of cash, and the promises of reduced waiting lists and waiting times on course to become the weakest part of the Executive's record by the 2003 election. He was awarded the *Herald* Politician of the Year award, on the same day that dire waiting time figures were published. The award was in recognition of making the best of a seemingly impossible job, and for his demeanour as a quiet, straight-talking politician, who enjoys a high degree of public trust. He treated the irony of the award's timing with his usual mixture of slightly awkward embarrassment and wry amusement. Despite a public persona as amiable but not particularly tough, the early days were marked by intervention by the Executive in the Beatson cancer centre in Glasgow, North Glasgow hospital trust and in Tayside Health Board's financial problems caused by an over-spend. He sought to sound pragmatic under early pressure to make more use of the private sector, as England was doing, and he seized the opportunity in 2002 to buy the private HCI hospital in Clydebank and turn it into a national centre designated to tackle waiting lists – at which it exceeded targets in its first year, but not without staffing problems.

Chisholm's conscience came back to give him considerable trouble with the second of two votes on the Iraq war in early 2003. While voting in support of Tony Blair's policy, he performed a remarkable u-turn two days later, when anti-war protestors turned up at his constituency surgery in Leith. He took their megaphone and expressed his regret at making an 'immoral' decision to back the war. His wife left the Labour Party over the Iraq war, while his constituency assistant was in Baghdad as a human shield. McConnell indulged him, so long as he made his point briefly and kept quiet about it thereafter, and Chisholm returned to the health post after the 2003 election. This meant legislation to abolish NHS trusts, boost the role of local health co-operatives, and to give ministers powers to intervene where hospitals are seen to be failing. This was a clear departure from Westminster's New Labour orthodoxy, where John Reid, a Scottish Labour MP, was steering through the reform of the NHS to create foundation hospitals. By the 2003 May re-shuffle, Chisholm was the only Labour minister with experience of Westminster.

MP

MARK LAZAROWICZ was born in Romford in 1953 and educated at St Benedict's School, London, then St Andrews University, where his MA was in moral philosophy and medieval history. As a mature student he gained a law degree from Edinburgh University in 1992. He was employed as an organiser for Scottish Education and Action for Development from 1978-80, and general secretary of the British Youth Council Scotland 1982-86, returning to SEAD from 1982-86. He was a solicitor from 1993-96, becoming an advocate from 1996. Before becoming an MP, Lazarowicz was well-known in Edinburgh politics, identified by his trademark high-speed talking, he had been on the district council from 1980-96 and again on the unitary council from 1999-2001. He was council leader from 1986-93 benefiting from a 'soft left' coup and settling it down after a tumultuous, confrontational time under a hard left administration led by Alex Wood, and leading it into some of the development decisions which would later help unleash its economic boom at the turn of the century. Later, in the unitary authority, he was transport convener, seeking to drive through controversial congestion charging plans.

He was also a member of the Scottish Labour executive from 1980-90, starting that period on the Bennite left but shifting to a softer left position focused on delivering services and campaigning. He was chair of the Scottish party in 1989-90, and contested Edinburgh Pentlands seat at Westminster in 1987 and 1992, losing to Malcolm Rifkind. Leaving the seat for Lynda Clark to win it in 1997, he made a late dash to fill the Cumbernauld and Kilsyth seat vacated in the final weeks before the 1997 election, but was beaten by Rosemary McKenna. His bid to become an MSP was rejected by the vetting panel, a process which he later criticised for concentrating too much power in small centrally-controlled committees. He had more luck, however, with the selection to replace Malcolm Chisholm when the MP of nine years stood down ahead of the 2001 election to concentrate on his Scottish Parliament role.

In 1990, Lazarowicz had been one of the prime movers in setting up the John Wheatley Centre, a Labour-oriented think tank which was influential in party circles pre-1997 in developing a policy programme for devolution, later moving to rebrand it as the Centre for Scottish Public Policy, to give it a more independent stance. As an author and pamphleteer, he has written a legal guide to the Scottish Parliament with a former leader of Glasgow City Council, Jean McFadden – an example of Glasgow-Edinburgh co-operation – and written in favour of proportional representation in local government. In Westminster, Lazarowicz voted against the Iraq war in February and March 2003. His select committee memberships reflect already-established interests, with seats on environment as well as food and rural affairs. His energetic, driven style, combined with an independent mind have allowed him to bounce back from setbacks but may well preclude him from Westminster advancement.

Edinburgh Pentlands

Predecessor Constituencies: none.

Socio-economic Indicators:

Constituency Pop. (16-64)	50,415
Claimant Count (May 2003)	2.3% (25.5% below average)
IBA/SDA Claimants	6.8%
Life Expectancy – Male	76.5 (3.1 years above average)
Life Expectancy – Female	81.6 (2.9 years above average)
Owner Occupied	74.1%
Social Rented	17.5%
Average Property Prices	£111,057 (2nd)
Average Gross Income	£31,478 (5th)
Low Birthweight Babies	147 (5.8%)
Teenage Pregnancy Rates	511 (4.8%)
No. of Lone Parent Households	2,986 (9.5%)

2003 Scottish Parliament Election

Electorate: 58,534   *Turnout*: 33,382 (57.0%)   *Turnout 1999*: 66.0%

Candidate	Party	Votes	Votes%	99 %	Change%
David McLetchie	Con	12,420	37.2	28.9	+ 8.3
Iain Gray	Labour	10,309	30.9	36.2	– 5.3
Ian McKee	SNP	5,620	16.8	22.2	– 5.3
Simon Clark	Lib Dem	3,943	11.8	12.7	– 0.9
Frank O'Donnell	SSP	1,090	3.3	–	–

Conservative majority: 2,111 (6.3%)   *Swing*: 6.8% Labour to Conservative

2001 General Election

Electorate: 60,484   *Turnout*: 38,932 (64.4%)

Candidate	Party	Votes	Votes%	Change%
Lynda Clark	Labour	15,797	40.6	– 2.4
Malcolm Rifkind	Con	14,055	36.1	+ 3.7
David Walker	Lib Dem	4,210	10.8	+ 0.8
Stewart Gibb	SNP	4,210	10.8	– 2.2
James Mearns	SSP	555	1.4	–
William McMurdo	UK Ind	105	0.3	+ 0.1

Labour majority: 1,742 (4.5%)   *Swing*: 3.1% Labour to Conservative

1945–97 Westminster

	Lab%	Con%	SNP%	Lib%	Other%	Turnout%
1997	43.0	32.4	13.0	10.0	1.6	76.7
1992	31.1	40.7	15.4	12.6	0.2	80.2
1987	30.0	38.3	7.2	24.5	–	77.6
1983	23.9	39.2	6.1	29.3	1.6	73.3
1979	36.6	39.3	11.0	13.1	–	76.8
1974O	30.9	33.9	24.6	10.6	–	75.5
1974F	30.8	41.2	12.4	15.6	–	80.9
1970	39.4	46.1	5.9	8.6	–	77.0
1966	44.8	45.0	–	10.2	–	80.5
1964	40.6	46.0	–	13.4	–	81.6
1959	39.7	60.3	–	–	–	80.3
1955	40.5	59.5	–	–	–	77.3
1951	42.3	57.7	–	–	–	83.3
1950	39.2	50.5	–	10.3	–	82.0

Edinburgh Pentlands has some of the most middle-class and prosperous parts of Edinburgh such as the detached villas of Colinton and Fairmilehead, as well as the stylish villages of Balerno and Currie. It also contains new private sector developments along the A70, as Edinburgh struggles to contain the fast growth of the last few years. The 'other side' of Edinburgh is present within the seat in the council scheme of Wester Hailes, which has witnessed extensive depopulation in the last two decades, both planned and unplanned, as well as smaller estates like Sighthill and Stenhouse. Edinburgh Pentlands' socio-economic profile illustrates the affluence and wealth of the majority of its inhabitants. Average property prices are the second highest in the country – 64.4 per cent above the national average and rose 89.1 per cent in the 1990s.

Pentlands has seen major public controversy in recent years in the more middle class, geographically semi-detached, commuter areas such as Balerno, Currie and Colinton over 'urban creep', as the growth of Edinburgh extends out and erodes the green belt. Edinburgh City Council also has major plans for the area with its privately-financed scheme for modernising the face of the city's state education system, with new schools at Broomhouse, South Morningside and St Joseph's, as well as developing a new 'smart school' out of Currie High.

The housing estates of Wester Hailes, Oxgangs and Sighthall have all experienced significant social problems over the last twenty years, and a large number of their residents have felt left out from the 'good times' of the Edinburgh boom. The Scottish Executive believes that anti-social behaviour, especially by young people in these areas, is a particular problem, and has proposed a number of initiatives to crack down on this. Wester Hailes Partnership, a multi-agency public body in place since 1989, has been given responsibility for advancing issues of urban regeneration and social inclusion in the area. One crucial factor for the future of Wester Hailes will be the outcome of the council's Housing Stock Transfer proposals which will, if successful, release sizeable funds for in public investment.

Pentlands should be and has been a traditional, safe Conservative seat, but of course this is Scotland. The seat was Conservative from its creation in 1950, but Labour came near at its Wilsonian high point of 1966, winning 44.8 per cent to the Conservatives' 45 per cent. Malcolm Rifkind held it in October 1974 in a three-way contest with Labour and SNP by a mere 1,257 votes and in a two-way contest with

Labour by 1,198 in 1979. This was not an auspicious base in which to start an unpopular period of Conservative Government. Rifkind's majority grew to 4,309 in 1983 and held at 3,745 in 1987 and 4,290 in 1992. He had by this point served an illustrious career as a Cabinet Minister through the Thatcher-Major Governments including a stint as Scottish Secretary of State from 1986-90, Transport Minister from 1990-92 and Defence Minister from 1992-97, before finally losing in 1997. He had become one of only three MPs to have served as ministers throughout the 18 Conservative years.

Lynda Clark, standing for the first time in 1997, put more than 5,000 on Labour's vote, while the Conservatives' fell by nearly 4,000, giving Labour a majority of 4,862. At the June 2001 Westminster election, there was a rematch of the 1997 contest between Lynda Clark and now knighted Sir Malcolm Rifkind. This was a battle which, for the Tories, was intrinsically interwoven with their sense of prestige and pride: namely how could Pentlands not be a Tory seat, and how could a class act like Rifkind fail to win? Despite Clark being unpopular with many voters and the best Tory efforts, Labour held on with a reduced majority of 1,742 – cutting Labour's majority in half on a 3 per cent swing – well short of the 5.3 per cent needed to win.

In the 1999 Scottish Parliament elections, the Conservatives reduced Labour's 1997 majority to 2,885. This translated into David McLetchie gaining a small swing of 1.67 per cent from Labour to Tory. Many may have thought this the Tories' best chance, but in May 2003 there was a rematch between McLetchie and Labour's Iain Gray, the enterprise and lifelong learning minister. A big local issue was the proposal by Edinburgh City Council to impose congestion charges around the city centre affecting many of the middle class commuter communities which inhabit Pentlands. McLetchie who had experienced a good four years in the Scottish Parliament as a regional list MSP and Tory group leader needed a 3.7 per cent swing to unseat Gray and he managed with a swing of 6.8 per cent and a majority of 2,111. In the regional list vote, the Conservatives won 27.8 per cent to Labour's 19.2 per cent with the SNP on 13.7 per cent, Greens on 11.7 per cent, Margo on 11 per cent, and the SSP on 3.4 per cent – their lowest vote in the Lothians regional seat.

The fact that Pentlands went Labour in the first place showed how far the Conservatives in Scotland had fallen by 1997 and they had not dug themselves out of it by 1999. That it took Labour from 1979 to 1997 to win this seat shows the lack of conviction with which it has embraced Labour. Pentlands was always likely to be the sort of place where the first green shots of Tory recovery would manifest itself, and so it has proven in the 2003 elections.

Boundary changes for Westminster see the constituency's expansion into Edinburgh South-West which is notionally Labour-held, but a Conservative target. The Conservatives will hope that David McLetchie's victory in 2003 is sustained at Holyrood and the first step back from being the kicking boys of Scottish politics which they had to endure for the 1980s and 1990s.

MSP

DAVID McLETCHIE was born in 1952 in Edinburgh and educated at Leith Academy and George Heriot's School, Edinburgh, followed by Edinburgh University where he studied law. He worked as an apprentice solicitor with Shepherd and Wedderburn from 1974-76, then specialising in how to handle the changes to inheritance tax law brought in by the then Labour Government. He was a solicitor with Tods Murray from 1976-80 and a partner from 1980, heading the department dealing with tax, estates and trusts. As an MSP, he continued to do some legal work with the firm.

McLetchie stood in the Edinburgh Central seat in the 1979 general election, losing to Robin Cook, and next stood 20 years later in the first Scottish Parliament elections, as Conservative candidate in

Edinburgh Pentlands. That year, being first on his party's Lothian list, he won a regional seat. He returned to fight the same seat in 2003 against the Labour incumbent, enterprise minister Iain Gray, and with his raised profile, his position in the party was strengthened by becoming one of its three constituency MSPs. He eschewed even an attempt to get into Westminster politics during the years of Conservative Government, later saying he did not want to hawk himself round constituencies, and found Westminster commuting unattractive once he had married and was parenting a son. His political involvement was in the party's voluntary wing. He was secretary of the party's national association in 1989-92, and president from 1994-97. After the 1997 election wipeout, he served on the Strathclyde Commission which reformed the party's structure and organisation. In September 1998, McLetchie was elected leader of the Scottish Conservative candidates, defeating former Ayr MP Phil Gallie. He surprised many by emerging from anonymity, beating off the first impressions of Edinburgh lawyerly greyness, to be a doughty and effective campaigner during the first Scottish Parliament election.

Irritated by repeated media reference to his political proximity to former Scottish Secretary and right-winger, Michael Forsyth, McLetchie set out once in the Parliament to give the Conservatives a moderate centre-right voice distinct from William Hague's populist agenda. He sought to show his independence of London with policies such as backing for government providing free personal care for the elderly, though there was discomfort within the party at such a statist policy. Under pressure from some MSPs to back more fiscal powers for the Parliament to bring about a more mature responsibility in its spending, he appeared sympathetic but could only achieve a consensus in London with the fudge of arguing for a royal commission to look into the issue.

During the first term, McLetchie faced a tough job in handling his own party, trying to convince them of the need to work within a Parliament they had strongly opposed, and which many continued to dislike after it was up and running. The leader's appeals were as much to his core vote to say it was important to have a voice in the new legislature, as it was to reach out to other voters. There was also skirmishing between MSPs and within the party at large, partly exploiting McLetchie's natural reticence and sometimes insecurity, which could make it difficult for him to crack the whip as leader. In the Parliament chamber, he used his legal skills and sharp wit to notable effect in unsettling First Ministers, and exposing Henry McLeish's evasions in particular. With John Swinney pulling his punches as McLeish stumbled over his constituency office expenses, McLetchie saw the opportunity to land the punches which were credited with felling the First Minister.

McLetchie also sought to pressure political opponents over the handling of the Holyrood building project, but found that public anger at the overspend was being reflected back on Tories as much as other MSPs. Although the party held Ayr, which it had won in a 2000 by-election, and gained Galloway and Upper Nithsdale as well as Edinburgh Pentlands, its total number of seats remained unchanged at 18 in the 2003 election.

McLetchie was widowed in 1995, and later remarried. His leisure pursuits include golf and regular attendance at Tynecastle as an enthusiastic supporter of Hearts.

MP

LYNDA CLARK was born in Dundee in 1949 and elected to Edinburgh Pentlands in 1997, ousting then Foreign Secretary Malcolm Rifkind. Educated at Lawside Academy, Dundee, St Andrews University and Edinburgh University where she obtained her PhD. Clark was a tutor and lecturer at Dundee University from 1971-76, and a practising advocate from 1977. She became one of Scotland's first female QCs in 1989, and was called to the English Bar in 1990. She was a member of the Scottish Legal Aid Board from 1991-94. Clark joined the Labour Party at the relatively late age of 34, unsuccessfully contesting North East Fife in 1992, after winning Edinburgh Pentlands in 1997, she took on the newly-created post of Advocate-General for Scotland in May 1999, the first woman law officer in Scotland.

There were rumours at points that she was unhappy with the life of a Scottish Labour Westminster MP and was considering standing down at the 2001 election, but she stood again and saw off Rifkind. She returned to the same job, overseeing Scottish legal affairs and occasional devolution issues from Whitehall's point of view, shifting in 2003 from the Scotland Office to the new Department of Constitutional Affairs, and working under Lord Falconer. This continued to involve a strange ritual of monthly questions lasting around five minutes, celebrated in the Commons for how little she gives away. The left-wing *Red Pepper* summed up her disdainful style by saying 'she mouths Blairite cliches with the passion of a senior QC'. She announced in early 2004, to the surprise of no one, that she would not stand again in the next general election.

Edinburgh South

Predecessor Constituencies: none.

Socio-economic Indicators:

Constituency Pop. (16–64)	54,726
Claimant Count (May 2003)	1.7% (45.9% below average)
IBA/SDA Claimants	5.7%
Life Expectancy – Male	75.3 (1.9 yrs above average)
Life Expectancy – Female	79.5 (0.8 yrs above average)
Owner Occupied	69.3%
Social Rented	13.9%
Average Property Prices	£126,749 (1st)
Average Gross Income	£30,952 (6th)
Low Birthweight Babies	127 (5.5%)
Teenage Pregnancy Rates	405 (3.5%)
No. of Lone Parent Households	2,539 (7.6%)

2003 Scottish Parliament Election

Electorate: 60,366   *Turnout*: 31,196 (51.7%)   *Turnout 1999*: 62.6%

Candidate	Party	Votes	Votes%	99 %	Change%
Michael Pringle	Lib Dem	10,005	32.1	22.3	+ 9.7
Angus MacKay	Labour	9,847	31.6	37.1	− 5.5
Geoffrey Buchan	Con	5,180	16.6	15.9	+ 0.7
Alexander Orr	SNP	4,396	14.1	23.5	− 9.4
Shirley Gibb	SSP	1,768	5.7	(other 1.2)	–

Lib Dem majority: 158 (0.5%)   *Swing*: 7.6% Labour to Lib Dem

2001 General Election

Electorate: 64,437   *Turnout*: 37,166 (57.7%)

Candidate	Party	Votes	Votes%	Change%
Nigel Griffiths	Labour	15,671	42.2	− 4.7
Marilyne MacLaren	Lib Dem	10,172	27.4	+ 9.7
Geoffrey Buchan	Con	6,172	16.6	− 4.7
Heather Williams	SNP	3,683	9.9	− 3.0
Colin Fox	SSP	933	2.5	–
Margaret Hendry	LCA	535	1.4	–

Labour majority: 5,499 (14.8%)   *Swing*: 7.2% Labour to Lib Dem

1945–97 Westminster

	Lab%	Con%	SNP%	Lib%	Other%	Turnout%
1997	46.8	21.3	12.9	17.6	1.3	71.8
1992	41.5	31.2	12.8	13.4	0.2	72.7
1987	37.7	33.8	5.1	22.5	0.9	75.7
1983	28.6	36.8	5.0	28.6	1.0	71.1
1979	34.3	39.7	8.4	16.4	1.2	77.3
1974O	28.2	35.9	21.7	14.2	–	74.2
1974F	27.6	41.7	12.8	17.9	–	80.8
1970	36.5	48.2	6.9	8.4	–	74.1
1966	39.5	53.2	7.3	–	–	77.6
1964	33.7	53.2	–	13.1	–	80.3
1959	28.5	57.6	–	13.9	–	81.2
1957B	30.9	45.6	–	23.5	–	65.8
1955	32.5	67.5	–	–	–	77.2
1951	27.4	72.6	–	–	–	81.4
1950	24.6	65.0	–	10.6	–	82.1
1945	29.2	70.8	–	–	–	66.4

Edinburgh South combines some of the most prestigious, sought after and exclusive areas found anywhere in urban Scotland. Neighbourhoods such as Morningside, Merchiston and Newington are home to the Scottish establishment from the private sector finance houses, to the civil service, legal profession and the city's universities. Average property prices are the highest house prices in Scotland – 87.9 per cent above the average, and rose 108.9 per cent in the 1990s. The constituency also contains post-war council estates such as Gilmerton and Liberton.

Edinburgh South contains the new Royal Infirmary of Edinburgh which opened in 2002 after being financed by a controversial £184 million private finance deal. The hospital, with 869 beds includes a range of state of the art facilities, including a biomedical research facility. However, embarrassingly for such a high profile project, there have been major problems with electricity supplies, a lack of ventilation and insufficient capacity. Opponents of public–private partnerships are concerned about these shortcomings, at the profits private contractors have made from the project, and about the out of town location.

In 2002, Lothian Primary Care Trust put on hold plans to sell Ashley Ainslie Hospital's northern grounds to allow for the development of a new secondary school. The southern part of the hospital's grounds will be used to develop a new hospital complex to replace the dilapidated buildings they currently inhabit. The council is planning extra investment in schools including turning Liberton School into a 'smart school', while, due to growth, there is over-crowding at the high-acheiving Boroughmuir High and James Gillespie's.

On first appearance, Edinburgh South looks like it should be a rock-solid Conservative seat. William Darling was Conservative MP from 1945-57 securing 70.8 per cent of the vote in 1945 and 72.6 per cent in 1951, representing the area until his resignation in 1957. He was followed by Michael Clark Hutchison who won a by-election in May 1957 and represented the seat until 1979. Gradually, his majority was whittled away until in October 1974 it was reduced to a mere 3,226 over Labour. Michael Ancram was elected for the first time in 1979, defeating a young Gordon Brown when Labour managed a 1.1 per cent swing from the Conservatives, reducing Ancram's majority to 2,460. Ancram held on in 1983 with an increased majority of 3,665 over the Liberal-SDP Alliance, before Nigel Griffiths jumped from third place, putting 5,500 on Labour's vote to seize the seat in 1987 with a majority of 1,859. In 1992, although a bad year for Labour and a relatively good year for the Conservatives in Scotland, Struan Stevenson could not win back any support and Labour held on, comfortably increasing its majority to 4,176. In May 1997 Nigel Griffiths increased Labour's vote by 4,500, while the Conservatives' fell by nearly 5,000 leaving Labour with an impressive majority of 11,452. In 2001 Griffiths' majority was slashed from to 5,499 on a 7 per cent swing from Labour to the Liberal Democrats and the Lib Dems moved from third to second.

In the 1999 Scottish Parliament election, Angus MacKay held on easily for Labour, despite seeing the party vote fall by 6,000. The SNP, energised by a strong campaign by Nationalist hero Margo MacDonald, emerged from nowhere, put on an extra 3,500 votes and 10.6 per cent, rising from fourth to second place, 5,424 votes behind Labour. The Liberal Democrats' Mike Pringle, then a popular local councillor, gained 1,000 votes after improving the Lib Dems' standing significantly in 1997. This left the Conservatives in a seat they had held until the previous decade reduced to fourth place and their vote reduced by 3,000 from 1997. At the 2003 elections, the Lib Dems' Mike Pringle – standing for the third time in Edinburgh South – finally overcame Labour's majority – jumping from third place to win by 158 votes. The extent to which the Margo MacDonald effect had helped Pringle is unclear – given she had been a popular SNP candidate in 1999, and her departure from the Nationalists and independent list candidature made Pringle the main challenger to Labour. The regional list voting gave Labour 19.7 per cent to Lib Dems 16.8 per cent and Greens 16.8 per cent – all within 1,000 votes of each other. The Conservatives won 15 per cent, MacDonald 12.3 per cent – her highest vote in the Lothian seat – the SNP 9.9 per cent and SSP 5.1 per cent.

Boundary changes at Westminster will see a new, enlarged Edinburgh South emerge which will lose Gilmerton and Newington, retain Morningside, and gain Colinton from Pentlands and Dalry from Central. This would, on current voting intentions, be a seat in which both the Conservatives and Liberal Democrats would think they stood a good chance of winning, yet past voting analysis suggests Labour would win. Edinburgh politics will be keenly contested, particularly between Labout and Lib Dem, and especially in this part of the capital.

MSP

MIKE PRINGLE was born in 1945 in Northern Rhodesia (now Zambia) where his father was a mining engineer, and was educated at Edinburgh Academy and Napier College. He qualified through the Scottish Institute of Bankers, and worked in Barclay's Bank in London and then moved to Edinburgh to work with the Royal Bank of Scotland from 1966-72. He set up his own business, TMM Ltd, wholesaling takeaway food under the name Munchies, and then a bakery business called Flour Power. He left that in 1992, when he became a councillor.

Pringle joined the Social Democrat Party in 1982 and was elected an Edinburgh district councillor from 1992-96, then to Lothian Region from 1994-6. He was a member of the unitary Edinburgh Council from 1995 until 2003, all that time being party group spokesman on sport and recreation. His preferred sport is rugby and he is a Hearts supporter, though his participation in sport is limited as a result of polio, which means he can usually be seen with a walking stick. He is also a collector of wine. He stood for the Edinburgh South seat at Westminster in 1997 and again in 1999 for the Scottish Parliament. At the top of the Lib Dems' regional list for Lothian in 2003, he stood a reasonable chance of taking the place vacated by the retiring Sir David Steel. A constituency victory over Labour astonished him about as much as anyone, and meant that no Lib Dem was elected from the Lothian list.

Following the 2003 election, he gained a place on the justice 2 and subordinate legislation committee and was made group spokesperson on equal opportunities while deputy spokesperson on justice.

MP

NIGEL GRIFFITHS was born in 1955 in Glasgow and has represented Edinburgh South since 1987, when he defeated Tory Michael Ancram (later to become MP for Devizes). Educated at Hawick High School, Edinburgh University and Moray College of Education, he has worked in a variety of advice and welfare rights posts, including a spell from 1979-87 as information and welfare rights officer of the North Edinburgh Action Group for people with disabilities.

Griffiths was an Edinburgh District councillor from 1980-87 and was chair of the housing committee, a member of Edinburgh Council of Social Services from 1984-87 and Edinburgh Health Council from 1982-87. A committed devolutionist without ever being on the nationalist wing of the party, Griffiths was secretary of Lothian Devolution Campaign in the 1979 referendum and a member of the cross-party Scottish Constitutional Convention, convening its finance committee.

After his 1987 election to the Commons, he was a Labour whip for two years, then spokesman on consumer affairs from 1989-97. The job suited him as one who had been inspired by the father of American consumer campaigning, Ralph Nader, and Griffiths specialised in energetically calling for the Conservative Government to hold lots of inquiries. Seen as an ally of Gordon Brown in opposition – *The Times* once said he was 'willing to carry Brown's bags through the gates of hell' – he was part of the Shadow Chancellor's charm offensive to win over business to New Labour, and in 1997 he became consumer affairs minister in the Department of Trade and Industry. However, he found the adjustment to office difficult, and suffered from poor relations with officials. A week before the first Blair reshuffle in July 1998, he was railing against 'a civil service coup' to get him sacked. Whether or not there was, his attack on them sealed his fate and he promptly lost his job. He then became a member of the Public Accounts Committee from 1999-2001. With the continued mentoring of Brown, he was one of those to whom Blair gave a second chance after the 2001 election, returning as small business and export controls minister, taking in the construction industry in 2003.

While he had problems with newspaper attacks on how he handled his own constituency expenses – owning his own office and charging the Commons for rent – the construction job apparently qualified him to comment unfavourably on the Scottish Parliament's handling of the Holyrood building project. This was partly to raise his profile after the loss of Edinburgh South constituency to the Lib Dems in the Scottish Parliament, as he busied himself with putting in defences for the next Westminster election. He also criticised the control Lib Dem ministers had over enterprise and transport briefs in the Scottish Cabinet, attacking his opponents' record in local government as 'very poor'.

Edinburgh West

Predecessor Constituencies: none.

Socio-economic Indicators:

Constituency Pop. (16-64)	49,790
Claimant Count (May 2003)	2.0% (36.1% below average)
IBA/SDA Claimants	5.3%
Life Expectancy – Male	75.8 (2.4 yrs above average)
Life Expectancy – Female	81.1 (2.4 yrs above average)
Owner Occupied	77.7%
Social Rented	15.2%
Average Property Prices	£100,130 (6th)
Average Gross Income	£32,139 (2nd)
Low Birthweight Babies	105 (4.5%)
Teenage Pregnancy Rates	389 (3.6%)
No. of Lone Parent Households	2,979 (8.8%)

CAB Enquiries

Issue	No. of cases	Percentage of total cases (%)
1. Benefits	928	25.5
2. Consumer	688	18.9
3. Employment	512	14.1
4. Other	445	12.2
5. Housing	393	10.8

2003 Scottish Parliament Election

Electorate: 60,136   *Turnout*: 33,301 (55.4%)   *Turnout 1999*: 67.3

Candidate	Party	Votes	Votes%	99 %	Change%
Margaret Smith	Lib Dem	14,434	43.3	36.5	+ 6.9
James Douglas-Hamilton	Con	8,520	25.6	25.4	+ 0.1
Carol Fox	Labour	5,046	15.2	21.3	− 6.2
Alyn Smith	SNP	4,133	12.4	16.8	− 4.4
Patricia Smith	SSP	983	3.0	–	–
Bruce Skivington	SPA	175	0.5	–	–

Liberal Democrat majority: 5,914 (17.8%)   *Swing*: 2.3% Conservative to Liberal Democrat

2001 Genral Election

Electorate: 62,503   *Turnout*: 39,478 (63.2%)

Candidate	Party	Votes	Votes%	Change%
John Barrett	Lib Dem	16,719	42.4	- 0.9
Elspeth Alexandra	Labour	9,130	23.1	+ 4.3
Iain Whyte	Con	8,894	22.5	- 5.5
Alyn Smith	SNP	4,047	10.3	+ 1.4
Bill Scott	SSP	688	1.7	-

Liberal Democrat majority: 7,589 (19.2%)   *Swing*: 2.6% Lib Dem to Labour

1945–97 Westminster

	Lab%	Con%	SNP%	Lib%	Other%	Turnout%
1997	18.8	28.0	8.8	43.2	1.2	77.9
1992	18.0	37.0	8.4	35.2	1.3	82.7
1987	22.2	37.4	5.6	34.9	–	79.3
1983	20.1	38.2	4.6	37.1	–	75.0
1979	28.2	45.4	9.2	17.2	–	77.8
1974O	25.2	38.2	20.2	16.4	–	76.6
1974F	24.4	44.2	9.9	21.5	–	82.2
1970	35.8	49.2	6.8	8.2	–	75.0
1966	39.0	48.2	–	12.8	–	78.7
1964	35.3	50.6	–	14.1	–	80.9
1959	30.5	56.5	–	13.0	–	80.3
1955	33.0	67.0	–	–	–	75.7
1951	34.0	66.0	–	–	–	83.1
1950	32.0	60.0	–	8.0	–	82.2
1945	44.9	47.3	–	7.8	–	67.5

Edinburgh West sits on the outskirts of the capital containing some of the finest areas of the Edinburgh middle classes and commuter towns outside the city. Its boundaries include Corstorphine, Cramond, Barnton and Blackhall, all highly exclusive and expensive. The slumbering, picturesque town of South Queensferry, on the Firth of Forth between the Forth Road and Rail Bridges, is also in West, having previously been in Linlithgow; Edinburgh Airport, is now also in West as with the villages of Ratho and Kirkliston. The seat also includes the run-down council estate of Muirhouse with major economic, crime and drug problems, which provided the setting for part of Irvine Welsh's cult hit *Trainspotting*.

The seat has 77.7 per cent owner occupation – the third highest in the country. Average property prices are 48.4 per cent above the average, and increased by 75.4 per cent in 1991-2001. The work of the local Citizens Advice Bureau, based in Pilton, reflects the poverty issues in the area – with benefit enquiries significantly ahead of consumer issues, and the number of debt enquiries, at 9.4 per cent, the highest of any Edinburgh CAB.

Edinburgh West, like most of the city, has seen major economic growth and numerous developments in recent years. One of the largest has been the massive business park and shopping complex in the South Gyle. There are improved rail links between the city centre and the Gyle, while the Scottish Executive is considering a major new rail hub at the airport.

Major housing developments are also a characteristic of this seat as Edinburgh's population grows, with Miller Homes planning a new estate near Corstorphine. The Royal High School, one of the most respected and successful state schools, has most of its catchment area in the seat, and this has a major effect on house prices. Edinburgh City Council recognises the increasing demands on services in the area, and is planning investment in Gylemuir Primary School and Queensferry High School.

It is not surprising that the seat is a Conservative-Liberal Democrat battleground. Edinburgh West was Liberal until 1929, then briefly won by Labour in that year, before turning to the Conservatives in 1931. Ian Clark Hutchison was Conservative MP from a by-election in 1941 until 1959, holding it over Labour by only 1,054 votes in 1945. However, as Labour's star waned in the seat in the affluent 1950s, the Conservative vote increased to a high of 67 per cent in 1955. James Stodart was MP from 1957 until October 1974 and was followed by Lord James Douglas-Hamilton, who was first elected with a majority of 5,202 over Labour in October 1974.

Post-1979, on three occasions, Douglas-Hamilton survived by narrow margins. In 1983 his majority fell from 7,351 to 498, rising to 1,234 in 1987 against the Liberal-SDP's Derek King. In 1992, Donald Gorrie, who had first stood as Liberal candidate in the seat in 1970, reduced the majority to 879. In 1997, he finally triumphed, despite boundary changes helping the Tories. Gorrie beat Lord James with a Liberal Democrat majority of 7,253 – polling 5,000 extra votes and seeing the Conservative support drop by 6,500. In June 2001, John Barrett succeeded Donald Gorrie as the Liberal Democrat candidate and increased his majority slightly to 7,589 on a reduced turnout, as Labour moved from third to second.

The 1999 Scottish Parliament elections were a good measure of the strength of the Lib Dems' support in terms of party versus Donald Gorrie's personal vote. Margaret Smith, an able, energetic councillor, had beaten Gorrie for the Lib Dems' nomination and held the seat with little difficulty. On a lower turnout, the Lib Dem vote fell by 5,000 and the Conservatives' by 3,000, producing a Lib Dem majority of 4,583. In the May 2003 election, Smith increased her majority to 5,914 and her vote share by 7 per cent. In the regional vote, the Lib Dems won 23.2 per cent to 21.9 per cent for the Conservatives, 15.7 per cent Labour, 11.4 per cent SNP, with 9.7 per cent for Margo MacDonald, 8.6 per cent Greens and 3.5 per cent SSP.

Boundary changes at Westminster see Edinburgh West divided between the new seats of Edinburgh West and Edinburgh North West. The new Edinburgh West will be very different in composition from the current seat, and will retain parts of Corstorphine, along with Queensferry and Kirkliston, while also gaining Balerno, Currie and Wester Hailes from Pentlands. Cramond and part of Corstorphine will go to the new North West seat. The new West seat will be a marginal one where both the Conservatives and Lib Dems have a decent chance, with the latter reckoned to be notional incumbents. The political contours of the existing West seat at the Scottish Parliament seem to suggest that the Lib Dems are well entrenched and have fortified their majority to the extent they can be confident of their ability to repel challengers.

MSP

MARGARET SMITH was born in 1961 in Edinburgh and educated at Broughton High School, Edinburgh, followed by Edinburgh University, where she graduated with an MA in general arts. She worked in pensions documentation in Guardian Royal Exchange from 1983-84, as an executive officer of Registers of Scotland (Land Register) from 1984-87, and then as Scottish officer of the United Nations Association from 1990-96. Elected to Edinburgh City Council in 1995, she was the Lib Dem spokesperson on transport from 1997-99. She became constituency organiser of Edinburgh West Lib Dems, in the run-up to the 1997 election and organised Donald Gorrie's winning campaign. She then surprisingly defeated Gorrie for the Lib Dem nomination for the Scottish Parliament, forcing him to seek an MSP seat on the Central Scotland list, which he did successfully,.

Smith took a high profile role as convenor of the health and community care committee throughout the first Parliamentary term, dealing with such controversies as the MMR (mumps, measles and rubella) vaccine, and leading the unanimous report which was influential in recommending Scotland should have free personal care for the elderly. At first, its findings were rejected, but after First Minister Henry McLeish indicated that might be revisited, Smith urged Lib Dems to seize the opportunity and push for full implementation. Despite some Labour opposition, including that of health minister Susan Deacon, her committee helped swing the Parliament behind the report's main recommendations. Smith was appointed Lib Dem spokesperson on equal opportunities in November 2000-01, then reverting to the health and community care spokespersonship until the election. She was one of the less rebellious Lib Dem backbenchers, perhaps thinking she was in line for ministerial promotion. Only once did she vote against the Executive, in January 2003, when it sought to railroad new procedures on the closure of fire stations. Following the election, with no ministerial job forthcoming, she lost the profile of a major committee convenership, instead becoming deputy convener of equal opportunities, and her party's spokesperson on justice, with a committee place on justice 1. Her main hobby is golfing. Smith's private life caused a small tabloid sensation just after the May 2003 election, when she announced, some time after her marriage had broken up, that she had become the partner of another woman.

MP

JOHN BARRETT was born in Hobart, Australia in 1954, and educated at Forrester High School, Edinburgh, Telford College and Napier Polytechnic. His career interest is primarily in film, since 1985 running his own company making training videos, ABC Productions. He has also been a board member of the Edinburgh International Film Festival from 1995-2001, plus the promotion agency for Edinburgh as a screen location. He was a City of Edinburgh councillor from 1995-2001, serving as a result as a director of the council's EDI property development arm, and was also election agent in Donald Gorrie's successful run for Westminster in the Edinburgh West seat in 1997. He contested the Linlithgow seat in the Scottish Parliament in 1999, coming a distant fourth, then winning the nomination to replace Gorrie at Westminster, once Gorrie had opted to stay in his other, Central Scotland list seat in the Scottish Parliament. Once in the Commons, Barrett became international development spokesperson for the Liberal Democrats. That put him in an awkward position when his constituency was proposed as the site for a refugee seekers' centre. In that role, he spent a week in early 2003 living with his family off a Red Cross food parcel, to publicise the African food crisis.

Falkirk East

Predecessor Constituencies: none.

Socio-economic Indicators:

Constituency Pop. (16-64)	49,455
Claimant Count (May 2003)	3.0% (5.1% below average)
IBA/SDA Claimants	9.1%
Life Expectancy – Male	74.4 (1.0 yrs above average)
Life Expectancy – Female	78.4 (0.3 years below average)
Owner Occupied	61.9%
Social Rented	32.3%
Average Property Prices	£53,708 (50th)
Average Gross Income	£25,619 (35th)
Low Birthweight Babies	118 (5.0%)
Teenage Pregnancy Rates	416 (4.3%)
No. of Lone Parent Households	3,262 (10.1%)

CAB Enquiries

Issue	No. of cases	Percentage of total cases (%)
1. Benefits	3547	24.8
2. Consumer	2901	20.3
3. Other	2302	16.1
4. Employment	2122	14.9
5. Legal	1136	8.0

2003 Scottish Parliament Election

Electorate: 56,175   **Turnout:** 27,559 (49.1%)   *Turnout 1999:* 61.4%

Candidate	Party	Votes	Votes%	99 %	Change%
Cathy Peattie	Labour	14,235	51.7	44.7	+ 7.0
Keith Brown	SNP	7,576	27.5	32.9	– 5.4
Thomas Calvert	Con	2,720	9.9	9.7	+ 0.2
Karen Utting	Lib Dem	1,651	6.0	7.1	– 1.1
Mhari McAlpine	SSP	1,377	5.0	(other 5.7)	–

Labour majority: 6,659 (24.2%)   Swing: 6.2% SNP to Labour

2001 General Election

Electorate: 58,201   *Turnout*: 33,702 (57.9%)

Candidate	Party	Votes	Votes%	Change%
Michael Connarty	Labour	18,536	55.0	- 1.1
Isabel Hutton	SNP	7,824	23.2	- 0.7
Bill Stevenson	Con	3,252	9.6	- 4.4
Karen Utting	Lib Dem	2,992	8.9	+ 3.7
Tony Weir	SSP	725	2.2	-
Raymond Stead	Soc Lab	373	1.1	-

Labour majority: 10,712 (31.8%)   *Swing*: 0.2% Labour to SNP

1983–97 Westminster

	Lab%	Con%	SNP%	Lib%	Other%	Turnout%
1997	56.1	14.0	23.9	5.2	0.8	73.2
1992	46.1	20.7	26.2	6.9	–	76.9
1987	54.2	18.7	15.4	11.7	–	74.8
1983	47.7	21.0	11.9	18.5	0.9	72.3

Falkirk East's socio-economic profile makes it marginally the better off of the two seats bearing the Falkirk name, although it does not include any part of Falkirk itself. Instead, this constituency is centred on the towns of Grangemouth, Bo'ness, Carron, Polmont and Stenhousemuir. The seat also contains some middle-class commuter areas such as Polmont which is located on the Edinburgh-Glasgow railway line. Average property prices are 20.4 per cent below the national average, but increased 46.4 per cent in the 1990s.

The Grangemouth area is a major petrochemical complex dominated by BP's oil refinery visible for miles which provides a particularly spectacular site at night. Other employers include BP Chemicals, Zeneca, Avecia and GE Plastics. There have been recent job losses at the BP refinery at Grangemouth – a result of their merger with Amoco – as well as local concerns raised by local MP Michael Connarty, about health issues connected with the plant.

Public–private partnerships have been used to develop new local facilities such as Polmont High School and for the rebuilding of Bo'ness Academy. There are widespread public concerns about health services being centralised in Stirling to the detriment of Falkirk, including the proposed down-grading of Falkirk Royal Infirmary. A major feat of modern engineering and one of the biggest visitor attractions in the country is the Falkirk Wheel – which links the Forth and Clyde Canal with the Union Canal. This is an £84.5 million British Waterways Millennium Link project which provides a coast-to-coast connection for the first time in Scotland in 70 years.

This seat has been through numerous boundary changes before the creation of Falkirk East. The Stirling and Falkirk Burghs seat (for full results see Stirling) elected Joseph Westwood from 1935 until his death in July 1948, during which time he served as Clement Attlee's first Secretary of State for Scotland. Harry Ewing became MP for the seat in a September 1971 by-election, despite a strong SNP challenge. For the February 1974 election, Grangemouth was added to the seat and the constituency's name.

Falkirk East was established in 1983 from parts of the old Stirling, Falkirk and Grangemouth seat and Stirlingshire East. The former seat's MP, Harry Ewing, stood for Labour in the new seat and secured a 10,061 majority over the Conservatives. Four years later, Ewing increased his majority to 14,023 over the Tories with 54 per cent of the vote. In 1992, Ewing announced his retirement and Michael Connarty was selected Labour candidate, becoming MP with a 7,969 majority over the SNP who surged into second place increasing their vote by 10.8 per cent.

In 1997 Connarty achieved a majority of 13,385. The 8.2 per cent swing from the SNP was indicative not only of the Labour landslide of that year, but also of the boundary changes in the seat. In the June 2001 election, Michael Connarty was easily re-elected with his majority cut from 13,385 to 10,712 – his percentage lead unchanged on a lower turnout – as Labour's vote fell by 5,000.

In the 1999 Scottish Parliament elections, the SNP recovered some support from 1997, gaining a 10.2 swing from Labour. However, this was not enough to stop Cathy Peattie securing the seat with a majority of 4,139. In the May 2003 election Peattie increased her majority over the SNP to 6,659, as Labour's vote rose by 7 per cent. In the regional list vote, Labour won 39.7 per cent to 25.6 per cent for the SNP, while the Greens won 5.2 per cent, Scottish Senior Citizens 5 per cent and SSP 4.2 per cent.

Boundary changes for Westminster will reduce the number of Falkirk seats from two to one, with parts of the existing Falkirk East seat joined with Linlithgow constituencies. Falkirk East in its short history has proven a safe Labour seat – with the party at Westminster securing over half the popular vote in three of the five contests, as well as the most recent Scottish Parliament election. The SNP has had hopes in this area, and polled decently in 1999, but their chances of over-turning Labour's majority here must be seen as medium to longer-term aspirations, and conditional on a major change in both parties' fortunes at a national level.

MSP

CATHY PEATTIE was born in 1951. She was educated at Moray Secondary School, Grangemouth, and had a number of occupations before becoming an MSP: she was a shop and factory worker from 1966-69, a training supervisor for the Scottish Pre-School Playgroup Association from 1970-75, field worker and training officer with the association from 1986-90, and then a development worker with the Volunteer Network in Falkirk. She was a community development worker and then manager of the Community Outreach organisation from 1991-93 and director of Falkirk Voluntary Action Resource Centre from 1993-99. She was also convenor of the Council of Voluntary Service Scotland, and remains chair of Linked Work Training Trust-Central as well as the Falkirk Women's Technology Centre. Peattie joined the Labour Party in 1974 and was a chair of the Scottish Labour women's committee, in addition to serving on the party's Scottish executive committee.

She started out the first Parliament on the rural affairs committee until December 2000 and became deputy convener of the education, culture and sport committee until the 2003 election. There she wrote a report on the issue of rural schools, many of which were coming under closure pressure. She also sat on the equal opportunities committee, as one of the leading Labour women driving the domestic abuse issue up the political agenda. As a well-known singer on the traditional singing and Burns circuit, she was allowed to bend Parliamentary protocol and sing her way through part of a debate on the national bard. With that interest, she was convenor of the cross party groups on traditional arts, culture and the media, as well as a member of numerous other groups. And she sang solo at Donald Dewar's funeral in Glasgow in 2000, singing Robert Burns' 'Aye Walkin', at the request of the late First Minister's family.

When Patricia Ferguson stepped down from her role as Deputy Presiding Officer in November 2001, to become Parliament affairs minister, Cathy Peattie emerged as the choice of new First Minister Jack McConnell to fill the vacated post. However, his unchallenged run for the top post and a cull of former ministers had left Labour MSPs resentful of his expectation that they would support him in this private ballot as well, so sufficient numbers of them voted for Conservative Murray Tosh instead. It was a vote that reflected much more on McConnell's tactics than Peattie's popularity or suitability, though she responded bitterly afterwards that the vote smacked of a prejudice against working class women.

Peattie showed a slightly more rebellious streak in 2003, with an abstention on the fire station vote the Executive lost in January of that year, and as one of six to vote against the Government's position on Iraq in the second vote on the subject in March. In the second Parliament, Peattie was selected by Labour to be convener of the equal opportunities committee.

MP

MICHAEL CONNARTY was born in Coatbridge in 1947. He was educated at St Bartholomew's and St Patrick's High, Coatbridge, and is a graduate of Stirling University in economics, later studying at Glasgow University and Jordanhill teacher training college. He worked as a special needs teacher, as well as teaching economics and modern studies, from 1976-92. He was a councillor on Stirling District from 1974-90 and Labour leader from 1980-90 in one of the closest fought councils in Scotland. In that role, he was also chair of Stirling Economic Development Company from 1987-90. He stood against Michael Forsyth in Stirling in 1983 and then attempted to win the East Kilbride nomination, losing to Adam Ingram in 1985, standing and losing again in Stirling in 1987. He was also a founder member of the Labour Co-ordinating Committee in Scotland, and took one of the more difficult modernising decisions for Scottish Labour in 1985, when he chaired the working party which accepted the sale of council house sales.

First elected to Falkirk West in 1992, he was Parliamentary Private Secretary to Tom Clarke as culture minister from 1997-98 and served on the European directives committee from 1993-97. He was chair of the Scottish Parliamentary Labour group at Westminster from 1998-99, and sat on the information committee and the European scrutiny committee. Amid wide-ranging interests from jazz to the Philippines, he also became chair of the all-party group for chemical industries – a clear constituency interest given the complex at Grangemouth. Connarty is one of the more vocal and articulate backbench MPs through the media, not least on devolution matters, being quick to criticise MSPs for straying into reserved territory. Yet he was critical of the Scottish Executive over its abolition of Section 28/Clause 2A – a far cry from his days as a leading left-winger and his time as leader of Stirling Council, where he was at the forefront of pioneering radical policies on equal opportunities and women's issues. In his council days, he had been one for courting controversy, once refusing to organise a civic reception for the RAF, instead granting one to a visiting delegation from Communist East Germany. He was also an enthusiastic writer of socialist pamphlets through the 1980s, acknowledging the influence on his thinking from Italian revolutionary Antonio Gramsci.

At Westminster, he was one of those to vote against the third reading of the Maastricht Treaty in 1993, and was an early and consistent opponent of war in Iraq in 2002-03. He also voted against the Blair Government's proposals on foundation hospitals in England in May 2003 and again in July 2003 – one of only three Scottish Labour MPs to do so. He abstained on the issue later in the year, and was one of five Scottish Labour MPs to vote against student top-up fees in January 2004. In November 2003 he was behind moves to bring together Scottish charities and propose an alternative to the Home Office run Dungavel Detention Centre for asylum seekers. He had hoped to become an MSP, but was warned off when named in the press as one of those the selection panel was intending to veto as being unsuitable. He withdrew from his bid to move north, and did not appear to suffer any harm to his Westminster career.

Falkirk West

Predecessor Constituencies: none.

Socio-economic Indicators:

Constituency Pop. (16–64)	44,956
Claimant Count (May 2003)	3.4% (9.2% above average)
IBA/SDA Claimants	10.0%
Life Expectancy – Male	73.1 (0.3 yrs below average)
Life Expectancy – Female	78.4 (0.3 yrs below average)
Owner Occupied	58.7%
Social Rented	34.0%
Average Property Prices	£56,763 (43rd)
Average Gross Income	£25,552 (37th)
Low Birthweight Babies	135 (6.0%)
Teenage Pregnancy Rates	400 (4.8%)
No. of Lone Parent Households	3,235 (10.7%)

CAB Enquiries

Issue	No. of cases	Percentage of total cases (%)
1. Benefits	3112	22.4
2. Consumer	2835	20.4
3. Other	2526	18.2
4. Employment	2056	14.8
5. Housing	1093	7.9

2003 Scottish Parliament Election

Electorate: 52,122   *Turnout*: 26,400 (50.7%)   *Turnout 1999*: 64.0

Candidate	Party	Votes	Votes%	99 %	Change%
Dennis Canavan	Falkirk West	14,703	55.7	55.0	+ 0.7
Michael Matheson	SNP	4,703	17.8	17.8	=
Lee Whitehall	Labour	4,589	17.4	18.8	– 1.4
Ian Mitchell	Con	1,657	6.3	5.6	+ 0.6
Jacqueline Kelly	Lib Dem	748	2.8	2.8	=

Falkirk West majority: 10,000 (37.9%)   *Swing*: 0.3% SNP to Falkirk West

2001 General Election

Electorate: 54,100   *Turnout*: 30,891 (57.1%)

Candidate	Party	Votes	Votes%	Change%
Eric Joyce	Labour	16,022	51.9	– 7.5
David Kerr	SNP	7,490	24.3	+ 0.8
Simon Murray	Con	2,321	7.5	– 4.6
Hugh O'Donnell	Lib Dem	2,203	7.1	+ 2.0
William Buchanan	Ind	1,464	4.7	–
Mhari McAlpine	SSP	707	2.3	–
Hugh Lynch	Ind	490	1.6	–
Ronnie Forbes	Soc Lab	194	0.6	–

Labour majority: 8,532 (27.6%)   *Swing*: 4.2% Labour to SNP

1983–2000 Westminster

	Lab%	Con%	SNP%	Lib%	Other%	Turnout%
2000B	43.5	8.3	39.9	3.2	5.1	36.2
1997	59.4	12.1	23.4	5.1	–	72.6
1992	49.8	19.6	24.3	6.3	–	76.8
1987	53.2	17.6	16.5	12.7	–	76.6
1983	45.6	21.0	13.0	20.4	–	74.0

Falkirk West contains the bulk of the town of Falkirk, along with the small towns of Denny, Larbert and Bonnybridge – the latter holding the proud title of Scotland's UFO capital. It is the poorer relation of the two seats which carry the Falkirk name. Average property prices are 15.8 per cent below the national average and rose 61.5 per cent in 1991-2001. A large number of Falkirk West's constituents are employed in the Grangemouth petrochemical complex, including BP's oil refinery.

Falkirk Council has undertaken a number of PPP ventures to invest and modernise in public services including the redevelopment of Larbert High School and opening of Carrongrange Special School. There are also concerns about Forth Valley NHS Trust's centralisation of services including the loss of acute surgical services at Falkirk Royal Infirmary to Stirling, while Falkirk gained maternity services.

Falkirk shares with Glasgow, Edinburgh and Dundee, the honour of having two teams in the Scottish Football League: Falkirk and East Stirlingshire. A national controversy erupted in 2003 when Falkirk Football Club, which had won the Scottish First Division, was prevented from promotion by the Scottish Premier League's rules. Falkirk took the SPL to court to challenge the decision, based on the rule requiring all Premier clubs to have 10,000 all-seated stadiums, claiming that they met this. Their established ground, Brockville, in the centre of Falkirk, did not meet these standards, but the team had entered into a ground sharing scheme with Airdrie to use their stadium for one year, while a new stadium was being built. Falkirk's appeal failed, with many left wondering what were the consequences of success and failure with Falkirk denied promotion and the bottom club in the Premier, Motherwell, saved from relegation.

Prior to its recent controversies, Falkirk West enjoyed a fairly undistinguished past as a safe Labour seat. Both the Falkirk seats were created in 1983, from the remains of the old Stirling, Falkirk and Grangemouth seat and in West's case, Stirlingshire West (see Stirling for results). Stirlingshire West first elected a Labour MP in 1922 and was continuously Labour from 1935. Thomas Johnston won the seat for Labour in 1929, lost it in 1931, and represented the area from 1935-45, rising to the position of Secretary of State for Scotland from 1941-45 in Churchill's wartime coalition. Dennis Canavan was selected Labour candidate for the October 1974 election, defeating Donald Dewar for the Labour nomination, a result which left a bitter taste and animosity which was to come back to haunt Labour twenty-five years later. Canavan only held the seat in the subsequent general election by the margin of 367 votes over the Nationalists, but this was to prove the high-water mark of the SNP's advance in this seat.

In the first election for Falkirk West in 1983 Canavan was elected Labour MP with an 8,978 majority over the Conservatives, and in 1987 he saw his majority rise to 13,552 with 53 per cent of the vote. In 1992, Canavan's majority fell to 9,812 as the SNP moved into second place as their vote rose by 8 per cent. Four years later, the normal patterns of Falkirk West Labour dominance continued, as Canavan was re-elected with a 13,783 majority over the Nationalists. This was not the sort of seat to excite much attention from commentators or psephologists.

However, everything changed in the period between the election of a Labour Government and the establishment of a Scottish Parliament. In those elections, it was the seat in which the Labour vote fell the furthest in the whole of Scotland, albeit in unique circumstances. The reason for this was the selection battle between the Labour Party hierarchy and the local CLP over the ability of the sitting Westminster MP, Dennis Canavan, to stand as Labour's candidate in 1999. Canavan had built up a substantial majority, was popular within his constituency and local party, but had developed a reputation as a maverick left-winger at Westminster. Definitely 'off-message' within New Labour and prone to acts of rebellion in the division lobbies at Westminster, Canavan was a candidate the Labour leadership did not want. So he stood as an independent at the Scottish election in 1999: appearing as MP for Falkirk West on the ballot paper, his subsequent victory was overwhelming and a humiliation for Labour. Significantly, Canavan not only swept his constituency but polled extremely well in the regional list for Central Scotland with 9,000 more votes than he achieved in the constituency.

He remained as a dual mandate member from his election in May 1999 until the end of 2000. During this period he had the power to cause a troublesome Westminster by-election for Labour at a time of his choosing. He did so in October 2000, and Labour delayed the vote until the week before Christmas: the first such Yuletide Scottish by-election since Inverness in 1954. In the event, Labour held the seat by the narrow margin of 705, a much less emphatic margin than had been widely predicted. The party's vote fell by 14,000 from 1997 on a turnout reduced by half, while the SNP's vote fell by over 1,000. In percentage terms, the party's vote fell 15.8 per cent, substantially more than in Glasgow Anniesland, but nowhere near the drastic fall of Hamilton South, while the SNP's increase of 16.5 per cent was a remarkable comeback after the Anniesland by-election results. The Scottish Socialists polled a respectable 5.07 per cent – their fourth saved deposit in five contests – signalling that they had become a permanent fixture on the Scottish political landscape.

In the June 2001 Westminster election Eric Joyce was re-elected with a much more comfortable majority of 8,532 over the Nationalists – though this still represented a significant fall from four years previously – with Labour's vote down 6,500 and 7.5 per cent. At the Scottish Parliament election of May 2003, Canavan was elected for the second time as an independent – winning a 10,000 majority over the SNP who moved into second place over Labour. In the regional vote, with 'the Canavan effect' removed – Labour finished on 40.7 per cent, ahead of the SNP on 24.6 per cent, Conservatives on 9 per cent, Scottish Senior Citizens 6.1 per cent, Lib Dems 5.8 per cent, Greens 5.2 per cent and SSP 4.8 per cent. Boundary changes for future Westminster seats see the number of Falkirk seats reduced from two to one, largely made up of Falkirk West.

MSP

DENNIS CANAVAN was MP for Stirlingshire West from October 1974 until 1983 and then became the member for Falkirk West. He was born in Cowdenbeath in 1942, educated at St Columba's High School, Cowdenbeath, and graduated from Edinburgh University, after which he became a maths teacher. He taught at St Modan's in Stirling from 1970–74 and was then assistant head of Holy Rood High School in Edinburgh. He was a councillor in Stirling from 1973–74 and became Labour group leader in 1974, before his election to Parliament later that year. At Westminster, Canavan was a member of the foreign affairs select committee from 1982-97 and then the international development select committee from 1997-99. In the Scottish Parliament, this specialism in international affairs was continued as he became a member of the European committee during both the first and second Parliaments.

He has long been a keen devolutionist, and seen as being on the nationalist and left wing of Labour. But he was also seen as independent-minded, and the Labour leadership in Glasgow and London decreed that such people were to be blocked from representing the party in the new Parliament. In early 1998, some MPs were dissuaded from putting themselves forward as candidates for the Scottish Parliament, some withdrew when it became clear they would be blocked, but Canavan pushed until he was rejected from the approved list. Before standing as an Independent, Canavan conducted a ballot of Falkirk West Constituency Labour Party and 95 per cent of party members wanted him to be able to stand as the Labour candidate. Like Mayor Ken Livingstone in London, he has found out that there is a blossoming life outside Labour; independence has only enhanced, rather than diminished him, he has assured for himself cast iron credentials as a community politician on the left, and he seems a safe bet for election to Falkirk West for as long as he wishes to stand.

On the second day of the Parliament in 1999, Canavan put himself forward as a candidate for First Minister, gaining three votes. After Donald's Dewar's election to the post, Canavan strode across the floor of the Parliament and shook hands with the new premier, much to the latter's obvious discomfort, and showing the Falkirk MSP's sense of Parliament as a place for theatre, more often demonstrated with a grandly delivered, passionate speech or a point of order carrying just the right amount of indignation.

A bizarre chain of events eventually led to Canavan resigning his Westminster seat. In October 2000, he announced his intention to resign his seat and force a Westminster by-election on Labour. However, events took an unexpected turn following Donald Dewar's death that month. In the subsequent election for a First Minister, Canavan stood again and won the same three votes, but engaged in a series of respectful asides with then winner Henry McLeish. Within weeks, after behind-the-scenes negotiations, Canavan called off his threat to force a by-election and re-applied to join the Labour Party. Two weeks later in November, Canavan announced he had changed his mind and was not re-applying to Labour, instead bringing a difficult by-election on them. The reason he gave was that he had found 'additional information' on why he was excluded from the list of approved candidates for the Scottish Parliament. A plausible reason could also have been that Canavan was genuinely shocked by many voters' reaction to his intention to rejoin Labour, which was one of regret and feeling let down at losing one of the few independent voices in the Parliament. Whatever the reasons in this strange chapter of events, Canavan emerged from it slightly diminished.

The first Parliament was not easy for Canavan. Although he worked with Tommy Sheridan and Robin Harper, the two lone representatives for the Socialist and Green parties, he was effectively shut out by the larger party whips' use of the committee system. He retained his support base in Falkirk, as shown by his majority in 2003, and ran a national campaign for pensioners of the Scottish Transport Group, stopping the Treasury from taking £126 million surplus out of it, and putting down successful amendments to the land reform legislation, to extend access to the Queen's estates.

Just after his 2003 re-election, he vociferously championed the cause of the town's football club believing it deserved promotion to the Scottish Premier League for winning the First Division. This formed the central theme of his speech in a fourth bid for First Ministership – becoming something of a tradition of pointlessness, this one even less successful than its predecessors. His life outside politics includes enthusiasm for his constituency's junior football clubs and running, while parenting his fourth child, Adam, born in May 2002, when his father was 59.

MP

ERIC JOYCE was born in 1960 in Perth and educated at Perth High School, Perth Academy, Perth FE College and Stirling University, where he did a BA in religious studies. He then did a teacher training degree at the West London Institute, qualifying as an RE teacher, and went on to do a masters degree at Bath University and an MBA at Keele University. He was a soldier in the Black Watch regiment from 1978-81 and an officer from 1987-99, much of that time spent at the Royal Military Academy, Sandhurst. He left military service in 1998, having fallen out with his superiors and being threatened with a court martial for writing a Fabian pamphlet – *Arms And The Man: Renewing The Armed Forces* – which criticised sexism, racism and class discrimination in the British military. He spent a year from 1999-2000 as a public affairs officer with the Commission for Racial Equality.

Joyce made it to Labour's panel of approved candidates for the Scottish Parliament in 1998, from 2004 as its deputy chair, and was a list candidate for Central Scotland. He has been a member of the Fabian Society executive since 1998 and was also editor of the Fabian pamphlet *Now's The Hour: New Thinking For Holyrood*.

He is a Blairite moderniser and an arch-Labour anti-nationalist who sees the SNP as an irrelevance in post-devolution politics. Having a short fuse and a sharp tongue, he criticised the writer Yasmin Alibhai-Brown in November 2000 for her 'superficial and confused analysis' which excluded other black voices in the media. In the 2000 by-election campaign, Joyce presented himself as an independent voice, emphasising his criticisms of the army and bringing attention to trouble at school when aged 15 for violent behaviour. In return, the SNP sought to rattle him with use of his Major title.

He became a member of the Scottish affairs select committee which looked into the Scottish media and came out strongly against the idea of an integrated BBC *Scottish Six* programme. With Tony Blair's build-up to war in Iraq, no backbench MP was more assiduous in supporting his leader in public debates and television studios, and he was repeatedly put up as a defender of the Government, even though not a member of it, throughout the Hutton inquiry when ministers were observing a period of media silence on its proceedings. In the aftermath of Hutton as the Blair Government reluctantly agreed to an inquiry into the intelligence services belief Iraq had Weapons of Mass Destruction, the integrity of the Prime Minister was more and more questioned by country and party. Joyce in these circumstances seemed to relish the unevenness of the fight and revel in using his military background. In his single-minded fanaticism and willingness to defend the indefensible he had something in common with true believer Thatcherite MPs who argued in 1990 that their heroine should go down in flames fighting in some kind of Wagnerian tragedy. The *Guardian* column 'Smallweed' commented that the only thing worse than the increasing tendency of the Government to refuse to put anyone up for *Today* or *Newsnight* was to put up Eric Joyce to defend it, noting his 'queasy green' facial colour and that he appeared 'as out of his depth as a kipper in a thunderstorm.' Roy Hattersley called him 'an embarrassing sycophant', emblematic of the decline of party politics, while Jon Snow once asked him on *Channel Four News*: 'Is there anything that the Government has done with which you disagree?'

He also took it upon himself to lead a campaign against Glasgow Kelvin MP and maverick George Galloway, criticising his opposition to the Labour leadership's stand on Iraq and accusing him of using Labour as 'a flag of convenience'. That culminated in Galloway's expulsion from the party. Having signalled his ambition with unabashed clarity, he took his first step on the Commons career ladder in 2003 by being made Parliamentary Private Secretary in the Foreign Office.

Fife Central

Predecessor Constituencies: Fife West (1945–70).

Socio-economic Indicators:

Constituency Pop. (16-64)	48,102
Claimant Count (May 2003)	4.8% (54.5% above average)
IBA/SDA Claimants	11.1%
Life Expectancy – Male	73.6 (0.2 yrs above average)
Life Expectancy – Female	78.7 (national average)
Owner Occupied	61.4%
Social Rented	31.2%
Average Property Prices	£43,841 (68th)
Average Gross Income	£23,487 (57th)
Low Birthweight Babies	146 (6.0%)
Teenage Pregnancy Rates	612 (5.8%)
No. of Lone Parent Households	3,657 (11.4%)

2003 Scottish Parliament Election

Electorate: 57,633   *Turnout*: 25,597 (44.4%)   *Turnout 1999*: 55.8%

Candidate	Party	Votes	Votes%	99 %	Change%
Christine May	Labour	10,591	41.4	57.3	– 15.9
Tricia Marwick	SNP	7,829	30.6	30.9	– 0.3
Andrew Rodger	Ind	2,258	8.8	–	–
Malcolm North	Con	1,803	7.0	5.8	+ 1.2
Elizabeth Riches	Lib Dem	1,725	6.7	5.9	+ 0.8
Morag Balfour	SSP	1,391	5.4	–	–

Labour majority: 2,762 (10.8%)   *Swing*: 7.8% Labour to SNP

2001 General Election

Electorate: 59,597   *Turnout*: 32,512 (54.6%)

Candidate	Party	Votes	Votes%	Change%
John MacDougall	Labour	18,310	56.3	– 2.3
David Alexander	SNP	8,235	25.3	+ 0.3
Elizabeth Riches	Lib Dem	2,775	8.5	+ 2.1
Jeremy Balfour	Con	2,351	7.2	– 1.8
Morag Balfour	SSP	841	2.6	–

Labour majority: 10,075 (31.0%)   *Swing*: 1.3% Labour to SNP

1945–97 Westminster

	Lab%	Con%	SNP%	Lib%	Other%	Turnout%
1997	58.7	9.0	25.0	6.4	0.9	69.9
1992	50.4	17.6	25.1	6.9	–	74.3
1987	53.4	16.7	14.7	15.2	–	76.2
1983	43.1	22.5	10.2	23.4	0.8	72.5
1979	58.0	20.2	19.3	–	2.5	77.4
1974O	51.9	12.3	33.4	–	2.4	73.9
1974F	53.3	19.8	22.5	–	4.4	79.2
1970	61.6	26.2	11.0	–	1.7	74.3
1966	63.0	19.3	14.1	–	3.6	76.8
1964	65.6	27.0	–	–	7.4	78.6
1959	56.2	24.7	–	–	19.1	81.3
1955	62.6	24.8	–	–	12.6	80.3
1951	64.9	24.6	–	–	10.5	85.5
1950	54.8	23.6	–	–	21.6	84.9
1945	37.7	20.6	–	–	42.1	75.4

Fife Central is based around the New Town of Glenrothes, established in 1948. It also includes smaller towns such as Buckhaven, Leslie, Leven, Markinch, Methil and Windygates. Parts of the old Fife coal mining industry and community are here, and in 2002 Longannet, Scotland's last deep coalmine whose seams go far underneath the Firth of Forth flooded and closed with the loss of over 500 jobs. Mining has always carried with it a sense of folklore and memory, and this loss had shockwaves across Scotland about the passing of an old industrial age, but the Fife economy has dramatically changed. Methil is the site of Kvaerner's oil fabrication yard, while Raytheon Defence Company are situated in Glenrothes, and Diageo have one of their largest and most successful plants in Leven. There have also been job losses in newer areas including Mitsubishi cutting its workforce at Glenrothes and ADC, a US telecommunications company, reversing a decision to establish its European operations in the area.

The biggest political issue in the last few years was the 'Officegate' scandal which saw the resignation of Henry McLeish as First Minister, then as local MSP. It centred on the financial arrangements and sub-letting by McLeish of his local constituency office in Glenrothes and the shady arrangements between the Labour Party, trade unions, local council and sympathetic businesses. McLeish came out of it a diminished, even broken man, whose competence was more in question than his honesty. Fife Council itself did not emerge unscathed although the first report into the matter found no major issues of concern. Many observers saw the 'Officegate' affair as having wider repercussions – revealing the secret Labour networks which govern so much of Scotland.

Willie Gallacher was MP for the seat, known as Fife West, from 1935-50 winning it in 1935 with a 593 majority over Labour – and being the only case in British politics of a Communist gain from the Unionists. He held on with a 2,056 majority over Labour in 1945, but as the Cold War began the Communists retreated and Gallacher was defeated in February 1950 by 13,445 by the Labour candidate, Willie Hamilton, who became a famous republican. This was the first of eleven Hamilton victories – with Labour easily holding out against the rise of the SNP in 1974 when the seat became Fife Central, and in 1979 winning a majority of 18,022 over the Conservatives in second place.

In 1983 boundary changes saw a majorly reconfigured Fife Central lose most of the old Fife coalfields to Dunfermline East, but Hamilton was still re-elected for what turned out to be the last time with a

7,794 majority over the Liberal–SDP Alliance. A young-left wing leader of Fife Regional Council called Henry McLeish had stood against Hamilton, for the Fife Central Labour nomination prior to the 1983 election and narrowly lost by 22 votes to 14. This encouraged Hamilton not to stand again in 1987 and McLeish won the seat with his majority doubled to 15,709 over the Conservatives. In 1992 McLeish was re-elected with a reduced majority of 10,578 over the SNP's Tricia Marwick as the Nationalist vote increased 10.3 per cent.

Five years later boundary changes saw the seat take in parts of the outskirts of Kirkcaldy and in the May 1997 Labour landslide, McLeish won with a 13,713 lead over Marwick. The Conservative candidate Jacob Rees-Mogg, son of William Rees-Mogg, a former editor of *The Times* was driven round the seat by his old nanny in a Rolls Royce and saw the Tory vote halved. In the May 1999 Scottish Parliament election, the third and final McLeish–Marwick contest saw Labour's lead fall to a still comfortable majority of 8,675 – as Labour polled an impressive 57 per cent and the SNP a creditable 31 per cent in second place.

In June 2001 Fife Central continued as a safe Labour seat as John MacDougall took over as Labour candidate for Westminster from Henry McLeish, elected with a majority of 10,075 as Labour's vote slipped by 5,000 and 2 per cent. 'Officegate' then brought down McLeish as First Minister and his retirement at the next election as an MSP. Christine May, leader of the local council, did not emerge unscathed from the episode and only narrowly won the Labour nomination. Labour faced the 2003 Scottish Parliament contest in Fife Central with trepidation, while the SNP's Tricia Marwick thought she had a chance of seizing the seat. In the end, Labour had a dismal result, but held on. The Labour vote fell by over 5,000 and 16 per cent, as the SNP could not capitalise on the situation with their vote falling 2,000 and remaining unchanged in percentage terms. Labour's majority fell from 8,675 to an uncomfortable 2,762 over the SNP, and Labour must hope that its most difficult years are behind it in this seat. In the regional vote, Labour won 38.9 per cent to the SNP's 27.7 per cent, while the SSP won 5.2 per cent and the Greens 3.8 per cent.

Boundary changes for Westminster do not alter the basics of this seat which is to be renamed Glenrothes. This is rock solid Labour terrain at Westminster, but at the Scottish Parliament, things are slightly more in doubt. The SNP has slowly built up a presence in this seat, and achieved solid second places in 1999 and 2003, but the fact it could not seize the opportunity offered by 'Officegate' points to their inability to make the final challenge.

MSP

CHRISTINE MAY was born in Dublin in 1948, and educated at Presentation Convent and St Mary's College of Catering, both in the Irish capital, qualifying with a diploma in institutional management. She worked in catering management in Dublin and London 1968-81, latterly for the Inner London Education Authority where she met her husband, and they moved to Kirkcaldy in 1984 when he got a job with Fife Regional Council. She took a family career break, and was a lecturer at Fife College from 1987-96, teaching public sector finance and management.

She joined the Labour Party at the late age of 39 in 1987, and was elected to Kirkcaldy District Council the next year, becoming leader of the council from 1993-96. Elected to the unitary Fife Council in 1995, she was deputy leader until 1998, and leader from 1998-2003. She was European affairs spokeperson for COSLA, with a special interest in structural funds, and was a member of the EU Committee of the Regions from 1997-2003, specialising in equality issues. She was also a bit of a Labour quangocrat as a member of the boards of Scottish Homes 1997-2003 as it wound up and became Communities Scotland, of Scottish Enterprise from 1998-2003, of the Kingdom of Fife Tourist Board

1996-2003 and of the Rosyth 2000 Initiative, from 1998–2003. That experience should help with her intention on entering Parliament in 2003 to focus on economic issues, and particularly ensuring public sector bodies work better together.

She was next in line to become an MEP as the fourth person on Labour's 1999 European elections list for Scotland, if Labour's David Martin had been successful in his bid to move to the Scottish Parliament, replacing Sam Galbraith, or to Westminster, if he had won the Midlothian nomination. But after tussles within the Labour Party, Martin stayed in Brussels, and so did May in Fife.

She had her own tussle to win the Central Fife nomination, after Henry McLeish declared he would not stand for re-election. Following the office expenses scandal that led to his resignation, there was a long-running police inquiry, which led eventually to no charges being brought. But while it was active, the executive of Scottish Labour refused to endorse his nomination, leading him to stand down at the 2003 election. The Labour candidacy was hard fought, with Donald Dewar's former spin doctor, David Whitton, coming within two votes of winning it. May was said by opponents to be damaged by evidence from an official inquiry that she had gone too far in trying to help McLeish through his troubles.

After the 2003 election, she took a place on the enterprise and culture committee as well as subordinate legislation. Being an experienced council leader, an effective networker and confident in Parliament as well as the media, she is one of the new intake more likely to make it to ministerial office.

MP

JOHN MacDOUGALL was born in 1947 in Dunfermline and educated at Rosyth Dockyard Technical College, followed by Glenrothes College and Fife Technical College, with qualifications in industrial management. He was a boilermaker from 1964 to 1978, and a full-time shop-steward from 1978-93, including time at Methil oilrig yard and at Rosyth dockyard. He left that job when council duties became full time. He was a councillor on Fife Regional Council from 1982-2001, rising through the ranks to become convener of the Region and unitary Fife Council from 1987-2001. He was leader of the controlling Labour group on COSLA in 1991-92, chairman of the East of Scotland European Consortium from 1993-96 and a bureau member of the Assembly of the European Regions in 1992, when he was also a member of the Scottish Constitutional Convention through his COSLA role.

With 14 years convening the council in what was a Labour fiefdom, he was naturally a serious contender in the hard-fought race to fill Henry McLeish's vacancy when the then First Minister was required to stand down from Westminster to concentrate (as he wrongly thought he would be doing) on the Scottish Parliament. However, this vintage car enthusiast had a formidable opponent in Alex Rowley, a former leader of Fife Region and then general secretary of the Scottish Labour Party, who had won that party job as Gordon Brown's man in head office, but who was quickly sidelined and sacked immediately after the 1999 election. Brown's efforts to have him installed in Fife Central were seen as his means of compensating Rowley, but it was telling that the Chancellor could not deliver such a vote in his own Fife backyard. MacDougall won the candidacy in May 2000, and once elected an MP, he took places on the Commons services, consolidation of bills and regulatory reform committees. He was unusual in signing an early day motion against war in Iraq in March 2002, and then voting with the government on its Iraq strategy a year later.

Fife North East

Predecessor Constituencies: Fife East (1945–79)

Socio-economic Indicators:

Constituency Pop. (16-64)	48,174
Claimant Count (May 2003)	1.7% (46.0% below average)
IBA/SDA Claimants	4.6%
Life Expectancy – Male	77.6 (4.2 yrs above average)
Life Expectancy – Female	82.3 (3.6 yrs above average)
Owner Occupied	69.2%
Social Rented	16.1%
Average Property Prices	£83,573 (11th)
Average Gross Income	£27,625 (17th)
Low Birthweight Babies	71 (3.9%)
Teenage Pregnancy Rates	263 (2.4%)
No. of Lone Parent Households	2,405 (7.7%)

2003 Scottish Parliament Election

Electorate: 58,695   *Turnout*: 29,282 (49.9%)   *Turnout 1999*: 59.0%

Candidate	Party	Votes	Votes%	99 %	Change%
Iain Smith	Lib Dem	13,479	46.0	37.8	+ 8.2
Ted Brocklebank	Con	8,424	28.8	23.7	+ 5.0
Capre Ross-Williams	SNP	3,660	12.5	17.7	– 5.2
Gregor Roynton	Labour	2,353	8.0	14.4	– 6.4
Carlo Morelli	SSP	1,366	4.7	(other 6.4)	–

Liberal Democrat majority: 5,055 (17.3%)   *Swing*: 1.6% Conservative to Liberal Democrat

2001 General Election

Electorate: 61,900   *Turnout*: 34,692 (56.0%)

Candidate	Party	Votes	Votes%	Change%
Menzies Campbell	Lib Dem	17,926	51.7	+ 0.5
Mike Scott-Hayward	Con	8,190	23.6	– 2.9
Claire Brennan	Labour	3,950	11.4	+ 1.1
Kris Murray-Browne	SNP	3,596	10.4	– 0.5
Keith White	SSP	610	1.8	–
Leslie Von Goetz	LCA	420	1.2	–

Liberal Democrat majority: 9,736 (28.1%)   *Swing*: 1.7% Conservative to Liberal Democrat

1945–97 Westminster

	Lab%	Con%	SNP%	Lib%	Other%	Turnout%
1997	10.3	26.5	10.9	51.2	1.2	71.2
1992	5.5	38.5	8.6	46.4	–	77.8
1987	7.4	41.2	6.6	44.8	–	76.2
1983	6.5	46.1	6.6	40.2	0.7	73.7
1979	19.9	43.0	14.1	23.0	–	79.0
1974O	16.9	38.8	31.7	12.6	–	73.7
1974F	15.0	47.9	19.5	17.6	–	78.8
1970	24.6	54.6	11.8	9.0	–	74.5
1966	24.6	51.5	14.4	9.5	–	76.1
1964	25.2	54.2	6.8	13.1	0.7	77.8
1961B	26.4	47.5	–	26.1	–	67.3
1959	30.1	69.9	–	–	–	75.2
1955	29.4	70.6	–	–	–	73.2
1951	29.4	70.6	–	–	–	78.7
1950	26.5	63.7	–	9.8	–	81.6
1945	30.6	69.4	–	–	–	70.8

Fife North East contains the ancient town of St Andrews, the coastal towns of Anstruther, Crail and Pittenweem, as well as the inland market towns of Auchtermuchty, Cupar and Falkland. This is country which has always been markedly different from the rest of the kingdom of Fife – the four other seats in the county are Labour-voting, industrial, urban areas, also shaped to different degrees by the legacy of mining, either directly or indirectly. Fife North East – covering the North Sea coast of the county between the Firths of Tay and Forth is shaped by farming, fishing, tourism and golf. Its profile underlines that this is one of the most prosperous parts of Scotland. Both male and females life expectancy rates are the highest in the county and the constituency also has the second lowest teenage pregnancy rate in Scotland after Orkney. Average property prices are 23.9 per cent above the national average and increased by 61 per cent in the 1990s.

St Andrews University – the oldest in Scotland – is a major attraction for English public school children who either cannot get into Oxbridge or prefer something different. The St Andrews Sloane image won a significant boost when in 2001, Prince William decided to come to the university. St Andrews is also the world home of golf and its Royal and Ancient Golf Club is the world authority for the game, with the exception of the US and Canada. St Andrews was a little surprised in 2003 when the *Idler* magazine in its guide to 'crap towns' rated it the seventh most awful place in the United Kingdom, partly on the grounds that it was stuffed with 'nauseating toffs'.

RAF Leuchers is a major employer and was given a huge boost in 1999 when the Ministry of Defence announced that the base was to become one of three UK bases to site the Eurofighter Typhoon jet, and three years later in 2002 it was decided that it would become home of the 56 (Reserve) Squadron, bringing with it 500 new jobs.

There are several other small towns and areas in the constituency including Auchtermuchty – childhood home of the legendary Proclaimers; Cupar; Falkland and its palace; Freuchie which has a notably successful village cricket team, and the villages of Newport and Tayport, nestling in on the Tay and sitting opposite Dundee. The East Neuk of Fife, which is the south-east extremity of the Fife coastline – 'neuk' meaning promontory – contains the picturesque seaside towns of Crail, Pittenweem and Anstruther and was voted in 2001 the most popular location for people wanting to buy a second home. This has had all kinds of knock-on consequences concerning affordable housing for local people in what has traditionally been an area with low incomes, but low costs.

This constituency was known as Fife East up until the 1979 election, and has had a long, glorious Liberal history. Henry Asquith held it from 1886 to 1918, sitting for the seat while he was Prime Minister from 1908-16. Asquith lost the seat in the 'coupon' election of 1918 which saw the beginning of the inter-war decline of the Liberals, losing to Colonel Sprot. The Liberals won the seat several times in the 1920s, but in 1931 the Liberal MP stood for the National Liberals – supporters of the Conservatives – and was returned. He died two years later and in the February 1933 by-election James Henderson Stewart won the seat easily for the Liberals with the novelist Eric Linklater standing for the National Party of Scotland.

Henderson-Stewart held the seat until his death in September 1961, and at the subsequent by-election John Gilmour was elected despite the Conservative vote falling by over 20 per cent. The Labour Party just managed to hold second place, despite a strong Liberal challenge. The Labour candidate was a young Glasgow University graduate standing for the first time called John Smith. He and Donald Dewar were seen as eager, right-wingers looking for seats and were named 'the seatseekers' by older Labour hands. Smith was to be the first of several Labour hopefuls who went on to higher things standing in the seat – others included Helen Liddell in October 1974 and Henry McLeish in 1979.

When John Gilmour won the seat in October 1974 he did so with a majority of 2,914, with the Liberals in fourth place, before retiring prior to the 1979 election. In the first contest between the Conservative Barry Henderson and Liberal Menzies Campbell in 1979, the Conservatives won with a majority of 9,355, but Campbell emerged in second place increasing the Liberal vote by 10.3 per cent. In 1983, with the seat now renamed Fife North East, Henderson's majority fell to 2,185 as Campbell put 14 per cent on the Liberal vote compared to 1979. Finally, in 1987 in the third contest between the two men, Menzies Campbell won the seat when he defeated Henderson with a majority of 1,447. In 1992, Campbell increased his majority to 3,308 over the Conservatives' Mary Scanlon, later to be an MSP.

In the May 1997 general election, Menzies Campbell was re-elected with a 10,356 majority over the Conservatives, with more than half of the vote, and the Conservatives reduced to just over a quarter. At the June 2001 election, Campbell's majority fell back slightly to 9,736 – increasing in percentage terms on a lower turnout. The Lib Dems vote rose to the highest Lib Dem share in the constituency, while the Conservatives fell back even further.

The first Scottish Parliament election of May 1999 showed the strength and resilience of the Lib Dems and weakness of the Conservatives. Iain Smith standing for the Lib Dems was elected on a smaller majority of 5,064 over the Conservatives, and saw the Lib Dems vote fall to 38 per cent – a decline of 13 per cent. However, the Conservatives could not make any inroads and their vote share fell back from 1997, with the SNP and Labour in third and fourth making gains.

The second Scottish Parliament election of May 2003 saw Smith re-elected with a 5,055 majority. Although the Lib Dems share of the vote recovered from four years previous, the Conservative vote share rose for the first time in the constituency in twenty years. In the regional vote list, the Lib Dems won 33.5 per cent to the Conservatives 24.1 per cent, while the Greens achieved an impressive 9 per cent and the SSP 4.4 per cent.

Fife North East already contains half of the acreage of the county of Fife, and is more populous than the rest of the Fife seats, and so is not radically altered in boundary changes for Westminster and looks set to remain a secure Lib Dem UK seat. The Liberals have turned the seat in less than twenty years into a formidable fortress where they now regularly poll over half the vote at Westminster and are near to similar levels at the Scottish Parliament. The Conservative decline has been steep and recent, before seeing a small recovery in 2003 – while they have a mere two seats on Fife Council. At future Scottish Parliament elections, Fife North East seems to have become a safe Liberal Democrat constituency, and one where the Conservatives have slipped too far to have any real hopes.

MSP

IAIN SMITH was born in 1960 in Gateside, near Cupar, and attended Bell Baxter High School, Cupar. He is a graduate of Newcastle University in politics and economics, and worked for Northumberland County Council in 1981. He became an advice worker and then manager at Bonnethill Advice Centre in Dundee from 1982-85 and was research assistant and agent for local MP Menzies Campbell, 1987-98, giving him a very strong knowledge of the party and support base, as that has by far the largest Lib Dem membership of any constituency in Scotland.

At the age of 22, he became a Fife Region councillor and secretary of the group, rising to the leadership of the main opposition group from 1995-99 on the unitary Fife Council – a period when Lib Dems were building their strength in the kingdom and poised to deny Labour the dominance it had long enjoyed. In 1998, his selection as a prospective candidate for the Scottish Parliament was the first of any party.

From the 1999 election to October 2000, he was deputy minister for Parliament as well as Liberal Democrat business manager and whip – a role in which he appeared to be unhappy and increasingly withdrawn, perhaps because he was encountering the hardball politics of his Cabinet boss Tom McCabe, Labour's chief whip and Parliament minister.

Smith would later accuse the Lanarkshire MSP of spreading rumours about his private life, saying private conversations and emails turned up in the *Daily Record* during the Section 28 controversy. He was removed from his ministerial post in 2000, partly due to dissatisfaction amongst party colleagues over his role in reforms to the committee system, which were introduced that December, and in which McCabe appeared to have done a deal with SNP business manager Mike Russell without Smith's involvement. Smith was appointed Lib Dem spokesman on local government in November 2000, and joined the local government committee of the Scottish Parliament in January 2001, arguing the party's case for voting reform. He introduced and steered through a new law allowing St Andrews University to offer an expanded range of courses in its school of medicine, linking that to improved local health services with the claim it would attract highly qualified doctors to work in North East Fife while studying for their medical degrees.

Smith was also chair of the Lib Dem's Westminster general election campaign in Scotland during 2000-01. Following the 2003 election, he became convener of the procedures committee while party spokesperson and committee member on local government and transport.

MP

MENZIES CAMPBELL was born in 1941 in Glasgow. He was educated at Hillhead High School, Glasgow, gained an MA and LLB from Glasgow University in the same era as Donald Dewar, David Steel, Neil McCormick and George Reid. He also studied at Stanford in the USA. He was an advocate from 1968, working as an advocate depute in the Crown Office from 1977-80 and becoming a QC in 1982. Campbell also distinguished himself as a sportsman, competing in the 100 metres at the Tokyo Olympics in 1964 and the Commonwealth Games in Jamaica in 1966. He was the UK athletics captain in 1965-66.

His politics took root in being 'captivated' by party leader Jo Grimond at the time of the Suez crisis. He was active in Liberal politics as a student and, at the invitation of new Borders MP David Steel, his activism was sparked once more in opposing the South African rugby tour of Scotland in 1970. He stood in Greenock and Port Glasgow in both 1974 elections, and was chair of the Scottish Liberals from 1975-77. He then stood in North East Fife in 1979 and 1983 before winning it in 1987. Since then, he has been a party spokesperson on arts, broadcasting and sport, Scottish legal affairs in the run-up to devolution, and defence and foreign affairs after 1999. He was a member of the trade and industry select committee from 1990-92 and the defence select committee from 1992-99.

It is on defence and foreign affairs that he built a strong reputation, being one of those likely to enter government if Tony Blair's would-be pact with Paddy Ashdown had come to fruition. Campbell was one of those confidantes closest to Ashdown through the period of that planning, and had one of five Lib Dem seats on Whitehall's joint cabinet committee in which the party sought common ground with the Labour Government from 1997-2001. Campbell was considered as a possible contender to succeed Ashdown in 2000, but although not particularly close to Charles Kennedy, he chose not to make it two Scots fighting for the post. He was later made deputy leader. With Blair fighting wars in Bosnia, Afghanistan and Iraq, Campbell developed a reputation as a wise counsel in the nation's broadcast studios, continuing to make regular appearances throughout 2003 even throughout his successful battle against lymph cancer. At the end of that year, he was knighted and, given a positive report by his doctors, he put himself forward for the next Westminster election.

Galloway and Upper Nithsdale

Predecessor Constituencies: Galloway (1945–79).

Socio-economic Indicators:

Constituency Pop. (16-64)	40,706
Claimant Count (May 2003)	2.9% (6.4% below average)
IBA/SDA Claimants	8.9%
Life Expectancy – Male	75.4 (2.0 yrs above average)
Life Expectancy – Female	79.4 (0.7 yrs above average)
Owner Occupied	61.6%
Social Rented	20.9%
Average Property Prices	£59,766 (37th)
Average Gross Income	£21,896 (68th)
Low Birthweight Babies	98 (5.7%)
Teenage Pregnancy Rates	382 (4.8%)
No. of Lone Parent Households	2,246 (7.7%)

CAB Enquiries

Issue	No. of cases	Percentage of total cases (%)
1. Benefits	7829	44.5
2. Consumer	2255	12.8
3. Employment	2081	11.8
4. Housing	1914	10.9
5. Other	1159	6.6

2003 Scottish Parliament Election

Electorate: 51,651   *Turnout*: 29,635 (57.4%)   *Turnout 1999*: 66.6%

Candidate	Party	Votes	Votes%	99 %	Change%
Alex Fergusson	Con	11,332	38.2	30.2	+ 8.0
Alasdair Morgan	SNP	11,233	37.9	39.3	– 1.4
Norma Hart	Labour	4,299	14.5	20.4	– 5.9
Neil Wallace	Lib Dem	1,847	6.2	10.1	– 3.9
Jocelyne Cherkaoui	SSP	709	2.4	–	–
Graham Brockhouse	SPA	215	0.7	–	–

Conservative majority: 99 (0.3%)   *Swing*: 4.7% SNP to Conservative

2001 General Election

Electorate: 53,254   *Turnout*: 35,914 (67.4%)

Candidate	Party	Votes	Votes%	Change%
Peter Duncan	Con	12,222	34.0	+ 3.5
Malcolm Fleming	SNP	12,148	33.8	−10.1
Thomas Sloan	Labour	7,258	20.2	+ 3.9
Neil Wallace	Lib Dem	3,698	10.3	+ 3.9
Andy Harvey	SSP	588	1.6	–

Conservative majority: 74 (0.2%)   *Swing*: 6.8% SNP to Conservative

1945–97 Westminster

	Lab%	Con%	SNP%	Lib%	Other%	Turnout%
1997	16.3	30.5	43.9	6.4	2.9	79.7
1992	13.0	42.0	36.4	8.6	–	81.7
1987	12.9	40.4	31.5	14.6	0.6	76.8
1983	11.4	44.7	30.8	13.1	–	75.8
1979	8.5	45.9	37.1	8.5	–	81.2
1974O	9.0	40.2	40.3	10.5	–	77.1
1974F	10.2	43.9	30.6	15.3	–	77.8
1970	20.3	50.4	20.5	8.8	–	72.0
1966	38.0	62.0	–	–	–	66.6
1964	23.2	52.8	–	24.0	–	73.8
1959	20.4	56.2	–	23.4	–	75.6
1959B	23.9	50.4	–	25.7	–	72.7
1955	33.1	66.9	–	–	–	69.1
1951	26.3	61.7	–	12.0	–	75.6
1950	34.4	65.6	–	–	–	63.0
1945	35.3	24.0	–	–	40.7	69.9

Galloway and Upper Nithsdale – the sixth biggest seat in the UK in land area – is positioned in the South West of Scotland, to the south of Carrick, Cumnock and Doon Valley and to the west of Dumfries. It combines the old Scottish counties of Kirkcudbrightshire and Wigtown which had their own councils up until the 1974 local government reorganisation. The seat, along with neighbouring Dumfries, was one of two Scottish parliamentary seats directly affected by the foot and mouth outbreak. This had knock-on effects on the tourist industry, vitally important in the area.

There are a number of small, attractive towns in the constituency including Castle Douglas, Newton Stewart and Whithorn. Many have a cultural flavour - Wigtown is Scotland's national book town which contains two dozen bookshops, and Kirkcudbright has a sizeable artistic community. The Isle of Whithorn is a small fishing village that suffered the loss of the Solway Harvester and is recognised as 'the cradle' of Christianity in Scotland where St Ninian settled in the 5th century. A movie watershed occurred in the constituency in 1973 when the cult film *The Wicker Man*, starring Edward Woodward and Britt Ekland, was filmed here. Based on the mythical Summerisle, it focused on the paganism of its local inhabitants. Scenes were filmed in Kircudbright's narrow wynds and lanes, while the spectacular ending where Woodward, a naïve constable from the mainland, is offered as a sacrifice to the gods was shot overlooking the Isle of Whithorn.

Apart from its fragile economy, the big local issue is transport, with the A75 between Stranraer and Dumfries carrying heavy Northern Irish traffic, and in need of a substantial upgrade. Dumfries and Galloway Council's plan to close a number of village schools in places such as Glenkens and Stewartry have encountered widespread local opposition. There are also serious pressures on health services and in 2001 the lack of GP services was addressed by a new health centre being opened in Kirkconnel. Affordable housing is a major issue in this rural constituency, and Dumfries and Galloway's council tenants voted in favour of a Housing Stock Transfer which will see new investment but also brings concerns of higher rents. Average property prices are 11.4 per cent below the Scottish average and rose 47.1 per cent in the 1990s.

Galloway has a long tradition of Conservative representation and in the last three decades has seen a Conservative-SNP battle for supremacy, typical of much of rural Scotland. It was represented by the Liberal Colonel Dudgeon from 1925 to 1931, who defected to Oswald Mosley's New Party and stood in its colours in the 1931 election polling a mere 3 per cent. The winner was John Mackie for the Conservatives who held the seat in 1945 as an Independent Unionist against the official Conservatives with a 1,825 lead over Labour. He then had the Conservative whip restored in March 1948 and was returned as an official Conservative from 1950 until his death in December 1958. In the resulting by-election in April 1959, four months before the general election, Henry Brewis held the seat for the Conservatives with the Liberals displacing Labour in second place. In 1970 the SNP emerged as the main non-Conservative challenger, and in September 1974 Brewis announced his retirement. In the October 1974 general election, the Nationalists, standing for only the third time in the seat, broke through and took the seat – George Thompson winning it from the Conservatives Kenneth Ross by a mere 30 votes.

Galloway was the second most marginal SNP seat and Ian Lang won it back with a majority of 2,922 – one of seven SNP seats won back by the Conservatives in 1979. The SNP kept their vote at 30 per cent in 1983 when the seat became Galloway and Upper Nithsdale, and in 1987, clearly remaining the main challengers to the Tories. In 1992, Lang's majority was cut to 2,468 as the SNP's Matt Brown put 3,000 votes on his party's support.

In May 1997, the SNP's Alasdair Morgan increased his vote by a further 3,000, while the Conservatives fell by 3,000 giving the Nationalists a 5,624 lead. There was some evidence of tactical voting as Labour's vote increased by a mere 1,000 votes and by half the Scottish average. Morgan also stood for and easily held the Scottish Parliament seat in 1999 despite the SNP slipping back by 4,500. The Conservatives fell by 2,000 on a lower turnout to give an SNP lead of 3,201. Labour polled creditably in third place increasing their support by over 300 votes.

At the June 2001 UK election, the Conservatives won back the seat, their only Scottish victory at that election, after having failed to win a single constituency seat in the previous two elections – all their MSPs being elected by the list in 1999. Peter Duncan, capitalising on BSE, foot and mouth and the crisis in farming, saw the Conservative vote fall by 603 votes on a lower turnout – an increase of 3.5 per cent. Malcolm Fleming standing for the SNP for the first time in the seat saw the Nationalist vote fall, resulting in a Conservative victory by the narrowest of margins: a mere 74 votes.

Many Nationalists accredited their defeat with the standing down of their A-team at Westminster post-devolution, but this was proven not to be the case by the 2003 Scottish Parliament election. In the second Alasdair Morgan–Alex Fergusson contest, the Conservative vote fell by 600 and the SNP by 3,500 to produce a Conservative majority one-third larger than two years before: 99 votes.

In the regional vote, the Conservatives won 34.2 per cent to the Nationalists 29 per cent – a Conservative lead of 1,548 votes – with the Greens on 4.8 per cent and SSP on 3.3 per cent.

Boundary changes for Westminster see the town of Dumfries linked with Kirkcudbrightshire and Wigtownshire to form the seat of Dumfries and Galloway which will be one of the closest fought seats in Scotland, with past vote analysis suggesting Labour would squeeze past the Conservatives. The Conservatives have recovered from the depths of the unpopularity they experienced in 1997 and 1999, but their victories in 2001 and 2003 were recorded against a backdrop of the most beneficial local circumstances to their cause – allowing the party to portray itself as the defenders of the country way of life. At future Scottish Parliament elections, this seat will undoubtedly see the Conservatives and SNP fight it out for supremacy.

MSP

ALEX FERGUSSON was born in 1949 in Leswalt, Wigtownshire, and educated at Eton and the West of Scotland Agricultural College. He worked as a farm management consultant from 1970-71, and as a farmer from 1971-99, running a 1,500-acre family farm. He was also a restaurant owner from 1981-86 and president of the Blackface Sheepbreeders' Association until 1999.

Fergusson stood for the Conservatives in the Galloway and Upper Nithsdale constituency in 1999 and was elected from the South of Scotland regional list. Standing there again in 2003, he beat the SNP's Alasdair Morgan by only 99 votes, in one of the Tories' two constituency gains that night. In the first Parliament, he was at first his party's deputy spokesman for rural affairs with special responsibility for fisheries. In 2001, he became convener of the rural affairs committee in succession to Alex Johnstone, and after the most difficult period in that job, steering through the bill banning hunting with dogs. After the 2003 election, he became spokesman on agriculture and forestry, with a place on the standards committee. An avuncular Kirk elder in Girvan, he took pride in tabling the 1999 motion which set up the multi-faith time for reflection each week in the Parliament. He is an enthusiast for rugby, curling and country dancing. And having admitted in 1999 that his greatest weakness was eating too much food, a further notable achievements from his first term was a sponsored diet, making him considerably leaner than when he entered Parliament.

MP

PETER DUNCAN was born in Kilwinning in 1961 and educated at Ardrossan Academy and Birmingham University. He worked as a project manager with Mackay's furniture stores in 1985-88, then from 1988-98 was a director of his family's 180-year old textiles wholesale firm, John Duncan & Son, going freelance as a business consultant in 1998-2001. A strapping Ayrshireman, he has a down-to-earth and affable style unlike Lord Ian Lang, the patrician and often distant Conservative who lost the seat in 1997, and he worked the constituency hard to win it back from the SNP, focusing on local issues, the most prominent one being the foot and mouth outbreak which immediately preceded his election. Although never having been elected to anything before, he was helped by being up against an inexperienced young Nationalist candidate Malcolm Fleming, standing in place of Alasdair Morgan, who was standing down.

One of his first acts as an MP was to back Iain Duncan Smith from the start of the leadership contest, writing to the *Daily Telegraph* with 13 other Tory MPs to say the strongly Euro-sceptic Chingford MP could unite the party on Europe. Despite that backing and despite being the only Scottish Conservative MP, the new leadership of Iain Duncan Smith did not see Duncan appointed to the front bench team in 2001, with Scottish affairs going to Jacqui Lait, while Duncan was made her Parliamentary Private Secretary in July 2002. He also won a place on the Scottish affairs select committee, and declared in August 2001 that he would not be voting on English-only legislation, as his party's response to the West Lothian Question about unbalanced MP powers. As Duncan Smith's leadership tottered in the aftermath of the party's 2003 Annual Conference, he decided to publish a diary of possible future events imagining how the Lib Dems could replace the Conservatives as the main opposition to Labour before the next election. Whether this was a helpful contribution to his party's prospects is open to question, but the arrival of Michael Howard as Conservative leader in November 2003 saw Duncan become the shadow Secretary of State for Scotland. He was to the fore in attacks on Scottish Labour MPs for voting in support of foundation hospitals and top-up student fees for England alone, when a majority of English MPs voted against, making a positive case out of his self-denying ordinance.

Glasgow Anniesland

Predecessor Constituencies: Glasgow Partick (1945), Scotstoun (1950–70) and Garscadden (1974–92).

Socio-economic Indicators:

Constituency Pop. (16-64)	39,308
Claimant Count (May 2003)	4.6% (48.1% above average)
IBA/SDA Claimants	15.7%
Life Expectancy – Male	70.0 (3.4 yrs below average)
Life Expectancy – Female	76.1 (2.6 yrs below average)
Owner Occupied	53.8%
Social Rented	38.4%
Average Property Prices	£67,353 (24th)
Average Gross Income	£22,835 (61st)
Low Birthweight Babies	168 (8.2%)
Teenage Pregnancy Rates	447 (5.2%)
No. of Lone Parent Households	4,653 (15.8%)

CAB Enquiries

Issue	No. of cases	Percentage of total cases (%)
1. Benefits	1452	28.7
2. Consumer	1046	20.7
3. Employment	672	13.3
4. Housing	533	10.6
5. Other	446	8.8

2003 Scottish Parliament Election

Electorate: 50,807   *Turnout*: 22,165 (43.6%)   *Turnout 1999*: 52.4%

Candidate	Party	Votes	Votes%	99 %	Change%
Bill Butler	Labour	10,141	45.8	58.8	–13.1
Bill Kidd	SNP	3,888	17.5	20.2	– 2.7
Bill Aitken	Con	3,186	14.4	10.6	+ 3.7
Charlie McCarthy	SSP	2,620	11.8	3.5	+ 8.3
Robert Brown	Lib Dem	2,330	10.5	6.3 (other 0.5)	+ 4.2

Labour majority: 6,253 (28.2%)   *Swing*: 5.2 % Labour to SNP

2001 General Election

Electorate: 53,290   *Turnout*: 26,722 (50.1%)

Candidate	Party	Votes	Votes%	Change%
John Robertson	Labour	15,102	56.5	− 5.3
Grant Thoms	SNP	4,048	15.1	− 2.0
Christopher McGinty	Lib Dem	3,244	12.1	+ 4.9
Stewart Connell	Con	2,651	9.9	− 1.5
Charlie McCarthy	SSP	1,486	5.6	+ 2.9
Katherine McGavigan	Soc Lab	191	0.7	–

Labour majority: 11,054 (41.4%)   *Swing*: 1.7% Labour to SNP

1945–2000

Scottish Parliament

	Lab%	Con%	SNP%	Lib%	Other%	Turnout%
2000B	48.7	10.6	22.1	6.8	11.8	38.3
1999	58.8	10.7	20.2	6.3	4.0	52.4

Westminster

	Lab%	Con%	SNP%	Lib%	Other%	Turnout%
2000B	52.1	10.8	20.8	8.1	8.2	38.4
1997	61.8	11.5	17.1	7.2	2.4	64.0
1992	64.4	11.5	19.0	4.9	0.2	71.3
1987	67.7	10.7	12.2	3.4	–	71.4
1983	56.2	15.4	10.2	17.6	0.6	69.1
1979	61.5	21.8	15.7	–	1.0	73.2
1978B	45.4	18.5	32.9	–	3.2	69.1
1974O	50.9	12.9	31.2	5.0	–	70.8
1974F	52.3	24.3	21.8	–	1.6	74.1
1970	57.5	31.4	9.3	–	1.8	70.5
1966	61.8	32.8	–	–	5.4	74.3
1964	61.6	38.4	–	–	–	77.2
1959	53.7	46.3	–	–	–	81.8
1955	49.4	50.6	–	–	–	79.5
1951	49.3	50.7	–	–	–	85.1
1950B	47.3	50.8	–	–	1.9	73.7
1950	46.0	46.5	–	4.9	2.6	84.6
1945	48.4	51.6	–	–	–	69.0

Anniesland is dominated geographically, culturally and in population by the massive post-war council estate of Drumchapel built in the 1950s Macmillan housing boom, with smaller estates such as

Knightswood and Yoker alongside. It is the Drum which defines the seat – a community situated on Glasgow's north-west frontier cheek-to-cheek with Bearsden with whom it shares little in common: economic prosperity, opportunities and even life expectancy are dramatically different in the two areas.

Socio-economic indicators help illustrate the extent of disadvantage and poverty in parts of the constituency. Incapacity and disability benefits are the sixth highest in Scotland and over one-fifth of the working age population are reliant on benefits. Anniesland is 53.8 per cent owner occupied and 38.4 per cent socially rented. Average property prices are only 0.1 per cent below the Scottish average, and the second highest in the city, only beaten by Kelvin, reflecting the desirable parts of the West End in the seat (Jordanhill, Kelvindale) and rose 68.4 per cent in the 1990s. Low birthweight babies are the third highest in the country and lone parent households 0.4 per cent above the average. This is the fifth most unhealthy constituency in Britain – only beaten by four other Glasgow constituencies.

The diverse nature of this seat is also illustrated by the variety of its educational establishments. There is Anniesland College, a further education institution with a student population of 9,000, mostly young people from more deprived parts of the seat; Jordanhill College, the teacher training college which is now part of Strathclyde University; Jordanhill School, a grant-aided school is not under local authority control to which several Labour politicians have sent their children, causing political controversy, and the High School of Glasgow, a co-educational independent school with 960 pupils.

Significant local issues include the controversial Glasgow housing stock transfer. In April 2002, the city's 82,000 council households voted narrowly to transfer from the city council to a not-for-profit housing association, the Glasgow Housing Association. This has major implications for residents of the Drum and other council areas such as Knightswood, with promises of investment and fears of rent increases. Another issue has been Glasgow City Council's public-private partnership proposals for schools in the city, from which Jordanhill School, after extensive consultation with governors and parents, has remained 'opted out'.

One of the biggest employers in the area is the BAE Systems Marine shipyard in Scotstoun situated in the neighbouring seat of Kelvin. In July 2001, the government announced that three Type 45 destroyers (out of a total twelve) would be built on the Clyde. Combined with orders for three Astute class submarines and two landing ships announced in the previous year, the future of the yards and its 1,200 jobs are safe for the next ten years.

Anniesland has, through its various incarnations, had a deep political attachment to the Labour Party, though that has, at points, wavered. In 1950 the then new seat of Scotstoun was captured with a 239 majority over Labour by the Conservative Sir Arthur Young (previously the Tory MP for Patrick from 1935-50), who died eight months later. In the subsequent by-election in October 1950 Conservative Colonel James Hutchison, an insurance broker (and another ex-Tory MP – this time for Glasgow Central from 1945-50), held on with a majority of 1,319 over Labour and retained the seat for the next two general elections, achieving ministerial office as Financial Secretary at the War Office, before retiring in 1959 when Labour won the seat.

William Small was the Labour victor in 1959 – a good year for Labour in Scotland as the nation swung left against the UK trend of Macmillan winning a third Tory term. Glasgow Toryism had past its peak in the 1950s, and would now experience an inexorable decline until the 1980s, when Glasgow became Tory-free at a parliamentary level. One of the reasons for Labour's victory in 1959 was the changing nature of the seat with a massive programme of council house building spanning Drumchapel, ironically spearheaded by Macmillan's commitment to build 300,000 houses a year.

Small held the seat for 19 years until his death in January 1978 forced a by-election on Labour in difficult circumstances. Donald Dewar, who had previously been Labour MP for Aberdeen South from 1966-70 stood in the famous April 1978 by-election when Labour and the SNP were battling for the political supremacy of Scotland, with Dewar campaigning on the implausible slogan 'Score with Dewar'. The by-election saw the SNP candidate Kevin Bovey court controversy with his pro-abortion and pro-CND views and Dewar restricted the swing to the SNP to 3.6 per cent. This, along with the Hamilton by-election a few months later in which George Robertson was elected, was seen as halting the SNP electoral bandwagon in the 1970s.

In the early 1990s, a new electoral threat arose to challenge the supremacy of Labour – Scottish Militant Labour, which made brief inroads at council level in 1992, nearly winning the Summerhill ward in that year's elections when Labour won 38.5 per cent to SML's 35.4 per cent.

In 1997, the reconfigured seat saw Dewar put 8.8 per cent on Labour's support from the 1992 notional result and the SNP marginally advanced in percentage terms while losing support in actual votes. The Conservatives continued to fall back losing 2,000 voters and declining to 11.5 per cent. In 1999, Labour's majority fell from 15,154 to 10,993, while the party's support fell by 4,000 votes on a reduced turnout. The SNP in a distant second place lost 241 votes and the swing from Labour to SNP of 3.1 per cent was the second lowest in Glasgow and one of the lowest in the country.

The unexpected death of Donald Dewar in October 2000 not only flung Labour into political and constitutional crisis, but left it facing two by-elections in the Anniesland seat, as Dewar represented the seat at both Westminster and in Edinburgh. The resulting by-elections in November 2000 saw Labour hold both seats but with drastically reduced majorities and turnouts. Labour's vote fell by over 10,000 in the Westminster by-election and by nearly 7,000 in the Scottish Parliament by-election, but on reduced turnouts these represented falls of respectively 9.7 per cent and 10.2 per cent, a considerable improvement on preceeding by-elections in Hamilton South and Ayr.

The 2001 Westminster election witnessed Labour nearly double its majority from the by-election to an impressive 11,054 over the SNP, although this was 4,000 down on four years previous. On a significantly reduced turnout, Labour's vote saw 6,000 disappear from the 1997 result, while the SNP's support declined 1,700. The main parties making headway were the Scottish Socialists and the Lib Dems who moved from fourth to third.

The second Scottish Parliament election of 2003 saw little change to Labour's hold over Anniesland, with Bill Butler's majority, a comfortable 6,253 over the SNP – a rise of nearly 1,000 since the November 2000 by-election, but a reduction of more than 4,500 votes from 1999. Both Labour and the SNP lost votes compared with Dewar's election: Labour 6,000, the SNP nearly 2,000. The winners were the other parties: the Conservatives gained 154 votes, the Scottish Socialists 1,600 and the Lib Dems, despite falling to fifth, rose 500. The pattern of second voting showed Labour's vote falling to 38.9 per cent, but no clear challenger emerging with the SNP on 15.2 per cent and SSP on 12.2 per cent, while the Greens finished on 7.2 per cent. Anniesland is not politically homogeneous, and at the 2003 council elections, the Lib Dems seized the Labour ward of Kelvindale.

Boundary changes for Westminster mean Glasgow loses three of its ten seats, and Anniesland is set to gain part of Kelvin to form what will be called Glasgow North West. It looks staunchly Labour. At future Scottish Parliament elections, Labour's hold on Anniesland seems secure and this part of Glasgow looks set to elect a Labour MP and MSP for some time to come.

MSP

BILL BUTLER was born in 1956 in Glasgow, and educated at St Mungo's High, Glasgow and at Stirling University. From 1980-2000, he was an English teacher in his native city. After 13 years as a city councillor, he was elected Labour MP for the seat in the November 2000 double by-election following the death of

Donald Dewar. He had won the Tollcross Ward in 1999, with 56 per cent of the vote, and during his final years in the city chambers, he held senior posts as convener of property services, vice-convener of policy and resources and secretary of the Labour group, as one of the leading contenders to become next Glasgow council leader. He was identified with the anti-Pat Lally faction during Lally's reign as leader of the council, and was suspended from the Labour group for six months in 1991 for poll tax non-payment.

Butler is Scottish secretary of the left-wing Campaign for Socialism group, which grew up out of the Labour left's opposition to Tony Blair's campaign to abolish Clause Four. He has opposed a raft of policies associated with the Blair Government and the Scottish Executive, including the housing stock transfer of Glasgow council houses and the introduction of electoral reform into local government. Butler won the selection contest for the Labour nomination in the by-election, easily defeating Donnie Munro, the ex-lead singer of Runrig, and Cumbernauld lawyer Ian Smart. However, he had, with some difficulty and embarrassment, to follow the official party line in the by-election campaign, declaring 'I am not New Labour. I am not Old Labour. I am middle-aged Labour'.

He is married to Patricia Ferguson, Labour MSP for Glasgow Maryhill, making them the only Labour couple out of three couples elected to the Parliament. She has also been identified with the left, but had to take a more pragmatic stance as a cabinet minister, chief whip and campaign manager in 2003, which means she has had a fight on her hands to persuade her husband to support the Executive's policy on introducing proportional representation for councils. In the March 2004 vote he abstained. In the absence of John McAllion since May 2003, Butler is de facto leader of the left in the Scottish Parliament, creating the potential for a broad range of interesting domestic tensions – even though a furious denunciation of Tony Blair's approach to Iraqi war in March 2003 was followed by a somewhat contradictory vote in the Labour leadership's favour. Butler became a member of the enterprise and life-long learning committee and the subordinate legislation committee of the Scottish Parliament in January 2001, and from 2003 has been on the justice 1 and standards committee. He was the mover of a parliamentary motion in early 2004 condemning Donald Gorrie's criticism of Donald Dewar over the escalating cost of the Holyrood Building Project, which was signed by 35 Labour MSPs. This showed Butler doing what he does best: invoking Labour tribalism while engaging in pointless political point-scoring with political opponents (and coalition partners).

MP

JOHN ROBERTSON was born in 1952 in Glasgow and educated at Shawlands Academy and Langside and Stow colleges where he trained as an electrical engineer. He was a telephone engineer and customer services manager with the GPO through its transformation into British Telecom and BT between 1973 and 2000, including activism in the Communication Workers Union. As chair of Glasgow Anniesland Labour Party, he got to know Donald Dewar well and positioned himself to replace him when he opted to leave Westminster to be elected to the Scottish Parliament. He had been selected for that Westminster seat, for the election anticipated in 2001 when Dewar would have stood down. But Dewar's sudden death brought that contest forward to a by-election in November 2000, in which Robertson faced no challenge to his candidacy. He was returned at the June 2001 election, becoming a member of the Scottish Affairs select committee, as well as the European scrutiny committee. With a constituency interest, and as secretary of the Glasgow Labour MPs, he voiced anxiety that Glasgow Airport faced downgrading in favour of Edinburgh. In the Iraq votes in early 2003, he backed the Government in February, but, influenced by the arguments put forward by Robin Cook, he switched sides to rebel in March.

Glasgow Baillieston

Predecessor Constituencies: Glasgow Camlachie (1945–55) and Provan (1959–92).

Socio-economic Indicators:

Constituency Pop. (16-64)	40,071
Claimant Count (May 2003)	4.5% (43.2% above average)
IBA/SDA Claimants	20.4%
Life Expectancy – Male	69.5 (3.9 yrs below average)
Life Expectancy – Female	75.2 (3.5 yrs below average)
Owner Occupied	51.3%
Social Rented	41.9%
Average Property Prices	£45,375 (66th)
Average Gross Income	£20,714 (69th)
Low Birthweight Babies	133 (8.0%)
Teenage Pregnancy Rates	485 (5.4%)
No. of Lone Parent Households	5,072 (19.1%)

CAB Enquiries

Issue	No. of cases	Percentage of total cases (%)
1. Benefits	1410	45.5
2. Consumer	722	23.3
3. Housing	275	8.9
4. Employment	199	6.4
5. Tax	158	5.1

2003 Scottish Parliament Election

Electorate: 46,347   Turnout: 18,270 (39.4%)   Turnout 1999: 48.3%

Candidate	Party	Votes	Votes%	99 %	Change%
Margaret Curran	Labour	9,657	52.9	47.6	+ 5.2
Lachlan McNeil	SNP	3,479	19.0	34.6	–15.6
James McVicar	SSP	2,461	13.5	7.9	+ 5.6
Janette McAlpine	Con	1,472	8.1	6.4	+ 1.6
David Jackson	Lib Dem	1,201	6.6	3.4	+ 3.1

Labour majority: 6,178 (33.9%)   Swing: 10.4% SNP to Labour

2001 General Election

Electorate: 49,268   *Turnout*: 23,261 (47.2%)

Candidate	Party	Votes	Votes%	Change%
James Wray	Labour	14,200	61.1	- 4.6
Lachlan McNeil	SNP	4,361	18.7	- 0.4
David Comrie	Con	1,580	6.8	- 1.0
James McVicar	SSP	1,569	6.7	+ 3.7
Charles Dundas	Lib Dem	1,551	6.7	+ 2.9

Labour majority: 9,839 (42.3%)   *Swing*: 2.2% Labour to SNP

1945–97 Westminster

	Lab%	Con%	SNP%	Lib%	Other%	Turnout%
1997	65.7	7.8	19.1	3.8	3.7	62.3
1992	66.5	7.8	21.7	4.0	–	65.3
1987	72.9	7.7	12.1	7.2	–	69.1
1983	64.4	10.8	8.8	15.0	0.9	65.2
1979	69.5	15.1	13.7	–	1.7	66.0
1974O	58.6	9.8	30.2	–	1.4	64.0
1974F	61.6	16.8	19.6	–	2.0	69.0
1970	60.9	27.9	9.8	–	1.4	65.6
1966	66.9	30.8	–	–	2.3	70.8
1964	65.8	30.8	–	–	–	75.7
1959	55.6	44.4	–	–	–	78.8
1955	50.3	49.7	–	–	–	74.7
1951	51.3	48.7	–	–	–	82.4
1950	51.5	48.5	–	–	–	80.7
1948B	42.1	43.7	–	1.2	13.0	56.8
1945	–	42.3	–	–	57.7	65.0

Baillieston is located in the north east corner of Glasgow and divided in two by the M8 Glasgow-Edinburgh motorway. It is dominated by the vast post-war estate of Easterhouse and includes smaller estates such as Barlanark, Queenslie and Gartloch, all of which were previously in Provan; Carntyne and Mount Vernon come from the old Shettleston. Easterhouse is one of the monuments to post-war planning that cover Glasgow. Built several miles outside the city centre with few leisure or social facilities, life has always been difficult even in times of high employment. It has had high levels of unemployment and poverty for three decades and its population has been in decline for the same period.

Unemployment has been a significant problem in Baillieston for over thirty years, and has contributed towards such social issues as poverty, exclusion, crime and drugs. The incapacity and disability claimant count is the third highest in Scotland, leaving one in four of the working age population reliant on benefits. Baillieston has 41.9 per cent social housing, of which 31.1 per cent was council housing, until the Glasgow stock transfer in 2003, a dramatic fall from the 61.4 per cent of ten years previously (then the third highest in Scotland). Average property prices are 32.7 per cent below the national average. Average gross income is the fourth lowest in the country. The percentage of lone parent households is the highest in the country and 82.1 per cent above the average. Local CAB enquiries reflect the reliance on the benefits system by a large part of the population and the problem of consumer debt – 18.2 per cent of enquiries involved debt issues. It has been rated the sixth most unhealthy constituency in Britain, with it only being beaten by five other Glasgow seats.

Easterhouse has, over the years, been frequented by high profile visits by the rich and famous, and various do-gooders. In 1968, Frankie Vaughan made a legendary trip to attempt to find a solution to gang warfare, while in 1993 the John Smith Commission on Social Justice made several visits. In 1999 Anita Roddick's Body Shop business opened Soapworks Ltd. based in the estate, a soap making and product packing facility, and most recently, the then Tory leader Iain Duncan Smith visited the area in early 2002 to give Toryism a human face. Easterhouse residents and community groups must suffer from media and celebrity fatigue as people trek through to the see how the 'other half' of the country gets by, with few of them staying long enough to do something about it.

Glasgow City Council faces difficult issues in this area with falling pupil rolls which led to proposals to merge three local primaries – St Colette's, St Clare's and St Benedict's – via an extension of the latter. This encountered widespread local opposition, and in April 2002, the council announced that it would build a new primary school, on the site of the former St Leonard's Secondary School.

Pre-Easterhouse, Glasgow's East End was represented by Camlachie, first won by Labour in the breakthrough election of 1922 by the Reverend Campbell Stephen, who held it until his death in 1948 (with a break after the 1931 debacle). In 1935 and 1945 Stephen had stood under the Independent Labour Party banner, following its breakaway from official Labour in 1932. In the by-election after his death the Conservatives squeaked home in what was previously inhospitable territory as both Labour and the ILP put up candidates and split the left vote; the Conservative C. S. McFarlane won Camlachie with a 395 majority, but Labour won back the seat in 1950.

The seat became Glasgow Provan from 1959 and has grown increasingly Labour since. Hugh Brown was first elected in 1964 and held the seat until his retirement in 1987. The challenge to Labour in the 1980s came increasingly from within the party, as the Militant Tendency had targeted Provan as an atrophied, inactive Labour Party, and Jimmy Wray came very close to losing the Labour nomination in 1987, but then won a 18,372 majority in the election. In the 1990s, Scottish Militant Labour elected two Independent Labour councillors in the 1992 council elections in Baillieston and Queenslie with 37.4 per cent and 64.1 per cent respectively; but both were defeated in the 1995 local elections.

1997 showed no real surprises with Labour increasing its majority from a notional 14,165 to 14,480. In 2001, Labour's Jimmy Wray was returned with a majority of 9,839 over the Nationalists. However, on a reduced turnout, Labour's vote fell by over 6,000, while the SNP's vote fell by 1,700 – as their vote remained stable in percentage terms. The SSP increased their support by 600 votes, more than doubling their percentage support, and finishing just 11 votes behind the third-placed Conservatives.

The 1999 Scottish Parliament election illustrated the fragility of Labour's hold on the constituency's political affections. Labour's majority fell from 14,840 to 3,072, while its vote was nearly cut in half on a much reduced turnout – 20,925 down to 11,289. Labour's fall in its vote was the third highest in Scotland (after Falkirk West and Shettleston) – declining 18.1 per cent, while the swing from Labour to SNP was the highest in the country at 16.8 per cent. The SNP increased its vote by 2,000 votes, while James McVicar, the Scottish Socialist candidate and previously one of the Scottish Militant Labour-supported councillors, put on nearly 1,000 votes compared with 1997. In the 2003 Scottish Parliament elections, Labour doubled their majority to a comfortable 6,178 votes, although Labour saw their vote fall by 1,600 on a reduced turnout. The Nationalists, without the assistance of Dorothy Grace Elder's enthusiastic campaigning, saw their vote more than halved – falling by more than 4,500 votes. The SSP gained 600 votes and finished in an impressive third place, while the Conservatives lost 54 votes, the Lib Dems gaining 400. On the second vote, Labour's support fell to 44.8 per cent, while the SNP won 18.5 per cent to the SSP's 13.4 per cent, with the Greens securing a negligible 3.7 per cent – their lowest support in Glasgow and finishing a distant sixth.

Bailieston's long Labour history looks likely to continue into the foreseeable future, after the brief shock of the 1999 Scottish Parliament elections, but the boundary changes for Westminster mean that it will gain a large part of neighbouring Shettleston to produce a new Glasgow East seat. The main political competition (and controversy) will arise from internal Labour jockeying for position and a possible selection contest between David Marshall and Jimmy Wray unless one of them considers early retirement. At future Scottish Parliament contest, Labour's dominance looks set to continue despite the atrophied state of local Labour politics and low turnout, with none of the opposition parties able to mount a credible challenge.

MSP

MARGARET CURRAN was born in 1958 in Glasgow and was educated at Our Lady and St. Francis School, Glasgow, and Glasgow University, gaining a degree in history and economic history and a certificate in community education. She was a welfare rights officer and community worker for Strathclyde regional council, before becoming a lecturer in community education at Jordanhill College, which became part of Strathclyde University.

Curran was a member of the left-wing Labour Co-ordinating Committee (Scotland) in the early 1980s and a founding member of the Scottish Labour Women's Caucus, which fought to advance gender balance in the Scottish Parliament. She was the third candidate in the first bitter ballot between Mike Watson and Mohammed Sarwar for the Glasgow Govan Labour nomination, and eventually became Sarwar's election agent in an attempt to heal party wounds. This move only brought her grief as a one-and-a-half-year investigation led to Sarwar being tried for electoral malpractice, and acquitted. Charges were also considered against Curran for election expense irregularities, though these were dropped. Before being elected to the Scottish Parliament, she was notable as a co-author of the 1996 *The Case Against a Referendum*, in the midst of a furious party row over Tony Blair's imposition of a vote on devolution.

She won the candidacy for Glasgow Baillieston by fighting off Margaret Lynch, then a prominent Labour activist who defected the next week to the SNP. In the 1999 election, Curran fought off a spirited challenge from the SNP's Dorothy-Grace Elder, she became convenor of the Scottish Parliament's social inclusion committee as well as co-convener of the cross party group on women. In the Scottish Parliament debate on Mike Tyson's coming to Scotland in May 2000, Curran's contribution was acknowledged by all sides, raising the issue of male violence against women while declining to make cheap political points.

Her ability was recognised by Henry McLeish in his first ministerial reshuffle in October 2000, giving her the post of deputy minister for social justice, working under Jackie Baillie, and getting involved in the tricky negotiations with Glasgow Council and private sector funders for the Glasgow Housing Stock Transfer. When Baillie was sacked by Jack McConnell in October 2001, her job was first offered to Susan Deacon, then to Iain Gray, who did it until a May 2002 reshuffle, and then it went to Curran.

The Ballieston MSP is credited with having ensured the stock transfer, including the tenants' referendum, was rescued from a parlous state and successfully completed, while settling down reform of

Scottish Homes into Communities Scotland. She led reform of Social Inclusion Partnerships, intended to direct finance at the most deprived parts of Scotland, but changed under her legislation to a new system of 'community planning'. Keeping a similar portfolio, reverting to 'communities minister' after the 2003 election, she faced several of the Executive's earliest challenges. Glasgow Council put up resistance to community planning, and joined others in furious opposition to the voting reform deal struck in coalition with the Liberal Democrats. Curran was put into the line of fire, along with Andy Kerr, whose finance portfolio includes local government.

She also faced a challenge from her former boss, Jackie Baillie, when Curran announced charity law reform, but refused to give a timetable. With a scandal about charity fund-raising then prominent in the press, Baillie's plans for a member's bill forced Curran into speeding up the legislation. With the start of the second term, McConnell also handed Curran the flagship legislation on tackling anti-social behaviour. Knowing the issues well from her own constituency experience, her colleagues credit her robust, no-nonsense style with getting things done, but without losing sight of her principles, and she is a significant representative in cabinet of both the left and feminist politics. This combined a very Old Labour sense of moral indignation with a dash of self-righteousness, which could sometimes be effective, and sometimes seem as though she had missed the point in its Labour tribalism. In particular, Curran's long journey through the institutions of Labour has meant that she has had nothing but contempt for what she sees as grandstanding, self-indulgent politics.

Curran as minister has worked in tandem with communities convener and close friend Johann Lamont, describing their relationship as 'a fearsome double act'. Both have attempted to take a political agenda many Labour men dismiss as 'middle class feminism' and put it in a language which connects to working class communities. In doing so on anti-social behaviour, Curran and Lamont have appropriated a feminist language of 'reclaiming the streets' in relation to disadvantaged communities, carrying dangers of a socially authoritarian agenda. Blunt and humorous, she is well suited to the art of the political put-down, and in particular taking on the enlarged group of Scottish Socialists. When not being political, her interests include cinema, *EastEnders*, reading feminist writing, country music and aiming to be 'a fun mother' to her two sons.

MP

JIMMY WRAY was born in 1935 in the Gorbals area of Glasgow. He was MP for Glasgow Provan from 1987-97 and has represented its successor, Glasgow Baillieston, since 1997. Educated at St Bonaventure's School in the Gorbals, Wray was a heavy goods vehicle driver and served as a Glasgow Corporation councillor from 1972-74 and on Strathclyde Region from 1974-87.

He beat off a challenge for the Labour candidacy in Provan from Militant Tendency's Jim Cameron, but only by 73 to 72 votes, with the assistance of party headquarters – even though the next year he co-sponsored a motion urging the rehabilitation of Leon Trotsky. As a member of the hard left Campaign Group, Wray stood up for retaining the old socialist Clause Four and opposed the Gulf War, saying John Major was 'the butcher of 10 Downing Street' and claiming: 'We built up this turkey [Iraq] and now we are being asked to vote for its killing'. He also took controversial stances on Irish republicanism, and intervened ineptly in the Monklands East by-election of 1994, while convener of the Scottish Labour group of MPs, at first criticising the party's candidate Helen Liddell for highlighting the Labour council's favouritism towards Catholic areas, and then being forced to retract.

He combines these various controversial themes with a conservatism on social issues such as abortion and gay rights – calling the Blair Government 'a gay mafia' over its proposals to abolish Section 28 and claiming 'the Scottish Parliament has misunderstood the morality of the Scottish people' when it sucessfully abolished Clause 2A north of the border. Wray has often been in the public eye due to his personal life, sacking his second wife as his constituency secretary, losing an industrial tribunal brought by her, and then suing and winning £60,000 from the *Mail on Sunday* over allegations she made that he assaulted her, punched her and threatened her with a knife. He welcomed Mike Tyson's decision to come to Glasgow for a boxing contest in May 2000, putting him at odds with the MSP for the seat, Margaret Curran, and won the dubious accolade in 2001 of being Britain's laziest MP, only voting 33 times that year. In November 2003, he made a rare Commons speech in the debate on fluoridation of water which he opposed, arguing that a 'socialist government' should be against 'mass medication'. Wray is king of the Scottish Labour 'Jimmy Tendency', known as 'the Jeweller' in the House of Commons for his entrepreneurial activities, and is treasurer of the all-party groups on boxing and on fairs and showmen. He is one of a select band of Scottish Labour MPs who does not have a constituency office. Wray, now aged 68 years old, suffered a mild stroke at the end of 2003 which reduced his political profile further.

Glasgow Cathcart

Predecessor Constituencies: none.

Socio-economic Characteristics:

Constituency Pop. (16-64)	41,112
Claimant Count (May 2003)	3.2% (2.3% above average)
IBA/SDA Claimants	14.4%
Life Expectancy – Male	71.2 (2.2 yrs below average)
Life Expectancy – Female	78.5 (0.2 yrs below average)
Owner Occupied	59.8%
Social Rented	29.5%
Average Property Prices	£57,999 (40th)
Average Gross Income	£24,699 (43rd)
Low Birthweight Babies	117 (6.0%)
Teenage Pregnancy Rates	391 (4.6%)
No. of Lone Parent Households	4,286 (14.9%)

CAB Enquiries

Issue	No. of cases	Percentage of total cases (%)
1. Benefits	5412	58.5
2. Consumer	881	9.5
3. Employment	632	6.8
4. Other	565	6.1
5. Housing	477	5.2

2003 Scottish Parliament Election

Electorate: 49,018   *Turnout*: 22,307 (45.5%)   *Turnout 1999*: 52.6%

Candidate	Party	Votes	Votes%	99 %	Change%
Mike Watson	Labour	8,742	39.2	48.1	– 8.9
David Ritchie	SNP	3,630	16.3	28.1	–11.9
Richard Cook	Con	2,888	12.9	12.3	+ 0.7
Malcolm Wilson	SSP	2,819	12.6	(other 3.4)	–
Thomas Henery	Lib Dem	1,741	7.8	8.1	– 0.3
Robert Wilson	Parent Ex	68	0.3	–	–

Labour majority: 5,112 (22.9%)   *Swing*: 1.5% Swing SNP to Lab

2001 General Election

Electorate: 52,094   *Turnout*: 27,386 (52.6%)

Candidate	Party	Votes	Votes%	Change%
Tom Harris	Labour	14,902	54.4	– 1.8
Josephine Docherty	SNP	4,086	14.9	- 5.4
Richard Cook	Con	3,662	13.4	+ 0.9
Thomas Henery	Lib Dem	3,006	11.0	+ 4.3
Ronnie Stevenson	SSP	1,730	6.3	+ 5.0

Labour majority: 10,816 (39.5%)   *Swing*: 1.8% SNP to Labour

1945–97 Westminster

	Lab%	Con%	SNP%	Lib%	Other%	Turnout%
1997	56.2	12.5	20.3	6.8	4.4	69.2
1992	48.3	24.5	18.1	7.8	1.3	75.4
1987	52.1	22.4	10.3	15.2	–	76.3
1983	41.4	30.5	5.6	22.5	–	75.7
1979	45.9	41.8	6.9	5.4	–	78.6
1974O	38.1	42.7	16.5	2.7	–	76.7
1974F	40.6	45.8	13.6	–	–	80.6
1970	45.0	54.2	–	–	0.8	74.6
1966	48.3	50.7	–	–	1.0	79.7
1964	47.1	52.9	–	–	–	79.3
1959	40.8	59.2	–	–	–	80.2
1955	27.4	72.6	–	–	–	75.7
1951	29.5	70.5	–	–	–	82.5
1950	27.3	64.8	–	7.9	–	83.8
1946B	37.1	52.5	10.4	–	–	55.6
1945	41.2	58.8	–	–	–	67.6

The Glasgow Southside seat is dominated by the council estate of Castlemilk which sits on a hill over-looking most of the rest of the seat. It also contains some of the most affluent areas of the city: King's Park, Mount Florida, Newlands and Cathcart. These areas include some of the most desirable and expensive detached houses in Glasgow. Just over one in six of the working age population is reliant on benefits. Cathcart has 59.8 per cent owner occupation (up from 48.6 per cent in 1991), and has the second highest owner occupation rates in the city. Average property prices are 4.5 per cent below the national average, and rose 24.6 per cent in the 1990s. Lone parent households are 41.7 per cent above the national average. Local citizens advice bureau figures show the highest number of benefit enquiries in Glasgow. It is also the healthiest constituency in Glasgow – rated at the dizzy heights of the nineteenth most unhealthy seat in Great Britain. Glasgow City Council's Housing Stock Transfer of council housing from local authority control to a not-for-profit housing association, the Glasgow Housing Association, will have massive consequences for Castlemilk estate, with promises of £4 billion investment over the next 30 years across the city. Another major local issue has been the future of the Victoria Infirmary, situated by Queen's Park. The hospital has been rocked over the last few years by a number of scandals about the standard of clinical care and cleanliness. At the end of 2001, the hospital was badly affected by a winter vomiting bug – a hospital acquired infection. In January 2002 Greater Glasgow Health Board announced plans for the Victoria to be transformed into an Ambulatory Care and Diagnostic hospital, whereby patients would be seen on a day care basis, which aroused wide opposition including the local MP and then Scottish Executive minister, Mike Watson.

One of the focal points of the constituency is Hampden Park – Scotland's national football stadium, as well as home to Queen's Park Football Club, the last amateur team to play in one of the UK's top leagues. Controversy arose when redevelopment of the ground went massively over budget and the Scottish Executive had to bail it out. The national stadium was also the centerpiece of Scotland's bid to host the European Championships in 2008, first initiated as a solo Scottish bid by Henry McLeish, then Jack McConnell with Mike Watson (at the time sports minister) made a joint bid with the seemingly reluctant Irish, which failed. Hampden did, however, successfully host the European Champions League Final in 2002. Cathcart was once a safe Conservative seat with Conservative representation from 1918-79. In 1955 in the Tories' peak year in Scotland, they polled 72.6 per cent in Cathcart to Labour's 27.4 per cent – a majority of 15,751. Slowly Labour began to eat into this majority as Glasgow swung to the left, culminating in 1979 when Labour's John Maxton, nephew of Jimmy Maxton, ILP firebrand, won the seat from Teddy Taylor, the man who would have been Mrs Thatcher's Secretary of State for Scotland. He became MP for Southend instead.

Cathcart has become a secure Labour seat since then. Labour turned a Conservative majority of 1,757 in October 1974 into a Labour one of 1,600 in 1979; this increased in 1983 to 4,230 and to 11,203 in 1987. In 1992 the Conservatives still held the wards of Newlands and King's Park on the local council with longstanding councillor John Young winning 58.7 per cent in Newlands; in 1995 he won 42.4 per cent in Cathcart, but, in 1999 Young stood for the Scottish Parliament, and not one Tory was returned to Glasgow City Council in the parliamentary seat of Cathcart. In the 1997 election, Maxton increased his vote to 56.2 per cent and his majority to 12,245 over the SNP. This once rock-solid Conservative seat saw the Tory vote plummet to 12.4 per cent, down 9.1 per cent on the notional 1992 result. In 2001, Maxton's retirement after 22 years in the Commons representing Cathcart, did not affect Labour's relatively recent hold on the seat with Tom Harris winning with a 10,816 majority.

Mike Watson, standing for Labour for the Scottish Parliament, saw Labour's support reduce by 6,000 votes, but even a 7.9 per cent swing from Labour to SNP could not do more than dent the party's majority reducing it to 5,374. The 2003 Scottish Parliament elections produced a good deal more interest and controversy in a six-party contest. Mike Watson faced local difficulties over plans to close services at the Victoria Hospital, including the candidature of Glasgow 'legend', ex-leader of the council and ex-Lord Provost, Pat Lally. Standing on a Local Health Campaign ticket, Lally polled respectably, but not sensationally, winning just under 11 per cent of the vote. He would have stood a better change of being elected on the Glasgow list. Watson, however, saw his vote fall by 4,200 votes on a reduced turnout and decline by 8.9 per cent – the second biggest fall for Labour in the city, leaving him with a still comfortable majority of 5,112. The SNP could not make any headway despite this, with their vote falling by nearly 4,000 votes – giving a notional swing from SNP to Labour of 1.5 per cent. The big gainers were the Scottish Socialists, who finished third with 2,819 votes. In the second vote, Labour won significantly more support than the constituency vote suggesting Watson's difficulties did hurt his support: Labour's 44.9 per cent was 5.7 per cent higher than the party's first vote, while the SNP won 15.4 per cent, the SSP 15.1 per cent, and the Greens 8.2 per cent – finishing fifth ahead of the Lib Dems.

Boundary changes for Westminster produce a new seat based on Cathcart called Glasgow South which will also include parts of nearby Govan. The politics of Cathcart have long left the era when it was a weathervane Labour–Conservative seat, instead producing a politics of Labour dominance over a fragmented field of opponents with the Conservatives reduced to a marginal status. This has allowed Labour's vote to fall to a perilously low level in the 2003 Scottish Parliament election without facing a serious threat, but the party cannot afford to let its vote fall any further, in case one opponent emerges from the pack of challengers.

MSP

MIKE WATSON was born in Cambuslang in 1949, but is a Dundonian at heart. He was educated at Dundee High School, Heriot-Watt University, where he did a BA Hons in economics and industrial relations, later recalling that Lenin had been one of his main influences in those days. In 1998, he took a DLitt at the University of Abertay, Dundee. He was a tutor and organiser with the Workers' Educational Association in the English East Midlands from 1974-77, and from 1978-89 was a full-time organiser with ASTMS, the so-called white collar trade union, (which became MSF, Manufacturing Science Finance).

Watson was MP for Glasgow Central from 1989-97, during which he opposed the Gulf War in 1991 and the Maastricht Treaty in 1993. Having first won the seat in a by-election, the constituency disappeared under boundary changes, and he lost the Labour nomination for the vacant Glasgow Govan seat to Mohammed Sarwar in June 1996, after a notoriously bitter internal party struggle. He also tried for the Kilmarnock and Loudoun candidacy ahead of the 1997 election, but was outmanoeuvred by Des Brown, a favourite of Donald Dewar and Gordon Brown. Watson was made a life peer after the 1997 election, titled Lord Watson of Invergowrie, though he is one of the downwardly mobile lordships, including Sir David Steel and James Douglas-Hamilton, who have chosen not to use such titles in the Scottish Parliament. Out of Westminster, he became a director of a public affairs company, PS Communications, with senior figures from other parties, including Denis Robertson Sullivan, the Lib Dem treasurer, and Struan Stevenson, later to become a Conservative MEP.

His first year in the Scottish Parliament, and his impressions of it, are chronicled in his book, *Year Zero: An Inside View Of The Scottish Parliament*, published by Polygon in 2001. He admits in it that he had hoped to be a minister from 1999, being one of few with Westminster experience, but he was not selected, and in the carve-up of committee convenerships, he got finance. He was also a member of the social inclusion, housing and the voluntary sector committee until December 2000. He was one of the first to use the members' right to propose bills, sponsoring the Protection of Wild Mammals Bill, which was to ban foxhunting with dogs, and as could have been expected, it caused much controversy. When he became a minister in November 2001, he had to hand the Bill over to the SNP's Tricia Marwick to pilot it through its final legislative stages, becoming law in February 2002.

Watson had been one of the team close to Jack McConnell during the 2000 and 2001 leadership battles, and was rewarded with a cabinet post, covering tourism, culture and sport, when McConnell became First Minister in November 2001. This was to raise the political profile of the tourism industry, which was troubled in the wake of 9/11 and the foot and mouth outbreak, and to raise the status also of culture and sport, which had failed to find a steady place within the devolved structures until then, despite Henry McLeish's enthusiasm for sport in particular. An early and difficult decision for McConnell and Watson was whether to continue McLeish's intention of a solo bid for the European football championships in 2008. Watson was thought to prefer going for it, but another option was a joint bid with Ireland, and in trying to reduce the liabilities and ambitions of the previous two years and to distance himself from the McLeish era, McConnell went for the Scottish-Irish option, leaving Watson to work on the details with the Scottish Football Association, including plans for new stadiums in

Dundee and Aberdeen. The bid was thought to be a strong one, though naive in its understanding of football politics, and in December 2002 the Celtic bidders lost out to Austria-Switzerland.

Watson got himself into political difficulties over the issue of Greater Glasgow Health Board's plans for rationalising acute hospital services, including the reduction of services at the Victoria Infirmary, serving Cathcart constituents, with the replacement accident and emergency department moved further away. With intense pressure building in the constituency, and mindful of the 7,000 votes hospital campaigner Jean Turner won in the Strathkelvin and Bearsden by-election in June 2001, Watson backed the local campaign. He attended public meetings about it with other MSPs working to oppose the move, including the SNP's Nicola Sturgeon, while voting for the rationalisation when his political opponents raised it in the Parliament and put it to a vote. McConnell answered the attacks, saying Watson had a duty to represent his constituents, but privately told the minister to keep out of the public campaign to save the Victoria. The issue put other south Glasgow MSPs under pressure, and forced Eastwood's Ken McIntosh to resign his unpaid post as a ministerial aide. After that, Watson tried to be loyal, not even causing difficulty over the Iraq war votes in early 2003, despite having opposed the 1991 war. But it seemed that either his performance or the hospital row cost him his ministerial job. The reshuffle after the 2003 election saw him ousted, and replaced in the tourism, culture and sport portfolio by Frank McAveety. Watson is author of two books on Dundee United, *Rags To Riches* and *The Tannadice Encyclopedia*, has played a leading role in the United for Change supporters' group and in August 2003 became a member of the Dundee United board of directors. He is a passionate music lover, and in his words, a bit of a 'white soul boy' and aficionado of the soul funkster James Brown.

MP

TOM HARRIS was born in Irvine in 1964 and educated at Garnock Academy, Kilburnie, Glasgow College and Napier College, Edinburgh, where he qualified with an HND in journalism. He was employed as a trainee reporter on the *East Kilbride News* from 1986-88, a reporter on the *Paisley Daily Express* from 1990-92, as press officer for the Scottish Labour Party from 1993-96 and then for Strathclyde Regional Council in 1996, before becoming senior media officer for Glasgow City Council from 1996-1998, PR manager for East Ayrshire Council from 1998-2001 and PR and marketing officer for the Strathclyde Passenger Transport Executive from 1998 until his election to Parliament in 2001. Being chair of Glasgow Cathcart Labour Party from 1998-2001, he was well placed to succeed John Maxton, when he stood down after 22 years as an MP.

A passionate opponent of proportional representation in any level of government, his maiden speech was used to argue against any link between declining turnout and electoral reform. In January 2002, he was one of those to write to the *Guardian*, putting the Euro-sceptic point of view from a Labour perspective, saying the debate about the euro is a 'costly distraction' from public services. Being more obvious about his ambitions than most, he got his foot on the ministerial ladder by becoming Parliamentary Private Secretary in the Northern Ireland Office in July 2003. Having been on the science and technology select committee, he lists astronomy among his interests.

Glasgow Govan

Predecessor Constituencies: Glasgow Tradeston (1945–51) and Craigton (1955–79).

Socio-economic Indicators:

Constituency Pop. (16–64)	40,881
Claimant Count (May 2003)	4.8% (54.5% above average)
IBA/SDA Claimants	15.4%
Life Expectancy – Male	69.8 (3.6 yrs below average)
Life Expectancy – Female	75.9 (2.8 yrs below average)
Owner Occupied	53.4%
Social Rented	30.3%
Average Property Prices	£63,913 (30th)
Average Gross Income	£24,697 (44th)
Low Birthweight Babies	182 (7.4%)
Teenage Pregnancy Rates	405 (5.6%)
No. of Lone Parent Households	3,562 (12.0%)

2003 Scottish Parliament Election

Electorate: 48,641   *Turnout*: 21,136 (43.5%)   *Turnout 1999*: 49.5

Candidate	Party	Votes	Votes%	99 %	Change%
Gordon Jackson	Labour	7,834	37.1	43.3	– 6.2
Nicola Sturgeon	SNP	6,599	31.2	36.7	– 5.4
James Scott	SSP	2,369	11.2	4.8	+ 6.4
Faisal Butt	Con	1,878	8.9	8.9	=
Paul Graham	Lib Dem	1,807	8.5	5.6	+ 3.0
Razaq Dean	Ind	226	1.1	–	–
John Foster	Com	215	1.0	0.7	+ 0.3
Asif Nasir	SPA	208	1.0	–	–

Labour majority: 1,235 (5.8%)   *Swing*: 0.4% Labour to SNP

2001 General Election

Electorate: 54,068   *Turnout*: 25,284 (46.8%)

Candidate	Party	Votes	Votes%	Change%
Mohammad Sarwar	Labour	12,464	49.3	+ 5.2
Karen Neary	SNP	6,064	24.0	-11.1
Robert Stewart	Lib Dem	2,815	11.1	+ 5.2
Mark Menzies	Con	2,167	8.6	– 0.2
William McGartland	SSP	1,531	6.1	+ 3.8

cont'd

Candidate	Party		Votes	Votes%	Change%
John Foster	Com		174	0.7	-
Badar Islam Mizra	Ind		69	0.3	-

Labour majority: 6,400 (25.3%)   Swing: 8.1% SNP to Labour

1945–97 Westminster

	Lab%	Con%	SNP%	Lib%	Other%	Turnout%
1997	44.1	8.8	35.1	5.9	6.1	64.7
1992	48.9	9.9	37.1	3.5	0.5	76.0
1988B	37.0	7.3	48.8	4.1	2.8	60.4
1987	64.8	11.9	10.4	12.3	0.6	73.4
1983	55.0	19.7	6.0	19.4	–	71.7
1979	67.9	18.5	13.6	–	–	69.1
1974O	49.5	7.1	41.0	1.9	0.5	71.7
1974F	43.2	12.7	40.9	3.2	–	74.9
1973B	38.2	11.7	41.9	8.2	–	51.7
1970	60.0	28.2	10.3	–	1.5	63.3
1966	67.9	28.1	–	–	4.0	67.5
1964	65.0	30.6	–	–	4.4	70.3
1959	60.3	34.8	–	–	4.9	75.0
1955	62.0	38.0	–	–	–	71.8
1951	49.7	50.3	–	–	–	84.9
1950	45.7	46.7	–	3.9	3.7	84.0
1945	66.1	33.9	–	–	–	63.9

Glasgow Craigton (1955–79)

	Lab%	Con%	SNP%	Lib%	Other%	Turnout%
1979	59.9	28.5	11.6	–	–	75.2
1974O	50.5	20.1	24.3	5.1	–	75.8
1974F	51.3	30.8	17.9	–	–	80.0
1970	55.7	36.4	7.9	–	–	75.1
1966	57.9	32.7	9.4	–	–	80.4
1964	58.4	41.6	–	–	–	80.9
1959	50.8	49.2	–	–	–	82.7
1955	49.7	50.3	–	–	–	79.1
1951	63.1	36.9	–	–	–	80.0
1950	62.9	37.1	–	–	–	78.8
1945	59.7	40.3	–	–	–	62.0

The seat ranges across some of the most different areas of urban Scotland to be brought together in the same seat, ranging from the old Govan heartland, stereotyped affectionately in the 'Rab C. Nesbitt' comedies, to Pollokshields, with its large Pakistani community making this Scotland's most ethnically diverse seat. Then there are the middle class areas of Shawlands, Strathbungo and Maxwell Park – the latter electing the solitary Tory on Glasgow City Council.

Govan is one of the most deprived parts of Scotland. The claimant count for incapacity and disability benefits is the ninth highest in Scotland and one in four of the working age population reliant on benefits. Govan has not changed dramatically in the last decade in housing tenure, owner occupation is up 5.2 per cent since 1991, and social housing is at 30.3 per cent, 17.9 per cent of which was council housing compared to 30.6 per cent in 1991. Average property prices are 5.2 per cent below the national average. It has been rated the eighth most unhealthy constituency in Britain, being beaten by six Glasgow seats and one part of Manchester in terms of ill-health.

The River Clyde shapes the identity of Govan, with the folklore and memories of the shipyards, and the different redevelopment plans that have been put forward for the riverfront. In the run-up to the May 1999 Scottish Parliament elections, Kvaerner announced that they would be putting the Govan shipyard up for sale, and this led after the election to the intervention of then Secretary of State for Scotland, John Reid. In July 1999, a deal was negotiated with GEC-Marconi buying the yard, but two years later in July 2001, 1,000 job losses were announced, and as a result in October, the government brought forward plans for two logistical landing ships to give the yards work. Just a short walk from the yards is Ibrox Stadium – home of Glasgow Rangers – one of the two main football clubs in Glasgow. Rangers have had an unsavoury reputation for sectarianism and connections by a small minority of their fans to the Northern Ireland Troubles. It took until 1989, when Graeme Souness became manager for Rangers publically to sign their first Catholic player, Mo Johnston, which caused anguish and heartache to 'the blue noses' – the most fervent Rangers fans.

The Glasgow waterfront site at Prince's dock – further upstream from the Clyde yards – was the site of the Glasgow Garden Festival in 1988 – seen as the forerunner of the Glasgow City of Culture success. However, after the exhibition, the site laid empty for years, as the various authorities could not agree on a single way forward. In June 2001, Glasgow Science Centre was opened with an Imax Cinema and spectacular revolving tower; the tower had to be closed in March 2002 due to faulty ball-bearings and in May of the same year it was announced the centre had an operating deficit of £500,000 due to lower visitor numbers. BBC Scotland, currently situated in cramped premises in the West End of the city, is to move to a new, purpose-built site on the Pacific Quay site, and has persuaded the public authorities to fund a specially-built bridge for the benefit of the media classes.

Govan gained near legendary political status due to two sensational by-elections, a bitter history of Labour-SNP competition and internal Labour conflict. Govan has also been exceptional in Glasgow terms – an island of fierce party contestability in a sea of Labour hegemony – and that alone has provided good copy over the years.

Govan's political history is even more interesting and diverse than its current battles. Daniel Turner Holmes, Tony Benn's maternal grandfather was Liberal MP for the seat from 1910-18; while the Tories won the seat in 1950 and 1951 by respectively 373 and 241 votes over Labour, returning Jack Nixon Browne. Jon Rankin, Labour MP for nearby Tradeston from 1945-55, won Govan in 1955 and represented it until his death in October 1973. In November 1973 the SNP's 'Blonde Bombshell' Margo MacDonald sensationally overturned a Labour majority of 7,142 over the Conservatives to produce a SNP majority of 571 over Labour's Harry Selby. With significant boundary redistribution in the February 1974 election, MacDonald narrowly failed to hold the seat against Selby, returning to political office in 1999 as Lothian MSP.

The first Govan by-election was a watershed in Scottish politics exposing the frailty of Labour's hold over the West of Scotland. Jim Sillars recalled in his autobiography, canvassing as a Labour MP in the 1973 campaign and see Labour blame everything on 'the boss class', leading to Willie Ross touring the seat with a loudhailer proclaiming: 'Noo's the day and noo's the hour for Govan to kick out Tory power' in a seat where the Tories were very much a minority. Govan then reverted to being a safe Labour seat with Labour's vote in 1987 under Bruce Millan rising to 64.8 per cent, its majority over the Liberal-SDP Alliance at 19,509, while the SNP were reduced to 10.4 per cent. However, all that changed when Millan resigned to take over as one of the two UK European Commissioners in 1988. Scottish politics were at this point in a combustible shape following 'the Doomsday Scenario' of the 1987 election when the Tories had lost half their Scottish seats, but been returned to government on English votes.

Jim Sillars, ex-Labour MP and one-time founder of the ill-fated Scottish Labour Party, had joined the SNP, became one of its leading lights and married Margo MacDonald. His decision to stand in Govan in November 1988 made a high-profile by-election even more so. Labour's candidate Bob Gillespie, an old-fashioned trade unionist (and father of rock group Primal Scream's Billy Gillespie), was no match for Sillars on the hustings and various TV debates, where he was spectacularly out-manoeuvred by Sillars on the finer points of European funding. Sillars turned a Labour majority of 19,509 into an SNP one of 3,500. Tony Benn, reflected on Sillars victory in his diaries: 'It revealed that if you don't offer people analysis they go for separatism, and it was also a reflection of our failure to discuss constitutional questions, which are at the core of the devolution argument.' However, Sillars like Margo before, could not hold on in the resulting election, losing in 1992 by 4,125 to Labour's Ian Davidson.

In 1997 Govan was once again faced with far-reaching boundary changes involving the abolition of Glasgow Central, where the MP was Mike Watson. Several of its wards came into Govan while Pollokshields, an area with a large Pakistani community and the base for Glasgow councillor Mohammad Sarwar, was added from Pollok. There was a long and bitter Labour selection battle between the two, resulting in Sarwar eventually winning a re-run ballot. In the 1997 election, Sarwar faced the young, energetic SNP candidate Nicola Sturgeon, who nearly halved Labour's majority from the notional 5,609 of 1992 to 2,914, winning a 3.2 per cent swing from Labour – one of the best SNP results in the election.

That was not the end, but only a pause in the controversy. Two weeks after the 1997 election, allegations were published of Sarwar trying to bribe an election opponent. Sarwar insisted the money was a loan and in the resulting trial in March 1999 was cleared of all charges. At the 2001 Westminster election, Sarwar, despite all the bad publicity and controversy was re-elected with ease, seeing Labour's vote fall by a mere 1,800 on a reduced turnout and increase 5.2 per cent from 1997, while the SNP vote fell by nearly half in votes – 5,000 and 11 per cent.

In 1999, after two years of adverse publicity, no one thought Labour had much of a chance holding the seat in the Scottish Parliament election, but hold it they did, Gordon Jackson winning with a reduced majority of 1,756 over the SNP's Nicola Sturgeon: the 1.2 per cent swing to the SNP was the lowest in Glasgow and one of the lowest in the country. In the Scottish Parliament elections of 2003, Labour approached them with even more anxiety, given the unrelenting negative coverage of Gordon Jackson, and the potential of the SNP to pose an electoral threat. In one of the most surprising Govan results of recent memory, Labour held off the threat of the Nationalists, achieving a reduced majority of 1,235 and restricting the Nationalists to a 0.4 per cent swing from Labour. Labour lost 3,500 votes compared to four years previous, and the SNP 3,000, as the SSP increased their vote by 1,000. In the second vote, the SNP finished ahead of Labour, winning 25.9 per cent to Labour's 25.2 per cent, a Nationalist lead of 138 votes, with the SSP on 15.3 per cent, and the Greens on 9.4 per cent in fourth place – ahead of the Conservatives and Lib Dems.

Labour's triumph in 2003 on the first vote illustrates the strength of Labour's dominance in the city of Glasgow, and how it can win in such unfavourable circumstances, but the second vote reveals that there is a shallowness and hollowness to Labour's strength which may return to haunt them.

Boundary changes for the next Westminster election see the dismemberment of Govan with its constituent parts scattered amongst neighbouring seats. Bits end up in the new seats of Central, South West and South. Many in the Labour Party will be more than happy to see Govan disappear from the political horizon at Westminster, but the seat may still have the ability to fascinate and shock at a Scottish Parliament level. Labour has held this seat in 1997, 1999 and 2003 with some of the worst possible backdrops of coverage imaginable, and this must give the party confidence in its ability to hold it in future. However, the Nationalists have been getting closer, and may eventually triumph.

MSP

GORDON JACKSON was born in Saltcoats in 1948 and was educated at Ardrossan Academy and St Andrews University. He is a Queen's Counsel, a member of the Faculty of Advocates and was previously an advocate-depute and private solicitor. Jackson has repeatedly been listed among the highest earning criminal defence lawyers in Scotland, the annual announcement of his legal aid payments proving something of a political embarrassment.

His invoicing of the public purse for the year 2002–03 came to £163,000, putting him in sixth position on the QC league table, despite being part-time. Other Labour MSPs might be rendered red-faced by such revelations, but Jackson appears to be unembarrassable. His habit of missing debates but turning up to vote just before 5 pm, fresh from the High Court, earned him the nickname 'Crackerjack', after the TV programme remembered for announcing its arrival with the words 'it's five to five...'. In at least one rape trial, his failure to turn up because of MSP work has not endeared him to the presiding judge either. He promised in May 2001 that he would give up the legal work to concentrate full-time on his tasks as an MSP, but he continued. He is his own man, generally loyal to Labour, but semi-detached and not given to kow-towing to individuals within it.

He was a surprise choice for Labour in Govan and an even more surprising victor, with the SNP targeting the seat where it had previously had two by-election successes. In the first Parliament, he sat on the justice and home affairs committee and then its justice 1 successor from January 2001 until the 2003 election, raising questions about conflict of interest while he continued to benefit from the legal aid system it was supposed to monitor. Subsequent committee roles included subordinate legislation and enterprise and lifelong learning, moving after the 2003 election to subordinate legislation and European and external relations. He has also convened the cross party group on shipbuilding.

The controversy of his legal work is one of the reasons given by members of his constituency Labour Party, the most fratricidal of any in Scotland, who have attempted to unseat him. In the run-up to the 2003 ballot, his abstention on the Iraq vote infuriated local members, particularly Muslim activists, who thought he had promised to vote against the Labour line. A no confidence motion was lodged a month before polling, but the party meeting was inquorate. Govan MP Mohammad Sarwar was seen to be struggling to hold the line with the Muslim community during that campaign, while Jackson went briefly on a family holiday in Spain two weeks before polling. The threadbare nature of the campaign was exposed by an undercover reporter for *Scotland on Sunday*. Having seen off yet another SNP challenge, the MSP returned to court work the day after the election, and was unsurprised to find that his talents continued to go unrecognised in the First Minister's announcement of his revamped ministerial team. He made his next parliamentary speech eight months later, to back the Blair government policy for England, but oppose Executive policy for Scotland, by expressing his support for top-up student tuition fees.

MP

MOHAMMAD SARWAR was born in Faisalabad, Pakistan in 1952. He was educated at Faisalabad University where he graduated with a BA in political science, English and Urdu. He had a taste for politics in his home country, rising to be president of the student wing of Zulfikar Ali Bhutto's Pakistan People's Party. He emigrated to Glasgow in 1976, and built up his businesses to become a cash and carry millionaire and company director, being reckoned to be the fifth wealthiest Asian in Scotland, with his investments estimated in 2003 at £19 million. He joined the Labour Party eight years after arriving in Scotland, and was elected to Glasgow District Council in 1992, winning the Pollokshields ward from the Tories (Labour's only council gain that year throughout Scotland), then continuing on the unitary Glasgow City Council from 1995-97.

Sarwar was selected as Labour candidate for Govan after an extraordinarily bitter selection battle with Mike Watson (then MP for Glasgow Central and losing his seat because of boundary changes, later to become Lord Watson and, in 1999, the MSP for Glasgow Cathcart). The battle between two camps involved allegations from both sides of malpractice by the other. In the first ballot, in December 1995, Watson won by 237 to 236 votes, with 52 votes declared invalid, 40 of which were for Sarwar. In the re-run ballot the following June, Sarwar triumphed by 279 to 197 votes. In March 1996, as champion of Glasgow's Pakistani community, he travelled to the Pakistani Punjab to rescue Glasgow-born Rifat and Nazia Haq who had been forced into arranged marriages against their will. Sarwar was criticised for using the family for his own publicity, while he also outraged Pakistani elders who felt he was undermining traditional values. That same year, with Blair's u-turn on the referendum for Scottish devolution, Sarwar came to the fore again in trying to persuade the Scottish Labour executive to support a three-question referendum; Blair's pre-legislation question and one on specific tax-raising plans, followed by a post-legislative referendum. This became Scottish Labour policy for one chaotic week, before George Robertson unilaterally overturned it.

In 1997, following Sarwar's election as Britain's first Muslim MP and substantial attention on him from Muslims in other parts of Britain, it was alleged that he had bribed another Pakistani candidate standing as an independent, with a £5,000 'bung' to 'ease off' his campaign. Sarwar's defence was that the money was merely a loan and part of Pakistani culture. He was suspended from the Parliamentary Labour Party and the procurator fiscal launched an investigation which led to him being charged, tried and acquitted in March 1999. Sarwar has been severely damaged by this long, drawn-out process and his political judgement brought into question, just as the Govan battle and the subsequent allegations brought Scottish Labour into disrepute; but then, Sarwar and his supporters, who included George Galloway MP before his expulsion from Labour, see the allegations and court case as evidence of widespread Islamophobia in Scotland.

With his religion giving him a UK and international profile, Sarwar was notable for backing the NATO action in Kosovo in 1999, also supporting military invasion as a means of stopping Serbian ethnic cleansing. He turned firmly against Tony Blair's approach to Iraq, signing the early day motion against war in Iraq in March 2002, and voting against war in the February and March 2003 Commons votes. He also reflected Muslim opinion being infuriated by the Iraq war, causing particular problems for Labour in the 2003 Scottish Parliament election. MSP Gordon Jackson took less than the wholehearted anti-war position local members expected of him, and Sarwar had to work hard to bring that part of the Govan community on-side for Labour once more. He is a member of the Scottish affairs select committee. He signed an early day motion criticising the government's policy of introducing top-up tuition fees for students in England, but voted to support it in January 2004.

Glasgow Kelvin

Predecessor Constituencies: Glasgow St Rollox (1945), Glasgow Woodside (1950–70), Glasgow Kelvingrove (1945–79) and Glasgow Hillhead (1945–92).

Socio-economic Indicators:

Constituency Pop. (16-64)	50,009
Claimant Count (May 2003)	4.0% (28.7 % above average)
IBA/SDA Claimants	10.8%
Life Expectancy – Male	70.0 (3.4 yrs below average)
Life Expectancy – Female	78.7 (national average)
Owner Occupied	49.7%
Social Rented	27.5%
Average Property Prices	£90,896 (10th)
Average Gross Income	£26,158 (31st)
Low Birthweight Babies	114 (6.7%)
Teenage Pregnancy Rates	269 (2.9 %)
No. of Lone Parent Households	2,961 (9.0%)

CAB Enquiries

Issue	No. of cases	Percentage of total cases (%)
1. Benefits	3651	31.1
2. Consumer	2391	20.4
3. Other	1394	11.9
4. Housing	1201	10.2
5. Employment	1031	8.8

2003 Scottish Parliament Election

Electorate: 56,072   Turnout: 22,080 (39.4%)   Turnout 1999: 46.3

Candidate	Party	Votes	Votes%	99 %	Change%
Pauline McNeill	Labour	7,880	35.7	44.8	– 9.1
Sandra White	SNP	4,591	20.8	29.3	– 8.5
Douglas Herbison	Lib Dem	3,334	15.1	13.1	+ 2.0
Andy Harvey	SSP	3,159	14.3	4.8	+ 9.5
Gawain Towler	Con	1,816	8.2	7.9	+ 0.3
Alistair McConnachie	Ind Green	1,300	5.9	(other 0.1)	-

Labour majority: 3,289 (14.9%)   *Swing*: 0.3% Labour to SNP

2001 General Election

Electorate: 61,534   *Turnout*: 26,802 (43.6%)

Candidate	Party	Votes	Votes%	Change%
George Galloway	Labour	12,014	44.8	- 6.1
Tamsin Mayberry	Lib Dem	4,754	17.7	+ 3.6
Frank Rankin	SNP	4,513	16.8	- 4.5
David Rankin	Con	2,388	8.9	- 1.9
Heather Ritchie	SSP	1,847	6.9	+ 5.7
Tim Strand	Green	1,286	4.8	–

Labour majority: 7,260 (27.1%)   *Swing:* 4.9% Labour to Lib Dem

1945-97 Westminster

	Lab%	Con%	SNP%	Lib%	Other%	Turnout%
1997	51.0	10.8	21.4	14.2	2.7	56.9
1992	38.5	17.1	16.5	26.2	1.8	68.8
1987	42.9	14.4	6.5	35.1	1.1	72.3
1983	33.3	23.6	5.4	36.2	1.5	71.9
1982B	25.9	26.6	11.3	33.4	2.8	76.4
1979	34.4	41.1	10.1	14.4	–	75.7
1974O	28.2	37.1	22.8	11.9	–	72.4
1974F	24.4	44.0	11.3	20.3	–	78.7
1970	30.5	61.3	8.2	–	–	69.6
1966	37.1	62.9	–	–	–	73.5
1964	36.0	64.0	–	–	–	74.7
1959	31.7	68.3	–	–	–	77.1
1955	32.4	67.6	–	–	–	72.9
1951	35.1	64.9	–	–	–	82.2
1950	33.8	60.8	–	5.4	–	82.2
1948B	31.6	68.4	–	–	–	56.7
1945	33.6	58.5	–	7.9	–	65.8

Glasgow Kelvingrove (1945–79)

	Lab%	Con%	SNP%	Lib%	Other%	Turnout%
1979	50.3	28.8	10.0	10.9	–	65.6
1974O	42.8	27.6	23.2	6.4	–	63.4
1974F	44.5	36.3	19.2	–	–	69.4
1970	53.7	46.3	–	–	–	60.2
1966	57.8	42.2	–	–	–	66.3
1964	54.0	46.0	–	–	–	67.3
1959	46.2	50.8	–	–	3.0	70.9
1958B	48.0	41.6	–	7.6	2.8	60.5

cont'd

	Lab%	Con%	SNP%	Lib%	Other%	Turnout%
1955	44.6	55.4	–	–	–	67.6
1951	47.6	52.4	–	–	–	78.6
1950	45.6	49.6	–	2.7	2.1	78.8
1945	46.0	45.7	4.9	3.4	–	61.7

Glasgow St Rollox (1945), Glasgow Woodside (1950–70)

	Lab%	Con%	SNP%	Lib%	Other%	Turnout%
1970	47.4	41.5	8.4	–	2.7	63.8
1966	50.5	41.8	7.2	–	0.5	73.0
1964	45.6	40.4	5.4	8.3	0.3	74.0
1962B	36.1	30.1	11.1	21.7	1.0	54.7
1959	43.1	49.2	–	7.7	–	75.2
1955	43.9	56.1	–	–	–	72.8
1951	46.6	53.4	–	–	–	80.9
1950	45.6	48.7	–	5.7	–	80.2
1945	62.9	37.1	–	–	–	61.1

Glasgow's West End is one of the most affluent and distinctive parts of urban Scotland, let alone Glasgow. Its inhabitants – the West End cognoscenti – revel in the character and uniqueness of the area. The transition from Hillhead to Kelvin has seen the seat move eastward into the city centre, losing parts of its west side to Anniesland. Kelvin includes within its boundaries some of the great cultural and civic symbols of Glasgow's wealth, past and present: BBC Scotland's headquarters at Queen Margaret Drive, Glasgow and Strathclyde Universities – which are major employers in the seat – Kelvingrove Park and Kelvingrove Museum and Arts Gallery, George Square and the Victorian marble opulence of the City Chambers. Kelvin also covers the more working class areas of Anderston, Partick and Scotstoun.

Kelvin's socio–economic profile reflects the affluence for which it is known, but also illustrates significant parts of poverty. The claimant count is the lowest in the city, meaning that nearly one in seven of the working age population is reliant on benefits. Female life expectancy is the highest in the city and the national average. Kelvin has 49.7 per cent owner occupation, and 27.5 per cent social housing (14.3 per cent of which was council housing). Average property prices are the highest in the city and 34.8 per cent above the national average, and rose 96.5 per cent in the 1990s; average gross income is the highest in the city and the only constituency where it is above the national average. Local CAB enquiries show a variety of issues: benefits being less prominent than other Glasgow seats, and sizeable numbers of consumer issues.

In 2002 it was announced that the Glasgow Beatson Oncology Centre was to move from its site at the Western Infirmary to a newly designed site by Gartnavel Hospital. It was, in 2001, hit by a number of crises with four top consultants resigning over lack of funding. At the same time, Greater Glasgow Health Board decided that the Western Infirmary will close in the next ten years and its services moved to Gartnavel as part of a modernisation and rationalisation of Glasgow hospital services.

The BAE Systems Marine shipyard at Scotstoun was helped by the government's decision in July 2001 to allocate three of the new type 45 destroyers to be built at the yard. Combined with orders for three Astute class submarines and two landing ships, these decisions safeguarded most of the jobs at the yard for the foreseeable future.

As Hillhead, this was once a traditional Conservative seat represented by the party continuously through the inter-war years, easily surviving, for example, the Red Clydeside election of 1922. James Reid, MP from 1937-48, held the seat in 1945 with a majority of 6,364. Thomas Galbraith won the 1948 by-election with a 8,641 majority over Labour and represented the seat until 1982. He won Hillhead in 1959 with a Tory vote of 68.3 per cent, which had fallen by 1979 to 41.1 per cent and a 2,002 lead over Labour: the last Tory seat in Glasgow, in the twentieth century at least.

Hillhead's name was put on the British political map with the March 1982 by-election. After the establishment of the Social Democratic Party in March 1981, Roy Jenkins had stood in Warrington and nearly won the once safe Labour seat; subsequently, in conjunction with the Liberals the SDP won spectacular by-election victories in Croydon North-West and Crosby with Shirley Williams. Jenkins stood again in Hillhead and in a three-way contest with the Tory Gerry Malone and Labour David Wiseman, he came out the winner with 33.4 per cent and a majority of 2,038 over the Conservatives.

Boundary changes ahead of 1983 abolished the Labour seat of Kelvingrove and the southern parts of the seat were joined to a more pro-Labour Hillhead. The contest for the new seat pitted Jenkins, now leader of the Social Democrats and the Alliance's candidate for Prime Minister, against Neil Carmichael, MP for Kelvingrove; Jenkins won with 36.2 per cent and a majority of 1,164 over Labour. However, in 1987 Jenkins faced Labour's George Galloway, and in a year in which Labour made gains all across Scotland, there was little Jenkins could do to stop Galloway winning with a majority of 3,251.

Post-Jenkins, Labour have tightened their hold, with Galloway gaining over half the vote in 1997 and the SNP establishing themselves in second place over the Lib Dems. In 2001 Galloway was safely returned for the fourth time achieving a reduced majority of 7,260 as Labour's vote fell 4,500 and 6.1 per cent, while the Lib Dems moved into second place holding on to their 1997 vote and seeing their share rise 3.6 per cent.

Labour's Pauline McNeill held the seat comfortably with a 6,408 majority in the first Scottish Parliament elections despite losing nearly 4,000 votes on a lower turnout; the SNP gained nearly 1,500 votes and secured their claim to second place. It is a measure of the changed political allegiances of the West of Scotland and Labour's current breadth of support that the two non-Labour parties which recently held Hillhead now poll derisory votes, the Lib Dems with 13 per cent and the Tories with 8 per cent.

The 2003 Scottish Parliament election witnessed six party candidates standing, and McNeill returned with a 3,289 lead over Sandra White of the SNP. Labour's vote fell by nearly 5,000 and 9.1 per cent – the biggest Labour fall in Glasgow, while the SNP fell back by nearly 4,000, while the SSP increased their vote by nearly 2,000. In the second vote, Labour's support fell to 26.5 per cent, and the SSP finishing second with 18.2 per cent – their highest vote in Glasgow outside Pollok (and only 2 per cent lower) showing the middle class base of some of the SSP vote, the SNP on 15.1 per cent, and Greens finishing fourth with 13.7 per cent, their highest vote in the city.

Boundary changes for Westminster will abolish Kelvin and scatter its remains between the seats of Central, North West and North. This had already presented George Galloway with selection problems, before his expulsion from the party in October 2003 for his comments on the Iraq war made him illegible for standing in official Labour colours. Galloway indicated that he will stand in England on an anti-war left ticket in the forthcoming 2004 European elections, which still leaves him the option of calling a difficult by-election for Labour in Kelvin before the next UK election, or waiting to stand in one of the new seats with a possibly diminished return. Kelvin has the appearance of a fairly safe Labour seat at the Scottish Parliament, but Labour's vote has fallen significantly in the 2003 election. If one clear challenger can emerge from the pack to challenge Labour, there is the prospect this seat could become interesting again, with or without the presence of George Galloway.

MSP

PAULINE McNEILL was born in Paisley in 1962 and educated at Our Lady's High School, Cumbernauld, and Glasgow College of Building and Printing where she qualified in print design and graphic illustration.

She later gained a law degree from Strathclyde University, where her contemporaries in Labour student politics included future MSPs and cabinet ministers Jack McConnell, Wendy Alexander, Sarah Boyack and Susan Deacon. She remains the closest MSP friend of Alexander, despite the abandonment of the enterprise minister's candidature for the Labour leadership in 2001 – a decision taken in McNeill's Glasgow West End flat.

McNeill was president of the National Union of Students-Scotland in 1986-88, remembered in student circles as Poll Tax McKnife for her non-payment position on that issue. From 1988-99, she was national organiser for GMB Scotland, which meant she became chair of the Glasgow health service joint trade union committee. She was on Labour's home rule wing, active in the Campaign for a Scottish Parliament and a founding member of Scottish Labour Action, the nationalist pressure group formed after the 1987 election defeat.

McNeill was deputy convenor of the petitions committee of the Parliament and a member of the justice and home affairs committee from May 1999 to December 2000, before joining the justice 2 committee as its convener. In that role, she was closely involved with passage of land reform legislation, working for a change to civil law benefiting asbestosis sufferers and others suing for compensation while suffering a terminal illness. She also sought to reform the law on rape to make the definition of 'consent' clearer. Her committee also carried out inquiries into the Crown Office and procurator fiscal service. She continued as convener of the justice 1 committee after the 2003 election, working on sentencing and police funding inquiries.

She was also deputy convenor of the Scottish Parliamentary Labour group in the first term, an important conduit between backbenchers and an Executive prone to top-down control politics. She shares with her constituency's MP, George Galloway, a passion for the Palestinian cause, convening that cross-party MSP group, and was one of six Labour MSPs to oppose moves towards war in Iraq in the March 2003 vote. From a musical family, as an enthusiastic guitarist and singer, and with experience of managing rock bands, she also convenes the MSPs' contemporary music group. McNeill's musical enthusiasms were perfectly captured in the 2003 campaign. In 1997 Labour had won a UK landslide to the backdrop of 'Things Can Only Get Better', but in 2003 McNeill played out of her car tannoy the Kylie Minogue classic 'Better the Devil You Know'.

MP

GEORGE GALLOWAY was born in Dundee in 1954 and was MP for Glasgow Hillhead from 1987-97 after winning the seat from Roy Jenkins. He has represented the successor seat of Glasgow Kelvin since 1997. Educated at Harris Academy, Dundee, Galloway worked for a brief period as a production worker in a Michelin tyre factory before becoming a party apparatchik.

At the age of 23, he became a highly controversial secretary organiser of Dundee Labour Party and at the same time stood in the 1977 council elections, losing a safe Labour ward with a sizeable Catholic community to the independent candidate Bunty Turley, apparently because he was cohabiting with his girlfriend. He aligned himself with the Bennite left, and was responsible for Dundee District Council flying the Palestinian flag and twinning the city with Nablus on the West Bank, despite 'Arabs' being more usually associated on Tayside with support for Dundee United. He was also drawn into police investigations of Dundee Labour Party of alleged fund-raising irregularities, alongside future Aberdeen MP Frank Doran and sitting Dundee MP Ernie Ross, though none of them was ever charged.

Known to friend and foes alike as 'gorgeous George' and immortalised in song by Edwyn Collins, ex-lead singer of Glasgow band, Orange Juice, he became chair of the Scottish Labour Party in 1981-82, and went south to become general secretary of War on Want from 1983-87, where his flamboyant character led to further controversy, including his admission of what he described as 'carnal knowledge' of two women at a conference in Greece. After his election in 1987, he was nearly de-selected in 1992, losing the ballot of party members and only scraping through due to the trade union block vote.

In 1994, on a visit to Iraq, he addressed Saddam Hussein with praise for 'your courage, your strength, your indefatigability' - later regretting that he had not used the Glaswegian word 'youse' as he claimed to mean the Iraqi people rather than the mass-murdering tyrant. Using a uniquely colourful, blood-curdling turn of phrase in the style of Arabic rhetoric, Galloway has been a consistent opponent of the West's policy of sanctions against Iraq, regularly visiting Baghdad under the Saddam regime, and bringing back a child for medical treatment as a means of highlighting the effect of post-1991 sanctions on healthcare. In 2001, he was the most travelled MP, making 12 foreign working trips, yet finding enough time also to win the *Spectator* award for Parliamentary debater of the year.

After the 9/11 attacks in the US, his profile rose as a ferocious critic of American foreign policy and Tony Blair's support of it, being one of 11 Labour MPs to vote against the attack on Afghanistan and bringing, among other harsh responses, an unusual sort of fatwa on him from Hollywood actor John Malkovich who bizarrely identified Galloway and the *Independent* correspondent Robert Fisk as the two people he would most likely to see dead.

The exchanges in the Commons and TV studios became more heated as war approached in Iraq, and once war began, Galloway gave an ill-judged interview for Abu Dhabi television in which he described Blair and President Bush as 'wolves', and appeared to urge other Middle East nations to rise up and defend Iraq against invading US and UK forces. The heat was turned up on Galloway when, as US forces reached Baghdad, the *Daily Telegraph* and *Christian Science Monitor* reported they had found documents appearing to show Galloway's links to the Saddam regime had been closer than previously thought with documents found in the Iraqi Foreign Ministry which appeared to show Galloway in the pay of Saddam's regime. Galloway countered that they were forgeries planted by Western intelligence forces to discredit him. Within days he was suspended by the Labour Party, making it almost impossible for him to fight for a Labour candidacy in one of the new Glasgow seats following boundary changes, and he widened the rift with the party by warning he would stand as an independent if not selected. The *CSM* claims were soon withdrawn, leading to a grovelling apology in court, and a sizeable payout to Galloway, while he denied the *Daily Telegraph* claims and sued. He was finally – after 36 years as a party member – expelled in October 2003 by a three-person panel of Labour's National Constitutional Committee. The panel found him guilty of four out of the five charges made against him, including inciting Arabs to attack British troops and urging UK forces to defy orders. Galloway denounced the decision as a 'political show trial' and immediately threatened legal action against the party, as well as threatening to stand as an independent left candidate as part of 'one movement of democratic liberation' against the Iraq war and Blairism in the forthcoming June 2004 Euro elections.

Galloway is a complex, contradictory person and politician – equally arrogant and vulnerable – and he had the potential to go far in Labour if he could have curbed his self-destructive streak. In his mixture of talents and over-inflated sense of himself he has similarities to a previous generation's equally talented Labour politician of whom great things were expected – Jim Sillars. He makes roughly as much money as a trenchant columnist for the *Mail on Sunday* as he does representing Glasgow Kelvin, and he has also financed a luxurious lifestyle, including his Portuguese bolt-hole, with a series of successful libel actions even before the Iraq war.

Glasgow Maryhill

Predecessor Constituencies: none.

Socio-economic Indicators:

Constituency Pop. (16-64)	42,346
Claimant Count (May 2003)	5.9% (88.3% above average)
IBA/SDA Claimants	20.1%
Life Expectancy – Male	67.9 (5.5 yrs below average)
Life Expectancy – Female	75.0 (3.7 yrs below average)
Owner Occupied	37.1%
Social Rented	49.0%
Average Property Prices	£60,824 (33rd)
Average Gross Income	£19,210 (71st)
Low Birthweight Babies	164 (8.7%)
Teenage Pregnancy Rates	513 (5.3%)
No. of Lone Parent Households	4,838 (16.1%)

CAB Enquiries

Issue	No. of cases	Percentage of total cases (%)
1. Benefits	1622	35.3
2. Consumer	974	21.2
3. Housing	490	10.7
4. Employment	471	10.2
5. Other	287	6.2

2003 Scottish Parliament Election

Electorate: 49,141   *Turnout*: 18,243 (37.1%)   *Turnout 1999*: 40.8

Candidate	Party	Votes	Votes%	99 %	Change%
Patricia Ferguson	Labour	8,997	49.3	49.8	– 0.5
Bill Wilson	SNP	3,629	19.9	31.0	–11.1
Donald Nicolson	SSP	2,945	16.1	6.2	+ 9.9
Arthur Sanderson	Lib Dem	1,785	9.8	7.8	+ 2.0
Robert Erskine	Con	887	4.9	5.2	– 0.3

Labour majority: 5,368 (29.4%)   *Swing*: 5.3% SNP to Labour

2001 General Election

Electorate: 55,431   *Turnout*: 22,231 (40.1%)

Candidate	Party	Votes	Votes%	Change%
Ann McKechin	Labour	13,420	60.4	- 4.6
Alex Dingwall	SNP	3,532	15.9	- 1.1
Stuart Callison	Lib Dem	2,372	10.7	+ 3.5
Gavin Scott	SSP	1,745	7.8	+ 6.6
Gawain Towler	Con	1,162	5.2	- 0.7

Labour majority: 9,888 (44.5%)   *Swing*: 1.8% Labour to SNP

1945–97 Westminster

	Lab%	Con%	SNP%	Lib%	Other%	Turnout%
1997	64.9	5.9	17.0	7.1	6.2	56.6
1992	61.6	10.3	19.1	7.0	1.9	65.2
1987	66.4	9.4	11.0	11.7	1.5	67.5
1983	55.2	14.8	7.1	22.2	0.9	65.4
1979	66.2	15.0	11.2	6.8	0.8	67.7
1974O	57.7	9.3	29.9	3.1	–	65.9
1974F	56.6	18.5	24.9	–	–	69.9
1970	65.6	23.0	11.4	–	–	63.9
1966	67.8	20.7	11.5	–	–	68.5
1964	68.4	27.6	–	–	4.0	70.5
1959	64.0	36.0	–	–	–	73.7
1955	62.8	37.2	–	–	–	69.9
1951	63.0	36.0	–	–	1.0	80.7
1950	61.2	32.2	–	6.6	–	80.0
1945	60.1	39.9	–	–	–	66.8

Maryhill's social mix includes the West End wards of Woodside and North Kelvinside with high numbers of students, and the more working class areas of Maryhill itself along with Milton, Possil and Summerston. The seat is ethnically diverse by Scottish standards, with the largest Chinese community in Scotland situated in North Kelvinside.

The socio-economic indicators underline the difficulties the area faces. The claimant count is the highest in the country, while incapacity and disability benefits the fourth highest in the country – resulting in over one in four of the working age population being dependent on benefits. Maryhill has the second lowest owner-occupation in the country. Average gross income is the third lowest in the country. Low birth-weight babies run at the second highest rate in the country, only beaten by Glasgow Shettleston. Maryhill has the third worst health record in Britain, only beaten by Shettleston and Glasgow Springburn.

Significant developments of public services are happening in Maryhill. Glasgow City Council plan via a controversial public–private partnership to build a £6 million school in Possil at Killearn Street which will be a 'super campus' and will ambitiously aim to bring non-denominational, Catholic, nursery and special needs schools under one roof. Such plans are being watched nervously by the Catholic hierarchy of the city. In the health service, Greater Glasgow Health Board has announced the closure of Ruchill Hospital which will be replaced by housing regeneration on the site.

Maryhill also includes within its boundaries the West of Scotland Science Park and Firhill Park – home of Partick Thistle Football Club – the third club in the city, and the poor relation to the 'Old Firm'. 'The Jags' as they are known, nearly went out of business a few years ago, but have since been put back on a sound financial footing thanks to support from the fans and local community. At a time when other Scottish clubs are going into receivership, Thistle have the lowest debt levels in the Scottish Premier.

Maryhill may have been Labour since 1935, but other areas incorporated into Maryhill have more diverse traditions. Woodside was a parliamentary seat from 1950-70 and was represented by the Conservatives from 1950 until Labour's Neil Carmichael won it in a 1962 by-election. Labour's vote in Maryhill reached a staggering 68.4 per cent in 1964, 66.2 per cent in 1979 and 66.4 per cent in 1987, the last two in four-party contests. Maria Fyfe was first elected in 1987, and saw her vote slip back in 1992, before climbing back in 1997 to 64.9 per cent and a majority of 14,242. The only exceptional thing about Maryhill in this election was the 2.19 per cent vote recorded by Lorna Blair, the Natural Law Party candidate. This was the highest vote recorded anywhere by the NLP in the UK, and twice the level of their next highest vote for no obvious reason, except perhaps for the growing number of student residences in the constituency. In the 2001 Westminster election, Labour's majority fell to 9,888 as Ann McKechin took over from Maria Fyfe, and Labour's vote fell by nearly 6,000. The SNP fell back by 1,500 on a reduced turnout – the fourth lowest in the UK.

Labour had a poor result here in the Scottish Parliament elections of 1999, with Patricia Ferguson seeing nearly 8,000 disappear from Labour's vote while its share declined by 15.2 per cent – the seventh worst in the whole of Scotland leaving Labour with a 4,326 lead. Labour's vote was the lowest it had ever been in a post-war election in Maryhill. In the 2003 Scottish Parliament election Maryhill had the second lowest turnout in the country. Patricia Ferguson increased Labour's majority to 5,368, as Labour's vote fell by 1,500 and the Nationalists by 3,500 and 11 per cent – their worst showing in the city and one of their worst results in the country. The SNP candidate Bill Wilson then decided to stand against John Swinney for the SNP leadership and won a similar level of support at the September 2003 SNP Conference. In the second vote, Labour won 38.3 per cent to the SSP's 17.8 per cent and SNP 17 per cent, with the Greens on fourth place on 9.2 percent.

Boundary Commission changes at a Westminster level see an enlarged Maryhill become Glasgow North, taking a chunk of the current Kelvin which is being abolished. That will not affect Labour's strong prospects. At future Scottish Parliament elections Maryhill looks set to remain reliably Labour, after having given it a small shock in 1999, which weakened, rather than dealt a fatal blow, to Labour's hold on the seat.

MSP

PATRICIA FERGUSON was born in 1958 in Glasgow, and educated at Garnethill Convent Secondary School, Glasgow and Glasgow College of Technology. She subsequently worked as a health service administrator in Glasgow and Lanarkshire, before becoming an administrator at the Scottish Trades Union Congress from 1990–94. Ferguson then became organiser for the Scottish Labour Party in the south-west of Scotland from 1994–96, before moving to Scottish party headquarters as Scottish officer of the party from 1996–99, where she worked with then general secretary Jack McConnell on some of the party's toughest times involving political rows and legal action in West Renfrewshire, Govan and Glasgow Council Labour group. Upon election to the Parliament, she became one of the two deputy presiding officers, making her a likely successor at one point to Sir David Steel as Presiding Officer.

A left winger, her apolitical duties gave her a low profile, which is where she appears to be most comfortable, but Jack McConnell plucked her from there, first to run his leadership campaign, then to become his Parliament business minister. He made her chief whip from October 2001, later giving her the task of co-ordinating the 2003 Labour re-election effort, for which she had almost no previous experience, provoking criticism of her from London HQ. After the 2003 election, she returned to the chief whip and Parliament minister role. This continues to put her in a fascinating position in trying to bring her husband into line on votes disputed within the Labour group. He is Bill Butler, secretary of the hard-left Campaign for Socialism, MSP for Glasgow Anniesland since a November 2000 by-election. In March 2003, he toed the party line on Iraq, despite a strong speech to the contrary, and in the second Parliament, he is a prominent opponent of council voting reform, to which she has to be committed as a coalition minister. Occasionally, she is put into the line of media fire with a particularly difficult issue, as with the Iraq war, despite being neither combative nor particularly persuasive. But that 1990s stint in party headquarters working with McConnell has stood her career in good stead, as he clearly values and trusts her.

MP

ANN McKECHIN was born in 1961 in Paisley and first elected to Parliament in 2001, following the retirement of Maria Fyfe. She was educated at Paisley Grammar School and Strathclyde University, where she studied in law. She was employed from 1983-86 as a solicitor with Pacitti Jones in Glasgow, then become a partner in the firm until 2000. She joined the Labour Party at the age of 30, having been involved in international development campaigning and being a member of the Muir Society of Labour Lawyers, a hothouse for party talent and aspiring Parliamentarians. She was on the co-ordinating committee of Jubilee Scotland, campaigning with churches and development agencies for the relief of international debt, and has been the Scottish representative on the Women's Development Movement from 1998 onwards.

McKechin was secretary of Glasgow Kelvin Labour Party from 1995-98, that being something of a fiefdom for George Galloway. She stood as a Labour list candidate in the West of Scotland at the 1999 Scottish Parliament election, and she benefited in her selection for Maryhill from it being an all-woman shortlist to replace Maria Fyfe who had chosen to retire close to the 2001 election. In a city where Labour politics reward age and machismo, she became the youngest Glasgow MP and its only female one. She was among those who signed a motion against war in Iraq in 2002, following up with votes against government policy in advance of the Iraq war in 2003. She won places on select committees covering Scottish affairs and information, while remaining active in several international development pressure groups.

Glasgow Pollok

Predecessor Constituencies: none.

Socio-economic Indicators:

Constituency Pop. (16-64)	38,894
Claimant Count (May 2003)	4.6% (48.2% above average)
IBA/SDA Claimants	16.7%
Life Expectancy – Male	69.6 (3.8 yrs below average)
Life Expectancy – Female	76.0 (2.7 yrs below average)
Owner Occupied	55.1%
Social Rented	37.8%
Average Property Prices	£49,594 (59th)
Average Gross Income	£20,412 (70th)
Low Birthweight Babies	145 (7.0%)
Teenage Pregnancy Rates	479 (5.3%)
No. of Lone Parent Households	4,845 (17.7%)

2003 Scottish Parliament Election

Electorate: 47,137   Turnout: 21,538 (45.7%)   Turnout 1999: 54.4%

Candidate	Party	Votes	Votes%	99 %	Change%
Johann Lamont	Labour	9,357	43.4	43.7	– 0.3
Tommy Sheridan	SSP	6,016	27.9	21.5	+ 6.4
Kenneth Gibson	SNP	4,118	19.1	25.9	– 6.8
Ashraf Anjum	Con	1,012	4.7	5.3	– 0.6
Isabel Nelson	Lib Dem	962	4.5	3.6	+ 0.9
Robert Ray	Par Ex	73	0.3	–	–

Labour majority: 3,341 (15.5%)   Swing: 3.4% Labour to SSP

2001 General Election

Electorate: 49,201   Turnout: 25,277 (51.4%)

Candidate	Party	Votes	Votes%	Change%
Ian Davidson	Labour	15,497	61.3	+ 1.4
David Ritchie	SNP	4,229	16.7	– 1.1
Keith Baldassara	SSP	2,522	10.0	– 1.1
Isabel Nelson	Lib Dem	1,612	6.4	+ 2.9
Rory O'Brien	Con	1,417	5.6	– 0.4

Labour majority: 11,268 (44.6%)   Swing: 1.3% SNP to Labour

1945–97 Westminster

	Lab%	Con%	SNP%	Lib%	Other%	Turnout%
1997	59.9	6.0	17.9	3.5	12.8	66.6
1992	43.4	15.8	15.6	5.9	19.3	70.7
1987	63.1	14.3	9.6	12.1	1.0	71.6
1983	52.3	20.5	9.9	17.4	–	67.2
1979	49.3	29.7	9.6	9.1	2.3	73.7
1974O	43.4	27.0	24.3	5.3	–	72.3
1974F	46.1	38.7	14.4	–	0.8	77.5
1970	46.3	44.8	8.9	–	–	72.6
1967B	31.2	36.9	28.2	1.9	1.8	75.7
1966	52.4	47.6	–	–	–	79.0
1964	44.6	43.9	–	11.5	–	77.8
1959	41.2	58.8	–	–	–	78.9
1955	38.7	61.3	–	–	–	75.5
1951	44.6	55.4	–	–	–	82.5
1950	38.8	56.4	–	4.8	–	81.3
1945	33.6	63.5	–	–	2.9	68.2

Pollok occupies the south-west corner of the city dominated by the post-war council estate of the same name. The new 1997 seat includes Pollok, Nitshill, Cowglen and Arden from the old Pollok, and Cardonald and Mosspark from the old Govan. The new Pollok seat has a mixture of affluence and poverty: the beauty of Pollok Park and House with the tourist attraction of the Burrell Collection, combined with some of Scotland's worst unemployment spots.

The claimant counts put just over one in four of the working age population on benefits. Average property prices are 26.5 per cent below the national average, having risen 59.8 per cent in 1991-2001; average gross income is the fourth lowest in the country. Lone parent households are 68.5 per cent above the average and the second highest across Scotland. Pollok has also been rated the fourth most unhealthy constituency in Britain – only beaten by three nearby Glasgow constituencies. There have been recent job losses by significant local employers such as Rolls-Royce at its Hillington plant which announced 150 job losses in March 2000, and then, 400 further losses in November 2001, representing one third of the workforce. However, employment growth has also been seen with Thomson, the UK's leading travel company announcing in 2000 that it would locate its new national call centre in Cardonald Park in Pollok. In July 2000 Barclays and Siemens business services decided that they would locate their new administration centre in Cowglen, bringing 600 new jobs to the area.

Pollok has a reputation as a safe Labour seat, but that is an unfair reading of its past and present. It was a Conservative seat continuously from 1918 until 1964, when it was first won by Labour in Harold Wilson's first election victory; it was then re-won in spectacular fashion in 1967 by the Conservatives' Esmond Wright thanks to an increase in the SNP vote damaging Labour; this was only months before Hamilton set Scottish politics alight and it played a contribution in those famous events. Pollok returned to the safe Labour fold in 1970 under James White who remained MP until 1987. Jimmy Dunnachie followed in 1987 by which point Labour's vote had risen to 63.1 per cent and a 17,983 majority over the Conservatives.

However, everything was not happy within the left-wing vote. In 1992, Tommy Sheridan stood under the banner Scottish Militant Labour (while in prison) and scored a significant success winning 6,287 votes and 19.3 per cent, causing Labour's vote under the dour Dunnachie to fall to 43.4 per cent and cutting Labour's lead to 7,883. The subsequent council elections were relatively bad results for Scottish Labour, coming one month after the unexpected re-election of the Conservative Government, and two SML councillors were returned in Glasgow, both in the Pollok seat: Sheridan in Pollok with 52.5 per cent and Nicky Bennett in South Nitshill with 44.3 per cent. Sheridan returned with 44.0 per cent in the Pollok ward in the 1999 elections. His vote could be compared with that of Jimmy Reid standing in Central Dunbartonshire for the Communists in February 1974 after the Upper Clyde Shipworkers' work-in; it was the highest vote up to that point in post-war politics gained by an independent who had not previously been an MP (beaten by Martin Bell in the 1997 election). It was thought Sheridan's star would wane, and in 1997 with boundary changes his vote fell to 11.1 per cent and Labour's majority climbed back to a respectable 13,791. In 2001, Labour's majority fell slightly to 11,268 as Ian Davidson saw Labour's vote on a reduced turnout fall by over 4,000, while the Nationalists slipped back by 1,500 and the Scottish Socialists without Sheridan by 1,000.

Any derisory judgement of Sheridan underestimated him, as he remained a hardworking, charismatic councillor, who nearly doubled his vote to 21.5 per cent in the 1999 Scottish Parliament elections, while Labour's vote fell by 8,000 and 16.2 per cent – Labour's fifth worst performance in the whole of Scotland – leaving Labour with a majority of 4,642 over the SNP. Both Sheridan and the SNP's Kenny Gibson were elected Glasgow list MSPs and many observers thought Sheridan often acted like he was 'MSP for Pollok'.

In the second Scottish Parliament election, Johann Lamont saw a slight decline in Labour's majority of 1,000 to 3,341, as her vote fell by 2,000, and the SSP's rose by 500 as they established themselves in second place, and the SNP fell by 2,500. Kenny Gibson, SNP candidate in 1999 and 2003, said at the count (after it became clear that he would not be re-elected as a Glasgow list MSP) that the SSP were 'a bunch of neds, housebreakers, drug dealers, thieves and scoundrels'. Some indication of the degree to which the SSP's vote is based on Sheridan's appeal can be seen in the second vote with Labour winning 43.3 per cent to the SSP's 20.2 per cent – 7.7 per cent below Sheridan's score in the constituency contest – with the SNP on 17.8 per cent and Greens on 3.9 per cent in sixth place – their second lowest vote in the city.

Boundary changes for Westminster have created out of Pollok a larger Glasgow South West constituency which also includes a sizeable part of Govan. At Scottish Parliament elections, Labour seem safe for the foreseeable future, with the Scottish Socialists and SNP splitting the anti-Labour vote. Unless the SSP can reinvent itself, or Sheridan can win on charisma alone, then their prospects of winning Pollok now look very slender.

MSP

JOHANN LAMONT was born in 1957 in Glasgow and was educated at Woodside Secondary School, Glasgow, then Glasgow University and Jordanhill College of Education. She worked as a history teacher in Rothesay and Glasgow, and has been involved in a number of community projects including education and social work developments in Castlemilk. Lamont has long been seen as being on the left of the Labour Party and as a campaigner on women's issues, voting against devolution in 1979 because it was a distraction from more important goals. Thatcherism changed her mind, but she retained a sharp-tongued disdain for nationalism and readily shows her contempt for political posturing. She was one of two women passed over in 1992 for the party's general secretary post, when that went to Jack McConnell, leaving little sign of warmth between the two Labour MSPs. She was involved in the left-wing Labour Co-ordinating Committee (Scotland) and as a founder member of the Scottish Labour Women's Caucus. This put her at the forefront of the battle for gender balance in the party's candidacies, alongside her friends Margaret Curran (MSP for Glasgow Baillieston) and Rosina McCrae. She was chair of the Scottish Labour Party in 1993-94, and as a member of Hillhead Labour Party in the run-up to the 1992 election, she was a vocal opponent of sitting MP George Galloway, playing a leading part in the unsuccessful attempt to deselect him.

Lamont was deputy convenor of the local government and equal opportunities committees of the Scottish Parliament from June 1999 until December 2000, before becoming convenor of the social justice committee the next month, where she dealt with the controversial Glasgow Housing Stock Transfer proposals. She has become one of Labour's more influential backbenchers. In the debate on the Abolition of Poindings and Warrant Sales Bill in April 2000, Lamont made one of the most impressive contributions to the debate, supporting the bill and indicating the strength of opinion amongst Labour MSPs: a difficult speech given that Tommy Sheridan, her arch-rival in Glasgow Pollok, was the Bill's sponsor. She has challenged some of the more conservative attitudes of the judicial system such as when Lord Abernethy commented after a high profile trial that 'sex without consent is not in itself rape.' She also voted against the 13.5 per cent MSP pay rise in March 2002.

Citing problems for her Pollok constituents, Lamont was to the fore in raising concerns about youth disorder and anti-social behaviour helping it become the central plank of Labour's 2003 election campaign. Following that election, she remained one of the abler Labour MSPs never to have been a minister, returning as convener of the communities committee again. She has worked closely with her friend and minister Margaret Curran on shaping anti-social behaviour policies, leading some observers to question her independence as committee convener when she is so closely associated with Executive policies. She admits to being a fan of mawkish country music and is a sometime Gaelic speaker.

MP

IAN DAVIDSON was born in 1950 in Jedburgh and was MP for Glasgow Govan from 1992-97, defeating the SNP's Jim Sillars in 1992. He avoided the worst of the selection battles that scarred Labour with the redrawing of boundaries and loss of a seat, winning the Pollok candidacy and the seat in 1997. Educated at Jedburgh Grammar School and Galashiels Academy, Davidson went to Edinburgh University and Jordanhill College of Education.

He was chair of the National Organisation of Labour Students in 1973, and worked as a researcher to Janey Buchan, MEP for Glasgow from 1978-85, and for Community Service Volunteers from 1985-92. He failed to get the Labour nomination in the 1988 Govan by-election, losing to trade unionist Bob Gillespie, who would go down disastrously in the campaign. Prior to becoming an MP, Davidson was a Strathclyde Region councillor from 1978-92, as convenor of the education committee, while also being convener of education for COSLA and chair of its negotiating committee on teachers' pay and conditions. With a breezy, abrasive style, he was willing to take on the Educational Institute of Scotland as a producer interest, and was keen to modernise education provision. He even incurred the wrath of the Catholic church by thinking out loud about integration of schools. At the time, he was a key figure for Labour in providing a bulwark against Conservative rule from the Scottish Office, while also showing how the party might govern if it won power nationally. Yet his subsequent reputation in Westminster would be as anything but a moderniser.

Davidson positioned himself as left wing, independently-minded and no friend of devolution. Yet he sought a seat in the Scottish Parliament, and in 1998, that off-message positioning led to the Labour leadership excluding him from the panel for consideration for the Scottish Parliament. One of the grounds cited was his informal attire at the interview. Davidson took this exclusion badly, explicitly stating that if his voting loyalty to the Government was rewarded thus, he would henceforth feel free to speak and act more freely. So he did, and does. He has grown into a formidable thorn in the Government's flesh, taking a leading role in vituperatively attacking the prospect of Britain joining the euro currency, and using his position on the Public Accounts Committee to question the cost of Britain's military presence in Iraq.

He voted twice against the Government in the build up to the Iraq war in early 2003, against foundation hospitals for England and student top-up fees for England. He also flexed Westminster muscles in the row over voting reform for councils, saying a special Labour conference might be necessary to bring Jack McConnell's administration into line with party policy on the issue, and suggesting: 'We reflect perhaps more accurately than MSPs do the views of the Labour Party in the country'.

Glasgow Rutherglen

Predecessor Constituencies: none.

Socio-economic Indicators:

Constituency Pop. (16-64)	41,597
Claimant Count (May 2003)	2.9% (8.6% below average)
IBA/SDA Claimants	15.1%
Life Expectancy – Male	72.5 (0.9 yrs below average)
Life Expectancy – Female	77.0 (1.7 yrs below average)
Owner Occupied	63.0%
Social Rented	30.4%
Average Property Prices	£58,166 (39th)
Average Gross Income	£23,559 (55th)
Low Birthweight Babies	108 (6.1%)
Teenage Pregnancy Rates	379 (4.4%)
No. of Lone Parent Households	4,009 (14.0%)

CAB Enquiries

Issue	No. of cases	Percentage of total cases (%)
1. Consumer	925	24.0
2. Benefits	885	23.0
3. Employment	587	15.2
4. Housing	412	10.7
5. Other	392	10.2

2003 Scottish Parliament Election

Electorate: 49,511　　Turnout: 23,554 (47.6%)　　Turnout 1999: 56.9%

Candidate	Party	Votes	Votes%	99 %	Change%
Janis Hughes	Labour	10,794	45.8	46.3	– 0.5
Robert Brown	Lib Dem	4,491	19.1	20.0	– 0.9
Anne McLaughlin	SNP	3,517	14.9	21.2	– 6.3
Gavin Brown	Con	2,499	10.6	8.0	+ 2.6
William Bonnar	SSP	2,259	9.6	2.9 (other 1.7)	+ 6.7

Labour majority: 6,303 (26.8%)　　Swing: 0.2% Lib Dem to Labour

2001 General Election

Electorate: 51,855   Turnout: 29,213 (56.3%)

Candidate	Party	Votes	Votes%	Change%
Thomas McAvoy	Labour	16,760	57.4	− 0.2
Anne McLaughlin	SNP	4,135	14.2	− 1.1
David Jackson	Lib Dem	3,689	12.6	− 1.9
Malcolm Macaskill	Con	3,301	11.3	+ 2.0
William Bonnar	SSP	1,328	4.5	+ 3.8

Labour majority: 12,625 (43.2%)   Swing: 0.5% SNP to Labour

1945–97 Westminster

	Lab%	Con%	SNP%	Lib%	Other%	Turnout
1997	57.5	9.3	15.3	14.6	3.4	70.1
1992	55.4	16.9	16.3	11.3	0.2	75.2
1987	56.0	11.5	8.1	24.4	–	77.2
1983	48.3	18.0	5.5	27.8	0.3	75.1
1979	46.7	26.5	8.4	18.4	–	80.4
1974O	44.4	24.0	25.3	6.3	–	78.8
1974F	47.6	37.2	15.2	–	–	82.6
1970	52.3	43.3	–	–	4.4	79.7
1966	54.1	39.5	6.4	–	–	84.2
1964	52.6	42.8	4.6	–	–	86.0
1964B	55.5	44.5	–	–	–	82.0
1959	47.9	52.1	–	–	–	85.8
1955	47.1	52.9	–	–	–	84.1
1951	49.5	50.5	–	–	–	87.7
1950	49.5	47.7	–	2.8	–	86.1
1945	59.6	40.4	–	–	–	76.4

Rutherglen was until recently an independent burgh, entirely separate from the city and council of Glasgow. It became part of Glasgow District Council in the local reorganisation of 1974, but did not entirely lose its independent state of mind – and in the 1995 local government reorganisation, part of the parliamentary seat was put into South Lanarkshire. The socio–economic profile of Rutherglen reflects the mixture of affluence and disadvantage which makes up this seat. This is the only Glasgow seat with a claimant count below the national average. Average property prices are 13.8 per cent below the national average, having risen 62.9 per cent in 1991-2001.

Rutherglen has, like most parts of Glasgow, suffered from job losses in recent years with anxieties and concerns over the less secure and less permanent nature of new jobs arising. In October 2001, the Hoover plant at Cambuslang announced job losses, but less than one year later its future looked secure when it won the contract to build a new generation of vacuum cleaners. However, in October 2003

Hoover announced it was shutting its Cambuslang plant with the loss of over 300 jobs after a 30 year presence. Future job worries also centre on the route of the M74 extension and the need for Morris Furniture to relocate. Significant developments are happening in the area including the decision for a £100 million housing development in Richmond Park, nearby Glasgow Green, involving 1,000 private homes as well as 250 rented homes. Rising social problems, including crime and drug problems, have seen a concerted attempt by public authorities to tackle them via such initiatives as the Rutherglen and Cambuslang Drugs Forum. South Lanarkshire Council has proposed building a new all-purpose community services, leisure and social work centre at Annan Drive, Cambuslang, which would see the closure of several local amenities.

Labour first won Rutherglen in the breakthrough year of 1922, before losing it in 1931, until 1945 when Gilbert McAllister won it back for Labour, holding it in 1950; Richard Brooman-White regained it for the Conservatives with a slender majority of 352 in 1951 and held it until his death in January 1964. George MacKenzie then retook it for Labour in a May 1964 by-election, just months before the October 1964 election, and held it continuously until his retirement in 1987.

In 1987, Thomas McAvoy increased Labour's vote to 56 per cent and again to 57.5 per cent in 1997. In 2001, McAvoy saw Labour's majority fall by 2,000 to 12,625 as Labour's vote fell by nearly 4,000 and the SNP fell back by over 1,000 producing, on a lower turnout, a tiny SNP to Labour swing.

Labour polled fewer votes in the first Scottish Parliament elections, while the SNP closed the gap between the two parties to 7,287 without threatening Labour's hold. In 2003 Labour's majority fell from 7,287 to 6,303 with their vote declining by 2,500, while the Nationalists fell back by 1,500, allowing the Lib Dems to win second place.

In the regional list vote, Labour won 38.3 per cent to the SNP's distant 14.5 per cent, the Lib Dems on 14.2 per cent and SSP on 10.8 per cent, with the Greens on 5.1 per cent in sixth place. Rutherglen has long had a strong Liberal tradition, reflecting the independent mind of the ancient burgh, but between 1983 and 1992 the Lib Dems saw their vote fall from 28 per cent to 11 per cent. Since then it has risen first to 14.5 per cent in 1997 and then to 20 per cent in 1999, but Robert Brown was unable to build on this in 2003 despite being a Glasgow list MSP.

Boundary changes for Westminster will move Rutherglen out of Glasgow with the exception of the Toryglen and King's Park wards which would be joined to the existing Cathcart seat in a new Glasgow South seat. The wards of Cambuslang and Halfway will form part of a new Rutherglen and Hamilton West seat along with parts of South Lanarkshire, while the remaining parts of the existing seat will be moved into East Kilbride. At a Scottish Parliament level, Labour's position in Rutherglen seems secure, with no opposition party able to gather enough support to mount a serious challenge.

MSP

JANIS HUGHES was born in 1958 in Glasgow and educated at Queen's Park School, Glasgow, and Glasgow Western School of Nursing. She subsequently became a nurse working in a variety of hospitals in the Greater Glasgow area, including the Victoria Infirmary, Royal Hospital for Sick Children, Western Infirmary and Belvedere Hospital from 1980-88. She was an administrator in the renal unit of the Glasgow Royal Infirmary from 1988-99.

With backing from the NUPE wing of Unison, of which she has been a member since 1980, she won the Glasgow Rutherglen candidacy, and had to rely on union backing again to secure it again for 2003, after becoming the only Labour MSP to lose the membership section of a re-selection ballot. Few MSPs enjoyed a lower profile than Hughes in the first Parliament, being at first deputy convenor of the procedures committee and then a member of the health and community care committee from January 2001.

A McConnell supporter in his leadership battles, she was made an unpaid aide to neighbouring MSP Mike Watson when he was tourism, culture and sports minister, and is a kenspeckle figure in the Parliament for sporting one of its two best perma-tans. She has shown some independent spirit, voting against the 13.5 per cent MSP pay rise and Greater Glasgow Health Board plans for re-shaping hospital services in the south of the city. Since the 2003 election, she has been deputy convener of the health committee. In 1999, she answered one questionnaire by claiming her preferred epitaph would be: she had some lovely shoes.

MP

TOMMY McAVOY was born in 1943 in Rutherglen and has been MP for Rutherglen since 1987. Educated at St Columbkilles Junior Secondary School, he worked as an engineering storeman and an engineering union shop steward. He became chair of Rutherglen Community Council in 1980 and a Strathclyde Region councillor from 1982-87. In the Commons, he was a whip from 1990-93 and 1996-97 and in Government became third in the Whips' Office in 1997 with the splendid title of Comptroller of HM Household. As such, he was one of only three Labour MPs on the government payroll who kept the same job from 1997 until at least 2004: the others were Tony Blair and Gordon Brown. Like several Catholic Scottish Labour MPs from the west of Scotland he is conservative on abortion, and embryo research, as well as opposing the 1992 Euthanasia Bill. Elected for four terms McAvoy's national profile is low, but he prides himself on his effectiveness as a local politician and in standing up for the interests of Rutherglen against Glasgow's designs for enlargement.

Glasgow Shettleston

Predecessor Constituencies: Glasgow Bridgeton (1945–70), Glasgow Gorbals (1945–70), Glasgow Queen's Park (1974–82) and Glasgow Central (1945–92).

Socio-economic Indicators:

Constituency Pop. (16-64)	37,769
Claimant Count (May 2003)	5.3% (70.5% above average)
IBA/SDA Claimants	27.6%
Life Expectancy – Male	63.9 (9.5 yrs below average)
Life Expectancy – Female	75.2 (3.5 yrs below average)
Owner Occupied	35.9%
Social Rented	51.4%
Average Property Prices	£39,539 (73rd)
Average Gross Income	£17,170 (73rd)
Low Birthweight Babies	154 (8.9%)
Teenage Pregnancy Rates	479 (6.6%)
No. of Lone Parent Households	4,742 (16.1%)

CAB Enquiries

Issue	No. of cases	Percentage of total cases (%)
1. Benefits	3023	43.5
2. Consumer	1259	18.1
3. Housing	615	8.9
4. Employment	523	7.5
5. Other	440	6.3

2003 Scottish Parliament Election

Electorate: 46,734   *Turnout*: 16,547 (35.4%)   *Turnout 1999*: 40.6

Candidate	Party	Votes	Votes%	99 %	Change%
Frank McAveety	Labour	9,365	56.6	54.0	+ 2.6
Jim Byrne	SNP	3,018	18.2	27.4	– 9.1
Rosie Kane	SSP	2,403	14.5	8.0	+ 6.5
Dorothy Luckhurst	Con	982	5.9	6.1	– 0.2
Lewis Hutton	Lib Dem	779	4.7	4.6	+ 0.1

Labour majority: 6,347 (38.4%)   *Swing*: 5.9% SNP to Labour

2001 General Election

Electorate: 51,557   *Turnout*: 20,465 (39.7%)

Candidate	Party	Votes	Votes%	Change%
David Marshall	Labour	13,235	64.7	- 8.5
Jim Byrne	SNP	3,417	16.7	+ 2.7
Rosie Kane	SSP	1,396	6.8	+ 5.0
Lewis Hutton	Lib Dem	1,105	5.4	+ 1.4
Campbell Murdoch	Con	1,082	5.3	- 0.2
Murdo Ritchie	Soc Lab	230	1.1	-

Labour majority: 9,818 (48.0%)   *Swing*: 5.6% Labour to SNP

1945–97 Westminster

	Lab%	Con%	SNP%	Lib%	Other%	Turnout%
1997	73.2	5.5	14.0	4.0	3.5	55.9
1992	60.6	15.0	19.1	5.3	–	68.9
1987	63.6	13.3	12.7	10.4	–	70.4
1983	54.2	19.1	7.9	18.5	0.3	67.4
1979	64.1	22.0	–	13.9	–	68.2
1974O	54.3	14.4	28.5	2.8	–	64.4
1974F	53.6	24.4	22.0	–	–	69.4
1970	59.9	26.7	13.4	–	–	63.7
1966	65.6	22.3	12.1	–	–	68.6
1964	68.0	32.0	–	–	–	71.4
1959	60.9	39.1	–	–	–	75.3
1955	57.8	42.2	–	–	–	69.3
1951	59.8	37.4	–	–	2.8	81.2
1950	56.6	36.8	–	–	6.6	79.9
1945	20.6	31.1	–	–	48.3	66.6

Glasgow Central (1945–92)

1992	57.2	13.9	20.8	6.3	1.8	63.1
1989B	54.6	7.6	30.2	1.5	6.0	52.8
1987	64.5	13.0	9.9	10.5	2.0	65.6
1983	53.0	19.0	10.3	16.7	1.1	62.9
1980B	60.4	8.8	26.3	–	4.1	42.8
1979	72.5	16.4	11.1	–	–	59.5
1974O	63.6	13.0	19.2	4.2	–	56.9
1974F	58.7	21.4	13.8	6.1	–	63.0
1970	66.1	19.9	14.0	–	–	59.2
1966	74.8	25.2	–	–	–	58.7
1964	70.1	29.9	–	–	–	62.4

cont'd

	Lab%	Con%	SNP%	Lib%	Other%	Turnout%
1959	64.6	35.4	–	–	–	67.4
1955	61.8	38.2	–	–	–	64.1
1951	58.3	40.2	–	–	1.5	74.3
1950	54.6	43.6	–	–	1.8	74.0
1945	36.9	44.0	–	5.0	14.1	59.6

Glasgow Gorbals (1945–70), Glasgow Queen's Park (1974–82)

	Lab%	Con%	SNP%	Lib%	Other%	Turnout%
1982B	56.0	12.0	20.0	9.4	2.6	47.0
1979	64.4	24.0	9.7	–	1.9	68.4
1974O	56.1	17.0	21.8	3.7	1.4	67.0
1974F	56.2	26.6	15.6	–	1.6	73.3
1970	69.3	20.8	7.4	–	2.5	59.8
1969B	53.4	18.6	25.0	–	3.0	58.5
1966	73.1	22.8	–	–	4.1	61.7
1964	71.4	23.0	–	–	5.6	64.5
1959	63.3	30.8	–	–	5.9	68.2
1955	61.1	32.1	–	–	6.8	65.2
1951	61.9	31.9	–	–	6.2	76.0
1950	58.0	31.4	–	–	10.6	77.3
1948B	54.5	28.6	–	–	16.9	50.0
1945	80.0	20.0	–	–	–	56.8

Glasgow Bridgeton (1945–70)

	Lab%	Con%	SNP%	Lib%	Other%	Turnout%
1970	62.9	21.6	8.8	–	6.7	56.3
1966	74.3	25.7	–	–	–	58.8
1964	71.6	28.4	–	–	–	63.6
1961B	57.5	20.7	18.7	–	3.1	41.9
1959	63.4	36.6	–	–	–	68.5
1955	57.7	34.9	–	–	7.4	66.0
1951	63.6	31.0	–	–	5.4	76.9
1950	59.4	32.3	–	–	8.3	76.9
1946B	28.0	21.6	13.9	–	36.5	53.3
1945	–	33.6	–	–	66.4	58.2

The socio-economic profile of Shettleston illustrates the poverty and disadvantage people in the area face. The claimant counts put one in three of the working age population on benefits. The gap between male and female life expectancy rates of 11.3 years is the highest in Scotland. There is 35.9 per cent owner occupation – the lowest in the country (up from 25.1 per cent ten years previous), and 51.4 per cent social housing. Average property prices are 41.4 per cent below the average, and join gross incomes as the lowest in the country. Low birthweight babies are 8.9 per cent of all live births – the highest rate in all Scotland, and lone parent households 53.6 per cent above the average. Citizens Advice Bureau enquiries reflect the reliance of a large part of Shettleston's inhabitants on state benefits and support. Shettleston has been rated the most unhealthy constituency in the whole of

Britain, narrowly ahead of neighbouring Springburn, and four other Glasgow seats which make up the top six.

Glasgow Shettleston is now a very different seat to the Shettleston prior to the 1997 boundary redistribution. This reconfigured the seat and the Shettleston which emerged is made up of exactly half of the old Central seat (24,693 voters) and half from Shettleston (24,665). Shettleston was previously the seat of the historic East End of Glasgow with its traditions of hard-working, radical and respectable working-class communities and culture. It is also the home of the legendary Glasgow Celtic FC, a team connected to the predominantly Catholic communities of the East End. The new Shettleston has now moved westward into the city centre and across the River Clyde taking in some of the most famous and evocative areas of Glasgow – the Gorbals and Hutchesontown – and reaching as far south as the once Tory and still gentrified terraces of Queen's Park.

Despite the grim statistics, there are signs of life in the new Shettleston. The legendary Gorbals now carries the word 'new' in front of it as a symbol of its comprehensive urban regeneration for the second time in just over a generation, as tenements, shops and tree-lined streets have been reintroduced in the Crown Street development. For the first time in decades, Glasgow's inner core has been reversing its population decline, seeing people and businesses come back into once declining areas – a symbol of Glasgow's capacity to reinvent itself.

Glasgow City Council has attempted to tackle some of the serious social problems, most prominently with the city-wide housing stock transfer, to be followed with large-scale refurbishment, development and demolition. The area will also be affected – for good or for ill – by the extension of the M74 into the Kingston Bridge. In March 2001, the council announced its intention to close Govanhill swimming pool with minimal consultation, its rationale being that the Victorian baths were dilapidated and new, first-class premises had opened in the Gorbals. The Labour council was caught unprepared for the power of the local community's response which involved an imaginative, energetic campaign touching a raw nerve about the decline of their area and its neglect by public agencies. The campaign eventually petered out, after police and sheriffs cleared protestors who had been barricading themselves around the building. Labour easily won the seat at the 2001 and 2003 elections, but a deeper damage had been done to peoples' trust in politics and governance.

Shettleston's Labour roots go back to the days of the Independent Labour Party. John Wheatley stood in the 'coupon' election of 1918 and just failed to defeat Rear Admiral Adair by 74 votes; he won the seat in Labour's watershed year of 1922 and went on to serve in the first Labour Government of 1924 as Minister for Health. He bequeathed Labour's claim to its first piece of significant legislation, with the Housing Act 1924 which brought in subsidies for council house building.

Wheatley's death in 1930 saw John McGovern become Labour MP from 1930-59, even managing to hold the seat in the debacle of 1931 when Labour was reduced to a mere seven seats across Scotland. Myer Galpern, MP from 1959-79, saw Labour's vote rise to 68.0 per cent in 1964; subsequently David Marshall became MP in 1979 winning 64.1 per cent in 1979 and a majority of 9,161; in 1987 this rose back up to 63.6 per cent, after dipping in 1983, while his majority increased to 18,981.

Labour's vote rose in 1997 to 73.2 per cent, while its majority rose from a notional 15,644 in 1992 to 15,868 in 1997. No significant opposition emerged as all the mainstream parties lost ground and the Scottish Socialists made little headway. In 2001, Labour's David Marshall saw his majority reduced from 15,868 to 9,818 as his vote fell by 6,000 and 8.5 per cent, while the SNP's vote fell by 331, allowing them, on a reduced turnout of 39.7 per cent (the third lowest in the UK), to put nearly 3 per cent on their vote.

The 1999 Scottish Parliament elections caused Labour a few problems. Frank McAveety, a young, popular and energetic city councillor, had become leader of the city council at the early age by Glasgow standards of 35. This involved him presiding over a series of year-on-year cuts in jobs and services, which attracted unpopularity, so his candidature in Shettleston was never going to be universally popular. McAveety was never going to lose Shettleston, but registered Labour's worst result in the elections (outside Falkirk West and its Dennis Canavan effect) with Labour's vote falling 19.2 per cent and its majority slashed from 15,868 to 5,467 and a swing of 16.3 per cent from Labour to SNP – the second highest in the country. In 2003, Labour's majority rose from 5,467 to 6,347 as Labour's vote fell by 1,700 – rising by 2.6 per cent on a lower turnout of 35.4 per cent (the lowest in Scotland). The Nationalists fell back by 2,500 and 9 per cent. Rosie Kane, standing for the third consecutive time in the seat for the SSP, increased her vote by 800 and 6.5 per cent.

In the regional list vote, Labour won 44.4 per cent to 17.6 per cent for the SNP, 15.5 per cent for the SSP, with the Greens on 4.6 per cent in fourth, just whisking ahead of the Tories and Lib Dems. The British National Party gained their highest Scottish vote in this seat, winning 1.6 per cent of the list vote.

Boundary changes for the Westminster Shettleston seat would see it abolished and its constituent parts distributed to the new seats of Glasgow North East, East and Central. At the Scottish Parliament level, Shettleston has shown its attachment to Labour, with the main challenge to the party's hold coming from increased voter apathy and disconnection.

MSP

FRANK McAVEETY was born in 1962 in Glasgow and educated at All Saints' Secondary School, Glasgow, and Strathclyde University, where he studied English and history. He then did teacher training at St Andrew's College of Education, Glasgow, teaching English in Glasgow and then Renfrewshire from 1985-98, and becoming a Glasgow councillor in 1988. Then aged 25, he was a breath of fresh air among the ranks of ageing Glasgow councillors. He became convenor of arts and culture from 1994-97. Then in 1997, at the age of 35, he became the youngest leader the council had ever had. This followed the 'junkets for votes' affair, which saw the demise and suspension of council leader Bob Gould and the suspension of other prominent councillors, as Labour headquarters acted to rid the city's Labour group of its long-running factionalism. Jack McConnell was then party general secretary, and worked to put McAveety in charge, with subsequent council leader Charlie Gordon as his deputy, and Andy Kerr (later the East Kilbride MSP) as MacAveety's unelected political minder. Although problems remain in Glasgow, this team was credited with putting Labour politics in Glasgow Council, which it dominates, on a new footing. McAveety has also been a board member of Glasgow Development Agency and was chair of the Glasgow Alliance.

McAveety's style as a fast-talking, wise-cracking showman, driven by his own obsessions and love for popular culture marked him out as a very different kind of Labour councillor in the hallowed chambers of Glasgow City Chambers, but have not transferred so easily to the Scottish Parliament. Having been the Labour Party's spokesman on housing in the 1999 elections, he became one of two deputies to Wendy Alexander – not a natural soulmate and a world apart in their political styles – with responsibility for local government. This put him directly into confrontation with his council successor Charles Gordon, who was unhappy about being forced into Glasgow's Housing Stock Transfer, and is not one of McAveety's bigger admirers. McAveety was also pushing at the time for a local government reform which would see directly-elected mayors, or provosts, of at least one big city, making little secret of how much he would like to be one himself, in Glasgow of course. But facing union opposition, and apparently fearing that Tommy Sheridan could do in Glasgow what Ken Livingstone was then doing to Labour in London, the idea was shelved.

That part of McAveety's ministerial career was brought to an abrupt end, following a notorious wobble during the 2000 Labour leadership race. Apart from his opponent, Jack McConnell, Henry

McLeish had the support of every minister with the exception of McAveety, and McLeish finally swung the Shettleston MSP away from the McConnell camp at the last minute, raising the animosity of both sides. The harsh reward for wobbling was to be one of McLeish's two sackings in the reshuffle which followed a few days later. As a wounded Labour backbench MSP, McAveety became at first a member of the health and community care committee, and the standards committee, similar to one he had set up in Glasgow Council.

The rise of Jack McConnell to First Minister did not bring him back into ministerial ranks – until, that is, Wendy Alexander abruptly left the cabinet in May 2002. McAveety was brought back as junior health minister under Malcolm Chisholm. Re-elected in 2003, he had a half-promotion, in that he took over tourism, culture and sport, with a junior minister's salary yet a place in cabinet. He quickly saw the photo opportunity potential, and got to work as one of Scottish politics' best entertainers and extroverts, though his appointment came just too late to go in his ministerial capacity to Seville to see his beloved Celtic play (and lose) in the UEFA cup final. One of his first major ministerial announcements was to decide the location of the national Theatre of Scotland with a £9.3 million budget in the Easterhouse Arts Factory. this decision was applauded by many in the world of arts and Galsgow's East End, but was also seen by others as reflecting McAveety's character: brash and liking the big gesture.

He is renowned for, and endlessly boasting about, the size of his record collection which fills his garage – hence the inevitable 'Frankie goes to Holyrood' references. However, in a series of rock profiles in *Holyrood* magazine, McAveety's choices embraced the dull certainties and conformities of the post-60s rock generation: Elvis, Dusty, the Sex Pistols, the Pixies (of course), Blue Nile, Big Star – a Gordon Brown favourite – and contained no genuine revelations (with the exception of Laura Nyro). Invited by the *Herald* to attend five Edinburgh Festival shows in one day, his prize pick was the 1970s has-been Dean Friedman, with McAveety declaring that he knew and could sing all the hits. Both of them.

MP

DAVID MARSHALL was born in 1941 in Glasgow, and educated at Larbert, Denny and Falkirk High Schools and Woodside Senior Secondary School, Glasgow. He has been MP for Glasgow Shettleston since 1979, described as one of 'the lost generation' for disappearing immediately and anonymously into Labour's opposition years. He was an office junior, a farm worker from 1956-59, a tram and bus conductor from 1960-69, and Scottish secretary of the Industrial Orthopaedic Society from 1971-79. He joined the Labour Party in 1962, became Labour organiser for Glasgow in 1969, before serving on Glasgow Corporation from 1972-74 and Strathclyde Regional Council from 1974-79, where he was convenor of its manpower committee.

As an MP, he opposed early attempts by the Michael Foot leadership to tackle Militant entryism, supporting Tony Benn's bid for the leadership in 1981. He introduced a backbench bill which became the Solvent Abuse (Scotland) Act 1983. He served on the Scottish Affairs select committee from 1981-83 and 1992-97 and the transport select committee from 1985-92, as its chair in the final five of those years, before being removed by Tory whips without even being told.

Marshall combines a mix of radical and conservative views not unusual amongst Scottish Labour MPs. He is sceptical about the European Union, voting against the Maastricht Treaty, was opposed to both Gulf wars while voting against Labour Government welfare benefit cuts twice in 1999, and opposing any reduction in the age of consent for male homosexuals in 1994 and again in 1999. He urged Donald Dewar to site the Scottish Parliament in Glasgow, in recognition of its poor health record. His own health is no doubt helped by numerous foreign trips on Commons business, helped by his chairmanship of the all party groups on aviation, Australia and New Zealand, Canada and the South Pacific.

Glasgow Springburn

Predecessor Constituencies: none.

Socio-economic Indicators:

Constituency Pop. (16-64)	44,145
Claimant Count (May 2003)	5.0% (58.7% above average)
IBA/SDA Claimants	21.1%
Life Expectancy – Male	66.6 (6.8 yrs below average)
Life Expectancy – Female	74.8 (3.9 yrs below average)
Owner Occupied	41.6%
Social Rented	48.0%
Average Property Prices	£40,928 (71st)
Average Gross Income	£18,848 (72nd)
Low Birthweight Babies	156 (7.5%)
Teenage Pregnancy Rates	576 (6.5%)
No. of Lone Parent Households	5,446 (16.5%)

2003 Scottish Parliament Election

Electorate: 49,557   *Turnout*: 18,573 (37.5%)   *Turnout 1999*: 43.8%

Candidate	Party	Votes	Votes%	99 %	Change%
Paul Martin	Labour	10,963	59.0	58.6	+ 0.5
Francis Rankin	SNP	2,956	15.9	26.2	- 10.2
Margaret Bean	SSP	2,653	14.3	4.7	+9.6
Alan Rodger	Con	1,233	6.6	5.3	+ 1.3
Charles Dundas	Lib Dem	768	4.1	5.3	` – 1.2

Labour majority: 8,007 (43.1%)   *Swing*: 5.4% SNP to Labour

2001 General Election

Electorate: 55,192   *Turnout*: 24,104 (43.7%)

Candidate	Party	Votes	Votes%	Change%
Michael Martin	Speaker	16,053	66.6	-
Sandy Bain	SNP	4,675	19.4	+ 2.9
Carolyn Leckie	SSP	1,879	7.8	+ 6.5
Daniel Houston	Scot Un	1,289	5.3	-
Richard Silverster	Ind	208	0.9	-

Speaker majority: 11,378 (47.2%)   *Swing*: n/a

1945–97 Westminster

	Lab%	Con%	SNP%	Lib%	Other%	Turnout%
1997	71.4	6.0	16.5	4.3	1.9	59.1
1992	67.7	8.7	19.5	4.1	–	65.7
1987	73.6	8.3	10.2	7.9	–	67.5
1983	64.7	13.1	8.1	14.1	–	65.1
1979	66.1	21.3	12.6	–	–	67.8
1974O	54.6	13.3	28.3	2.7	1.1	66.5
1974F	53.7	22.1	22.8	–	1.4	70.4
1970	64.3	19.6	14.3	–	1.8	61.3
1966	67.8	19.1	9.4	–	3.7	66.6
1964	65.3	21.8	9.2	–	3.7	69.2
1959	58.8	36.7	–	–	4.5	72.6
1955	57.5	37.0	–	–	5.0	69.1
1951	62.4	37.6	–	–	–	78.0
1950	59.7	31.9	–	4.3	4.1	76.9
1945	65.0	35.0	–	–	–	63.6

Springburn stretches from the northern boundary of the city close to the city centre and East End. It includes Riddrie and Lethamhill, the striking tower blocks known as the 'Red Road' flats, recently used to house Kosovo Albanian refugees, and the tenements and parks of Dennistoun and Alexandra Parade. The socio-economic profile reflects the disadvantage of the area. The claimant counts put just over one in four of the working age population on benefits. Average property prices are 39.3 per cent below the national average, having risen 52.1 per cent in the 1990s; average gross income is the second lowest in the country only beaten by Shettleston. Lone parent households are 57.1 per cent above the average. It has been rated the second most unhealthy constituency in Britain after Shettleston.

The biggest political controversy affecting Springburn in the last few years has been the UK Government's policy of dispersing asylum seekers. Glasgow City Council has taken over 8,000 asylum seekers, placing 1,500 of them in the Sighthill area of Springburn. With a vulnerable community which feels it has little influence or voice with the powers that be, tensions and conflict burst into the open as a result. Local people felt ignored and that asylum seekers were getting preferential treatment, while some felt it permissible to voice racist opinions. In August 2001 this reached a climax when Firsat Dag, a 22 year old Kurdish man from Turkey was stabbed to death in Sighthill.

Another major issue was the decision announced in January 2000 by Greater Glasgow Health Board to open a secure unit for mentally ill offenders at Stobhill Hospital in the constituency. Two months later, in March, the Scottish Parliament's health committee forced the Board to consult the local community with 43,000 people signing a petition against the proposals. In June 2001, Jean Turner, a former Stobhill doctor won second place in the neighbouring Strathkelvin and Bearsden by-election, eventually winning the seat in the resulting 2003 election. In January 2002, the Board confirmed its decision to open a medium secure facility. Plans were also announced to turn Stobhill hospital into an Ambulatory Care and Diagnostic hospital where people will be seen on a day care basis. Barlinnie Prison, Scotland's most infamous prison is situated in the constituency, and in March 2002 it was announced that it would reduce its size to house 530 prisoners.

Springburn, like several of the Glasgow seats, was first won by Labour in 1922, by George Hardie, half-brother of Labour leader and legend, Keir Hardie. It was later lost by him in the National Government landslide of 1931 by the most slender of margins (34 votes) and rewon in 1935. Post-war Springburn was represented first by John Forman, from 1945-64, then by Richard Buchanan from 1964-79, followed by Michael Martin from 1979 to the present day. Martin drove Labour's vote up to 73.6 per cent in 1987 – the highest in Glasgow and one of the highest in the UK. In 1997, Martin polled 71.4 per cent, just being outpolled by neighbouring Shettleston for the highest Labour vote share in Scotland. He later became Speaker of the House of Commons with the convention that he should therefore stand unopposed without party label broken by the SNP and SSP. His vote fell by 6,000.

In the 1999 elections, the MP's son Paul, a local councillor, became Springburn MSP. Martin Junior was elected with 8,000 fewer votes on a lower turnout and a majority reduced from 17,326 to 7,893; the SNP established a respectable second place, but still 32 per cent behind Labour. In 2003, Paul Martin increased Labour's majority by 114 votes and 11 per cent on a reduced turnout of 37.5 per cent (the third lowest in Scotland), as Labour's vote declined by 3,000 and the Nationalists by over 3,000 – seeing their vote half and fall by 10 per cent – their second highest fall in the city. The Scottish Socialists in third place put 1,500 votes on their support and increased their share by 10 per cent. In the regional list vote, Labour won 47.1 per cent to 14.5 per cent for the SSP and 14.3 per cent for the SNP, with the Greens in a distant fourth place on 5.4 per cent.

Boundary Commission changes at Westminster have produced a larger Springburn which will take parts of neighbouring Shettleston to form a new Glasgow North East expected to have the Speaker as candidate. Springburn's future political configuration in the Scottish Parliament is unlikely to throw up any major surprises, beyond the lack of enthusiasm voters seem to have for all the political choices on offer. Such a prospect will suit what threadbare Labour machine there is in Springburn – but one which is still infinitely superior to anything the rival parties can offer – allowing Labour to remain dominant for years to come.

MSP

PAUL MARTIN was born in 1967 in Glasgow and educated at All Saints Secondary School, Glasgow, and Barmulloch College, Glasgow, without having had a career outside politics. First elected a councillor on Glasgow District Council in a 1993 by-election for the Alexandra Park ward, he became a councillor on Glasgow City Council in 1995 for Royston. On the council, Martin held a variety of economic development posts. In the battle for Glasgow seats ahead of the 1999 election, he had something of an advantage with his father, Michael, the long-time MP for Glasgow Springburn, who would become Speaker of the Commons in 2000.

In the Scottish Parliament, Martin joined the justice 1 committee in January 2001, and facing persistent constituents' complaints about anti-social behaviour and youth offending, he was prominent in pushing within his party for the Executive to take the issues more seriously. Allied with Johann Lamont in Glasgow Pollok, the pressure paid off when Jack McConnell adopted the cause as the main plank of the 2003 election campaign and post-election legislative programme.

In the early period as an MSP, Martin's most significant achievement had been to campaign successfully to block Greater Glasgow Health Board's attempts to put a secure unit at Stobhill Hospital in his constituency. More often, he is an arch-Labour loyalist not given to rocking the backbench boat. His reward in the first Parliament was to sit on a record four committees simultaneously by the time of its dissolution; audit, justice, standards and procedures, and in 2002, he became Parliamentary aide to finance minister Andy Kerr. Following the 2003 election, his committee work was limited to the local government and transport committee, but his party loyalty was tested by the coalition adopting voting reform for councils. In the March 2004 vote on the issue, he abstained. Martin became chair of a Labour group including MSPs, MPs and trade unionists who wanted to stop the measure.

MP

MICHAEL MARTIN was born in Glasgow on 3 July 1945, two days before the 1945 general election, and has been MP for Glasgow Springburn since 1979. Educated at St Patrick's Boys' School, Glasgow, he served on Glasgow Corporation from 1973-74 and Glasgow District Council from 1974-79. Originally a sheet metal worker, he was active in the 1970s campaigns against the closures of the Upper Clyde Shipyard and Hillington Rolls Royce plant where he was an AUEW shop steward from 1970-74 before becoming a NUPE full-time organiser from 1976-79.

After being elected an MP in 1979, he was an early opponent of the Tory policy of selling off council houses, calling it 'irresponsible', and had to fight off a Militant entryist challenge in Springburn before being re-selected for the 1983 election. He was Parliamentary Private Secretary to Denis Healey, when Healey was deputy leader of the Labour Party from 1981-83, a member of the services committee from 1987-91 and finance and services committee from 1992-97 as well as chair of the administrative committee from 1992-97. In 1997, he became a Deputy Speaker and deputy chair of Ways and Means. One of Scottish Labour's Catholic MPs, he is conservative on social issues such as abortion and homosexuality. In 1983, he petitioned to ban doctors from giving prescription contraceptives to girls under the age of 16, voted for the Alton abortion-limiting bill in 1988, was one of only six Labour MPs to vote against the lowering of the age of consent for male homosexuals in 1994, later abstaining on the issue in 1998. In 1989, he alleged a 'fascist element in the Scottish National Party which the leadership will do absolutely nothing about', which 'encouraged young children to throw stones at Labour cars'.

When Betty Boothroyd announced her intention to retire as Speaker of the House of Commons, Martin became one of the leading candidates to succeed her. In the contest, arranged on the first day of the new Parliamentary session on 23 October 2000, and presided over by the father of the house, Sir Edward Heath, a dozen candidates competed for the post. After Menzies Campbell canvassed opinion, and appeared to have the support of Tony Blair but then withdrew, the main contest was between Martin, supported by many Labour members, and Sir George Young, the Eton-educated Conservative MP, who was Tony Blair's next choice and that of several prominent ministers. Martin won the vote easily, becoming the first Catholic Speaker since the Reformation, while breaking with the convention that the Speakership alternated between the major parties. His authority was challenged by Tory ridicule, and there were reports he found his Parliamentary officials snobbish towards him. There was even more trouble from Parliamentary sketch-writers, who made cruel fun of his accent, with the nickname 'Gorbals Mick', questioning his intelligence and credentials for the job. He hit back at the campaign to undermine him, and having seen off Nationalist and Scottish Socialist candidates in his constituency he was acclaimed as Mr Speaker after the 2001 election, without any opposition.

Gordon

Predecessor Constituencies: Aberdeenshire and Kincardineshire Central (1945) and Aberdeenshire West (1950–79).

Socio-economic Indicators:

Constituency Pop. (16-64)	50,803
Claimant Count (May 2003)	1.2% (60.1% below average)
IBA/SDA Claimants	4.7%
Life Expectancy – Male	76.3 (2.9 yrs above average)
Life Expectancy – Female	81.4 (2.7 yrs above average)
Owner Occupied	73.0%
Social Rented	17.0%
Average Property Prices	£73,796 (18th)
Average Gross Income	£29,484 (9th)
Low Birthweight Babies	129 (5.3%)
Teenage Pregnancy Rates	247 (2.4%)
No. of Lone Parent Households	2,020 (6.4%)

2003 Scottish Parliament Election

Electorate: 60,727   *Turnout*: 28,798 (47.4%)   *Turnout 1999*: 56.5%

Candidate	Party	Votes	Votes%	99 %	Change%
Nora Radcliffe	Lib Dem	10,963	38.1	36.7	+ 1.3
Nanette Milne	Con	6,892	23.9	19.6	+ 4.3
Alasdair Allan	SNP	6,501	22.6	24.3	− 1.7
Ellis Thorpe	Labour	2,973	10.3	11.8	− 1.4
John Sangster	SSP	780	2.7	(other 7.6)	–
Steven Mathers	Ind	689	2.4	–	–

Liberal Democrat majority: 4,071 (14.1%)   *Swing*: 1.5% Liberal Democrat to Conservative

2001 General Election

Electorate: 60,059   *Turnout*: 35,001 (58.3%)

Candidate	Party	Votes	Votes%	Change%
Malcolm Bruce	Lib Dem	15,928	45.5	+ 2.9
Nanette Milne	Con	8,049	23.0	− 3.0
Rhona Kemp	SNP	5,760	16.5	− 3.5
Ellis Thorpe	Labour	4,730	13.5	+ 3.2
John Sangster	SSP	534	1.5	–

Liberal Democrat majority: 7,879 (22.5%)   *Swing*: 3.0% Conservative to Liberal Democrat

1945–97 Westminster

	Lab%	Con%	SNP%	Lib%	Other%	Turnout
1997	10.3	26.0	20.0	42.6	1.1	71.9
1992	11.3	37.0	14.3	37.4	–	73.9
1987	11.5	31.9	7.2	49.5	–	73.7
1983	8.5	42.0	5.7	43.8	–	69.4
1979	15.3	40.9	8.3	35.5	–	75.9
1974O	12.2	35.7	22.2	29.9	–	76.5
1974F	10.5	38.9	15.4	35.2	-	81.0
1970	15.5	46.7	5.3	32.5	-	75.8
1966	17.1	39.7	–	43.2	-	76.3
1964	20.4	46.4	–	33.2	-	77.4
1959	31.5	68.5	–	–	-	72.1
1955	27.2	59.0	–	13.8	-	72.6
1951	22.6	55.2	–	22.2	-	78.3
1950	23.1	55.5	–	21.4	-	80.9
1945	26.6	52.3	–	21.1	-	68.3

Gordon constituency is located to the north-west of the city of Aberdeen and includes a large part of commuter territory and Aberdeen hinterland, as well as rural towns and settlements such as Ellon, Huntly, Inverurie, Keith, Old Meldrum and Turriff to the north-west of the granite city. It was one of the largest seats in the United Kingdom prior to the boundary changes which preceeded the 1997 election. From an electorate of 81,097, the new seat was reduced to 56,716 voters. Their socio-economic profile reflects the prosperity of the seat. The claimant count is the second lowest in the country, while incapacity and disability benefits are the third lowest. Average property prices are 9.4 per cent above the national average and rose 50 per cent in the 1990s.

Gordon has been changed by the oil boom of the 1980s, bringing new jobs and services. However, this has brought problems as well as opportunities, with the 1990s slide in the price of oil affecting the growth of the industry. Farming is still important, but was hit by the BSE crisis and the restrictions on cattle movements imposed to deal with the foot and mouth outbreak in 2001. The industry was already in trouble before these body-blows with Arthur Simmons, the pig breeder, going out of business, while the Aberdeen and Northern Marts Thainstone Agricultural Centre has had to diversify from agricultural auctions into other activities such as car boot sales. The Scottish Executive has proposed to establish a Nitrate Vulnerable Zone in the Ythan area to tackle nitrate pollution of ground water, but farmers have concerns that this could restrict the fertilisers they can use.

Rapid expansion has brought with it a housing boom and with it pressures on housing, education, hospitals and roads – the kind of problems one associates with the South East of England. There is a lack of affordable housing in the area, and the growth of towns such as Ellon and Inverurie has changed them radically. The pressure on roads has seen calls for the A90 and A96 roads from Aberdeen to Ellon and Inverness respectively, to be upgraded to dual carriageways, but this has only happened over stretches. A crossrail link to Aberdeen and Stonehaven is planned.

A major local issue in the last five years has been the rising cost of building a new secondary school at Oldmeldrum to meet the needs of the growing population and funded by PFI/PPP. The Scottish Executive has been unwilling to come to the aid of rising costs and Aberdeenshire Council have been left with a large part of the extra bill. The council has also incurred the wrath of local residents by introducing a policy of charging for children's transport to rural schools if they live within a two mile radius for primaries and three miles for secondaries.

As Aberdeenshire West and its predecessors, Conservatives held this seat for most of the inter-war period – winning it in 1924 from the Liberals. In 1950, the Conservative Major Spence – who had been MP for the predecessor seat of Aberdeen and Kincardine in 1945 – held the seat with a 10,252 majority over Labour, and kept the seat until the 1964 general election. In 1966, James Davidson won the seat for the Liberals, but only succeeded in holding it for one term, losing to the Conservatives in 1970. The Conservative he lost to was no backroom, faceless Tory but Lt. Col. Colin Mitchell, who went by the nickname of 'Mad Mitch' and 'the hero of Aden' for his military exploits in the 1960s. The February 1974 election saw Russell Fairgrieve succeed Mitchell, holding on in October with a 2,468 majority over the Liberals. In the 1979 contest, despite a revival in the Scottish Conservatives fortunes which saw them make six net gains and their vote rise nationally, Fairgrieve faced the Liberal Malcolm Bruce and won with a 2,766 majority. In 1983 the seat became Gordon, Fairgrieve retired and Bruce won the seat against the Conservative James Cran by a margin of 850 votes as the Liberal-SDP Alliance vote rose by 13 per cent.

Bruce was safely re-elected in 1987 with a large majority of 9,519 over the Conservatives and winning nearly half the vote. However, in 1992 as another Scottish Conservative recovery got underway – this one a small one – Bruce nearly lost his seat, winning by the margin of 274. After 1992, following extensive boundary changes to Gordon because of the rapid growth of the population in the seat, it was predicted that Gordon would become safely Conservative in 1997. The boundary changes involved the transfer of around 20,000 Gordon voters in the Liberal Democrat voting Aberdeen suburbs to the Aberdeen North constituency, while Turriff, with no Liberal Democrat tradition and a predominantly Conservative electorate, was transferred into Gordon. However, a notional Conservative majority of approximately 8,500 was turned on its head by the Conservative wipeout at the 1997 election. The Liberal Democrats emerged as winners again, with Malcolm Bruce triumphing comfortably with a majority of 6,997. John Major commented in his autobiography of a visit to this constituency in 1997: 'After a few minutes in the town I was certain we would not win there – and if not Gordon, what would be won in Scotland?' In June 2001 Malcolm Bruce was re-elected with a majority of 7,879 over the Conservatives.

The Liberal Democrats sucessfully held the seat in the 1999 Scottish Parliament elections with a 4,195 lead over the SNP. The Conservative decline continued at the 1999 election, and the party's fall from grace was underlined by the fact that it came third behind the SNP and saw the Tory vote fall to just under 11 per cent. At the 2003 Scottish Parliament election, Nora Radcliffe successfully defended the seat retaining a 4,071 majority over the Conservatives who replaced the SNP in second place compared with four years previous. In the regional vote, the Lib Dems won 28.3 per cent to the Conservatives 23.1 per cent and Nationalists 22.7 per cent – while the Greens won 5.4 per cent and SSP 2.9 per cent.

Boundary changes for Westminster mean Gordon will regain Dyce and Bridge of Don, but lose Turriff, Fyvie-Methlick and Upper Ythan. Liberal Democrat strength would suggest they have a good chance in any reconfigured seat, and at the Scottish Parliament, Gordon has become a relatively safe Lib Dem seat. The decline of the Conservatives electoral support in this seat has been sharp and of recent origin – winning 42 per cent as recently as 1983 when Bruce first won the seat, but reduced to 23.4 per cent in the last two elections. This follows a familiar pattern to Conservative support across Scotland – once they lose a seat, their organisation and electoral base withers away, making the seat impossible to recapture.

MSP

NORA RADCLIFFE was born in Aberdeen in 1946, educated at Aberdeen High School for Girls and is a graduate of Aberdeen University. She worked in the hotel and catering industry from 1967-73, did some part-time work from 1973-88 while raising two children, and worked on developing primary care for Grampian Health Board from 1988-98. She was a councillor in Gordon District from 1988-92, where she was vice-chair of the environmental health and economic development committees. She also sat as a member of the Scottish Constitutional Convention.

In the first Parliament, Radcliffe became Lib Dem spokesperson on the environment (her main political interest) and Europe, and was deputy convener of the transport and environment committee. Until December 2000, she was on the equal opportunities committee, where she was a reporter on the sub-group tackling the issue of sexual orientations, and in 2000, she took a prominent role in arguing on behalf of the party for the repeal of Section 28. She was active in the passage of the Water Environment and Water Services Act and pressed successfully for clauses on wildlife crime to be included in the Criminal Justice Act. While an authentic slice of the North East, she is not always one to inspire confidence in her Parliamentary contributions, and she can be somewhat timid in the cut and thrust of debate - perhaps because she had five different spokeswomanships over her first four years as an MSP, including health, equal opportunities, environment, Europe, transport and the environment.

In the second Parliament, she won a place on the environment and rural development committee, while also her group's spokesperson on those areas. As a non-rocker of boats, a good broker of compromises and not seen as angling for promotion, she also replaced George Lyon as Lib Dem group convener.

MP

MALCOLM BRUCE was born in Birkenhead in 1944. He was educated at Wrekin College and has an MA from St Andrews University, in economics and political science as well as an MSc in marketing from Strathclyde. In the 1990s, perhaps foreseeing the potential loss of his seat with the boundary changes, he studied law at the Inns of Court in London and became a barrister, though the voters of Gordon saved him from the second oldest profession. Before his election in 1983, he had a varied career, starting as a journalist with the *Liverpool Daily Post and Echo*, then a buyer for Boots 1968-69 and working for the North East of Scotland Development Agency 1971-75. He became director of Noroil Publishing and was then co-founder and editor of Aberdeen Petroleum Publishing. He fought North Angus and Mearns for the Liberals in October 1974 against the Conservatives' Alick Buchanan-Smith. In 1979, he contested Tory-held West Aberdeenshire, later to become Gordon. He was first elected an MP in 1983 and has held a variety of Liberal, Alliance and then Lib Dem portfolios at Westminster. He has been a spokesperson for energy, education, employment, trade and industry, environment, Scotland and Treasury issues, the latter from 1994-99. The Scottish role included leadership of the Scottish party from 1988-92, defeating Archy Kirkwood for the post, and being replaced by Jim Wallace. It was in that role that he was one of those party leaders to take part in the famous Usher Hall devolution debate in January 1992, handling it rather better than Donald Dewar. He was also chair of the Lib Dem Parliamentary group from 1999-2001. When David Steel stepped down as party leader in 1988, he was considered as having an outside chance of replacing him, but became Paddy Ashdown's campaign manager instead. He was a member of the Treasury Select Committee from 1997-99 and sat on the select committee on standards and privileges. He was also elected to the rectorship of Dundee University from 1986-89. His policy interests stress environmentalism, speaking for the Lib Dems on environment, food and rural affairs and, most recently, trade and industry. He has learned sign language, as one of his daughters is deaf, commenting: 'When I started, my daughter fell about laughing because I'd learned English signs, not Scottish'.

Greenock and Inverclyde

Predecessor Constituencies: Greenock (1945–70) and Greenock and Port Glasgow (1974–92).

Socio-economic Indicators:

Constituency Pop. (16–64)	39,731
Claimant Count (May 2003)	4.9% (57.8% above average)
IBA/SDA Claimants	14.2%
Life Expectancy – Male	70.3 (3.1 yrs below average)
Life Expectancy – Female	77.5 (1.2 yrs below average)
Owner Occupied	61.0%
Social Rented	31.8%
Average Property Prices	£51,556 (55th)
Average Gross Income	£23,848 (52nd)
Low Birthweight Babies	129 (6.6%)
Teenage Pregnancy Rates	423 (5.1%)
No. of Lone Parent Households	3,552 (12.9%)

2003 Scottish Parliament Election

Electorate: 46,045   *Turnout*: 23,781 (51.6%)   *Turnout 1999*: 59.0%

Candidate	Party	Votes	Votes%	99 %	Change%
Duncan McNeil	Labour	9,674	40.7	41.3	– 0.6
Ross Finnie	Lib Dem	6,665	28.0	26.2	+ 1.8
Thomas Chalmers	SNP	3,532	14.9	23.6	– 8.8
Patricia McCafferty	SSP	2,338	9.8	3.0	+ 6.8
Charles Dunlop	Con	1,572	6.6	5.9	+ 0.7

Labour majority: 3,009 (12.7%)   *Swing*: 1.2% Labour to Liberal Democrat

2001 General Election

Electorate: 47,884   *Turnout*: 28,419 (59.3%)

Candidate	Party	Votes	Votes%	Change%
David Cairns	Labour	14,929	52.5	– 3.6
Chic Brodie	Lib Dem	5,039	17.7	+ 3.9
Andrew Murie	SNP	4,248	14.9	– 3.6
Alister Haw	Con	3,000	10.6	– 0.9
David Landels	SSP	1,203	4.2	–

Labour majority: 9,890 (34.8%)   *Swing*: 3.8% Labour to Liberal Democrat

1945–97 Westminster

	Lab%	Con%	SNP%	Lib%	Other%	Turnout%
1997	56.2	11.5	18.6	13.8	–	71.1
1992	58.0	11.7	19.0	11.4	–	73.7
1987	63.9	9.6	8.5	17.9	–	75.4
1983	46.8	9.8	6.8	36.3	0.3	74.2
1979	53.0	10.8	7.6	28.2	0.4	73.7
1974O	48.2	11.3	21.1	19.4	–	71.1
1974F	48.3	18.5	11.5	20.6	1.1	69.3
1970	53.7	–	–	44.7	1.6	76.0
1966	57.2	17.5	–	23.2	2.1	73.6
1964	55.1	18.2	–	25.4	1.3	76.5
1959	50.6	22.6	–	26.8	–	78.9
1955B	53.7	46.3	–	–	–	75.3
1955	51.4	48.6	–	–	–	77.9
1951	57.1	42.9	–	–	–	83.0
1950	50.6	–	–	28.7	20.7	83.2
1945	47.0	23.6	–	17.2	17.2	68.0

The central focus of this seat, the town of Greenock, can be found at the mouth of the River Clyde, situated in the picturesque plain between the Clyde and nearby hills. Other towns in the seat include Port Glasgow, Gourock and Wemyss Bay. Statistics show that this is not among the most prosperous parts of Scotland. Average property prices are 23.6 per cent below the average. The seat is the eleventh most unhealthy constituency in Britain and eighth in Scotland and won the accolade of being the most unhealthy place to live in Scotland outside Glasgow.

There are serious social problems in parts of the constituency including crime, drugs and anti-social behaviour. In 2001, the Inverclyde area had the highest proportion of heroin users in Scotland with as many as five people in every 100 registered heroin users and 560 people known to be heroin addicts. This side of Greenock life was portrayed in Ken Loach's film *Sweet Sixteen* which showed the pressures and lack of choices for young people growing up in the area where organised crime, gangs and a world funded by drugs were seen as viable career choices. MP David Cairns criticised the film when it was being made as portraying the negative side of Greenock life, but when it came out he praised its 'wisdom, insight and hope'.

Greenock has, in the last 20 years, attempted to reinvent itself by bringing new industries into the area such as IBM and National Semi-conductors, Fullarton Computer Industries and Telecom Service Centres. However, many of these companies are now suffering from the worldwide over-capacity in the electronics sector with Mitsubishi announcing 350 job losses and National Semi-Conductors 600 job losses from their Greenock plant in 1998. There is a thriving and prosperous marina in the centre of the town. New developments in the area include Clydeport creating a five acre site next to Greenock Ocean Terminal, the modernisation of Gourock and Wemyss Bay piers, a new passenger ferry service connecting Greenock, Dunoon and Rothesay with the Braehead shopping complex. Sizeable commuter communities in Gourock and Wemyss Bay are reliant on the poor quality rail services from Glasgow Central station.

Greenock, as it was then simply called, has had a long tradition of Liberal support which allowed it to differentiate itself from the metropolis of Glasgow. It was first won by Labour in a 1936 by-election with a 2,604 majority over the National Liberals. Hector McNeil then held the seat for Labour from 1941-55, retaining it in 1945 with a majority of 8,089 over the Conservatives, as the Communists polled a respectable 17.2 per cent. He was Clement Attlee's third and final Secretary of State for Scotland from February 1950 to October 1951. McNeil's death shortly after the 1955 election forced a by-election which Dickson Mabon won for Labour with 53.7 per cent to the Conservatives' 46.3 per cent. Fifteen years later in 1970, the Conservatives unusually allowed the Liberals a free run against Mabon – who saw his majority slashed to 3,000. In 1974, the seat became Greenock and Port Glasgow and in October 1974 Mabon survived the challenge of the SNP with a lead of 11,955, which in 1979 became a 11,282 majority over the Liberals.

Dickson Mabon defected to the Social Democrats and stood in the Renfrew West and Inverclyde seat in 1983. Norman Godman became Labour candidate in Greenock and Port Glasgow and held it with a majority of 4,625 over the Liberal-SDP Alliance who increasing their vote by 3,000. However, in 1987 the Alliance could not keep up this momentum and their vote collapsed, falling by more than half to leave Labour with a colossal 20,055 majority. By 1992, Godman's main challenger was the SNP, 14,979 votes behind Labour, with the Liberal Democrats now in a distant fourth place.

Boundary changes prior to the 1997 election created the Greenock and Inverclyde constituency and the resulting election saw Godman increase Labour's vote by 1,000 on the notional 1992 result, while the SNP held their vote and retained second place 13,040 votes behind Labour. Godman retired prior to the 2001 UK election and David Cairns was selected as the Labour candidate – winning the seat with a reduced majority of 9,890 on a reduced turnout and a slightly reduced percentage lead. The main change was the move of the Liberal Democrats from third to second place, displacing the Nationalists.

In the 1999 Scottish Parliament elections, Ross Finnie resuscitated the Lib Dems' cause by cutting the Labour majority to 4,313. In the process, he increased the Lib Dem vote by 2,500 and saw Labour's support fall by 7,500, while the SNP vote remained static. In the second Scottish Parliament election, Duncan McNeil and Ross Finnie went head-to-head for the second time, with Finnie's position as a Scottish Executive minister for four years giving him a high profile and an outside chance of causing an upset. Labour's lead was cut to 3,009, while the Scottish Socialists finished in a strong fourth place ahead of the Conservatives.

In the regional vote, Labour won 33.2 per cent to the Lib Dems 23.2 per cent – with the SSP on 9.1 per cent and Greens on 4 per cent. At a local government level, the Lib Dems swept to overall control at the 2003 elections winning 42.6 per cent to Labour's 31.3 per cent aided by the unpopularity of Labour's proposals on public-private partnerships to secure extra investment in schools in the area, compared to four years previous when Labour had won 37.5 per cent to the Lib Dems' 34.6 per cent.

Boundary changes for Westminster will see the removal of Port Glasgow and Kilmacolm from West Renfrewshire into a new Inverclyde seat which could see either David Cairns or Jim Sheridan, MP for West Renfrewshire, as Labour candidate. Labour are safe at Westminster in any new seat, and while Labour's hold on the Scottish Parliament seat is much less sure with a significant Liberal Democrat profile and base – the seat looks likely to return a Labour MSP for the foreseeable future.

MSP

DUNCAN McNEIL was born in 1950 in Greenock, and educated at Mount School in the town followed by Reid Kerr College, Paisley. He worked as a boilermaker in Cartsdyke shipyard from 1965-79, making him one of the few MSPs with experience of working within traditional heavy industry, where his roots in the GMB union go deep. He was employed for two years in unemployed workers' centres, becoming a full-time official in the GMB union from 1981-99, where he was responsible for membership in the construction, distribution and whisky industries. McNeil was chair of Inverclyde Rights and Advice Centre, chair of the Scott Lithgow Charity Committee, and a member of the Scottish Labour executive.

His role as an MSP has been as a party loyalist with a particular understanding of the culture, nuances and feel of the Labour and trade union movement. He also has a particular appetite for and skill at noising up and ridiculing Nationalists and Scottish Socialists in the debating chamber. That explains why he was entrusted with the non-ministerial tasks of being a Labour whip and deputy member of the Scottish Parliamentary bureau and the Corporate Body. Continuing in his Corporate Body role after the 2003 election, he had special responsibility for personnel, allowances and procurement, along with a place on the health committee.

MP

DAVID CAIRNS was born in 1966 in Greenock and educated at Notre Dame High School, Greenock, then training for the Catholic priesthood at the Gregorian University, Rome and the Franciscan Study Centre at Canterbury. He became a priest in 1991 and worked in that role until 1994 at St Mary's Church, Clapham. His experience of inequality and poverty forced him to reconsider the limitations on political involvement placed on priests, becoming co-ordinator of the Christian Socialist Movement from 1994-97. He was research assistant to English MP Siobhain McDonagh from 1997-2001. During this time, he became a Labour councillor in Merton Borough Council from 1998-2001, becoming chief whip in 1999.

Having been selected to fight the Inverclyde seat, it became clear that the Catholic Church still considered him a priest, even if he did not, and there was a legal bar on priests being MPs. The Removal of Clergy Disqualification Act was passed in 2001 to allow him to sit in the Commons. In representing his constituency in 2002, he criticised Ken Loach's film *Sweet Sixteen* when the director was scouting in Greenock as the setting for a grim film about drugs culture. Yet he chose also to draw attention to the town's drug problems, in a campaign to get the Foreign Office to take the supply of opium from Afghanistan more seriously. He was one of few in the Christian Socialist Movement to support Tony Blair in his lead-up to war in Iraq, and was rewarded in June 2003 by being made a Parliamentary Private Secretary in the Department of Works and Pensions. Given a top slot in the private members' bill lottery in 2002-03, he got a piece of legislation to his name, bringing Scottish retail workers into line with those in England and Wales in having the right to refuse to work on Sunday.

Hamilton North and Bellshill

Predecessor Constituencies: Bothwell (1945-79) and Motherwell North (1983-92).

Socio-economic Indicators:

Constituency Pop. (16-64)	45,989
Claimant Count (May 2003)	4.0% (27.6% above average)
IBA/SDA Claimants	13.3%
Life Expectancy – Male	72.4 (1.0 yrs below average)
Life Expectancy – Female	78.0 (0.7 yrs below average)
Owner Occupied	60.2%
Social Rented	33.7%
Average Property Prices	£60,114 (35th)
Average Gross Income	£25,605 (36th)
Low Birthweight Babies	141 (6.2%)
Teenage Pregnancy Rates	423 (4.3%)
No. of Lone Parent Households	3,698 (12.9%)

CAB Enquiries

Issue	No. of cases	Percentage of total cases (%)
1. Benefits	3544	35.7
2. Consumer	2194	22.1
3. Employment	1189	12.0
4. Housing	773	7.8
5. Legal	693	7.0

2003 Scottish Parliament Election

Electorate: 51,965   *Turnout*: 24,195 (46.6%)   *Tirnout 1999*: 57.8%

Candidate	Party	Votes	Votes%	99 %	Change%
Michael McMahon	Labour	12,812	53.0	48.8	+ 4.2
Alex Neil	SNP	4,907	20.3	30.8	−10.5
Charles Ferguson	Con	2,625	10.8	10.3	+ 0.6
Shareen Blackhall	SSP	1,932	8.0	–	–
Siobhan Mathers	Lib Dem	1,477	6.1	6.7	– 0.6
Gordon McIntosh	SPA	442	1.8	(other 3.4)	–

Labour majority: 7,905 (32.7%)   *Swing*: 7.4% SNP to Labour

2001 General Election

Electorate: 53,539   *Turnout*: 30,404 (56.8%)

Candidate	Party	Votes	Votes%	Change%
John Reid	Labour	18,786	61.8	- 2.2
Chris Stephens	SNP	5,225	17.2	- 1.9
Bill Frain-Bell	Con	2,649	8.7	- 1.7
Keith Legg	Lib Dem	2,360	7.8	+ 2.7
Shareen Blackall	SSP	1,189	3.9	-
Steve Mayers	Soc Lab	195	0.6	-

Labour majority: 13,561 (44.6%)   *Swing*: 0.2% Labour to SNP

1945-97 Westminster

Westminster

	Lab%	Con%	SNP%	Lib%	Other%	Turnout%
1997	64.0	10.4	19.1	5.1	1.5	70.9

Motherwell North (1983–92)

	Lab%	Con%	SNP%	Lib%	Other%	Turnout%
1992	63.4	11.4	20.3	4.9	–	76.7
1987	66.9	11.1	14.0	8.0	–	77.3
1983	57.8	15.5	12.6	14.1	–	74.9

Bothwell (1945–79)

	Lab%	Con%	SNP%	Lib%	Other%	Turnout%
1979	55.0	23.4	10.8	10.8	–	78.6
1974O	47.8	17.9	24.5	8.9	–	76.5
1974F	46.8	26.7	14.1	11.2	1.2	81.2
1970	54.8	32.5	12.7	–	–	75.5
1966	61.0	36.3	–	–	2.7	78.0
1964	60.4	39.6	–	–	–	80.4
1959	54.7	45.3	–	–	–	82.2
1955	54.2	45.8	–	–	–	78.9
1951	56.3	43.7	–	–	–	86.0
1950	56.7	43.3	–	–	–	84.5
1945	65.8	34.2	–	–	–	73.0

Lanarkshire North (1945–79)

	Lab%	Con%	SNP%	Lib%	Other%	Turnout%
1979	55.5	31.5	13.0	–	–	79.7
1974O	46.2	22.5	26.9	4.4	–	79.5
1974F	48.4	33.1	18.5	–	–	82.7

cont'd

	Lab%	Con%	SNP%	Lib%	Other%	Turnout%
1970	51.8	40.0	8.2	–	–	77.9
1966	60.9	30.1	–	–	–	79.2
1964	60.6	39.4	–	–	–	82.0
1959	58.7	41.3	–	–	–	82.8
1955	57.9	42.1	–	–	–	81.5
1951	58.2	41.8	–	–	–	85.4
1950	58.3	39.0	–	2.7	–	84.7
1945	59.6	40.4	–	–	–	73.3

Hamilton North and Bellshill does not include the town of Hamilton – containing only a few northern outskirts. Instead, the main settlements which make up the seat are Bellshill, Bothwell, Holytown and Uddingston – situated just to the east of the Glasgow conurbation and within its travel-to-work region. Average property prices are 10.9 per cent below the national average. It was ranked the twentieth most unhealthy constituency in Britain, and was the second most unhealthy seat in Scotland outside Glasgow.

The most pressing issues in the constituency focus on employment issues, with several employers recently announcing large job losses, including Daks Simpson, based in Larkhall, which has shifted a sizeable portion of its clothing business overseas to reduce costs. Housing developments are another important issue with a number of private developments springing up around Uddingston. There are significant commuter towns in this seat, and the M74 and M9 are vitally important for people to get to work easily and efficiently in Glasgow.

This seat has a number of connections with Scottish football. Bothwell, tucked into the west bank of the River Clyde, is now the home of choice of several of Glasgow Celtic's and Rangers' most expensive and famous international footballers – providing proximity to Glasgow with a degree of privacy. The other, more illustrious football connection is provided by the working class town of Bellshill. It has provided many of Celtic's greatest football legends and is the birthplace of Billy McNeill, captain of the Celtic team which won the European Cup in 1967 – the first British team to do so. It is also the birthplace of Scottish pop star of the 1980s, Sheena Easton, who later went on to work with Prince.

As Bothwell, Labour first won the seat in a 1919 by-election, lost narrowly in the 1931 debacle, and won back again in 1935 – the beginning of nearly seventy years of continuous Labour dominance. John Timmons won the seat in 1945 with a 12,162 majority over the Unionists, and held the seat until his retirement in 1964. His successor, James Hamilton, first took the seat in 1964 and won the seat seven times, first as Bothwell, and then, from 1983 as Motherwell North, before announcing his retirement prior to the 1987 election.

John Reid was selected as the Labour candidate to succeed Hamilton for the 1987 election and held the seat with a massive 23,595 majority over the SNP. With 67 per cent of the vote, this was Labour's highest post-war vote in the constituency. In Labour's missed election victory year of 1992 – when the party saw its vote slump in Scotland – Reid still won a 18,910 majority over the SNP.

In the May 1997 election, Reid was re-elected for the new seat of Hamilton North and Bellshill with a 17,067 majority over the Nationalists. In the June 2001 UK election his majority was 13,561 – slightly reduced on a lower turnout compared to four years before – but with none of the opposition parties making any inroads.

In the first Scottish Parliament election, Michael McMahon was elected Labour MSP with a much narrower 5,606 majority over the SNP, who polled a respectable 31 per cent in the seat. In the May 2003 Scottish Parliament election, Michael McMahon increased his majority by over 2,000 to 7,905 over the

SNP, but in percentage terms saw a significant shift as his lead increased from 18 per cent to 33 per cent, as the SNP vote fell by over 10 per cent. In the regional list vote, Labour won 43.7 per cent to 18.8 per cent for the Nationalists, while the SSP won 8.5 per cent, the Scottish Senior Citizens 6.9 per cent and the Greens 4.1 per cent.

Hamilton North and Bellshill has proven itself one of the safest Labour seats in the United Kingdom. Boundary changes for future Westminster elections see the abolition of Hamilton North and Bellshill with its constituent parts split fairly evenly between the four surrounding seats. At the Scottish Parliament, Labour has increased its hold on the seat and the SNP surge of 1999 has not been repeated. Labour's Lanarkshire dominance should continue into the medium to longer-term.

MSP

MICHAEL McMAHON was born in 1961 in Bellshill. He was educated at Our Lady's High School, Motherwell, and worked as a welder with Terex Equipment in Motherwell from 1977-92, gaining wide experience of GMB trade union activism, including the 1986 national youth award. In 1992, he became a full-time student, gaining a degree in social sciences, politics and sociology from Glasgow Caledonian University in 1996. He worked as a political researcher from 1996-99, and held various offices in his local Labour Party including constituency party secretary. In the first Scottish Parliament, he served on the equal opportunities committee, moving to local government and transport as well as the petitions committee after the 2003 election.

On the socially conservative wing of the party, McMahon played a crucial role in the Section 28 debate, proposing in the education committee in May 2000 an amendment recognising the importance of marriage. This specific proposal was defeated, but marked out McMahon as one of the Lanarkshire group of Labour MSPs who were most unhappy about the Section 28 debate and keenest for compromise. He was loyal to the Jack McConnell camp, supporting him in the 2000 leadership contest, nominating him the following year and becoming his parliamentary aide from February 2002 to April 2003. In March 2002, he was one of the 15 MSPs who voted against giving themselves a 13.5 per cent pay rise. His achievements after four years focussed on his constituency case load, supporting constituents affected by anti-social behaviour, opposing telecom masts and unwelcome housing and industrial planning, and seeking to reduce emissions from an animal waste facility. Early in the second Parliament, the possible siting of a psychiatric unit caused him problems with a vocal constituents' campaign. With intense pressure and even death threats, he eventually came out against the siting of the unit in Bothwell.

MP

DR JOHN REID was born in Bellshill in 1947, and has been an MP since 1987, representing Motherwell North from 1987 and then its successor seat, Hamilton North and Bellshill, since 1997. He was educated at St Patrick's Secondary School, Coatbridge and has degrees in history from Stirling University, including a doctorate on economic history entitled 'Warrior Aristocrats in Crisis: The political effects of the transition from the slave trade to palm oil commerce in the Kingdom of Dahomey'. He also has enjoyed a less academic sideline as a rock musician with a band called the Graduates in the 1960s who were on the fringes of pop success. He continues to enjoy guitar playing.

Reid joined Labour in 1968, was president of Stirling Student Association in 1972, and then vice-chair of the National Union of Students-Scotland the following year. He was a member of the Communist Party from 1973-75, rejoining Labour in 1976. Having done so, he was employed as a research officer of the Scottish Labour Party from 1979-83, becoming involved in Neil Kinnock's successful campaign for the leadership in 1983, having been convinced by the party's 1983 humiliation of its need to renew and modernise. Reid then worked for two years in Kinnock's office as a political adviser, before becoming Scottish organiser of Trade Unionists for Labour from 1985-87. He remained an enthusiastic backer of Kinnock once in Westminster, also taking a carefully worded position against legislation which would have restricted abortion law.

In Government, Reid was armed forces minister at the Ministry of Defence from 1997-98, then Minister of State responsible for transport under Deputy Prime Minister John Prescott from 1998-99. As power was devolved to the Scottish Parliament and Executive, he moved to become Secretary of State for Scotland from 1999-2001. He was noted there for seeking to flex the non-devolved muscles of the new government structure, fighting turf wars with First Minister Donald Dewar. This began weeks after the Parliament in Edinburgh gained its new powers, over the proposed closure of Kvaerner Govan shipyard, with Reid claiming credit for brokering a deal which would keep the yard open, helped with prospect of new MoD work. This passage with Donald Dewar created bad feeling and was not helped by the revelations of so-called Lobbygate, in which Reid's son, Kevin, was heavily implicated, as one of two young public affairs executive caught by an undercover journalist trying to sell access to the Scottish Executive though Labour Party channels. There was significant tension and disagreement between Reid and Dewar over this, and it led to a heated public scene between the two at Scots night at the UK Labour conference in 1999. Henry McLeish, when First Minister, did not think much of Reid either, describing him to Helen Liddell, unknowingly into a live radio station microphone, as 'a patronising bastard'. Reid would go on to claim that he had been asked to become Scotland's First Minister after Donald Dewar's sudden death.

Reid's tough demeanour and combative nature hide a formidable intellectual and political brain. He was convinced of the need for Labour to transform itself long before the words 'New Labour' were ever invented. He is capable of putting forward a compelling case for the need to modernise and for the rationale of New Labour, combining traditional principles with a revisionist understanding in a manner that is a combination of Blair and Brown. He was noted by Tony Blair as a good man to help out with presentation in a crisis, frequently presenting the government's case on difficult issues such as the petrol blockade in September 2000 and returning to the fray in duffing up the BBC over its reporting of the 'dodgy dossier' used to justify war in Iraq. It was on the latter issue that Reid over-stretched the Government's case by warning of 'rogue elements' within the intelligence services trying to undermine the government, in what subsequently appeared to be a reference to the then unnamed weapons expert Dr David Kelly. Blair has seen Reid as valuable for the way in which he speaks New Labour language with an Old Labour accent, and that helps explain why Blair kept giving Reid new cabinet jobs, in response to a series of cabinet crises. In 2001, when Peter Mandelson was forced to resign from the Cabinet for a second time, Reid became Northern Ireland Secretary, the first MP to start with the distinct advantage of understanding sectarian politics as it operates – in a less dangerous context – in Lanarkshire.

With Blair facing growing trouble in diminishing trust in his Government, and opposition to his modernising policies from within the Labour Party, Reid was moved in 2002 to become Minister without Portfolio, also holding the new post of Blair-appointed Party chair. That lasted about three months, until Robin Cook's departure in protest at the Iraq war saw Reid replace the Livingston MP as Leader of the House of Commons. Two months later, with Alan Milburn's unexpected departure from the Cabinet for personal reasons, Reid was moved to replace him as Health Secretary – his fourth cabinet job in a year. His appointment raised a variation on the West Lothian Question once more, about Scottish MPs running English affairs, and one of his early tasks was to sort out the dispute with consultants in England over their new contract. The tougher job was to turn around the NHS's slowness to respond to injections of vast amounts of additional funding. Despite so many ministerial jobs, Reid took over the health job – something of a poisoned chalice – with limited experience at cabinet level of running a large spending department. He faced a difficult relationship with Gordon Brown, controller of the purse-strings, the two Scots having a long history of mutual mistrust.

In 2000, Reid, along with fellow Labour MP, John Maxton (who retired in 2001), faced an embarrassing investigation by the House of Commons Commissioner for Standards, Elizabeth Filkin. She found that they had acted improperly in misusing Westminster parliamentary allowances for Scottish Labour purposes in the Scottish Parliament elections – using parliamentary staff for party work. A subsequent inquiry by the Commons standards committee reported in December 2000 and did not uphold the complaints against Reid and Maxton. Labour spin doctors presented this as both of them being 'cleared', much to the anger of opposition MPs on the committee who insisted their verdict was more accurately one of 'not proven'. Reid faced a battle to retain a seat in the Commons, with the reduction in the number of Scottish seats removing his. He broke Labour ranks in an unsuccessful challenge to the Boundary Commission draft plans, but the new boundaries have forced him to fight on neighbouring turf, in a county which lends itself to bitter political in-fighting.

Reid remarried in 1999 – after the death of his first wife – to Brazilian filmmaker Carine Adler, and has let it be widely known that he sleeps with a copy of Gramsci's *Prison Notebooks* by his bedside.

Hamilton South

Predecessor Constituencies: Hamilton (1945–92).

Socio-economic Indicators:

Constituency Pop. (16-64)	39,824
Claimant Count (May 2003)	3.4% (7.7% above average)
IBA/SDA Claimants	14.7%
Life Expectancy – Male	72.5 (0.9 yrs below average)
Life Expectancy – Female	76.7 (2.0 yrs below average)
Owner Occupied	61.7%
Social Rented	32.1%
Average Property Prices	£49,790 (58th)
Average Gross Income	£23,620 (54th)
Low Birthweight Babies	131 (6.8%)
Teenage Pregnancy Rates	357 (4.2%)
No. of Lone Parent Households	3,434 (13.7%)

CAB Enquiries

Issue	No. of cases	Percentage of total cases (%)
1. Benefits	1577	28.5
2. Consumer	1463	26.4
3. Employment	758	13.7
4. Housing	452	8.2
5. Legal	415	7.5

2003 Scottish Parliament Election

Electorate: 45,749   *Turnout*: 20,518 (44.8%)   *Turnout 1999*: 55.4%

Candidate	Party	Votes	Votes%	99 %	Change%
Tom McCabe	Labour	9,546	46.5	54.4	– 7.9
John Wilson	SNP	4,772	23.0	26.7	– 3.7
Margaret Mitchell	Con	2,601	12.7	11.3	+ 1.4
William O'Neill	SSP	1,893	9.2	–	–
John Oswald	Lib Dem	1,756	8.6	7.7	+ 0.9

Labour majority: 4,824 (23.5%)   *Swing*: 2.1% Labour to SNP

2001 General Election

Electorate: 46,665　　　　　　　　　　　　　　*Turnout*: 26,757 (57.3%)

Candidate	Party	Votes	Votes%	Change%
Bill Tynan	Labour	15,965	59.7	– 5.9
John Wilson	SNP	5,190	19.4	+ 1.8
John Oswald	Lib Dem	2,388	8.9	+ 3.8
Neil Richardson	Con	1,876	7.0	– 1.6
Gena Mitchell	SSP	1,187	4.4	–
Janice Murdoch	UK Ind	151	0.6	–

Majority: 10,775 (40.3%)　　　　　　　　　*Swing*: 3.9% Labour to SNP

1945–97 Westminster

	Lab%	Con%	SNP%	Lib%	Other%	Turnout%
1999B	36.9	7.2	34.0	3.3	18.6	41.6
1997	65.6	8.6	17.6	5.1	3.0	71.1
1992	55.2	17.6	19.7	7.5	–	76.2
1987	59.7	14.4	12.7	13.2	–	76.9
1983	52.4	19.2	8.2	20.1	–	75.7
1979	59.6	23.8	16.6	–	–	79.6
1978B	51.0	13.0	33.4	2.6	–	72.1
1974O	47.5	9.5	39.0	4.0	–	77.2
1974F	48.0	20.1	31.9	–	–	79.7
1970	52.9	11.4	35.1	0.6	–	80.0
1967B	41.5	12.5	46.0	–	–	73.7
1966	71.2	28.8	–	–	–	73.3
1964	71.0	29.0	–	–	–	77.5
1959	66.1	27.7	6.2	–	–	79.9
1955	67.4	32.6	–	–	–	76.1
1951	68.7	31.3	–	–	–	80.6
1950	70.0	30.0	–	–	–	81.7
1945	73.5	26.5	–	–	–	70.0

Hamilton South lies to the south-east of Glasgow and is based on the town of Hamilton, which has contributed richly to the theatre and excitement of Scottish politics over the last thirty-five years. Hamilton South has changed dramatically in the last twenty years as the traditional heavy industries have passed into folklore and been replaced by new, hi-tech industries located at Hamilton's International Technology Park. The nature of public services is a controversy here as elsewhere in Scotland, and South Lanarkshire Council have embraced private finance as a way to modernise and invest in the area's state schools. The council plans to merge two schools – Earnock High and Blantyre High – to create an £18 million educational complex, but this is opposed by residents in both areas. Health is another sensitive issue with a shortage of Accident and Emergency consultants in the area which has been addressed by the Health Board using 'flying doctors' between hospitals, much to the horror of local groups.

The socio-economic profile reveals that the constituency is significantly poorer than the neighbouring Hamilton North and Bellshill seat. Average property prices are 26.2 per cent below the Scottish average. Hamilton South is ranked as the 34th most unhealthy constituency in Britain, significantly better than Hamilton North and Bellshill – which was ranked 20th. Hamilton contains a number of areas of poverty and hardship affected by crime, drugs and anti-social behaviour and was a pilot for developing curfews for preventing young people aged 16 and under being outdoors unsupervised after 9pm. The scheme was introduced in 1997 and in the first year a total of 280 youngsters, some as young as four years, were returned to their homes.

Hamilton has a long, proud Labour history, first being won by the party when the seat was created in 1918, while also having a proven track record of surprises and shocks. Labour's first victory was the beginning of nearly 50 years unbroken Labour dominance, with the party's strength so powerful in the area that it even managed to hold on to it in 1931 with a 2,053 majority over the Unionists – at a time when Labour in Scotland was reduced to seven seats. Tom Fraser won it in a January 1943 by-election held two days before the German surrender at Stalingrad, and held it in 1945 with a 12,789 majority over the Unionists. Fraser served as Minister for Transport in the first Wilson Government in 1964, but after Wilson won his 1966 landslide victory, Fraser was offered the chairmanship of the North of Scotland Hydro-Electric Board.

In the resulting by-election in November 1967, sixteen days before the Wilson Government gave in to economic pressure and humiliatingly devalued the British pound, Winnie Ewing overturned a substantial Labour majority, entering the seat and Mrs Ewing into Nationalist mythology. Ewing won 18,397 votes which gave her 46 per cent of the vote to Labour's 16,598 votes and 41.5 per cent as she overturned Labour's huge majority in its second safest seat in Scotland to produce a 1,799 majority. On her arrival at Westminster, she commented: 'As I took my seat it was said by political pundits that 'a chill ran along the Labour back benches looking for a spine to run up.'

Richard Crossman, Labour cabinet minister and chronicler wrote in his diary immediately after the result: 'Tam [Dalyell] had been working here a great deal and said that the way Tom Fraser, like Bowden [Labour MP for Leicester 1945–67], went off to a highly-paid job had caused great resentment among the miners and a boost for the Scot Nat movement. This, of course, follows the Scot Nat success in Pollok, more Welsh nationalist success in Rhondda and absolute success in Carmarthen. I was reminded of how Ted Heath had said last week at the Broadcasting Committee meeting that nationalism is the biggest single factor in our politics today.'

Scottish politics were never to be the same again, and no Scottish by-election or SNP gain ever had such a dramatic impact. Crossman, unlike nearly all his other Labour ministerial colleagues, understood that something fundamental was afoot in Scotland and Wales. Tony Benn, for example, his competitor as a comprehensive recorder of every mood and nuance in Cabinet, made no mention of Hamilton or the rise of Scottish Nationalism in the 1960s.

Winnie Ewing's hold on Hamilton was short-lived, as Labour's Alexander Wilson – who had stood and lost in the by-election – won the seat back by a comfortable margin at the 1970 election, but the influence of Ewing's victory lived on for years. In October 1974, the SNP's high tide nationally, Wilson held on with a majority of 3,332 over the Nationalists. His premature death in March 1978 threw Labour into another difficult by-election, but whereas lightning was prepared to strike twice in Glasgow Govan, this was not the case in Hamilton. The May 1978 contest pitched Labour's George Robertson, a GMWU trade union organiser, against the victor of the first Govan by-election, Margo MacDonald. The timing of the election came as the political tide was turning against the Nationalists – the previous month Donald Dewar held Garscadden – and the Scotland Act was near to completing its parliamentary passage. Labour's triumph, with Robertson winning over half the vote, was seen at the time as the passing of a political moment.

Hamilton returned yet again to being a safe Labour seat. Robertson was elected in 1979 with a 14,799 majority over the Conservatives with the SNP reduced to a dismal third place. In subsequent elections Robertson's majority grew to 21,662 over the Conservatives in 1987, and in 1997 in the new Hamilton South seat, he was re-elected for the last time with a 15,878 majority with the Nationalists.

Robertson had been Defence Secretary for the first two years of Blair's government, and in 1999 he was appointed Secretary-General of NATO and elevated to the House of Lords as Lord Robertson of Port Ellen, precipitating another by-election. Held in September 1999 – during the SNP Annual Conference to dilute the party's efforts – Labour found itself rudely awakened by the voters. Labour with a combative candidate, Bill Tynan, saw its vote collapse, losing two-thirds of its previous 21,709 vote – a decline of 29 per cent. The SNP candidate, Annabelle Ewing, daughter of Margaret Ewing, victor at Hamilton thirty-two years previous, increased the party's vote by 16 per cent and came within 556 votes of winning the seat on a 23 per cent swing. The contest was also noteworthy for the support recorded by the Scottish Socialists who finished third and won 9.5 per cent, their highest ever vote at this point outside Pollok, while a Hamilton Accies candidate protesting about the state of the club polled an impressive 5.5 per cent, ahead of the Lib Dems.

In the June 2001 Westminster election normal Labour dominance was resumed as Bill Tynan increased his majority to a more comfortable 10,775 over the SNP. Labour's vote fell by nearly 6,000 and 6 per cent, but still left the party with 60 per cent, while the Nationalists increased their vote in percentage terms and still ended up polling under 20 per cent.

In the Scottish Parliament election of May 1999 Tom McCabe was elected with a more slender, but still comfortable majority of 7,176. In the second Scottish Parliament election in May 2003, McCabe's majority fell to 4,824 over the SNP as Labour's vote fell 4,500 and the SNP's by over 2,000. In the regional list vote, Labour won 40 per cent to the SNP's 18.9 per cent, while the Scottish Senior Citizens won 8.1 per cent, SSP 8 per cent and Greens 4.8 per cent.

Boundary changes for Westminster see the abolition of the neighbouring Hamilton North and Bellshill seat. There can be no doubt that any future Westminster seat will be Labour by an emphatic margin, although the party must wonder whether this seat's tradition of throwing up difficult Westminster by-elections will continue. At the Scottish Parliament, Hamilton South looks certain to remain a safe Labour citadel, and one in which the highest aspiration of any of the opposition parties is to finish a credible second.

MSP

TOM McCABE was born in Hamilton in 1954. He was educated in the town at St Martin's School and Bell College of Technology, where he gained a diploma in public sector management. He then worked for Hoover plc at its Hamilton plant from 1974-93 where he was a senior shop steward, and formed relationships within the AEEU engineering union, later Amicus, which would be important to him politically. He worked as a welfare rights officer for Strathclyde Regional Council from 1993-96 and in North Lanarkshire from 1996-99. He was a councillor in Hamilton District Council from 1988-96 where he was chair of housing from 1990-92 and leader of the council from 1992-96. With the reorganisation of local government, he was elected to South Lanarkshire Council in 1995 and was its leader from 1995-99. He also served as vice-convenor of Strathclyde Joint Police Board and was a member of Lanarkshire Development Agency over this period.

McCabe's leadership of Hamilton and South Lanarkshire councils gained him a reputation as something of a moderniser, at least by Lanarkshire standards, though it was filled with controversy, such as the decision to back curfews for young people in his home town. He was also involved in South Lanarkshire in a political row in January 1999 when allegations of bullying and intimidation were made against him. The Rev Stuart McQuarrie, then secretary of the Labour group, accused McCabe and his deputy, Eddie McAvoy, of 'the most vicious foul-mouthed verbal threats I have ever experienced'. The matter was investigated by Alex Rowley, then Labour general secretary, and McCabe was cleared, but there were several resignations from the party and McQuarrie stood down at the 1999 council elections.

With McCabe leaving the council as well, he won the Hamilton South seat which, while twinned with neighbouring Clydesdale, had him and Karen Gillon selected with no opposition: an unusual occurrence, particularly with the vicious internal Labour battle for neighbouring constituencies. Perhaps McCabe's ability shone through Lanarkshire's murky politics, perhaps he had a stranglehold on Hamilton, or perhaps it was his air of quiet menace which helped. McCabe had come to know Donald Dewar through having a place on the Scottish Labour executive. During the Scottish Parliament election campaign, Dewar made him spokesman on home affairs and government and then chose him as a member of Labour's five-strong coalition negotiating team. Having become the first person to be returned as an MSP on the historic night of May 6th 1999, McCabe was appointed minister for parliament and Labour's business manager, playing an important role in getting the institution's working arrangements up and running. His combative style was sometimes cited as symptomatic of an Executive wanting to see the Parliament take a small-minded, municipalist approach, illustrated with tense exchanges between the business manager and Presiding Officer Sir David Steel. The alternative view is that the Hamilton MSP brought ability and tough-minded negotiating skills to dealings with other parties, while keeping important links open to unions, councillors and women MSPs. His role in trying to make the coalition work led to only one defeat on his watch – a foul-up over a fisheries vote, when too many Labour MSPs were allowed to leave early – but did not endear him to his Liberal Democrat colleague Iain Smith, who criticised him after leaving the deputy's minister post. His role in the Section 28/Clause 2A debate came under scrutiny, with McCabe seen as one of the influential 'Big Macs', along with Jack McConnell and Henry McLeish, who were acutely sensitive to the concerns of the Keep the Clause campaign, partly driven by vocal, socially conservative forces within Lanarkshire Labour politics in opposition to the Scottish Executive's policy.

With Donald Dewar's illness in summer 2000, McCabe played a strange game of trying to resolve an internal cabinet dispute over distribution of that year's Executive underspend by presenting himself as the incapacitated leader's approved conduit to the outside world. After Dewar's death, McCabe was one of the prime movers in Henry McLeish's successful campaign to become Labour leader and First Minister, and he would remain one of his closest, most loyal colleagues. The second First Minister gave McCabe responsibility for strategic communications and presentation – not always an easy task under McLeish, and at odds with McCabe's uncomfortable and in one case litigious relationship with the media. This was while retaining his post as parliament minister, chief whip, and overseeing the Executive's policy review, unofficially entitled 'dump the crap'. McCabe was occasionally put out to brief the media, his strategy coming unstuck in the first week of 2001, when his call for the Executive to be known as a 'government' started a row, and provoked a backlash from Westminster MPs who saw this as a sign that the McLeish administration was getting above itself.

Having been so close to McLeish, it surprised nobody that he was ousted by Jack McConnell amid the purge that followed the election of the third First Minister. McCabe took quietly to the backbenches and finance committee membership, and showed his party loyalty by leading for Labour in defence of the party line on Iraq in an SNP debate on January 2003. The May election was followed by a return to favour, first with a place in Labour's coalition negotiating team – the only person to have been retained from the 1999 team – and then returning to ministerial office as deputy to health minister Malcolm Chisholm, where McCabe provided a hard-edged complement to the cabinet minister's easy-going manner.

MP

BILL TYNAN was born in 1940 in Glasgow and educated at St Mungo's Academy, Glasgow and at Stow College as a mechanical engineer. He was a toolmaker from 1961-88 and was a key shop steward in the Caterpillar sit-in and 103 day occupation in 1986-87. He then became a union official and served as a political officer with the AEEU engineering union from 1988-99. He had been a union activist from 1977 and joined Labour in 1969. His union role put him in a key funding position for Scottish Labour, as chair of the Scottish Trade Union-Labour Liaison Committee from 1997-98. Before his 1999 election to Westminster, Tynan had lost out to Jack McConnell in the candidate selection for Motherwell and Wishaw at the Scottish election in 1999, in a hard and close-fought Labour battle, with only two votes separating the contenders, leaving elements in the constituency party which are bitter to McConnell and his rise to become First Minister. Their antipathy has gone deeper with McConnell's agreement to introduce electoral reform for local councils. Tynan became one of those running the First Past the Post Group campaigning against the move, and warning that a special Labour conference might be called to force the Scottish Executive coalition to back down or break up.

When George Robertson was ennobled and became secretary-general of NATO, Tynan stood in the resulting by-election, being run close by the SNP's Annabelle Ewing (who would go on to be Perth MP). Once in the Commons, he was quickly moved into influential positions, reinforcing his reputation as an arch-fixer of political deals and a kingmaker: he became treasurer of the AEEU Parliamentary group and convener of the Scottish group of Labour MPs in 2002. At first, he was on the Scottish affairs select committee, moving to European scrutiny and Northern Ireland after the 2001 election. He voted against war in Iraq in both Commons debates in 2003.

Inverness East, Nairn and Lochaber

Predecessor Constituencies: Inverness (1945–79) and Inverness, Nairn and Lochaber (1983–92).

Socio-economic Indicators:

Constituency Pop. (16–64)	54,930
Claimant Count (May 2003)	2.2% (29.8% below average)
IBA/SDA Claimants	6.9%
Life Expectancy – Male	75.2 (1.8 yrs above avereage)
Life Expectancy – Female	80.4 (1.7 yrs above average)
Owner Occupied	68.2%
Social Rented	18.0%
Average Property Prices	£66,664 (26th)
Average Gross Income	£24,774 (42nd)
Low Birthweight Babies	150 (5.6%)
Teenage Pregnancy Rates	476 (4.8%)
No. of Lone Parent Households	3,045 (8.4%)

CAB Enquiries

Issue	No. of cases	Percentage of total cases (%)
1. Benefits	7454	31.0
2. Consumer	3753	15.6
3. Employment	3020	12.6
4. Other	2755	11.5
5. Housing	2527	10.5

2003 Scottish Parliament Election

Electorate: 66,694   *Turnout*: 34,795 (52.2%)   *Turnout 1999*: 63.1%

Candidate	Party	Votes	Votes%	99 %	Change%
Fergus Ewing	SNP	10,764	30.9	33.1	– 2.1
Rhoda Grant	Labour	9,718	27.9	32.0	– 4.0
Mary Scanlon	Con	6,205	17.8	14.6	+ 3.2
Patsy Kenton	Lib Dem	5,622	16.2	20.3	– 4.2
Steven Arnott	SSP	1,661	4.8	–	–
Thomas Lamont	Ind	825	2.4	–	–

SNP majority: 1,046 (3.0%)   *Swing*: 1.0% Labour to SNP

2001 General Election

Electorate: 66,452   *Turnout*: 42,459 (63.2%)

Candidate	Party	Votes	Votes%	Change%
David Stewart	Labour	15,605	36.8	+ 2.9
Angus MacNeil	SNP	10,889	25.6	– 3.4
Patsy Kenton	Lib Dem	9,420	22.2	+ 4.7
Richard Jenkins	Con	5,653	13.3	– 4.2
Steven Arnott	SSP	892	2.1	–

Labour majority: 4,716 (11.1%)   Swing: 3.1% SNP to Labour

1945–97 Westminster

	Lab%	Con%	SNP%	Lib%	Other%	Turnout%
1997	33.9	17.5	29.0	17.5	2.1	72.7
1992	25.1	22.6	24.7	26.0	1.5	73.3
1987	25.3	23.0	14.8	36.8	–	70.9
1983	14.4	29.8	9.8	46.1	–	70.6
1979	20.6	24.8	20.6	33.8	0.2	74.4
1974O	15.6	22.0	29.6	32.4	0.4	70.5
1974F	16.6	26.8	17.9	38.7	–	76.7
1970	23.0	31.5	7.1	38.4	–	72.3
1966	27.7	32.9	–	39.4	–	72.1
1964	26.3	33.9	–	39.8	–	71.4
1959	22.8	44.3	–	32.9	–	71.6
1955	19.9	41.4	–	38.7	–	67.6
1954B	22.6	41.4	–	36.0	–	49.2
1951	35.5	64.5	–	–	–	69.3
1950	31.8	45.5	–	22.7	–	68.6
1945	34.6	–	–	22.2	43.2	59.0

Inverness East, Nairn and Lochaber is the second largest seat in the United Kingdom covering a total of 750,000 hectares. It ranges across a wide array of contrasting settlements and environments, containing most of the city of Inverness, but ranging from the rugged North Atlantic coastline to the Moray Firth on the North Sea coast.

Inverness gained city status in 2000 and is one of the fastest growing cities in the United Kingdom. The city along with its surrounding region bid unsuccessfully for the title of European City of Culture for 2008, but it illustrated the ambition and drive which characterises the area. This can be seen in a variety of initiatives and developments such as the University of the Highlands and Islands – a multi-venue venture aiming to expand access and opportunity across the region. New jobs and employers are setting up in the area including Inverness Medical which began business in 1995 and has now expanded to 1,000 staff, resulting in it being bought by the American firm Johnson and Johnson. Westminster

Healthcare, a nursing home agency relocated its administrative headquarters from London to Inverness to reduce costs. The Scottish Executive as part of its dispersal policy decided to relocate the public agency Scottish Natural Heritage from Edinburgh to Inverness, but this has met with staff resistance and a question mark over the sense of the Executive's dispersal programme.

European Union funds have been crucial to the development of the Highlands and Islands and in 1999 the region was awarded £213 million in structural funds over a seven year period lasting up to 2006 following on a smiliar tranche of Objective 1 money. However, the European Union expansion in 2004 to bring in the ex-Communist countries mean the bonanza days of European Union funding days are over. Transport links are another crucial issue with the Aberdeen-Inverness rail link needing investment, but substantial progress is happening in places. The Scottish Executive is finally upgrading the A830 Mallaig road. The Chancellor of the Exchequer, Gordon Brown's decision in 2000 to abolish Air Passenger Duty on flights from the Highlands and Islands assisted the area, but duties are still charged on flights into the region.

Traditional industries such as crofting and fishing are still important in this part of Scotland in such small communities such as Arisaig, Mallaig, and the islands of Rhum, Canna, Muck and Eigg. The Land Reform (Scotland) Act allows communities the right to purchase their estates. The islanders of Eigg have already succeeded in collectively purchasing their island following a high-profile campaign against their absentee landlords. Tourism is another important earner – as this is a constituency with some of the most spectacular landscapes in the United Kingdom – and is home to the legendary Loch Ness Monster and Ben Nevis, the highest mountain in the UK. Historic landmarks include Glencoe, site of the infamous massacre of the MacDonalds by the Campbells in 1692.

The ambitions of Inverness can be seen in the fortunes of Inverness Caledonian Thistle – which only entered the Scottish Football League in 1994-95 from the Highland League. They famously put Celtic out of the Scottish Cup in February 2000, costing then Celtic manager John Barnes his job, and regularly sit near the top of the Scottish First Division, challenging for a place in the top flight.

Inverness has a long and respected Liberal tradition and was won by Murdoch Macdonald for the Liberals in 1922. He continued to hold the seat under the banner of the National Liberals who aligned themselves with the Conservatives from 1931 onward. John MacCormick, one of the founding fathers of the modern Nationalist movement, stood three times in the seat – in 1931 and 1935 for the National Party of Scotland and then for the fledgling SNP winning 14 and 16.1 per cent of the vote. He then fell out with the party leadership and stood for the Liberals in 1945 winning a more impressive 22.2 per cent in 1945 before going off to establish his National Covenant scheme for a Scottish Parliament.

Macdonald retired prior to the 1950 election, and the Conservatives Lord Malcolm Douglas-Hamilton won the seat with a 4,820 majority over Labour. He stood down four years later forcing a December 1954 by-election in the week before Christmas which Neil McLean won with a slender 1,331 lead over the Liberals and held in the next two general elections which were won nationally by the Conservatives. However in 1964, as the UK tide turned against the Conservatives, the Liberal Russell Johnston defeated McLean in a three-party contest with Labour polling significantly.

Johnston did what Liberals do and dug in deep at a local level and in October 1974 faced a serious SNP challenge which saw him hold on by 1,134 votes. He increased this to a safer 4,157 over the Conservatives in 1979. With the creation of the Liberal-SDP Alliance in 1981, Johnston increased his vote to 46 per cent in 1983 and a 7,298 lead over the Conservatives in the newly created seat of Inverness, Nairn and Lochaber, before seeing it fall slightly to 5,431 over Labour's David Stewart in 1987.

In the 1992 Westminster election, in a year which saw the Lib Dems suffer some high-profile reverses and scares to their MPs, Johnston's vote fell by 11 per cent and Labour's David Stewart – standing for the second time and unable to increase his own vote – came within 458 votes of taking the seat. This was the closest four-party contest ever seen in Scotland with a mere 1,741 votes separating the four candidates, and the Lib Dem winning share of 26 per cent representing the lowest winning percentage in any post-war election in Scotland at Westminster or the Scottish Parliament.

The seat became Inverness East, Nairn and Lochaber in 1997 and notionally a more marginal seat where the Lib Dems would have had a 736 lead over the SNP with all four main parties in competition. With Johnston retiring from the Commons, the seat became a Labour–SNP battleground, with the Lib Dems running a poor third. David Stewart, standing for Labour for the third time, finally took the seat, coming from a notional fourth in 1992 to increase his support by 11 per cent, while the Nationalists' Fergus Ewing put 4 per cent on his vote resulting in a Labour majority of 2,339. In June 2001, David Stewart was re-elected with his majority doubled to 4,339 over the SNP, as Labour's vote fell back by 500 votes on four years previously, while the SNP declined by 3,000.

In the first Scottish Parliament election, both Labour and SNP fancied their chances of winning the seat and Fergus Ewing finally triumphed in the seat increasing the SNP vote by 4 per cent and achieving a narrow 441 majority over Labour. The constituency was one of only three seats to change hands in the 1999 election – the other two being Aberdeen South and Falkirk West. In 2003, Ewing confirmed this seat as a split Westminster/Scottish Parliament constituency, doubling his majority to 1,046, as the Nationalist vote fell 3,000 and Labour's vote by 3,500. In the regional list vote, Labour won 25.9 per cent to the SNP's 23.2 per cent – a Labour lead of 917 votes – while the Greens won an impressive 9.5 per cent and the SSP 5.2 per cent.

Boundary changes at Westminster will see the city of Inverness reunited in the same seat and extended to include Badenoch and Strathspey to the south and east, while losing Lochaber. In a seat as marginal and close to call as this any change could affect the political make-up. Future Inverness East, Nairn and Lochaber contests for the Scottish Parliament now seem destined to be Labour-SNP affairs with the Lib Dems and Conservatives having wilted since their failure to win in 1992. Both the Labour Party and the SNP have built up effective organisations in the seat over the last decade. This will be a seat to keep an eye on in the future, and one where organisation, the quality of representation and candidates, may make all the difference to the result.

MSP

FERGUS EWING was born in Glasgow in 1957. He was educated at Loretto School, Edinburgh and is a graduate in law from Glasgow University. He was employed as a solicitor until his election in 1999, from 1985- 2000 running his own firm, and from 2001 working part-time as a partner in Leslie Wolfson and Co, for which he had previously worked from 1981-85. Part of a political dynasty, his mother Winnie is a Nationalist icon, having represented Highlands and Islands in the Parliament's first term and in the European Parliament, and victor of the famous 1967 Hamilton by-election breakthrough. His wife, Margaret, represents Moray as an MSP and did so as an MP from 1987-2001. His sister Annabelle, represents Perth in the Commons. He is one of those championing the sizeable small business element within the SNP, being on the more business-friendly wing of the party and seen as conservative on many issues.

After two attempts to win the Inverness-shire seat, in 1992 and 1997, he was elected in 1999. No-one can doubt his hard work in the Parliament, if that is measured by asking the largest number of written questions – more than 1,500 in the first term – many on environmental and constituency issues, and those asked orally being notable for the carefully calculated discomfort they cause ministers. That lawyerly, forensic approach to questions has also caused unease for those in the Holyrood Building

Project, of which he has been one of the most prominent critics. At first on the enterprise and lifelong learning committee, he later joined the rural development committee, and various campaigns saw him take up the plight of Scottish Bus Group pensioners and those with osteoporosis. He was prominent in the passage of land access and national parks legislation, being a keen hill walker and member of his local mountain rescue team. Following the 2003 election, John Swinney appointed him spokesman on finance and public services, in opposition to Labour's Andy Kerr. He is also deputy convener of the finance committee, which puts him in a strong position to continue his pursuit of the Holyrood Building Project, in particular his questions about the Flour City contract, which lost at least £6 million.

MP

DAVID STEWART was born in 1956 and educated at Hyndland Secondary School, Glasgow, and Paisley College where he studied social science, followed by social work at Stirling, and management with the Open University. He was a social worker from 1981-87 in first Dumfries and then moved to the Highlands, working in Dingwall and becoming a Highland Regional Council social work manager from 1987–97. He served as a councillor in Nithsdale District Council from 1984-86 and subsequently on Inverness District Council from 1988-96. Meanwhile, he was a member of the Scottish Labour executive from 1985-95, and stood twice in the Inverness seat before being successful. In 1992, he came within 458 votes of unseating the long-time Lib Dem incumbent, Russell Johnston. In his 1997 maiden speech, he stressed his campaign on high fuel prices in the Highlands.

Stewart was a member of the Scottish affairs select committee from 1997-99, resigning after he admitted leaking a report to Donald Dewar. He has campaigned on improving services for diabetics, calling in 1988 for a national screening programme and becoming secretary of the all-party diabetes group in 2000, from where he welcomed Government plans to introduce free needles for people who need insulin. Soon after being first elected, he also became chairman of the Parliamentary Labour Party's agriculture committee, again reflecting his constituency's priorities, and in 2001 became secretary of the Scottish Labour group of MPs. In 2001, he won back a select committee place, this time on work and pensions, and two years later he was made a Parliamentary Private Secretary in the Scotland Office. In June 2003 he signed a Commons motion condemning Scottish Executive plans to introduce proportional representation in local government. He is a member of the Tribune Group, which says more about the deradicalised nature of Tribune than it does about this ultra-loyalist.

Kilmarnock and Loudoun

Predecessor Constituencies: Kilmarnock (1945–79).

Socio-economic Indicators:

Constituency Pop. (16-64)	51,271
Claimant Count (May 2003)	4.6% (46.8% above average)
IBA/SDA Claimants	10.4%
Life Expectancy – Male	73.1 (0.3 yrs below average)
Life Expectancy – Female	77.1 (1.6 yrs below average)
Owner Occupied	62.2%
Social Rented	30.5%
Average Property Prices	£51,579 (54th)
Average Gross Income	£25,143 (40th)
Low Birthweight Babies	154 (6.3%)
Teenage Pregnancy Rates	483 (4.6%)
No. of Lone Parent Households	3,455 (10.3%)

CAB Enquiries

Issue	No. of cases	Percentage of total cases (%)
1. Benefits	2489	28.7
2. Consumer	2176	25.1
3. Employment	1335	15.4
4. Housing	823	9.5
5. Other	538	6.2

2003 Scottish Parliament Election

Electorate: 61,056   Turnout: 31,520 (51.6%)   Turnout 1999: 64.0

Candidate	Party	Votes	Votes%	99 %	Change%
Margaret Jamieson	Labour	12,633	40.1	44.1	– 4.0
Daniel Coffey	SNP	11,423	36.2	37.1	– 0.8
Robin Traquair	Con	3,295	10.5	11.7	– 1.2
Ian Gibson	Lib Dem	1,571	5.0	7.2	– 2.2
Colin Rutherford	SSP	1,421	4.5	–	–
Mary Anderson	Ind	404	1.3	–	–
Matthew Donnelly	Ind	402	1.3	–	–
Lyndsay McIntosh	SPA	371	1.2	–	–

Labour majority: 1,210 (3.8%)   Swing: 1.5% Labour to SNP

2001 General Election

Electorate: 61,048   *Turnout*: 37,665 (61.7%)

Candidate	Party	Votes	Votes%	Change%
Desmond Browne	Labour	19,926	52.9	+ 3.1
John Brady	SNP	9,592	25.5	- 9.1
Donald Reece	Con	3,943	10.5	- 0.3
John Stewart	Lib Dem	3,177	8.4	+ 4.4
Jason Muir	SSP	1,027	2.7	-

Labour majority: 10,334 (27.4%)   *Swing*: 6.1% SNP to Labour

1945–97 Westminster

	Lab%	Con%	SNP%	Lib%	Other%	Turnout%
1997	49.8	10.8	34.5	4.0	0.9	77.2
1992	44.8	19.0	30.7	5.5	–	80.0
1987	48.5	19.6	18.2	13.7	–	78.0
1983	43.6	24.7	9.0	22.7	–	75.6
1979	52.6	29.1	18.3	–	–	81.1
1974O	45.7	18.9	30.2	5.2	–	80.4
1974F	47.2	27.7	15.3	9.8	–	83.2
1970	59.3	27.8	6.9	6.0	–	79.2
1966	68.5	31.5	–	–	–	79.0
1964	62.3	26.7	–	11.0	–	82.8
1959	62.7	37.3	–	–	–	82.4
1955	60.9	39.1	–	–	–	81.1
1951	60.7	39.3	–	–	–	86.7
1950	56.6	35.8	–	5.4	2.2	86.2
1946B	59.7	32.5	7.8	–	–	68.4
1945	59.4	40.6	–	–	–	76.1

Kilmarnock and Loudoun is based on the town of Kilmarnock with its distinctive and marked sense of independent and smaller settlements such as Stewarton, Kilmaurs, Galston, Newmills and Darvel. This is East Ayrshire country – a mixture of urban living in and around Kilmarnock with small villages which were once dominated by the textile industry. Average property prices are 23.5 per cent below the national average, and rose 50.4 per cent in the 1990s. Kilmarnock is the home of the world famous Johnnie Walker Scotch whisky and also the location for some of Kilmarnock-born William McIlvanney's novels – characterised as the town of Graithnock – a working class town where the hero, Laidlaw, is unsure of himself and his emotions. It has also been the location for the first private prison in Scotland, based at Bowhouse outside the town, which has attracted much negative press and political hostility.

Kilmarnock has suffered from the contraction of the textile industries in the 1980s and 1990s, but also seen new jobs growth and in May 2001 a new technology centre opened at Rugby Park, home of Kilmarnock Football Club, in partnership with Kilmarnock College. Significant job losses have occurred. Blackwood Carpet Yards which has traded in the area since 1847 and was one of the largest carpet yarn exporters to Europe in the UK, closed with the loss of 300 jobs. The Kilmarnock-based Rowallan Creamery, which had been in business for over 110 years and supplied products to the baking industry, closed with the loss of over 100 jobs. And there have been concerns over the future of Kilmarnock abattoir which was badly hit by the foot and mouth outbreak in 2001.

Kilmarnock has a long Labour pedigree and was first won by Labour in 1923, although it was also won by that creation of Ramsay MacDonald 'National Labour' in 1931 and 1935 after the Labour MP switched sides with MacDonald. Clarice Shaw won it back for Labour in 1945 with a 7,537 majority over the Unionists but was MP for just over a year – resigning in October 1946 and forcing a by-election. Her successor was Willie Ross who won the December 1946 by-election with a majority of 10,217 (with the Attlee government enjoying six years of office without losing a single Labour seat in a by-election) while the SNP came a distant third with 7.8 per cent. Ross was to stand successfully and be returned for Kilmarnock ten times spanning 33 years and was twice Secretary of State for Scotland from 1964-70 and 1974-76. Ross earned the nickname 'hammer of the Nats' for his hostility to the SNP and the idea of a Scottish Parliament, believing that he could win a better deal out of Whitehall than any elected institution sitting in Scotland could. However, as a pragmatic politician, Ross changed his views in 1974 as Labour was forced to come round to accepting the need for devolution – driven by Wilson's worries over the electoral threat of the SNP.

Labour's vote rose to an all-time high of 68.5 per cent in 1966, but in the two elections of 1974 it dipped for the first time below 50 per cent. On the last occasion Ross stood in the seat, in October 1974, the Nationalists moved into a strong second place with 30.2 per cent and 14,655 votes. This still left Ross with a comfortable majority of 7,529, but it was a sign that Kilmarnock was changing. William McKelvey was selected as Labour candidate in 1979 and could not have been more different – a hard left Bennite from Dundee Labour Party – who won with a 11,467 majority over the Conservatives. In subsequent elections he was returned with majorities of 8,800 in 1983 and 14,127 majority in 1987, on both occasions over the Conservatives, while in the latter contest the SNP in third place putting 9 per cent on their vote. In 1992 McKelvey faced a strong challenge from the SNP's Alex Neil who gave the Nationalists their best-ever vote in the constituency up until then – 30.7 per cent – and cut Labour's lead to 6,979.

McKelvey was forced to announce his retirement in March 1997 two months prior to the general election when he suffered a stroke. The proximity of the UK general election allowed the Labour NEC to impose a truncated selection process on the constituency with an NEC approved shortlist of eight candidates, from which advocate and Donald Dewar friend, Des Browne, emerged as the Labour candidate. Browne was elected with a 7,256 majority against the SNP's Alex Neil with both parties increasing their percentage support. In the June 2001 UK election Des Browne increased his majority to 10,334 over the SNP and nearly doubled it in percentage terms as the Nationalist vote fell back.

In the first Scottish Parliament election, Alex Neil stood for the third and probably final time in the constituency, and while not winning the seat, succeeded in turning it into a highly contestable Labour-SNP marginal, cutting Labour's majority from 7,256 to 2,760. At the second Scottish Parliament election, Labour's Margaret Jamieson saw her majority cut in half again falling to 1,210 over the Nationalists. Lyndsay McIntosh, a Conservative list MSP for Central Scotland in the first Parliament who had stood four years before in Kilmarnock, defected to the right-wing Scottish People's Alliance and secured a paltry 371 votes – 1.2 per cent of the votes cast. In the regional list vote Labour won 37.2 per cent to the SNP's 27.3 per cent while the SSP secured 5.6 per cent to the Greens 4.3 per cent and Scottish Senior Citizens 4.2 per cent. Although the constituency moved towards to the Nationalists, East Ayrshire Council swung back to Labour from the SNP with Labour winning 49.3 per cent of the vote to the Nationalists 35.3 per cent, whereas four years previous Labour won 47.8 per cent to the Nationalists 40.8 per cent.

Kilmarnock and Loudoun has followed increasingly divergent paths for Westminster and the Scottish Parliament – remaining a fairly safe Labour seat in the former, and becoming a very marginal Labour seat and key SNP target in the latter. SNP progress has been slow and steady rather than spectacular, but is all the stronger for it; even though there have been internal party rifts. The new Westminster seat of Kilmarnock,

Stevenson and Cumnock will reinforce Labour's hold. However, at Holyrood, Kilmarnock and Loudoun is the sort of seat the Nationalists must win if they are to challenge Labour as a party of government.

MSP

MARGARET JAMIESON was born in Kilmarnock in 1953 and educated at Grange Academy, Kilmarnock and Ayr College. She worked in public sector catering as a cook with Arran Health Board and then Strathclyde Regional Council from 1969 until becoming a pioneering female official for the National Union of Public Employees (later Unison) in 1979. Having political responsibility for women, health, local government and further education, she held this position for nearly 20 years until her election to the Scottish Parliament, where she went on to be chair of the Unison branch of parliamentary employees. She was also a former chair of Scottish Labour's women's committee.

In the first Parliament, Jamieson sat on the audit committee and was deputy convener of the health and community care committee. In that role, she gained unwelcome publicity for her involvement in the Parliament's industry liaison group, gaining experience working with the drugs company Pfizer. This involved a visit to the United States in 2002, where she signed a ten-year confidentiality agreement, which was perceived by many as compromising her independence on the health committee. If there were arguments in her favour, she failed to make them in public. The episode was symbolic of a difficult relationship between MSPs and lobbyists, at least when reported in the media, with her experience putting a chill on further such industry links by others. Her next unwelcome publicity was for claiming the highest expenses of any MSP, some of which was due to a vast order for pre-paid envelopes, apparently because of an 'over-zealous' assistant. After re-election in 2003, she sat on the audit committee.

MP

DES BROWNE was born in 1952 in Stevenson and was educated at St Michael's Academy, Kilwinning followed by Glasgow University where he studied law. He practised as a solicitor from 1976 and became an advocate in 1993, working for Ross Harper and Murphy. In 1992, he contested Argyll and Bute, and came a distant fourth. He subsequently represented the Labour Party in court, successfully preventing an episode of *Panorama* which included an interview with then Prime Minister John Major being broadcast in Scotland immediately before the Scottish local government elections in 1995. Before becoming an MP, Browne also served on the Scottish Catholic Bishops' Conference working party on child sexual abuse and the Scottish Office consultative committee on child law. He was chair of the Children's Rights Group from 1981-86 and a council member of the Law Society of Scotland from 1988-92.

Browne was elected to Westminster in 1997 after the retirement of Willie McKelvey led to a last-minute selection battle. From a short-list of eight drawn up by head office, this bright, loyal moderniser won through, with the backing of Donald Dewar and Gordon Brown. At Westminster, Browne served on the Northern Ireland affairs select committee in 1997-98, before getting his feet on the ladder of ministerial promotion with his appointment as a Parliamentary Private Secretary to Donald Dewar at the Scottish Office from 1998-99. With Dewar's move to the Scottish Parliament, Browne shifted briefly to provide PPS support to Adam Ingram at the Northern Ireland office. He then returned to the back benches and sat on the select committee on public administration.

Following the 2001 election, he was made a junior minister at the Northern Ireland office, until the 2003 summer reshuffle, when Tony Blair appointed him minister of state at the Department of Work and Pensions. In April 2004, he was handed the poisoned chalice of sorting out the Government's asylum mess, after the resignation of Beverly Hughes.

Kirkcaldy

Predecessor Constituencies: Kirkcaldy Burghs (1945–70) and Kirkcaldy (1974–79).

Socio-economic Indicators:

Constituency Pop. (16-64)	40,157
Claimant Count (May 2003)	5.4% (71.9% above average)
IBA/SDA Claimants	9.9%
Life Expectancy – Male	74.1 (0.7 yrs above average)
Life Expectancy – Female	78.9 (0.2 yrs above average)
Owner Occupied	60.8%
Social Rented	30.9%
Average Property Prices	£46,660 (60th)
Average Gross Income	£24,239 (46th)
Low Birthweight Babies	124 (6.3%)
Teenage Pregnancy Rates	469 (5.9%)
No. of Lone Parent Households	3,138 (10.7%)

2003 Scottish Parliament Election

Electorate: 49,653   *Turnout*: 21,939 (44.2%)   *Turnout 1999*: 54.9%

Candidate	Party	Votes	Votes%	99 %	Change%
Marilyn Livingstone	Labour	10,235	46.7	48.1	– 1.5
Colin Welsh	SNP	5,411	24.7	32.4	– 7.7
Alexander Cole-Hamilton	Lib Dem	2,417	11.0	9.2	+ 1.8
Mike Scott-Hayward	Con	2,332	10.6	10.3	+ 0.4
Rudi Vogels	SSP	1,544	7.0	–	–

Labour majority: 4,824 (22.0%)   *Swing*: 3.1% SNP to Labour

2001 General Election

Electorate: 51,559   *Turnout*: 28,157 (54.6%)

Candidate	Party	Votes	Votes%	Change%
Lewis Moonie	Labour	15,227	54.1	+ 0.5
Shirley-Ann Somerville	SNP	6,264	22.2	– 0.7
Scott Campbell	Con	3,013	10.7	– 3.0
Andrew Weston	Lib Dem	2,849	10.1	+ 1.5
Dougie Kinnear	SSP	804	2.9	–

Labour majority: 8,963 (31.8%)   *Swing*: 0.6% SNP to Labour

1945-97 Westminster

	Lab%	Con%	SNP%	Lib%	Other%	Turnout%
1997	53.6	13.7	22.9	8.7	1.2	67.0
1992	46.0	21.8	22.5	9.6	–	75.1
1987	49.6	21.3	11.7	17.4	–	76.5
1983	40.3	26.3	9.0	24.3	–	71.9
1979	53.9	26.2	19.9	–	–	77.4
1974O	45.4	16.5	32.0	6.1	–	75.0
1974F	47.0	27.3	25.7	–	–	79.3
1970	56.1	32.1	11.8	–	–	74.5
1966	59.6	27.0	13.4	–	–	75.4
1964	60.0	29.1	10.9	–	–	77.2
1959	58.3	32.5	–	9.2	–	80.5
1955	59.3	40.7	–	–	–	75.2
1951	60.6	39.4	–	–	–	84.6
1950	60.0	40.0	–	–	–	84.8
1945	45.0	29.5	17.0	–	8.5	76.2

This is a Fife county seat made up of coastal and inland communities including the royal burgh of Kirkcaldy and the surrounding coastal towns of Wemyss, Buckhaven, Burntisland and Kinghorn. Kirkcaldy – 'the lang toun' was made a royal burgh in 1644 – and is the birthplace of Adam Smith, the author of *The Wealth of Nations* and the architect Robert Adam, as well as the childhood home of the Chancellor Gordon Brown. It is also the birthplace of one of Scotland's greatest-ever entertainers, the accordionist, band leader and music hall draw, Jimmy Shand, who recently passed away at the age of 92. Daniel Defoe passing through the town on his tour of Britain in the early 18th century found it 'a very well built town, with clean and well-paved streets.' It is also the home of Raith Rovers Football Club. Kirkcaldy used to be the main port servicing the Fife coalfields, but they have now gone completely. It was the linoleum capital of the United Kingdom – and legend has it that visitors will be able to detect a distinct and not unpleasant smell in the air – hence Mary Campbell Smith's famous lines - 'For I ken masel' by the queer-like smell/That the next stop's Kirkcaldy.'

The last coal mine in the constituency shut with the closure of Seafield colliery, and job losses have continued with Alcan Chemicals, the town's biggest employer shedding 120 out of 500 local jobs as part of a global restructuring, while BT closed its call centre in Kirkcaldy. The constituency has the fourth highest claimant total in Scotland. Average property prices are 30.8 per cent below the national average, and rose 39.5 per cent in the 1990s. Fife Health Board has faced opposition to its plans to locate accident and emergency services in Kirkcaldy's Victoria Hospital rather than the Dunfermline Queen Margaret Hospital. Neither side was happy with the fifteen month consultation process. Another major issue has been flood defences at East and West Wemyss and Dysart.

Labour first captured Kirkcaldy in a 1921 by-election and has held it at every election since 1923, with the exception of the National Government landslide of 1931 – an 80-year affiliation which looks set to continue long into the future. Thomas Hubbard first won the seat for Labour in a war-time by-election in February 1944 at which the Nationalists' Douglas Young cut Labour's majority to 1,136 and won 41.3 per cent – one of the best performances at the time by the SNP. Labour's majority increased to a safer 5,302 over the Unionists in 1945 with Young winning 17 per cent for the SNP: their best result after

Motherwell in the 1945 election. Hubbard retired in 1959 and Harry Gourlay easily won the seat, becoming a Labour Whip and then Deputy Speaker, holding on effortlessly even at the SNP high point of October 1974 with a majority of 6,101. Gourlay won in the four-party system of Scotland in 1983 on a mere 40.3 per cent of the vote – which still gave him a 5,331 lead in 1983 over the Conservatives – before announcing he was not standing at the next election. Lewis Moonie was chosen to replace Gourlay and doubled his majority over the Tories to 11,570 in 1987.

Moonie was safely re-elected in 1992 with a reduced majority of 9,126, as the SNP's Stewart Hosie put 11 per cent on the party's vote. Five years later, in a Moonie-Hosie rematch, Labour increased its majority to 10,710 as Moonie put 8 per cent on his notional 1992 vote. In June 2001, Moonie's majority fell to 8,963 over the SNP on a lower turnout which remained unchanged in percentage terms.

In the May 1999 Scottish Parliament election, Marilyn Livingstone was elected with her majority halved to 4,475 as Hosie's third candidature in the constituency saw him put nearly 10 per cent on the SNP vote. In just over a decade, Hosie had taken the SNP from a poor fourth in the constituency with just over 11 per cent to offering a serious challenge to Labour with 32 per cent. In the 2003 Scottish Parliament election, Livingstone was re-elected with her majority slightly increased. The SNP vote fell back 8 per cent to 25 per cent, losing much of the momentum built up over the previous decade. In the regional list vote, Labour won 36.7 per cent and the Nationalists 22.4 per cent, while SSP won 6.1 per cent and the Greens 5.5 per cent.

Kirkcaldy has been a safe Labour seat for 80 years, with the exceptions of 1931 and wartime by-elections. In short, it seems to take extraordinary circumstances to threaten Labour's hold in this seat. Until the 2003 Scottish Parliament the seat seemed to be developing a split personality between Westminster where it has been unwaveringly loyal to Labour, and the Scottish Parliament, where the SNP had made impressive in-roads. This pattern has been checked by the SNP's reverses in 2003. Boundary changes for Westminster would see the creation of a new seat called Kirkcaldy and Cowdenbeath, in which it is highly likely Gordon Brown will stand, because of the abolition of his seat. As for future Scottish Parliament elections, Kirkcaldy looked like it was going to become an interesting seat and one party managers would have to pay attention to. Instead, the voters of the town and its surrounding areas seem to have indicated, for now, that they are content to remain loyal to Scottish Labour and its Fife brand.

MSP

MARILYN LIVINGSTONE was born in 1952 and educated at Viewforth Secondary and Fife College. She was a councillor in Fife and also head of the Fife College's business school in Glenrothes, before her election in 1999. Outside work, her community activities focussed on women's groups, highlighting sexual abuse problems in Fife and later convening the MSPs' cross-party group on childhood sexual abuse.

An enthusiast for the Co-operative Party wing of Labour, she was a member of the enterprise and lifelong learning committee in the first Parliament, and convenor of the Labour MSPs' group. In the latter role, she had an important part in the Abolition of Warrant Sales Bill debate in April 2000, alerting ministers to backbench opinion. She has quietly earned a reputation as someone who is a hard worker, trusted by all sides, and backing both those who emerged as First Ministers when the job became vacant in 2000 and 2001. However, there are those in the group who believe she never let it become the forum for political debate it could have been in the first four years. She was replaced as group convener after the 2003 election and took a place on the equal opportunities committee.

Ministers put her as a Labour representative on the Kerley Committee, tasked with devising a detailed plan for reforming local government, including its voting system. Along with Sandra Osborne, Labour MP for Ayr, she submitted a minority report making the case for retention of first-past-the-post.

MP

LEWIS MOONIE was born in 1947 in Dundee, and was first elected MP for Kirkcaldy in 1987. He was educated at Nicolson Institute, Stornoway and Grove Academy, Dundee, before studying medicine at St Andrews and Edinburgh Universities. He was briefly, while at university, a Conservative supporter 'partly because it was the unconventional thing to do', and then joined the Communist Party in 1971, remaining a member for four years. He worked in psychiatry from 1973-75 before becoming a clinical pharmacologist and medical adviser with a range of pharmaceutical companies in the UK, the Netherlands and Switzerland from 1975-80. He moved back into the NHS, training as a community medic, and working for Fife Health Board in that area of public health from 1984-87. That medical background was later to help inform his contributions to the debate on abortion, arguing against restrictive legislation.

In politics, Moonie only joined the Labour Party in 1979, aged 32, three years later becoming a regional councillor in Fife, where he served until 1987. At Westminster he was a member of the social services committee from 1987-88 and the Treasury select committee from 1989-90. He became Opposition front-bench spokesman on technology from 1990-92, science and technology from 1992-94, industry 1994-95, and was national heritage spokesman on broadcasting from 1995 to 1997. As an old-fashioned Labour moderate, Moonie seemed to have missed out with the creation of New Labour, and the transition from opposition to government saw him dropped from the front-bench. He may not have helped his career prospects with a report during the 1997 campaign that he was in favour of stripping BBC governors of their powers, which was quickly rubbished by a nervous Labour leadership.

Instead, he became chair of the finance and services select committee briefly in 1997, a member of the House of Commons Commission from 1997 and of the Treasury Select Committee from 1998. He complained at that time of backbenchers with not enough to do and the discouragement of independent thinking by MPs. His ministerial time came at last in January 2000, with the resignation of Peter Kilfoyle protesting about the political direction and priorities of New Labour. Moonie won a junior ministerial post in the Ministry of Defence, responsible for veterans. He visited UK troops in Kuwait just before the Iraq war began in 2003, commenting one month before hostilities that war seemed 'pretty damn inevitable'. It was another comment which went down badly in Downing Street - so he lost his ministerial job in the bungled reshuffle of June 2003. He was one of the first to announce his retirement from the Commons ahead of boundary changes and a reduced number of seats, making way for Gordon Brown to take over Kirkcaldy and Cowdenbeath.

Linlithgow

Predecessor Constituencies: Linlithgowshire (1945) and West Lothian (1950–79).

Socio-economic Indicators:

Constituency Pop. (16-64)	46,647
Claimant Count (May 2003)	2.8% (9.1% below average)
IBA/SDA Claimants	10.5%
Life Expectancy – Male	72.9 (0.5 yrs below averaege)
Life Expectancy – Female	77.9 (0.8 yrs below average)
Owner Occupied	59.1%
Social Rented	35.3%
Average Property Prices	£58,864 (38th)
Average Gross Income	£26,629 (27th)
Low Birthweight Babies	162 (6.8%)
Teenage Pregnancy Rates	426 (4.7%)
No. of Lone Parent Households	3,123 (10.4%)

CAB Enquiries

Issue	No. of cases	Percentage of total cases (%)
1. Benefits	2020	25.8
2. Consumer	1527	19.5
3. Employment	1358	17.3
4. Housing	760	9.7
5. Legal	627	8.0

2003 Scottish Parliament Election

Electorate: 54,113   *Turnout*: 27,645 (51.1%)   *Turnout 1999*: 63.3%

Candidate	Party	Votes	Votes%	99 %	Change%
Mary Mulligan	Labour	11,548	41.8	45.1	– 3.4
Fiona Hyslop	SNP	9,578	34.6	36.5	– 1.8
Gordon Lindhurst	Con	3,059	11.1	9.4	+ 1.7
Martin Oliver	Lib Dem	2,093	7.6	7.8	– 0.3
Steven Nimmo	SSP	1,367	4.9	(other 1.2)	–

Labour majority: 1,970 (7.1%)   *Swing*: 0.8% Labour to SNP

2001 General Election

Electorate: 54,603   *Turnout*: 31,655 (58.0%)

Candidate	Party	Votes	Votes%	Change%
Tam Dalyell	Labour	17,207	54.4	+ 0.2
Jim Sibbald	SNP	8,078	25.5	– 1.3
Gordon Lindhurst	Con	2,836	9.0	– 3.6
Martin Oliver	Lib Dem	2,628	8.3	+ 2.4
Eddie Cornick	SSP	695	2.2	–
Helen Cronin	Rock 'n' Roll	211	0.7	–

Labour majority: 9,129 (28.8%)   *Swing*: 0.8% SNP to Labour

1945–97 Westminster

	Lab%	Con%	SNP%	Lib%	Other%	Turnout%
1997	54.1	12.5	26.8	5.9	0.7	73.8
1992	45.0	17.5	30.3	7.2	–	78.7
1987	47.3	14.8	24.9	12.6	0.3	77.5
1983	45.1	19.1	18.4	17.0	0.5	75.2
1979	54.9	19.7	24.8	–	0.6	78.1
1974O	45.3	10.0	40.9	3.4	0.4	78.8
1974F	45.3	19.0	35.0	–	0.7	80.6
1970	52.9	18.1	28.2	–	0.8	76.7
1966	52.4	11.2	35.3	–	1.1	79.6
1964	50.3	18.0	30.4	–	1.2	79.5
1962B	50.9	11.4	23.3	10.8	3.6	71.1
1959	60.3	39.7	–	–	–	77.9
1955	59.7	40.3	–	–	–	75.4
1951	60.5	39.5	–	–	–	84.9
1950	60.6	35.6	–	–	3.8	79.1
1945	64.1	35.9	–	–	–	73.2

Linlithgow is centred on the ancient burgh of the same name situated between Glasgow and Edinburgh with an old-fashioned, quaint High Street, a magnificent palace and loch. The rest of the seat follows the path of the M8 motorway and carries with it the traditions and scars of ex-mining areas: Bathgate, Blackburn and Whitburn – with the landscape still shaped by the dramatic slag heaps or 'pit bings' which remain from decades of shale-mining. Bathgate was the site of a well-known British Motor Corporation plant opened in 1961 to replace the employment of the mines, but it closed in the 1980s. The socio-economic profile of Linlithgow shows that this is an above average area in terms of wealth and prosperity. Average property prices are 12.7 per cent below the national average, and have increased 59 per cent in 1991-2002, with West Lothian the fastest growing part of Scotland.

The area has been doing relatively well in the last decade through the jobs in neighbouring Livingston's technology sector, but was dealt a huge blow in April 2001 when Motorola, the American mobile phone company announced plans to close its East Inch site near Bathgate with the loss of 3,200 jobs – the most significant loss of jobs in Scotland since Ravenscraig a decade earlier. This was despite having pocketed £17 million of UK government investment to locate and invest in the site and showed that the Scottish Enterprise backed strategy of the early 1990s of attracting inward investment was proving only a short-term success. The agency was successful in helping locate nearly all those made redundant, reflecting the buoyancy of the Lothian job market.

Linlithgowshire – as it then was - was first won by Labour's Manny Shinwell in 1922, who lost it in 1924 and 1931, before George Mathers won it back in 1935 and held it until 1950. He was then elected for the reconfigured seat of West Lothian in the February 1950 election with a 11,237 majority over the Unionists before announcing his retirement at the next election. John Taylor, who had been Scottish Labour General Secretary for 1939-51 – making him the Helen Liddell of his period – was selected Labour candidate and was elected with a majority of 10,052 over the Unionists on an 84.9 per cent poll. He then represented the seat from 1951-62 rising to be Deputy Chief Whip from 1959-61.

His death in March 1962 caused a by-election which, along with Bridgeton months before, signalled the profound changing of Scottish politics. It pitted Tam Dalyell against the SNP's William Wolfe for the first of seven contests; this was in many ways the start of the modern SNP as Wolfe polled 9,450 votes, representing 23.3 per cent of the vote. Slowly over the next six contests Wolfe chiselled away at Labour's majority, reducing it to 2,690 in October 1974 when he won 24,977 votes to Dalyell's 27,687 votes. This was seen at the time as proof of the forward march of Nationalism, but was to be as near as the SNP would get and in 1979, in the last Dalyell-Wolfe contest, Labour's majority grew to 20,082.

The seat was renamed Linlithgow in the 1983 redistribution and contests have not been as exciting since. Dalyell has gone on with majorities of 11,361 in 1983 and 10,373 in 1987; the latter seeing a heavy-weight contest between Dalyell and Jim Sillars, standing for the first time under the SNP's banner, but he made little impression on Labour's majority. In 1992, Dalyell's majority fell to 7,026 over the SNP's Kenny MacAskill; in 1997 a rematch between the two saw Dalyell re-elected for the eleventh time with Labour's majority increasing to 10,838 as the SNP slipped again. In the June 2001 UK election, Dalyell was re-elected for the twelfth time – more than any other MP in the current House - with a similar majority to four years previously. The only highlight was the 211 votes recorded for Helen Cronin standing for the Rock 'n' Roll Loony Party.

In the 1999 Scottish Parliament election, Labour's candidate Mary Mulligan saw her vote fell by 5,000 while Stewart Stevenson saw the SNP vote rise by 1,700 to reach its highest vote since October 1974 and reduce Labour's majority to 2,928. This still left Labour with a 8.7 per cent lead – much larger than 25 years before – but gave the SNP hope. In the May 2003 Scottish Parliament election, Mulligan faced a determined challenge from Fiona Hyslop, an SNP Lothian list MSP. Mulligan emerged victorious with her majority cut by 1,000 to 1,970 – as on a lower turnout Labour's vote fell by 3,750 and the Nationalists by 2,750. In the regional vote, Labour won 32.8 per cent and the SNP 27.3 per cent, while Margo MacDonald won 7.5 per cent, the Greens 6.7 per cent and SSP 4.6 per cent.

Linlithgow has long been an SNP target seat, combining as it does Nationalist history and folklore with the local government base of a sizeable SNP group on West Lothian Council. At future Westminster elections, Labour have strengthened their grip winning 54 per cent in the last two contests, and boundary changes are unlikely to weaken Labour's hold in the new Linlithgow and Falkirk East seat. The Scottish Parliament contest promises a very different kind of politics here with the SNP slowly working itself back into contention and reducing Labour's majority to 7.1 per cent in 2003 – the best SNP performance since William Wolfe in 1974. The SNP have to win seats such as Linlithgow to remain a viable electoral force in Scottish politics, and to be taken seriously as a challenger to Labour.

MSP

MARY MULLIGAN was born in 1960 in Liverpool, and educated at Notre Dame High School, Liverpool, and Manchester University, where she gained a degree in economic and social studies. She worked as an assistant staff manager in British Home Stores from 1981-82 and as an assistant manager in the Edinburgh Woollen Mill from 1982-86, becoming active in USDAW, the shop workers union.

Mulligan was elected to Edinburgh District Council from 1986-96, where she was chair of housing from 1992, and was then a member of Edinburgh City Council from 1995-99. In the Scottish Parliament, Mulligan was convener of the education, culture and sport committee, which got involved in investigations into Scottish Opera and the rebuilding of Hampden Park without getting to grips with educational issues – until, that is, the Scottish Qualifications Authority fiasco broke over the Executive and Parliament. In Henry McLeish's first ministerial reshuffle in October 2000, Mulligan became parliamentary aide to the First Minister, though there is little evidence that she achieved much in handling the confused relations McLeish had with his party group. Under Jack McConnell's leadership, she was appointed deputy minister for health and community care, working under Malcolm Chisholm. Following the 2003 election, she was moved to be deputy to Margaret Curran as communities minister. She presents the more cheerful face of Labour politics, while falling some way short of being one of its heavy hitters.

MP

TAM DALYELL was born in 1932 in Edinburgh and served as MP for West Lothian from 1962 until 1983, first winning the seat in a 1962 by-election. Since boundary changes, taking effect in 1983, he has been MP for Linlithgow. He was educated at Edinburgh Academy and Eton. He did national service, in which he failed to make it to officer grade in the very Royal Scots Greys regiment founded by one of his forefathers. This is linked by his biographer Russell Galbraith with explaining much of his subsequent political life's most pronounced characteristics - doggedness and anger. He went on to study at King's College, Cambridge, where he toyed with Conservative politics, and then Moray House teacher training college, Edinburgh. He was first employed as a teacher in Bo'ness Academy from 1957-61 and as deputy director of studies on the ship-school Dunera from 1961-62.

On entering Parliament, Dalyell became a member of the Public Accounts Committee from 1962-66, Parliamentary Private Secretary to Richard Crossman from 1964-65 and 1967–70, vice-chair of the PLP from 1974-76 and Opposition spokesman on science from 1980-82, losing his job for refusing to back Labour's position in support of the Falklands War. The latter was Dalyell's only frontbench experience in his long Commons career, with regret obvious that he never made it to be a minister. The scientific interest, however, was a theme through his Commons career, as a long-running columnist also for the *New Scientist*. He was also, for one year from 1985-86, a member of Labour's NEC, elected on the hard left Campaign Group ticket. This was an unlikely alliance that ended in tears, or at least in the group discovering their man was more independently-minded than they had realised.

Dalyell's background of Eton and Cambridge and being the tenth baronet of the Binns – his home near Linlithgow, which is open to the public through the National Trust for Scotland – has given him the confidence to plough a lonely, obsessional course. Such single-mindedness may be in the blood: one of his ancestors is the last person ever to escape from the Tower of London. In the 1960s, he made his name in successfully fighting the environmental cause of Aldabra, an Indian Ocean island, when a major air base was planned there. He was active also in foreign and defence policy, and in questioning germ warfare research at Porton Down. In the 1974–79 Parliament, he doggedly pursued his own government over its devolution plans, predicting the United Kingdom as a unitary state could not accommodate legislative devolution to Scotland without ending the union. He wrote a book on the subject, *Devolution: The End of Britain?*, where the question mark seemed a little superfluous, and gave birth to 'the West Lothian Question' named after his constituency – so titled by Enoch Powell. This asked why he, as a Scottish MP after devolution, would be able to vote on education in Bath, but the MP for Bath would not be able to vote on education in Bathgate.

Post-1979, he was a constant thorn in Mrs Thatcher's flesh: over the sinking of the Argentinian cruiser Belgrano, the Westland helicopter crisis which saw Heseltine and Leon Brittan resign from Thatcher's Cabinet, and the bombing of Pan Am flight 103 over Lockerbie. The return of a Labour Government in 1997 seemed to emphasise his other-worldliness and blunt his effectiveness. His criticisms of Labour's proposals on Scottish devolution ('a motorway without exit') lacked the force of two decades previous. He did not play an active role in the 'no' vote campaign, and the little he did say on the subject angered many in the party.

There was talk of trying to deselect him if he could not be persuaded to retire. But anyone who knew his personality would know such a rumour was bound to backfire. With the support of a constituency party which holds him and his idiosyncrasies in some affection, he returned in 2001, to become a particularly cantankerous Father of the House, declaring that of all the Prime Ministers he had watched in the House of Commons, Tony Blair was the worst, for the damage he had done to parliamentary democracy. He was not particularly impressed by Blair as a warrior Prime Minister, voting against the Afghan and Iraq wars. In answer to his own West Lothian question, he took a self-denying ordinance not to vote on devolved issues where the policy in England did not affect his constituents. That did not include this Edinburgh University rector from voting against student top-up fees in January 2004. In the same month he announced his decision to stand down at the next election.

Livingston

Predecessor Constituencies: created anew from Midlothian and West Lothian in 1983.

Socio-economic Indicators:

Constituency Pop. (16-64)	58,940
Claimant Count (May 2003)	2.7% (14.1% below average)
IBA/SDA Claimants	8.4%
Life Expectancy – Male	73.3 (0.1 yr below average)
Life Expectancy – Female	78.1 (0.6 yrs below average)
Owner Occupied	65.8%
Social Rented	28.5%
Average Property Prices	£67,230 (25th)
Average Gross Income	£28,043 (13th)
Low Birthweight Babies	211 (6.1%)
Teenage Pregnancy Rates	602 (5.0%)
No. of Lone Parent Households	3,872 (11.1%)

2003 Scottish Parliament Election

Electorate: 65,421   *Turnout*: 30,557 (46.7%)   *Turnout 1999*: 58.9%

Candidate	Party	Votes	Votes%	99 %	Change%
Bristow Muldoon	Labour	13,227	43.6	47.3	– 3.7
Peter Johnston	SNP	9,657	31.6	36.7	– 5.1
Lindsay Paterson	Con	2,848	9.3	8.2	+ 1.1
Paul McGreal	Lib Dem	2,714	8.9	7.8	+ 1.1
Robert Richard	SSP	1,640	5.4	–	–
Stephen Milburn	SPA	371	1.2	–	–

Labour majority: 3,670 (12.0%)   *Swing*: 0.7% SNP to Labour

2001 General Election

Electorate: 64,852   *Turnout*: 36,033 (55.6%)

Candidate	Party	Votes	Votes%	Change%
Robin Cook	Labour	19,108	53.0	– 1.9
Graham Sutherland	SNP	8,492	23.6	– 3.9
Gordon Mackenzie	Lib Dem	3,969	11.0	+ 4.3
Ian Mowat	Con	2,995	8.3	– 1.1

cont'd

Candidate	Party		Votes	Votes%	Change%
Wendy Milne	SSP		1,110	3.1	-
Robert Kingdon	UK Ind		359	1.0	-

Labour majority: 10,616 (29.5%)　　　　　　　　　　*Swing*: 1.0% SNP to Labour

1983–97 Westminster

	Lab%	Con%	SNP%	Lib%	Other%	Turnout%
1997	54.9	9.4	27.5	6.7	1.5	71.0
1992	44.4	19.4	26.6	8.6	1.0	74.6
1987	45.6	18.7	16.6	19.1	–	74.1
1983	37.3	23.9	13.3	25.4	–	71.6

Livingston is one of Scotland's post-war New Towns which housed Scotland's over-spill from its urban centres in a grand plan of socialist and modernist social engineering. It was a magnet for families from across the Central Belt, Glasgow and Edinburgh. Around it are the ex-mining villages such as Broxburn and Uphall and communities such as Calder, all with long Labour traditions and memories. Livingston is one of the newest seats in Scotland, only appearing on the electoral map in 1983. Average property prices are 0.3 per cent below the national average, and increased 85 per cent in the 1990s, reflecting rapid population growth in West Lothian, due to jobs there and Edinburgh's expansion.

Economic growth in this area has seen numerous hi-tech companies in the electronics and communications sectors establishing themselves. Job losses have also been seen in this sector, and in 2001 NEC shut its Livingston plant with the loss of 1,260 jobs, while Shin Estu, who employ 550 people at their Livingston location, announced the contraction of their plant. At the same time, Motorola's announcement of its closure of its nearby Bathgate plant in the neighbouring constituency of Linlithgow was a big blow in Livingston where many workers lived. In February 2002, the Scottish Executive announced that the Inland Revenue was moving to Livingston with 360 new civil service jobs being created.

The growth of this area is reflected in the decision by the Edinburgh-based Meadowbank Thistle to transform itself into Livingston Football Club and relocate to the area. Whereas Meadowbank, as Edinburgh's third team, struggled, Livingston prospered in an expanding New Town which had not had a senior football team. After entering the Scottish Football League in 1995-96 they were promoted from the Third Division to the Premier League in six seasons and achieved third place in 2001-2 – their first season, placed behind the big guns Celtic and Rangers. At the beginning of 2004, Livingstone had to face the trauma of going into administration. However, despite this, they still managed to win the League cup – the club's first ever major trophy.

The constituency's creation in 1983 came from the bringing together of parts of Midlothian and West Lothian to create a new super-safe Labour seat. Robin Cook, MP for Edinburgh Central from February 1974, faced with a more marginal seat because of boundary changes decided to do a 'chicken run' by shifting to the comparative safety of Livingston. Cook's calculations were proved correct as Labour lost Edinburgh Central, while he won Livingston with 37.3 per cent, 4,551 ahead of the Liberal-SDP Alliance with 25.4 per cent of the vote and the Conservatives on 23.9 per cent. In 1987, Cook increased his majority to 11,105 over the Liberal-SDP Alliance, falling back in 1992 to 8,105 over the SNP, whose vote rose by 10 per cent.

In the 1997 UK election Robin Cook saw Labour's vote rise to 54.9 per cent – an increase of 9 per cent – and its majority to 11,747 over the SNP. In 2001, Cook's vote held firm, giving him a comfortable majority over the SNP.

In the 1999 Scottish Parliament elections, Bristow Muldoon saw Labour's vote fall by 6,000, while the SNP picked up just under 2,000 votes and 9 per cent, reducing Labour's majority to 3,904. However, in the second Scottish Parliament election, Muldoon was safely re-elected with a 3,670 majority over the Nationalists as both Labour and the SNP votes fell back. In the regional list vote Labour won 33.9 per cent to the Nationalists 24.9 per cent, while Margo MacDonald won 8.9 per cent, the Greens 6.5 per cent and the SSP 5.2 per cent.

As a relatively new seat, Livingston does not have the Labour-SNP history of neighbouring Linlithgow, but is otherwise similar, politically and socio-economically. The Nationalists have not had the history or depth of support here that they have in Linlithgow. Instead, they have slowly gained strength in the 1999 and 2003 Scottish Parliament elections, polling an impressive 36.7 per cent in the first election, and in a poor national showing in 2003, managing to keep in contention, winning 31.6 per cent. Boundary changes for Westminster are not expected to affect Labour's hold in a new, expanded Livingston seat. At the Scottish Parliament, the SNP must harbour hopes that if the national tide turns towards them – and some of their historic target seats fall – other seats such as Livingston will topple as well.

MSP

BRISTOW MULDOON was born in 1964 and educated at Cumbernauld High School, Strathclyde University, where he studied chemistry, and the Open University. Muldoon worked in a range of InterCity railway posts between 1986 and the privatisation of its parent company, British Rail; starting as a management trainee, working out of London Paddington and Euston, then as a catering manager and train manager based in Edinburgh. Post-privatisation, in 1996-97, he was a train services manager for GNER, followed by a period as a business analyst in the year before being elected an MSP.

He was elected to Lothian Regional Council from 1994-96 and became vice-chair of the economic development committee from 1994-96 and a councillor on the unitary West Lothian Council from 1995-99. He was convenor of community services there from 1995-99. Muldoon was eased into the Labour candidacy for Livingston by having been election agent for Robin Cook, having long been a strong local supporter of the former Foreign Secretary. As an MSP, Muldoon began as a member of the subordinate legislation committee and was a member of the local government committee. With committee reform from the start of 2001, he joined the transport and environment committee, taking over as its convener in late 2001, replacing Andy Kerr when the latter became finance and public services minister. With Muldoon in the chair, the committee delivered a toughly-worded report on the state of railways in Scotland, while his other backbench activities saw him an enthusiastic backer of the fox hunt ban law.

With the change of committee remits, he became convener of the local government and transport committee in 2003, and was soon challenging the Green and Scottish Socialist Party attempts to block the M74 extension through Glasgow. That committee faced legislation in 2004 involving extensive local government reform, including contentious changes to the voting system, followed by a review of local government finance. Amid the Labour MSP group's tribal wars in the first Parliament, Muldoon backed Henry McLeish in the 2000 leadership contest, and then was one of those to nominate McConnell the following year. His wife is a member of West Lothian Council.

MP

ROBIN COOK was born in 1946 in Bellshill and elected MP for Edinburgh Central from 1974-83 and for Livingston since 1983. Educated at Aberdeen Grammar School, Royal High School, Edinburgh, and Edinburgh University, where he originally planned to study divinity and become a minister, but instead found politics and studied English literature, failing to complete a PhD on Charles Dickens. He was briefly a teacher in Bo'ness Academy from 1969-70 and a tutor-organiser for the Workers' Educational Association from 1970-74. He was elected to Edinburgh Corporation from 1971-74. Cook first contested Edinburgh North in 1970 and won Edinburgh Central by 961 votes on his 28th birthday in February 1974.

He was a prominent opponent of devolution, voting against Labour's devolution plans during the 1974-79 Government and campaigning energetically for a 'no' vote in the 1979 referendum alongside Brian Wilson and Tam Dalyell. Unlike them, he changed his mind on the issue as a result of the Thatcher Government's treatment of Scotland – the conversion coming on election night in 1983. He later said: 'Unkind commentators have said that this shows what you can get out of anyone if you keep them awake until 4 o'clock in the morning and shine bright lights in a TV studio in their eyes.' However, he was to cause problems for Labour's devolution plans in 1992, when he observed that a Scottish MP could not serve as a UK minister on devolved issue such as health, leading to a retraction under instructions from then leader Neil Kinnock.

In the Commons, he was Treasury and economic affairs spokesman from 1980-83, and after Labour's defeat in 1983 was Neil Kinnock's campaign manager for the party leadership. He was subsequently elected to the Shadow Cabinet, holding frontbench posts from 1983-97, and in 1993 and 1994 finished top of the PLP ballot. He was European Community affairs spokesman from 1983-85, handled trade and industry from 1986-87, health and social security from 1987-89 and health from 1989-92, and he successfully moved to amend the Criminal Justice Bill to legalise male gay sex in Scotland, 13 years after England and Wales. In 1992, after Labour's fourth defeat, Cook took the role of John Smith's campaign manager in his bid for the leadership and became trade and industry spokesman from 1992-94 and Shadow Foreign Secretary from 1994-97. He was also chair of the Parliamentary Labour Party in 1997.

With election victory in 1997, he moved into the Foreign Office and immediately declared an end to Conservative xenophobia, particularly on Europe, and an 'ethical foreign policy' – a phrase that would come back to haunt the Labour Government. After the 2001 election, with tensions growing between Cook and Tony Blair, and with Gordon Brown successful in forcing Cook out of the key decisions on the euro referendum on which Cook had been relatively europhile, he was shifted to become Leader of the House of Commons, taking his time to decide if he would accept the demotion. There he achieved limited reform to the House's practices, most notably in its hours, and struggled less successfully to drive through Lords reform, getting little support from Blair and finding his proposals blocked in a Commons voting fiasco of multiple, inconclusive divisions. As Blair moved towards war in Iraq, Cook's discontent was known though not explicit. He backed Blair in the February 2003 vote, still dependent on seeking UN approval for war, but when that diplomatic process failed and just before hostilities began, Cook resigned on 17 March and issued a typically withering and personal denunciation of Blair's Iraq strategy from the backbenches, followed by telling interventions in the months that followed, as Blair came under intense pressure over the Hutton inquiry and policy in Iraq began to unravel. On student tuition top-up fees, he backed a rebellious early-day motion, and abstained in the knife-edge January 2004 vote.

Over Labour's long years in opposition, Cook gained a reputation as a combative debater in the House who was both feared and respected by the Conservatives. His demolition of Conservative ministers over the 'arms to Iraq' affair and the subsequent Scott Report was a particular high point. He was never fully signed up for the Blair and Brown modernising agenda, and was viewed as a potent threat in leading the left's cause. That role was undermined, at first with women MPs, by the nature of his humiliating split with his first wife Margaret in favour of his secretary, Gaynor, and then, more generally by his arrogant treatment of backbenchers. He has long had an uneasy relationship with Gordon Brown, despite the two having worked together on *The Red Paper on Scotland* in the 1970s, where Cook wrote about housing. The two worked together on another volume, *Scotland: The Real Divide*, published in 1983, which is thought to be the source of their conflict from then on. The tensions between them mirror those between Brown and Blair; Cook is the senior of the two, and was eventually outshone by Brown, upon his later arrival in the House in 1983.

Cook's isolation in the Labour Government made some suggest in the Scottish Parliament's first year and a half that he could have been a likely successor to Donald Dewar as First Minister. Such speculation ended with the death of Donald Dewar and the election of Henry McLeish as First Minister, when it became clear how difficult it would be to parachute someone like Cook into the Scottish Parliament. Cook has been the subject of a biography by journalist John Kampfner, and he is notable in his spare time for his expertise as a horse racing tipster. In October 2003, Cook published a book of memoirs, seven months after his resignation, *The Point of Departure*. These examined his experience in government from June 2001 and his increasing differences with Tony Blair, as Leader of the House over Lords reform and the Iraq war. Cook, along with Brown, has taken part in Sue Lawley's *Desert Island Discs* choosing as his first and second records, 'Mr Tambourine Man' by Bob Dylan and 'Dirty Old Town' by Ewan McColl and Peggy Seeger. Other choices by Cook included Wagner, Spartacus and Gershwin, while the one book he would take to his island along with Shakespeare would be the *National Hunt Form Book*.

Midlothian

Predecessor Constituencies: Midlothian and Peeblesshire Northern (1945), Midlothian and Peeblesshire Southern (1945) and Midlothian and Peebles (1950–1).

Socio-economic Indicators:

Constituency Pop. (16-64)	40,609
Claimant Count (May 2003)	1.9% (39.9% below average)
IBA/SDA Claimants	8.7%
Life Expectancy – Male	74.3 (0.9 yrs above average)
Life Expectancy – Female	78.8 (0.1 yr above average)
Owner Occupied	61.5%
Social Rented	31.6%
Average Property Prices	£76,731 (16th)
Average Gross Income	£25,938 (33rd)
Low Birthweight Babies	138 (6.1%)
Teenage Pregnancy Rates	454 (5.5%)
No. of Lone Parent Households	2,909 (11.1%)

CAB Enquiries

Issue	No. of cases	Percentage of total cases (%)
1. Benefits	2719	28.8
2. Consumer	2505	26.5
3. Employment	1096	11.6
4. Housing	890	9.4
5. Legal	558	5.9

2003 Scottish Parliament Election

Electorate: 48,319   *Turnout*: 23,556 (48.8%)   *Turnout 1999*: 61.5%

Candidate	Party	Votes	Votes%	99 %	Change%
Rhona Brankin	Labour	11,139	47.3	48.6	−1.3
Graham Sutherland	SNP	5,597	23.8	30.1	− 6.3
Jacqueline Bell	Lib Dem	2,700	11.5	10.7	+ 0.8
Rosemary Macarthur	Con	2,557	10.9	8.6	+ 2.3
Robert Goupillot	SSP	1,563	6.6	(other 2.1)	–

Labour majority: 5,542 (23.5%)   *Swing*: 2.5% SNP to Labour

2001 General Election

Electorate: 48,625   *Turnout*: 28,724 (59.1%)

Candidate	Party	Votes	Votes%	Change%
David Hamilton	Labour	15,145	52.7	– 0.8
Ian Goldie	SNP	6,131	21.3	– 4.2
Jacqueline Bell	Lib Dem	3,686	12.8	+ 3.7
Robin Traquair	Con	2,748	9.6	– 1.3
Robert Goupillot	SSP	837	2.9	–
Terence Holden	Pro-Life	177	0.6	–

Labour majority: 9,014 (31.4%)   *Swing*: 1.7% SNP to Labour

1950–97 Westminster

	Lab%	Con%	SNP%	Lib%	Other%	Turnout%
1997	53.5	10.9	25.5	9.2	0.9	74.1
1992	43.9	20.1	21.9	13.1	1.0	77.9
1987	48.3	18.2	10.6	22.0	0.9	77.2
1983	42.7	21.9	6.2	29.2	–	75.0
1979	47.8	26.4	16.8	9.0	–	77.8
1974O	41.5	16.0	35.6	6.9	–	77.4
1974F	44.6	28.4	27.0	–	–	81.6
1970	52.9	31.5	15.6	–	–	75.6
1966	56.7	27.0	16.3	–	–	77.5
1964	61.3	38.7	–	–	–	78.9
1959	60.2	39.8	–	–	–	81.3
1955	60.2	39.8	–	–	–	78.1
1951	55.3	44.7	–	–	–	83.8
1950	52.8	38.7	–	8.5	–	82.9

Midlothian and Peeblesshire, Southern (1945)

	Lab%	Con%	SNP%	Lib%	Other%	Turnout%
1945	55.8	32.4	–	11.8	–	73.5

Midlothian and Peeblesshire, Northern (1945)

	Lab%	Con%	SNP%	Lib%	Other%	Turnout%
1945	45.7	47.9	–	–	6.4	70.1

Midlothian is situated south of Edinburgh and contains a host of small, traditional working-class towns and villages such as Bonnyrigg, Dalkeith, Loanhead and Newtongrange. Prior to the 1983 boundary redistribution, Midlothian had grown to 101,000 voters, unheard of by the normal size of Scottish constituencies and making it one of the largest seats in the UK, let alone Scotland, and it was reduced in size with the creation of the new seat of Livingston.

Employment patterns have changed dramatically in Midlothian in the last twenty years with the demise of the coal mining industry in the area. The names of the collieries, Bilston Glen and Monktonhall, are deeply etched in the memory of the community and evoke the bitter division and brave defiance of the miners' strike of 1984-85. Post-coal mining, new jobs and industries have come, while commuter culture has also arrived bringing the area into the Edinburgh travel-to-work region.

In the last few years the textile industry has suffered an international downturn which has hit Midlothian hard. In 2000 Dawson International shut its Bonnyrigg site with the loss of 95 jobs, most of which were relocated to other factories in Scotland. Later the same year, Dawson sold Pringle to a Hong Kong based knitwear company, and shut Laidlaw and Fairgrieve, a mill they owned in Dalkeith, with the loss of 190 jobs. Transport links to Edinburgh are a major issue and in March 2002 the Scottish Executive announced that it was going to bring forward plans to reopen the railway line from the Borders to Edinburgh which would involve the reopening of the local station at Gorebridge.

Midlothian still contains significant parts of the constituency with council housing which make 24.3 per cent of all housing, and in 2002 an audit report identified Midlothian Council as the worst in the country in terms of rent arrears with 13.3 per cent of its council tenants thirteen weeks or more behind with their rent. Average property prices are 13.8 per cent above the national average, and rose 91.5 per cent in 1991-2001.

William Ewart Gladstone, Liberal Prime Minister four times in the late 19th century, stood in the constituency in the 1880 general election which gave birth to his legendary Midlothian campaign which he called a 'festival of freedom' and which saw him address numerous packed and enthralled meetings. He was returned as MP for the area and went on to become Prime Minister as the Liberals in Scotland routed the Unionists – winning 52 out of 58 seats and 70 per cent of the vote on a limited franchise.

Post-war Labour representation has been shaped by the politics of the mining industry. In 1945, when there were two Midlothian and Peebles seats, one Conservative and one Labour, the Northern Division was held by Lt. Col. Lord John Hope with a 1,177 lead, the Southern Division by David Pryde, a former miner by 6,496. The seat was renamed Midlothian and Peebles in February 1950 and returned Labour's Pryde with a majority of 7,188. He held the seat until his death in August 1959. James Hill, another miner and local councillor, followed from 1959-66 and was followed by Alex Eadie, a third former miner from 1966-92. Labour was never under threat in these years, but their vote began to decline slowly as Scottish politics moved from the Labour-Conservative two-party battle of the 1950s to a much more fragmented party system in the 1970s. Labour won 60 per cent plus in the period 1955-64, seeing its vote slump below 50 per cent in the 1974 elections and a low of 41.5 per cent in October of that year, with Eadie's majority cut to 4,048 over the SNP.

In 1983 Midlothian lost some voters to the new Livingston seat and Balerno and Currie to Edinburgh West, but Labour's hold on the seat remained secure, with Eadie securing a 6,156 lead over the Liberal-SDP Alliance. Eadie won again in 1987 and announced his retirement before the 1992 election with Labour's fourth post-war miner Eric Clarke chosen to replace him. Clarke secured victory with 43.9 per cent, while the SNP moved into second place adding 5,000 votes to their support and reducing Labour's majority to 10,334. In 1997, Clarke increased Labour's vote by just over 1,000 and was returned with a 9,870 majority. Prior to the June 2001 election, Eric Clarke announced his retirement and David Hamilton, Labour's fifth successive miner, was selected in his place. Hamilton was safely elected with a 9,014 majority over the SNP, as the Nationalists slipped back 4.2 per cent.

In the 1999 Scottish Parliament election, Labour broke the mould and selected a non-miner and because of twinning arrangements, a woman. Rhona Brankin saw the Labour vote fall by more than 4,000, while the SNP's remained static on a reduced turnout, leaving Labour with a 5,525 majority. In the May 2003 Scottish Parliament election, Brankin saw her majority hold at 5,542 – an increase of 17 actual votes from four years before, but a percentage increase from a 18.6 per cent lead to 23.5 per cent.

In the regional vote, Labour won 35.6 per cent to the Nationalists 19.1 per cent with Margo MacDonald on 11.3 per cent – the ex-SNP independent's second highest vote in Lothian – the Greens on 7.1 per cent and the SSP 4.2 per cent.

Boundary changes for Westminster will see an enlarged Midlothian seat take back Penicuik from Tweeddale, Ettrick and Lauderdale, some areas of East Lothian and Musselburgh from Edinburgh East and Musselburgh. At future Scottish Parliament elections, the Labour Party's hold over Midlothian currently looks very strong in the light of the 2003 elections, but this masks the shift towards the SNP in the previous decade which was not completely reversed in the most recent contest. In 1983, the SNP polled a mere 6.2 per cent in Midlothian, whereas in the 1999 Scottish Parliament election they won 30.1 per cent. Despite this impressive advance, the question remains whether the SNP can build on its successes in seats like Midlothian in positioning itself as the main opposition challenger to Labour, and go on and take the seat. Recent reverses throw major doubt on whether the Nationalists can ever realistically break through in seats such as Midlothian, which could have major implications for the state of Scottish politics.

MSP

RHONA BRANKIN was born in 1950 and educated at Jordanhill College School, Glasgow, Aberdeen University, Northern College, Dundee, and Moray House, Edinburgh. She worked in a variety of teaching and learning support posts while spending much of her adult life in the Highlands: in Dingwall Primary from 1975-77, Invergordon Academy from 1983-84, South Lodge Primary, Invergordon, from 1984-88, Alness Academy from 1988-90 and Inverness High School from 1990-94. She then became a lecturer in special educational needs at Northern College, Dundee, from 1994-99.

Brankin was chair of the Scottish Labour Party in 1995-96 and has been associated with the Blairite purge of leftish opponents of the leadership in the run-up to the 1997 election, leading into membership of 'The Network', a Blairite group which sought to continue that job between 1997-99. She was also a member of the Scottish Constitutional Convention. She won the Midlothian candidacy through gender twinning, facing unhappiness in the former mining communities that locally popular men were effectively ruled out. In the 1999 campaign, she was spokesperson on health, sports and arts, and after the elections was given the post of deputy minister for culture and sport as deputy to the minister for children and education, which she held until October 2000, putting together a rather timid arts strategy, at a time when her boss in that department, Sam Galbraith, was working to protect the national companies, and Scottish Opera in particular. In Henry McLeish's first ministerial reshuffle in October 2000, Brankin became deputy minister for rural development, working as deputy to Ross Finnie, and specialising in fisheries. She faced a stormy time there, even having her effigy burned in a Peterhead quayside protest in March 2001, at the height of protests against the Executive's vessel decommissioning policy. With time, she appeared to be winning the trust of the industry, even though her decommissioning scheme was the subject of one of the Executive's few defeats in Parliament – more due to whips' ineptitude than her management of the issue.

Brankin's face fitted less well with Jack McConnell and she was sacked as a minister. From the back-benches, she took on the role of Nationalist-baiter in debates, while joining the enterprise and lifelong learning committee. Post-2003 election, she became a member of the education and the audit committees. The first Parliament was marred for her when diagnosed with breast cancer, from which she recovered fully. Her second marriage is to Peter Jones, Scotland and north of England correspondent of *The Economist*.

MP

DAVID HAMILTON was born in Dalkeith in 1950, and was first elected in 2001. He was educated at Dalkeith High School, and was employed as a miner from 1965-85, rising in the National Union of Mineworkers to become leader of 3,500 Lothian miners in 22 pits in the bitter 1984-85 strike. He was jailed for the role he played, and after the strike, the NCB refused to reinstate him, despite his winning a tribunal. He also led a campaign to prevent the closure of Monktonhall Colliery in 1992, enabling it to be taken over by its own workers with the investment of £10,000 of redundancy money each, but they had to be bailed out by a private company in 1995 and the pit was finally closed in 1997. Hamilton by that time was the councillor seeking to redevelop the site for a new purpose. Out of the industry, he became an employment training scheme supervisor for Midlothian Council from 1987-89, placing training officer with the Craigmillar Festival Society from 1989-92 and he was chief executive of Craigmillar Opportunities Trust from 1992-2000. He was elected a Midlothian councillor from 1993-2001, and was COSLA spokesperson for economic development and tourism from 1999-2001. Among his early signs of being independently-minded in the Commons was joining with other Labour MPs to throw out the plans for reform of select committees, finding himself sitting on those for broadcasting, procedures, Scottish affairs and one of the European standing committees. He signed a motion against war in Iraq in March 2002, and followed up with rebellions against the government line in February and March 2003. He abstained on the December 2003 foundation hospital vote, and backed the government on student top-up tuition fees.

Moray

Predecessor Constituencies: Moray and Nairn (1945–79) and Banff (1945–79).

Socio-economic Indicators:

Constituency Pop. (16-64)	50,481
Claimant Count (May 2003)	2.0% (37.1% below average)
IBA/SDA Claimants	6.0%
Life Expectancy – Male	74.8 (1.4 yrs above average)
Life Expectancy – Female	79.6 (0.9 yrs below average)
Owner Occupied	63.2%
Social Rented	22.0%
Average Property Prices	£55,686 (45th)
Average Gross Income	£25,254(39th)
Low Birthweight Babies	137 (5.5%)
Teenage Pregnancy Rates	374 (3.9%)
No. of Lone Parent Households	1,975 (6.1%)

CAB Enquiries

Issue	No. of cases	Percentage of total cases (%)
1. Benefits	1726	27.7
2. Employment	1076	17.2
3. Consumer	964	15.5
4. Legal	590	9.5
5. Relationships	588	9.4

2003 Scottish Parliament Election

Electorate: 58,290   *Turnout*: 26,981 (46.3%)   *Turnout 1999*: 57.9%

Candidate	Party	Votes	Votes%	99 %	Change%
Margaret Ewing	SNP	11,384	42.2	38.8	+ 3.4
Timothy Wood	Con	6,072	22.5	25.6	– 3.1
Peter Peacock	Labour	5,157	19.1	26.5	– 7.4
Linda Gorn	Lib Dem	3,283	12.2	9.1	+ 3.1
Norma Anderson	SSP	1,085	4.0	–	–

SNP majority: 5,312 (19.7%)   *Swing*: 3.2% Conservative to SNP

2001 General Election

Electorate: 57,898   *Turnout*: 33,223 (57.4%)

Candidate	Party	Votes	Votes%	Change%
Angus Robertson	SNP	10,076	30.3	-11.2
Catriona Munro	Labour	8,332	25.1	+ 5.3
Frank Spencer-Nairn	Con	7,677	23.1	− 4.5
Linda Gorn	Lib Dem	5,224	15.7	+ 6.8
Norma Anderson	SSP	821	2.5	-
Bill Jappy	Ind	802	2.4	-
Nigel Kenyon	UK Ind	291	0.9	-

SNP majority: 1,744 (5.3%)   *Swing*: 8.3% SNP to Labour

1983–97 Westminster

	Lab%	Con%	SNP%	Lib%	Other%	Turnout%
1997	19.8	27.6	41.6	8.9	2.1	68.2
1992	11.9	38.1	44.3	5.7	–	72.5
1987	11.3	35.0	43.2	10.5	–	72.7
1983	7.3	39.2	35.2	18.3	–	71.1

Moray and Nairn (1945–79)

	Lab%	Con%	SNP%	Lib%	Other%	Turnout%
1979	8.7	40.1	38.9	12.3	–	77.5
1974O	9.7	40.0	41.2	9.1	–	74.7
1974F	7.0	43.7	49.3	–	–	79.8
1970	22.8	49.4	27.8	–	–	72.2
1966	34.1	48.1	–	17.8	–	68.0
1964	27.3	50.8	–	21.9	–	69.4
1959	25.0	52.7	–	22.3	–	73.6
1955	39.4	60.6	–	–	–	67.9
1951	39.8	60.2	–	–	–	74.5
1950	40.1	59.9	–	–	–	75.0
1945	38.4	61.6	–	–	–	61.8

Banff (1945–79)

	Lab%	Con%	SNP%	Lib%	Other%	Turnout%
1979	14.2	44.6	41.2	–	–	72.5
1974O	7.3	37.9	45.9	8.9	–	72.5
1974F	6.4	34.5	46.1	13.0	–	75.7
1970	17.4	38.7	22.9	21.0	–	68.9
1966	24.3	41.3	–	34.4	–	65.1
1964	26.6	47.8	–	25.6	–	67.8

cont'd

	Lab%	Con%	SNP%	Lib%	Other%	Turnout%
1959	29.4	70.6	–	–	–	63.3
1955	30.2	69.8	–	–	–	54.7
1951	29.1	70.9	–	–	–	65.6
1950	26.3	58.1	–	15.6	–	74.1
1945	20.9	49.5	–	29.6	–	66.5

Moray contains a number of small towns, villages and settlements along the North East coast of Scotland, and others further inland along the River Spey. These include the cathedral town of Elgin, Buckie, Burghead, Forres, Lossiemouth – birthplace of Ramsay MacDonald, Labour's first Prime Minister – plus a large part of Speyside. Given its association with the Ewing SNP dynasty for the last thirty years, it is only apt that there is a town called Dallas on the banks of the River Lossie. Average property prices are 17.4 per cent below the national average, and increased 49.6 per cent in the 1990s.

Moray's position, situated by the Moray Firth, gives it a relatively warm climate and it is not uncommon to see dolphins swimming in the sea nearby. This is an area with significant religious and spiritual history and belief, from the Pluscarden monastery run by Benedictines to the more recent arrival in the early 1960s of the Findhorn Foundation, a new age settlement situated near to RAF Kinloss.

The Royal Air Force has a big presence in the constituency with two bases – Kinloss and Lossiemouth. Kinloss is the main northern base for Nimrod planes monitoring and protecting the United Kingdom's air defences.

The Scotch whisky industry is crucial to Moray's economy, containing more than half of all Scotland's distilleries including the world-famous Glenlivet and Glenfiddich brands. it is responsible for bringing in many of the area's tourists. Fishing has been traditionally important to the small ports of Lossiemouth, Buckie, Burghead, and Hopeman. The North East fishing fleet has been particularly hit by fishing restrictions in the last few years caused by over-fishing in the North Sea.

As Moray and Nairn, the seat has a long Conservative tradition and was won by them in 1923 when James Stuart captured it from the Liberals and went on to hold the seat until 1959. In this period he rose through his party's ranks to become Secretary of State for Scotland from 1951-57 under the premierships of Winston Churchill and Anthony Eden. He was succeeded as Conservative MP by Gordon Campbell in Macmillan's election triumph of October 1959 and he too became Secretary of State for Scotland, in Ted Health's 1970-74 Government.

In the February 1974 general election Winnie Ewing – the SNP victor in the 1967 Hamilton by-election – stood in the seat and defeated the sitting Conservative Secretary of State Gordon Campbell. In October 1974, Ewing surprisingly saw her majority reduced to a mere 367 votes over the Conservative Alexander Pollock – with a Liberal intervention taking votes from the SNP. Ewing was a prominent figure in the SNP parliamentary group at Westminster from 1974-79 and in the May 1979 electoral whirlwind the Nationalists faced, she would conventionally have stood little chance. However, Pollock, standing again for the Conservatives only beat her by a margin of 420 votes.

In 1983 the constituency became Moray, as it lost the town of Nairn and gained parts of western Banffshire. Pollock increased his majority to the relative comfort zone of 1,713 as the Nationalists fell further back in the seat by 3.4 per cent from the 1979 notional result. If Pollock thought he could enjoy the long tenure of his Conservative predecessors, Stuart and Campbell, he was to be proven wrong by the SNP mini-revival of 1987 where they captured three North East rural seats from the Conservatives. The SNP candidate was Margaret Ewing who had, as Margaret Bain, been MP for Dunbartonshire East and had now married into the Ewing family. She achieved the biggest majority in the seat since 1970 – winning by 3,685 votes and putting an impressive 8 per cent on the SNP vote.

Ewing held on in 1992 with a reduced majority of 2,844 which in May 1997 widened to 5,566 – in both cases over the Conservatives. In the latter case both the SNP and Conservative votes fell and Labour's vote rose by 8 per cent. Ewing also stood in the first Scottish Parliament election in May 1999 where this trend continued and her vote slipped back by 2.8 per cent as she was returned with a 4,129 majority. Labour continued to make ground – displacing the Conservatives to gain second place and see their vote rise by 7 per cent. The SNP share of the vote, 38.8 per cent, was their lowest since 1970, while Labour's share, 26.5 per cent was their highest since Wilson's landslide of 1966.

Angus Robertson was chosen as SNP candidate to replace Margaret Ewing for the 2001 UK election. He was returned with his majority drastically cut from 5,566 to 1,744, winning a mere 30.3 per cent of the vote. The SNP's vote fell back by 6,500 votes and 11 per cent – the biggest fall in any of the six SNP-held Westminster seats – while Labour moved from third to second place increasing their support by 450 votes and 5 per cent.

In the 2003 Scottish Parliament election Margaret Ewing increased her majority to 5,312 – a rise of 1,000. The Conservatives moved from third to second place despite losing 3 per cent of their support, as Labour's vote fell back by 7 per cent, reversing the recent trend in this seat of Labour building a base at Westminster and Scottish Parliament elections. In the regional list vote, the Nationalists won 30.9 per cent to 21.3 per cent for the Conservatives and 20.5 per cent for Scottish Labour, with the Greens on 6.5 per cent and SSP on 3 per cent.

Moray is located in the Highlands and Islands region of the Scottish Parliament list system, but at a local government level Moray was until 1995 part of Grampian region. SNP strength at a local government level on Moray Council has dissipated in recent years. In 1995 the Nationalists won 50.2 per cent of votes for the council and had 13 out of 18 councillors. In 1999 their vote fell to 30 per cent and two councillors, as Independents swept the board and Labour made significant gains in towns such as Elgin. This position did not fundamentally alter in 2003, with the party winning 25.2 per cent of the vote and three council seats. This cannot augur well for future Nationalist success at Westminster and Scottish Parliament elections. Boundary changes for future Westminster elections see the town of Keith and its outlying areas returned to Moray after being shifted to Gordon prior to 1997. This will probably not adversely affect the Nationalists. They have enough to worry about at future Westminster elections with the erosion of their vote which must put the seat up for grabs. At a Scottish Parliament level the seat is more securely Nationalist, particularly as long as Margaret Ewing is their candidate.

MSP

MARGARET EWING was born in Lanark in 1945, was educated at Biggar High School and has degrees from Glasgow and Strathclyde universities and a teaching diploma from Jordanhill College. Before becoming an MP, she was a special needs teacher and also worked as a freelance journalist. She had two spells at Westminster, first as MP for Dunbartonshire East from October 1974 to 1979, winning the seat by only 22 votes, and then as MP for Moray from 1987 to 2001. Married in 1983 to Fergus Ewing, MSP for neighbouring Inverness East, Nairn and Lochaber, she is daughter-in-law of Winnie Ewing, the SNP president, and sister-in-law of Annabelle Ewing, the Perth MP.

At Westminster she was a member of the select committee on European legislation from 1992-98 and a member of the European scrutiny committee. She has held a number of positions within the SNP, including deputy leader from 1983-87, and SNP Parliamentary group convener – in Westminster from 1987-99 and in the Scottish Parliament from 1999. She joined the rural development committee in January 2001, and European and external relations from 2003.

Ewing, then Margaret Bain, was one of the leading left-wing firebrands of the SNP in the 1970s, but has mellowed with age. She was defeated by Margo MacDonald in a bid for the deputy leadership in 1977, and led an attempt to withdraw the SNP from support of the 1978 devolution legislation, after the notorious 40 per cent 'yes' vote threshold was tacked on to it. She opposed the left-wing '79 Group after the 1979 election accusing them of 'rent-a-mob' tactics in trying to promote civil disobedience. After her election as MP for Moray in 1987, Ewing proved to be a hard-working constituency MP and latterly MSP, supporting local campaigns to retain Lossiemouth and Kinloss RAF bases. In 1989, she was one of the team, with Jim Sillars and Gordon Wilson, which opted not to take the party into the Scottish Constitutional Convention, having profound consequences for the party and Scottish politics. Steering the party to a more fundamentalist position, it ended the electoral honeymoon which had followed Sillars' November 1988 Govan by-election victory.

She stood against Alex Salmond for the national convenorship of the SNP in 1990, and despite starting as favourite, was defeated by a margin of 486 to 186 votes. As Parliamentary leader of the SNP at Westminster in 1993, she negotiated a deal with the Conservatives to gain extra Scottish places on the European Committee of the Regions, in return for SNP votes backing the Conservatives over the Maastricht treaty. This was widely seen as a misjudgement.

Her profile and influence in the party has not recovered since she lost the party leadership contest to Salmond, and despite her undoubted abilities she is not fully utilised by the party leadership. Her first term in the Scottish Parliament saw her shadow rural affairs while deputy convener of the rural affairs committee, while her mischievous sense of humour made for some of the better quality barracking in the chamber. But that term was also blighted by cancer, from which she recovered, but it left her visibly weakened and her health is seen as the reason she had no front bench post after the 2003 election.

MP

ANGUS ROBERTSON was born in London in 1969, making him one of the youngest MPs elected in 2001. He was educated at Broughton High School in Edinburgh and at Aberdeen University where he studied politics and international relations. He was employed as a news editor in the Austrian Broadcasting Corporation from 1991-99, being the main radio reporter for the BBC based in Vienna from 1991-2001. He was also a consultant in media and presentation skills and political affairs with Communication Skills International. This unusual early career path for a Nationalist is explained by Robertson being half German, and being fluent in both German and French.

He joined the SNP aged 16 and became active in the student and youth wings, becoming national organiser of the Federation of Nationalist Students in 1988. As a trusted member of Alex Salmond's campaign team, he dealt with the substantial foreign media presence at the 1999 Scottish Parliament election, while also standing unsuccessfully in Midlothian. He was European adviser to the SNP group in the Scottish Parliament, and was the staffer with the task of keeping the party's internationalist outlook active. On his election to Westminster, he immediately became the SNP's spokesperson on foreign affairs, defence and Europe in the Commons, his defence interest being a crucial issue for a constituency which is home to two large RAF bases. With the SNP group split on how to handle the Afghanistan war, he was among the three out of five who voted in November 2001 against the US-UK action, followed by voting against action in Iraq in 2003. He became a member of the European scrutiny select committee.

Motherwell and Wishaw

Predecessor Constituencies: Motherwell (1945–70), Motherwell and Wishaw (1974–9) and Motherwell South (1983–92).

Socio-economic Indicators:

Constituency Pop. (16-64)	42,820
Claimant Count (May 2003)	4.1% (30.0% above average)
IBA/SDA Claimants	15.4%
Life Expectancy – Male	70.9 (2.5 yrs below average)
Life Expectancy – Female	77.8 (0.9 below average)
Owner Occupied	50.9%
Social Rented	43.0%
Average Property Prices	£45,704 (64th)
Average Gross Income	£22,778 (64th)
Low Birthweight Babies	142 (6.3%)
Teenage Pregnancy Rates	503 (5.4%)
No. of Lone Parent Households	3,818 (13.0%)

CAB Enquiries

Issue	No. of cases	Percentage of total cases (%)
1. Benefits	5401	31.6
2. Consumer	3860	22.6
3. Employment	2325	13.6
4. Other	1507	8.8
5. Housing	1268	7.4

2003 Scottish Parliament Election

Electorate: 51,785   *Turnout*: 25,388 (49.0%)   *Turnout 1999*: 57.1%

Candidate	Party	Votes	Votes%	99 %	Change%
Jack McConnell	Labour	13,739	54.1	46.0	+ 8.2
Lloyd Quinan	SNP	4,480	17.7	29.2	–11.6
Mark Nolan	Con	2,542	10.0	12.2	– 2.2
John Mulligan	SSP	1,961	7.7	(other 6.2)	–
John Swinburne	Scot Senior	1,597	6.3	–	–
Keith Legg	Lib Dem	1,069	4.2	6.2	– 2.0

Labour majority: 9,259 (36.5%)   *Swing*: 9.9% SNP to Labour

2001 General Election

Electorate: 52,418   *Turnout*: 29,673 (56.6%)

Candidate	Party	Votes	Votes%	Change%
Frank Roy	Labour	16,681	56.2	– 1.2
Jim McGuigan	SNP	5,725	19.3	– 3.2
Mark Nolan	Con	3,155	10.6	– 0.4
Iain Brown	Lib Dem	2,791	9.4	+ 3.0
Stephen Smellie	SSP	1,260	4.2	–
Claire Watt	Soc Lab	61	0.2	–2.0

Labour majority: 10,956 (36.9%)   *Swing*: 1.0% SNP to Labour

1945–97 Westminster

	Lab%	Con%	SNP%	Lib%	Other%	Turnout%
1997	57.4	11.0	22.5	6.4	2.8	70.1
1992	57.1	16.0	20.4	6.2	0.4	76.2
1987	58.3	14.5	15.3	11.3	0.6	75.5
1983	52.4	20.0	9.8	17.8	–	72.9
1979	56.9	28.9	12.3	–	1.9	77.8
1974O	44.6	18.2	31.9	2.9	2.4	75.4
1974F	46.7	30.6	20.0	–	2.7	77.0
1970	53.2	32.2	9.9	–	4.7	73.7
1966	60.8	35.2	–	–	4.0	74.7
1964	58.8	37.3	–	–	3.9	78.9
1959	53.7	43.0	–	–	3.3	81.1
1955	53.9	46.1	–	–	–	76.5
1954B	56.4	39.3	–	–	4.3	70.5
1951	57.3	42.7	–	–	–	84.7
1950	54.3	34.0	9.3	–	2.4	84.5
1945	52.7	20.6	26.7	–	–	72.8
1945B	48.6	–	51.4	–	–	54.0

Motherwell and Wishaw can be found to the south east of Glasgow and is shaped by the two towns which give the constituency its name. These are situated in the Clyde Valley and are part of North Lanarkshire Council. This is an area with large concentrations of poverty and disadvantage. The seat has 43 per cent social housing, including 37.2 council housing – a far cry from the 62.5 per cent of 1991, but still putting Motherwell top of the league for council housing. Average property prices are 32.2 per cent below the average while Motherwell is the 25th most unhealthy constituency in Britain, the 14th most unhealthy in Scotland and the fourth worst outside of Glasgow.

Motherwell was once dominated by the Ravenscraig steel works and is still shaped by the physical presence of its derelict site. For over a decade after the Conservatives came to power in 1979 the symbolism of Ravenscraig drew on the heartstrings of a wide Scottish coalition from the Labour Party and SNP to church leaders. Ravenscraig was opened in 1961 by political decision and the Macmillan Government's need to have a regional policy, and it stayed open under the Thatcher administration due to politics, as she felt she had a loyalty to them for remaining open through the 1984–85 miners' strike. Its closure was announced on 8 January 1992 when its political guarantees ran out under the privatised British Steel Corporation which had no choice but to shut it. The Scottish media expected the Conservatives to pay the price in the subsequent April general election, but Ravenscraig had already been discounted. The economic slack has been taken up with service sector jobs, such as call centes and Silicon Glen employment, some of which is proving to be short-lived in Lanarkshire.

North Lanarkshire Council is still recovering from the collapse of its Direct Labour Organisation in 1999 after losses of £6 million and 1,000 job losses. The scandal revealed malpractice, cronyism and corruption with members of the DLO able to claim outrageous overtime expenses, and the whole episode seemed to many an apt summary of the narrow world of Lanarkshire Labour. The Scottish Executive had to wind up the DLO via a Section 19B order of the Local Government Planning and Land Act.

Another national scandal was the outbreak of E.coli 0157 food poisoning which resulted in the death of 21 victims in the Wishaw area – most of them elderly citizens. The deaths started in late 1996 and were sourced to Wishaw butcher John Barr, who provided the food for a church lunch in the town attended by several of the people who subsequently died. This scandal traumatised the community and was the worst such outbreak ever seen in the United Kingdom.

Motherwell Football Club have struggled to compete in the Scottish Premier League and were not helped by having to call in the receiver in 2002, even after John Boyle, chairman of the club, had invested £11 million of his own money. Motherwell had to cancel all their existing contracts with players to reduce debts, and in the 2002-3 season finished bottom of the league. However, they were not relegated as Falkirk, who won the First Division, did not meet the stadium criteria for the SPL and despite court action this was upheld. Motherwell fans were mightily relieved, but some commentators wondered about the merits of a league which was uncompetitive at the top due to 'Old Firm' dominance and at the other end did not have relegation.

Motherwell was very briefly held by the Communist J. Walton Newbold who won the seat in 1923 with 33.3 per cent in a four-way contest only to lose the seat the following year, despite increasing his vote to 37.4 per cent. A crucial factor had been the decision of Motherwell Trades Council to support the Communist candidate, once it could not find a suitable Labour one.

The Reverend James Barr won the seat for Labour in 1924 and while he was defeated in the National Government landslide in 1931, the next major shock did not come until the end of the Second World War. In a by-election on 12 April 1945, Robert McIntyre sensationally seized Motherwell for the Scottish Nationalists, winning 11,417 votes to Labour's Alexander Anderson's 10,800 – an SNP majority of 617. McIntyre found the gentlemanly atmosphere of the House of Commons an inhospitable place and when he arrived he had no MPs to sponsor him and the House voted 273 to 199 not to allow him in such circumstances to take his seat. The next day McIntyre accepted sponsors, but said, 'I do this under protest', leading Harold Nicolson in his diaries to conclude, 'He is going to be a sad nuisance and pose as a martyr.' In the July 1945 UK election, Anderson retook the seat with a Labour majority of 7,809 votes over McIntyre – who polled 26.7 per cent – their highest vote in any contest in the national election.

McIntyre went on to be one of the folk heroes of the modern Scottish Nationalist movement, standing in a succession of elections and the 1971 Stirling and Falkirk by-election before passing away in 1998 at the age of 84. Anderson, the Labour MP for the seat from 1945, passed into obscurity, holding the seat until his death in February 1954. He was followed by George Lawson who easily held the seat in an April 1954 by-election until February 1974 when it became known as Motherwell and Wishaw. He announced his retirement before the October 1974 election. His replacement, Jeremy Bray, won the seat with a majority of 4,962 over the SNP while Labour's vote dipped below 50 per cent, an all-time low in the constituency.

This was the first and so far only post-war SNP challenge in the seat as Bray increased his vote to 56.9 and majority to 10,937 in 1979. The seat became Motherwell South in 1983 but this did not affect the political complexion of the seat and Bray was returned both in 1983 and 1987 with over half the vote and five figure majorities. Bray announced his retirement before the 1997 election and Frank Roy, previously a Ravenscraig steelworker, was selected as Labour candidate for the new seat of Motherwell and Wishaw with a 12,791 majority over the Nationalists. In June 2001 Frank Roy was re-elected with a 10,956 majority.

The Scottish Parliament election of May 1999 underlined that Jack McConnell's biggest challenge had been winning the Labour nomination, which he only did by the margin of two votes – securing the seat with a majority of 5,076, less than half the margin of two years previous. McConnell, who shares a constituency office with Roy, became First Minister shortly after the 2001 UK election, and in the May 2003 Scottish Parliament election he nearly doubled his majority to 9,259, improving his lead from 18 per cent to 36.5 per cent. The Nationalist Lloyd Quinan, who had been a West of Scotland list MSP, saw his party's support collapse by 11.6 per cent, from 29 per cent in 1999. John Swinburne, standing for the Scottish Senior Citizens Party as their leader, in their only constituency contest, polled a respectable 6.3 per cent and won enough support across the Central Scotland region to be elected a list MSP. In the regional vote, Labour won 44.1 per cent and the SNP 17.1 per cent, while the Scottish Senior Citizens polled an impressive 10.5 per cent – their highest vote in the region, the SSP 8.2 per cent and the Greens 3.6 per cent.

Boundary changes for Westminster will not challenge Labour's prospects in this part of the country, nor in the new Motherwell and Wishaw seat. At future Scottish Parliament elections, Lanarkshire man and woman have shown the strength of their allegiance to the Labour Party through good times and more stormy waters, some caused by the actions of the local Labour council. It is a matter of weighing the Labour vote in this part of the country.

MSP

JACK McCONNELL was born in Irvine in 1960, but after his family moved to the Isle of Arran to run a sheep farm and tea room, he grew up there and attended Arran High School, Lamlash. He is a graduate of Stirling University where he gained a BSc in Mathematics, followed by a teacher training qualification. He was president of Stirling students' association from 1980-82, becoming vice-president of NUS-Scotland from 1982-83. It was a time when slightly younger Labour students were rising to prominence in campus associations and were also destined to become MSPs, including Wendy Alexander, Susan Deacon, Jackie Baillie, Sarah Boyack, Andy Kerr, Frank McAveety and Tommy Sheridan. McConnell worked as a maths teacher at Lornshill Academy in Alloa from 1983-92, and was elected as a councillor in Stirling District from 1984-93 where he was chair of the leisure and recreation committee from 1986-87 and the equal opportunities committee from 1986-90. He served as council treasurer from 1988-92 and leader from 1990-92. He also stood in Perth and Kinross in the 1987 election, winning 15.9 per cent of the vote and finishing fourth.

As a Stirling councillor and leader of the council he was at the forefront of developing innovative policies on delivering services. Throughout the 1980s, McConnell was a leading figure in the Labour Co-ordinating Committee (Scotland), the then Bennite group formed to develop a radical policy prospectus in the party. After Labour's election defeat in 1987, he was a founder member of Scottish

Labour Action, the pro-home rule nationalist pressure group, where he was instrumental in pushing for greater autonomy for the Scottish party and developing the 'dual mandate' thesis, which argued that Scottish Labour would use a Scottish election victory as a mandate for unilateral action while also fighting to win at UK level.

He was appointed general secretary of the Scottish Labour Party after the election defeat of 1992, a move which was seen as dampening down demands for a more autonomous and pro-devolution approach. In that post, he had to deal with a host of internal managerial and resource difficulties and post-1997, address a number of disciplinary problems associated with Labour scandals in the West of Scotland. With his role in co-ordinating the Scottish Labour campaigns for the 1997 election and referendum prominent in his curriculum vitae, McConnell resigned from Keir Hardie House in 1998 to focus his attention on winning a seat in the new Parliament, starting up a short-lived public affairs branch of the Uddingston-based public relations company, Beattie Media. His judgement was called into question in 1998, when he began to serialise his memoirs of his period as general secretary in *Scotland on Sunday*, this at a time when Labour faced an uphill and chaotic struggle to prepare for the imminent election. He pulled out of the serialisation after only one week. The public affairs connection was to cause him trouble and embarrassment when the 'Lobbygate' scandal blew up in September 1999. In this, two young Beattie Media executives, one of them the son of Lanarkshire MP John Reid, were caught on a hidden camera pitching to an undercover journalist posing as a potential client. McConnell by this time was finance minister, and they claimed to have privileged access to him. The MSP was fully cleared of any impropriety by the resulting enquiry, though it made him more cautious and careful about his previously open relations with journalists. Despite an Arran background and a base in Stirling politics, he had opted to fight for a safe Labour seat in Lanarkshire. This became a fierce and bitter fight for Motherwell and Wishaw with local union official Bill Tynan, who later became the MP for Hamilton South. McConnell won the ballot in November 1998 by two votes – 270 to 268 – with five spoilt ballot papers and 20 out of 180 postal ballots (mostly thought to be for Tynan) ruled out. The bitterness would come back to bite McConnell once he had become First Minister, as his critics inside the local party sought to undermine him with leaks of fund-raising irregularities, involving £11,000. This sought to taint him by association, helped by the fresh memory at that time of the expenses fiasco that led to Henry McLeish's downfall, but it failed to get beyond a smear.

Ahead of the election, Donald Dewar made him campaign spokesperson on the environment. Post-election, he became minister for finance, responsible for finance and budgets, negotiations with the Treasury, as well as Europe and modernisation of government. This gave McConnell a considerable platform for developing influence across departments, with ministers, and to take a lead he would keep in later jobs in developing Scotland's links to continental Europe. He was one of the first to enter the battle over list MSPs versus constituency ones, driving through a funding mechanism which gave constituency MSPs, most of them Labour, more resources than others. In June 2000, there was a spat with Susan Deacon, the health minister, over distribution of underspent funds from the previous financial year, which left sourness between the two. He was also on the other side from his female and more liberal cabinet colleagues, as one of 'the Big Macs', along with Tom McCabe and Henry McLeish, who urged caution and compromise on repealing Section 28/Clause 2A concerning homosexuality and the school curriculum – this apparently because he faced strong local pressure from those in his constituency party who were critical of the Executive's position.

Dewar's sudden death in October 2000 forced the barely concealed succession battle out into the open. The party leadership, most notably Gordon Brown, the Chancellor, would have preferred to have had no contest, instead anointing Henry McLeish. But McConnell resisted the pressure and stood for the leadership. Without the backing of a single ministerial colleague, McConnell fought a carefully focused campaign touching on a number of key themes: worries about unspecified 'interference' from the UK party and backbench anger about lack of consultation by the Executive. This nearly paid its reward, as McConnell clearly won a majority of backbench MSPs and lost to McLeish by the narrow margin of 44:36 in the ad hoc electoral arrangements which gave a vote only to Labour MSPs and Scottish party executive members. McConnell had won the right to increased seniority in the cabinet, to which McLeish responded by making him minister for education, Europe and external relations (the latter at his insistence) with responsibility for pre-school and school education, children and young people. This had two tough tasks; first in reaching a deal between teachers unions and their council employers, which was required to avert the threat of major disruption in schools: and second, in sorting out the mess and management fiasco that was the Scottish Qualifications Authority in the previous three months, for which Sam Galbraith had been education minister and taken the publicity heat. McConnell delivered on both, moving swiftly on the SQA to clear out the discredited management. It remained a matter of debate, however, as to whether the teachers' pay and conditions deal was good value for the taxpayer. On the external relations front, McLeish was to work with McConnell to sign up to a new grouping of European regions with legislative powers, including Catalonia, Bavaria and Flanders. This was reported to have caused consternation in the Foreign Office when they found out that the Scottish Executive was running its own embryonic foreign policy, asserting sub-state regions' rights against those of EU member states. In their discussions with McLeish and McConnell, it was later claimed the education minister had secured both an enhanced role in the 2001 Westminster election campaign and a special adviser working solely for McConnell. Neither promise came to anything in the following year.

Having fought and lost in autumn 2000, McConnell was clearly established as the strongest contender to replace McLeish when the time came. McConnell and his sizeable band of backbench fans were quietly confident that time would not take long, and they were right. McLeish's demise in November 2001 – from which McConnell stood well back to avoid association – created another emergency Labour leadership election. McConnell was again ready to hit the ground running, his supporters quick to rubbish Wendy Alexander, who emerged as the 'Stop Jack' candidate. She was favoured in London, with those backing her alarmed that McConnell would gain the levers of power in Scotland. Facing the start of a strong attack through the media, and for her own personal reasons, Alexander let her supporters down, including several exposed cabinet colleagues, when she withdrew from the race only two days after making it clear she was ready to run. There was one day when Malcolm Chisholm made public soundings on a run against McConnell, but he quickly withdrew. That left the way open for the education minister to step up as Labour leader and First Minister, except for one large obstacle in his way: reports about to surface in the media of an extra-marital affair with a former party colleague. He took pre-emptive action with an extraordinary press conference, sitting beside his wife Bridget, at which he confessed to having had an affair six years before. It played to the image he had as Jack the Lad, but with his wife stating that he had 'betrayed my trust', it also emphasised the question that emerged from two leadership elections: why is it that so many contemporaries in senior positions in the Labour Party were so keen to ensure that he did not become party leader and First Minister? Could it have to do with broader issues of trust? The press conference was painful and humiliating, the subject matter seedy, but it did the trick in killing off the threat of another media mugging.

As First Minister, McConnell's first act was to mislead his colleagues into a false sense of security about their jobs. In one November 2001 morning in Bute House, 'Jack the Knife' saw off all his Labour colleagues with the exception of an isolated Wendy Alexander, burdening her with a ministerial workload in enterprise, lifelong learning and the addition of transport. This was to lead to her disillusion and resignation the following May. His MSPs quickly sent him a warning that he could not take them for granted, with a secret ballot in which many voted against his choice of Cathy Peattie as deputy presiding officer. The mantra of his early months was to 'do less, but do it better', paring down priorities to health, education, crime, jobs and transport. It was pointed out this accounted for 64 per cent of Executive spending, so it was not much of a prioritisation, especially when he indicated he would personally be raising the profile of environmental policy as well. However, it was accompanied by a marked change in the Executive's handling of the media, in which the First Minister's newly-appointed spin doctor took a much lower profile than predecessors, the day-to-day briefing being carried out by civil service officials. There was a less haphazard, unpredictable leadership style, with a ministerial team keenly aware of the new boss's ruthlessness with those whose loyalty to him was in any doubt. Those who had lost their ministerial jobs could have caused trouble from the backbenches, but their dissent was stifled by the prospect of the 2003 election. It was suggested by some of them that it was no coincidence that the destabilising media briefing and leaks had ended once McConnell was in the top job.

McConnell set about a strategy which made as clear a demarcation as possible between his administration and that led by his two predecessors. It appeared Dewar and McLeish had been all but airbrushed from history, with McConnell contrasting the unhappy image of drift, division and ineptitude under them with an image he sought to project of being closer to 'people's priorities'. In spring of 2002, this began with a move towards a tougher rhetoric on crime, particularly youth crime and anti-social behaviour, which would come to dominate his 2003 election campaign and the early months of the post-election administration.

The high-profile McConnell gave to tackling anti-social behaviour saw him condemn 'ned culture' and the antics of irresponsible young people, parallel with the assault on 'yob culture' envisaged by UK Home Secretary David Blunkett. Whatever critics in the party thought, McConnell had found a policy popular with Labour voters, particularly older, working class ones, which found a startling 90 per cent support from the public. He also used his stand to distance the image of Labour toughness on crime with the Liberal Democrats' liberalism, personified by justice minister Jim Wallace. McConnell was alert to the Lib Dem electoral threat by claiming credit for good news from the Executive, while rarely being held to account for the bad news, and he moved to bypass them where he could. He left Wallace to tackle the awkward issue of prison estates renewal, first proposing the closure of Peterhead prison and then being forced into a u-turn. In August, the First Minister also put pressure on Ross Finnie, the Lib Dem environment minister responsible for the water industry, when a water safety scare in Glasgow was whipped up by opposition and media into a political storm.

Two speeches at that time also marked out distinctive elements in what was taking shape as McConnellism. In August, he set out a much more radical environment agenda than his predecessors, partly through his own long-standing interest as a member of Friends of the Earth-Scotland, and partly through seeking to define it as more of an economic justice and urban issue of interest to Labour heartlands than had been the case. He followed up with a visit to South Africa to attend the Earth Summit in September 2002. The same month, he delivered another speech which put economic growth at the top of the agenda for Scotland, even though the devolved institutions had limited powers to tackle the economy's sluggishness. This reflected Silicon Glen losing thousands of jobs as manufacturing moved overseas, the economy moving into technical recession, and the issue of population decline increasingly being seen as a major problem facing Scotland and its economy.

The 2003 election campaign was explicitly set out as McConnell's time to win his own personal mandate, having become First Minister through such a circuitous route. It began with considerable nervousness about the impact of the Iraq war – on which McConnell had struggled to hold a line which reflected strong anti-war feeling in his Scottish party, including dissent from health minister Malcolm Chisholm, without being disloyal to Tony Blair. The war problems were dissipated by election day, and the big issue from the Labour leader was a strengthened message on youth crime, not least because this was the biggest difference with Lib Dems. McConnell also found through the campaign he was facing ferocious public hostility to the Holyrood Parliament Building Project, which he deflected mid-campaign by announcing an independent inquiry into the management and costs. The election result, with six seats lost to the SNP, Tories, a Lib Dem and hospital campaigner, saw any talk of a mandate dropped. McConnell emerged as First Minister once more, but chastened by the message from the electorate and low turn-out. He turned in subsequent months to ever tougher talk on crime and anti-social behaviour, believing it to be the best way of rebuilding that link to voters' priorities. In a BBC forum in August 2003 to analyse falling turnout, he would admit that the manifesto had 'failed to set the heather on fire', and that he was disturbed by a persistent 10 per cent gap between the votes won by Labour at Scottish elections and those won in Scotland at Westminster elections. The coalition deal with Lib Dems was hard to portray as a Labour success story, particularly with talk of 'four years of war' with Labour-controlled local authorities, after Lib Dems won their demand for the single transferable voting system to be introduced by the next council elections.

Being First Minister, McConnell's background and personal life is better known than that of any other MSP. For instance, he has talked in media interviews of the importance of a large extended family to him, which he cites as his main way of spending time outside politics, while golf is his main leisure interest. In marrying Bridget McLuckie in 1990, he adopted her two children by a previous relationship, about whom he speaks with an unusual emotional intensity. He also said in a Radio Scotland interview it was important for his relationship with them that he did not father his own children. He spoke of the pressure his marriage had faced as a result of his affair, and the prejudice he faced from being married to someone of a different Christian denomination. His wife is a senior official with Glasgow Council and a professionally trained musician.

MP

FRANK ROY was born in 1958 in Motherwell, and elected an MP in 1997. He was educated at St Joseph's High School, Motherwell, and was a steelworker at Ravenscraig from 1977-91, responding to its closure as the local community had to do, by retraining and finding a new future. He gained an HNC in marketing from Motherwell College and a degree in consumer and management studies from Glasgow Caledonian University. He was election agent for Dr Jeremy Bray in Motherwell South in 1987 and 1992, before being part of Helen Liddell's by-election team in 1994, then becoming her constituency assistant.

He would later become Parliamentary Private Secretary to her at the Scottish Office in 1998-99, then to John Reid at the Scotland Office from 1999-2001. Roy was then briefly Helen Liddell's Parliamentary Private Secretary when she replaced Reid in the Cabinet post, before a bizarre incident in which Roy took it upon himself to warn the Irish Prime Minister, Bertie Ahern, that it would be unsafe to visit his Lanarkshire constituency to unveil a memorial at the Carfin Grotto to Irish emigrants amid the post-match sectarian tension of an Old Firm match day. The Irish government took his advice, but it left Roy a damaged, diminished figure for advertising his constituents as intolerant and lawless. He had to resign from his PPS role for having given the impression he spoke with Liddell's authority in his faxed warning to the Irish consul-general in Edinburgh. This reputation for clangers was not helped with a controversy about his betting on the election of Michael Martin as the Speaker, using his inside knowledge of the way Labour MPs would vote to win £3,400.

One of Roy's more important roles is as political minder in Westminster for Jack McConnell, who lacks other close associates in the Scottish Labour MP group. Roy is credited with swinging the selection vote for McConnell in 1998, and McConnell remained loyal through the Carfin Grotto row, saying nothing about the affair even though he was then the Scottish Executive minister responsible for external relations. Roy was on the select committee on social security from 1997-98 and on defence since 2001.

Ochil

Predecessor Constituencies: Clackmannan and East Stirlingshire (1945–79) and Clackmannan (1983–92).

Socio-economic Indicators:

Constituency Pop. (16-64)	48,950
Claimant Count (May 2003)	2.9% (5.9% below average)
IBA/SDA Claimants	10.2%
Life Expectancy – Male	74.1 (0.7 yrs above average)
Life Expectancy – Female	78.8 (0.1 yr above average)
Owner Occupied	61.5%
Social Rented	30.2%
Average Property Prices	£69,117 (21st)
Average Gross Income	£27,823 (16th)
Low Birthweight Babies	156 (6.7%)
Teenage Pregnancy Rates	448 (4.1%)
No. of Lone Parent Households	3,221 (10.4%)

CAB Enquiries

Issue	No. of cases	Percentage of total cases (%)
1. Benefits	2270	41.2
2. Consumer	827	15.0
3. Employment	582	10.6
4. Housing	578	10.5
5. Other	409	7.4

2003 Scottish Parliament Election

Electorate: 55,596   *Turnout*: 30,416 (54.7%)   *Turnout 1999*: 64.6%

Candidate	Party	Votes	Votes%	99 %	Change%
George Reid	SNP	11,659	38.3	38.2	+ 0.1
Richard Simpson	Labour	11,363	37.4	41.7	− 4.4
Malcolm Parkin	Con	2,946	9.7	11.3	− 1.6
Catherine Whittingham	Lib Dem	2,536	8.3	8.8	− 0.5
Flash Gordon Approaching	M R Loony	432	1.4	-	-
William Liddell	Ind	378	1.2	-	-

SNP majority: 296 (1.0%)   *Swing*: 2.3% Labour to SNP

2001 General Election

Electorate: 57,554   *Turnout*: 35,303 (61.3%)

Candidate	Party	Votes	Votes%	Change%
Martin O'Neill	Labour	16,004	45.3	+ 0.3
Keith Brown	SNP	10,655	30.2	- 4.2
Alasdair Campbell	Con	4,235	12.0	- 2.6
Paul Edie	Lib Dem	3,253	9.2	+ 4.0
Pauline Thompson	SSP	751	2.1	-
Flash Gordon Approaching	Monster Raving Loony	405	1.2	-

Labour majority: 5,349 (15.2%)   *Swing*: 2.3% SNP to Labour

1945–97 Westminster

	Lab%	Con%	SNP%	Lib%	Other%	Turnout%
1997	45.0	14.6	34.4	5.2	0.9	77.4
1992	49.1	17.3	26.9	6.7	–	78.3
1987	53.7	14.9	20.9	10.5	–	76.7
1983	45.8	18.0	19.0	17.2	–	75.6
1979	41.9	18.0	40.1	–	–	81.7
1974O	36.4	10.4	50.7	2.5	–	81.8
1974F	36.4	19.5	43.5	–	0.6	82.6
1970	50.7	28.2	15.5	5.6	–	75.7
1966	55.3	24.6	20.1	–	–	77.5
1964	57.2	30.6	12.2	–	–	79.8
1959	59.3	40.7	–	–	–	80.7
1955	58.7	41.3	–	–	–	79.8
1951	58.7	41.3	–	–	–	85.7
1950	56.5	33.5	–	10.0	–	83.4
1945	62.9	37.1	–	–	–	71.7

Ochil contains Clackmannanshire, – the Wee County – the smallest council in size and population in mainland Scotland, and parts of Stirlingshire and Kinrosshire. This includes the towns of Alloa, Clackmannan and Tullibody, the towns of Alva, Dollar, Menstrie and Tillicoultry, known as the Hillfoots because they sit on the southern fringe of the Ochil Hills, as well as to the west the University of Stirling and Bridge of Allan. The seat extends eastwards to Kinross and Loch Leven and crosses the River Forth taking in a number of small towns such as Cowie, Fallin and Plean. Average property prices are 2.5 per cent above the national average and rose 46.6 per cent in the 1990s.

This part of Scotland has changed dramatically in the past two decades with the disappearance of coal mining which used to be the biggest employer in Alloa, Clackmannan and Dollar. New jobs have included the rapid expansion of Epoint, based in Alloa, which supplies equipment for printing digital photographs, while Tesco announced it was opening a new Alloa store in 2002 creating 350 jobs. Job losses have been seen in the textile industry with Coats Viyella closing its Alloa plant with the loss of 200 jobs, followed by Paton and Baldwin shutting its Alloa textile factory with 220 jobs lost.

Transport issues are important in this seat of many small settlements, and a major campaign has been focused on reopening the Alloa to Stirling rail link which would significantly boost the local economy. The Scottish Executive has promised support and has given a commitment to fund a variety of improved transport links. Glenochil Prison is located within the constituency and in June 2000 a drugs seizure resulted in a riot by inmates, indicating the growing problem of drugs in prison.

Labour first won this seat when it was known as Clackmannan and East Stirlingshire in 1922, lost it in the 1931 debacle, before winning it back in 1935. Arthur Woodburn then held the seat for Labour in a by-election held six weeks after the outbreak of war in October 1939, winning 93.7 per cent of the vote against a pacifist candidate who won 6.3 per cent. Woodburn faced a little more opposition when he was re-elected in 1945 achieving a 10,100 majority over the Unionists, and went on to become Attlee's Secretary of State for Scotland from 1947-50. Woodburn lasted long after the Attlee Government and the age of austerity had passed into history continuing to represent the area until his retirement in 1970.

In 1970 Dick Douglas retained the seat for Labour, but he did not hold it long, losing in February 1974 to the SNP's George Reid. In the October 1974 election, Reid won the seat with 25,998 votes and 50.1 per cent of the vote to Labour's Dick Douglas support of 18,657 and 36.4 per cent – an SNP majority of 7,341. However, in the 1979 electoral disaster for the Nationalists, even Reid could not buck the trend and lost narrowly to Labour's Martin O'Neill by a margin of 984 votes.

In 1983 the constituency became known as Clackmannan, and O'Neill held the seat with increasingly comfortable majorities of 9,639 in 1983 and 12,401 in 1987 – in both cases over the Nationalists. In 1992, in the last contest in Clackmannan O'Neill was re-elected with a 8,503 majority over the SNP, as Labour increased its vote by 4.7 per cent and the SNP by 6 per cent.

For the May 1997 election, a new constituency was created – Ochil – which as well as Clackmannan, Alloa and Dollar, included parts of Stirlingshire and Kinrossshire. O'Neill found himself facing a serious challenge from George Reid once more. Labour's vote rose by 2 per cent compared to the notional 1992 result, while the SNP vote rose by 8.3 per cent. Labour's majority was cut to 4,652. Ochil – which as Clackmannan had become a safe Labour seat in the 1980s – was now back as a Labour-SNP marginal. In the June 2001 UK election Martin O'Neill increased his majority to 5,349 as Labour's vote fell.

In the first Scottish Parliament elections in May 1999, Reid stood again for the SNP and faced Labour's Richard Simpson. Reid required a 5.3 per cent swing to win the seat, but could only manage a 3.6 per cent swing as he cut Labour's lead back to a narrow 1,303 margin. At the same time in the local government elections, the SNP polled strongly in Clackmannanshire Council, winning 44.55 per cent of the vote to Labour's 44.54 per cent and winning one more seat – enough to give them control. Labour also lost the university ward of Logie on Stirling Council in the 1999 election which used to be held by Jack McConnell. In the second Scottish Parliament election, Richard Simpson and George Reid squared up to a rematch: Simpson as a Labour ex-minister who had resigned over his injudicious remarks about the firefighters' strike, and Reid after four years as Deputy Presiding Officer of the Parliament. Both the Labour and SNP votes fell in actual numbers – Labour by 4,000, the Nationalists by 2,400 – as Simpson's majority of 1,303 translated into one for Reid of 296. The left field candidate – Flash Gordon Approaching – stood for the second time for the Monster Raving Loony Party polling 432 votes.

In the regional vote, Labour won 35.3 per cent to the SNP 28.3 per cent – a Labour lead of 1,466 – suggesting that George Reid gained significant numbers of tactical votes either because of who he was or cast against Richard Simpson. The Greens won 6.5 per cent and the SSP 4.5 per cent. At council level, the SNP fell back, and Labour regained control with 44.3 per cent to the SNP's 41.2 per cent.

Boundary changes at Westminster will see Ochil expanded northwards to become Ochil and South Perthshire. It will be very hard fought between Labour, SNP and Conservatives. At the Scottish Parliament, the capture of Ochil by the Nationalists was a rare moment of joy for Nationalists on a difficult night – along with the triumphs of Aberdeen North and Dundee East. A crucial issue in terms of their longer-term significance will be the SNP's ability to hold these at the 2007 elections.

MSP

GEORGE REID was born in Tullibody in 1939. He was educated at Dollar Academy, St Andrews University, studying history, and Union College in the USA, doing Russian and international studies. In 1960, he was on the first post-war visit to the Soviet Union by a Scottish student group, along with Donald Dewar and David Steel. Reid worked as a journalist with the *Daily Express* from 1962-64, STV from 1964-66, and Granada from 1966-69. He was then head of news and current affairs at STV from 1969-74.

Having previously been a Labour supporter, he was elected SNP MP for Clackmannanshire and East Stirling from February 1974-79, as one of the eleven SNP members who had such a dynamic effect on that decade's politics in Scotland. He took a leading role for the SNP in the 'yes' campaign in the 1979 devolution referendum, his nationalism being of the firmly pragmatic, gradualist variety, while being both strongly pro-European Community and social democratic before either was accepted policy for the SNP. After being ousted from Westminster with most of the SNP group in 1979, his next electoral outing was in 1997 and again in 1999. In the meantime, he returned to journalism as a TV and radio presenter with the BBC until 1984, and then became public affairs director with the International Red Cross in Geneva until 1996, followed by a period as a consultant and working his way back into SNP politics. He was the vice-convenor of fundraising for the SNP and also their external affairs spokesperson until the 1999 election, while put on the cross-party Constitutional Steering Group, set up by Donald Dewar and chaired by devolution minister Henry McLeish, to draw up the working procedures for the new Parliament. Reid was influential with his wide international political experience, and pushed for an effective system of public petitions.

Fighting the SNP target seat of Ochil, Reid was narrowly beaten by Labour's Dr Richard Simpson, but he was elected as a Mid-Scotland and Fife list MSP from the second position on the list. As the SNP's most respected elder statesman, he was elected Deputy Presiding Officer in the first Parliament, creating the Conveners' Liaison Group informally and then having it formally recognised as one of the key bodies in the Parliament. He continued to nurse the Ochil seat, most notably championing the cause of the villagers of Blairingone, who were angered by the spreading of foul-smelling slurry on nearby land. Using the petition and committee system, Reid was able to claim a victory in stopping the practice. That helped him unseat Simpson in 2003 by only 296 votes, as one of the SNP's three constituency gains, helped by Simpson's reported comment, while deputy justice minister, that the striking fire-fighters were 'fascist bastards'. Reid drew on his extensive humanitarian crisis experience and speech-making skills in a notable speech made both to party council, and to the Parliament, later to be used in an election broadcast, which powerfully made the case against the Iraq war.

As Deputy Presiding Officer, Reid had antagonised Labour by coming down hard on ministers wanting to trail announcements in the media, in 2001 deflating Angus MacKay, then finance minister, by refusing to let him make a statement because it had been in that morning's papers. It was clear many Labour MSPs did not want to let him become Presiding Officer. They were also reluctant to see a Nationalist represent the Parliament in the considerable representation and diplomatic work the post requires with foreign visitors. But Labour MSPs' hopes of installing one of their own, most likely Trish

Godman, had to be abandoned when the Labour-Lib Dem majority following the 2003 election was too small to allow any one MSP to be sacrificed to a non-party, non-voting role. Although Conservative Murray Tosh and Annabel Goldie were seen as possible opponents, Reid's qualifications for the job and the respect in which he was widely held ensured that no-one else stood against him. Yet seven MSPs voted against him and nine abstained, meaning he was elected the Parliament's second Presiding Officer, and removed from SNP party politics. Reid made it clear early on that he was keen to see reforms of debating and question time, while putting more emphasis on the Parliament's scrutinising role. He wanted to take a liberal approach to the unorthodox politics of the 'rainbow Parliament' which had emerged on 2 May 2003, while stressing also that 'majorities have rights too'. And he brought a new determination to bring the budget of the Holyrood building project under control, starting by getting consultants to cap their fees. Reid indicated too that he intended to serve only one four-year term in the post, with a view to some caravanning round Europe with his wife in the summer of 2007.

MP

MARTIN O'NEILL was born in 1945 and educated at Trinity Academy, Edinburgh, then at Heriot-Watt University, where he studied economics, and Moray House College of Education. He worked as an insurance clerk from 1963-67 before going to university. He spent a year as president of the Scottish Union of Students in 1970-71, and then 1971-73 in the Estates Duty Office of Scotland. He taught modern studies in Edinburgh secondary schools in 1974-79, and became an Open University tutor from 1976-79.

O'Neill unsuccessfully contested Edinburgh North in the October 1974 general election, and was first elected for Stirlingshire East and Clackmannan in 1979, replacing the SNP's George Reid. His seat became Clackmannan in 1983-97 and Ochil since 1997. He was in the thick of the battles for the soul of Labour in the early 1980s, on the centrist side, as a member of Labour Solidarity though abstaining on the crucial vote between Tony Benn and Denis Healey in 1981. His local party censured him for failing to back Benn. He was a frontbench Labour spokesperson for defence from 1988-92 as the party moved painfully under the Neil Kinnock leadership from its previous unilateralist stance on nuclear weapons and abandoned its opposition to Trident – a position finally reached in 1991. In 1988, he accused Labour MPs of deluding themselves if they thought cancelling Trident would release billions of pounds for public services, and dismissed the 1989 Scottish Labour vote against Trident as 'an outdated slap on the wrist'. In 1990, he was the defence spokesman who gave Labour backing to the action against Iraq for invading Kuwait.

For his soft-left revisionism, he was never elected to the shadow cabinet during his defence years, but he did well under Kinnock's patronage and remained on the front bench after Kinnock's departure, holding the energy portfolio from 1992-95. He became more distant from Tony Blair through publicly sticking to a policy of coal renationalisation, while Blair was moving away from it. His next gaffe was to hint that Labour could abandon opposition to nuclear power, at a time when Blair was trying to reassure the coal industry. That helps explain why he did not shift into government when Labour won power in 1997. He had already, in 1995, become chair of the select committee on trade and industry, retaining a high media profile. One notable report from the committee came in 1998, with the recommendation that more nuclear power stations should be built, with O'Neill dismissing safety worries about Dounreay as 'scaremongering'. He is opposed to Labour introducing proportional representation in local government. O'Neill also caused problems when he signed a motion criticising the government's policy on top-up tuition fees for students in England, but supported it in the crucial January 2004 vote. That same week, he announced he would not contest Ochil's successor seat at the next election.

Orkney and Shetland

Predecessor Constituencies: none, but separated for Scottish elections and joined at Westminster.

Socio-economic Indicators:

Orkney and Shetland:

Constituency Pop. (16-64)	26,274
Claimant Count (May 2003)	1.9% (38.0% below average)
IBA/SDA Claimants	4.8%

Orkney:

Life Expectancy – Male	74.8 (1.4 yrs above average)
Life Expectancy – Female	82.2 (3.5 yrs above average)
Owner Occupied	72.1%
Social Rented	14.0%
Average Property Prices	£45,947 (63rd)
Average Gross Income	£23,290 (60th)
Low Birthweight Babies	18 (3.9%)
Teenage Pregnancy Rates	48 (1.9%)
No. of Lone Parent Households	566 (6.8%)

CAB Enquiries

Issue	No. of cases	Percentage of total cases (%)
1. Benefits	492	28.4
2. Consumer	310	17.9
3. Employment	241	13.9
4. Other	155	9.0
5. Housing	141	8.1

Shetland:

Life Expectancy – Male	75.4 (2.0 yrs above average)
Life Expectancy – Female	81.3 (2.6 yrs above average)
Owner Occupied	63.4%
Social Rented	25.8%
Average Property Prices	£46,494 (61st)
Average Gross Income	£27,260 (22nd)
Low Birthweight Babies	32 (4.5%)
Teenage Pregnancy Rates	88 (3.2%)
No. of Lone Parent Households	816 (9.0%)

CAB Enquiries

Issue	No. of cases	Percentage of total cases (%)
1. Benefits	663	23.6
2. Consumer	584	20.8
3. Other	367	13.0
4. Employment	362	12.9
5. Relationships	248	8.8

2003 Scottish Parliament Election (Orkney)

Electorate: 15,487   *Turnout*: 8,004 (51.7%)   *Turnout 1999*: 57.0%

Candidate	Party	Votes	Votes%	99 %	Change%
James Wallace	Lib Dem	3,659	45.7	67.4	−21.7
Christopher Zawadski	Con	1,904	23.8	15.6	+ 8.2
John Mowat	SNP	1,056	13.2	10.3	+ 2.9
John Aberdein	SSP	914	11.4	–	–
Richard Meade	Labour	471	5.9	6.7	– 0.8

Liberal Democrat majority: 1,755 (21.9%)   *Swing*: 14.9% Liberal Democrat to Conservative

2003 Scottish Parliament Election (Shetland)

Electorate: 16,677   *Turnout*: 8,645 (51.8%)   *Turnout 1999*: 58.8%

Candidate	Party	Votes	Votes%	99 %	Change%
Tavish Scott	Lib Dem	3,989	46.1	54.5	– 8.3
Willie Ross	SNP	1,729	20.0	14.3	+ 5.7
John Firth	Con	1,281	14.8	8.7	+ 6.1
Peter Hamilton	Labour	880	10.2	22.5	–12.3
Peter Andrews	SSP	766	8.9	–	–

Liberal Democrat majority: 2,260 (26.1%)   *Swing*: 7.0% Liberal Democrat to SNP

2001 General Election (Orkney and Shetland)

Electorate: 31,909   *Turnout*: 16,733 (52.4%)

Candidate	Party	Votes	Votes%	Change%
Alistair Carmichael	Lib Dem	6,919	41.3	– 10.6
Robert Mochrie	Labour	3,444	20.6	+ 2.3
John Firth	Con	3,121	18.7	+ 6.4
John Mowat	SNP	2,473	14.8	+ 2.1

cont'd

Candidate	Party		Votes	Votes%	Change%
Peter Andrews	SSP		776	4.6	–

Liberal Democrat majority: 3,475 (20.8%) | *Swing*: 6.5% Liberal Democrat to Labour

---

1945–97 Westminster

	Lab%	Con%	SNP%	Lib%	Other%	Turnout%
1997	18.3	12.2	12.7	52.0	4.9	64.0
1992	19.8	22.0	11.2	46.4	–	65.5
1987	18.7	23.3	–	41.7	16.3	68.7
1983	13.1	25.6	15.4	45.9	–	67.8
1979	17.5	21.3	4.8	56.4	–	67.2
1974O	12.4	14.2	17.2	56.2	–	66.8
1974F	15.4	22.6	–	62.0	–	71.1
1970	21.1	31.9	–	47.0	–	68.0
1966	18.6	22.3	–	59.1	–	65.2
1964	17.4	20.0	–	62.6	–	72.8
1959	17.3	18.5	–	64.2	–	71.3
1955	15.8	20.4	–	63.8	–	66.1
1951	16.3	26.2	–	57.5	–	69.0
1950	21.3	31.9	–	46.8	–	67.7
1945	29.8	36.0	–	34.2	–	55.5

Orkney and Shetland comprise the two island groups to the north of Scotland. Each is distinct in character from Scotland and from each other, due to their geography, political affiliations and Norse past. While Orkney is relatively near to the Scottish mainland – separated by the narrow Pentland Firth – Lerwick, capital of Shetland is 204 miles north of Aberdeen, but just 234 miles west of Bergen, Norway.

Orkney and Shetland have the fourth lowest claimant total of incapacity and disability benefits. Orkney has the second highest female life expectancy in the country. Low birthweight babies and teenage pregnancies are the lowest in Scotland. Shetland has the joint fourth highest male and female life expectancy.

In the last thirty years the islands have been transformed by the discovery and exploitation of North Sea oil with massive oil terminal facilities sited at Flotta in Orkney and Sullom Voe in Shetland having a significant economic and employment impact. The fishing industry is still vitally important, much of it dependent on quotas set in Brussels negotiations. With neighbouring Norway out of the European Union, Shetland has a particularly euro-sceptic streak.

Orkney and Shetland have for long had a very distinct political identity compared to mainland Scotland. They became Scottish in 1468-49, but have never lost a suspicion of Edinburgh rule. This suspicion was illustrated in the 1979 devolution referendum when the two islands voted against the Callaghan Government proposals by a margin of three to one. Even in the 1997 referendum, Orkney and Shetland were the least supportive parts of Scotland. Orkney showed the least enthusiasm of anywhere for a Parliament – with 57.3 per cent supporting it. On the tax raising powers Shetland joined Dumfries and Galloway in voting against, 52.6 per cent voting 'no'. Islanders regard the Scottish Executive decision to abolish the North of Scotland Water Authority in favour of an all Scotland Water Authority as symptomatic of the centralisation they feared would occur under devolution.

Tourism is a growing income earner with Skara Brae pre-historic village and the Ring of Brodgar standing stones in Orkney, plus popular diving sites, and the Norse Settlement in Shetland. The islands have also seen a wide spectrum of more recent military history based on the British Royal Navy's northern anchorage at Scapa Flow in Orkney. In June 1919 after Germany surrendered, the might of the German naval fleet was scuttled, and twenty years on, six weeks into the Second World War, HMS Royal Oak was sunk by a German U-boat, U-47, with the loss of 833 lives.

Orkney and Shetland have a long Liberal tradition going back to the 19th century. The Conservative Basil Spence won the seat in 1935 from the Liberals and held it until 1950 when he was defeated by Jo Grimond by 2,956 votes. Grimond was leader of the Liberal Party from 1956-67 and led the recovery of the party, first in a series of by-elections, but also at the 1959 and 1964 elections. Grimond last stood in 1979 winning 56.4 per cent of the vote and a 6,810 majority over the Conservatives.

In 1983, Grimond retired from the House of Commons and a young, eager 28-year-old Liberal candidate, Jim Wallace, replaced him. Despite facing a challenge from the SNP's Winnie Ewing, he was elected with 45.9 per cent and a 4,150 majority over the Conservatives. In 1987, Wallace saw his vote fall to 41.7 per cent, but was protected by the fragmented nature of the opposition, including an Orkney and Shetland Movement candidate on 14.5 per cent, and had a 3,922 majority over the Conservatives. Five years later, Wallace increased his vote to 46.4 per cent and gained a 5,033 lead over the Conservatives.

In May 1997 Wallace, standing for the fourth time won a majority of the vote – 52 per cent – and achieved a 6,968 majority over Labour as the Conservatives slipped from second place which they had occupied since 1950 to fourth. In the first Scottish Parliament election of May 1999 Orkney and Shetland were split into two seats, with Jim Wallace, Scottish Lib Dem leader standing in Orkney and winning a resounding 67 per cent and 4,619 majority over the Conservatives. Tavish Scott, standing for the Lib Dems in Shetland, won an equally impressive 54.5 per cent and 3,194 majority over Labour.

In the June 2001 UK election Alistair Carmichael took over from Jim Wallace as Liberal Democrat candidate and saw his majority cut in half to 3,475 as his vote fell by 3,800. All the opposition parties gained ground from this. Labour in second place increased its vote by 2.3 per cent, the Conservatives moved from fourth to third putting 6.4 per cent on their vote, and the SNP, despite falling to fourth, put 2.1 per cent on their support. In the May 2003 Scottish Parliament election, Jim Wallace success-fully held Orkney, but saw his majority slashed to 1,755 as his vote fell by over 2,000 and by 21.7 per cent. The Conservatives in second place picked up 8.2 per cent, while the Scottish Socialists finished fourth with 11.4 per cent, ahead of Labour. In the regional vote the Lib Dems won 29.6 per cent to the Conservatives 20.5 per cent, while the Greens won an impressive 10 per cent, and the SSP a respectable 9.3 per cent.

In the Shetland contest, Tavish Scott saw his majority reduced – but much less sensationally – to 2,260 as his vote declined by 1,500 and 8.3 per cent, the SNP moved into second place from third, putting 5.7 per cent on their vote, while the Conservatives increased their support by 6.1 per cent. In a disastrous set of results on the islands Labour finished fourth, seeing their vote halved as it fell by 12.3 per cent. In the regional vote, the Lib Dems won 28.6 per cent to the SNP's 17.3 per cent, with the SSP on 11.7 per cent and Greens on 9 per cent.

Orkney and Shetland's special status ensures the constituency remains unchanged at Westminster, due to Section 86 of the Scotland Act 1998 which declares that they cannot be combined within any other local authority area in a parliamentary seat. Schedule 1 Clause 81 of the 1998 Act also guarantees separate parliamentary representation of the two sets of islands in the Scottish Parliament. The Lib Dems have enjoyed an unbroken run of local success for more than 50 years, and their local roots go back much further and deeper. They have easily managed the transition from one popular MP to another Liberal twice – from Jo Grimond to Jim Wallace and now to Alistair Carmichael – and there is every reason to believe they can do so again at Westminster and at the Scottish Parliament.

MSP for Orkney

JIM WALLACE was born in Annan in 1955. He was educated at Annan Academy, Downing College, Cambridge, and Edinburgh University, where he did an LLB in law, becoming an advocate in 1979 and a Queen's Counsel in 1997, as part of the convention of awarding the title to lawyer MPs. Having toyed with the wettish wing of the Conservatives at Cambridge University – belonging to the same Progressive and Economic Social Toryism group then chaired by Keith Raffan (now Mid-Scotland and Fife Lib Dem MSP) – Wallace joined the Liberals while still a student and was chair of the Edinburgh University Liberal Club from 1976-77, and then a member of the party's Scottish executive committee from 1976-85.

He contested the Dumfries constituency in the 1979 general election, quickly followed by the South of Scotland seat at the European Parliament elections of that year. With some help from then Scottish party chairman Ross Finnie, he was selected to replace Jo Grimond in Orkney and Shetland – one of the party's few safe seats – winning it in 1983. He was chief whip from 1987-92, and then replaced Malcolm Bruce as leader of the Scottish Liberal Democrats, speaking on Scottish affairs for the party in the Commons. This was hardly the most coveted of posts in the Lib Dem group of MPs at the time: Bruce had wanted out of it. It meant that Wallace was a key figure in the Scottish Constitutional Convention, negotiating on it with Scottish Labour leader George Robertson and Scottish Labour general secretary Jack McConnell. He became a member of the Consultative Steering Group which drew up the draft standing orders and procedures of the Scottish Parliament in 1998.

Having successfully lobbied at Westminster for the Scotland Act to create two constituencies in the Scottish Parliament from his single northern isles seat in the Commons, he stood for Orkney, where his family has been based since 1983, and won with the largest share of the vote of any MSP in Scotland. A sure-footed, if charismatically-challenged campaigner, the Lib Dem campaign became dominated by the promise to abolish student tuition fees in a way Wallace had not intended, making it politically essential that he do so in government. His failure to eradicate tuition payments entirely came to feature in his media interviews in the 2003 campaign, putting him on the defensive on an issue for which he was claiming credit. With a group of 17 MSPs elected on 6 May 1999, Wallace entered coalition talks with Labour demanding an agreed programme for government, but not taking enough time to hammer out the detail, to hold out for more ministerial posts or a tougher wording to ensure council voting reform (something that was nailed down thoroughly when they returned to the issue in 2003). The subsequent impression was that Wallace had been rushed by Labour and only eight days after the election, he signed the agreement, along with Labour leader Donald Dewar, at the new Museum of Scotland in Edinburgh. As a result of the deal, Wallace became Deputy First Minister, the first Liberal in peacetime government since 1922. In the first Parliament, he also held the justice portfolio, and after the 2003 election – and with a new programme for government being negotiated in much more detail and at greater length – his responsibility shifted to enterprise and lifelong learning. Questioned on what qualified him for the economic portfolio, he claimed he had experience of the private sector through being a self-employed advocate and he was dogged by criticism that he was failing to inspire much confidence in his handling of the new brief.

To the astonishment of some Labour MSPs, Wallace also became acting First Minister when Donald Dewar underwent heart surgery in the summer of 2000, and he took over again after Dewar's death in October 2000, until the election of Henry McLeish. For a third time in November 2001, he became acting First Minister, when McLeish resigned and Labour had to find a new leader. Wallace won widespread acclaim for his sure-footed handling of question time, as the SNP sought unsuccessfully to drive wedges between him and the Labour MSPs who found themselves cheering him on. He joked that having had the post three times, like the Jules Rimet World Cup, he should be allowed to keep it. Instead, he had to be happy with the *Herald* naming him Politician of the Year in 2000.

As leader of the junior coalition partner, Wallace set many of the precedents for how devolved government would operate, tending to use a good, personal working relationship with the Labour leaders to smooth over tensions and leaving partisan politics to his awkward squad of backbenchers. There was acknowledgement, after the 2003 election, that he had had insufficient support to cover the full range of Executive activities and paperwork, and that support was increased. As justice minister, he drove a liberal reforming agenda and a heavy workload of legislation, including the Adults with Incapacity Act, with criminal justice reform, insisting on a more open Freedom of Information Act than was being passed at Westminster, reforming the appointment of judges, and with long-delayed reforms of land ownership and family law. He also handled the implications of the European Convention on Human Rights being incorporated into Scots law, and he steered through the first piece of legislation in the Scottish Parliament: an emergency measure in September 1999 responding to a loophole in the law which allowed a dangerous patient, and potentially others, out of Carstairs State Hospital.

His reputation took a bit of a stumble after Jack McConnell became First Minister, determined to ensure more distance between Labour and Lib Dems by the time of the 2003 election. Several justice policies suffered a public and media backlash, in which the new Labour leadership was happy to see Wallace taking the flak. This included, in 2002, his plans to outlaw the smacking of toddlers, a pilot to extend the Children's Panel system to 16 and 17-year olds, and his plan to renew dilapidated Scottish prisons with privately-run jails. He was forced into high-profile u-turns on all these, including a reprieve for Peterhead prison and its sex offenders unit. McConnell also talked tough on dealing with youth offending, giving the lead role on it to education and young people's minister Cathy Jamieson – even though Lib Dems refused to let all the Labour plans through. McConnell was determined Labour should have the justice ministry after the 2003 election, handing that to Jamieson. Indeed, he had attempted to shift Wallace away from justice in May 2002, when Wendy Alexander resigned from the enterprise portfolio, but Wallace refused to take over from her, and Labour's Iain Gray did so instead.

In the run-up to the 2003 election, Wallace brought criticism from other Lib Dems for refusing to talk about a coalition deal with the SNP. This was partly because he did not want to talk them up, and partly because he was determined not to give ground on their demand for an independence referendum. But some on his own side thought he was tying himself too closely to Labour. So, facing internal party pressure, he changed the tone of his plans to say he would work with the largest party to find common ground for a coalition, and would be willing to walk away from talks if he did not get what he wanted. He refused, however, to say which policy or policies would make him do this, declining to make council voting reform 'non-negotiable', even though it was. Because there was little distance between Labour and Lib Dem on the big issues, much attention was focused on the areas where they did differ, including Wallace's describing Labour's plans for jailing the parents of persistent young offenders as 'unworkable'. His language was more cautious than in 1999, with a view to avoiding hostages to fortune in the coalition negotiations he expected to follow. His Lib Dem campaign lacked much lustre, gaining Edinburgh South off Labour, and returning 17 MSPs as before, when he had said he expected at least 20. But it left Wallace in an unchallenged position as party leader, and able to choose the time of his departure, so that he can spend more time with his wife Rosie, playing golf or on horseback.

MSP for Shetland

TAVISH SCOTT was born in Inverness in 1966 and grew up on Shetland, attending Anderson High School in Lerwick, and graduating from Napier College in 1989 with a degree in business studies. He worked for local MP Jim Wallace in the House of Commons 1989-90, followed by a stint as press officer for the Scottish Liberal Democrats in 1991-92, giving him more confidence than most in dealing with the media, as witnessed by his fronting of the coalition negotiating team in 2003. Moving back to Shetland in 1992, he ran the 760 hectare family farm in Shetland and became a local councillor in

Lerwick from 1994–99. He was vice-chair of Shetland Council's roads and transport committee, chair of Lerwick Harbour Trust and a director of Shetland Islands Tourism.

At the start of the first Parliament, he was Lib Dem spokesperson for transport, the environment and Europe, and sat on both the European and transport and environment committees in 1999-2000. Tavish Scott steered the first member's bill through the Scottish Parliament, with a strong constituency flavour to it, tidying up the law of the seabed in a way Westminster had insufficient time to do, with the Sea Fisheries (Shellfish) (Amendment) Bill amending the Sea Fisheries (Shellfish) Act of 1967. This did not receive much media attention, but was a landmark for both Scott and the Parliament's legislative processes.

A confident Parliamentary performer trusted by Wallace, Scott was rewarded in October 2000 with promotion to the ministerial job of Lib Dem whip, or more formally the deputy minister of Parliament and Lib Dem business manager with a role on the Parliamentary Bureau, replacing Iain Smith. This came to an abrupt end only five months later, with the first of two major quota reduction and decommissioning packages required by Brussels of the Scottish fishing fleet during the first Parliamentary term. Pressure was exerted by the fishermen's leaders, with SNP support, for the Executive to fund a tie-up scheme, but this was resisted by the Lib Dem cabinet minister responsible for fisheries, Ross Finnie. With fishing communities furious at his refusal, and deputy fisheries minister Rhona Brankin burned in effigy in Peterhead, Scott came under intense, personalised pressure in Shetland. That helps explain his odd tactics, in that he voted to support the Executive and immediately resigned in protest at the policy he had just supported.

On the backbenches from 2001-3, he took more of a role as Lib Dem strategist and adviser for Wallace, and was spokesman on enterprise and lifelong learning and the Highlands and Islands. Better able than ministers to distance himself from the Executive, he proposed the Lib Dem motion opposing the Iraq war in March 2003. After being re-elected in that year's election, Wallace chose him as his first lieutenant in the coalition negotiations, doing most of the media fronting as they went on, and successfully getting the message out that Lib Dems had done significantly better out the talks than Labour. With five ministerial posts instead of four, Scott was the new addition to the Lib Dem team, returning to the role of deputy Parliamentary Business minister. In November 2003, Scott tested McConnell's latitude to the extreme, when twice within a week he stated that the European Union Common Fisheries Policy should be 'abolished', which was not the policy of the Scottish Executive. He was faced with no choice but to recant, announcing that he believed the policy should be reformed. Although he works closely with Nicol Stephen, the two are seen as potential rivals for the party leadership when Wallace chooses to stand down. Scott lists his interests as including the islands' wild winter festival of Up Helly Aa.

MP

ALISTAIR CARMICHAEL represents both Orkney and Shetland, and has done so since 2001. He was born in Islay in 1965 and attended Islay High School and Aberdeen University, where he studied law. He was a hotel manager in 1984-89, a procurator fiscal depute from 1993-96 and a solicitor in private practice in Turriff from 1996-2001, while a prominent activist in the Gordon Lib Dem party.

On his election, he became his party's deputy spokesperson on Northern Ireland and on energy in Scotland, and secured a place on the Scottish affairs select committee, where he regretted the committee's decision not to favour a BBC *Scottish Six* news programme – a source of some controversy at the time, in which Labour saw the idea as the thin end of a nationalist wedge. He delivered a well-received speech at the 2001 Liberal Democrat autumn conference, days after the 9/11 attacks, at which he urged that poverty be tackled as a key cause of terrorism, saying: 'Poverty leads to war which leads to poverty', and that 'we have bombed and shot our way to the brink of disaster', concluding that 'war challenges our liberalism'. He combines eldership in the Church of Scotland with a taste for amateur dramatics.

Paisley North

Predecessor Constituencies: none.

Socio-economic Indicators:

Constituency Pop. (16-64)	39,466
Claimant Count (May 2003)	4.2% (35.5% above average)
IBA/SDA Claimants	15.4%
Life Expectancy – Male	71.4 (2.0 yrs below average)
Life Expectancy – Female	76.7 (2.0 yrs below average)
Owner Occupied	58.8%
Social Rented	32.8%
Average Property Prices	£43,270 (70th)
Average Gross Income	£22,807 (62nd)
Low Birthweight Babies	157 (7.6%)
Teenage Pregnancy Rates	451 (5.9%)
No. of Lone Parent Households	3,610 (13.0%)

CAB Enquiries

Issue	No. of cases	Percentage of total cases (%)
1. Consumer	2908	26.4
2. Benefits	2150	19.5
3. Employment	1859	16.8
4. Housing	1074	9.7
5. Other	1071	9.7

2003 Scottish Parliament Election

Electorate: 44,999   *Turnout*: 22,206 (49.3%)   *Turnout 1999*: 56.6%

Candidate	Party	Votes	Votes%	99 %	Change%
Wendy Alexander	Labour	10,631	47.9	48.6	– 0.7
George Adam	SNP	6,321	28.5	32.0	– 3.5
Allison Cook	Con	1,871	8.4	8.1	+ 0.3
Brian O'Malley	Lib Dem	1,705	7.7	7.7	=
Sean Hurl	SSP	1,678	7.6	3.6	+ 3.9

Labour majority: 4,310 (19.4%)   *Swing*: 1.4% SNP to Labour

2001 General Election

Electorate: 47,994   Turnout: 27,153 (56.6%)

Candidate	Party	Votes	Votes%	Change%
Irene Adams	Labour	15,058	55.5	- 4.0
George Adam	SNP	5,737	21.1	- 0.8
Jane Hook	Lib Dem	2,709	10.0	+ 3.1
Craig Stevenson	Con	2,404	8.9	- 0.7
Jim Halfpenny	SSP	982	3.6	-
Robert Graham	Pro-Life	263	1.0	- 0.6

Labour majority: 9,321 (34.3%)   *Swing*: 1.6% Labour to SNP

1983–97 Westminster

	Lab%	Con%	SNP%	Lib%	Other%	Turnout%
1997	59.5	9.6	21.9	6.9	2.2	68.7
1992	50.7	16.4	23.3	8.2	1.4	73.4
1990B	44.0	14.8	29.4	8.3	3.6	53.7
1987	55.5	15.8	12.9	15.8	–	73.5
1983	45.6	21.4	8.0	23.7	1.3	68.5

Paisley North is slightly less well off on a majority of indicators compared to Paisley South. Average property prices are 35.9 per cent below the national average and rose 32.7 per cent in the 1990s Paisley North has been ranked the 30th unhealthy constituency in Britain and 16th in Scotland, just ahead of South in terms of unhealthiness. Paisley is situated on the south side of the Clyde between the parliamentary seats of West Renfrewshire, which was to play an important role in Paisley politics in the 1990s, and the Glasgow seats of Govan and Pollok. It is currently Scotland's fifth largest town and in the 19th century had the third largest population in Scotland, ahead of Aberdeen and Dundee. Paisley North includes parts of Paisley, along with Renfrew, Linwood and Hillington.

Paisley has a proud tradition but in recent years has seen hard times. Linwood car plant was opened to great fanfare in 1963 by the Rootes Group to build the Hillman Imp and kept open with Labour Government support when it was threatened with closure in 1975. It was finally shut in 1981. While new jobs are being created in electronics, communications and the service sector, other jobs are being lost and in 2001 Rolls Royce announced they would make 400 job cuts at their Hillington factory. Glasgow Airport is located within the constituency and has dramatically expanded in recent years. The airport, like Edinburgh's, has been restricted by the lack of a city centre–airport rail connection and the Scottish Executive has agreed to give support and funding to such a link. However, there are concerns that it is losing ground to the growth of Edinburgh Airport, which has better ground transport links.

Paisley High Street has been drastically hit by the opening of the nearby Braehead Shopping Centre, situated on the border between Renfrewshire West and Glasgow. Paisley shops have seen a drastic downturn in trade and many businesses have closed, leaving empty retail units in the town centre.

Paisley North does not have many areas of affluence, and some of its poorer areas are amongst the most disadvantaged in Scotland. Ferguslie Park became a by-word in the 1980s for a failing estate and was chosen under the Conservatives as one of their four main Areas of Priority Treatment. It was also affected by widespread flooding when the River Clyde broke its banks in 1994 with large numbers of residents too poor to have insurance. As a recipient of significant government, local council and public agency money, it was the centre of serious allegations about corruption, malpractice and misuse of public money which emerged in conjunction with the infighting in the local Labour Party post-1997. The Scottish Executive's social justice strategy has seen a number of initiatives to try to turn the area round and tackle the lack of opportunities, poor health, crime and drugs. Widespread demolition of some of the worst housing stock has been undertaken.

In 1983, Paisley was split into two seats – North and South – with North taking a slightly smaller part of the old Paisley seat. In the resulting general election, Allen Adams, previously elected for the Paisley seat in 1979, held the new seat with a 7,587 majority for Labour, and doubled his majority to 14,442 in 1987 – on both occasions over the Liberal-SDP Alliance. Paisley politics were then thrown into shock by the deaths within a month of both of the town's MPs, Adams and Norman Buchan. The subsequent by-elections held on 29 November 1990 were marked by the resignation of Margaret Thatcher as Prime Minister seven days before polling and the election of John Major. Both by-elections returned Labour MPs with sharply reduced majorities; Irene Adams, widow of Allen, being returned in North with a majority of 3,770 over the SNP.

The 1992 election increased Labour's majority to 9,321 over the SNP. Boundary changes translated this into a notional majority of 10,414, which Labour widened to 12,814 over the Nationalists in 1997. Irene Adams increased Labour's support by 1,000, while the SNP vote fell by 1,000 and the Conservatives' by 2,500. In the June 2001 UK election, Irene Adams was re-elected with a 9,321 majority over the SNP, as Labour's support fell by 5,000 and the Nationalists by 1,750.

The 1999 Scottish Parliament elections saw Wendy Alexander, sister of Douglas Alexander, MP for South, returned with a majority of 4,616, the Labour vote falling by nearly 7,000, while the SNP's support increased by 1,400. In the second Scottish Parliament contest in 2003, Alexander was returned with a majority of 4,310 over the Nationalists. In the regional vote, Labour won 37.3 per cent to the SNP's 26.1 per cent, while the Scottish Socialists won 8.2 per cent and Greens 4.6 per cent.

Boundary changes for Westminster see the number of seats covering Paisley and Renfrewshire fall from three to two. They all look fairly safe Labour seats. Labour's main problems at Westminster will come from managing the internal Labour selection contest of three MPs into two seats. At the Scottish Parliament, Paisley North is a significantly safer Labour seat than South, and the SNP have not managed in the seat's 20 year history to pose a serious challenge.

MSP

WENDY ALEXANDER was born in 1963 in Glasgow and educated at Park Mains High School, Erskine, with a scholarship to Lester B. Pearson College, Vancouver. At Glasgow University, she began as a medical student but switched to history, where her undergraduate thesis on medical missionaries was published. Masters degrees followed at Warwick University and INSEAD business school, France. She was chair of Glasgow University Labour Club from 1984-85 and a member of Scottish Labour Action, the pro-home rule pressure group, along with a number of future Labour MSPs: Sarah Boyack, Susan Deacon, Jackie Baillie and Jack McConnell. She was Parliamentary assistant to George Galloway, the Glasgow MP, from 1987-88 and research officer to the Scottish Labour Party from 1988-92. When Jack McConnell became general secretary, she left party headquarters at Keir Hardie House to study for her business qualification, followed by a management consultant's post at Booz Allen and Hamilton from

1994–97. She continued to contribute to the devolution debate and became special adviser to Donald Dewar, as Secretary of State for Scotland from 1997, where she had special responsibility for the legislation to establish the Scottish Parliament.

In the 1999 Scottish Parliament election, Alexander was campaign spokesperson on the economy, but after the election, rather than get the enterprise portfolio as widely expected, she became cabinet minister for communities, then including social justice, housing and local government. Alexander is acknowledged as being bright and driven – not words always associated with Scottish Labour politicians – but her people skills and her patience in managing colleagues and officials have gained her a bad reputation. As one of her Labour MSP colleagues put it: 'In Wendy's world, everybody else is in primary five'. In her first year as a minister, she was involved in one of the biggest political controversies in Scotland for years, after she announced, during a Glasgow University speech, the Executive's intention to abolish Section 28, which had since 1988 banned the 'promotion' of homosexuality in schools. Alexander drew the wrath of the Catholic Church and of Brian Souter, millionaire owner of Stagecoach with strong religious beliefs, who bankrolled a virulent campaign, with extensive tabloid support, and a private referendum intended to show the level of opposition to the Executive's policy. Section 28 was eventually abolished, but at much cost to the Executive's political capital, to Alexander personally, and with the result that the Parliament was driven towards a more socially conservative caution.

In Henry McLeish's first ministerial reshuffle in October 2000, Alexander was given the post she had wanted, minister for enterprise and lifelong learning, where she was author of the 'smart, successful Scotland' strategy. Facing major job losses in Silicon Glen – most notably in a successful campaign to place 3,200 redundancies at Motorola in West Lothian, many into Edinburgh's finance sector – this moved enterprise policy sharply away from dependence on inward investment and towards support for high-tech developments of university expertise. The Scottish Tourist Board was reformed into VisitScotland, in response to poor performance in the industry. McLeish tried to get her to take responsibility for the water industry, including substantial major reform, but she angrily refused, saying she was too busy with her other work, including the key role she was playing in running the 2001 election campaign, along with her brother, Douglas, who was managing it from London with Gordon Brown. Her behaviour, including the allegation of throwing a 'tantrum' over the water request, was seen as a sign of both McLeish's weakness and the difficulty others faced in working with her, with stories surfacing in the media of unreasonable treatment of civil servants. When Jack McConnell became First Minister, Alexander was to lose responsibility for tourism, but gained transport, steering it away from the environmental brief with which it had been linked, and orienting it more towards economic growth.

Alexander was spoken of, while Donald Dewar was First Minister, as a potential successor to him, and seen by many as his preferred candidate. However, her prospects were not aided by the Section 28/Clause 2A debacle, and Dewar's death came too soon for her to put her name forward. She backed Henry McLeish against Jack McConnell in the October 2000 leadership contest. When McLeish went, she made it clear she would challenge McConnell as front runner, drawing on the support of his Labour cabinet colleagues. But two days after the campaign unofficially began, she decided against standing, for what she said were personal reasons of not wanting to take such a high profile, and perhaps because she knew how unlikely she was to win. It was a move which alienated her from former supporters, who were left exposed. Those same cabinet colleagues were ousted from the cabinet in McConnell's reshuffle, leaving her a lone figure in the new team, and privately complaining of being overworked and undersupported. In May 2002, she suddenly resigned from being 'minister for everything', damaging the Executive's attempts to build trust in the business community.

Following that, she became a member of a justice committee until the 2003 election, and joined the finance and education committees following it. Her formidable energy and intellect found an avenue as a visiting professor at the Fraser of Allander Institute based at Strathclyde University, initiating a series of lectures about Scotland's economic future given by what she called the Real Madrid of internationally-renowned economists. In December 2003, she married Professor Brian Ashcroft, policy head of the Institute.

Alexander is a contributor to a wide range of books and publications, ranging from *The World Is Ill-Divided*, where she wrote about the first women medical graduates at Glasgow University, to the IPPR collection, *The State And The Nations* and *A Different Future: A Moderniser's Guide To Scotland*. In 2003 she published a pamphlet, *Chasing the Tartan Tiger: Lessons from a Celtic Cousin?* with the Smith Institute. She contributes to Labour Party strategic thinking from a modernisers' point of view which, unusually for MSPs, keeps links both to Blairites and to the Gordon Brown team in Whitehall. She remains politically close to her brother, Douglas Alexander, MP for Paisley South and Cabinet Office minister, who similarly straddles the Blair-Brown camps in London.

MP

IRENE ADAMS was born in 1947 in Paisley and elected for Paisley North in a November 1990 by-election, succeeding her late husband, Allen Adams, who had been MP for Paisley from 1979-83 and for Paisley North during 1983-90. She was educated at Stanley Green High School, Paisley, and was the youngest woman councillor when elected, aged 24, to Paisley Town Hall from 1970-74. The following year, she became the youngest ever Justice of the Peace. She served on Renfrew District Council from 1974-78 and Strathclyde Regional Council from 1979-84, replacing her husband in representing his ward at the time he was elected to Westminster. Having also been his constituency worker from 1984-90, she was selected in 1989 to fight the Argyll and Bute constituency at the following election, but her husband's death and subsequent by-election changed that plan.

Adams is on the pro-devolution left wing of the party and after Labour's unexpected defeat in 1992 was one of the main supporters of the cross-party initiative 'Scotland United', along with Labour MPs George Galloway and John McAllion. She was one of five Labour MPs who drew attention to the home rule cause in July that year by attempting to prevent the removal of the Commons mace after a Conservative debate. As one of very few Scottish Labour women MPs, at least when elected, she has argued against quotas and positive discrimination for women, forming Labour Supporters for Real Equality, along with Gwyneth Dunwoody and Llin Golding. In 1993, she scored unexpectedly well in the shadow cabinet elections, with 88 votes. On touchstone Commons votes, she has shown an independence of mind and lack of predictability. She opposed the Gulf War in 1991, but supported the government in votes on the Iraq war in February and March 2003, and she voted against the Maastricht Treaty on its third reading in 1993. She was appointed chair of the Scottish Affairs Select Committee in 1997, which came under criticism in the wake of devolution for not having the busiest of schedules leading into the 2001 election. She is also vice-chair of Scottish Labour MPs, and chairs the Scotch Whisky All Party Group.

After the 1997 election she became involved in a bitter dispute with neighbouring Labour MP Tommy Graham, tied up with the suicide of Paisley South MP Gordon McMaster that autumn. It resulted in Graham being expelled from the party and Adams' position in Renfrewshire's bruising politics was strengthened. The positions she has taken on tackling drugs have also resulted in threats to her from local dealers.

Paisley South

Predecessor Constituencies: Paisley (1945–79).

Socio-economic Indicators:

Constituency Pop. (16-64)	42,820
Claimant Count (May 2003)	4.1% (31.7% above average)
IBA/SDA Claimants	13.0%
Life Expectancy – Male	70.6 (2.8 yrs below average)
Life Expectancy – Female	77.5 (1.2 yrs below average)
Owner Occupied	59.7%
Social Rented	32.3%
Average Property Prices	£45,608 (65th)
Average Gross Income	£24,034 (50th)
Low Birthweight Babies	179 (7.9%)
Teenage Pregnancy Rates	458 (5.4%)
No. of Lone Parent Households	3,632 (12.1%)

2003 Scottish Parliament Election

Electorate: 49,818   *Turnout*: 24,984 (50.2%)   *Turnout 1999*: 57.2%

Candidate	Party	Votes	Votes%	99 %	Change%
Hugh Henry	Labour	10,190	40.8	45.3	– 4.6
Bill Martin	SNP	7,737	31.0	30.7	+ 0.3
Eileen McCartin	Lib Dem	3,517	14.1	9.7	+ 4.4
Mark Jones	Con	1,775	7.1	7.9	– 0.8
Frances Curran	SSP	1,765	7.1	(other 6.4)	–

Labour majority: 2,453 (9.8%)   *Swing*: 2.4% Labour to SNP

2001 General Election

Electorate: 53,351   *Turnout*: 30,536 (57.2%)

Candidate	Party	Votes	Votes%	Change%
Douglas Alexander	Labour	17,830	58.4	+ 0.9
Brian Lawson	SNP	5,920	19.4	– 4.0
Brian O'Malley	Lib Dem	3,178	10.4	+ 1.0
Andrew Cossar	Con	2,301	7.5	– 1.1
Frances Curran	SSP	835	2.7	–
Patricia Graham	Pro-Life	346	1.1	–

cont'd

Candidate	Party	Votes	Votes%	Change%
Terence O'Donnell	Ind	126	0.4	–

Labour majority: 11,910 (39.0%)　　　　　　　　　*Swing*: 2.4% SNP to Labour

1945–97 Westminster

	Lab%	Con%	SNP%	Lib%	Other%	Turnout%
1997B	44.2	7.0	32.5	11.0	5.3	43.4
1997	57.5	8.7	23.4	9.4	1.1	69.1
1992	50.7	15.9	24.1	9.1	0.3	75.0
1990B	46.1	13.4	27.5	9.8	3.1	55.5
1987	56.2	14.7	14.0	15.1	–	75.3
1983	41.4	20.7	13.0	24.1	0.7	72.6
1979	55.8	26.1	15.7	–	–	72.8
1974O	44.8	15.6	33.1	6.5	–	72.2
1974F	48.4	30.3	21.3	–	–	75.2
1970	54.1	32.4	7.3	6.2	–	71.5
1966	60.0	23.2	–	16.8	–	76.5
1964	52.9	13.2	–	33.9	–	79.8
1961B	45.4	13.2	–	41.4	–	68.1
1959	57.3	42.7	–	–	–	78.9
1955	56.4	43.6	–	–	–	76.2
1951	55.3	31.0	–	13.7	–	84.4
1950	56.1	36.5	–	7.4	–	84.0
1948B	56.8	–	–	43.2	–	76.0
1945	55.6	32.7	–	10.0	1.7	73.9

Paisley South comprises the southern part of the town of Paisley, along with the nearby village of Johnstone which was previously in Renfrewshire West. Paisley is only seven miles from Glasgow, but prides itself on its distinctiveness – it has an Abbey, a proud grammar school and a football team which once played in the top league. It was once famous for its cotton mills with their imperial links to India obvious in the Paisley pattern. In 1983 the division into Paisley North and South saw the latter seat take 51 per cent of the old Paisley seat. Paisley South is the slightly better off of the two. Average property prices are 32.4 per cent below the average and rose 17.8 per cent in 1991-2001. Paisley South has been rated the 36th most unhealthy constituency in Britain and 19th in Scotland, just behind Paisley North.

Paisley South contains Paisley Grammar School – one of the most prestigious state schools in Scotland – which became a major centre of political controversy in the 1980s. Strathclyde Regional Council announced in 1988 it was planning to close it and Conservative minister Michael Forsyth intervened to save the school. Margaret Thatcher in her memoirs calls it 'a popular school of high academic standards and traditional ethos' and believed it was because of this that the 'Scottish left-wing establishment' wanted to close it. Renfrewshire Council now sees Paisley Grammar as a model of success and plans to extend and upgrade it.

Health provision is a major concern with local anxieties over waiting times at the Royal Alexandra Hospital in Paisley, while the Scottish Executive funded project, 'Have a Heart Paisley' has looked at ways of improving the health and living standards of people in the area. There are significant areas of poverty and hardship in the constituency and credit unions are active in the towns of Glenburn and Johnstone, providing support and low interest credit to people on low incomes.

Paisley has a proud Liberal tradition and in 1920 Liberal leader and the former Prime Minister, Herbert Asquith, won the burgh seat in a by-election, representing the area until he was defeated by Labour in 1924. The Liberals rewon it in 1931 – Labour's wipeout year – and succeeded in holding it until 1945 when Labour's Viscount Corvedale won the seat with a 10,330 majority. In December 1947, he became Earl Baldwin of Bewdley when his father Stanley Baldwin, former Conservative Prime Minister, died. In the resulting by-election in February 1948, Labour's Douglas Johnston was faced with a formidable challenge from John MacCormick standing as a National Liberal candidate with Conservative support on a pro-home rule ticket based on the Scottish Convention. Labour saw its majority cut to 6,545 in a two-horse race. The bitterness of the contest, and the possibility MacCormick might win the seat, was a contributory factor in the Attlee Government becoming more hostile both to the Convention and the idea of a Scottish Parliament. MacCormick in his memoirs wrote of his campaign allowing Conservative and Liberal members to 'unite against the centralising policies of the Labour government' and noted with pleasure the support he gained from Tories such as Walter Elliot, Lady Tweedmuir and others who had been 'immovable opponents of Scottish Nationalism'. The unholy nature of this alliance does not seem to have crossed MacCormick's mind.

Johnston remained Labour MP for Paisley until 1961 when he became a Court of Session judge forcing another by-election on the seat. In the resulting contest in April 1961, John Robertson, Labour's candidate faced a strong Liberal challenge, and saw his majority slashed, but in the subsequent general election in October 1964, the Liberal threat waned. Robertson was elected in October 1974 with a 5,590 lead over the SNP and in 1976 established the devolutionary Scottish Labour Party with Jim Sillars. However, Robertson chose not to stand again in 1979 and Labour's Allen Adams was elected with a 13,755 lead over the Conservatives.

In 1983, the creation of South saw Norman Buchan returned with a 6,529 majority over the Liberal-SDP Alliance, which he widened to 15,785 in 1987. The death of Buchan in 1990 came close to that of Allen Adams, MP for North, and produced the unusual situation of two by-elections on the same day in adjoining constituencies. Gordon McMaster held South for Labour with a 5,030 majority over the SNP's Iain Lawson, previously a Conservative candidate, and this majority increased to 9,549 over the SNP in 1992.

Boundary changes before 1997 gave Labour a notional 10,469 majority over the SNP. In the May 1997 contest, McMaster increased Labour's vote by 1,000, as the SNP's vote fell by the same amount, resulting in a 12,750 majority over the SNP. McMaster was a bright, able MP who had been leader of Renfrew District Council and would have had a good chance of holding ministerial office. However, three months after the May election triumph, he committed suicide. This turned Paisley politics upside down. It revealed the dark side of local politics, with Paisley nick-named 'a town called malice'. McMaster had believed Tommy Graham, MP for West Renfrewshire, had been carrying out a campaign of rumour and invective to undermine him, and, after a party investigation, Graham was expelled from the Labour Party.

The November 1997 by-election was a difficult contest for Labour, but Douglas Alexander held the seat relatively easily. On a 43.4 per cent turnout, Labour's vote was more than halved, falling by 11,000 as the SNP achieved an 11 per cent swing, but saw their own vote fall by 1,000 votes, reducing Labour's majority to 2,731. The June 2001 UK election saw Alexander safely re-elected with a 11,910 majority over the SNP – as the Labour vote increased in percentage terms by just under 1 per cent, and the SNP fell back 4 per cent from four years previous – proof if it were needed of Labour's strength and endurance in this part of the country.

The 1999 Scottish Parliament elections increased Labour's lead over the SNP to 4,495. Hugh Henry saw Labour's vote fall 7,000 from the May 1997 total on a reduced turnout, as the SNP vote rose by 700. Both the Lib Dems and Conservatives increased their shares and Paul Mack, an ex-Labour councillor, polled respectably as an independent. The May 2003 Scottish Parliament election saw Henry re-elected, but his majority nearly halved to 2,453 over the SNP: the kind of majority which must give the Nationalists hope for the future. In the regional vote, Labour won 37.3 per cent – exactly the same share it won in Paisley North – and the Nationalists 27.2 per cent, with the SSP on 7.7 per cent and Greens on 4.5 per cent.

Boundary changes for Westminster will see the number of seats for Paisley and Renfrewshire reduced from three to two – Paisley and Renfrewshire North, and Paisley and Renfrewshire South – which look solidly Labour, but which may involve some intensely contested internal Labour selection contests. At the Scottish Parliament, Labour's hold on this seat is less secure than at Westminster, and if or when the party sees a downturn, Paisley South is just the sort of seat that could be vulnerable, provided the SNP are able to capitalise on the situation. Labour will hope that it has been through the worst in recent years and that a period of calm will benefit the incumbents.

MSP

HUGH HENRY was born in Glasgow in 1952 and educated at St Mirin's Academy, Paisley, the University of Glasgow and Jordanhill College of Education. He worked as an accountant for IBM from 1973-75 and then became a teacher with Strathclyde Region from 1976-79. Henry switched after this to becoming a welfare rights officer in social work from 1979-93 and a community care manager with community enterprise in Strathclyde from 1993-96.

Henry's politics were on the far left, as a Trotskyite and member of Militant Tendency, which was then trying to take over the Labour Party by entryism and which is now transformed into the core of the Scottish Socialist Party. He was elected a councillor on Renfrew District Council from 1984-96 and Renfrewshire Council from 1995-99, where he was council leader for four rather turbulent years of Labour-SNP attrition and police being called to the council chamber. He was also COSLA's spokesperson on European and international affairs from 1996-99. That set him up, in the first Scottish Parliament, to be the first convenor of the European committee. He was also, at first, a member of the health committee.

Amid the many reshuffles of the first Parliament, Henry was plucked from the backbenches by Jack McConnell in November 2001, having nominated the Motherwell and Wishaw MSP for leader. At first, he was deputy health and community care minister, taking the place of Malcolm Chisholm after the Leith MSP was promoted to that cabinet post. Henry became deputy justice minister in 2002, after Richard Simpson admitted to having called firefighters 'fascist bastards' in the middle of their strike. There is no risk of 'Hangdog Henry' being so inflammatory or flamboyant, as his presentational skills can be almost comically dull, masking what is said to be a ministerial talent. He was useful to McConnell in pushing a harder line inside the justice department while Lib Dem leader Jim Wallace was its cabinet minister, and he was one of two deputy ministers tipped for promotion, to replace Wallace after the 2003 election – that job going instead to Cathy Jamieson. Henry remained in the deputy's position but with much delegated power.

MP

DOUGLAS ALEXANDER was born in 1967 in Glasgow and was returned as MP for Paisley South in a November 1997 by-election. Educated at Park Mains High School, Erskine, and on a scholarship to Lester

B. Pearson College, Vancouver, like his older sister Wendy (see Paisley North). He went to Edinburgh University, with another scholarship year in North America, this time at Pennsylvania University. Alexander was a member of Gordon Brown's close-knit team in opposition, a relationship which has helped and also overshadowed him in subsequent years. He opted out of that to do legal training at Edinburgh University while doing some politics lecturing, and was admitted as a solicitor in 1995, working for Brodies and then Digby Brown law firms. That year, he stood in the 1995 Perth and Kinross by-election in what was a key Conservative-SNP seat and tested some of New Labour's emerging themes: trying out the concept of 'Middle Scotland' and running a combative, aggressive anti-SNP campaign that lifted Labour from third to second place, adding 3,000 to Labour's vote as the SNP won the seat.

Alexander stood again in the 1997 general election, and while he finished third behind the Conservatives, yet again improved Labour's share of the vote. After the 1997 election, he developed, with Brown, Scottish Labour's more unionist strategy for the Scottish Parliament elections. This saw Alexander and Brown pen a pamphlet *New Scotland, New Britain*. Alexander was installed at a late stage in the 1999 Scottish election campaign, and is credited both with giving it discipline and strategy where previously it had been in trouble, and also with a hard anti-Nationalist line under the banner 'Divorce is an Expensive Business'. That shocked many in the party, including Donald Dewar, but worked so well that it was recycled for 2003. However, his imprint on the campaign was less clear that year, as Jack McConnell is supposed to have ensured Alexander's role was more limited. His performance and ability in mixing an acute strategic sense with an understanding of campaign techniques at every level won him appointment by Tony Blair as joint co-ordinator of the 2001 Westminster election campaign, alongside Gordon Brown. He was appointed again in 2003 to prepare the ground for the next Westminster election, expected in 2005 and given one of the three NEC places at the Prime Minister's disposal – thus leading to Gordon Brown's exclusion.

His reward for such a key role in the second landslide was to be made third in command of the Department of Trade and Industry and minister for e-commerce and competitiveness – in parallel at the time with his sister's portfolio in the Scottish Executive. He was subsequently moved to the Cabinet Office, working alongside Lord Gus MacDonald, as a progress chaser on public services reform and the minister most closely aligned with the Prime Minister's Delivery Unit. This proved him to be a rare example of an arch-Brownite who appears to be close to Tony Blair as well. With MacDonald's retirement in 2003, Blair's botched reshuffle of June that year saw Alexander move up the pecking order while still just outside the cabinet, installed instead as Chancellor of the Duchy of Lancaster. Such Cabinet Office work takes him out of the public eye and away from the despatch box, while putting him at the heart of government. However, his profile remains high as one of the most active writers and strategists for the modernisers' cause, in doing much of the thinking about difficulties in engaging voters, and in trying to find a means of renewing Labour in the face of weak opposition in both Scotland and Westminster. His fingerprints were clearly on the 'Big Conversation' initiative launched by Blair in late 2003, attempting to open a dialogue with the public. He is also one of the leading members of his generation of MPs to be tipped for the top, for example identified by *The Times* after the 2001 election, but with the caveat that 'he still looks 10'. He has all the necessary ambition, talent and belief to go far, though he tends not to help his cause among colleagues by his rush to do so.

Perth

Predecessor Constituencies: Perth and East Perthshire (1945–79).

Socio-economic Indicators:

Constituency Pop. (16–64)	50,070
Claimant Count (May 2003)	2.1% (31.9% below average)
IBA/SDA Claimants	7.3%
Life Expectancy – Male	75.5 (2.1 yrs above average)
Life Expectancy – Female	80.7 (2.0 yrs above average)
Owner Occupied	64.6%
Social Rented	21.2%
Average Property Prices	£73,246 (19th)
Average Gross Income	£26,977 (23rd)
Low Birthweight Babies	174 (6.8%)
Teenage Pregnancy Rates	404 (4.0%)
No. of Lone Parent Households	2,951 (8.5%)

CAB Enquiries

Issue	No. of cases	Percentage of total cases (%)
1. Benefits	5336	32.7
2. Consumer	3014	18.5
3. Employment	2624	16.1
4. Other	1511	9.3
5. Housing	1383	8.5

2003 Scottish Parliament Election

Electorate: 61,957   Turnout: 31,614 (51.0%)   Turnout 1999: 61.3%

Candidate	Party	Votes	Votes%	99 %	Change%
Roseanna Cunningham	SNP	10,717	33.9	36.3	– 2.4
Alexander Stewart	Con	9,990	31.6	30.9	+ 0.7
Robert Ball	Labour	5,629	17.8	23.2	– 5.5
Gordon Campbell	Lib Dem	3,530	11.2	9.5	+ 1.7
Philip Stott	SSP	982	3.1	–	–
Thomas Burns	Ind	509	1.6	–	–
Kenneth Buchanan	SPA	257	0.8	–	–

SNP majority: 727 (2.3%)   Swing: 1.6% SNP to Conservative

2001 General Election

Electorate: 61,497   *Turnout*: 37,816 (61.5%)

Candidate	Party	Votes	Votes%	Change%
Annabelle Ewing	SNP	11,237	29.7	- 6.7
Elizabeth Smith	Con	11,189	29.6	+ 0.3
Marion Dingwall	Labour	9,638	25.5	+ 0.7
Vicki Harris	Lib Dem	4,853	12.8	+ 4.8
Frank Byrne	SSP	899	2.4	–

SNP majority: 48 (0.1%)   *Swing*: 3.5% SNP to Conservative

1945-97 Westminster

	Lab%	Con%	SNP%	Lib%	Other%	Turnout%
1997	24.8	29.3	36.4	8.0	1.5	73.9
1995B	22.9	21.4	40.4	11.8	3.4	62.1
1992	12.5	40.2	36.0	11.4	–	76.9
1987	15.9	39.6	27.6	16.9	–	74.4
1983	9.9	40.2	25.1	24.7	–	72.3
1979	13.4	41.9	35.5	9.2	–	77.3
1974O	13.6	38.9	40.8	6.7	–	73.8
1974F	15.1	47.3	27.2	10.4	–	78.3
1970	23.8	52.0	17.0	7.2	–	73.6
1966	27.9	56.5	15.6	–	–	72.3
1964	24.7	57.9	17.4	–	–	75.6
1959	18.2	58.2	23.1	–	–	75.6
1955	20.5	56.7	22.8	–	–	73.5
1951	25.7	59.4	14.9	–	–	78.3
1950	26.4	56.1	9.3	8.2	–	81.6
1945	32.6	63.1	4.3	–	–	65.3

The Perth constituency is made up of the picturesque town of Perth sitting on both banks of the River Tay and the smaller towns of Auchterarder, Crieff, Comrie, Bridge of Earn and Glencarse. The seat no longer contains Kinross, which was transferred to Ochil before the 1997 election, but the Perth seat does contain a significant amount of territory to the west of Perth.

The Perth area has a variety of employment – with insurance, banking and a number of call centres setting up in the area – while agriculture and tourism support many jobs. BSE and foot and mouth, along with the delay in removing export restrictions on British beef, hit the Perth countryside badly. Perth Auction Mart is particularly reliant on exports and winning back export orders will be crucial to farming recovering its fortunes. Tourism is a vital income earner. The constituency contains a variety of attractions ranging from Gleneagles with its international hotel and golf course to a host of whisky attractions including the 'Famous Grouse' Glenturret distillery with its new £2.5 million 'whisky experience'. The constituency is very much part of affluent Scotland, but contains elements of poverty and disadvantage in its borders. Average property prices are 8.6 per cent above the average and rose 55.6 per cent in the 1990s.

One of the most controversial local issues in recent years has been the proposed closure of maternity and paediatric departments at the Perth Royal Infirmary (PRI) which gave birth to a 'Hands Off PRI' campaign. In the face of a concerted campaign of opposition, Tayside Health Board instituted a review of acute services which resulted in the Royal Infirmary becoming a centre for a new midwife-consultant partnership project which would maintain maternity care. The Health Board has been plagued with problems of financial mismanagement, and in July 2001 the audit committee of the Scottish Parliament produced a critical report into the way the board was run, which led to the resignation of the chief executive.

Perth was once true blue Scottish Tory territory where inter-war years candidates, with names such as Lord Scone, were elected on the Conservative ticket. In 1945, Colonel Alan Gomme-Duncan won the Perth and Kinross seat for the Conservatives with a 10,867 majority over Labour with the SNP in third place on 1,547 votes and 4.3 per cent. At the 1950 election the seat was renamed Perth and East Kinross-shire, and Gomme-Duncan was elected with a similar majority. The various incarnations of the Perth constituency are the only place in Scotland where the SNP has contested every UK election since 1945 – and in the hostile environment of the early 1950s it won 14.9 per cent in 1951 with Robert McIntyre as candidate, taking second place as early as 1955. Gomme-Duncan retired prior to the 1959 election and his successor Ian MacArthur held the seat with the SNP in second place, winning an impressive 23.1 per cent of the vote.

MacArthur remained MP for the seat until the election of October 1974 when he was defeated by the SNP candidate Douglas Crawford and a majority of 793 votes. Crawford became one of the most prominent Nationalist MPs at Westminster in the 1974-79 Parliament, and held most of his support in the 1979 general election, only 300 votes down. Bill Walker, the new Conservative candidate, increased his vote by 3,500 to give him a majority of 3,103.

In 1983 boundary changes produced two very different seats – Tayside North – which Walker chose to fight – and Perth and Kinross – which Nicholas Fairbairn, the Conservative MP for Kinross and West Perthshire, chose to fight. Perth and Kinross was the successor seat to the old Perth and East Perthshire seat, and Fairbairn, a flamboyant and controversial Conservative figure with a love of the good life, held the seat with a 6,733 majority over the SNP's Crawford. In 1987, Fairbairn was re-elected by a 5,676 margin, but in 1992 encountered stiff opposition from Roseanna Cunningham who increased the SNP vote by 8.4 per cent and more than halved his majority to 2,094 votes. Fairbairn eventually succumbed to the effects of the good life and in the resulting by-election in May 1995, Cunningham captured the seat for the SNP with a 7,313 majority over Labour's Douglas Alexander who pushed Labour into second place ahead of the Conservatives John Godfrey whose vote had fallen by half.

The subsequent May 1997 general election saw the seat become simply Perth. All three main parties put up the same candidates and Cunningham won by the narrower margin of 3,141 over the Conservatives, with Labour in third place increasing its vote again. This was surprisingly the first time in the SNP's history that a by-election victor had held the seat at the following general election – and marked a shift in the SNP's support from transitory by-election victories which galvanised Scottish politics, but which then had little lasting effect on the party, to less sensational victories gained on a deeper and longer-term support. Cunningham stood in the 1999 Scottish Parliament election, and there was little doubt she would be returned. However, a harbinger of future trouble for the Nationalists was her narrowing majority, reduced to 2,027 over the Conservatives who saw their vote rise by 1.5 per cent.

In the June 2001 election, Annabelle Ewing replaced Roseanna Cunningham as SNP candidate and the party was given a very unpleasant surprise. The Nationalist vote fell on a lower turnout by 5,000 and

6.7 per cent, while the Conservatives fell by just under 2,000 meaning a rise in share of 0.3 per cent. This resulted in Ewing's majority falling to a mere 48 votes. Labour polled 25.5 per cent in this election – its highest vote in the seat since 1951. This result was more than a shift from the SNP A team to its B reserves at Westminster – as Cunningham's result in the 2003 Scottish Parliament showed the weakness of the Nationalists appeal. The SNP's vote fell by 2.4 per cent, while the Conservatives saw their share rise by 0.7 per cent to leave Cunningham with only one-third of her previous majority – a lead of 727 votes. In the regional vote, the Conservatives won 27.1 per cent to the SNP's 25 per cent – a Conservative lead of 678 votes – with the Greens on 7.8 per cent and SSP on 4 per cent.

Boundary changes for Westminster mean an enlarged Perth seat which takes in parts of Tayside North to become Perth and North Perthshire which the SNP would be favourites to win, but which the Conservatives have a decent chance in. At future Scottish Parliament contests, Perth has shown that it has the capacity to be too close to call, with well-organised, professional SNP and Conservative electoral machines, both capable of getting their vote out. Both parties are entrenched on Perth and Kinross Council and in 2003 the SNP won 35.6 per cent to the Conservatives 28.4 per cent, representing a slight shift to the SNP in votes since 1999. A worrying sign for the Nationalists has been that despite holding Perth and its predecessor seat since 1995, they have not been able to gather most of the anti-Tory vote around them. This can be seen most clearly in the rise of the Labour vote up to the 2001 election. With the SNP and Conservatives so evenly matched, it is perhaps in the size of the Labour and Lib Dem votes, that the fate of the seat will be sealed.

MSP

ROSEANNA CUNNINGHAM was born in Glasgow in 1951 and emigrated to Perth, Australia as an eight-year-old child, returning in 1973 as a student with her Scottish Nationalist politics already developed from her time in exile. She has a degree in politics from University of Western Australia, and trained as a lawyer at Edinburgh and Aberdeen universities. She worked for the SNP as a researcher before becoming a solicitor, working the courts in Dumbarton and then Glasgow. She became an advocate in 1990.

Cunningham was a supporter of the '79 Group set up after the SNP's electoral humiliation in the 1979 election to push for a more left-wing position. In 1982, the party leadership proscribed the group, expelling leading members including Alex Salmond, and then reducing the sentences to suspension. Her brother, Chris Cunningham, was one of the seven prominent members of the '79 Group who was suspended and he never rejoined the party.

Following the death of Conservative maverick Sir Nicholas Fairbairn, the 1995 Perth and Kinross by-election was called, for which Cunningham fought off a strong challenge for the party's candidacy from Alasdair Morgan, later to become MP and MSP for Galloway and Upper Nithsdale. That selection battle also dragged up old, personal animosities with party president Winnie Ewing. At that by-election, the candidate's republican views generated some controversy, as she styled the monarchy 'the pinnacle of the British class system'. However, Perth and Kinross was not as royalist as the Conservatives thought and 'Republican Rose' swept into Westminster at that election. Noted for crossing her fingers as she took the Commons' oath of allegiance, she kept her republican views quiet until after the 2003 election, when she re-opened the party's debate on whether it should retain a monarchist stand during a TV interview. Being part of a small Westminster group, she was spokeswoman on a wide range of issues, including environment, land reform, arts, broadcasting, employment and women.

She was elected Perth's MSP in the Scottish Parliament, holding a dual mandate in both legislatures until the 2001 Westminster election. In the Scottish Parliament, she was the convenor of the justice and home affairs committee from 1999-2000 until the reshuffle which followed John Swinney's rise to the party leadership in September 2000. Her committee work included one of the heavier workloads, resulting in two justice committees being formed. Cunningham began the first committee-based legislation, aimed at tackling domestic violence. She remained the SNP's spokesperson on justice, equality and land reform, despite leaving the committee. One of the SNP's abler Parliamentary performers, she has a significant following within the party, shown by her victory over Lothian MSP Kenny MacAskill and grass roots activist Peter Kearney in the September 2000 deputy leadership contest.

In the 2003 election campaign, her national profile was lower, as she has not been treated by Swinney as one of his inner circle. Wary of the possibility of her mounting a challenge to him, Swinney was quick to draw her publicly into his leadership defence in 2003 when challenged by Bill Wilson. The 2001 Westminster result, which nearly saw Perth return to the Tories, also forced her to concentrate on her constituency – not an easy task when her home is in Glasgow and she does not drive. Wanting out of doing justice, her role after the 2003 election is as the SNP front bencher dealing with environment, rural affairs, culture and sport. Her hobbies are mildly unorthodox: she is a renowned *Star Trek* fan, as well as other sci-fi, and is a devotee of the martial art of aikido.

MP

ANNABELLE EWING was born in 1960 in Glasgow, daughter of Winnie Ewing, who would seven years later be elected the SNP MP for Hamilton, becoming a Nationalist icon and founding a sort of dynasty. One of Annabelle's two brothers, Fergus, is MSP for Inverness, East, Nairn and Lochaber and Fergus's wife, Margaret, is MSP for Moray. Joining the party aged 15 probably seemed the natural thing to do. Annabelle studied law at Glasgow University, and also attended the Bologna Centre of John Hopkins University along with the Amsterdam University Europa Institute. She was an apprentice lawyer in 1984-86 with Ruth Anderson & Co, then worked as an official for the European Commission from 1987. While her mother was the Highlands and Islands MEP, she was a solicitor specialising in European Union in Brussels from 1987-97, then becoming a partner in her brother's law firm, Ewing & Co, from 1998-2001, giving her the opportunity to get back into Scottish domestic politics.

She stood in Stirling in the 1999 Scottish Parliament elections, and took a higher profile in running Labour to within 556 votes of a major upset in the Hamilton South by-election in September 1999, which was caused by the resignation of George Robertson to head up NATO. Winning Perth in 2001 by only 48 votes, she was made spokesperson in the Westminster group shadowing the work and pensions and home affairs, with the grand title of the SNP's shadow minister for social security. She was also given the crucial task for SNP MPs of handling their side of the legislation to amend the Scotland Act, with the Government wanting to limit the amendment to retaining the number of MSPs at 129, while the SNP wanted to open up the Act for more widespread amendment.

Ross, Skye and Inverness West

Predecessor Constituencies: Ross and Cromarty (1945–79) and Ross, Cromarty and Skye (1983–92).

Socio-economic Indicators:

Constituency Pop. (16-64)	45,803
Claimant Count (May 2003)	2.9% (6.2% below average)
IBA/SDA Claimants	7.8%
Life Expectancy – Male	72.8 (0.6 yrs below average)
Life Expectancy – Female	79.5 (0.8 yrs above average)
Owner Occupied	65.2%
Social Rented	22.6%
Average Property Prices	£60,252 (34th)
Average Gross Income	£23,964 (51st)
Low Birthweight Babies	111 (5.0%)
Teenage Pregnancy Rates	431 (4.9%)
No. of Lone Parent Households	2,910 (9.5%)

CAB Enquiries

Issue	No. of cases	Percentage of total cases (%)
1. Benefits	8079	31.3
2. Consumer	3795	14.7
3. Employment	3390	13.1
4. Other	2955	11.4
5. Housing	2596	10.0

2003 Scottish Parliament Election

Electorate: 55,777   *Turnout*: 28.971 (51.9%)   *Turnout 1999*: 63.4%

Candidate	Party	Votes	Votes%	99 %	Change%
John Farquhar Munro	Lib Dem	12,495	43.1	32.9	+10.2
David Thompson	SNP	5,647	19.5	22.6	– 3.1
Maureen Macmillan	Labour	5,464	18.9	28.6	– 9.7
Jamie McGrigor	Con	3,772	13.0	9.5	+ 3.6
Anne MacLeod	SSP	1,593	5.5	(other 6.5)	–

Liberal Democrat majority: 6,848 (23.6%)   *Swing*: 6.7% SNP to Liberal Democrat

2001 General Election

Electorate: 55,915   *Turnout*: 34,812 (62.3%)

Candidate	Party	Votes	Votes%	Change%
Charles Kennedy	Lib Dem	18,832	54.1	+15.4
Donald Crichton	Labour	5,880	16.9	-11.8
Jean Urquhart	SNP	4,901	14.1	- 5.5
Angus Laing	Con	3,096	8.9	- 2.0
Eleanor Scott	Green	699	2.0	–
Stuart Topp	SSP	683	2.0	–
Philip Anderson	UKIP	456	1.3	–
James Cranford	Country	265	0.8	–

Liberal Democrat majority: 12,952 (37.2%)   *Swing*: 13.6% Labour to Liberal Democrat

1945–97 Westminster

	Lab%	Con%	SNP%	Lib%	Other%	Turnout%
1997	28.7	10.9	19.6	38.7	2.1	71.8
1992	15.3	23.0	18.6	41.6	1.6	73.9
1987	19.1	19.7	11.8	49.4	–	72.7
1983	14.0	33.7	13.8	38.5	–	72.8
1979	20.1	42.4	23.6	13.9	–	76.4
1974O	16.8	38.9	35.7	8.6	–	69.5
1974F	19.8	36.1	23.0	21.1	–	75.1
1970	26.0	33.2	11.7	29.1	–	71.7
1966	30.4	27.6	–	42.0	–	71.2
1964	27.7	32.1	–	40.2	–	69.4
1959	29.1	47.2	–	23.7	–	65.3
1955	37.7	62.3	–	–	–	61.9
1951	35.8	64.2	–	–	–	57.5
1950	37.4	–	–	–	62.6	63.1
1945	37.2	–	–	–	62.8	61.9

Ross, Skye and Inverness West is the largest constituency in the United Kingdom covering a total of nearly two and million acres in which fewer than 56,000 electors live. It stretches from the rugged West Coast to the East Coast and includes the Isle of Skye, the Wester Ross wilderness, Cromarty and the Black Isle and includes a sizeable part of the fast growing capital of the Highlands, Inverness. Average property prices are 10.7 per cent below the national average and increased 45.6 per cent in the 1990s.

The Highlands and Islands have been aided in recent years by funding from the European Union's structural funds, but these will dry up in 2006 and are unlikely to be renewed due to European enlargement into central and eastern Europe. A major issue of local complaint is the high cost of fuel and transport, and there has been much anger about the the privately financed Skye Bridge and the high price of its tolls. In May 2002, campaigners submitted a lengthy petition to the Queen asking her to wave convictions against 125 people who have been prosecuted for not paying the bridge tolls. Lib Dem John Farquhar Munro promised he would back a judicial review of the tolls and in 2003 secured a coalition agreement to remove them.

Another controversy has been over GM trials of oilseed rape at Roskill Farm on the Black Isle. Numerous environmental campaigners have been arrested for repeatedly trying to vandalise the trial site, and in April 2002 the Transport and Environment Committee of the Scottish Parliament narrowly recommended abandoning GM crop trials, but the Scottish Executive has refused to abandon GM trials, claiming it has to tolerate them under European law.

This constituency contains some of the most beautiful and striking countryside anywhere to be found in Scotland. The Highlands are now increasingly a popular tourist and mountain sports destination for international visitors. This seat includes such diverse attractions as Skye's *raison d'etre* – the Red Cuillins and Black Cuillins, the acclaimed Three Chimneys restaurant and Jean Urquhart's wonderfully idiosyncratic Ceilidh Place in Ullapool, scene of many a cultural and political gathering of writers, commentators and thinkers.

As Ross and Cromarty, the constituency has a long Liberal tradition, and a varied, contradictory political history. Liberal or National Liberal for most of the inter-years it was won in a 1936 by-election by Malcolm Macdonald, son of Ramsay Macdonald, standing under the National Labour banner his father had created to legitimise his alliance with the Conservatives. Macdonald won the seat with a 2,982 majority over official Labour, but did not stand in 1945. Instead Jack MacLeod stood as an Independent Liberal and defeated Labour by 4,102 votes. MacLeod was elected as an Independent again in 1950 before taking the National Liberal and Conservative banner in 1951 and representing the seat until 1964.

In 1964 Alistair Mackenzie won the seat for the Liberals from the Conservatives, but in 1970 Hamish Gray regained the seat in Ted Heath's 1970 electoral victory and served as a whip in the Conservative Government. In October 1974 as the SNP surged into a powerful second place, Gray saw his majority reduced to a mere 663 votes, but five years later his majority increased to 4,735 over the Nationalists. Gray then became Minister of State for Energy in the first Thatcher government, but had to cope with not only the emerging unpopularity of Thatcherism north of the border, but boundary changes in 1983 which added the Isle of Skye. Gray faced a 23-year-old Glasgow University graduate called Charles Kennedy who was selected by the Liberal-SDP Alliance at the last minute, and who produced the only Conservative loss in Scotland in 1983 – winning the seat by 1,704 votes as the Alliance vote increased 17.4 per cent on the 1979 notional result. This was the only Social Democrat Party gain in the whole of the 1983 election, excluding former Labour MPs who had switched sides. Kennedy increased his majority to a healthy 11,319 in 1987 and won just under half the vote, which fell to a still comfortable 7,630 in 1992 – on both occasions with the Conservatives in second place.

In May 1997, the seat took its present name as it lost parts of Easter Ross to Caithness and Sutherland, but gained part of Inverness. The UK election of that year was to provide Kennedy with his greatest challenge so far, at the hands of Labour's Donnie Munro, the former Runrig singer. Munro increased Labour's vote by nearly 10 per cent and moved from fourth to second, cutting Kennedy's majority to 4,019, while the Conservatives fell from second to fourth on a mere 11 per cent of the vote. In June 2001, as party leader, Kennedy was emphatically returned as Lib Dem MP for the constituency as his vote increased by 3,400 and 15.4 per cent. This was – Romsey apart, where the Lib Dems had sensationally won a by-election from the Conservatives – the biggest increase in Lib Dem support across the entire United Kingdom. Labour, on the back of their excellent 1997 and 1999 results, went into reverse and lost 5,500 votes and 11.8 per cent of their support. This produced a gigantic 13.6 per cent Labour to Lib Dem swing – which would have been enough nationally to give the Lib Dems a powerful bargaining position with Tony Blair – but instead Kennedy had to be content with his own majority tripled and an all-time post-war high number of Lib Dem colleagues.

In the 1999 Scottish Parliament election, Donnie Munro lost to John Farquhar Munro by a narrower margin of 1,539 votes: an unusual mainland contest between two native Gaelic speakers. Labour's surge of support was partly a result of Donnie Munro's popularity as a candidate, but was also a product of Labour's rural popularity in certain parts of Scotland and the support of the *West Highland Free Press*, a widely-read newspaper on the west coast. Labour polled very well in 1997 in both Inverness seats. At the second Scottish Parliament election, John Farquhar Munro built on Kennedy's success increasing his majority to 6,848 – putting 800 votes and 10.2 per cent on Lib Dem support, while the SNP moved from third to second, despite losing 3.1 per cent, and Labour fell back 9.7 per cent in third place.

In the regional vote, the Lib Dems won 26.7 per cent to the Nationalists 19.7 per cent, with the Greens on an impressive 11 per cent – their highest showing in the Highlands – and SSP on 5 per cent.

Boundary changes for Westminster will see the seat take in Lochaber, Charles Kennedy's home turf, but lose Inverness, creating a seat the Lib Dems would easily hold. At future Scottish Parliament contests, the Lib Dems look relatively secure for the foreseeable future, but Labour's strong showings in 1997 and 1999 show the potential of this seat to throw up surprises.

MSP

JOHN FARQUHAR MUNRO was born in 1934 in Glen Sheil, and educated in Plockton High School and at the Sharpness sea training college in Gloucestershire. He served in the Merchant Navy from 1951-61, then worked in road construction from 1961-65, becoming manager of a contracting company from 1965-75, and then a self-employed quarrying contractor and bus operator from 1975-93. He also ran his croft near Kyle of Lochalsh from 1971-97.

He was a councillor for 33 years, serving on Inverness-shire County Council from 1966-74, on Skye and Lochalsh District Council from 1974-95, where he was council convener from 1984-95, and on Highland Regional Council from 1978-82. He served one term on the unitary Highland Council from 1995-99, where he was Lib Dem group leader, while chair of the roads and transport committee and the Highland Council Rail Network Partnership. In the Scottish Parliament, he became a member of the equal opportunities and rural affairs committees until December 2000, before joining the transport and environment committee in January 2001. He became the Lib Dem spokesperson on Gaelic from 2000, continuing what is one of the less arduous roles after the 2003 election.

Farquhar Munro is an independent-minded Liberal Democrat MSP and was one of only three (with Donald Gorrie and Keith Raffan) who voted against going into coalition with Labour in May 1999. He remained a difficult man for Lib Dem whips to figure out, let alone control, and most Labour colleagues have all but given up even trying to understand his mysterious Highland ways. He has about him the air of a modern-day Lochalsh chieftain; canny, enigmatic, often getting by with a sly wink and a mischievous smile before he disappears behind a cloud of pipe smoke. He is a native and fluent Gaelic speaker and has been an active campaigner for land reform in the Parliament, sponsoring a debate on the sale of the Black Cuillin and pushing the Executive to take a more radical stance on land reform.

He rebelled against the Executive line on fishing boat decommissioning in 2001, contributing to a lost vote, and was one of four Lib Dems in January 2003 to help defeat ministerial plans for changing procedures on the closure of fire stations. In the 2003 coalition agreement, he secured a stronger promise than in 1999 to get rid of Skye Bridge tolls, the most prominent of several constituency transport issues on which he campaigns. Having been on the public petitions committee from 2001, he remained on it after the 2003 election. In March 2004 he was the only Lib Dem MP to rebel when he abstained on a Scottish Executive motion allowing the commercial growing of GM crops – reducing the coalition's majority to a mere one vote. With his wife Celia watching his political patch closely, they are also careful to look after Charles Kennedy's interests, while the Lib Dem leader is busy with UK duties. The two men are politically very close.

MP

CHARLES KENNEDY was born in Inverness in 1959, went to Lochaber High School, Fort William and was first elected to this seat in 1983, as Westminster's youngest MP. He joined the Labour Party at the age of 15, but at Glasgow University decided to join the Social Democrat Party soon after it was formed, partly after hearing Roy Jenkins speak, but also because the Labour Club, unlike the Social Democrats, did not engage in debating. Kennedy was also president of Glasgow University Union, where he became known as 'Taxi Kennedy' due to his propensity to get numerous taxis across the campus, incurring substantial expenses by student standards.

He won the *Observer* Mace debating contest in 1982, was a journalist with BBC Highland in Inverness in 1982 before heading to university in Indiana, and was set to continue his doctoral studies there, until he was told by Kenny Macintyre, a friendly reporter at BBC Highland, that there was a chance of moving the centre party vote from fourth to first place. With only a few weeks to go to the election, he blew the 500 dollars in the bank on a return ticket to get to the selection meeting, spoke at the hustings and was told two weeks later he had won. Macintyre was proven right, as Kennedy unseated Conservative energy minister Hamish Gray by campaigning round the vast constituency with his father, a noted fiddle player, going ahead to provide entertainment whenever the candidate was late for a meeting.

Kennedy has been SDP and Liberal Democrat spokesperson for a range of policy areas. He was Liberal-SDP spokesman on health and social services, as well as Scotland from 1983-87, election spokesman on social security from January to June 1987, Liberal Democrat interim joint spokesman on social security in 1988, trade and industry spokesman 1988-89, health spokesman 1989-92, Europe spokesman 1992-977, followed by agriculture and rural affairs spokesman from 1997-99. He has also been a member of the select committee on social services from 1985-87, the select committee on House of Commons televising in 1998 and the standards and privileges committee from 1997-99.

He was a pro-merger SDP MP when it joined the Liberal Party, and was Liberal Democrat president from 1990-94. He was not particularly close to Paddy Ashdown while the latter was party leader, especially on Ashdown's work with Tony Blair to create an anti-Conservative alliance after the 1997 election, and he distanced himself after Lord Roy Jenkins delivered a fudged report on Commons electoral reform in 1998. Kennedy was one of the more sceptical party MPs about working with Labour, though he made it less obvious than Simon Hughes. When Ashdown stood down in 1999, leaving a lengthy period for party campaigning, Kennedy was favourite from the start in a contest against Hughes, but had to work hard to impress the relatively large party membership in the south of England, and particularly to attack the popular image of 'Chatshow Charlie' making regular, humorous appearances on TV. He won the leadership by 28,425 to Hughes' 21,833, by which time Ashdown's cabinet committee work with the Labour Government was on ice. It remained that way until 2001 when it was finally killed off - helped by the publication of Ashdown's memoirs, showing how far Blair had gone in risking his own party's position.

As Liberal Democrat leader, Kennedy faced what he called a 'devilishly difficult' Westminster election campaign in Scotland in 2001, as for the first time his party was defending a record in government in Scotland but attacking Labour's record at Westminster. The campaign worked very well for the party leader, as voters responded to his laid-back, non-spun, straight-talking style in contrast to the highly-spun Blair and the Conservatives' William Hague, who proved a massive turn-off with voters. Kennedy took much of the credit for the Liberal Democrat group in the Commons rising from 46 to 52, the largest third party presence since 1929. Portraying his party as 'the effective opposition', and careful to avoid talk of displacing the Conservatives as the official Opposition, in 2003 he opposed Blair's moves to war in Iraq, speaking at the massive demonstration in London and leading his party twice into voting against the Government, when the Conservatives were not doing so. The shine began to come off his laid-back leadership after the war began, when he was attacked as an opportunist in voicing support for British troops.

Having been questioned by *Newsnight*'s Jeremy Paxman on his drinking habits – a line of questioning for which the presenter later apologised – malicious attacks were renewed in summer 2003, backed by a whispering campaign against him, as it appeared the strain of leadership was beginning to show, largely focussed on his non-appearance at the Chancellor's major set-piece announcement about the euro currency in June. However, he ended the summer on a high, with a huge Labour majority in Brent East by-election being overturned with a Lib Dem victory only three days before his party conference. A sign of his success as leader was that strong poll ratings contributed to a sense of danger for Conservatives in particular, with Kennedy coming under unusually strong attack in the *Sun* for some of his party's less mainstream policies. Iain Duncan Smith's inept leadership of the Conservatives from 2001-03 provided the Lib Dems with a golden opportunity to make the case for replacing the Conservatives as the official Opposition to Labour, and the ascendancy of Michael Howard to the Conservative leadership may reduce the chances of the Lib Dems gaining ground in the run-up to the next UK election. That became all the more likely in March 2004, when Kennedy's health and 'sociability' again dominated headlines, as a result of a no-show on budget day and a sweaty, uneasy speech at his party's Southport conference.

Roxburgh and Berwickshire

Predecessor Constituencies: created anew in 1983 from Roxburgh, Selkirk and Peebles.

Socio-economic Indicators:

Constituency Pop. (16-64)	35,976
Claimant Count (May 2003)	2.0% (47.4% below average)
IBA/SDA Claimants	7.3%
Life Expectancy – Male	76.0 (2.6 yrs above average)
Life Expectancy – Female	80.8 (2.1 yrs above average)
Owner Occupied	57.8%
Social Rented	25.7%
Average Property Prices	£57,428 (41st)
Average Gross Income	£23,632 (53rd)
Low Birthweight Babies	87 (5.8%)
Teenage Pregnancy Rates	217 (3.2%)
No. of Lone Parent Households	1,938 (7.4%)

CAB Enquiries

Issue	No. of cases	Percentage of total cases (%)
1. Benefits	1311	31.3
2. Consumer	743	17.8
3. Employment	722	17.3
4. Housing	354	8.5
5. Other	342	8.2

2003 Scottish Parliament Election

Electorate: 45,625   Turnout: 22,511 (49.3%)   Turnout 1999: 58.5%

Candidate	Party	Votes	Votes%	99 %	Change%
Euan Robson	Lib Dem	9,280	41.2	40.6	+ 0.6
Sandy Scott	Con	6,790	30.2	27.8	+ 2.4
Roderick Campbell	SNP	2,816	12.5	16.9	– 4.4
Simon Held	Labour	2,802	12.4	14.7	– 2.3
Graeme McIver	SSP	823	3.7	–	–

Liberal Democrat majority: 2,490 (11.1%)   Swing: 0.9% Liberal Democrat to Conservative

2001 General Election

Electorate: 47,515   *Turnout*: 28,797 (60.6%)

Candidate	Party	Votes	Votes%	Change%
Archy Kirkwood	Lib Dem	14,044	48.8	+ 2.3
George Turnbull	Con	6,533	22.7	– 1.2
Catherine Maxwell-Stuart	Labour	4,498	15.6	+ 0.7
Roderick Campbell	SNP	2,806	9.7	– 1.6
Amanda Millar	SSP	463	1.6	–
Peter Nelson	UK Ind	453	1.6	+ 1.0

Liberal Democrat majority: 7,511 (26.1%)   *Swing*: 1.7% Conservative to Liberal Democrat

1983–97 Westminster

	Lab%	Con%	SNP%	Lib%	Other%	Turnout%
1997	15.0	23.9	11.3	46.5	3.3	73.9
1992	8.6	34.3	10.2	46.9	–	77.6
1987	8.8	37.2	4.8	49.2	–	76.8
1983	7.4	39.6	2.7	50.3	–	75.0

Roxburgh and Berwickshire is a predominantly rural constituency covered in part by the Southern Uplands and much farmland along with the Borders towns of Hawick, Jedburgh, Melrose and Kelso – famous for their ancient abbeys and rugby teams. The seat was created from the division of David Steel's old seat, Roxburgh, Selkirk and Peebles, into two seats in the 1983 boundary redistribution. Steel chose to stand in the Tweeddale, Ettrick and Lauderdale seat and Archy Kirkwood in Roxburgh and Berwickshire.

The most important political issue in this area in recent years has been the controversy over Scottish Borders Council's education cuts. The council initially proposed massive cuts of £5.9 million, sparking widespread local opposition and campaigns which led to the council withdrawing cuts in curriculum support for primary schools and outdoor education services. Its plans to hand over seven swimming pools to private firms also met with massive opposition and anger and had to be withdrawn. Feelings heightened in February 2002 when the council proposed a 10 per cent council tax increase and cuts of £5.5 million, including education services, which had been reprieved. This resulted in a vote of confidence in the council leader, Drew Tulley, and his subsequent resignation, and then replacement by John Ross Scott, a Liberal Democrat who formed an alliance with the SNP. In the 2003 elections, the Conservatives made sweeping gains across the council – with Independents gaining 30.4 per cent of the vote to the Conservatives 28.6 per cent, Lib Dems 26.3 per cent and SNP's 11.5 per cent. The Conservatives ended up with ten seats, gaining a net total of seven from the other three main political groupings and an Independent/Conservative coalition has been formed.

This part of the Borders has the tweed, cashmere and knitwear industries as large employers, and in February 2000 there was local and national anxiety when the Pringle business was sold by Dawson International to the Hong Kong based Fang Brothers Knitting Ltd for £10 million. Pringle is still an internationally recognised and successful brand, but the firm employs fewer and fewer people in the constituency. It used to employ 2,000, but now employs fewer than 300. In 2002, the Hawick based cashmere firm, Tendrahealth, went into liquidation as a result of falling orders.

Farming has been particularly hit by BSE and the foot and mouth outbreak with the area severely affected by the draconian restrictions imposed on the movement of livestock. Further local jobs could also be lost by the Scottish Parliament's decision to outlaw fox hunting in the Wild Mammals (Scotland) Act 2002. The Borders is a traditionally strong fox hunting area with five major Borders hunts including the Buccleuch hunt of the Duke and Duchess of Roxburghe. There are also concerns about how cross-border hunts such as the Otterburn Hunt will be managed while the law is different north and south of the border.

In December 2001 Scottish Borders tenants voted in a Housing Stock Transfer ballot to transfer their homes from local authority control to a not-for-profit housing association with the promise of greater investment and Scottish Executive support. There is a scarcity of affordable housing in large parts of the constituency, particularly small villages and rural areas. Proposed property developments often met opposition from conservation campaigners. For instance, in 2002, Rivertree Developments announced plans to build 300 new houses on the site of a former psychiatric hospital by Dingleton, increasing the local community by 50 per cent and putting a strain on existing public services.

Roxburgh and Berwickshire's creation saw an intriguing contest in 1983 between Archy Kirkwood, the Liberal-SDP Alliance candidate and the Conservative Iain Sproat, who was MP for Aberdeen South and had assessed the Borders seat was a safer prospect after boundary changes. This was a complete misjudgment as the Conservatives held Aberdeen South, while Kirkwood defeated Sproat by 3,396 votes. Kirkwood then marginally increased his majority over the Conservatives to 4,008 in 1987 and 4,257 in 1992.

In 1997, Kirkwood increased his majority to 7,906. As the Lib Dem vote rose marginally in numbers and percentage, the Conservatives declined by 3,000 and Labour moved from fourth to third, picking up 2,000 in their support. In June 2001, Kirkwood was returned with a 7,511 majority over the Conservatives who returned their lowest vote ever in the seat.

The 1999 Scottish Parliament election resulted in the Lib Dems winning the seat with a 3,585 majority over the Conservatives – the Lib Dem vote fell by 5,000, while the Conservatives slipped by 500 and the SNP rose by 1,000 moving into third ahead of Labour. The Lib Dems' victory with 40.6 per cent was the lowest vote they have achieved in five contests in the seat, while the Conservative share in 1999 was the first time their vote rose in percentage terms. The May 2003 Scottish Parliament contest saw Euan Robson re-elected with a reduced majority of 2,490, as Sandy Scott increased the Conservatives vote. In the regional list vote, the Conservatives won 28.4 per cent to the Lib Dems 26.7 per cent – a Conservative lead of 425 – with the Greens on 7.6 per cent and SSP on 3.6 per cent.

Roxburgh and Berwickshire, in its twenty-year history, has displayed an impressive loyalty to the Liberal Democrats, and has become in recent Westminster and Scottish Parliament elections much more secure than the neighbouring Tweeddale, Ettrick and Lauderdale. Boundary changes for future Westminster elections will see the creation of an enlarged Berwickshire, Roxburgh and Selkirk which would take the latter from Tweeddale, Ettrick and Lauderdale and be even safer Lib Dem territory, although the other Lib Dem Border seat will disappear. At future Scottish Parliament contests, the Lib Dems are in a weaker position than at Westminster elections and the Conservatives have recovered slightly in the 1999 and 2003 elections. The Tories can take heart from their recovery and strong showing on the 2003 regional list vote.

MSP

EUAN ROBSON was born in 1954 in Corbridge, Northumberland, and schooled at Trinity College, Glenalmond, before studying history at the University of Newcastle-upon-Tyne, and then Strathclyde

University, gaining a masters degree in political science. He worked as a teacher at the King Edward VI School, Morpeth, from 1976–79, was deputy secretary of the Gas Consumers' Northern Council from 1981–86, and Scottish manager of the Gas Consumers' Council from 1986–99, where he had a public profile in providing the consumers' voice at times of privatised Scottish Gas and Transco controversies. Robson was also a councillor on Northumberland County Council from 1981–89 and was secretary to the council's Liberal-SDP Alliance Group from 1981–87. He contested the Northumberland seat of Hexham in 1983 and 1987.

Elected to the Scottish Parliament in 1999, he was Lib Dem spokesperson for rural affairs and team leader on fisheries until the start of 2001, when he became spokesperson on justice. He steered through one of the first member's bills, allowing civil marriages to take place outside registry offices, and was one of the Lib Dem Borders MSPs and MPs fighting to protect the cashmere industry from punitive trade tariffs through the so-called Banana Wars between the US and EU. After starting on both audit and justice committees until December 2000, he then uniquely served on both justice 1 and 2 committees until the call came to occupy one of the Lib Dems' four first-term ministerial posts. That was in March 2001, with the resignation of deputy Parliament minister Tavish Scott, over a constituency clash with Executive policy on fisheries. In his new role, Robson deputised first for Tom McCabe and then Patricia Ferguson, taking a very low public profile perhaps because he is not one of the great media communicators, but at least enjoying less troublesome times than his two predecessors in whipping the Lib Dem group. While representing the Lib Dems on the Parliamentary Bureau, he did much of the unglamorous work handling the legislative programme and managing cross-cutting policies as well as assisting with strategic communications. After the 2003 election, he was shifted to become deputy minister for schools and young people, with Peter Peacock his boss at cabinet level.

A keen angler around his Kelso home, he is also an expert on Scottish art. He authored *George Houston: Nature's Limner*, which was published in 1997, and he contributed to *Kirkcudbright: One Year: An Artist's Colony*, published in 2000.

MP

SIR ARCHY KIRKWOOD was born in 1946 in Glasgow and has been MP for Roxburgh and Berwickshire since 1983. Educated at Cranhill School and Heriot-Watt University, he qualified as a pharmacist and then as a solicitor. A supporter of nuclear disarmament, he joined the Labour Party in the late 1960s and was a branch secretary and delegate to the UK annual conference in 1970, leaving it the following year because he found it 'too right-wing'. He then worked as an aide to David Steel MP from 1971–75 and 1977–78, while in between he was youth campaign director of Britain in Europe at the time of the 1975 referendum.

Kirkwood was Liberal spokesman on health and social sciences from 1985–87, Liberal-SDP Alliance spokesman on overseas development in 1987, and Scottish whip from 1987–88. In 1988, he lost a contest with Malcolm Bruce for leadership of the Scottish Liberal Democrats, by 2,690 to 1,396 votes. He became the party's convener on welfare, health and education from 1988–89, deputy chief whip and spokesman on welfare and social security from 1989–92, chief whip from 1993–97 and spokesman on community care from 1994–97. He has been Liberal Democrat social security spokesperson from 1997 and chair of the social security select committee 1997-2001, and its successor work and pensions select committee following the 2001 election, being an assiduous tabler of written questions on the subject and building up an expertise which has won him admirers. In 1998, he welcomed the thrust of Labour's welfare strategy, then shifted to say the Government was rushing complex changes. That backbench seniority helps explain the rare case of an opposition MP knighthood, awarded in the 2003 New Year honours list, for services to Parliament.

Stirling

Predecessor Constituencies: Stirlingshire West (1945–79), Stirling, Falkirk and Grangemouth (1974–79) and Stirling and Falkirk Burghs (1945–71).

Socio-economic Indicators:

Constituency Pop. (16-64)	45,333
Claimant Count (May 2003)	2.3% (25.1% below average)
IBA/SDA Claimants	8.3%
Life Expectancy – Male	75.5 (2.1 yrs above average)
Life Expectancy – Female	79.7 (1.0 yr above average)
Owner Occupied	68.1%
Social Rented	21.3%
Average Property Prices	£92,145 (7th)
Average Gross Income	£28,417 (11th)
Low Birthweight Babies	106 (5.1%)
Teenage Pregnancy Rates	324 (3.8%)
No. of Lone Parent Households	2,632 (8.9%)

CAB Enquiries

Issue	No. of cases	Percentage of total cases (%)
1. Benefits	1510	27.8
2. Consumer	1360	25.0
3. Employment	917	16.9
4. Housing	466	8.6
5. Legal	355	6.5

2003 Scottish Parliament Election

Electorate: 52,087   *Turnout*: 29,647 (56.9%)   *Turnout 1999*: 67.7%

Candidate	Party	Votes	Votes%	99 %	Change%
Sylvia Jackson	Labour	10,661	36.0	37.8	– 1.8
Brian Monteith	Con	7,781	26.2	25.6	+ 0.7
Bruce Crawford	SNP	5,645	19.0	26.7	– 7.6
Edward Kenyon Wright	Lib Dem	3,432	11.6	9.5	+ 2.1
Margaret Stewart	SSP	1,486	5.0	(other 0.4)	
Keith Harding	SPA	642	2.2		

Labour majority: 2,880 (9.7%)   *Swing*: 1.3% Labour to Conservative

2001 General Election

Electorate: 53,097   *Turnout*: 35,930 (67.7%)

Candidate	Party	Votes	Votes%	Change%
Anne McGuire	Labour	15,175	42.2	- 5.2
Geoff Mawdsley	Con	8,901	24.8	- 7.8
Fiona Macauley	SNP	5,877	16.4	+ 3.0
Clive Freeman	Lib Dem	4,208	11.7	+ 5.5
Clarke Mullen	SSP	1,012	2.8	–
Mark Ruskell	Green	757	2.1	–

Labour majority: 6,274 (17.5%)   *Swing*: 1.3% Conservative to Labour

1983–97 Westminster

	Lab%	Con%	SNP%	Lib%	Other%	Turnout%
1997	47.5	32.5	13.4	6.2	0.5	81.8
1992	38.5	40.0	13.7	7.0	0.8	82.3
1987	36.5	37.8	10.7	14.9	–	78.1
1983	27.9	40.0	8.2	23.9	–	75.7

Stirling and Falkirk Burghs (1945–71); Stirling, Falkirk and Grangemouth (1974–79)

	Lab%	Con%	SNP%	Lib%	Other%	Turnout%
1979	56.5	26.6	16.9	–	–	78.9
1974O	43.2	14.1	39.8	2.9	–	79.4
1974F	41.9	23.6	34.5	–	–	81.2
1971B	46.5	18.9	34.6	–	–	60.0
1970	50.7	34.8	14.5	–	–	73.1
1966	52.7	31.2	14.4	–	1.7	77.1
1964	52.4	37.6	10.0	–	–	79.9
1959	49.6	43.8	6.6	–	–	81.1
1955	48.2	45.1	6.7	–	–	79.7
1951	52.3	47.7	–	–	–	86.1
1950	49.0	45.5	3.7	–	1.8	84.4
1948B	49.0	42.8	8.2	–	–	72.9
1945	56.1	43.9	–	–	–	71.5

Stirlingshire West (1945–79)

	Lab%	Con%	SNP%	Lib%	Other%	Turnout%
1979	47.7	25.7	18.3	8.3	–	82.0
1974O	39.0	18.4	38.2	4.4	–	80.7
1974F	40.8	29.5	29.7	–	–	82.7
1970	48.9	29.7	21.4	–	–	79.0
1966	48.6	25.4	26.6	–	–	82.4
1964	58.8	41.2	–	–	–	81.2

cont'd

1959	57.5	42.5	–	–	–	83.6
1955	54.6	45.4	–	–	–	80.4
1951	56.0	44.0	–	–	–	86.7
1950	55.6	44.4	–	–	–	85.7
1945	54.4	45.6	–	–	–	75.0

The Stirling constituency includes the town of Stirling, which became Scotland's sixth city in 2002, marking the Queen's Jubilee and defeating competition from Paisley, Dumfries and Ayr. It also includes a hinterland of 800 square miles ranging from the banks of Loch Lomond in the west to the Trossachs, including Loch Katrine and Loch Tay. There are numerous small towns and villages including Aberfoyle, Callander, the inspiration for Tannochbrae in the legendary *Dr Finlay's Casebook*, Doune, Dunblane, Killin and Lochearnhead.

The constituency contains some of the most powerful and potent symbols of Scottish history and identity. Dominating the Forth Valley is Stirling Castle which proudly sits on top of a massive outcrop of basalt rock with clear views across the river plain for miles. Daniel Defoe compared Stirling Castle to Windsor, viewing it 'more than Windsor in strength and somewhat less in greatness', while the editor of Fullarton's 1843 Gazetteer was reminded of 'Athens, Golcondah [in India] and the old town of Edinburgh'. The other striking attraction is the Wallace Monument which was built in the 1860s on the nearby Abbey Craig in recognition of one of Scotland's most important and romanticised patriots. Numerous famous battles took place in this strategically important terrain – at Stirling Bridge Wallace defeated numerically superior English forces in 1297 and at Bannockburn Robert the Bruce defeated the English in 1314. These sites are part of Scotland's heritage industry, with a visitor centre nearby the Bannockburn battle site which is visited by vast numbers of international tourists.

Stirling is one of the most prosperous parts of Scotland. Average property prices are 36.6 per cent above the national average and increased 71.1 per cent in the 1990s. The Stirling economy in recent years succeeded in attracting a host of new businesses into the area aided by the opening in 1996 of Stirling Castle Business Park. Scottish Amicable, the Bank of Bermuda and Scotia Pharmaceuticals have located there, as has the Scottish Environment Protection Agency (SEPA). A major controversy arose in September 2001 when St Mary's Episcopal Primary School in Dunblane – one of only two Scottish schools to use the Conservative government's self-governing legislation – was returned by the Scottish Executive to local authority control, despite the opposition of parents and local groups. Dunblane, sadly became internationally infamous on 13 March 1996 when Thomas Hamilton entered Dunblane Primary School and shot dead 16 schoolchildren, leading to legislation being passed banning handguns.

Prior to the creation of the Stirling seat the area was represented by Stirling and Falkirk, which was first won by Labour in 1922 and represented by Joseph Westwood from 1935 – Attlee's first Secretary of State for Scotland from 1945-47 – until his death in 1948. Malcolm MacPherson won the seat for Labour in an October 1948 by-election with a narrow 2,175 majority over the Unionists, and represented the area until his death in May 1971. At the subsequent by-election in September 1971, Labour's Harry Ewing faced a strong challenge from the Nationalist Robert McIntyre, the previous victor in the 1945 Motherwell by-election. McIntyre's campaign, a year before the launch of the 'It's Scotland's Oil' campaign, saw the SNP slash Ewing's majority and the beginning of the SNP's second wave of the 1970s.

In February 1974, boundary changes meant the seat became Stirling, Falkirk and Grangemouth, and Ewing held the seat in October of that year with a 1,766 over the irrepressible McIntyre, but this expanded to a much more comfortable 15,618 over the Conservatives in 1979, with the SNP reduced to third place. Further boundary changes in 1983 saw parts of Stirling, Falkirk and Grangemouth, along with sizeable sections of Stirlingshire West and Kinross and West Perthshire create a new and highly marginal seat of Stirling. The 1979 notional result put the Conservatives ahead of Labour by 1.6 per cent, and Ewing drew the appropriate lesson and moved to nearby Falkirk East. In the event Michael Forsyth, a young, intelligent and right-wing Conservative won the seat against Michael Connarty, then leader of Stirling Council, by the relatively large margin of 5,133 votes and 12.1 per cent.

Forsyth became Mrs. Thatcher's favourite Scottish Conservative, in her own words, 'the real powerhouse for Thatcherism at the Scottish Office', as well as in folklore a popular hate figure of the Scottish chattering classes. In 1987, in a rematch with Connarty he held on by the margin of 548 votes as Labour's vote rose by 8.4 per cent, and in 1992 he widened his lead over Labour's Kate Phillips to 703 votes, as both main parties increased their support by 2,000 votes. His success was in part due to his assiduous work as a local MP as well as his ability to mobilise support in the rural areas, small towns and the Conservative parts of Stirling. The 1997 Labour landslide was to overwhelm Forsyth, despite his prominence as Secretary of State for Scotland and his belated attempts to humanise the public face of Scottish Toryism. Forsyth was one of three Cabinet ministers to lose their seats in Scotland on 1 May – the others being Malcolm Rifkind and Ian Lang, both of whom had also served as Secretaries of State for Scotland. Labour's candidate – Anne McGuire – chosen early from an all-women shortlist to allow her to focus her energy and time campaigning – won with a 6,411 majority over Forsyth, the largest victory yet seen in the new seat of Stirling on an impressive 81.8 per cent turnout, the highest in Scotland and third highest in the United Kingdom. In June 2001, McGuire held this once-proud Conservative seat with a majority of 6,274, as Labour's vote fell by 5,000 and the Conservatives by 5,000, with the Lib Dems and SNP both gaining votes. In the 1999 Scottish Parliament election, Labour's Sylvia Jackson easily won the seat despite Labour's vote falling by nearly 10 per cent, as the SNP's Annabelle Ewing surged into second place, increasing her party's support by 13.3 per cent. That produced a Labour majority of 3,981. The Conservatives, despite a high profile candidate in Brian Monteith, managed to come a disappointing third with their vote falling back to 25.6 per cent in a seat where until recently they had prided themselves on their organisation and ability to get their vote out. The May 2003 Scottish Parliament election saw Jackson returned for Labour with a slightly reduced majority of 2,880, Monteith moved up to second place, more because of the fall in the SNP vote than any inroads he was able to make. Keith Harding, a Conservative list MSP for Mid-Scotland and Fife and ex-leader of Stirling Council, defected to the right-wing populist Scottish Peoples' Alliance, but failed to impress, securing 642 votes. In the regional vote list, Labour won 25 per cent to the Conservatives 23.9 per cent – a Labour lead of 329 – with the Greens on 10.6 per cent and SSP 4.7 per cent.

Stirling has become a safe Labour seat at Westminster since Labour's emphatic triumph in 1997 and should look to remain so in future elections despite boundary changes for Westminster which will enlarge the seat, taking in voters from the old Ochil seat but not changing its fundamental political character. At the Scottish Parliament, it is less securely Labour with the Conservatives decent showing in 2003 giving them hope that that may be able to mount a serious challenge. They cite as grounds for optimism that this is a seat where they managed to defy the predictions and resist the incoming anti-Tory tides of the 1980s and 1990s much longer than anyone thought possible. Conservative supporters believe that when Labour becomes more unpopular at a Scottish and UK level, they will have a chance of winning.

MSP

SYLVIA JACKSON was born in 1946 in Lincolnshire and schooled at Brigg High School for Girls. She is a chemistry and education graduate of Hull University, with a PhD in education from Stirling University. She was a chemistry teacher, education researcher and lecturer, before her election, at Moray

House teacher training college and an adviser in Lothian and Edinburgh. She remained an adviser with Clackmannanshire Sports Council, listing running and walking as her main leisure pursuits. She was formerly chair and secretary of Central Region Labour Party, a member of the Scottish Policy Forum, and chair of Labour's local government committee in Scotland.

She continued that interest as deputy convener of the Parliament's local government committee from 2000-03, joining the local government and transport as well as subordinate legislation committees after being re-elected. She was also convener of the cross-party group on renewable energy in the first Parliament. Jackson was an unpaid ministerial aide to health minister Malcolm Chisholm, appointed in 2001. Despite being one of the best qualified MSPs in any party, with her particular skills as an educational researcher, along with exhibiting no sign of marked rebelliousness or awkwardness, the ever-cheerful MSP has been repeatedly passed over for ministerial office.

MP

ANNE McGUIRE was born in 1949 in Glasgow and educated at Our Lady of St Francis Secondary School, Glasgow, Glasgow University, where she studied politics and history, and later Notre Dame College of Education in Glasgow. She worked from 1971-74 in Glasgow University administration, then from 1983-85 as a secondary teacher, from 1985-93 she was development officer of Community Service Volunteers, becoming its Scottish national officer from 1988-93, and then deputy director of the Scottish Council for Voluntary Organisations from 1993-97. She joined Labour in 1967, at a time of unpopularity in Government and when the SNP was breaking through across Scotland. She was a Strathclyde Regional Councillor from 1980-82 and was shortlisted for a number of seats, including the Govan by-election in 1988, finding her obvious talent was overlooked in favour of male candidates – disastrously in the case of Govan. McGuire was election agent to Norman Hogg in Cumbernauld and Kilsyth in the 1983, 1987 and 1992 elections, became a member of the Scottish Labour executive from 1984-97, and was chair of the party from 1992-93.

She was also one of three candidates for consideration as Labour's Scottish general secretary after the 1992 election defeat, the others being Johann Lamont and Jack McConnell, with the latter appointed. There was widespread criticism of the appointment at the time, because two able women had been passed over and Scottish Labour was having severe problems selecting women candidates in winnable seats.

When she was finally selected in Stirling, it was from an all-female shortlist. She was identified as one of the leading figures in 'The Network', seen by some on the left of the party as a sinister organisation, but by its supporters as an attempt to bring Blairite modernisation to the party north of the border. After the 1997 election, this became known as Scottish Labour Forum, and her loyalty sometimes became sycophancy, as with the Commons question: 'Does the Prime Minister recognise that our emphasis over the past year on the economy, health and education has kept faith with the voters?'

At Westminster, she was a member of the European legislation committee from 1997-98 and was Parliamentary Private Secretary to Donald Dewar at the Scottish Office from 1997-98. She became an assistant whip in 1998-2001, a whip from 2001-02, and then replaced George Foulkes at the Scotland Office as deputy to Helen Liddell, taking rather less of the flak than her boss in the struggle to justify their workload. With Liddell's departure in the 2003 summer re-shuffle, McGuire found herself in the odd position of being deputy to two Cabinet ministers; Alistair Darling, who was Scotland Secretary while based at the Department of Transport, and Lord Falconer at the newly-created Department for Constitutional Affairs. That left her likely to be a key figure in the amendment of the Scotland Act to retain the number of MSPs at 129.

Strathkelvin and Bearsden

Predecessor Constituencies: Dumbarton District of Burghs (1945) and Dunbartonshire East (1950–79).

Socio-economic Indicators:

Constituency Pop. (16–64)	52,401
Claimant Count (May 2003)	2.0% (37.0% below average)
IBA/SDA Claimants	6.8%
Life Expectancy – Male	76.2 (2.8 yrs above average)
Life Expectancy – Female	80.3 (1.6 yrs above average)
Owner Occupied	79.6%
Social Rented	16.4%
Average Property Prices	£81,974 (12th)
Average Gross Income	£30,581 (8th)
Low Birthweight Babies	103 (5.3%)
Teenage Pregnancy Rates	273 (2.4%)
No. of Lone Parent Households	3,006 (9.5%)

CAB Enquiries

Issue	No. of cases	Percentage of total cases (%)
1. Consumer	1639	23.4
2. Benefits	1585	22.6
3. Employment	1060	15.1
4. Other	911	13.0
5. Housing	635	9.1

2003 Scottish Parliament Election

Electorate: 61,905 *Turnout*: 35,336 (57.1%) *Turnout 1999*: 67.2%

Candidate	Party	Votes	Votes%	99 %	Change%
Jean Turner	Ind	10,988	31.1	(other 1.0)	–
Brian Fitzpatrick	Labour	10,550	29.9	50.7	–20.9
Joanne Swinson	Lib Dem	4,950	14.0	9.8	+ 4.2
Fiona McLeod	SNP	4,846	13.7	22.1	– 8.4
Rory O'Brien	Con	4,002	11.3	16.4	– 5.0

Independent majority: 438 (1.2%) *Swing*: n/a

2001 General Election

Electorate: 62,829   *Turnout*: 41,486 (66.0%)

Candidate	Party	Votes	Votes%	Change%
John Lyons	Labour	19,250	46.4	– 6.5
Gordon Macdonald	Lib Dem	7,533	18.2	+ 8.4
Calum Smith	SNP	6,675	16.1	– 0.2
Murray Roxburgh	Con	6,635	16.0	– 4.1
Willie Telfer	SSP	1,393	3.4	–

Labour majority: 11,717 (28.2%)   *Swing*: 7.4% Labour to Liberal Democrat

1945–2001

Scottish Parliament

	Lab%	Con%	SNP%	Lib%	Other%	Turnout%
2001B	37.0	12.1	15.5	17.2	18.2	66.2
1999	50.7	16.4	22.1	9.8	1.0	67.2

Westminster

	Lab%	Con%	SNP%	Lib%	Other%	Turnout%
1997	52.9	20.1	16.3	9.7	1.0	71.0
1992	42.3	36.0	12.5	9.1	0.2	82.3
1987	38.1	33.4	7.1	21.4	–	82.1
1983	25.6	36.4	9.2	28.7	–	79.3
1979	37.8	34.1	20.6	7.5	–	83.
1974O	30.3	31.2	31.2	7.3	–	80.7
1974F	29.6	36.7	22.3	11.4	–	85.0
1970	44.7	37.0	11.3	4.7	2.3	77.8
1966	52.2	36.4	9.0	–	2.4	80.6
1964	55.0	42.0	–	–	3.0	82.5
1959	51.1	44.9	–	–	4.0	84.2
1955	48.7	46.4	–	–	4.9	81.6
1951	51.3	44.6	–	–	4.1	86.6
1950	52.6	43.4	–	4.0	–	86.0
1945	65.2	34.8	–	–	–	73.2

Strathkelvin and Bearsden is situated north of Glasgow, and along with Eastwood to the south of the city is the main middle class commuter centre of the West of Scotland. Its main middle class centre is Bearsden, while the towns of Bishopbriggs and Kirkintilloch are more working class.

The middle class part of this constituency is very prosperous with a large number of people travelling into the Glasgow city area to work in professional and managerial jobs in a variety of sectors – working in the city and using its services, but choosing to live outside and not contribute to the city's council tax revenue. The working class side of the constituency is less reliant on commuting and more on local employment, with the major employer in the seat being the health service. Kirkintilloch town centre was recently voted by the architectural magazine *Unlimited* the most 'dismal town centre in Scotland'. The constituency has 79.6 per cent owner-occupation – the second highest in the country after Eastwood. Average property prices are 21.5 per cent above the national average and rose 43.3 per cent in the 1990s.

The constituency has been dominated politically in recent years by the future of Stobhill Hospital – which is actually located in Glasgow Springburn, but is used by many residents of Strathkelvin and Bearden. Greater Glasgow Health Board decided to downgrade acute services at Stobhill while orthopaedic services were transferred from it to the Glasgow Royal Infirmary. At the same time there were also plans to site a medium security unit for sex offenders at Stobhill which met with widespread local opposition including a 43,000 strong petition, but were given approval in January 2002. All of this triggered Jean Turner's independent candidature in the June 2001 Scottish Parliament by-election and ultimate victory in the May 2003 Scottish Parliament election. Other major local issues have included the closure of Low Moss Prison in Bishopbriggs which is a medium-secure unit housing prisoners on remand or at the end of their sentences. Plans are afoot to demolish the current facilities and build a new privately run prison.

This seat was first the Dumbarton District of Burghs and won by the ILP campaigner David Kirkwood in 1922 and was even held by Labour in its wipeout of 1931 when Kirkwood held on by 997 votes. The constituency became Dunbartonshire East in 1950 and was won by Kirkwood for the first and last time that year, before C. R. Bence won it in October 1951 with a 3,426 majority over the Unionists. Bence represented the seat until 1970 when Hugh McCartney won it for Labour only to lose it to the Conservative Barry Henderson in a three-way split with the Nationalist. Henderson was MP for just over seven months, as in October 1974 the SNP's Margaret Bain – later to become Margaret Ewing, MP and MSP for Moray – took the seat in an even tighter three-way contest, where the main candidates were 429 votes apart. Bain won with a 22 vote margin over Henderson and achieved victory on a perilous 31.2 per cent of the vote. There was little chance of Bain holding the seat in the climate of the 1979 election debacle the Nationalists experienced, but Labour retook the seat after the twin defeats of 1974. Norman Hogg achieved a 2,324 majority over the Conservative Michael Hirst, with Bain in a distant third place.

In 1983, the constituency became a much more Conservative seat called Strathkelvin and Bearsden and Hogg decided to decamp to the safer Cumbernauld and Kilsyth. The new seat was won by Hirst with a 3,700 majority over the Liberal-SDP Alliance with Labour reduced to third place, and Margaret Bain, the previous MP reduced to fourth place and less than one-tenth of the vote.

Four years later, 1987 was Scottish Labour's year of triumph and neurologist Sam Galbraith defeated Hirst with a majority of 2,452. This showed the difference between 'Bearsden man' and 'Basildon man' – Scottish Labour's ability to win middle-class support versus the inability of English Labour, particularly in the South, to win significant numbers of middle class voters. In 1992 Galbraith broke the pattern of volatility, holding the seat with an increased majority of 3,162 over the Conservatives. The 1997 boundary changes increased Labour's majority to a notional 6,948, and in the 1997 election Galbraith was returned with a vastly increased majority of 16,292 over the Conservatives. Labour's vote rose by 2,500, while the Conservatives fell by nearly 7,000.

Galbraith was the Labour candidate in the 1999 Scottish Parliament election and saw a 5,000 fall in Labour's vote, while the Nationalists moved from third to second place, their vote increasing by more than 1,000. Labour's majority over the SNP was an impressive 12,121, and Galbraith became a prominent figure in the first Executive administration. In the June 2001, UK election John Lyons who had been chosen to replace Sam Galbraith for Labour at Westminster, was returned with an 11,717 majority. The Lib Dems moved from fourth to second and doubled their vote in percentage terms, with the SNP in third, forty votes ahead of the Conservatives – who had held the seat only 16 years before.

It looked as if Strathkelvin and Bearsden was making that well-worn shift into becoming a safe Labour seat, but even as Lyons celebrated his victory, movements were occurring which were to challenge Labour's hold on the seat. In a 2001 by-election for the Scottish Parliament, Labour candidate Brian Fitzpatrick, an ex-adviser to Donald Dewar, saw the party's majority fall to 7,829 and Jean Turner, a retired local GP finish, second on the issue of closing services at Stobhill Hospital. Turner polled 7,572 or 18.2 per cent, narrowly finishing ahead of the Lib Dems and SNP.

This was a warning Labour chose to ignore over the next two years. Fitzpatrick's personal style seemed to grate on voters, while Jean Turner began putting together a more serious and organised campaign as feelings about Stobhill and other health service changes intensified. Turner put another 3,500 votes on her by-election support, while Labour vote fell by a further 4,500 – representing a total fall of 21 per cent since 1999 – giving Turner a famous victory by 438 votes. After her victory, Turner drew a broader lesson from her victory, 'I think there is a move afoot where people are beginning to realise they should stand up for themselves and not be bullied by a minority government.'

In the regional list vote, without any Jean Turner campaign, Labour won 31.4 per cent – only 1.5 per cent above Fitzpatrick's constituency vote – while the Conservatives finished second with 16.2 per cent, while the Greens won 6.7 per cent and SSP 6.5 per cent

Strathkelvin and Bearsden has become in a relatively short time a safe Labour seat at Westminster, despite the fact that is not natural territory for Labour. However, in the 1980s and early 1990s Scottish Labour was able to appeal successfully to middle class voters as the defender of the public good against Thatcherism and position itself on the national question. Boundary changes for Westminster would see the creation of a new seat called East Dunbartonshire, where Labour will have to fight off the Conservatives and Lib Dems, who are putting down roots in the council. The fragility of Labour's hold on this seat has been revealed by Jean Turner. What this seems to indicate is that at a Scottish Parliament level, the fortuitous circumstances which produced Scottish Labour's broad coalition in the 1980s are coming to an end in places which came late to it. Voters no longer see Labour as automatically the defenders of the public sector, and are more ambiguous in how they see the national question. Strathkelvin and Bearsden's recent results could herald a shift in Scottish politics where Labour is viewed as the incumbent and punished as a result when voters see fit.

MSP

JEAN TURNER was born in Glasgow in 1939, and educated at Hillhead High School, Glasgow, before studying medicine at Aberdeen University. She worked for ten years in hospital medicine in Glasgow and Aberdeen, including six years at Glasgow's Southern General and eight years as an anaesthetist. For 25 years, she was a GP in Springburn, Glasgow. She also did some part-time vocational studies tutoring for Glasgow University medical students.

She entered politics in retirement and by an unorthodox route, protesting at the downgrading of Stobhill Hospital. She chose to highlight the issue with an independent candidacy in the by-election caused by the mid-term retirement of Sam Galbraith from Strathkelvin and Bearsden, scaring the Labour Party by winning 7,000 votes after only three weeks of campaigning, coming second to Labour's Brian Fitzpatrick.

Hospital issues have become more of an issue in politics across Glasgow (also bringing former Lord Provost Pat Lally out of retirement to stand against Mike Watson in Glasgow Cathcart on the hospital closures issue), and candidates stood to protest closures in Dunfermline constituencies and Mid-Scotland and Fife list as well. In October 2002, Turner announced she would stand again at the 2003 election in the same constituency. There were expectations that the different style of a general election would disadvantage her, but she received favourable local media publicity, and astonished Labour by defeating Fitzpatrick.

Once elected, she won a place on the health committee, and admitted she had to find out what other issues matter, alighting first on Scottish Water and the lack of leisure facilities in her constituency. She sits in the chamber as an ominous reminder of three things; what major party MSPs can expect if they fail to listen to constituents, the ability of insurgent political forces to unseat those in power at a time of growing antipathy to mainstream politics, and the power of nimbyism, particularly in the local politics of health and anxieties over hospital closures.

MP

JOHN LYONS was born in 1949 in Glasgow and educated at Woodside Secondary School, Glasgow, West Middlesex Polytechnic and Stirling University, where he did a masters degree in human resource management in 2000. He was employed from 1971-99 as a mechanical engineer and from 1988-2001, he was regional officer of NUPE, which then merged to form Unison. During 1999-2001, he was a member of Forth Valley Health Board. He became a Labour candidate for Westminster after Sam Galbraith announced he was standing down from Westminster. He had been on a secret list of candidates approved by the big Scottish union barons, but his selection did not go as smoothly as others on that list. In the first selection ballot, Lyons lost by only two votes to Doug Maughan, an airline pilot based in Stirling. But after claims of irregularities in the process, headquarters ordered a second ballot which Lyons won easily. After his election he quickly secured places on three of the more significant select committees politically; public accounts, Scottish affairs and broadcasting. He was one of the Labour MPs to sign a motion against war in Iraq in March 2002, and voted against it in February and March the following year.

Tayside North

Predecessor Constituencies: Kinross and West Perthshire (1945–79)
and Perth and Kinross (1983–95).

Socio-economic Indicators:

Constituency Pop. (16-64)	47,705
Claimant Count (May 2003)	1.9% (38.0% below average)
IBA/SDA Claimants	6.2%
Life Expectancy – Male	75.9 (2.5 yrs above avereage)
Life Expectancy – Female	80.6 (1.9 yrs above average)
Owner Occupied	62.2%
Social Rented	21.5%
Average Property Prices	£70,814 (20th)
Average Gross Income	£25,402 (38th)
Low Birthweight Babies	98 (4.7%)
Teenage Pregnancy Rates	377 (4.2%)
No. of Lone Parent Households	2,637 (7.8%)

CAB Enquiries

Issue	No. of cases	Percentage of total cases (%)
1. Benefits	6240	32.4
2. Consumer	3479	18.0
3. Employment	3182	16.5
4. Other	1866	9.7
5. Housing	1599	8.3

2003 Scottish Parliament Election

Electorate: 62,697   *Turnout*: 33,343 (53.2%)   *Turnout 1999*: 61.6%

Candidate	Party	Votes	Votes%	99 %	Change%
John Swinney	SNP	14,969	44.9	44.1	+ 0.8
Murdo Fraser	Con	10,466	31.4	33.1	– 1.7
Gordon MacRae	Labour	3,527	10.6	15.1	– 4.5
Bob Forrest	Lib Dem	3,206	9.6	7.8	+ 1.9
Roseanne Adams	SSP	941	2.8	–	–
George Ashe	SPA	234	0.7	–	–

SNP majority: 4,503 (13.5%)   *Swing*: 1.2% Conservative to SNP

2001 General Election

Electorate: 61,645   *Turnout*: 38,517 (62.5%)

Candidate	Party	Votes	Votes%	Change%
Peter Wishart	SNP	15,441	40.1	– 4.8
Murdo Fraser	Con	12,158	31.6	– 4.2
Thomas Docherty	Labour	5,715	14.8	+ 3.6
Julia Robertson	Lib Dem	4,363	11.3	+ 3.2
Rosie Adams	SSP	620	1.6	–
Tina MacDonald	Ind	220	0.6	–

SNP majority: 3,283 (8.5%)   *Swing*: 0.3% SNP to Conservative

1945-97 Westminster

	Lab%	Con%	SNP%	Lib%	Other%	Turnout%
1997	11.3	35.7	44.9	8.2	–	74.3
1992	7.1	46.7	37.5	8.7	–	77.6
1987	8.8	45.4	32.9	12.9	–	74.7
1983	5.4	51.0	24.3	19.2	–	72.6
1979	8.5	50.5	29.4	11.6	–	79.6
1974O	7.7	41.7	41.5	9.1	–	75.1
1974F	9.9	52.8	23.1	14.2	–	77.8
1970	15.2	57.3	18.6	8.9	–	74.1
1966	18.7	60.8	20.5	–	–	73.5
1964	18.8	66.6	14.1	–	0.5	75.0
1963B	15.2	57.3	7.3	19.5	0.6	76.1
1959	16.8	68.2	15.0	–	–	71.0
1955	24.8	75.2	–	–	–	70.5
1951	23.8	76.2	–	–	–	73.2
1950	18.6	55.4	–	26.0	–	76.9
1945	32.0	68.0	–	–	–	67.4

Tayside North contains a number of attractive small towns and settlements such as Pitlochry, Forfar, Brechin, Edzell, Kirriemuir, Blairgowrie, Coupar Angus, Dunkeld, Blair Atholl and Aberfeldy. At its western side the constituency skirts the foothills of the Grampians and is covered with lochs and woodland and has the largest river system in the United Kingdom as well as the Angus Glens, and Schiehallion, 'the hill of the fairies'.

Tayside North contains numerous historical and tourist attractions including Killiecrankie, where the Jacobite commander John Graham of Claverhouse – better known as 'Bonnie Dundee' – defeated the English in 1689 losing his own life in the process, the historic town of Scone, with Scone Palace, site of the enthronement of Scottish kings and queens and Glamis Castle, birthplace of the late Queen Mother. The small town of Kirriemuir is the birthplace of Bon Scott, the original lead singer of the hard rock band AC/DC. It is better known as the birthplace of J. M. Barrie, creator of Peter Pan, and a contributor to the kailyard school of literature. 'The Kirriemuir career' is a phrase which described the experience of the 19th century 'lad o'pairts' who excelled at a country school and then went off to university and the world: while more myth than reality it reinforced Scottish ideas of the power of education and egalitarianism.

The constituency has a large farming community. Raspberry growers are experiencing difficult times due to competition from cheap imports and in 2001 the Scottish Soft Fruit Growers, the trade organisation for producers went out of business. There have been calls from the industry for government assistance to bring together an agency to properly promote Scottish soft fruit at home and abroad. A significant blow to the local economy was also the announcement in March 2000 of the closure of RAF Edzell which had been home to two generations of US intelligence operations, with the loss of 200 jobs and many more indirect ones.

The changing nature of health services has been a major issue in the constituency. Tayside Health Board's reduction of services at Stracathro Hospital and their recommendation to close the facility and replace it with a community hospital met fierce resistance with 25,000 people signing a local petition to save the hospital. Perth and Kinross Council in May 2002 unveiled a large public-private partnership programme which would see the creation of six new primary and five secondary schools including new schools in Aberfeldy, Blairgowrie and Kinross, but would involve the closure of several older, dilapidated schools.

This part of rural Scotland has had a long, eventful Conservative tradition. As Kinross and West Perthshire, it was Conservative for the entire inter-war period. It was represented for most of these years by the Duchess of Atholl – the first Scottish woman MP – who first won the seat in 1923 and became known as 'the Red Duchess' when in April 1938 she resigned the Conservative whip over British non-intervention in the Spanish Civil War. Her Conservative Association voted 273 to 167 to look for a new candidate and she resigned her seat, forcing a by-election where she stood as an independent with the support of the Labour and Liberal Parties. Held days before Christmas with the backdrop of Chamberlain's Munich agreement, the Duchess narrowly lost by 1,313 to the Conservative William McNair Snadden.

Snadden was returned in 1945 by the much larger majority of 8,754 over the Liberals and represented the seat until his retirement in 1955. His successor Gilmour Leburn won the seat in 1955 and 1959 by massive majorities, although the Nationalists stood for the first time in the latter contest winning 15 per cent of the vote. Leburn died in August 1963 producing a by-election where the selected Conservative candidate George Younger, later to be MP for Ayr from 1964–92, stood down to allow Sir Alec Douglas Home to become the candidate. To be eligible to stand, Douglas-Home had to renounce his peerage . He won the November 1963 contest effortlessly, with Labour a very distant second: this was the first parliamentary contest the young Gordon Brown campaigned for Labour. Douglas-Home went on to sit for less than a year in the seat as Prime Minister, losing the October 1964 general election to Harold Wilson, but he remained leader of the Conservative Party until July 1965. He remained MP for the seat until October 1974, and served in the 1970-74 administration of Ted Heath as Foreign Secretary, before becoming Lord Home of the Hirsel. He was a model of Tory loyalty to the leaders that followed him – an example that was to be lost on Conservative leaders that came after.

In October 1974 the Conservatives choose Nicholas Fairbairn as their new candidate and the SNP vote rose by 18.4 per cent, leaving Fairbairn the victor by a mere 53 votes. Five years later, Fairbairn was returned by a more comfortable 6,478 over Labour. The boundary changes which came about in 1983 saw Kinross and West Perthshire become Tayside North, while Perth and East Perthshire became Perth and Kinross. Confusingly the sitting Conservative MPs swapped seats with Fairbairn fighting Perth and Kinross, and Bill Walker, MP for Perth and East Perthshire since 1979, standing in Tayside North. Walker, an uncompromising right-winger won the new Tayside North by the margin of 10,099 over the SNP, but in 1987 his majority was halved to 5,016 with the Nationalists making a recovery increasing their vote by 8.6 per cent. In the 1992 election, Walker faced a challenge from a young, ambitious SNP candidate, John Swinney who further increased his party's vote by 4.5 per cent and cut the Conservative majority to 3,995.

In 1997 there were further boundary changes,which saw Tayside North gain Brechin and Edzell from Angus, slightly aiding the Nationalists. Walker faced a further challenge from Swinney. In the 1992-97 Parliament, Walker had gained a high profile as one of the leading Euro-sceptics who had harried John Major's battered government over the Maastricht Treaty and supported the right-wing challenge from John Redwood to Major's leadership in 1995. Swinney, on the other hand, had quietly and effectively worked his way up the SNP hierarchy without becoming known to the wider public. The result was an impressive SNP victory by 4,160 as the Conservative vote fell back 10.6 per cent on the notional 1992 result. Two years later, in the May 1999 Scottish Parliament election, Swinney held the seat by a similar margin of 4,192 votes with the SNP holding their 1997 vote in percentage terms, while the Conservatives fell back by a further 2.6 per cent.

In June 2001, Pete Wishart was selected as SNP candidate as John Swinney's replacement at Westminster and was elected with a 3,283 majority over the Conservatives – with the SNP vote down 5,000 and the Conservatives down 4,000 on four years before. In the second Scottish Parliament election of May 2003, John Swinney, standing for the first time as SNP leader, was faced again by Murdo Fraser, who had become a list MSP for Mid Scotland and Fife in 2001. Swinney was safely returned with a 4,503 majority, but did not receive any major leader's bonus as his vote crept up 0.8 per cent on a lower turnout. In the regional list vote, the SNP won 35.8 per cent versus the Conservatives 28.7 per cent, with the Greens on 6.5 per cent and SSP 3 per cent.

The SNP have built up an impressive position in Tayside North – which is all the more impressive when one considers that they never held the seat prior to 1997, However, boundary changes for Westminster will see Tayside North disappear from the map, much of it going into Perth and North Perthshire, which the SNP will have good hopes of laying claim to. At the Scottish Parliament, the SNP should have every confidence that Tayside North looks relatively safe for as far as one can see with the party well rooted in the local constituency.

MSP

JOHN SWINNEY was born in Edinburgh in 1964, grew up in the western suburb of Corstorphine and was educated at the capital's Forrester High School and Edinburgh University, from which he has a degree in politics. He was employed as a researcher on the Scottish Coal Project at Napier University, as an economic consultant in the consultancy company, Development Options Ltd, run by future leadership rival Alex Neil, and then as a strategic planner with Scottish Amicable before his election to Westminster in 1997. He joined the SNP aged 15, becoming interested in politics and current affairs through the Boys' Brigade and becoming a Nationalist from a sense of injustice as a 14 year old, when BBC commentators credited Scottish success at the Commonwealth Games to Britain, while Scottish failings remained Scottish. Joining the party at a time when it went into organisational meltdown, in the wake of the 1979 election defeat and the rows over the '79 Group of left-wingers being suspended, a whole generation was drifting away from the party, leaving the way clear for Swinney's generation to take senior office at a young age. Swinney thus became SNP national secretary aged 21, when he was still at university. He served in that post from 1986-92 and was then publicity vice-convener from 1992-97. He immediately showed his appetite for modernising the party platform, proposing the conference motion which ended the SNP policy on nationalisation.

He contested Tayside North for the first time in 1992, but saw it retained by the long-standing Conservative MP, Bill Walker. He won the seat five years later and was elected deputy leader, after MEP

Allan Macartney died in 1998. Swinney was a protégé of Alex Salmond throughout the latter's leadership, rewarding the trust placed in him with strong organisational skills, being campaign co-ordinator in the 1999 election, and taking on some challenging public tasks in party debate. However, even Swinney's organisational skills could not counter-balance the chaotic 1999 election campaign, largely run by Salmond and chief executive Mike Russell by the seat of their pants, going badly off course under intense media pressure and memorable among SNP activists for putting independence tenth on a list of pledges. Swinney vowed he would never let any of that happen again.

Once an MP, from 1997, he quickly made his mark in the Commons. With the 1999 Budget, and Gordon Brown's promise to cut the basic rate of income tax by one penny in 2000, it was Swinney, as the group's finance spokesperson, who was central to the rapid change of policy and election strategy. He announced the decision in the Commons, and a week later made the case to the national conference in Aberdeen, for the party to campaign for 'A Penny for Scotland'. This was to reinstate the penny 'tax bribe' Brown was promising to make, while promising ill-defined extra spending on public services, only six weeks out from the first Scottish Parliament election. Many voters, with Labour's encouragement, saw this as a tax increase, and it was acknowledged that such a rapid change of a central plank of the election platform could not be introduced at such a late stage.

Swinney was one of seven constituency MSPs returned in 1999, out of the 35-member group, settling down as deputy leader to Salmond, and given the convenership of the enterprise and lifelong learning committee. This was an important signal that the SNP was willing to use the committee system in the 'new politics' style for which it had been designed, even though many of its other tactics were old-style oppositionism. Swinney was credited with running the committee imaginatively, working with enterprise and lifelong learning minister Henry McLeish on shared agendas to do with enterprise agencies and a national tourism strategy. The committee was also notable for establishing links with the business community, through its sponsorship of 'business in the chamber' in 1999, which featured business representatives debating economic development policy within the Scottish Parliament chamber for a day. Swinney and McLeish jointly won an award from the *Herald* in 1999 in recognition of their consensual approach – little realising that they would be First Minister and opposition leader a year later.

In July 2000, Alex Salmond suddenly sprung his resignation on the party, giving Swinney less than two days advance warning. Swinney was clearly the front runner, strong enough to dissuade all of those who had been Salmond loyalists to leave the way clear, and bringing in the rest of the new generation of Nationalists by appointing Nicola Sturgeon his leadership campaign manager. His one opponent was Alex Neil, MSP for Central Scotland, from an older generation and the left wing, who had been, and arguably remained, on the party's 'fundamentalist' wing. Swinney won at the September 2000 conference in Inverness, by a margin of 67 per cent to 33 per cent, stating in his acceptance speech: 'I stand here as the first leader in the history of the SNP who has a hard-headed opportunity to lead our party into government and our country on to independence'. The effect of the campaign was to force Swinney to show he was as committed to independence as Neil, closing down the chance that devolution could move the party to more of an accommodation with the British state and an embrace of post-nationalist politics. The subsequent and difficult 2001 and 2003 elections were to reinforce that. The more Swinney's position was questioned, the more he had to present himself as putting independence first.

The early leadership stages were tough for Swinney, facing the death of Donald Dewar within two weeks of becoming leader, and then by-elections in Glasgow Anniesland and Falkirk West. He was only months away from the Westminster election, at which the SNP would be fighting for the first time on new strategic ground, with most of its resources and focus elsewhere. The results were far from good, losing Galloway and Upper Nithsdale to the Conservatives, nearly losing Perth as well, while safer seats registered sharply reduced SNP majorities. He turned down a £32,000 pay rise recommended for the leader of the largest opposition party, but voted for the 13.5 per cent pay rise for MSPs. In the Parliament chamber, he struggled to pin anything on Henry McLeish because of the First Minister's mercurial answers, and as the fiasco of McLeish's office sub-lets unfolded, the SNP leader hesitated rather than pressing home the case, leaving the credit for McLeish's downfall with Conservative leader David McLetchie. Swinney found Jack McConnell easier to engage but a doughty opponent in question time jousts. Swinney's approach was to grind down the Executive with statistical barrages continuing over weeks and months, succeeding with this approach on deferred hospital waiting lists, but lacking the dramatic edge the weekly event can demand.

Swinney's main strength remained his methodical approach and his organisational aptitude, bringing in his old Boys' Brigade chum, Peter Murrell, as party chief executive, while running concurrent reviews of head office, of party finance, and of policy, all aimed at ensuring the mistakes of the 1999 campaign were not repeated. The 'Penny For Scotland' policy was abandoned, in favour of sending a tax-cutting signal through a reduction in business rates to become more competitive than England. Andrew Wilson MSP and party treasurer Jim Mather undertook a boardroom and media offensive to impress on outsiders the party was serious about business and cutting tax to grow the economy, while Swinney had to lean on other front benchers to rein in their enthusiasm for spending commitments. With Sturgeon as campaign manager and Fiona Hyslop in charge of policy, the end result, for the 2003 election, was an ultra-safe platform, with an ultra-slick launch, and an attempt to harness the most modern campaigning methods. Nothing was sprung on the electorate at a late stage while populist messages about higher-paid nurses, smaller primary school classes and more police officers were high-lighted. Swinney was particularly keen to ensure a stronger message about fighting crime (parallel to Labour's) and there was emerging a more sceptical stance on Scotland's place in the European Union, presenting a more ambiguous SNP position as the 2004 European elections approached.

The 2003 campaign, in short, was much better than anything the SNP had produced before, making it all the more difficult and awkward to explain why the party did so badly. Those outside the party questioned whether the independence message is the big problem, and Labour's scare tactics about it seemed to work with voters. There was a question mark over Swinney's leadership, and whether he had enough charisma to project his friendly, engaging personality beyond the political-media village and out to the public. He tended too often to be speaking a political language divorced from common usage, and hardly ever tried to project himself as a man of the people. He could seem, as with his handling of the McLeish 'Officegate' scandal, too keen to be respectable and appear the cautious leader of a government-in-waiting. The voting system also worked against the SNP, and will probably continue to do, with Swinney offering the explanation the day after polling that the party had been caught in midstream between being a party of protest and becoming a party of government. The protest voters left in large numbers to other parties, particularly with the second vote and most notably favouring Greens and the SSP. But Swinney argued there was still some way to go to make the party a credible alternative government, and challenged the party to let him continue that mission at least until the 2007 election. Whatever the reason, the 2003 result left the SNP further away from its challenge to Labour, any realistic sense of power and its ultimate goal of independence.

That was the background to Bill Wilson, a little-known activist from Glasgow and unsuccessful candidate in Glasgow Maryhill in 2003, emerging as the standard bearer for the disaffected fundamentalists and left wing of the party, announcing in July 2003 he was challenging Swinney for the leadership. This announcement came a day before the leader's marriage to BBC journalist Elizabeth Quigley (he has two children from his first marriage), and diverted his energies for the next two months. He was attacked over the poor electoral performance, for allegedly playing down the independence message and over internal reforms which Swinney intended to spread power away from branch delegates and towards the ordinary party members. Swinney's victory was a foregone conclusion, but the internal fighting that accompanied the contest damaged the party and opened up rifts from pre-devolution days. Swinney emerged from the September 2003 conference in Inverness with a stronger mandate than expected, both for his leadership (he won 84 per cent of the votes cast) and for his internal party reforms. He had plans to draw up a new, draft constitution for the SNP due to be considered at a special party conference in spring 2004, including a move to one-member-one-vote selection of list MSP candidates and of the leader and deputy leader, while it was expected there would also be a higher threshold required for leadership challenges.

MP

PETE WISHART was born in 1962 in Dunfermline, and in 2001 became the first Member of Parliament to have been a professional rock musician – and a reasonably successful one at that, with a claim also to be the first MP ever to have appeared on BBC's *Top Of The Pops*. He was educated at Queen Anne High School, Dunfermline and Moray House College of Education, becoming a community education worker from 1984-85. He was a drummer with Dunfermline-rooted band Big Country around 1981, leaving just before it hit major UK and US success. He was then asked to join the Skye-rooted rock group Runrig, which was already a phenomenon in Gaeldom, fronted by the Gaelic singing of Donnie Munro. Wishart was with the band from 1985 until months before his election in 2001 as it gathered a non-Gaelic speaking and international following, and played a small but significant part in the cultural renaissance of Scotland and Gaelic during those years. At the height of its success, it was playing to vast crowds on Loch Lomondside, and for several nights to 7,000-strong crowds on Edinburgh Castle esplanade.

Wishart, who is not a Gaelic speaker, counted himself as a socialist and was a member of the Labour Party, but left it to join the SNP in 1997, over Labour's dithering about home rule. That year, he became a member of the National Executive Council, and became vice-convener for fundraising in 1999. He was also on the Scotland Against Drugs campaign committee from 1997-99. His conversion to the Nationalist cause exacerbated growing antagonism, at least over politics, which had opened up with Donnie Munro, a keen Labour supporter and part of the team loyal to Brian Wilson MP. Under Wilson's tutelage, Munro put up a spirited fight to unseat Charles Kennedy from Inverness, Nairn and Lochaber in 1997 and again failed to win the same seat in the 1999 Scottish Parliament election. It was therefore Wishart, the unassuming rhythm section, who made it to Parliament before his band's front man. He became whip of the five-member SNP group, and used his maiden speech to talk of the importance of music as 'the soundtrack of political change'. He was responsible in 1999 for putting together a SNP fundraising album called *A New Sang: Twelve Songs for Scottish Independence* which contained the dulcet tones of Alex Salmond, Winnie Ewing, Margo MacDonald, Andrew Wilson and others singing a variety of Scottish classics. It was not enough to finish Wishart's political career, but it should finish his musical one.

Tweeddale, Ettrick and Lauderdale

Predecessor Constituencies: Roxburghshire and Selkirkshire (1945–51) and Roxburgh, Selkirk and Peebles (1955–79).

Socio-economic Indicators:

Constituency Pop. (16-64)	41,675
Claimant Count (May 2003)	1.6% (47.4% below average)
IBA/SDA Claimants	6.5%
Life Expectancy – Male	76.0 (2.6 yrs above average)
Life Expectancy – Female	80.2 (1.5 yrs above average)
Owner Occupied	66.0%
Social Rented	22.9%
Average Property Prices	£74,449 (17th)
Average Gross Income	£26,599 (28th)
Low Birthweight Babies	116 (5.8%)
Teenage Pregnancy Rates	301 (3.7%)
No. of Lone Parent Households	2,176 (7.8%)

CAB Enquiries

Issue	No. of cases	Percentage of total cases (%)
1. Benefits	3159	28.6
2. Consumer	2179	19.7
3. Employment	1744	15.8
4. Housing	1037	9.4
5. Other	828	7.5

2003 Scottish Parliament Election

Electorate: 50,912   *Turnout*: 26,700 (52.4%)   *Turnout 1999*: 65.4%

Candidate	Party	Votes	Votes%	99 %	Change%
Jeremy Purvis	Lib Dem	7,197	27.0	35.8	− 8.9
Christine Grahame	SNP	6,659	24.9	22.5	+ 2.4
Catherine Maxwell Stuart	Labour	5,757	21.6	22.4	− 0.8
Derek Brownlee	Con	5,686	21.3	19.3	+ 2.0
Norman Lockhart	SSP	1,055	4.0	–	–

cont'd

Candidate	Party	Votes	Votes%	99 %	Change%
Alexander Black	SPA	346	1.3	–	–

Liberal Democrat majority: 538 (2.0%)   *Swing*: 5.6% Liberal Democrat to SNP

2001 General Election

Electorate: 52,430   *Turnout*: 33,217 (63.4%)

Candidate	Party	Votes	Votes%	Change%
Michael Moore	Lib Dem	14,035	42.3	+11.0
Keith Geddes	Labour	8,878	26.7	– 0.7
Andrew Brocklehurst	Con	5,118	15.4	– 6.7
Richard Thomson	SNP	4,108	12.4	– 4.7
Norman Lockhart	SSP	695	2.1	–
John Hein	Liberal	383	1.2	+ 0.2

Liberal Democrat majority: 5,157 (15.5%)   *Swing*: 5.9% Labour to Liberal Democrat

---

1945–97 Westminster

	Lab%	Con%	SNP%	Lib%	Other%	Turnout%
1997	27.4	22.1	17.1	31.2	2.1	76.6
1992	10.8	31.7	17.0	39.9	0.6	78.1
1987	11.4	29.6	9.1	49.9	–	76.5
1983	7.6	28.9	5.0	58.5	–	77.0
1979	8.5	31.3	7.1	53.1	–	82.0
1974O	8.9	27.4	20.0	43.7	–	79.2
1974F	6.3	33.6	8.0	52.1	–	86.1
1970	9.6	41.1	6.8	42.3	0.2	80.8
1966	13.6	40.8	–	45.6	–	84.9
1965B	11.3	38.6	–	49.2	0.9	82.2
1964	15.8	42.8	2.5	38.9	–	82.2
1959	21.0	50.2	–	28.8	–	80.0
1955	20.2	47.7	–	32.1	–	80.8
1951	20.8	40.6	–	38.6	–	84.9
1950	24.7	36.4	–	39.4	–	82.1
1945	28.9	37.9	–	33.2	–	73.6

Tweeddale, Ettrick and Lauderdale can be found in the Scottish Borders, between Lothian and the city of Edinburgh to the north and Roxburgh and Berwickshire to the south. Its main towns include Galashiels, Peebles, Selkirk, and Penicuik in Midlothian. Average property prices are 10.4 per cent above the national average and rose by 55.6 per cent in the 1990s.

The biggest local issue of the last few years, as with neighbouring Roxburgh and Berwickshire, has been Scottish Borders Council's proposed education cuts of £5.9 million as a result of a £3.9 million overspend in the education budget. Teaching cuts made up £2 million of the planned savings which would have seen 125 education jobs lost. A motion of no confidence was put forward in Drew Tulley, who resigned and was replaced by John Ross Scott, Liberal Democrat councillor, who established a 'rainbow alliance' with the SNP. The 2003 local elections saw the Conservatives make gains from Independents, Lib Dems and SNP.

In 1998 the closure of Viasystems, an American based company which made electronic circuit boards, with the loss of over 1,000 jobs at their Galashiels and Selkirk plants, showed the vulnerability of the new economy to changes in the international market. Traditional industries such as knitwear have also been in decline in recent years with Dawson International which then owned Pringle, closing factories in Galashiels and Selkirk with the loss of 720 jobs. However, since Dawson sold Pringle to the Hong King based Fang Brothers Knitting Ltd, Pringle has begun to enjoy an international comeback. Farming has been badly hit by the twin crises of BSE and foot and mouth, while the passing of the Wild Mammals (Scotland) Act banning fox hunting could have an adverse impact on an area which has traditionally supported several fox hunts.

Transport issues are of vital importance to this part of Scotland and there are hopes that the Scottish Executive's plans to reopen the Edinburgh-Borders rail line will bring jobs to the area. The rail line was shut by Dr. Beeching in January 1969, and the influential Campaign for Borders Rail have been campaigning for its reopening ever since. Any new service would use the Waverley line from Galashiels into central Edinburgh and provide a boost to the Borders, Midlothian and Edinburgh. The proposed link has been costed by the Scottish Executive at £126 million, but by the 2003 Scottish Parliament election, an appropriate business plan had not been presented, which was essential if the work was to begin by 2006.

As Roxburghshire and Selkirkshire, and then Roxburgh, Selkirk and Peebles, this seat has long Conservative traditions. It was represented by the Earl of Dalkeith from 1923 until 1935. He was then succeeded by Lord William Scott, the son of the 7th Duke of Buccleuch, who held it with the narrow majority of 1,628 over the Liberals in 1945. However, in 1950 the unthinkable happened and the Conservatives narrowly lost the seat to the Liberal Archibald MacDonald with a majority of 1,156 – one of two Liberal gains in Scotland that year – the other being Orkney and Shetland which Jo Grimond won. The Liberals' ascendancy was to be brief and in October 1951 the Conservatives Commander Charles Donaldson won it back with a slender majority of 829.

From May 1955, the constituency became known as Roxburgh, Selkirk and Peebles, and Donaldson held the seat in three subsequent general elections until his death in December 1964. This precipitated a by-election which was held in March 1965 where a 26-year-old David Steel won the seat from the Conservatives and this setback, while the Conservatives were in opposition, encouraged opponents of Alec Douglas-Home's leadership to challenge him, resulting in Ted Heath becoming leader. Steel as a young MP courageously brought forward a Private Member's Bill in the controversial area of abortion, which became the Abortion Act 1967. In 1970, after a whole Parliament of prominently supporting a swathe of Sixties liberal legislation and causes – gay rights and anti-apartheid as well as abortion – Steel's majority was cut to 550 votes. He increased his majority to 7,443 over the Conservatives in October 1974 and became Liberal Party leader in 1976, taking his party into the Lib-Lab pact which propped up Jim Callaghan's ailing Labour government from 1977-78. His majority rose to 10,690 over the Conservatives in 1979.

In 1983, two Borders seats were created and the northern and western part became Tweeddale, Ettrick and Lauderdale which Steel decided to stand in. By this time, Steel had been central to the creation of the Liberal-SDP Alliance, the most credible third force in post-war British politics, which very nearly supplanted the Labour Party in terms of votes in 1983. Steel was re-elected in 1983 with an 8,539 majority, which fell to 5,942 in 1987 – on both occasions over the Conservatives. Steel resigned as

Liberal Party leader in 1988, seemingly exhausted by trying to 'break the mould' of British politics and by tensions within the Alliance with the Social Democrat Party leader David Owen. In 1992 he got an unpleasant shock when his vote fell by 10 per cent, and his majority tumbled to a vulnerable 2,520 over the Conservatives. This result could be seen in the context of a number of Lib Dem reverses across Scotland – most notably Malcolm Bruce narrowly holding Gordon, and Russell Johnston in Inverness, Nairn and Lochaber. Several commentators put this down to voters disapproval of Labour-Lib Dem co-operation in the cross-party Scottish Constitutional Convention from 1989.

Steel announced his retirement at Westminster, later elected Lib Dem list MSP for the Lothians in the 1999 Scottish Parliament election, becoming the first Presiding Officer of the new institution. Steel's successor, Michael Moore, looked like he was faced with a tough prospect to hold on to the seat in the 1997 general election. He was not helped by boundary changes which brought 13,000 voters from Penicuik and surrounding Midlothian into the seat, helping Labour and hindering the Lib Dems – and producing a notional Lib Dem lead of 1,735 over the Conservatives. Moore was returned with a 1,489 majority over Labour's Keith Geddes who increased his party's vote by 11 per cent, and moved from a notional fourth to second. The Lib Dem share of the vote, 31.2 per cent, was their lowest in the seat since 1959 and the lowest vote for any winning candidate in the 1997 election. In the June 2001 UK election, Michael Moore was re-elected with his majority increased by a factor of three to 5,157. Labour's Keith Geddes managed to retain second place, but could not build on his 1999 vote.

The 1999 Scottish Parliament contest was a very competitive four-party contest. Lib Dem Ian Jenkins, a local teacher, won the seat relatively comfortably with a 4,478 majority. The SNP surged into second place, closely followed by Labour. In January 2002 Ian Jenkins announced he would not stand again for the Scottish Parliament and the Lib Dems selected Jeremy Purvis as their new candidate. In the 2003 election, Purvis was returned with a narrow 538 margin over the SNP's Christine Grahame as the Lib Dem vote fell by 5,000 votes and 9 per cent. The Lib Dem share of the vote – 27 per cent – was the lowest winning percentage in the 2003 election and the second lowest in post-war Scottish politics – only ever bested by Inverness, Nairn and Lochaber in 1992. In the regional list vote, the Conservatives finished ahead on 21 per cent to the Liberal Democrats 20.3 per cent – a Conservative lead of 186 – with the Greens on 10.2 per cent and SSP on 5.4 per cent.

Tweeddale, Ettrick and Lauderdale has gone through a number of different political periods – even in its 40 year recent history as first a Liberal and now Lib Dem seat. At points it has looked like becoming a safe seat, and at others, a hyper-marginal, but the last Westminster election indicated a strengthening of the Lib Dem position, after a run of difficult results. However, boundary changes for Westminster will see the creation of one entirely Borders seat with Selkirk joining Roxburgh and Berwick to become Roxburgh, Berwick and Selkirk, while the rest of the seat joins with parts of Clydesdale in Peebles, Clydesdale and Annandale in what looks like unlikely Lib Dem territory. At Scottish Parliament contests, the current constituency has confirmed its vulnerable status and unpredictability with the SNP now emerging as the main challengers to the Lib Dems, whereas in 1997 it had been Labour and in 1992 the Conservatives. The Lib Dems' hold on this seat is perilous in the extreme and the challenge for the Nationalists will be whether they can build on their recent success – or whether like Labour and the Conservatives in the last decade – having come so far they will fall back.

MSP

JEREMY PURVIS was born in 1974 in Berwick, and educated in Berwick-upon-Tweed High School and Brunel University, where he did a BSc (Hons) in politics and modern history. He is one of the newish breed of politician whose entire working life has been inside politics, legislatures and public affairs, having worked as a research assistant to Sir David Steel while a student and then as personal assistant to the then MP in the House of Commons in 1996-97, moving to work in the Lords with him in 1997-98, after his boss became Lord Steel of Aikwood. He then worked in a Parliamentary affairs company from 1998-2001, and was co-director of a strategic communications consultancy from 2001-03.

Taking his place in the Lib Dem Parliamentary group after narrowly winning Tweeddale, Ettrick and Lauderdale in 2003, he became spokesperson for finance while having a place on the finance committee, where he made an early impression with an interrogation of the chief executive Paul Grice over the Holyrood Building Project. As with Sir David Steel, he is a classic cars enthusiast.

MP

MICHAEL MOORE was born in 1965 and elected MP for Tweeddale, Ettrick and Lauderdale in 1997. Educated at Strathallan School, Jedburgh Grammar School and Edinburgh University, where he studied politics and modern history, he worked as a research assistant to Archy Kirkwood from 1987-88 and as a chartered accountant from 1991-97, becoming a manager in corporate finance practice at Coopers and Lybrand from 1993-97.

He had joined the Social Democrat Party in 1983, and once at Westminster, he became the Liberal Democrats' Scottish spokesman on business and employment from 1995-97, spokesman on the economy and health from 1997, and a member of the Scottish affairs select committee. He voted with 21 other Lib Dems against Labour's ban on hand guns in 1997, and voted against foxhunting the same year. He led a delegation to St Louis, Missouri in 1998, in an unsuccessful attempt to prevent the Viasystems factory in Galashiels from shutting and moving to North East England. He also visited the United States the next year to lobby against US sanctions hitting knitwear products from the Borders as part of the American approach to fighting the European Union on trade in the so-called 'banana wars'.

He was the campaign manager of the Lib Dems for the Scottish Parliament elections in 1999, and despite being an MP, was on the Lib Dems' five-member negotiating team with Labour on agreeing a coalition government. He was Scottish spokesman of the Lib Dems from 1999-2002, when he became deputy spokesman on foreign affairs under Menzies Campbell, often deputising for Campbell during the Iraq war while the North East Fife MP was fighting cancer.

West Renfrewshire

Predecessor Constituencies: Renfrewshire West (1945–79) and Renfrew West and Inverclyde (1983–92).

Socio-economic Indicators:

Constituency Pop. (16-64)	44,647
Claimant Count (May 2003)	2.9% (7.1% below average)
IBA/SDA Claimants	11.0%
Life Expectancy – Male	73.0 (0.4 yrs below average)
Life Expectancy – Female	78.6 (0.1 yrs below average)
Owner Occupied	75.3%
Social Rented	18.9%
Average Property Prices	£79,784 (14th)
Average Gross Income	£30,658 (7th)
Low Birthweight Babies	104 (5.0%)
Teenage Pregnancy Rates	292 (3.2%)
No. of Lone Parent Households	2,656 (10.0%)

CAB Enquiries

Issue	No. of cases	Percentage of total cases (%)
1. Consumer	2908	26.4
2. Benefits	2150	19.5
3. Employment	1859	16.8
4. Housing	1074	9.7
5. Other	1071	9.7

2003 Scottish Parliament Election

Electorate: 50.963   *Turnout*: 28,302 (55.5%)   *Turnout 1999*: 64.9%

Candidate	Party	Votes	Votes%	99%	Change%
Patricia Godman	Labour	9,671	34.2	37.3	– 3.2
Bruce McFee	SNP	7,179	25.4	28.8	– 3.5
Annabel Goldie	Con	6,867	24.3	21.2	+ 3.0
Alison King	Lib Dem	2,902	10.3	7.8	+ 2.4
Gerard McCarthey	SSP	1,683	5.9	(other 4.7)	–

Labour majority: 2,492 (8.8%)   *Swing*: 0.2% SNP to Labour

2001 General Election

Electorate: 52,889   *Turnout*: 33,497 (63.3%)

Candidate	Party	Votes	Votes%	Change%
James Sheridan	Labour	15,720	46.9	+ 0.4
Carol Puthucheary	SNP	7,145	21.3	– 5.2
David Sharpe	Con	5,522	16.5	– 2.1
Clare Hamblen	Lib Dem	4,185	12.5	+ 4.8
Arlene Nunnery	SSP	925	2.8	–

Labour majority: 8,575 (25.6%)   *Swing*: 2.8% SNP to Labour

1945–97 Westminster

	Lab%	Con%	SNP%	Lib%	Other%	Turnout%
1997	46.6	18.6	26.5	7.7	0.7	76.0
1992	36.6	32.9	20.2	10.0	–	80.3
1987	38.7	29.8	10.1	21.4	–	80.5
1983	29.0	32.7	8.7	29.5	–	78.0
1979	44.5	31.0	13.1	11.4	–	81.2
1974O	38.5	26.8	28.6	6.1	–	80.1
1974F	40.3	35.4	15.2	9.1	–	82.9
1970	48.0	43.2	8.8	–	–	79.5
1966	54.3	45.7	–	–	–	81.6
1964	46.1	43.8	–	10.1	–	82.9
1959	46.5	53.5	–	–	–	82.6
1955	44.8	55.2	–	–	–	83.0
1951	46.2	53.8	–	–	–	84.9
1950	46.1	53.9	–	–	–	77.6
1945	48.8	44.9	6.3	–	–	70.2

West Renfrewshire is situated between Greenock and Inverclyde and the two Paisley seats and includes a variety of small and medium towns such as Port Glasgow – the working class part of the constituency – and more middle class, commuter settlements such as Erskine, Houston, Bridge of Weir, Bishopton and Kilmacolm. It is a relatively affluent constituency where average property prices are 18.3 per cent above the national average and increased 58 per cent in 1991-2001.

The area received a boost when it was announced in 2002 that Port Glasgow was to be the recipient of £5 million of European Union Structural Funds to revitalise the town's declining waterfront, along with Clydebank. The regeneration of the East Glen shipyard in Port Glasgow requires a Scottish Executive traffic order to temporarily reroute the A8 dual carriageway and there have been concerns about delays jeopardising the project. This was welcome news in an area which has seen recent job losses in electronics: Compaq have cut their Erskine staff by 700, and Selectron, which produces IBM circuit boards, closed its Port Glasgow plant.

Fergusons' Lower Clyde shipyard at Port Glasgow is still a major employer, and in 2002 they won a high-profile £8 million contract to build a Scottish Fishery Protection Agency vessel, but lost an order for Caledonian MacBrayne ferries to English based competitors. In May 2002 BAE announced it was planning to close its Bishopton Royal Ordinance plant – the last propellant facility in the United Kingdom which could produce tank and navy shells, and in particular, the Royal Navy's Sea Wolf anti-aircraft missile system. Local campaigners became concerned about the loss of local jobs, but an even more serious issue was, once the plant closed, who would pick up the bill for the environmental damage and cleaning of the huge 2,300 acre munitions complex.

Renfrewshire West was first won by Labour in 1922, lost in 1924, regained in 1929 and emphatically lost in the debacle of 1931. Robert Forgan, who was elected Labour MP in 1929, defected to Oswald Mosley's New Party and stood under its banner in 1931, polling a mere 4 per cent. Tom Scollan regained the seat for Labour in 1945 by a majority of 1,214 over the Conservatives. However, in the February 1950 election, the Conservative John Maclay won the seat back, defeating Scollan by 3,102 votes and in October 1951 defeating a young Bruce Millan by 2,963 votes. Maclay went on to become Minister of State at the Colonial Office from 1956–57 and then Secretary of State for Scotland for most of Macmillan's premiership from 1957–62.

Maclay held the seat until Norman Buchan won it for Labour in 1964 and Labour slowly began to build up their hold over the constituency, winning it by 5,300 over the SNP in October 1974 and 8,572 over the Conservatives in 1979. The 1983 boundary redistribution created Renfrew West and Inverclyde which was notionally a marginal seat. Local MP Norman Buchan moved to the safety of Paisley South, and Dickson Mabon, Labour MP for Greenock since 1955, stood in Renfrew West under the Liberal-SDP Alliance banner. The result was a three-way cliffhanger. Anna McCurley won for the Conservatives, with a 1,322 majority over Mabon, and Labour in third place 200 votes behind. In 1987 Tommy Graham, hardly an obvious choice in a marginal seat, took Labour from third place to first, increasing the party's vote by 5,000 and beating McCurley by 4,063 votes despite the Conservative support falling by a mere 100 votes. Mabon stood again for the Liberal-SDP Alliance and saw his support decline by 2,500.

In 1992 a strong performance by the Conservative Annabel Goldie cut Graham's majority in half to 1,744 as she put nearly 2,000 on the Conservative vote, while the SNP moved from fourth to third, putting 5,000 on their support. The 1997 boundary changes made the new West Renfrewshire a more secure seat for Labour with a notional 6,046 majority. In 1997, Graham put an additional 1,000 votes on Labour's vote, while the SNP re-established themselves in second place increasing their vote by 2,000, as the Conservative vote fell by nearly 4,000 leaving Graham with a comfortable 7,979 majority.

Post-1997 there were two years of allegations and scandal centred on local Labour politics in the wake of the suicide in July 1997 of Gordon McMaster, Labour MP for Paisley South. Tommy Graham was implicated for spreading rumours about McMaster's sexuality. He was immediately suspended from the party, pending the allegations being investigated, expelled a year later in September 1998 and political oblivion, rather than martyrdom, was the result. Graham sat as an Independent Labour MP for the rest of the 1997–2001 Parliament, but wisely decided not to stand again in 2001. In June 2001, James Sheridan stood as Labour candidate, having been selected to replace the disgraced Graham. Sheridan held the seat with an 8,575 majority over the SNP who fell back in second place seeing their vote fall 5.2 per cent.

The May 1999 Scottish Parliament elections were awaited by Labour with unease, and came as something of a relief. Patricia Godman, wife of Norman Godman, the then MP for Greenock and Inverclyde, was elected with 2,893 majority over the Nationalists' Colin Campbell. She saw a fall in Labour's support of nearly 6,000 votes, while the SNP vote marginally declined and the Conservatives' Annabel Goldie managed the feat of holding on to most of her 1997 vote. Neal Ascherson, the well-known writer, commentator and ardent home ruler, stood for the Lib Dems and polled a paltry 2,659 votes. Allan McGraw, standing as an Independent on a pro-Graham ticket, polled 1,136 votes. The May 2003 Scottish Parliament election saw Godman re-elected by the same margin as four years before, winning a 2,492 majority over the SNP as both main parties saw their votes fall back by similar amounts. In the regional vote, Labour won 29.5 per cent to the SNP's 22.5 per cent, while the SSP won 6.2 per cent and the Greens 5.9 per cent.

Renfrewshire Council had been bitterly fought between Labour and the SNP for much of the 1990s – and a source of many of the controversies and scandals which have tarred the reputation of Renfrewshire politics. Neither party emerged unblemished in this, but a major contributory factor to the intensity of distrust between the two parties seems to have been that Renfrewshire was until 1992 a safe Labour council with relatively little opposition, and in that year the SNP broke through in significant numbers. The resulting dynamic saw West of Scotland politics at its worst, but was actually the product of a culture of one-party politics being faced with serious opposition. In the 2003 elections, the Nationalists won 39.3 per cent to Labour's 36.8 per cent, but Labour emerged with 21 seats to the SNP's 15, and a Labour majority of two.

Boundary changes for Westminster will see Paisley and Renfrewshire's three constituencies reduced to two – Paisley and Renfrewshire North, and Paisley and Renfrewshire South – that might cause some conflict in internal Labour politics – something this area has seen lots of in the last decade. At the Scottish Parliament, this seat has in two consecutive elections underlined its character as a near-marginal with Labour's dominance more based on the fragmentation of their opponents votes, than the strength of Labour's appeal. Both the Nationalists and Conservatives are well placed to offer a serious challenge to Labour in this seat, and if one of these parties can establish itself as the principal opposition, Labour's hold on the seat could be shaky.

MSP

PATRICIA GODMAN was born in 1939 and educated at St Gerard's Senior Secondary and Jordanhill College, where she gained her social work qualification. She has worked as a social worker and bank clerk, and was elected to Strathclyde Regional Council and Glasgow City Council where she served as vice-convenor of the social work resources committee. Godman is married to Norman Godman, MP for Greenock and Inverclyde from 1983 to his 2001 retirement, for whom she used to work as a researcher. Prior to the 1992 election, she stood in the Glasgow Kelvin Labour selection against sitting MP George Galloway, winning 57 per cent of party members, but losing due to the trade union block vote.

In the first Scottish Parliament, Godman was convenor of the local government committee, starting each meeting by greeting 'comrades', and building a sure, quiet authority, notably in the hearings she conducted over the repeal of Section 28 on homosexuality being 'promoted' in schools. A committee report on the future of local government finance went badly adrift, however. She was widely touted as a deputy presiding officer in October 2002 when Patricia Ferguson vacated the post to become Parliament minister, but the new First Minister favoured Cathy Peattie, his intervention having the effect of losing the opportunity for both women, as it went instead to the Conservatives' Murray Tosh. She was then even more widely touted as a successor to Sir David Steel as Presiding Officer from 2003-07. But the unexpectedly slim coalition majority emerging out of the 2003 election meant that Labour was not in a position to sacrifice one of its MSPs to the post, leaving it open and uncontested for the SNP's George Reid. Godman took a confused position over the Iraq war votes in 2003, saying she was against invasion and then voting for the Labour 'pro-war' position.

MP

JIM SHERIDAN was born in Glasgow in 1952 and educated at St Pius Secondary School in the city. He worked in Beaverbrook's *Daily Express* print plant in Glasgow from 1967-70, then moving to Barclay Curle shipyard, next to Yarrow's, from 1970-78. He worked as a machine operator at Bowater Scott packaging company from 1978-82, until it closed and he was unemployed for two years. From 1984-99, he worked in the stores of Barr and Stroud, the Govan defence optronics firm, taken over by Pilkington and more recently part of Thales. Throughout his period there, he was convener of the Transport and General Workers Union, becoming a full-time official of the union from 1999-2000. He also became chair of the union's national power and engineering committee. Despite coming through the classic route for a union activist becoming a Labour politician, he did not join the party until the age of 32.

Sheridan became chair of West Renfrewshire Constituency Labour Party in the wake of the ructions which accompanied Tommy Graham's political self-destruction after the 1997 election. Sheridan was also a councillor and vice-convener of social work on Renfrewshire Council from 1999 to 2001 until elected MP for West Renfrewshire in 2001. He campaigned to safeguard Bishopton Royal Ordnance Factory when it came under closure threat in 1998-99, arguing that it was essential for Britain to have its own capacity for manufacturing missile propellants for national security reasons, rather than import them. But having lost that battle, attention shifted to the mechanics of cleaning up the heavily-polluted 2,300-acre munitions complex. Sheridan signed a Commons motion in March 2002 against the moves towards war in Iraq, yet voted with the government in both the vital votes on war in 2003. He became a member of the broadcasting select committee and is chair of Westminster's Scottish Football Group.

Western Isles

Predecessor Constituencies: none.

Socio-economic Indicators:

Constituency Pop. (16–64)	16,254
Claimant Count (May 2003)	3.5% (11.6% above average)
IBA/SDA Claimants	7.8%
Life Expectancy – Male	72.6 (0.8 yrs above average)
Life Expectancy – Female	80.2 (1.5 yrs above average)
Owner Occupied	71.9%
Social Rented	17.3%
Average Property Prices	£40,719 (72nd)
Average Gross Income	£22,185 (67th)
Low Birthweight Babies	12 (4.7%)
Teenage Pregnancy Rates	66 (2.1%)
No. of Lone Parent Households	1,143 (10.1%)

CAB Enquiries

Issue	No. of cases	Percentage of total cases (%)
1. Benefits	2852	53.1
2. Consumer	535	10.0
3. Employment	531	9.9
4. Other	483	9.0
5. Housing	353	6.6

2003 Scottish Parliament Election

Electorate: 21,043   *Turnout*: 12,387 (58.9%)   *Turnout 1999*: 62.3%

Candidate	Party	Votes	Votes%	99 %	Change%
Alasdair Morrison	Labour	5,825	47.0	51.9	– 4.9
Alasdair Nicholson	SNP	5,105	41.2	36.9	+ 4.3
Frank Warren	Con	612	4.9	7.9	– 2.9
Conor Snowden	Lib Dem	498	4.0	3.3	+ 0.8
Joanne Telfer	SSP	347	2.8	-	-

Labour majority: 720 (5.8%)   *Swing*: 4.6% Labour to SNP

2001 General Election

Electorate: 21,706   *Turnout*: 13,159 (60.6%)

Candidate	Party	Votes	Votes%	Change%
Calum MacDonald	Labour	5,924	45.0	–10.6
Alasdair Nicholson	SNP	4,850	36.9	+ 3.5
Douglas Taylor	Con	1,250	9.5	+ 2.9
John Horne	Lib Dem	849	6.5	+ 3.4
Joanne Telfer	SSP	286	2.2	–

Labour majority: 1,074 (8.2%)   *Swing*: 7.0% Labour to SNP

1945–97 Westminster

	Lab%	Con%	SNP%	Lib%	Other%	Turnout%
1997	55.6	6.7	33.4	3.1	1.3	70.1
1992	47.8	8.5	37.2	3.4	3.2	70.4
1987	42.7	8.1	28.5	20.7	–	70.1
1983	30.1	9.6	54.5	5.8	–	66.5
1979	32.3	10.6	52.5	4.6	–	67.5
1974O	24.7	8.3	61.5	5.5	–	61.5
1974F	19.1	6.9	67.0	–	6.9	67.4
1970	38.4	18.5	43.1	–	–	64.8
1966	61.0	20.2	–	18.8	–	61.5
1964	55.1	14.0	–	30.9	–	66.9
1959	53.6	46.4	–	–	–	64.2
1955	57.3	42.7	–	–	–	59.6
1951	48.7	40.7	5.0	5.6	–	60.5
1950	53.2	–	–	44.1	2.7	55.7
1945	45.7	21.3	–	33.0	–	53.3

The Western Isles constituency was created as a single seat for the 1918 general election, and has remained so ever since. The seat stretches for 130 miles and includes the two large isles of Lewis and Harris which make up the Outer Hebrides, North and South Uist, Barra and Benbecula and a host of smaller isles. Its main towns are Stornoway, Tarbert and Lochmaddy, though Stornoway has the largest share of the population by far. The Western Isles socio-economic profile shows the lack of material wealth in this part of Scotland. Average property prices are the second lowest in the country, only beaten by Glasgow Shettleston, at 39.6 per cent below the national average. Local Citizens Advice Bureau enquiries show the frailty of the local economy with 53.1 per cent of enquiries dealing with benefits issues – one of the highest figures in the country.

The biggest issue facing the Western Isles is depopulation, as younger people have moved elsewhere for education and employment. Traditional areas of employment such as fishing, farming, and Harris Tweed have faced serious problems for a significant time.

The Western Isles has a culture very different from mainland Scotland. The north of the seat is dominated by the Free Church of Scotland, commonly known as the 'Wee Frees', while the south is characterised by Catholic beliefs. In the north, this contributes to a powerful religious sentiment and sabbatarian outlook where the Sabbath is still universally obeyed with all social amenities – shops, bars, hotels, restaurants, golf clubs closed. The decadent mainland life of Sunday shopping and loose living – whether it be gambling, sex outside marriage or homosexuality – is not viewed positively, but departing from God's way. Many hotel owners would like to relax the Sunday taboo, as it means tourists tend to depart on Saturday. This is now being slowly eroded with Loganair running Sunday flights from Edinburgh and Inverness to Stornoway since October 2002, despite local opposition. Iain MacDonald, Scottish Secretary of the Lord's Day Observance Society viewed that the new service was 'a breach of God's law'.

The Western Isles is the heart of the Gaidhealtachd with, on the latest 2001 census figures, 71.6 per cent of local inhabitants speaking Gaelic. The preservation of the ancient language has become a key issue in the cultural life of Scotland, with the number of native speakers falling, but significant monies have now been allocated to it, particularly in broadcasting. Some critics suggest that a language spoken by a mere 93,282 people in Scotland is a form of political correctness, while others allege that a 'Gaelic mafia' of public sector quangocrats has made life for themselves very cushy out of presenting themselves as advocates for the language.

Labour first won the seat in 1935 when journalist Malcolm Macmillan won it from the National Liberals who were allies of the Conservatives. In that contest, the SNP standing for the first time polled an impressive 28.1 per cent of the vote. After such a good showing, the Nationalists waited until 1951 to stand again, and then until 1970. Macmillan represented the seat for an impressive 35 years – first standing when Clement Attlee first led Labour into an election in 1935, and last standing as an official Labour candidate in 1970 when Harold Wilson was seeking re-election as Prime Minister.

In 1970, at his first attempt, the SNP's Donald Stewart won the seat, defeating Macmillan. This was the first time the SNP had ever won a parliamentary seat at a general election, and it was a defeat Macmillan did not take too well. In 1972 he was expelled from the Western Isles Labour Party after they rejected his candidacy and he stood in the February 1974 election as a United Labour Party candidate and polled a disappointing 6.9 per cent of the vote, while Donald Stewart secured his highest ever vote – 67 per cent.

Stewart was leader of the SNP Parliamentary Party from 1974–79, and held the constituency in 1979 – one of only two SNP survivors in that year. He held it again in 1983, before announcing his retirement. In the resulting 1987 election the SNP's vote collapsed, falling by 26 per cent as Labour's Calum MacDonald swept to victory with an impressive majority of 2,340. In 1992 this was reduced to 1,703 votes as Labour's vote rose by 5.1 per cent, but the Nationalists put on 8.7 per cent. However, in May 1997 MacDonald increased his vote to 55 per cent and his majority to 3,576 with Anne Lorne Gillies for the SNP, slipping by nearly 4 per cent. In the 2001 UK election, MacDonald witnessed his majority slip back as Labour's vote fell back by 3,000 and 10.6 per cent, and the SNP's Alasdair Nicholson put 3.5 per cent on his support.

In the 1999 Scottish Parliament contest, Labour's Alasdair Morrison faced a tough challenge from the Nationalist Alasdair Nicholson and saw Labour's majority cut to 2,093. The second Scottish Parliament election of 2003 showed a similar political trend with Morrison facing a challenge from Nicholson – standing in his third consecutive election. Labour, defending a more vulnerable seat than its Westminster equivalent, saw its vote fall by 1,400 and 4.9 per cent, as the SNP vote fell by 50 votes on a lower turnout, but increased by 4.3 per cent. The end result was a Labour majority reduced by two-thirds to 720 votes, and a seat that has become a hyper-marginal between Labour and the Nationalists. For the first time, the Western Isles found itself with the highest turnout of a Scottish constituency – 58.9 per cent - as voting fell by less here than in Central Scotland seats.

In the regional vote, the Labour Party won 38.7 per cent and the SNP 33.6 per cent – a Labour lead of 508 – with the Greens on 8.1 per cent and SSP on 4.3 per cent. The Western Isles with its 21,205 electors is by far the smallest electorate to be represented at Westminster – less than one-third of the electoral quota for English seats of 69,934. Despite this, the Boundary Commission decided to recognise its unique status and leave it well alone. Their only change for Westminster elections is a name change to Na h-Eileanan An Iar. The Western Isles has, through much of its history, valued personality and incumbency, with both MacDonald and Morrison benefiting from their local status and their ability to speak Gaelic. In recent years things look like they have begun to change. Labour enjoyed a very good result here in 1997, but since then its position has slowly deteriorated, and at both Westminster and the Scottish Parliament, Labour seem vulnerable to a challenge again from the Nationalists.

MSP

ALASDAIR MORRISON was born on North Uist in 1968, the Gaelic-speaking son of a Free Presbyterian manse, and he was educated at the Nicolson Institute in Stornoway and Glasgow Caledonian University. From 1991-99, he was a broadcaster with the BBC, mainly in Gaelic – a career his brother John still pursues for BBC network news. From 1997-99, he was editor of the Gaelic newspaper *An Gaidheal Ur*. With the support of Brian Wilson, the Cunninghame North MP who has newspaper and family interests in the Hebrides and is an influential figure in Highland Labour circles, Morrison won the Labour candidacy and saw off SNP hopes of the well-known Gaelic singer Anne Lorne Gillies.

Donald Dewar made him Henry McLeish's deputy minister for enterprise and lifelong learning, with special responsibility for the Highlands and Islands, tourism and Gaelic. This made him, having just turned 30 the previous year, the youngest minister, but it put him in the awkward position with his constituents of having to explain why the Executive was not pushing, at that time, for secure legal status for Gaelic. He continued in the enterprise role when Wendy Alexander took over cabinet responsibility for it, but gained much unwelcome publicity in the midst of the foot and mouth outbreak, allied to a crisis in rural tourism, when he went on a family holiday in Tuscany. On becoming First Minister, Jack McConnell sacked him, which he accepted with the same casual nonchalance with which he had been minister, joining the justice 2 and rural development committees. The pre-election period in 2003 saw him under pressure on the Executive's doubted commitment to retaining air services to the Isle of Barra, though he was able to claim victory on that battle in time for the ballot. He took places on both the environment and rural development committees, as well as that for Europe and external relations.

MP

CALUM MacDONALD was born in 1956 in Stornoway, the son of a crofter and weaver. He was educated at Bayble School and Nicolson Institute, Stornoway, and studied political philosophy at Edinburgh University and the University of California, Los Angeles. He has been both a crofter, following in his father's footsteps, and an academic, having been a teaching fellow in political philosophy at the University of California from 1982-85, as well as working in his brother's local retail business selling kitchen and bathroom fittings from 1986-87. He was elected to the Commons in 1987, being helped to dislodge Nationalists from the Hebridean seat by Kenneth Macmillan, the son of Malcolm

Macmillan, who was Labour MP for the area from 1935-70. MacDonald was a member of the select committee on agriculture from 1987-92.

After Labour gained power, he was Parliamentary Private Secretary to Donald Dewar at the Scottish Office in 1997, before becoming Parliamentary Under-Secretary of State in the Scottish Office from December that year until the devolution election, having responsibility for housing, transport and European affairs. His tenure in housing was significant for initiating the Housing Stock Transfer programme, saying that at one stroke, it put Labour on the side of the consumer instead of the producer. He also introduced the last pre-devolution Bill, the Scottish Enterprise Bill, in January 1999. However, devolution meant the number of Scottish Office jobs at Westminster was cut, and he took quietly to the backbench life once more. MacDonald has an eclectic range of political perspectives which make him difficult to categorise: pro-European (he was one of only five Labour MPs to vote in favour of the Maastricht Treaty in 1993), urging intervention in Serbia in 1992 and taking a conservative Christian approach (as constituents would expect) against abortion and embryo experimentation. He is a Blairite moderniser, a supporter of the Gaelic language, and he falls within the orbit of Brian Wilson's substantial influence, whose enthusiasm for land reform he has shared.

Regional Seats and MSPs

The Scottish Parliament's electoral system divides the country into 73 First Past The Post seats and eight regions each of which elect seven additional members providing a total of 56 'top up' MSPs. Voters have two votes – one for their FPTP constituency and one for a party list in their regions. The seven regional seats in each area are divided between the parties according to the relative strengths of their regional vote, to give as proportional a result as possible for the whole Parliament.

This means there is a relationship between how many seats a party wins under FPTP and how many it wins via the regional seats. Thus, Labour does relatively well under FPTP and so does not win many 'top up' seats, whereas the Conservatives and SNP who are under-represented via FPTP do well out of the regional seat system. This complex system means that whether a party wins or loses a FPTP seat has consequences for the regional seat allocation, e.g., Labour's success in winning all the Glasgow seats means it did not win any top-up seats in the city. This results in a Scottish Parliament which much more accurately reflects the wishes of the Scottish electorate than would have been possible under a purely FPTP system.

On the following pages, the Scottish Parliament election results show the number of seats each party won in 1999 and 2003, with the number of First Past The Post seats in brackets. There then follows a short description of the political geography of each of the eight regional seats, followed by profiles of the seven regional MSPs for each area.

Central Scotland

Scottish Parliament Election Results

	Lab	SNP	Con	Lib Dem	SSP	Green	SSCUP	Ind
1999	(9)	5	1	1	–	–	–	(1)
2003	(9)	3	1	1	1	–	1	(1)

Constituency Vote

	Lab	SNP	Con	Lib Dem	SSP	Green	Others
1999	46.5	29.8	9.6	6.6	0.3	–	7.1
2003	45.3	25.1	9.3	5.6	6.5	–	8.2
Diff.	-1.2	-4.7	-0.3	-1.0	+ 6.2	–	+ 1.1

Regional Vote

	Lab	SNP	Con	Lib Dem	SSP	Green	Others
1999	39.3	27.8	9.2	6.2	1.7	1.8	4.1
2003	40.4	22.5	9.2	5.9	7.2	4.7	10.2
Diff.	+1.1	-5.2	=	-0.3	+5.5	+2.9	-2.9

The Central Scotland regional seat runs from Ayrshire to the River Forth, from Kilmarnock and Loudoun in the west, skirting the south-east of Glasgow and through Lanarkshire to Falkirk East. This is solid Labour territory and in 1992 and 1997, Labour won every one of the ten Westminster seats. In the 1997 election, Labour won 59.4 per cent of the vote to the SNP's 23.4 per cent, with the Conservatives winning 10.4 per cent and the Liberal Democrats 5.2 per cent.

In the first-past-the-post section of the 1999 Scottish Parliament elections, Labour polled 46.5 per cent to the SNP's 29.8 per cent. The large fall for Labour since 1997 was largely explained by former Labour MP Dennis Canavan standing as an independent, and securing the largest majority in Scotland. He also polled well in the regional list vote, winning significant support outside his constituency as a popular protest against mainstream Labour's decision to bar him from representing the party in the election, for being 'not good enough'. As he had already won a constituency seat, his second votes were redistributed in such a way that the SNP benefited as did the Conservatives and Lib Dems, in a region where both smaller parties are particularly poorly organised.

A 2000 Westminster by-election in Falkirk West, resulting from Canavan's resignation from his first Parliamentary seat, saw Labour's Eric Joyce win it for the party. In 2001, Labour returned to a clean sweep of all ten Westminster seats, with 56.6 per cent of the vote, to the SNP's 21.6 per cent. The 2003 election, saw no change in constituency representation, even though the SNP ran Labour close in Cumbernauld and Kilsyth. Labour had 45.3 per cent of the constituency vote to the SNP's 25.1 per cent. With Canavan not on the regional list, there was a different pattern to the second vote share. Labour was up slightly to 40.4 per cent, while the SNP fell from its 1999 level by 5.2 points to 22.5 per cent. The result saw the Lib Dem taking a poor sixth position in the top-up ballot behind the Scottish Senior Citzens, while the Greens had their poorest performance in Scotland, with 4.7 per cent of the vote winning them no seats.

LINDA FABIANI (SNP) was born in Glasgow in 1956. She was educated at Hyndland School, Glasgow and has an HND from Napier University along with a housing diploma from Glasgow University. She worked as a housing administrator in Glasgow from 1982-85, Clydebank from 1985-88, Bute Housing Association from 1988-94, and was then director of East Kilbride Housing Association from 1995 until her election in 1999. She contested the East Kilbride constituency in 1999 and came second. She stood against Labour's Andy Kerr again in 2003, registering a tiny swing from Labour to SNP. She was elected on the Central Scotland list, having been one of the beneficiaries of the strongly criticised Nationalist ranking system which saw off the party's finance spokesman Andrew Wilson in the same Central Scotland Region.

In the first Parliament, Fabiani sat on the transport and environment committee and was then on the equal opportunities committee. She was deputy spokesperson for transport and environment, and then for justice, housing and cities from September 2000 until the 2003 election. Thereafter, she became number two to Bruce Crawford as deputy business manager and whip, while sitting on the petitions committee. She has been prominent in raising international development, asylum and justice issues, including a visit to East Timor as a UN election observer, and has risked the wrath of the anti-abortion lobby by her strong views on the subject. She has also been at the centre of the much-criticised Holyrood Building Project, as one of three MSPs on the Progress Group, her presence limiting the ability of her own party to criticise the overspend. The job of chairing that group was intended to go to George Reid, when he was deputy presiding officer, but the party leadership would not allow one of its MSPs to take the risk of being linked to the project's unpopularity, with Fabiani emerging as a compromise under a Labour convener.

DONALD GORRIE (Liberal Democrat) was born in India in 1933, and still has something of the Raj about him. He was educated at Hurst Grange, Stirling, Oundle School and Corpus Christi College, Oxford. He worked as a school teacher at private schools including Gordonstoun and Marlborough, and was a researcher at Edinburgh University. He was a long-standing full-time councillor in Edinburgh and Lothian, first elected in Corstorphine in 1971. He went on to hold the same ward until the 1997 general election. He was both a district and regional councillor for the area and Liberal/Liberal Democrat group leader on each council. He stood for Parliament in Edinburgh West in 1970, February and October 1974 and 1992, before winning it in 1997 from Lord James Douglas-Hamilton, who had held it for the Tories for 23 years. However, he was not selected to fight his Westminster seat in the Scottish elections - local councillor Margaret Smith was - and had to settle for the Central Scotland regional list. While a councillor, he was also a notable activist for the arts and children on numerous boards of arts and voluntary organisations.

He has proved in the Parliament to be a highly independent, principled politician and thus a nightmare for his party's managers. He was a forceful and vocal critic of the coalition negotiations between Labour and Lib Dems, being one of three Lib Dem MSPs to vote against the 1999 deal, along with John Farquhar Munro and Keith Raffan. Gorrie has also, along with the equally single-minded Margo McDonald, been one of the most consistent questioners and critics of the escalating costs of the Holyrood Building Project. In the first Scottish Parliament, he was on the procedures, finance and then justice 1 committees, while being party spokesman on local government, justice and the voluntary sector, switching to the deputy convenership of the communities committee after the 2003 election, while also on the standards committee and the Lib Dem spokesperson on communities, culture and sport.

Among many dogged campaigns, he took the issue of outlawing sectarianism from a ridiculed notion into the mainstream, with Executive backing and a clause in the criminal justice act, and was among the first in the Parliament to push the issue about Scotland's alcohol problems up the political and media agenda. On numerous issues, he pushed the Executive by talking through policy questions at length in Lib Dem group meetings, portraying himself as the liberal conscience of the group, and helped in that role by having no ambition for ministerial office. He was one of two Lib Dem MSPs to vote against the 13.5 per cent pay increase in March 2002, and was one of those in January 2003 to defeat the Executive on its plans to change procedures for closing fire stations.

CAROLYN LECKIE (SSP) was born in 1965, and educated at Adelphi Secondary, in Glasgow's Gorbals area. After a break from formal education, she trained as a midwife at St James College of Nursing and Midwifery, starting in 1992. She was a steward for the National Association of Local Government Officers (NALGO, later part of Unison) for three years from the age of 17, including strike action taken in support of striking miners, until she had the first of two daughters.

Leckie worked as a midwife in Rutherglen maternity unit and in Unison, where she became branch secretary, leading a number of strikes and campaigns for health workers in north Glasgow hospitals, including a strike by 300 ancillary workers against Sodexho, the French multinational which includes the Parliament canteen among its contracts. When the Rutherglen unit closed, she joined the SSP, becoming an organiser of the new East Kilbride branch and a candidate in Central Scotland in 1999, where the SSP won 1.74 per cent of the vote.

In the SSP, she was elected health spokesperson, becoming co-chair of the party in 2001, and standing against the Speaker of the House of Commons, Michael Martin, in the 2001 Westminster election – breaking with the convention that the Speaker is elected unopposed by other parties. She stood against Labour's Andy Kerr in East Kilbride in 2003, winning fourth place on 2,736 votes – an 8 per cent share. She won her Central Scotland seat in 2003 with 19,016 votes (7.2 per cent), the second best SSP performance in Scotland after Glasgow. Once in the Parliament, as the SSP group health spokesperson, she accused the larger parties of working together to keep her off the health committee, and was described in a *Sunday Herald* profile as being 'flamboyant, shabbily glamorous and possessed of a sharp wit'.

MICHAEL MATHESON (SNP) was born in 1970 in Glasgow, educated at John Bosco Secondary School and then gained a BSc in Occupational Therapy from Queen Margaret College in Edinburgh, as well as a BA and diploma in applied social sciences from the Open University. He worked as an occupational therapist for Highland Regional Council from 1991-93, then with Central Regional Council from 1993-97 and subsequently with Stirling Council from 1997 to 1999. He joined the SNP in 1989 and stood first in the Hamilton North and Bellshill constituency at the 1997 election, and then in Falkirk West in 1999, where the entire vote was skewed by the success of Dennis Canavan as an independent candidate. Standing again against Canavan in the same constituency in 2003, Matheson moved the SNP into second place, overtaking Labour.

Once elected from number three on his party list in 1999, he became the SNP's deputy spokesman for justice and equality and sat on the justice committee until December 2000, transferring into its justice 1 successor, the dual role giving him an important role in the scrutiny of a substantial legislative workload, particularly on land reform. He took credit for forcing the Lord Advocate to open up evidence before the Dunblane inquiry which had been previously been placed under a 100 year secrecy rule. He was also convener of the disability cross-party group. For the 2003 election, he secured second position in a bitterly contested internal party battle, helping to oust front bencher Andrew Wilson from the

Parliament. The second Parliament saw him continue on the justice 1 committee, while remaining as deputy justice spokesperson, with European affairs added to his brief.

While deputy to Roseanna Cunningham in handling the justice brief, in 2000 he managed her successful campaign for the post of party deputy leadership then being vacated by John Swinney. Although canny about his positioning within the party, he is usually associated with the more fundamentalist wing of the SNP. In his non-political life, he is something of a travel adventurer, a keen mountaineer and member of Ochil Mountain Rescue Team.

MARGARET MITCHELL (Conservative) was born in 1952 in Coatbridge, and educated at Coatbridge High School, doing teacher training at Hamilton 1971-4, and working as a primary teacher until 1992 in Airdrie, Bothwell, Shotts and Craighead special school, Blantyre. She studied for a BA degree through the Open University from 1986-90, then doing a certificate in media studies at Jordanhill College, from 1990-91, and training as a lawyer at Strathclyde University from 1992-95. She is a South Lanarkshire Justice of the Peace and a member of the Hamilton crime prevention panel. Mitchell was special adviser to the Conservative MSPs for Lothian, David McLetchie and Lord James Douglas-Hamilton, during the first Parliament. She stood in 2003 in Hamilton South, coming third to Labour's Tom McCabe, with 12.8 per cent of the vote. She had, however, secured top place on the Central Scotland list, ousting first term Conservative Lyndsay McIntosh, who left the party as a result and stood, unsuccessfully, for the Scottish People's Alliance. Elected from that top slot, Mitchell said her main interest as an MSP is in justice, which fits with her justice 1 committee place and a deputy spokesperson's role on justice and home affairs.

ALEX NEIL (SNP) was born in 1951 in Irvine, and was educated at Dalmellington High School, Ayr and at Dundee University where he studied economics. He worked as a researcher for the Labour Party in its Glasgow headquarters in 1975-76, before joining the breakaway, strongly pro-home rule Scottish Labour Party with Jim Sillars in 1976. He was general secretary of the party from 1977-79, among other things fighting off the entryist attentions of the International Marxist Group and people such as Charlie Gordon, later to re-emerge as Labour leader of Glasgow City Council post-1999. Neil was a marketing manager from 1979-83, living part of that time in New Hampshire, then basing himself in Ayr and working for Cumnock and Doon Enterprise Trust in 1983-87. He ran his own company, Network Scotland Ltd, from 1987-93, and was an economic consultant from 1993-99, including much work for local enterprise companies. He also worked for the Prince's Scottish Youth Business Trust.

Neil joined the SNP in 1986, and was a leading fundamentalist within the party alongside Sillars. He fought the Glasgow Central by-election in 1989 followed by the Kilmarnock and Loudoun constituency, all unsuccessfully, in 1992, 1997 and 1999. In the 1992 general election, as a party vice-convener, he had been architect of the 'Free by '93' campaign – widely seen as triumphalist and out of touch with the electorate's sense of priorities, and leading to a disappointing result. In 1996, in a typically electrifying speech, he caused controversy when at the SNP conference he compared George Robertson, then Shadow Scottish Secretary, to Lord Haw Haw, the Nazi collaborator. He was made one of three SNP members on the executive of the cross-party Scotland Forward 'yes-yes' referendum campaign in 1997, as a means of tying the more fundamentalist wing of the Nationalists into the campaign. In the 2003 election, he shifted to Hamilton North and Bellshill, his party critics eagerly pointing out that the result saw one of the sharpest collapses of SNP support anywhere in Scotland. Once in the Parliament, being semi-detached from the Salmond leadership as the fundamentalists sought to redefine the agenda, he sat on the social inclusion committee of the Scottish Parliament and was the party's social security spokesperson until September 2000, this despite it being a reserved issue which could have been better dealt with by one of the dual mandate MPs/MSPs at that time. Neil used a member's bill to push the Executive towards making quango and other public appointments more open, though not getting his wish to see them scrutinised by Parliamentary committees.

As the SNP's vice-convener for policy, he contested the party leadership after Alex Salmond suddenly resigned in summer 2000, the only other candidate being the deputy leader John Swinney. Following his defeat, by a margin of two to one, Neil opted not to hold any frontbench post, instead becoming convener of the enterprise and lifelong learning committee, a post previously held by Swinney. That became part of the consensus which saw the SNP back the 'smart, successful Scotland' strategy of the Executive, and there was also a major report into the future of higher education, which went down a strongly statist path under Neil's convenership. He was also prominent in raising the issues of population decline. After the 2003 election, he was not offered a front bench post or a significant committee post, and took a seat on the standards committee. He was the first MSP to table a bill after the 2003 election, taking on Michael Russell's stalled member's bill on achieving secure status for Gaelic – although the Executive had agreed in the 2003 coalition agreement to legislate for this.

The challenge to Swinney's leadership launched in July 2003 by little-known Glasgow activist Dr Bill Wilson saw several Swinney supporters openly accuse the candidate of being a stalking horse for Alex Neil. The Central Scotland MSP was in Australia during the early weeks of the campaign, refusing to say how he would vote, and issuing threats of legal action and party disciplinary proceedings against former MSPs Andrew Wilson and Duncan Hamilton. It appeared the challenge raised by Bill Wilson could have harmed any hopes Neil had of another attempt at the leadership, as it seemed likely the rules for such a challenge would change, and the party was likely to have a limited appetite for another challenge as soon as a year after Wilson's. Choosing not to back Wilson, Neil risked losing ground as the leading figure on the hardline wing of the party, in particular to Campbell Martin, the West of Scotland MSP who went out on a limb to attack Swinney. Neil chose to focus his attention instead on plans for an independence convention, building links with other pro-independence parties including the Scottish Socialist Party.

JOHN SWINBURNE (Scottish Senior Citizens Unity Party) was born in Pennsylvania in 1930, his parents bringing him back to Scotland aged seven, where he was educated at Dalziel High School. He worked as a mechanical engineer, a freelance journalist and as press officer and commercial manager of Motherwell football club, of which he wrote the club history, published in 1999. He claims not to have missed a home game at Fir Park since 1947, and has based his party headquarters at the stadium. While a director of the club, he - or at least his consultancy business, the Swinburne Agency – continues to work on behalf of Motherwell Football Club in drumming up sponsorship and advertising money, declaring annual earnings ranging between £15,000 and £50,000.

Swinburne has claimed that it was politicians who drove him into politics, giving voice to a popular public frustration at the species. He formed his party in early 2003, after hearing a politician say that it would become necessary in future for people to work until they are 70. He contacted the Electoral Commission, registered the party name – eclipsing the Pensioners' Party, which was already established and standing candidates – and scored an impressive publicity coup by getting veteran heroes Billy McNeil from Celtic and Eric Caldow of Rangers to support him, with McNeil number three on the Central Scotland list and Caldow number four. Swinburne also gained publicity by standing against Jack McConnell in Motherwell and Wishaw, securing 1,597 votes, or 6.29 per cent and taking fifth place ahead of the Liberal Democrat. He won his Central Scotland list place with 17,146 votes, or 6.5 per cent of the second votes cast.

Having worked the football press at Motherwell, Swinburne is a savvy media operator, with a knack for a well-turned, indignant soundbite. And while championing the poor downtrodden senior citizen, there is nothing poor or downtrodden about his suave style. He claimed to have done his sums on the candidacy, in terms of the potential support for a senior citizens' representative in the increasingly aged demographics of Central Scotland, though his 2003 win came as something of a surprise to others. He seemed not to have done so much homework on the issues, as most of the arguments he made in his campaign and in the second Parliament were about pensions and welfare payments, these being reserved issues for Westminster. This put him in a near-nationalist position, of demanding that the Scottish Parliament should have more powers so that his desired reforms could be brought about. Yet he also says the 'Unity' in his party's title refers to the United Kingdom, and brought forward a plan for electing ten regional list MSPs, three of whom would be sent to Westminster to deal with reserved issues. Holding his first national conference weeks after the election, he said he was hoping to branch out to the ethnic minority vote, particularly in Glasgow. He was also reported early on as having made some intolerant comments about gays during his campaign, which he denied having made. He found that by making outrageous statements in Parliament, he could easily gain media attention, starting with his attacks on the Holyrood Parliament building, saying it would be better to brick up window spaces even if that were not aesthetic, rather than spend more money on their installation. With a fine line in political incorrectness, he angered fellow MSPs during a row about the proposed siting of a secure psychiatric unit near Bothwell, stirring up fear and declaring that those placed in it would be 'two pills short of flipping'.

Glasgow

Scottish Parliament Election Results

	Lab	SNP	Con	Lib Dem	SSP	Green
1999	(10)	4	1	1	1	-
2003	(10)	2	1	1	2	1

Constituency Vote

	Lab	SNP	Con	Lib Dem	SSP	Green	Others
1999	49.3	27.9	7.7	8.1	6.3	-	0.7
2003	45.9	19.3	8.7	9.4	14.5	-	2.1
Diff.	-3.5	-8.6	+1.0	+1.3	+8.2	-	+1.4

Regional Vote

	Lab	SNP	Con	Lib Dem	SSP	Green	Others
1999	43.9	25.5	7.9	7.2	7.2	4.0	4.3
2003	37.7	17.1	7.5	7.3	15.2	7.1	8.0
Diff.	-6.2	-8.4	-0.4	+0.1	+8.0	+3.2	+3.7

Glasgow as a Parliamentary region is comprised of all ten Glasgow constituencies, one of which, Glasgow Rutherglen, is partly in the South Lanarkshire Council area. In 1992, 1997, 1999, 2001 and 2003, Labour won all the seats. The last time it did not have such dominance of Glasgow was after the 1988 Govan by-election, won by the SNP but lost by them four years later. Govan continued to be the city seat the SNP targeted, but with a frustrating lack of success. At the 1997 high point for Labour, it won 60.4 per cent of the vote to the SNP's 19.2 per cent, the Conservatives 8.5 per cent and the Liberal Democrats 7.3 per cent. In the 1999 election, despite another Govan challenge, Labour's clean sweep made Glasgow one of two regions in which it won all the first-past-the-post constituencies, the other being West of Scotland. Labour won 49.3 per cent of the constituency vote to the SNP's 27.9 per cent. In the regional vote, Labour won 43.9 per cent to the SNP's 25.5 per cent which calculated into top-up seats for all the other parties bar Labour.

In 2001, the Labour dominance continued, with 50.9 per cent of the vote to the SNP's 17.2 per cent. This apparent ten point drop in the Labour vote was largely down to Michael Martin in Springburn standing as The Speaker of the House of Commons. In 2003, Labour's position was greatly strengthened when a respectable showing at constituency level for the SSP was largely at the expense of the SNP, leaving Labour with enhanced majorities. Labour won 45.9 per cent of a sharply reduced turnout in the region, with the SNP on 19.3 per cent and the SSP on 14.5 per cent – up from 6.3 per cent in 1999. The SNP took second place everywhere except Glasgow Pollok, where Tommy Sheridan was runner-up, and Rutherglen, where Lib Dem Robert Brown boosted the party's showing. The regional vote had Labour on 37.7 per cent to the SNP's 17.1 per cent and the SSP's 15.2 per cent, with only 3,778 second votes separating the latter two. The SNP's Dorothy Grace

Elder had stood down ahead of the election, having fallen out with her party group and Kenny Gibson failed to be re-elected.

BILL AITKEN (Conservative) was born in 1947 in Glasgow and educated at Allan Glen's School, Glasgow, and Glasgow College of Commerce. After training with the Association of Chartered Insurance, he worked at Eagle Star and NEM Insurance as an insurance underwriter. Joining the Conservative youth wing in 1970 and becoming national chairman from 1975-77, Aitken was first elected to Glasgow City Council in 1976 and served for 23 years – a period which saw the steady decline of Conservatism in Scotland and particularly in Glasgow. The experience has left him with a doggedness, a dry, wry, sarcastic, adenoidal humour, and experience of shadowing the workings of the Glasgow Labour mindset, all of which mean he is often at his best in the face of adversity. From 1977-79, he was convenor of the city licensing committee and vice-convenor of the personnel committee during the last period the Conservatives were running the city. Known as Baillie Bill, he was later leader of the Tory opposition from 1980-84 and 1992-96, with the Conservative group down to five councillors in the latter period. When Aitken stood down from his Kelvinside ward in 1999 to stand instead as an MSP, they were reduced to one seat.

Aitken contested the Anniesland constituency for the Scottish Parliament against Donald Dewar, and was elected the sole Conservative from the Glasgow regional list. Upon his election, he became his party's deputy business manager, and a deputy member of the Scottish Parliamentary bureau. Other roles in the first four years were as deputy spokesman on local government and housing, membership of the social justice committee, followed by two years as deputy convener of one of the justice committees, linked to party deputy spokesmanship on justice and social affairs. In the latter, he even made the cover of *Newsweek* magazine as well as, unusually, capturing the attention of the London media, with his provocative claim that the Executive's land reform legislation of 2003 was a landgrab of which Zimbabwe's Robert Mugabe would have been proud: 'little short of a deadly cocktail of restriction, inhibition to investment and downright legalised theft'. Of course, he also dealt with Glaswegian issues for the party, in which role he enthusiastically backed the Executive's Housing Stock Transfer. Re-elected to a Glasgow list seat in 2003, again the only Conservative from the city, he was appointed the party's business manager and chief whip, with a raised political profile in the media and in co-ordinating the party's debating effort.

ROBERT BROWN (Liberal Democrat) was born in 1946 in Newcastle-upon-Tyne and educated at Gordons School, Huntly, and Aberdeen University where he studied law. He worked as a law assistant at Edmonds & Ledingham in Aberdeen from 1969-72, as deputy procurator fiscal in Dumbarton from 1972-74, and as assistant, then partner specialising in civil law at the major Glasgow-based firm Ross Harper & Murphy, from 1974-99.

Brown was elected to Glasgow District Council from 1977-92 and was leader of the Liberal/Lib Dem Group for all that time. He has stood seven times for the Glasgow Rutherglen seat – five Westminster elections – October 1974, 1979, 1983, 1987 and 1997, and both Scottish Parliament elections – getting himself elected instead for the Glasgow region in both 1999 and 2003. In the 2003 vote, his doggedness showed a modest reward as he moved into second place behind Labour. In the first Parliament, his membership of the Scottish Parliament corporate body put him into the thick of the Holyrood Building Project, having to defend its mismanagement to the finance committee and in public. Lacking much in the way of charisma, he has nevertheless proved a solid and thoughtful Parliamentary performer. He was the party's spokesman on communities and housing, and was on the social justice committee. From there, he focussed on passage of the Housing Act, winning changes which reformed the right to buy, sought to tackle homelessness and focussed on children. Following the 2003 election, he took on one of the most significant backbench posts as convener of the education committee, while continued membership of the corporate body saw him take special responsibility for finance and governance issues including freedom of information.

Brown has also been convenor of the Scottish Lib Dem policy committee from 1996-99, meaning a leading role away from the public view in drawing up the Scottish Lib Dem manifestos in 1997, 1999 and 2003, where his strategic sense is valued by the party leadership. He has gained a reputation for local campaigning and advocacy and was chair of Rutherglen and Cambuslang Citizen's Advice Bureau from 1983-88 and from 1993-98. He became embroiled in the heated south Glasgow debate over a council decision to close Govanhill swimming pool, where he encountered Charlie Gordon, Labour leader of Glasgow City Council, whose passionate support for the first-past-the-post electoral system leads to disdain for list MSPs.

PATRICK HARVIE (Green) was born in 1973 in Vale of Leven, educated at Dumbarton Academy and left Manchester Metropolitan University after three years with no degree. His mother ran and still runs a re-cycling campaign, which saw him spend childhood Saturday mornings bundling newspapers for pulping. He once told her he wanted to be the first Green Prime Minister. His working life has included jobs as an Inland Revenue worker, and as part of the gay men's services team of the sexual health agency PHACE from 1997-2003, in Strathclyde and then as development worker in Lanarkshire. This included counselling and assertiveness training.

He joined the Labour Party in 1994, hopeful that Tony Blair's new leadership would rid the party of 'outdated socialist doctrine' in favour of more 'social radicalism', but found within a year it was not going to be as he imagined, so he let his membership lapse. He joined the Greens after hearing Robin Harper give his support to repeal of Section 28, which had banned promotion of homosexuality in schools, and rose fast through its slim ranks, becoming justice and social justice portfolio on the party's council in 2001-02 and justice spokesperson in 2002-03. He was the Green representative on the Coalition For Justice Not War, set up to oppose war in Iraq.

Posing for photographers with his mum, he became the new Green contingent's early star in the second Parliament, and signalled early – featuring on the front page of the *Sun* – his intention to bring in family law changes which would recognise civil partnerships between gay, lesbian and unmarried heterosexual couples. This may have backfired, as the harsh reaction seems to have scared the Executive off doing anything so radical (though it had wanted to), at least until Westminster deals with it. He was made his party's spokesperson on justice and social inclusion, while a member of the communities committee. His interests remain in sexual health, as well as media, technology, freedom of information, citizenship and 'food culture'.

ROSIE KANE (SSP) was born in 1961 in Glasgow, and was educated at Lourdes Secondary School, Glasgow, where she admits to having truanted most of the last two years, leaving with no qualifications. Her education was taken up again in her early thirties, doing an access to university course in social science, and doing most of her first year of the degree, until finance and child care problems forced her to give up. She has done various shop and sports work, teaching swimming and keep fit, working in a laundry and in the years before her election, she was a youth worker in Drumchapel, Glasgow, and sometime telephone councillor with Childline Scotland.

Having been withdrawn and depressed, she got involved in politics from 1996 through the campaign against the M77 motorway extension. She stumbled across the Pollok Free State while visiting her mother nearby, and soon become one of the protestors, living in the tree branches at the protest site at the height of the protests. Meeting up with activists from the Scottish Socialist Alliance, she joined up, and became environment spokesperson for the successor Scottish Socialist Party, arguing the issue must be made relevant to people's lives and get away from too much science. She has criminal convictions for her anti-nuclear protests at Faslane and chaining herself to the railings as part of the long-running protest at the closure of Glasgow's Govanhill swimming pool in 2001.

She stood in Glasgow Shettleston in 1999, 2001 and 2003, on the most recent occasion getting 2,403 votes, 14.5 per cent of the vote, and coming third. She was, however, elected as number two on the Glasgow list to Tommy Sheridan – that being the only part of Scotland to have two SSP representatives – Kane quickly became a national media star and talking point, when she said on election night that the new SSP group would bring 'madness and craziness' to the Parliament, and it would become like Channel Four's *Big Brother* house, so that people would want to tune in and find out what happen next. She caused a small sensation and grabbed every very front page by turning up to be sworn in wearing jeans and a shoulder-baring colourful top, described as 'butterflies on the windscreen', and having had one of her teenage daughters write 'My oath is to the people' on the palm of one hand. Her style is never short of refreshingly direct and breezily subversive. She claims to be feisty and determined, and is much sharper at mainstream politics than she likes to let on. One of her many ambitions as an MSP is to ensure that she never fits in to the Parliament's debating chamber: 'There seem to be a pile of unspoken rules and I neither know nor want to know them'. 'Her quick wit can condense socialism into soundbites and make it sound like fun at the same time,' said the *Sunday Herald*, though it also reported her first few months as an MSP had involved so much talking that she was under medical advice to rest her throat. She appeared on the UK-wide *Question Time* in November 2003 – a sign of the growing profile of the SSP – and even managed to charm the Conservative Lord Strathclyde – proof, if it were needed of her personal and political talents.

With Executive ministers declaring a tough line on anti-social youth behaviour, Kane began a debate on whether it was demoralising to call young people 'neds', which led to a sharp exchange with communities minister Margaret Curran, in which the new MSP may have discovered Parliamentary life might not be as easy as she had thought. With a seat on the local government and transport committee, she promised also to campaign against the M74 northern extension, for women's refuges and for women in prison, while campaigns can also be expected to oppose fluidisation of water, GM crops and toxic dumping. This is helped by being a columnist in the *Sunday Mail*.

Kane suffered a return of depression after being criticised in Parliament by SNP MSP Stewart Stevenson, who estimated she had contributed 5,000 words in six months at a cost of £5.59 per word. She came off the local government and transport committee and announced she was taking a month off from what she called the 'macho boys' club' of the Parliament. At the turn of the year, as she slowly increased her activities, she publicly talked about her history of problems with mental ill-health, and thanked her fellow SSP MSP, Carolyn Leckie and the general public for the support she had received.

TOMMY SHERIDAN (SSP) was born in 1964 in Glasgow and educated at Lourdes Secondary School, Glasgow, followed by Stirling University, where he studied economics and politics. He held a number of jobs while a teenager and student; a sales assistant at Burtons menswear aged 16, a Pickfords removal labourer aged 17, a health instructor (he remains a fitness fanatic and keen amateur footballer), and a team leader on a programme to tackle hypothermia. Inspired by his mother, who campaigned against domestic abuse, and a book she gave him about John Maclean, Sheridan became a member of the Labour Party when he went to Stirling, soon joining the Trotskyite Militant Tendency. Through the vicious battles within the party in the mid-1980s, he was on the other side to those who would become Labour MSPs; Jack McConnell, also at Stirling, and Sarah Boyack, Wendy Alexander, Susan Deacon and Frank McAveety, who would become his opponent also on Glasgow Council.

He came to public attention as one of the leading organisers against the poll tax in the late 1980s and as president of the Anti-Poll Tax Federation. In October 1991, he was involved in a street protest which prevented a warrant sale in Glasgow and, for tearing up a court order to desist, he was charged and detained at Saughton Prison, Edinburgh. His jail sentence covered the period of the 1992 election, in which Sheridan stood for the Glasgow Pollok seat, his home turf, as a Scottish Militant Labour candidate, winning 19.2 per cent of the vote. A month later, he was still in jail when he was elected councillor for Pollok ward on Glasgow City Council, winning 52 per cent of the vote. He continued to represent the ward until the 2003 election, when Keith Baldassara, from the same party as Sheridan, retained it by a narrower margin. He stood for the Glasgow seat in the 1994 European elections and in Pollok in the 1997 general elections. By then a much altered seat, he won 11.1 per cent of the vote for the newly-named Scottish Socialist Alliance.

With the setting up of the Scottish Socialist Party in 1999, Sheridan became the national convenor, and with jibes that it was a one-man band, he won election to the Scottish Parliament in May that year. He stood again in the Pollok seat, winning 21.5 per cent, and was elected, though with 7.3 per cent – not a large margin – as a list MSP for Glasgow. This gave him prominence as one of the three individual MSPs, along with Robin Harper for the Scottish Greens and Denis Canavan, the independent member for Falkirk West. The three worked closely together through the first term, to ensure their motions were seconded, with Sheridan taking more of the limelight than the others. In 2003, Sheridan stood in Pollok again, moving into second place ahead of the SNP's Kenny Gibson, and rising from 21 per cent to 28 per cent of the vote. But with a 3,341 majority and 15.5 per cent lead for Labour's Johann Lamont, Sheridan was still some way off a constituency breakthrough at what might have been his best chance.

He became one of the stars of the first Parliament by pioneering the backbench bill on the Abolition of Poindings and Warrant Sales, relating directly to the anti-poll tax campaign that had made his name. Sheridan steered this through its pre-legislative committee stages, successfully making it all but impossible for Executive ministers to demand that coalition backbenchers oppose the bill when it reached its stage one reading in April 2000. The revolt by backbenchers that day was the only really significant one of the first term, showing the way the committees could work independently, and also the danger to ministers of not taking backbenchers with them. Sheridan was later to be disappointed, however, by the alternative system for debt collection, on which he worked with ministers at first but then resigned from the working party in protest at the shape the replacement was taking.

He tried the same tactics with his second member's bill of the first term, which would have seen universal provision of free school meals, at an annual cost of more than £180m. This time, Sheridan was careful to bring on board children's and educational pressure groups and representatives, to build an alliance much broader than his hard left base. It was less successful in Parliament, although some left-wingers backed him, and by this time, he was causing major difficulties to the SNP, which tried to develop its own policy on the issue rather than handing all the credit to Sheridan, realising too late the danger the SSP posed to the Nationalists. Following the election, the SNP was split over whether to build a pan-nationalist alliance, including the pro-independence SSP and Greens, with six and seven seats respectively, or to be more effective in seeing off the threat they posed.

Sheridan also created problems for the SNP over the Iraq war, taking a harder line against it under any conditions, and winning over their more radical support. New supporters included headline-grabbing celebrities Dougray Scott, Peter Mullan and Elaine C. Smith. The fall of Saddam Hussein days before the election turned the tide of public opinion, and may have diminished the SSP momentum. The result, adding five more SSP MSPs, took the pressure off him, and killed off the jibe that the party was a one-man band. But it also threatened to change the face of the SSP, making it seem less disciplined and less austere.

Tommy Sheridan spent a second period in jail with a week behind bars immediately before Christmas 2000 in Greenock Prison, and in August 2003 in Barlinnie. The reason on both occasions was Sheridan's refusal to pay a £250 fine for breach of the peace after an anti-nuclear protest at Faslane nuclear submarine base. Sheridan turned the first event, like most things he is involved in, into a publicity success and wrote a 'Prison Diary' for the Sunday papers which underlined his celebrity status. He stood for the rectorship of St Andrews University in early 2000, and polled respectably, narrowly losing to Andrew Neil, broadcaster and right-wing publisher of the *Scotsman*.

Sheridan is a throwback to a Red Clydeside tradition of articulate, passionate, charismatic, working-class radicals, whose wide appeal perplexes his political opponents. He had one of the worst voting records in the first Parliament, balancing the role of campaigner, Parliamentarian and Glasgow councillor. He was absent, for instance, on the landmark vote to repeal Section 28 on the promotion of homosexuality in the classroom, although strongly in favour of repeal. He takes about £24,000 of the MSPs' salary, representing the average skilled worker, and giving the rest to the SSP. He is also a kenspeckle figure for his trademark tan, a sign of vanity he readily admits but also a source of instant recognisability. And high on the glamour stakes with his air steward and trade unionist wife Gail, they honeymooned and continue to holiday in Cuba, to signify his support for the socialist regime, Fidel Castro and Che Guevara, and to top up their tans. Sheridan took Rosie Kane's place on the local government and transport committee when she took a month off at the end of 2003 due to mental ill-health.

Sheridan has written an autobiography, *A Time to Rage*, with journalist Joan McAlpine, now deputy editor of the *Herald*. He also co-authored with Alan McCombes *Imagine: A Socialist Vision for the 20th Century* published at the end of 2000, which outlines the revolutionary socialist case for Scotland. His status was enhanced by James Kirk, ex-bass player of Orange Juice penning a eulogy to Sheridan, 'Get on Board', which saluted his anti-nuclear protests with the chorus, 'Mr Sheridan, he's all right. Each generation picks up the fight.'

NICOLA STURGEON (SNP) was born in 1970 in Irvine and educated at Greenwood Academy, Irvine, and the University of Glasgow where she studied law. She was a trainee solicitor in Glasgow from 1993-95, a solicitor in Stirling from 1995-97 and a solicitor at Drumchapel Law Centre, Glasgow from 1997-99.

Sturgeon joined the SNP in 1986, and rose to a key party position of publicity vice-convener in 1997-99, leading up to the first devolution election. Already on the party's national executive, she first stood at the age of 21 in Glasgow Shettleston in the 1992 election, and then in the Labour-SNP marginal of Glasgow Govan in 1997 where she succeeded in nearly halving Labour's majority to 2,914. She stood again in Govan in the Scottish Parliament elections and – though she further reduced Labour's majority to 1,756 – had been everyone's favourite to win after two years of constant Labour scandals. Instead, Labour's Gordon Jackson won, and she was elected as a regional list member through her top spot on the SNP's Glasgow list. Thus, 2003 was her third attempt at Govan – twice a scene of SNP by-election victories. Standing as incumbent, Jackson had problems with his Labour activists in coming out to support him, he had difficulties with Muslim voters over the Iraq war, he gained much adverse publicity both for going on holiday in the middle of the campaign and for going back to his ultra-lucrative court work the day after the election. But still Sturgeon could not make it, facing the same Glasgow problems that other SNP MSPs suffered, of much of their vote shifting to the SSP. Labour's majority was cut to 1,235, but the SNP share of the vote was down by five points to 31 per cent, inviting jibes from Labour that if she could not make it after three tries, they should get to keep her for the mantlepiece. More seriously, with Sturgeon as her party's campaign co-ordinator – a task John Swinney had also handed her in 2001, following her role as his own campaign manager in the 2000 leadership election – her own loss in Govan spoke of a more deep-seated problem for the SNP in breaking through, particularly in the West of Scotland.

Sturgeon has covered the three biggest portfolios during her time in the Scottish Parliament. At first, she continued her pre-1999 role as SNP spokesperson on children and education, moving to health and community care in 2000 when John Swinney became leader and reshuffled his team. She held positions in the relevant committees during that time. Dealing with education, she faced Sam Galbraith, and on health, it was Malcolm Chisholm, who used first a patronising and then a relaxed style to get the better of her serious, brittle approach which often has her characterised as 'a nippy sweetie'. She claims credit for pushing for free long-term care for the elderly and for exposing the deferred hospital waiting lists which the Executive was forced to end. Following the 2003 election, she became justice spokeswoman, giving her party's support to much of the anti-social behaviour legislation the Executive was proposing. Her political proximity to Swinney, just as she was very close to Salmond before, established her as de facto deputy leader even though Roseanna Cunningham may beg to differ. However, it was noted that she played a lower profile role in Swinney's defence of his leadership against a grassroots challenger in 2003. Her role at that year's conference was more notable for successfully moving that all the party's MSPs and MPs should donate £250 per month to the party.

SANDRA WHITE (SNP) was born in 1951 in Govan, Glasgow, and educated at Garthamlock Secondary School, Glasgow College and Cardonald College, Glasgow. Having worked as a clerk and been a mature student, she was elected to Renfrewshire Council from 1989 until 1999, a time when it was riven with sometimes unruly disputes between Labour and the SNP. While working for the William Wallace Society, she was a full-time councillor and convenor of the property and construction services committee, as well as being her party group's deputy housing spokesperson.

White joined the SNP in 1983, contested Glasgow Hillhead in 1992 and Glasgow Kelvin in 1997. In the 1999 Scottish Parliament election, she stood again in Glasgow Kelvin, losing to Labour's Pauline McNeill, and was elected from the number four spot on the SNP Glasgow top-up list. She stood in Kelvin again in 2003, and lost again while cutting McNeill's majority to 3,289, but also seeing the SNP share of vote cut from 29.3 per cent to 20.8 per cent. She was even surer of a regional list seat in 2003, taking top Glasgow slot by beating Nicola Sturgeon and Kenny Gibson (who lost his list seat in 2003), largely thanks to the party's membership being strongest in her Kelvin political base. This was a prime example of the SNP's internal system for list selection rewarding those who act locally with little national profile, while punishing talented politicians who played a prominent national role.

In the first Parliament, White was SNP deputy spokesperson on equality and race relations and SNP deputy whip, while on the local government committee from January 2001. After the 2003 election, she was made deputy health and social justice spokesperson. She takes a generally left-wing position, voting against the 13.5 per cent pay rise for MSPs in March 2002, then having lost the vote, she said she would donate the difference to Women's Aid. She was at odds with the party leadership when it shifted away from opposition to support for the Glasgow Housing Stock Transfer. White was among those Glaswegians who stuck with their opposition. She also gained a high profile in Glasgow for her campaign against lap dancing bars being licensed in the city, and she was convener of the cross-party MSP committee on older people and ageing. She played a cautious political game at the time of the 2003 challenge to John Swinney's leadership, first welcoming the debate that it sparked but swinging late on behind the incumbent. She also made unhelpful waves for the party leadership supporting the idea of an independence convention, and welcoming the SNP examining ways of working with the Scottish Socialists.

Highlands and Islands

Scottish Parliament Election Results

	Lab	SNP	Con	Lib Dem	SSP	Green
1999	3 (1)	2 (2)	2	(5)	-	-
2003	2 (1)	2 (2)	2	(5)	-	1

Constituency Vote

	Lab	SNP	Con	Lib Dem	SSP	Green	Others
1999	27.4	28.5	14.3	28.3	-	-	1.6
2003	22.7	26.6	16.4	27.9	5.2	-	1.2
Diff.	-4.7	-1.9	+2.1	-0.4	-	-	-0.4

Regional Vote

	Lab	SNP	Con	Lib Dem	SSP	Green	Others
1999	25.5	27.7	14.9	21.4	0.9	3.7	6.0
2003	22.3	23.4	16.0	18.8	5.3	8.3	6.0
Diff.	-3.2	-4.3	+1.1	-2.7	+4.5	+4.5	=

The Highlands and Islands is perhaps the most easily identifiable region of Scotland, with its distinctive political culture well established. It includes three island seats, the three giant mainland seats in Highland Council area, encompassing also Argyll as far south as Kintyre and into the commuter area for Glasgow, and on the other flank, it incorporates Moray which would otherwise seen as being more oriented towards the North East. The pattern of party competition varies considerably from the politics of the Central Belt. There is a four-party system at play, with the Liberal Democrats successfully tending, at Parliamentary level, to mop up the spirit of independence that keeps the mainstream parties out of control in all the region's councils except Moray. In the 1997 election, less than 2,000 votes separated the Liberal Democrats, Labour and the SNP, who all won around 27 per cent of the Westminster vote, with the Conservatives in fourth place on 16.2 per cent. The Lib Dems won four seats to Labour's two and the SNP's one, with the only constituency changing hands being Inverness East, Nairn and Lochaber, with the retirement of Lib Dem Russell Johnston making way for Labour's David Stewart.

In 1999, it was the most interesting region to watch, not only because the three leading parties were again separated on the constituency vote by 2,000 votes, with the SNP this time finishing top with 28.5 per cent, but also because the lack of incumbency – an important factor in Highlands and Islands politics – put several constituencies into play that might not otherwise have been hard contested. Lib Dems did well to turn incumbency at Westminster into fresh victories for the Scottish Parliament. It was the four-way marginal of Inverness East, Nairn and Lochaber which changed hands again, in favour of the Nationalists – making it one of only two seats at that time to be represented by different parties in the two Parliaments (excluding Dennis Canavan in Falkirk West). So the Lib Dems had five constituencies to the SNP's two and Labour's one. On the regional vote, the SNP finished in the lead again with 27.7 per cent, ahead of Labour's 25.5 per cent and the Lib Dems 21.4 per cent. Labour proved, as it would do in 2003, that where it has some chance of winning top-up seats, it is reasonably good at hanging on to its first vote supporters. Thus, the composition of regional members was very different from the rest of the country, with Labour winning its only top-up seats. In 1999, this was the only part of Scotland where any party other than Labour – in this case the Lib Dems – did so well at winning constituencies that even after the compensating factor intended to feed through the top-up mechanism, it was still had a disproportionately strong representation.

In 2001, no seats changed hands, and the SNP saw its share of the vote drop since the 1997 election from 26.7 to 22.9 per cent while Labour held steady on 27 per cent and Lib Dems pushed up from 27.7 to 30.3 per cent. By the 2003 election, incumbency played a part in making the constituency battles much less interesting than four years before, with the Lib Dems coming ahead of the SNP and Labour, with 27.9 per cent, 26.6 per cent and 22.7 per cent respectively. It was expected this was the area in which the Greens stood their best chance of adding to their one Lothian seat, and they did indeed register their second best second vote result after Lothian, with 8.3 per cent. The SNP saw their share of the regional vote drop to 23.4 per cent – losing the standard bearer they previously had in party veteran and icon Winnie Ewing, as well as the youngest MSP, Duncan Hamilton, both of them choosing to stand down. They still remained ahead of the other parties – albeit more narrowly with Labour on 22.3 per cent – making this the only region other than North East Scotland where they outpolled Labour in the top-up section. The end result was a loss of Rhoda Grant's Labour top-up seat.

ROB GIBSON (SNP) was born in 1945 in Glasgow, and educated in the High School of Dundee, Dundee University and Dundee College of Education, where he trained as a geography and modern studies teacher. He quickly switched into being a guidance teacher at Invergordon Academy from 1974–77 and principal teacher of guidance at Alness Academy from 1977-95. He then left teaching to become a writer and researcher, having his book *Plaid and Bandannas*, about the links between Highland drovers and the Wild West cowboy culture, published by Luath Press in 2003. That explains a motion put down early as an MSP commemorating the Battle of Little Bighorn.

He joined the SNP in 1966, and was president of the Federation of Nationalist Students from 1970-73. He was a Westminster candidate in Inverness-shire in 1974, and in Ross, Cromarty and Skye in 1987 and 1992 where Charles Kennedy was the incumbent. He was a Ross and Cromarty district councillor from 1988-96, and when the SNP created a shadow cabinet, he was its environment spokesperson from 1992-94. His main political interests through these years were in land reform, traditional arts (he is a singer), the environment and affordable Highland housing. His interests in environmental matters also blossomed into his relationship since 1994 with Eleanor Scott, also elected a Highlands and Islands list MSP in 2003, but for the Green Party. They live together in Evanton, Ross-shire, with Gibson claiming to be on the green wing of the Nationalists and Scott saying she is on the nationalist wing of the Greens.

Standing in Caithness, Sutherland and Easter Ross in 2003, Gibson won 3,692 votes and 17.5 per cent, down substantially in vote and share on 1999. But with the oldest and youngest of the 1999-2003 MSPs – Winnie Ewing and Duncan Hamilton – standing down from the SNP list in the Highlands and Islands, Rob Gibson benefited from winning second place on the list, after Jim Mather. He was not given a spokesmanship, and became a member of the environment and rural development committee.

JAMIE McGRIGOR (Conservative) was born in 1949 in London and educated in Argyll, at Eton College, and Neuchatel University in Switzerland, where he studied commercial French. He worked in shipbuilding insurance for J & A Gardner Shipping and Steamship Mutual Insurance Company, then as a stockbroker for Laurence Trust & Co from 1971-74. In 1975, he returned to Scotland to become a hill farmer of beef cattle and blackface sheep on Loch Awe-side in Argyll, as well as diversifying into fish farming. This would give him some credibility on fisheries and the rural economy when he came to speak on these in the Scottish Parliament. With his Argyll farming, he retained his Etonian image from another era, managing to be both aloof and gregarious, and both fey and focussed at the same time. He is a member of various private members' clubs, including Whites, the Turf Club, the Chelsea Arts Club and the Royal Company of Archers, while also declaring himself a Mason when the issue of secret societies became part of a procedures committee report. He is also a member of the Scottish Landowners Federation, Scottish Crofters Union and National Farmers Union Scotland. Closer to home, he became a trustee of the Awe Fisheries Trust, founding chairman of the Loch Awe Improvement Association and a council member of the Atlantic Salmon Trust, while his spare time is often devoted to guitar-playing and his ambition of becoming 'the next Bob Dylan'.

He stood for the Conservatives at the 1997 general election in the Western Isles and contested the same seat in 1999, winning less than 8 per cent of the vote. He was, however, number one on the Conservative list for the Highlands and Islands, and became a regional MSP in 1999. He was deputy spokesman on rural affairs during the first Parliament, while a member of the rural development committee from 2001-03. In that position, he built up a specialism in fisheries and was noted for his particular enthusiasm on the subject of nephrops, or prawns. He was also convener of the cross-party group on children and young people. In 2003, he fought Lib Dem-held Ross, Skye and Inverness West, retaining the Conservatives' fourth place, but turning out more voters than 1999 and raising the party's share of the vote to 13 per cent. He again had top place on the Tory regional list and was returned as a Highlands and Islands list MSP, with a place on the procedures committee and the Tory spokesmanship for tourism, culture and sport.

MAUREEN MacMILLAN (Labour) was born in 1943 in Oban and was educated at Oban High School, Edinburgh University and Moray House teacher training college. She was a community councillor and English teacher for many years, as a supply and part-time teacher from 1976-83 then at Millburn Academy, Inverness from 1983-99, where she became a senior teacher. She was also involved in the women's movement in the Highlands as a founder member and director of Ross-shire Women's Aid refuge and vice convenor of the Highland Domestic Abuse Forum.

That background helps explain the close interest she took in the passage of the Protection from Abuse (Scotland) Act 2001, the first bill to be passed which had started its life as a committee initiative, with MacMillan sitting on the justice committee at the time. From the start of 2001 until the 2003 election, she sat on the transport and environment committee, then joining both the communities and environment and rural development committees. At the 2003 election, as with her fellow Labour MSPs for the Highlands, the party rules were bent to allow her to stand for both a constituency and the list. Contesting Ross, Skye and Inverness West, where the singer Donnie Munro had stood in a then Labour target in 1999, MacMillan saw the Labour vote drop sharply from 28.6 per cent to 18.9 per cent of the vote, with the SNP pushing Labour into third place while Lib Dem John Farquhar Munro increased his grip on the seat.

She was elected in 2003 as second on the Labour list after Peter Peacock, while Rhoda Grant, who had been elected as number three in 1999, lost her seat. Being one of the first three list MSPs for Labour, MacMillan has been in the minority position of arguing within the party for proportional representation at council level as well. MacMillan was prominent among the mourners for Henry McLeish's career, tearfully telling waiting journalists outside the Labour group meeting which saw him off that he had been murdered by the media. Having regained her composure five days later, she was one of those to nominate Jack McConnell as Scottish Labour leader. Fluent in French and less so in Gaelic, her Labour links are a family affair, with her husband Michael, the Highland councillor for Dingwall North, a leading Highland solicitor and a former European Parliament candidate, while her daughter Anna, one of a family of four, worked as a press officer in Glasgow Labour headquarters until the end of 2003.

JIM MATHER (SNP) was born in 1947, and educated at Paisley Grammar and Greenock High, followed by Glasgow University as part of his chartered accountancy training. He worked as a chartered accountant at first, then in marketing for electronics giant IBM in 1973-83, and as an IT company director from 1983-96, which helped young entrepreneurs launch commercial ventures. His knack as an enthusiastic salesman is reputed to have made a sizeable pile of cash, before taking his enthusiasm and sales techniques into full-time politics.

He was a candidate for the SNP in 1999, fighting Ross, Skye and Inverness West, he then fought the Ayr by-election in 2000, where he moved the party into second place behind the Tories, and 2,100 votes clear of Labour, which had previously held the seat. He also fought the 2001 Westminster election in Ayr, coming third and being knocked back slightly from the 1997 position, then returning to the Highlands to fight Argyll and Bute in 2003. The SNP had seen this as a target, but its vote slumped and Mather took a disappointing third place. He won a list seat, however, as top on the party's Highlands and Islands list, a position occupied in 1999 by the party president, Winnie Ewing. Following a bruising battle over the party finances and treasurership, Mather took on the treasurer post in 2000 with the backing of Alex Salmond and John Swinney, and the bitterness died down. From 1998, he was also a director of Business for Scotland, the semi-independent group set up to win business friends and funders for the party.

Mather had already made his mark as the most promising newcomer of 2003, having spent much of the previous two years working assiduously with the party's finance spokesperson, Andrew Wilson, to persuade the business community and media of the case for independence as a means to cutting tax and growing the Scottish economy. It was noted by many commentators that this was an essentially right-wing agenda, and in many ways at odds with the more leftist, dominant thinking through much of the rest of the party, but it was done with the full backing of the party leadership. Once elected, Mather was given a place on the finance committee, and was the only SNP newcomer to be given a front-bench role, and a crucial one for the party of handling enterprise and the economy. This replaced Andrew Wilson, who lost his seat in 2003, and was another signal that Swinney was nudging the party's core policies in a rightward direction.

PETER PEACOCK (Labour) has born in 1952 in Edinburgh and educated at Hawick High School and Jordanhill College of Education, where he obtained a diploma in youth work and community service. He was a councillor, elected as an independent, in Highland Region and then Highland Council from 1982-99, including a spell as deputy leader of the regional council, and then leader of the unitary Highland Council from 1995-99. Through his vice-presidency of COSLA, he was also a member of the European Union's Committee of the Regions. In 1998, he circulated a paper to other independent councillors, considering the possibilities of getting elected to the Scottish Parliament without party affiliation, he and Argyll's Dick Walsh being the two most likely contenders at that time. However, the chances were not good, particularly in the Highlands and Islands, where Lib Dems portray themselves as independent Highlanders. Peacock was at least as close to joining the Lib Dems, but after talks with Donald Dewar, he joined the Labour Party, less than a year before the Scottish Parliament elections. With Dewar's help and by a contentious selection method, his placing on the Highlands list in the pole position by the party leadership practically guaranteed his election, causing widespread local resentment, not least because he had spent years on the council running rings around its other councillors.

His non-political work was as a community education worker in Orkney from 1973-75, as Citizens' Advice Scotland area officer for the Highlands from 1975-87, and as a business and training consultant as a partner in the Apt Partnership until his election in 1999. He was also a board member of Scottish Natural Heritage. Once an MSP, he was appointed deputy to Sam Galbraith, as minister for children and education in the Scottish Executive, involving him in the tortuous negotiations towards a teachers' pay and conditions settlement, known as the McCrone settlement. He became deputy minister for finance and local government in 2000, where he remained until the 2003 election, doing much of the less glamorous, lower profile work on legislation, finance bills and local government finance. He set the record for the first term, by taking ten bills through the Scottish Parliament, involving numerous careful, well prepared, safe and rather tedious appearances before committees and the chamber debate stages. Given his background and a low-key manner, he has not been one to take public attention from old Labour hands, but is well connected within the Scottish policy community, such as it is.

In the 2003 election, ad hoc Labour rules guaranteed him the same top placing on the Highlands and Islands party list, ensuring him a return even though the number of Labour MSPs returned from that list reduced from three to two. However, party rules were bent by the party's executive to let him and the other two list MSPs fight Highland seats, which he did in Moray, taking Labour from second to third place as the Conservatives overtook him, and Labour's share of vote fell from 26.5 per cent to 19.1 per cent. He found his talents rewarded after the 2003 election, when Jack McConnell promoted him to the cabinet as schools and young people's minister, responsible for legislation to allow ministers to take control of schools deemed by HM Inspectors to be failing, but without that post's previous responsibility for tackling youth crime and disorder. Amid all the First Ministerial changes, ministerial shuffling and changes of direction, Peacock has shown himself to be a survivor.

MARY SCANLON (Conservative) was born in 1947 in Dundee. She was educated at Craigo School, Montrose and worked for three years as a civil servant before becoming a full-time mother. She later studied economics and politics at Dundee University, graduating as a mature student in 1982. She has a postgraduate diploma in personnel management, and worked at Perth College, Dundee Institute of Technology and then Inverness College as a lecturer in business administration and economics before her election in 1999.

Scanlon stood in a number of seats before election as a list MSP, including North East Fife in 1992, and Inverness East, Nairn and Lochaber at the 1997, 1999 and 2003 elections, taking 17 per cent of the 2003 vote, and pushing Lib Dem Patsy Kenton into fourth place. Elected on the Highlands and Islands list from 1999, Scanlon moved from timidity to blossoming confidence, mainly as a result of being made Conservative spokesperson on health and social work, sitting on the health and community care committee in the Scottish Parliament, and consistently getting the Conservative message out to the public with numerous media appearances. She wrote a committee report on the MMR (mumps, measles and rubella) vaccine, at a time it was being shunned by some parents because of an alleged link to autism. This caused tension with the Executive, when she alleged the chief medical officer was trying to undermine her. She later cited this report as her main achievements in 1999-2003, in that she helped ensure parents fears be taken into account, helping secure more information and choice for them.

Scanlon was credited with a bold move for a Conservative, with which many disagreed, in throwing the party's weight behind free personal care for the elderly, going further than the Executive originally intended to go, and further also than Whitehall went. This changed the Parliamentary arithmetic and helped move the Executive towards adopting the policy in 2001. She criticised the Executive, however, for not adopting all the health committee's report on the subject. Such Scanlonite Conservatism is a notably centrist, sometimes statist variety. It is liberal too, absenting herself from her party line against repeal of Section 28, which banned homosexuality being promoted in the classroom. And it can be puzzling, as with her vice-convenership of the MSPs' cross-party group on Cuba.

Returned on the Highlands and Islands Conservative list in 2003, Scanlon took an effective demotion from the health portfolio to cover the communities brief. Her comments to Grampian TV soon after the 2003 election showed the Conservative group of MSPs were not united in opposition to council voting reform, indicating that she and some others could vote in favour of proportional representation. This again changed the Parliamentary arithmetic and forced Labour MSPs to accept the reform would go through with their opponents' combined votes even if they were to refuse to buckle to Lib Dem pressure and attempt their own minority administration.

ELEANOR SCOTT (Green) was born in 1951 in Inverness, moving to Glasgow aged nine, and she was educated at Bearsden Academy and Glasgow University, where she graduated with a medical degree in 1974. She worked in hospital and GP jobs in the north before becoming a community paediatrician specialising in special needs children, until her election to the Scottish Parliament in 2003.

She joined the Scottish Green Party in 1989, at a time the party had won 15 per cent of the UK vote in the European elections, and stood for election at different levels at least seven times, along with working on campaigns on waste strategy, incinerators near Inverness, GM crops and the Iraq war. Highland opposition to crop trials near Munlochy on the Black Isle during the first Parliament helped raise the Greens' profile, and the party secured 8.3 per cent of the vote at the 2003 ballot. In October 2002, Scott was elected convener of the Scottish Green's council, she was registered leader with the Electoral Commission and convener of the Parliamentary group, though this left some confusion as to whether she took precedence over Robin Harper, the Lothian MSP who had been an MSP since 1999, and was given the grand title of 'shadow First Minister' after the 2003 election to get the party out its impasse. Scott was made deputy convener of the environment and rural development committee.

She is partner of Rob Gibson, an SNP list member for the Highlands and Islands, commenting on election night: 'We will discuss things in an intelligent and civilised manner, and I'm sure we will fight, but I think we will cope'.

Lothians

Scottish Parliament Election Results

	Lab	SNP	Con	Lib Dem	SSP	Green	Ind
1999	(8)	3	2	1 (1)	–	1	–
2003	(6)	2	1 (1)	(2)	1	2	1

Constituency Vote

	Lab	SNP	Con	Lib Dem	SSP	Green	Others
1999	40.2	26.9	15.9	15.7	0.7	–	0.6
2003	35.4	21.1	18.1	19.1	6.0	–	0.3
Diff.	-4.8	-5.8	+2.2	+3.4	+5.3	–	-0.3

Regional Vote

	Lab	SNP	Con	Lib Dem	SSP	Green	Others
1999	30.2	25.7	15.8	14.4	1.6	6.9	5.2
2003	24.5	16.2	15.1	11.0	5.4	12.0	15.6
Diff.	-5.7	-9.5	-0.6	-3.4	+3.9	+5.1	+10.4

The Lothian seat includes the six Edinburgh constituencies plus Midlothian and two in West Lothian, having the makings of a greater Edinburgh conurbation and already having a sort of political culture through having had its own Lothian Regional Council until 1996. Despite the name, however, it does not include East Lothian, which lies within the South of Scotland region. In 1997, Lothian reflected Labour's growing dominance in Scottish politics, while the Conservatives declined, losing two Westminster seats, and the SNP suffered from its historic weakness in the capital, while its long-standing roots in West Lothian made it a contender, albeit unsuccessful.

In 1997, Labour won 45.9 per cent of the vote to the Conservatives 19.2 per cent, while the SNP won 18.4 per cent and the Liberal Democrats 14.9 per cent. Labour won eight out of the nine seats, gaining Edinburgh Pentlands from the Conservatives, while the Liberal Democrats gained Edinburgh West from the Tories. In the 1999 Scottish Parliament elections, on constituency votes Labour won 40.2 per cent to the SNP's 26.9 per cent with no seats changing hands, although the SNP polled respectably in both Linlithgow and Livingston. On the regional vote, Labour won 30.2 per cent to the SNP's 25.7 per cent with the additional members distribution including Britain's first Green Parliamentarian. In 2001, only the Lib Dems increased their vote share, moving with ominous significance into second places in Edinburgh South and Edinburgh Central. With a growing presence on the city council, they were poised for one of the biggest upsets of the 2003 elections, in which they took Edinburgh South from Labour, while Tory leader David McLetchie took Edinburgh Pentlands from Labour as well. The dominance Labour enjoyed in the region in 1997 was quickly disappearing. But of more significance in the regional vote was the success of the Robin Harper in winning more Green votes – 12 per cent of the regional vote, which was more than double the proportion his party won in the four least verdant parts of the country. There was also the considerable presence of Margo MacDonald. She had topped the SNP list in 1999, and fallen out with her party list, so she was standing as a one-woman list in 2003. As with Dennis Canavan in Central Scotland in 1999, her 10.2 per cent of the vote distorted the result so that it looked unlike any other result in Scotland. Labour lost 9.9 per cent of its support between first and second votes, to 24.5 per cent, by far its worst second vote showing. It was also the worst falling away of first votes in Scotland for the SNP, down by 4.9 per cent to only 16.2 per cent of the second votes. And it was the only part of Scotland where the SSP did worse on the second vote than the first winning 5.4 per cent. The end result saw the Conservatives paying for their success in Pentlands by losing a regional seat.

MARK BALLARD (Green) was born in 1971, and spent some of his early years in India and Pakistan, where his mother was researching women's healthcare. He was educated at Lawnswood Comprehensive School in Leeds and Edinburgh University, where he got an MA (Hons) in economic and social history. He worked for European Youth Forest Action in Edinburgh and Amsterdam from 1994-98, and was editor of the *Reforesting Scotland* journal from 1998-2001, turning it into a forum for a broader range of environment-related articles than forestry. He also edited *Climax*, a newspaper for the international youth climate campaign. From 2002-03, he set up and ran a graphic design and environmental communications consultancy.

His political interests began through his parents' involvement in the Anti-Nazi League and peace movement, becoming involved in Youth CND and the Labour Party from the age of 15. He was active in the Labour Party, joining the Militant Tendency and campaigning against the poll tax. He left the Labour Party in 1991, resigning as secretary of the Edinburgh University Labour Club, and shifting interest to green politics, helping found the Scottish Green Student Network in 1992. He stood as number five on the Green list for the Lothians in the 1999 Scottish Parliament election, rising to number two for 2003. In 2000-02, he was convener of the Scottish Greens' national council and national secretary since 2002. A conviction along with two others, carrying a £125 fine, for destroying some GM crop trials in Midlothian in 1999 was quashed in March 2003, after the sheriff took too long to produce a report about the case. Ballard was the only Green elected from the number two slot on a regional list anywhere in Scotland, with the party winning 31,908 votes, or 12 per cent of second votes in Lothian. He was allocated a place on the procedures committee while being the Green member of the Parliamentary Bureau and spokesman for the Green group on finance, public services and Parliamentary affairs.

LORD JAMES DOUGLAS-HAMILTON (Conservative) was born in 1942 in Strathaven, and elected MP for Edinburgh West from October 1974 until defeated by Donald Gorrie of the Lib Dems in 1997. He stood in the 1999 Scottish Parliament elections in Edinburgh West, again defeated by the Lib Dems, and was elected as number two, after David McLetchie, on the Lothians regional seat. Douglas-Hamilton was educated at Eton and Balliol College, Oxford where he studied modern history and won a boxing blue, and then Edinburgh University where he qualified in Scots law. He was called to the Scottish bar in 1968 and was a Tory councillor from 1972-74.

As a Westminster MP, he was a Scottish Conservative opposition whip from 1977-79 and a Government whip from 1979-81. He worked for Malcolm Rifkind as Parliamentary private secretary, first at the Foreign Office, and then as Scottish Secretary over the period 1983-87. In 1987, with the Scottish Conservative representation cut in half, he became Scottish Office minister with responsibility for home affairs and environment, then from 1992-95 handled education and housing, and from 1995-97, he was health and home affairs minister. In the Scottish Parliament, he became Conservative chief whip and business manager, while a member of the Scottish Parliamentary Bureau and of the standards committee.

His style is a one-off; aristocratic yet tentative, he specialises in surprising people by being much more on top of things than he appears. His impeccable old world politeness proves a superb way of disarming political opponents. He won an award for the best speech of the Scottish Parliament's first year, with a denunciation of the anti-Catholic 1703 Act of Settlement. Having been a justice spokesman in the first Parliament, David McLetchie shifted him onto the education brief after the 2003 election, while he is also deputy convener of the education committee. He contested that election in the Edinburgh West he represented for 23 years, losing ground to Margaret Smith of the Lib Dems, with a 3.4 per cent swing from Tory to Lib Dem, and was then elected as the only Lothian Conservative returned from the regional list.

Lord James is the second son of the 14th Duke of Hamilton, famous for being the man who Rudolf Hess apparently flew to meet on his ill-fated peace mission of May 1941. Douglas-Hamilton has written a book on the subject, *The Truth about Rudolf Hess*, as well as histories of his father's pioneering flight over Mount Everest and the Battle for Malta. He fought a complex legal battle with a cousin to inherit the title of Earl of Selkirk, though he chose not to use it, preferring when he won in 1996 to remain a member of the House of Commons and avoid a by-election, so his eldest son is the Earl instead. He was made a life peer in John Major's dissolution honours list in 1997, which entitles him to a seat in the House of Lords.

COLIN FOX (SSP) was born in 1959 in Motherwell, the brother of Carol Fox, who stood for Labour in Edinburgh West in 1999 and 2003. He was educated at Our Lady's High School, Motherwell and did an HND in accounting at Bell College, Hamilton. He was a political activist from those years, joining Labour Party Young Socialists in 1978, quickly identifying with the Militant Tendency, taking part in the Caterpillar occupation of 1987-88 in Uddingston for its 103 days, and treating the Militant-run Liverpool City Council as his second home throughout the 1980s. He lived in London from 1988-95, and returned to Edinburgh in 1995, where he worked as Lothian organiser for the SSP's forerunner, remaining in that post until his election in 2003. He re-founded the Edinburgh People's Festival in 2002, and is author of *Motherwell is won for Moscow: The Story of Walter Newbold: Britain's first Communist MP* and *Lenin's Man in Motherwell*, published by Scottish Militant Labour in 1992.

He stood for the SSP as number one on the Lothian list at the 1999 election, which won only 1.6 per cent of the second votes, far behind Arthur Scargill's Socialist Labour. His 2003 election victory – with 14,448 votes (5.4 per cent) – was by a very slim margin, resulting in a celebratory hurdle with reverse twist and double air-punch in the Meadowbank counting centre. This became one of the images of the smaller parties' successful morning on 2 May, and was in character for the ebullient Fox. He described his victory as 'an absolute roller coaster', and marked his taking of the oath on the first day of the new Parliament by attempting to sing Robert Burns' 'A Man's A Man for A' That', despite Sir David Steel's repeated interventions. He is an enthusiast also for Motherwell Football Club, golf and horse-racing.

Early in the second Parliament, Fox proposed a bill which would abolish prescription charges. He was made his party's spokesperson on justice, tourism and sport, and took a place on the justice 2 committee.

ROBIN HARPER (Green) was born in 1940 in Thurso and, with his father in the military, his childhood involved several homes. He was educated at St Marylebone Grammar School, Elgin Academy and Aberdeen University, where he took an MA in 1962, followed by Edinburgh University where he qualified as a teacher. In 1992, he would further qualify with an advanced teaching diploma from Heriot-Watt University. He has been a teacher of, at different times, English, history, science, drama and modern studies, working at Crookston Castle Secondary School, Glasgow, from 1962-63, Braehead School from 1964-68 and Kolanya School, Kenya from 1968-70. From 1972-99, Harper taught modern studies and was a guidance teacher at Boroughmuir High, Edinburgh, and earned the rare honour of a fellowship of the Educational Institute of Scotland. He has also been an actor, musician and guitar teacher for Fife and Edinburgh local authorities and is a former music director of the Edinburgh Children's Theatre Workshop. He took a year out of teaching in 1970-71 to try acting full-time, and was the impresario behind a multi-party MSPs' charity show on the Edinburgh Fringe in 2000 and again in 2003. Harper was also on Lothian Children's Panel from 1985-88 and Lothian Health Council from 1990-95. He is on the board of the Traverse Theatre and was, from 2001-03, a diligent rector of Edinburgh University.

Harper has stood in numerous elections for the Scottish Greens – he reckons he lost his deposit at least ten times – including Edinburgh Central in 1992 and Edinburgh Pentlands in 1997. He also stood in the 1989 and 1994 European elections as well as the 1998 North East Scotland Euro by-election. He credits his 1999 Lothian list place to getting himself well enough known through his various work and spare time interests, winning a wide circle of friends and admirers in the environmental movement and beyond with his refreshingly non–politician style and gentle eccentricity, best seen in his Doctor Who hat and scarf. He is the first Green representative ever to have been elected to a UK Parliament, followed by English Green MEPs from June 1999, and a seven-member Green group in the Scottish Parliament from 2003. That success owes much to his ability to project that avuncular style to an electorate fed up with cloned politicians and warming to his bumbling ability to get across both the message that Greens could be the conscience of the Parliament and that they wanted only second votes, as none of them were standing in constituencies.

In the first Parliament, he sat on the transport and environment committee and on 27 cross-party groups – complaining that there were too many such groups. He was criticised as the 2003 campaign began, for not having done enough to mark out his party's ground – at least in comparison with Tommy Sheridan, who sat also as the lone representative of his party and worked closely with Harper to second each other's motions. The Green leader countered that he had used a member's bill to push the Executive into a promise of a target for improving the extent of organic farming and produce. He also harried rural development minister Ross Finnie on his refusal to block genetically-modified crop testing, becoming a champion of the GM protests around Scotland, and particularly on the Black Isle.

There was some early confusion about his leadership status after the 2003 election, when Eleanor Scott was elected to the Highlands and Islands, already having the position of principal speaker and legally designated leader with the Electoral Commission. The Green group attempted to resolve this by making Harper the 'shadow First Minister', while Scott was 'principal spokesperson'. He gained an impressive 23 votes when he stood as Deputy Presiding Officer and then stood for First Minister against Jack McConnell winning six votes, delivering a furious and passionate speech as if to make up for being so nice for the previous four years. Harper also got a bit ahead of himself, when responding to media speculation that the Greens could form part of a 'traffic light coalition' with Labour and the Lib Dems. Jack McConnell made mischievous overtures to him, leaving Harper speculating in public on the likely conditions he would require. Along with his ambiguous leadership role, he became his party's education and young people's spokesman, with a place on the audit committee.

FIONA HYSLOP (SNP) was born in 1964 in Irvine and educated at Ayr Academy, then Glasgow University, where she studied economics and sociology, and the Scottish College of Textiles, where she did a diploma course in industrial administration. She worked in a variety of posts in sales and marketing for Standard Life Assurance from 1986-99, most recently as a marketing manager, putting her skills to use in the SNP. Her home and political base is in Linlithgow, where she lives with her husband and two children. Having been in charge of SNP candidate vetting, she did not stand there in 1999, winning election on the Lothian list instead. She did, however, challenge Labour's Mary Mulligan in Linlithgow in 2003, registering a fall in SNP support and share of vote, but a tiny swing of 0.77 per cent from Labour to SNP reducing Labour's majority to 1,970.

Hyslop joined the party in 1986 and was first elected to its national executive four years later. She stood for Westminster in 1992 in Edinburgh Leith, and in 1997 in Edinburgh Central. In the Scottish Parliament, she was SNP spokesperson on housing and social justice. From September 2000, with the rise of John Swinney to the leadership, she was the party's policy vice-convener, charged by the new boss with an overhaul of party policy, and being one of the three or four MSPs in his inner team. That appeared to make her one of the party's rising stars, though the success of that revamped policy platform along with professional marketing ploys in the campaign, resulted in a very poor 2003 result for the party, which may not help Hyslop's career.

In the first Parliament, she was on the social justice committee, clashing early on with the convener, Labour's Margaret Curran, over whether Curran had allowed a committee report on Housing Stock Transfers to be amended by the Executive. The issue came back to cause Hyslop problems, as her party at national level relented in its opposition to the Glasgow stock transfer, while Nationalists in the city remained firmly opposed. This encounter, however, showed off her combative abilities, which continued to be displayed in occasional TV confrontations. However, from 2001, Swinney handed her the job of party business manager along with membership of the Parliamentary Bureau, meaning that her two main roles took her out of the public eye. After that unhappy 2003 election experience, Swinney handed her the front bench role as spokeswoman on education and lifelong learning.

KENNY MacASKILL (SNP) was born in 1958 in Edinburgh, and educated at Linlithgow Academy and Edinburgh University where he trained as a lawyer. He subsequently became a solicitor, working as a senior partner of an Edinburgh law firm from 1984-2000, and as director of a legal services agency. MacAskill joined the SNP in 1981, walking quickly into a prominent position in the bitter SNP civil war which had followed the party's 1979 election defeat. He became one of the leading lights in the left-wing '79 Group and was one of its seven prominent members who were expelled as a result of the SNP leadership's proscription of it in 1982; this was commuted to suspension. He then became, after the 1987 election, the SNP spokesperson on the poll tax where his mixture of charm and enthusiasm was interpreted outside and inside the SNP as a bit over-enthusiastic, lacking good judgement or a subtle touch.

He has also been a vice-convenor for policy and SNP treasurer, which saw him deliver some of the best and funniest of party conference fund-raising speeches, even if eyebrows were raised at his full-blooded anti-Englishness. This was MacAskill's persona as one of the Tartan Army's most ardent squaddies, who missed out on Scotland's match against England at Wembley in the European championship play-off in November 1999, after being judged by the Metropolitan Police to be best suited to a few hours in their cells. He can also prove to be a thoughtful and imaginative political thinker and sayer of the unsayable, even if it tends to be said at full volume. In 1999, he began a brave and sometimes lonely transformation from fundamentalist to the most gradualist wing of the party, losing many of his friends in the process. In September 2000, he stood for the post of deputy leader (or senior vice-convener), losing to Roseanna Cunningham partly because he had alienated his former 'fundie' friends. Alex Salmond and John Swinney rewarded his move with key front bench roles, including transport and environment 1999-2000, enterprise and lifelong learning 2000-01, and transport, tourism and telecommunications from 2001. In the latter role, he championed the cause of improved Scottish air links, particularly for Inverness, but he also proved to be something of a liability for committing the SNP to massive spending projects.

Being a Lothians-based Nationalist, he has ploughed an unfertile electoral furrow. He contested Livingston in the 1983, 1987 and 1992 Westminster elections, and Linlithgow in 1997. In the 1999 election, he stood in Edinburgh East and Musselburgh, losing to Labour's Susan Deacon, and was elected from second place on his party's Lothian regional list. He returned to Edinburgh East in 2003, but lost ground and a lot of votes, while retaining second place. Following the infighting surrounding the SNP's 2003 regional lists, he secured first place in Lothian, retaining his MSP seat. He was much quicker than others to open up debate in the wake of the election defeat about the directions the SNP should be taking. He argued for 'parking' the independence issue for some time in order to bed down devolution first, and argued against the 'hell mend you' approach of Nationalists who thought the Scottish electorate deserve the worst if they remained unpersuaded of the case for independence. MacAskill also argued for close integration between an independent Scotland and the rest of the UK, including energy and rail, and he said the party needed a modernised defence policy, in which an independent Scottish military would be closely integrated with European defence forces. In the 2003 leadership election, he backed Swinney, while attacking opponents as entryists who had failed to change the Labour Party and were intent on damaging the SNP instead.

MARGO MacDONALD (Independent) was born in 1943 in Hamilton, and educated at Hamilton Academy, with training as a physical education teacher at Dunfermline College. She taught from 1963-65, and was a barmaid and mother from 1965-73, where a larger-than-life personality won friends ranging from Billy Connolly to the upper echelons of the Scottish National Party. She joined the SNP in 1966 and first stood in Paisley in the 1970 general election, winning 7.3 per cent of the vote. In November 1973, she became a nationally-recognised figure, as the 'Blonde Bombshell' who won a by-election in Glasgow Govan. This was the first breakthrough by the party into any Scottish city, and in a time of political ferment, it was a pointer to the electrifying effect the SNP was about to have on 1970s Scottish politics, winning eleven constituencies the next year. None of those, however, was Margo McDonald's. One of the more remarkable aspects of her political impact is that it occurred with less than four months spent at Westminster, before being turfed out at the February 1974 general election. Even that was enough to make MacDonald a Nationalist icon alongside Winnie Ewing and Jim Sillars, to whom she was married in 1980. Her appeal, however, has sometimes been stronger outside the party than in it, particularly as it professionalised and became more tightly controlled from the top, in a drive to present itself as an alternative administration.

MacDonald won the deputy leadership in 1977 against Margaret Bain (later Ewing, who was then an MP and later the Moray MSP), retaining that post until 1979. She stood again in the Hamilton by-election in 1978, losing to Labour's George Robertson (later Defence Secretary and NATO General Secretary). The SNP's defeat that night was one of the significant events in their electoral retreat in the 1970s. MacDonald was prominent in the campaign for a 'yes' vote in the 1979 devolution referendum, and was one of the leading figures of the left-wing '79 Group, established after the party's 1979 electoral disaster to appeal to Central Belt Labour voters with a radical, socialist agenda. The establishment of this group made it possible for Sillars, the ex-Labour MP and founder of the short-lived breakaway, the

Scottish Labour Party, to join the SNP. In 1982, the SNP hierarchy acted against the '79 Group by suspending seven prominent members. MacDonald resigned from the party in disgust and did not rejoin it until after the 1992 election.

After losing her seat in 1974, MacDonald became a freelance writer and journalist, director of Shelter (Scotland) from 1978-81, a Radio Forth broadcaster, becoming editor of topical programmes from 1981-85, and a political and current affairs reporter for Scottish Television from 1985-91, in which she won cross-party friendships, one of her programmes being called, presciently, *Mayhem With Margo*. In 1991, she went to Tory minister Michael Forsyth with her idea of a series of helplines offering specialist services – including Drugline, Smokeline, National AIDS Helpline – and got his backing, becoming chief executive of Network Scotland from 1991-94.

Back in the SNP but treated with some caution by the Salmond leadership team, MacDonald contested Edinburgh South, where she lives, in the 1999 elections. Her personal profile ensured she did well by coming second with 23.5 per cent of the vote, losing to Labour's Angus MacKay. She was elected a Lothian list MSP, having secured top spot on the SNP's regional list. She sat in the Parliament on the European committee and enterprise and lifelong learning committee until December 2000, before becoming convener of the subordinate legislation committees from January 2001 until the 2003 election. It was not glamorous work, she conceded, but she tried to ensure its members had some fun in doing it.

From the outset in the new Parliament, MacDonald's skill at staying off-message was going to cause problems with the leadership. She disagreed with the SNP's support of devolution, arguing it posed dangers to the cause of winning independence. She said on television that she had stood for election to make sure the Salmond leadership 'didn't sell the jerseys'. She was slightly less hostile to John Swinney's leadership, but she remained her own woman, revelling in what she called her 'bad girl' image. She shrugged off disciplinary action taken against her for speaking to the media about an SNP group meeting, and her scepticism about the party's direction was never far from the surface. She ploughed her own furrow, on issues which mainstream politicians were scared to touch, including a legislative proposal for councils to designate prostitution tolerance zones, and a commission on decrim-inalising the use of cannabis for medicinal use – an issue which has become more mainstream since she began to push it. She counted one of her chief achievements of the first four years as having secured more specialist PE teaching in schools, and she was among the first to tap into a rich vein of public disaf-fection with mainstream politicians, by asking consistently awkward questions about the Holyrood Building Project. Having been a journalist, she used the media expertly to further these campaigns, though sometimes her contrary ways and courting of controversy backfired, as with comments in 2002 about extreme right French presidential candidate, Jean-Marie Le Pen which appeared to be positive, and were slapped down by John Swinney.

In May 2002, the SNP balloted through its delegate system for the priorities on the regional lists, dumping MacDonald in an unwinnably low number five position for Lothian, where she had previously been number one. She responded with a cleverly drawn-out, will-she-won't-she drama about her inten-tions, which raised the profile of her various campaigns, but also led to a campaign to discredit her, including the briefing of journalists that she had mild Parkinson's Disease. In autumn 2002, she announced she would not stand again for the SNP, and ruled out suggestions she might join the SSP. In late January 2003, she announced she would stand as an independent on the Lothian list.

Her low-budget campaign, the subject of a documentary broadcast after the election, focussed on making sure people knew she was standing, and also on the Holyrood project. Happily for her, this is what voters seemed to want to talk about as well, and having begun her campaign with the partial leak of a private report into the project for the Auditor General, her call for an independent inquiry was met with a publicity coup mid-way through the campaign, when Jack McConnell told the Sunday papers –

coincidentally on her 60th birthday – that he was writing to her to announce he intended to support her call and arrange for one. McConnell had an interest in causing maximum damage to the SNP campaign, but it was also a favour to a friend he had known since student days at Stirling University. It is typical of MacDonald that she tends to get on better with such political opponents than with fellow Nationalists. Although an accomplished politician in many ways, she is not always a good team player.

Her 2003 result – 27,144 votes, or 10.2 per cent of Lothian second votes – was nearly good enough to elect a second MSP, though she was the only person on her list. Back for the second term and re-invigorated, she stood for First Minister winning two votes, and Dennis Canavan, another candidate, offered if he won to job share the post with her. The profile of her Holyrood criticisms as well as her other campaigns was boosted by her return. She returned to the cause of prostitution tolerance zones. With nine grandchildren, health worries and a retreat in Portugal, she began her time as MSP by saying her ambition was 'to retire gracefully'. There were few signs of that happening.

Mid-Scotland and Fife

Scottish Parliament Election Results

	Lab	SNP	Con	Lib Dem	SSP	Green
1999	(6)	3 (2)	3	1 (1)	–	–
2003	(5)	2 (3)	3	1 (1)	–	1

Constituency Vote

	Lab	SNP	Con	Lib Dem	SSP	Green	Others
1999	36.4	31.4	18.6	12.8	–	–	0.8
2003	29.8	27.4	19.2	14.1	4.5	–	5.0
Diff.	-6.6	-4.1	+0.7	+1.3	–	–	+4.2

Regional Vote

	Lab	SNP	Con	Lib Dem	SSP	Green	Others
1999	33.4	28.7	18.6	12.7	1.0	3.9	1.8
2003	25.3	23.0	17.6	12.0	4.6	6.9	10.7
Diff.	-8.1	-5.6	-1.0	-0.7	+3.5	+3.0	+8.9

Mid-Scotland and Fife covers the rural seats of Tayside North and Perth through Stirling and Ochil to the Kingdom of Fife. In 1997, Labour won 40 per cent of the vote to the SNP's 25.3 per cent, while the Conservatives won 21.1 per cent and the Liberal Democrats 12.6 per cent. The Conservatives had at the 1992 election held three seats in this area and lost all three of them in 1997; Tayside North and Perth to the SNP and Stirling to Labour. The SNP also polled a strong second in the Labour seat of Ochil, leaving Labour with six seats to the SNP's two and one for the Lib Dems, who have built up a stronghold in formerly-Tory North East Fife.

In the 1999 Scottish Parliament elections, Labour won 36.4 per cent of the constituency vote to the SNP's 31.4 per cent. However, despite the SNP running Labour so close, no constituency changed hands and the best the Nationalists had to show was their reduction of the Labour majority in Ochil to 1,303.

In the 2001 election, none of the seats changed hands, though the Conservatives came within 48 votes of taking Perth from the SNP. Otherwise, they have found it harder to win back former seats in this region than they have in the South of Scotland, as Labour has dug in its Stirling seat and the SNP's John Swinney in Tayside North. The SNP's George Reid won Ochil from Labour for the first time since he had represented its predecessor seat 24 years before – though he soon left the party group to become Presiding Officer. While Labour and SNP saw sharply reduced second vote shares in 1999 – 33.4 per cent to 25.3 per cent for Labour – four years later there was only one change in the share of regional seats, with the SNP seeing a 4.4 per cent fall away of its first vote support to its second vote result. This was its worst differential in one of the defining patterns of the 2003 election, outside the exceptional election in Lothian. The SSP won 4.6 per cent, their second lowest support across all of Scotland, and did not win any representation.

TED BROCKLEBANK (Conservative) was born in St Andrews in 1942 and grew up in the Fife burgh, where he attended Madras College. He trained as a journalist, at first with D. C. Thomson in Dundee from 1960-63, and then moved into television. He worked the as a freelance journalist from 1963-65, then with Scottish Television 1963-70, and moved to Grampian Television. Based in Aberdeen, he became an on-screen reporter and documentary-maker, making his name with programmes about the oil industry, gaining a BAFTA award and a series carried on Public Broadcasting Service in the USA. At Grampian, he was a reporter from 1970-76, head of news and current affairs from 1977-85 and head of documentaries and features from 1985-95. He then went into freelance television production, with his own St Andrews-based company, Greyfriars Productions, during which he continued to work with his long-time associate, Selina Scott, and did a series of high-profile celebrity profiles.

He claims to have had invitations to join and stand for several parties, before plumping for the Conservatives. He stood for them in Fife North East in 1999, coming second, while he was fifth on the party list for Mid-Scotland and Fife. He stood again for the Westminster Banff and Buchan seat in 2001, and tried again for the third time in the Lib Dems' North East Fife stronghold in 2003. He won 28.8 per cent of the vote, almost holding the Tory vote, with a 1.5 per cent swing to the Lib Dems' Iain Smith. In the battle for the Conservative list for Mid-Scotland and Fife, he took third place, seeing off a long-time Stirling stalwart of the party and first term MSP, Keith Harding, and pushing him into an unwinnable place. This prompted Harding to quit the party to fight for his seat under the Scottish People's Alliance banner. Brocklebank made an early impression in Parliament, with a natural confidence and gravitas giving him a good start in fisheries debates and questions.

BRUCE CRAWFORD (SNP) was born in Perth in 1955 and educated at Kinross High School and Perth High School. He worked for the Scottish Office from 1974 until 1999, while being elected councillor with Perth and Kinross District and then its successor Perth and Kinross Council from 1988 until 1999, in one of the parts of Scotland where the SNP has done best in local government. He was convenor of the environmental health committee from 1988-92 and then council leader from 1996-99, remaining SNP group leader in Perth some time after being elected to Edinburgh. He was also a board member of Scottish Enterprise Tayside and several other local bodies in the area.

In the Scottish Parliament he was SNP chief whip from 1999-2000 before becoming front bench spokesman on transport and environment following the first Swinney reshuffle of September 2000. In the 2001 election, the SNP was strongly criticised for its environmental policy, favouring cuts in fuel duty and with more road building. In a further reshuffle, Swinney took the transport brief away from Crawford, in the hope that more focus could be brought to the party's environmental position. With that role, Crawford made some impact in tackling the Executive's and Ross Finnie's record on water safety, during the 2002 cryptosporidium outbreak affecting Glasgow, but the party's improved environmental position by the 2003 election was not enough to avoid major losses to the Green Party.

Within the first Parliament, Crawford sat on the European committee from 1999 to 2000 before joining the transport and environment committee in 2000. The 2003 election saw him contest Stirling, a Labour-Conservative marginal held by Labour's Sylvia Jackson, in which the SNP share of vote dropped from 26 per cent in 1999 to 19 per cent. In the second Parliament, Swinney returned Crawford to the chief whip role, while also making him the SNP's business manager – positions which allow him to use a natural authority, particularly given that the generation gap in the SNP left so many of his generation out of politics, with much of the MSP group being younger than him.

MURDO FRASER (Conservative) was born in Inverness in 1965, and was educated at Inverness Royal Academy and Aberdeen University, where he trained as a lawyer. He worked from 1987-89 for Philip and Kemp solicitors in Aberdeen, 1989-90 for Ross Harper and Murphy in Edinburgh and from 1990-2001 was an associate partner in Ketchen and Stevens, also in the capital, where he specialised in commercial and agricultural law.

His politics were influenced by former Scottish Secretary of State Michael Forsyth, having been chairman of the Scottish Young Conservatives in 1989-91, at a time of the most vicious internal warfare between Forsyth's wing, when the then Stirling MP had been appointed Scottish party chairman by Margaret Thatcher, and that of Malcolm Rifkind, who was then Scottish Secretary. In 1991-92, he was chairman of the UK Young Conservatives. Fraser remains on the dessicated dry right wing of the party, at least on economic affairs, and close to Brian Monteith, another Forsythite and also a member of the right-wing Tuesday Club. Both of the MSPs favour greater fiscal powers for the Scottish Parliament, arguing it needs to take more responsibility for the funds it raises as well as the money it spends. Fraser wrote a pamphlet arguing the case in 1998, published by the Tuesday Club, as well as the case against Scotland being in the euro zone, published in 1999. As a member of the Conservative Christian Fellowship, he has authored an essay on *Defending Britain's Heritage*, published by Keep Sunday Special in 1993.

Fraser stood for East Lothian in 1997 and in Tayside North in the 1999 Scottish Parliament elections as well as the June 2001 Westminster elections. His break came in August 2001, when Nick Johnston resigned, having been elected in the second spot of the 1999 Tory regional list for Mid-Scotland and Fife, and angrily citing his differences with the direction of the Conservative group under David McLetchie. He was automatically replaced by the next Conservative on the 1999 list who had not been elected. This was Murdo Fraser, ranked fourth and the first such replacement without a by-election, only adding to Labour constituency MSPs' unhappiness with the electoral system their party intro-duced in the Scotland Act. In 2003, Fraser stood again for Tayside North, which had been a safe Conservative seat at Westminster until 1997, but found the gap secured by John Swinney widened, winning 31 per cent against the SNP leader's 44 per cent.

The legal brain and ability of this munro-bagging Rangers fan is feared by his opponents, as evidenced by Scottish Enterprise in summer 2002, when Maureen McAlpine, head of public affairs wrote an internal memo – subsequently leaked – gathering opinions on how to counter the Tory assault, following a *Business am* article by Fraser which contained strong criticism of the quango. This seemed to illustrate a number of the shortcomings of Scottish politics: the narrow 'village' nature which precludes large areas of life from public debate and the neurotic nervousness of Scottish Enterprise, the country's biggest quango.

Coming late to the first Parliament, Fraser spent 2001-03 as deputy spokesman on education, culture and sport and was on the subordinate legislation committee. But, being relatively close to McLetchie, Fraser was rewarded for his skills after the 2003 election, when he took on enterprise and lifelong learning, a crucial portfolio for Tories. He also became a member of the enterprise and culture committee.

TRICIA MARWICK (SNP), was born a miner's daughter in Cowdenbeath in 1953, and worked as a public affairs officer for Shelter from 1992 until her election in 1999. She contested the Fife Central constituency at the 1992, 1997, 1999 and 2003 elections, making her something of an expert in the incumbent Labour Party's problems at the time Henry McLeish's constituency office problems began to unravel his leadership and tenure in the seat. With Labour's weakness, Marwick secured a 7.8 per cent swing from Labour to SNP in 2003, but failed to beat the Labour candidate to replace McLeish, Christine May.

Marwick was the SNP's deputy business manager in the Parliament until September 2000 when she became business manager, replacing Mike Russell and allowing her to make the most of her appetite for mixing it with Labour. She was a member of the standards committee which dealt with the Lobbygate hearings in autumn 1999, becoming deputy convener. With experience of justice and equal opportunities committees, she became convener of the standards committee after the 2003 election, walking straight into controversy over a complaint against her by former SNP MSP Dorothy-Grace Elder. This required her to stand down temporarily, and when the issue was held over, she launched an intemperate public attack on fellow committee members, which brought into question whether she could return to the convener's chair with the trust of other MSPs. On that count, in October 2003, she was forced to stand aside permanently fom the convener's post. Having an interest in animal welfare campaigning, she took a high profile as co-sponsor of the anti-fox hunting bill, taking over the leadership role on the legislation after Labour's Mike Watson had to move aside from it on his appointment to the Executive. In 2002, she also introduced a bill which would have introduced voting reform for councils, intended to flush out Liberal Democrats from their coalition loyalties. It did not succeed in flushing them out, but it put the coalition under pressure. Following a further complaint, Marwick with an obvious sense of irritation and lack of grace resigned from the post of convener of the committee.

BRIAN MONTEITH (Conservative) was born in 1958 in Edinburgh and educated at Portobello High School, Edinburgh, and Heriot-Watt University. He was a full-time sabbatical at Heriot-Watt's student association and a researcher at the Centre for Policy Studies in 1981-82. Between 1983-99, he worked in public relations, including two stints for Michael Forsyth Associates, Dunseath Stephen in 1984-85, then becoming his own boss as managing director of Leith Communications from 1986-91. He was PR director of Forth Marketing Ltd 1991-95, and from 1995-96, he was Scottish account director for the Communication Group plc, and then proprietor of Dunedin Public Relations from 1996-99. He has a colourful right-wing past within the Conservative Party, as chairman of the Federation of Conservative Students in 1982-83, at a time it was gaining notoriety for its radical, ultra-Thatcherite ideas and rowdy conference behaviour, later to lead to its disbandment by party chairman Norman Tebbit. Monteith was also chairman of the Scottish Young Conservatives from 1987-88, putting him in a prominent position in support of Margaret Thatcher and her Scottish acolyte Michael Forsyth.

With the 1997 election disaster, other Conservatives were weary and running scared, with the party declining to commit itself any more to the anti-devolution cause. But Monteith, not being afraid of lost causes, filled the vacuum, as lead organiser of the 'Think Twice' campaign arguing for a 'no' vote in the 1997 devolution referendum. He had also founded a student organisation against devolution in 1978, using slogans such as 'Nice Girls Say No'.

Having lost the 1997 vote, he was one of the first Conservatives to get on board for an MSP seat, contesting the Stirling constituency in 1999 in which his political associate Michael Forsyth had been defeated two years before. The result was a disappointing third to both Labour and the SNP, but his third place on the Conservative list for Mid-Scotland and Fife saw him elected. Completely untroubled by the position of working in a Parliament the existence of which he had been prominent in opposing, he was made Conservative spokesman for education, arts, culture and sport, sitting on the education committee in the Parliament, and playing a prominent role in asking awkward questions of the Executive after the 2000 Scottish Qualifications Authority meltdown. He tried for Stirling again in 2003, this time beating the SNP into second place. And having seen off Keith Harding, the former Tory leader on Stirling Council and first term MSP, by beating him in the party list, Monteith took second place on the list, after Murdo Fraser, and was re-elected. In 2003, he became convener of the audit committee and was made spokesperson on finance, local government and public service reform.

He remains radical and provocative in his thinking, and willing to mix it with his own party, infuriating MSP colleagues at least as much as political opponents, and bringing a public rebuke in June 2000 from Murray Tosh for stirring up trouble. Group leader David McLetchie appears by turns to fear Monteith's trouble-making capacity while welcoming his imaginative, creative flair for presentation and policy ideas. Monteith has been at the forefront of trying to steer McLetchie and the rest of the party to arguing for more taxation powers for the Scottish Parliament, to enhance fiscal responsibility, and to let Scottish Conservatives have a wider range of tax-cutting options. His appointment by McLetchie as finance spokesman would suggest he is pushing at an open door. Since 2001 and the arrival of Murdo Fraser as an MSP, Monteith has found a political soulmate within the MSP group.

Sporting a flamboyant dress sense, often accompanied by extravagant cigars, he is one of the more readable and trenchant of MSP newspaper columnists, mainly in the *Edinburgh Evening News*, also commenting on his beloved Hibernian Football Club as a one-time organiser of a 'Hands On Hibs' movement, protesting the management's alleged under-investment. He is a member of the Society for the Protection of the Unborn Child and organises the Tuesday Club, a right-of-centre dining society.

KEITH RAFFAN (Liberal Democrat) was born in 1949 in Aberdeen, and schooled at Robert Gordon's College, Aberdeen, and Glenalmond, and studied then at Corpus Christi College, Cambridge. He worked as a Conservative Central Office researcher and in Scottish HQ 1968-70, then researched a biography of One Nation Tory Iain MacLeod, famed for being 'too clever by half'. For four years, on a Rowntree Trust Fellowship, he was full-time chairman of the centre right Pressure for Economic and Social Toryism (PEST – an apt acronym, according to some colleagues). Writer Matthew Parris remembers him from that time as 'slinkily plausible'. In the February 1974 general election, he stood for the Tories in Dulwich and in October, in Aberdeenshire East, which he lost to the SNP's Douglas Henderson. From then until 1983, Raffan was a journalist as a Westminster sketch writer and diarist, mainly on the *Daily Express* and *Sunday Express*. Then, he was elected as Conservative MP for Delyn in North Wales from 1983-92, sitting on the Welsh Affairs select committee throughout his tenure at Westminster. He was far from being a Thatcherite and was pro-devolution, hence part of the reason for his departure from the Conservatives to the Lib Dems after leaving Westminster in 1992, accusing them of being class-ridden and appealing only to a narrow sectional interest.

From then until 1994, he worked as a PR consultant in New York, and from 1994-99 as a presenter and interviewer with HTV in Wales. He stood for the Lib Dems at the North East Scotland European Parliamentary by-election in November 1998 and then stood as a regional list candidate in Mid-Scotland and Fife in 1999. In the Scottish Parliament, he has the reputation of being flamboyant, outspoken and independently-minded. He was also one of only three Liberal Democrat MSPs who voted against entering a coalition with Labour, the others being Donald Gorrie and John Farquhar Munro. Raffan was then the only Lib Dem MSP who did not vote for Donald Dewar in the subsequent First Ministerial election, abstaining instead.

In the first Parliament, he sat on the finance and social inclusion committees until December 2000 and joined the audit committee from January 2001 until the 2003 election. He was the Lib Dem spokesman for health and community care from November 2000 to January 2001, but resigned as part of the process of forcing Labour's front bench into fully funding long-term care for the elderly. In any case, he preferred to be free of portfolio responsibilities so that he could pursue his own interests. These have primarily been around drug misuse (he is convener of the cross-party MSP group on that) and prisons policy, on both of which he takes a well-researched, liberal and often radical stance. When

Labour ministers cut funding to the Airborne Initiative in February 2004, a Lib Dem revolt created a coalition crisis, though Raffan was the only one to follow through his protest and vote against the initiative. Though experienced and able, he is seen as not enough of a team player to become a minister.

MARK RUSKELL (Green) was born in 1972 in East Anglia. The son of an engineer/inventor and a massage therapist, he was educated at Edinburgh Academy and Stevenson College, Edinburgh, before doing a BSC Hons in environmental science with biology at Stirling University. While there, he was a founder member of a range of environmental groups, including Green Action Movement and Green Publishing Co-op, campaigning on campus issues such as woodlands, cycle facilities, recycling, as well as developing country debt, whaling and being active in the Scottish Green Student Network. Local politics involved a campaign which took 15 per cent of the vote in Stirling Council's Logie ward against then council leader Jack McConnell. He also did an MSc in sustainable agriculture at Aberdeen University/Scottish Agriculture College, worked as a community development worker at Falkirk Voluntary Action Resource Centre from 1997-2000, as a regeneration officer for Midlothian Council from 2000-02, and as project officer, for the Soil Association Scotland from 2002-03. He worked for LETSlink Scotland, an umbrella body for local currency schemes, setting up the Stirling Local Exchange Trading System, as well as a food co-operative, a project linking low-income farmers with deprived urban communities, and protesting against the M77 and Forthside road in Stirling.

Ruskell stood in the 1999 Scottish Parliament elections, in second place on the Mid-Scotland and Fife list, and then in 2001, standing for the Stirling seat at Westminster, where he won 757 votes or 2.1 per cent of the vote. He worked with Robin Harper on the Organic Farming Targets Bill in the first Parliament. Being elected in 2003, he took the agriculture portfolio for the Green group.

North East Scotland

Scottish Parliament Election Results

	Lab	SNP	Con	Lib Dem	SSP	Green
1999	(4)	4 (2)	3	(3)	-	-
2003	2 (2)	1 (4)	3	(3)	-	1

Constituency Vote

	Lab	SNP	Con	Lib Dem	SSP	Green	Others
1999	26.2	33.1	17.8	21.2	0.7	-	1.0
2003	21.6	30.3	17.5	24.3	3.2	-	0.4
Diff.	-4.6	-2.8	-0.3	+3.1	+2.5	-	-0.6

Regional Vote

	Lab	SNP	Con	Lib Dem	SSP	Green	Others
1999	25.5	32.3	18.3	17.5	1.1	2.8	2.6
2003	20.2	27.3	17.4	18.8	4.2	5.2	7.0
Diff.	-5.3	-5.1	-0.9	+1.3	+3.1	+2.4	+4.4

North East Scotland includes Aberdeen and Dundee with most of their rural hinterlands, which are distinctive in their culture and their politics, and comprised of rich farmland and Scotland's major fishing communities. The regional seat, like the neighbouring Highlands and Islands, stands proudly apart from the political patterns of the Central Belt, reflecting an often genuine and closely-fought four-party system, with the SNP notable for being at its strongest. In 1997, Labour came out on top, particularly in the two cities, winning 30.9 per cent of the vote to the SNP's 26.1 per cent, with the Conservatives on 22.4 per cent and the Liberal Democrats 18.9 per cent. The electoral map, as elsewhere in Scotland, was shaped by Conservative losses with Aberdeen South, which they won in 1992, retaken by Labour, and Aberdeenshire West and Kincardineshire won by the Lib Dems. Gordon, a 'notional' Conservative seat in 1992, was also 'lost' to the Lib Dems – leaving Labour with five seats to two each for the Lib Dems and the SNP.

In November 1998, the SNP convincingly retained the North East Scotland European constituency in a by-election, with 48 per cent of the vote, while Labour was pushed into third place. In the 1999 Scottish Parliament elections, the SNP polled well here, but not well enough to make a break out from its Banff and Buchan and Angus strongholds, winning 33.1 per cent of the constituency vote to Labour's 26.2 per cent. The SNP's rise in popularity saw it run Labour close in Aberdeen North and Dundee West, but win no extra constituency seats. The only seat to change hands was the three-way marginal Aberdeen South which was won by the Lib Dems, while held by Labour at Westminster. In the regional vote that year, the SNP won 32.3 per cent to Labour's 25.5 per cent and the Conservatives 18.3 per cent.

With the SNP grip on Banff and Buchan confirmed in a 2001 by-election, that year's Westminster election saw no change of party representation. But the 2003 Scottish Parliament result saw the SNP break through in two urban seats: Aberdeen North and Dundee East, though failing to break through as they had hoped in Dundee West or in Dundee City Council. Lib Dem Nicol Stephen was also notable for a sharply increased vote in retaining the previously marginal Aberdeen South. There were expectations that a Fishing Party candidate could use a high media profile to win a regional seat, but because the SNP and Conservatives were giving strong support to the fishing industry at a time of major decommissioning and quota cuts, this challenge to the mainstream parties came to merely 2.3 per cent of the vote. Having lost two constituencies, Labour only dropped by 1.4 per cent from its constituency vote to its regional vote, thus picking up its first top-up seats outside the Highlands and Islands. In both regions, it avoided the pattern elsewhere of seeing a sharp drop in support between first and second vote. It was the Lib Dems who registered the most notable drop from first to second vote, with a difference of 5.5 per cent – almost precisely the vote share won by the Greens to win a top up seat with 5.2 per cent. The Scottish Socialists secured 4.2 per cent – their worst regional vote and across Scotland and one of three regions they failed to win any seats. With the SNP representing four of the nine constituencies, it paid for its two gains with the loss of most of its regional seats, falling from four to one top-up seats.

SHIONA BAIRD (Green) was born in 1946, and was educated at Hereford High School, moving to Mary Erskine's School, Edinburgh aged 16, and then Edinburgh University, where she studied social science, including psychology. She trained as a social worker, and worked in West Lothian for two years, then becoming a farmer of 55 acres of Angus, near Dundee, and mother to four sons and a daughter. Three of the sons now work in partnership on the farm, and she is on the board of green company Tayside Recyclers.

She joined the Ecology Party in the early 1980s, and contested several elections, mainly at local level, standing for Westminster in Dundee East in 1992 when she won 295 votes, and the Scottish Parliament in 1999. Placed at the top of the Greens' North East Scotland list in 2003, Baird won 5.2 per cent of the second vote, the lowest percentage of any of the Greens elected in six regions. Early on, she declared her intention to focus on rubbish, and all issues to do with waste minimisation and management. She gained a place on the equal opportunities committee and became Green spokesperson on enterprise and lifelong learning.

RICHARD BAKER (Labour) was born in 1974 in Edinburgh, the son of two Anglican vicars. He counts choral singing and the Anglican church among his leisure interests. He was educated at primary school in Cowdenbeath and St Bees School, Cumbria, followed by an MA in English literature at Aberdeen University. Active in student politics, he joined Labour in 1992 and became deputy president and then president of the National Union of Students Scotland, from 1997-2000, campaigning to abolish tuition fees and restore grants. He worked as press officer for Help the Aged from 2000-02, campaigning for free personal and nursing care. Both these campaigns were later claimed as coalition victories for Lib Dems. Baker went on to work as senior research officer for Scottish Labour from 2002-03.

He stood in Aberdeen South, a seat held by Labour's Anne Begg at Westminster but by the Lib Dems' Nicol Stephen in the Scottish Parliament. His result against Stephen was very poor, with a 10.77 per cent swing from Labour to Lib Dem. However, with constituency losses by Labour in Aberdeen North and Dundee East, the party picked up two list seats, to the evident astonishment of Baker, in second place to Marlyn Glen.

He got a place on the enterprise and culture committee (being a keen amateur actor) as well as sitting on procedures. Early signs after the 2003 election were of continuing his previous interests in tertiary education and financial exclusion of elderly people, as well as taking up issues to do with the oil and gas industry.

DAVID DAVIDSON (Conservative) was born in 1943 in Edinburgh and educated at Trinity Academy, Edinburgh. He trained as a pharmacist at Heriot-Watt University and business administration at Manchester Business School, then managed a north of England chain of pharmacies from 1969-93, while overseeing a family livestock farm in Perthshire. He was also a director of Unichem and founder chairman of the Association of Scottish Community Councils. He was a local councillor in Stirling Council from 1995-99 before standing in the North East and fighting the Banff and Buchan constituency at the first Scottish Parliament election. He was deputy convener of the audit committee, and his first term place on the finance committee gave him a prominent role in asking some of the most probing and awkward questions about the Holyrood building project. He caught the Parliament's attention by telling movingly of his family's experience of eating disorders, successfully raising the profile of the issue, along with that of mental health.

At the 2003 election, he stood in the Conservative target seat of Aberdeenshire West and Kincardine, held by the party at Westminster before 1997. Mike Rumbles of the Liberal Democrats held on, with a 5.3 per cent swing from Conservative to Lib Dems. However, the Conservatives won three regional list seats in North East Scotland, with Davidson topmost among them, as he was in 1999. The second Parliament saw him promoted to the health and community care spokesmanship – one of the Conservatives' most prominent, which goes with a place on the health committee, but it also requires the steering of a tricky line between the party's Westminster view on health and a distinctive view in Scotland. Davidson has a family of five, all grown up, he is suave but lacks charisma, and has admitted his greatest weakness is being 'too polite'.

MARLYN GLEN (Labour) was born in Dundee in 1951, and educated at Kirkton High School, Dundee, and at St Andrews University, followed immediately by a diploma in education from Dundee University. She gained a special education diploma in 1986, and an honours degree also from the Open University in 1987, followed by yet another degree, this time in psychology, in 2000. She has taught in Liverpool, then as assistant principal of English at Ravenspark Academy, Irvine, and more recently, she was principal for support of learning at Baldragon Academy in Dundee, while also a prominent activist in the Educational Institute of Scotland.

She was a councillor in Dundee City Council from 1993-96, representing the Blackshade ward, where her victory in a by-election was a significant check in the planned advance of Militant outside Glasgow. She was a member of Labour's Scottish executive as well as convener of Scottish Labour Women's Caucus, being one of those foremost in pushing for the gender balance used in the 1999 election. She was caught in a disputed selection contest in Dundee East, when John McAllion stood down as MP in 2001, creating a vacancy. Glen secured nominations to take his place from each of the party's branches in the seat, plus five union nominations, but was at first blocked from standing by party headquarters. This was despite having won a place on the approved candidates list for the Scottish Parliament in 1999. The selection contest was run twice, and won eventually by Iain Luke, who went on to become the MP. Her main interests include lifelong-learning and the environment, and in 2003, she was appointed to positions on both the justice 1 and the equal opportunities committee.

ALEX JOHNSTONE (Conservative) was born in 1961 in Stonehaven, educated at Mackie Academy, Stonehaven and was a dairy and arable farmer before his election in 1999. Inspired by the North East's centre-left Conservative hero, the late Alick Buchanan-Smith, he contested the Gordon constituency for the party in 1999, and went on to contest Angus in 2003, taking second place. He saw a swing in his favour from the SNP's Andrew Welsh of 1.7 per cent, but with 22 per cent of the vote, still won less than half of Welsh's votes.

Despite his cheerful, bucolic appearance, he is a driven political operator, seeing his role as holding 'the thin blue line against the ranks of the politically correct loony left who would turn Scotland into the new Cuba'. He first showed his talents as his party's spokesperson on rural affairs, while also convening the rural affairs committee. This double role, present in other committees and with other parties, was criticised for endangering the impartiality of the committee convener, and Johnstone found it a tough balancing act while seeing through much of the committee stage of the bill to ban fox hunting with dogs. He used his casting vote against that, after much private dispute in the committee, but their decision was subsequently overturned by the Parliament.

In 2001, David McLetchie handed the rural affairs committee job to Alex Fergusson, and Johnstone became business manager and member of the Parliamentary bureau. This meant a lower profile for the Kirk elder and Led Zeppelin fan, but he was credited with shaping a more distinctive position for the Conservative group, working closely with McLetchie. Post-2003 election, he was given rural development and environment as his brief. He lists his leisure interests as including information technology.

RICHARD LOCHHEAD (SNP) was born in Paisley in 1969, and educated at Williamwood High School, Clarkston, and Glasgow Central College of Commerce, doing business studies. He worked at the South of Scotland Electricity Board for two years before returning to full-time education, to study for a degree in politics at Stirling University. After graduating, he was constituency assistant and then office manager for Alex Salmond in Banff and Buchan, and also worked as an economic development officer with Dundee City Council before the 1999 election.

Building up his political credentials as a north-easterner, he stood in Gordon at the general election of 1997, followed by Aberdeen Central in 1999. He made that into a Labour-SNP marginal, with a 2,696 majority for Labour's Lewis Macdonald, and returned in 2003 with hopes of his party taking both Central and Aberdeen North seats. While the North seat fell to the SNP, Lochhead managed a 2.1 per cent swing in Central, but not enough to defeat Macdonald, who had a majority of 1,242 votes, or 5.9 per cent of turnout.

Lochhead was, throughout the first Parliament and into the second, the SNP's deputy spokesperson for rural affairs. He made his mark with his responsibility for fisheries, ensuring that the SNP's voice was loud on the issue. In March 2001, he tabled a motion favouring a tie-up scheme for boats which became the first of three motions on which the Executive was defeated – though that was as much down to Labour whips' ineptitude as it was Lochhead's tactics of drawing in Lib Dem dissenters. The vote was re-run the following week, and the Executive won. He infuriated ministers and Executive back-benchers during the December 2002 Brussels negotiations, where his running commentary was seen as undermining the UK position. And on some of the trickier votes, he prefers to abstain, including the Section 28 vote in April 2000, which concerned homosexuality being promoted in the classroom, and on the 13.5 per cent pay rise for MSPs in March 2002.

He sat on the rural development committee and was, during the first year, a member of the European Committee. He was to return to that position after the 2003 election, as its convener and with an expanded remit to deal with external relations, promising to make more waves with the committee than it achieved under Labour convenership.

NANETTE MILNE (Conservative) was born in Aberdeen in 1942 and has lived all her life there, being educated at Aberdeen High School for Girls, then qualifying as a doctor at Aberdeen University in 1965, and doing a post-graduate degree in anaesthetics in 1969. Her medical career was largely part-time, initially in training posts in Aberdeen hospitals, and later taking a career break to raise her family. She returned to part-time research work in oncology, including chemotherapy trials for gynaecological cancer.

Side-tracked from medicine into politics, and joining the Conservative Party in 1974, Milne was an Aberdeen city councillor from 1988-99, standing down so that she could stand for the Scottish Parliament that year. She was a director of Grampian Enterprise and on Aberdeen and Grampian Tourist Board. She remains a trustee of Aberdeen International Youth Festival, and is on the court of Aberdeen University. She was also a vice-chairman of the Scottish Conservative Party from 1989-93, through some of its most turbulent times, which helps explain the OBE in 1994.

In 1999, she came third as Conservative candidate in Aberdeen South, and she lost out in fifth place in her party's North East list. The 2001 Westminster election saw her contest Gordon constituency against Lib Dem Malcolm Bruce, in which there was a 3 per cent swing from Conservatives to the Lib Dems. She stood in 2003 in the Gordon seat again, where she came second to Lib Dem Nora Radcliffe, with 6,892 votes and 23.9 per cent. That meant a 1.5 per cent swing from Lib Dem to Conservative, but still left a 4,071 majority. Elected to the Scottish Parliament in 2003, she was a newcomer to position three on the party's list for North East Scotland following the departure of former army major Ben Wallace, who had been one of the party's young hopes in the first Parliament but left in the hope of winning a Cumbrian seat at Westminster. She said she intended to focus on health issues and David McLetchie appointed her deputy to fellow north-easterner David Davidson as a Conservative spokesman on health and community care.

South of Scotland

Scottish Parliament Election Results

	Lab	SNP	Con	Lib Dem	SSP	Green
1999	(6)	3 (1)	4	(2)	-	-
2003	(5)	3	2 (2)	(2)	1	1

Constituency Vote

	Lab	SNP	Con	Lib Dem	SSP	Green	Others
1999	37.0	25.6	22.8	14.6	-	-	-
2003	35.2	20.2	26.7	12.6	4.8	-	0.4
Diff.	-1.7	-5.4	+3.9	-2.0	-	-	-

Regional Vote

	Lab	SNP	Con	Lib Dem	SSP	Green	Others
1999	31.0	25.1	21.6	12.0	1.0	3.0	6.2
2003	30.0	18.4	24.2	10.3	5.4	5.7	5.9
Diff.	-1.1	-6.8	+2.6	-1.7	+4.4	+2.7	-0.3

The South of Scotland regional seat extends across Scotland from Ayr and the Ayrshire coast, skirting the south of Glasgow to the Firth of Forth and the East Lothian eastern boundary of Edinburgh, encompassing along the way the Scottish Borders and Dumfries and Galloway. In 1997, this area voted Labour 43.4 per cent, Conservative 22.6 per cent, SNP 19.1 per cent and Liberal Democrat 13.4 per cent. The Conservatives lost both Dumfries and Ayr to Labour, and Galloway and Upper Nithsdale to the SNP. This gave an overall result of Labour winning six seats, the Lib Dems two and the SNP one. In the 1999 Scottish Parliament elections, Labour won 37 per cent of the constituency vote, while the SNP won 25.6 per cent and the Conservatives 22.8 per cent. In that election, no constituencies changed hands from the 1997 result, though the Conservatives came within 25 votes of taking Ayr. The top-up regional vote delivered four seats to the Conservatives, their strongest presence in Scotland, with the SNP taking three seats.

In a 2000 by-election, Labour lost Ayr to the Conservatives, and in the 2001 Westminster election, the SNP lost Galloway and Upper Nithsdale to the Tories, in the only seat to change hands that year. That pattern helped make the region the most interesting one to watch in the run-up to the 2003 Scottish Parliament election, helping explain the 52.3 per cent turnout as the second highest regional turnout in Scotland. Several seats were in play. Conservative John Scott retained Ayr and his party turned the screw on the SNP in the South-West by gaining Galloway and Upper Nithsdale from the Nationalists while coming a good second to Labour in Dumfries. The SNP's Christine Grahame put up a strong, personal showing in Tweeddale, Ettrick and Lauderdale – an area where Nationalists had very little previous track record of support. The regional vote outcome saw the Conservatives lose two top-up seats as the price for gaining two constituencies, even though this was the only region of Scotland in which they outpolled the SNP on the second vote. The SNP stayed on three list MSPs but because of their internal battles over list priorities, it lost Mike Russell, one of the party stars from the first Parliament.

The Green Party and SSP both squeezed through the voting system to take a seat each with 5.7 per cent and 5.4 per cent respectively.

CHRIS BALLANCE (Green) was born in 1952 in Worcester and was educated at St Andrews. He has been resident in Scotland since moving to Fife as a student, and is now based in Wigtown, Galloway. He worked as a self-employed drama writer from 1993-2003, including part-time creative writing teaching at Glasgow University's Crichton campus in Dumfries. He is an executive member of the Writers' Guild of Great Britain, a member of the Scottish Society of Playwrights and he is a lapsed member of Equity actors' union. Since 1999, he has been part-owner of a second-hand bookshop. Before then, he was manager of a mental health charity in Glasgow, was co-founder of the Carbeth Hutters' Association, and worked for SCRAM, the Scottish Campaign to Resist the Atomic Menace, as well as protesting against nuclear waste dumping in the Galloway hills. He has been successful in putting Wigtown on the map of the book world, as chair of the Wigtown Book Festival and a director of the Wigtown Booktown Company.

He joined the Scottish Green Party in 1980, signalling his politics by being attired in green, right down to his shoes, and he was top of the party's West of Scotland list in the 1999 election, where the party registered only 2.6 per cent of second votes and still fell short of winning a seat in 2003. His victory from the top of the South of Scotland was a narrow one. He was given responsibility for transport, culture, sport and tourism after the 2003 election, and his main green interests include waste and litter, and improved public transport campaigns.

ROSEMARY BYRNE (SSP) was born in 1948 in Irvine and educated at Irvine Royal Academy followed by a teacher training qualification at Craigie College, Ayr. Her teaching career culminated in being principal teacher of learning support at Ardrossan Academy from 2000-03. Her political activism has seen campaigning against the poll tax, in demos against Timex and apartheid, backing the firefighters 2002-3 strike, and as secretary of Irvine and North Ayrshire Trades Union Council. In the 2003 election, she gained a respectable 2,677 votes and 11.8 per cent in Cunninghame South, putting her in third place while Irene Oldfather won the seat for Labour. Winning a list seat in South of Scotland was probably the toughest of the SSP's six seats to win. This grandmother and crossword enthusiast is her party's spokesperson on education and young people, and has a seat on the education committee.

PHIL GALLIE (Conservative) was born in 1939 in Portsmouth and educated at Dunfermline High School, Rosyth Dockyard Technical College and Kirkcaldy Technical College. He worked as an apprentice electrical fitter in Rosyth naval dockyard, from 1955-60, as an electrical engineer in the merchant navy for Ben Line from 1960-64, and in several power stations in Scotland and England from 1964-92. He returned to working in business during two subsequent years out of Parliamentary politics, 1997-99, when he was a business adviser for Ayrshire Enterprise.

Having been a Cunninghame district councillor, Gallie was Conservative MP for Ayr from 1992-97, inheriting the long-time highly marginal seat from the late George Younger (Viscount Younger of Leckie) in 1992. Against expectations, he held it that year with a majority of 85 votes. Gallie had previously stood for Westminster, contesting Cunninghame North in 1983 and Dunfermline West in 1987. As an MP, he was a member of the Scottish Affairs Select Committee from 1992-97. After losing his Westminster seat in 1997, he was on the Strathclyde Commission, which reshaped the Scottish party structures. With a leadership vacuum in the absence of any Scottish MPs, Gallie was one of only two contenders for the leadership of the Scottish Conservatives candidates group in September 1998, losing to David McLetchie.

He stood in the Ayr seat in the Scottish Parliament 1999 election, losing to Labour's Ian Welsh by only 25 votes. Gallie was subsequently elected as a list MSP for the South of Scotland. When Ian Welsh resigned later in 1999, Gallie was tempted to win his old seat back in a by-election which favoured the Conservatives. But as he would have had to stand down from his list seat in order to stand for a constituency, the candidacy went to John Scott, who would go on to win, in the first Scottish Conservative by-election gain since Glasgow Pollok in 1967. Gallie made little pretence that he would still like to return to Westminster, and contested the Ayr seat in the 2001 general election, losing again to Labour's Sandra Osborne but with a sharply reduced majority. In the 2003 election, with John Scott defending Ayr, Gallie fought Carrick, Cumnock and Doon Valley against deputy Labour leader Cathy Jamieson, securing a 3 per cent swing from Labour to Conservative and pushing the SNP into third place. He was returned again on the South of Scotland list.

In the first Parliament, he was at first Conservative spokesperson on home affairs, was a member of the justice and home affairs and public petitions committees until the 2003 election. Then, he joined the European and external relations committee, while taking on a new spokesman's brief of constitutional affairs and Europe – reserved issues for Westminster, but tailored, it seems, to suit Gallie's interests and strengths. It was with such an interest in international affairs that McLetchie chose him to lead for the party in the 2003 Iraq debates.

Gallie says Margaret Thatcher was one of his greatest influences. He is a populist right-wing working-class Tory in the Sir Teddy Taylor mould, increasingly rare in the Scottish and UK party. In the Commons, he was associated with the right-wing Eurosceptic tendency of the party, but did not rebel on any major votes, being more of a party loyalist than an ideologue. He abstained on the vote which gave MSPs a 13.5 per cent pay rise. His mixture of populism and verbal pugnaciousness – he describes his treatment of the Executive as 'bullying' – adds liveliness and a certain unpredictability to Conservative ranks in the Parliament.

CHRISTINE GRAHAME (SNP) was born in 1944 in Burton-on-Trent and educated at Boroughmuir High School, Edinburgh, Edinburgh University and Moray House College of Education. She worked as a secondary teacher at Woodmill High School in Fife and at Whithorn Secondary School from 1966 to 1982. She then took some years out 'for motherhood' and retrained as a solicitor, at which she worked from 1985-99; as a partner in Alan Dawson, Simpson and Hampton, moving to J. & R. A. Robertson where she was senior litigation assistant, and then to Dickson, McNiven & Dunn from 1998-99.

Grahame stood for the SNP in Tweeddale, Ettrick and Lauderdale in 1992 and in the South of Scotland seat in the 1994 European elections. In 1999, she stood in Tweeddale again, taking third place, and was elected for the South of Scotland region, under her previous married name of Christine Creech. Her experience was of working round the perception from the party leadership that she was too much on the party's fundamentalist wing, by proving herself with little help from the leadership. She was SNP spokesperson for older people for the first year, then becoming spokesperson on the reserved issue of social security. Having started on both public petitions and justice committees, the leadership gave her convenership of the justice 1 committee, which she chaired with the formidable presence one might expect of a teacher-turned-lawyer.

She also showed herself an impressive local campaigner, nursing the Tweeddale, Ettrick and Lauderdale seat, which had never previously been promising turf for Nationalists. Ever present in the local media, she was a strident critic of the local council when education overspending plunged it into crisis, seeking to link the dominant independent group of councillors with the Lib Dem group which had been supporting them. She was also careful to associate herself with the Borders rail link, although that has multi-party backing, and she sought to get herself off the hook of voting for the 13.5 per cent MSP pay increase by saying she would donate the rise to Borders charities.

While the council saw considerable turnover in the 2003 election, Grahame took on the new candidate Jeremy Purvis, replacing the retiring Ian Jenkins, and registered a swing of 5.6 per cent from Lib Dem to SNP, cutting the majority from 4,478 to 538. Having played the internal party politics required to secure a high placing on the SNP regional priorities, Grahame came top of the South of Scotland list, and was one of those to demote Michael Russell down the list, so that one of the party's biggest fish failed to secure re-election. Carrying gravitas from her previous committee role, but not being part of John Swinney's policy team, Grahame was handed the convenership of the health committee, following the 2003 election. She claims to be 'a gardening bore', saying her garden is her favourite place in the world.

ADAM INGRAM (SNP) was born in 1951 in Kilmarnock and educated at Kilmarnock Academy and Paisley College where he gained a degree in business economics. He was a manager in A. H. Ingram and Son, the family bakery firm, from 1971-76, senior economic assistant with the Manpower Services Commission from 1985-86, then a researcher and lecturer at Paisley College from 1987-88, before becoming an economic development consultant from 1989-99.

Ingram stood in the Carrick, Cumnock and Doon Valley constituency for the SNP in 1999, losing to Labour, and was elected for the South of Scotland regional seat. He stood there again in 2003, experiencing one of the worst SNP results that night, knocked into third place by Tory Phil Gallie, down from 26 per cent of the vote to 17 per cent. In the Parliament – recognisable by his lugubrious, undertaker's air – this father of four was on the left, formerly fundamentalist wing of the party, and managed Alex Neil's campaign for the SNP leadership in autumn 2000. He was one of those to welcome the debate brought about by the challenge to John Swinney's leadership in summer 2003.

He was his party's deputy finance spokesperson for a year, and then deputised as spokesman on enterprise and lifelong learning from 2001-03, sitting also on both transport and environment and enterprise and lifelong learning committees for most of the first Parliament. He piloted one of the first member's bills through Parliament, modernising leasehold laws to block the so-called Raider of the Lost Titles from snapping up property. Ingram was also convener of the cross-party group on mental health. He was one of those who emerged successfully out of the vicious infighting which characterised the SNP's regional list elections, and returned to Parliament by that means in 2003, this time having no party spokesmanship, and sitting on the education committee.

ALASDAIR MORGAN (SNP) was born in 1945 in Aberfeldy and educated at Breadalbane Academy, Aberfeldy, and the University of Glasgow where he obtained an MA in mathematics and political economy, before going to Moray House College of Education and the Open University where he studied for a bachelors degree in history. The maths teaching career only lasted from 1973-74, before Morgan switched to being a computer analyst with Shell from 1974-80 and with GEC from 1980-84. He was then a computer systems team leader with Fife Regional Council, followed by Lothian Region and then West Lothian Council from 1984-97. Morgan was national treasurer of the SNP through difficult years from 1983-90 and senior vice-convenor (deputy leader to Alex Salmond's first year of leadership) in 1990-91, being seen as a safe pair of hands and a pro-leadership loyalist. He was the SNP leadership's preferred choice as candidate in the important 1995 Perth and Kinross by-election instead of Roseanna Cunningham, but lost out to her in the selection battle.

Elected to represent Galloway and Upper Nithsdale in the House of Commons in 1997, he claimed the scalp of Ian Lang, then a senior cabinet minister at the Department of Trade and Industry. He retained the seat with the first Scottish Parliament election, standing down by choice from his Commons seat at the following general election. In the meantime, Alex Salmond got Morgan to take charge of Westminster affairs from 1999-2000, as all the MPs had dual mandates. In the Scottish Parliament, he was made party spokesperson on rural affairs, while deputy convener of the rural affairs committee, where he fought for toughened wildlife crime legislation. From 2001-03, he was finance spokesman, with a place on the finance committee.

At the 2001 Westminster election, Morgan watched as his old seat – fought by party researcher Malcolm Fleming and badly affected that year by the foot and mouth outbreak – was lost by a margin of only 74 votes to Conservative Peter Duncan. That was the only Scottish constituency to change party hands that night, and gave the Conservatives their only Scottish seat in the Commons. It was a warning of what was to befall Morgan in 2003, as the Tory list MSP Alex Fergusson ousted him from the constituency. Morgan was elected, however, as number two on the South of Scotland SNP list. He became convener of the SNP Parliamentary group and convener of the enterprise and culture committee, which early on set about inquiries into renewable energy and the effect on Scotland of Whitehall plans for university top-up fees.

DAVID MUNDELL (Conservative) was born in 1962 in Dumfries and educated at Lockerbie Academy, Edinburgh University, where he trained as a lawyer, and Strathclyde Business School, where he gained an MBA. He worked as a corporate lawyer with Biggart, Baillie and Gifford in Glasgow from 1989-91, as group legal adviser with BT Scotland from 1991-98 and as head of national affairs from 1998-99. He was criticised after becoming an MSP for retaining a BT consultancy role, which he promptly ended.

Mundell was elected as a Conservative to Annandale and Eskdale District Council from 1984-86 and Dumfries and Galloway Council from 1986-87. He stood in the Dumfries seat in 1999, losing to Labour's Elaine Murray, and was elected from the South of Scotland regional list. An amiable and centrist Conservative, not given to inter-party bickering, he nursed the seat through the first Parliament, and did well to secure a 3 per cent swing from Labour to Conservative, cutting Murray's majority from 3,654 to 1,096. In the first Parliament, he was deputy spokesman on education from 1999-2001, and then deputy spokesman on enterprise and learning until 2002, becoming spokesman on transport and planning from 2002-03. He sat on the enterprise and lifelong learning committee from 2001-03, and took a place on the local government and transport committee after the 2003 election, with the new party role as spokesman on transport, IT and telecommunications.

Moffat-based Mundell is a former member of the board of the International Teledemocracy Centre, is convener of the grandly titled cross party group on information, knowledge and enlightenment, and is an accredited alternative dispute resolution mediator.

West of Scotland

Scottish Parliament Election Results

	Lab	SNP	Con	Lib Dem	SSP	Green	Ind
1999	(9)	4	2	1	–	–	–
2003	(8)	3	2	1	1	–	(1)

Constituency Vote

	Lab	SNP	Con	Lib Dem	SSP	Green	Others
1999	43.5	26.9	16.4	11.3	0.6	–	1.4
2003	38.3	20.9	15.1	13.5	5.9	–	6.3
Diff.	–5.2	–6.0	–1.2	+2.3	+5.3	–	+4.9

Regional Vote

	Lab	SNP	Con	Lib Dem	SSP	Green	Others
1999	38.5	25.9	15.7	11.0	1.9	2.6	4.3
2003	32.6	19.6	15.7	12.3	7.2	5.7	6.9
Diff.	–5.9	–6.3	=	+1.3	+5.3	+3.0	+2.6

The West of Scotland seat includes nine constituencies all to the west of Glasgow on both the north and south banks of the Clyde. It stretches north towards Argyll and includes the Isle of Arran, but its population is dominated by Labour heartlands on Clydeside and North Ayrshire along with the leafy outlying suburbs of Glasgow where the Conservatives can rely on some of the truest blue enclaves in Scotland. In short, it is not a region with much of a unifying political identity. In 1997, this area voted Labour 51.3 per cent to the SNP's 19.9 per cent, with Conservatives on 18.2 per cent and Liberal Democrats on 9.2 per cent. Labour won all nine seats in 1997, gaining Eastwood from the Tories, and retained them all in 2001.

In the 1999 Scottish Parliament elections, Labour won 43.5 per cent of the constituency vote to the SNP's 26.9 per cent and took all nine of the Westminster seats it represented. In the regional vote, Labour won 38.5 per cent of the vote to the SNP's 25.9 per cent and Conservatives 15.7 per cent. By 2001, Labour's share of the vote stood at exactly 50 per cent to the SNP's 17.5 per cent, the Tories' 15.7 per cent and the Lib Dems' 13.2 per cent, meaning the Lib Dems had made a modest gain, while the other parties had lost ground slightly.

In the 2003 Scottish Parliament elections, Labour retained all the constituency seats but its regional vote fell from 38.5 per cent to 32.6 per cent. The SNP won 19.6 per cent and dropped one of its four seats, with the three list members elected being newcomers to the party's group in the Scottish Parliament. This change was largely a result of the vicious internal battling for placings on the party's list. Their lost seat went to the SSP, which more than trebled its regional vote since 1999, winning 7.2 per cent of the regional vote while the Greens on 5.7 per cent failed to win a seat – one of only two regions where this happened. An interesting occurrence happened in Press Association reporting of the regional count with 40,000 votes mysteriously added to the Lib Dems from nowhere boosting their regional vote, and in most subsequent press reports distorting the entire national result in percentage terms.

FRANCES CURRAN (SSP) was born in Glasgow in 1961, and educated at St Brendan's High, Linwood and St Andrew's High, Carntyne in Glasgow. From a family of politicised women, she joined Labour in 1979, becoming involved in the Young Socialists, quickly being elected to the regional and then national committees. She was working at that time in Strathclyde Region finance division, and studying accountancy. At the height of the internal warfare within Labour, aged only 24, she moved to London where she had been elected a member of Labour's national executive committee, working with the Bennite Campaign Group of MPs, and later associated with the Militant Tendency, which helps explain her split with Labour. She worked also with campaigns such as the artists' Red Wedge movement, including Billy Bragg and Paul Weller, campaigning against the poll tax and in Youth Against Racism in Europe. She returned to Glasgow in 1995, and was involved in launching the Scottish Socialist Alliance, later to become the SSP, and has been its international officer from the early days. She has taken part in various campaigns to retain public services, including a blockade of Glasgow City Chambers and occupation of a community centre and schools.

This bingo and caravan enthusiast was, unsuccessfully, in second place to Tommy Sheridan on the SSP's Glasgow list in 1999, and in the eighth, final place on the party's European list that year. She contested Paisley South for the SSP in 2003, winning 1,765 votes and 7.1 per cent, taking fifth place, and being elected as a list MSP for West of Scotland. She became the party's spokesperson on enterprise and lifelong learning, with membership of the equal opportunities committee.

ROSS FINNIE (Liberal Democrat) was born in 1947 in Greenock and educated at Greenock Academy. He worked as an audit assistant with Arthur Anderson from 1970-73, as manager of corporate finance, British Bank of Commerce from 1973–74, manager of corporate finance at James Findlay Bank from 1974-86, director of Glasgow corporate finance for Singer and Friedlander from 1986-91, and set up his own chartered accountancy practice in 1991, allowing him more easily to mix business with politics.

He served on Inverclyde District Council from 1977-96 and Inverclyde Council from 1995-99, and was planning convener on the former from 1977-80, his party's group leader from 1988-96, and opposition leader from 1995-99. A small, long-time oasis of Lib Dem strength in the West of Scotland, Inverclyde returned to Lib Dem control in the 2003 elections. Finnie was chair of the Scottish Liberal Party from 1982-86, a time when it helped to put his future party leader, Jim Wallace, into the winnable Orkney and Shetland candidacy after Jo Grimond vacated the seat in time for the 1983 election. Finnie chaired the general election committee from 1995-97 and was chair of the Scottish candidates vetting panel from 1997-99. He stood in West Renfrewshire in the 1979 general election and in Stirling in 1983. Having nursed the Greenock and Inverclyde seat in Westminster elections, he stood there also in the 1999 elections, polling respectably, with 12 extra percentage points added on the Lib Dem vote. Although Labour lost control of the council to the Lib Dems in 2003, and with the Lib Dem candidate's high profile, Finnie could only achieve a modest additional swing in his direction from Labour's incumbent MSP, Duncan McNeil.

Elected on the West of Scotland regional list in 1999, Finnie was one of the five-strong Lib Dem coalition negotiating team with Labour, and joined Jim Wallace as the other Lib Dem in Donald Dewar's first cabinet. Although from an urban background, Finnie took the rural affairs post, later known as rural development, to which he would add environment and responsibility for reforming the water boards in 2001. To widespread surprise – including, apparently, his own – he retained his job after the 2003 coalition deal was struck, though this time he was not part of Jim Wallace's core team of negotiators.

A comically low voice, his sense of the ridiculous and more than a passing resemblance to Captain Mainwaring of *Dad's Army*, have helped this churchman and rugby enthusiast become one of the best known faces and voices in the Scottish Parliament. Events have helped raise his profile as well, as he first had to deal with the later stages of the BSE 'mad cow disease' episode, including the ban on selling beef on the bone, which he lifted ahead of the UK. He was then face of the Scottish Executive dealing with the foot and mouth outbreak in 2001, giving him a reputation as a sound chap in a crisis – particularly when compared with Whitehall's mismanagement of England's outbreak. Crises followed, with a water safety scare in Glasgow in summer 2002 spilling into his lap, at a time the Labour-supporting *Daily Record* began to target him personally as a way of distancing Labour from Lib Dems. He did not help his reputation by calling at a business dinner the head of the CBI Digby Jones, 'an English prat'. Responsible for fisheries, he tended to leave much of that work to his deputies, though had to work with UK fisheries minister Elliot Morley in negotiating two very difficult quota reduction and decommissioning agreements in Brussels. That link, with the agriculture department in Whitehall, put Finnie and his department into one of the most difficult of the devolved relationships, repeatedly having to remind ministers in London they had to take Scottish differences into account.

He has faced criticism from within the Lib Dems and environmental groups for failing to support his own party's policy objecting to genetically-modified crop farm tests, preferring to stick to officials' and legal advice. Crofters have also accused him of being too close to the National Farmers Union and big farming interests. It was revealed in January 2004 that Finnie would undergo a double heart bypass operation and take three months off to recover. In this period, his deputy, Alan Wilson, would sit in the cabinet.

ANNABEL GOLDIE (Conservative) was born in Glasgow in 1950 and educated at Greenock Academy and Strathclyde University where she gained an LLB. She has been self-employed as a partner in law firms since 1978 and was a partner in the Glasgow firm Donaldson, Alexander, Russell and Haddow. She is a member of the Royal Faculty of Procurators in Glasgow, the Law Society and the Scottish Law Agents Society. Goldie has a long record of involvement in voluntary organisations and has been a director of the Prince's Scottish Youth Trust, a member of the West of Scotland Advisory Board of the Salvation Army, Strathclyde University court and a Church of Scotland elder. She has held a number of posts in the voluntary wing of the Scottish Conservatives: vice-chair in 1992, deputy chairman 1995-97 and acting chairman from 1997-98. She was in that position on the morning of 2 May 1997, about the only Conservative still standing and willing to speak for it at its lowest point. In September 1988, she became deputy when David McLetchie was elected leader of the Scottish Conservatives.

Goldie stood in Renfrew West and Inverclyde in 1992 and in West Renfrewshire in 1999. She stood in 2003 in the same seat, losing ground in the latter vote, ending in third place to Labour and the SNP. She was elected in both 1999 and 2003 from the top of the Conservative regional list for West of Scotland. In the first Scottish Parliament, Goldie was party spokeswoman on the economy, industry and finance, becoming deputy convener of the enterprise and lifelong learning committee. She quickly established a reputation as an effective debater, skilled in out-manoeuvring ministers and opponents, often using her strong sense of humour, both self-deprecating and cutting; in one debate she challenged Wendy Alexander, then communities minister, and many years her junior, with the words 'as one spinster to another'. However, given her deputy leader position, the first Parliament saw her falling somewhat short of high expectations of the difference she could make. Goldie was talked about as a successor to Sir David Steel as Presiding Officer in 2003, but did not stand for that or the deputy post held by Conservative colleague Murray Tosh. Following the 2003 election, McLetchie appointed her justice and home affairs spokeswoman. Her pastimes include walking and bird–watching, and she has defined her personal ambition as 'making a meal for eight without a flap'.

BRUCE McFEE (SNP) was born in Johnstone in 1961 and educated at Johnstone High School. He was export manager and then customer services manager with Pest Protection Services (Scotland) from 1991-2003, as the man who pushed its expansion to the Falklands and Estonia (where he met his wife), selling 'the products, expertise and training to tackle the world's pest problems'. He was a councillor on Renfrew District Council and then Renfrewshire Council from 1988-2003, becoming group leader after only four years, and remaining in that position for eleven turbulent years from 1992-2003. This was a period when Labour in Renfrewshire was suffering its own internal warfare, and the council chamber was notorious for its rowdy meetings, with police being called from their station across the road on several occasions to calm the aggro between SNP and Labour councillors. The latter was led until 1999 by Hugh Henry, later Labour MSP for Paisley South, and the SNP group included Sandra White, who would become a Glasgow MSP. Leading his group from the front with disruptive tactics and strenuous accusations of Labour sleaze, McFee was given a police escort from meetings on at least five occasions, most recently in October 1998. He was one of the 13 Renfrewshire SNP councillors (out of 15) who backed Alex Neil in the 2000 leadership contest, and was among the first to support the challenge by Glasgow activist Bill Wilson in 2003 – at least in that it opened up a party debate about the route to independence.

McFee was hot favourite to be the SNP candidate in the 1997 Paisley North by-election, even until the day before selection, but pulled out on the day of the vote in favour of outsider Ian Blackford, who was favoured by headquarters. To McFee's credit, while he stood down from the council in 2003, the SNP won more votes than Labour in the council election, but lost out in the number of seats. He stood in the Scottish Parliament election against Tricia Godman in Renfrewshire West, and won 25.3 per cent of the vote along with a tiny 0.1 per cent swing from Labour to SNP. He had, meanwhile, been one of the three newcomer SNP members who had played the party's internal electoral system to their advantage and saw off the incumbents from the first Parliament, with McFee seen as having ousted former headteacher Colin Campbell. Not a favourite of the Swinney leadership, the new MSP got a place on the local government and transport committee.

CAMPBELL MARTIN (SNP) was born in 1960 in Irvine, and was educated at first in Ardrossan Academy. He did a craft apprenticeship at ICI in Stevenston, Ayrshire from 1976-80, and from 1980-93, he did various jobs, including labourer, club DJ, club steward, taxi and coach driver, returning to full-time education to study at James Watt College, Greenock from 1993-94. He was a buyer on British Aerospace's Jetstream aircraft project at Prestwick from 1995-97, was in purchasing liaison at the same company's Avro International subsidiary in Manchester from 1997-99, and with the election of the first Scottish Parliament, he became assistant to Kay Ullrich, then SNP whip, who stood down in 2003.

He has taken left-wing positions within the SNP, with direct action against the poll tax and in campaigning against nuclear weapons. He was an Ardrossan councillor on Cunninghame District Council from 1992-96, and fought Cunninghame North's Westminster seat in 2001 and the Scottish Parliament seat in 2003, taking a creditable second place to Labour's Allan Wilson. Martin registered a 1.25 per cent swing from Labour to the SNP, winning 27.1 per cent of the vote, against Wilson's 38.9 per cent. He secured a place on the equal opportunities committee, but early signs that he was far from being in with John Swinney's leadership circle, emphasised when he was among the first to voice support for the challenge mounted to Swinney in July-September 2003, saying the leader had lost touch with grass roots members. This earned him a personal rebuke without being named by John Swinney at the SNP annual conference.

STEWART MAXWELL (SNP) was born in 1963 and educated at King's Park Secondary in Glasgow, and Glasgow College of Technology, from 1981-85, doing a BA Hons degree in social sciences. A varied career took him through a hypothermia campaign for Strathclyde Region 1985-86, working for Wilmax, the family wholesale butchers from 1987-88 and 1991-92, as an administrator for the Scottish Training Foundation from 1988-91, and from 1993-2003 in Strathclyde Fire Brigade, working mainly in its command and control centre and rising to become principal administrative officer.

His interest in politics was sparked as a boy by having an uncle, David Torrance, on the joint shop stewards committee during the Upper Clyde Shipbuilders work-in, in 1971. As a student, he was a campaigner in support of striking miners, CND and the anti-apartheid movement, joining the Labour Party in the mid-1980s but leaving after a few years.

He joined the SNP in 1992, standing in 2001 for the Westminster seat of Eastwood, and for the same constituency's Scottish Parliament seat in 2003, falling to fourth place with 4,736 votes and 12.2 per cent – a heavy loss from the 1999 SNP vote. He was elected from third place in the West of Scotland SNP list, with the other two also newcomers in 2003, suggesting they had worked the internal selection machinations of the SNP better than previous Nationalist incumbents. Maxwell's declared positioning with the SNP is mainstream, even though he is not seen as one of John Swinney's inner circle, and he stresses his interest in council voting reform, opposition to nuclear power and weapons, plus a commitment to organic farming. Following the 2003 election, he became deputy convener of the justice 1 committee, with a place also on subordinate legislation.

MURRAY TOSH (Conservative) was born in 1950 in Ayr and educated at Kilmarnock Academy, Glasgow University and Jordanhill College of Education. He worked as a history teacher at Ravenspark Academy, Irvine 1975-77, as principal teacher of history at Kilwinning Academy from 1977–84 and at Belmont Academy, Ayr, from 1984-89. Tosh first stood for national office for the Liberal Party in Ayr in the October 1974, and first stood with the Conservatives in Glasgow Hillhead in 1983, coming third to the SDP's Roy Jenkins. He was elected to Kyle and Carrick District Council from 1987-96 and was deputy leader of the Conservative group from 1992-96, convener of the housing committee and vice-convener of the planning and development committee. In the 1999 elections, Tosh stood in the Cunninghame South seat, and was returned for the South of Scotland region as a list MSP, having been in third position. For 2003, he said he was standing down in what appeared to be an example of a politician preferring the appeal of local politics, where South Ayrshire Council showed signs of becoming Conservative-controlled. But then, having become Deputy Presiding Officer, he changed his mind and moved, uniquely, to a different region, standing as a no-hope candidate in the Dumbarton seat, coming fourth, and being elected as a West of Scotland regional MSP as number two on the Tory list after deputy leader Annabel Goldie.

In the first Parliament, he began as his party's spokesman on transport and environment, while on the transport and environment committee in 1999-2001, and was for four years convenor of the procedures committee, even after being elected Deputy Presiding Officer. In the latter role, he led the committee towards a major report into the workings of the Parliament, with many recommendations for reform in its second term, published just before its 2003 dissolution.

Tosh has gained a reputation for being an open-minded, pragmatic, schoolmasterly politician, a Tory trade union member interested in getting things done. He has a short fuse when having to put up with party ideologues. His dislike of Brian Monteith became public in June 2000, with Tosh penning a furious letter to the *Scotsman* denouncing the Mid-Scotland and Fife Tory MSP for trying to stir up trouble within the party. Being respected across the chamber, he became deputy to Sir David Steel, when Labour's Patricia Ferguson vacated that post to become Parliament Minister in November 2001. There were moves to have Labour's Tricia Godman stand for the post, but having just been elected First Minister, Jack McConnell made his first mistake by trying to bounce his party into electing Cathy Peattie. This being a private ballot, his own MSPs and others rebelled, and Tosh came out the victor by 68-45 votes. The Conservative might have been a compromise choice for Presiding Officer, if Labour had followed through on the mission of some of its MSPs to stop George Reid, but that campaign fizzled out with Labour's disappointing election result and reduced coalition majority with the Lib Dems in 2003. Tosh stood for the deputy's post, winning 43 votes, while Tricia Godman came second with 59, being elected one of the two Deputy Presiding Officers when Green Robin Harper pulled out after the first round.

Scotland's MEPs

Scotland has eight MEPs, elected in June 1999 using the whole country as a single multi-member constituency and using the single transferable vote system. At the previous election in 1994, there had been the same eight regional constituencies which would subsequently be used in the 1999 Scottish Parliament election for the top-up party vote. The shift in voting system meant Labour's representation was cut from six to three, while the SNP remained on two, having already represented the Highlands and Islands and North East Scotland. The Conservatives gained two and the Liberal Democrats one. They were elected for a five year term, and by the June 2004 election, the number of Scottish seats was due to be cut to seven as a result of EU enlargement and the influx of MEPs from new EU members, meaning the UK complement of MEPs falls from a total of 87 to 78.

ELSPETH ATTWOOLL (Liberal Democrat) was elected first in 1999, with only 9.8 per cent of the vote. She was born in Chiselhurst in 1943 and educated at Tiffin Girls' School, Surrey, then at St Andrews University where she gained an MA in politics and philosophy, and an LLB. She was a lecturer in jurisprudence and comparative law at Glasgow University from 1966-98, and is married to an academic historian. She was a prominent party activist, including the presidency of Scottish Women's Liberal Democrats since 1998, while a member of the party's executive in Scotland since 1996. She stood five times in unpromising territory for the Lib Dems of Glasgow Maryhill constituency in October 1974, 1979, 1983, 1987 and 1997 and also contested the Glasgow Euro-constituency in 1979. She speaks fluent French and respectable German, with some Dutch and modern Greek. Within the European Parliament, she became a member of the committees on fisheries, employment and social affairs, and as a substitute member on agriculture and rural development. She is her party's co-ordinator on public health and consumer policy. She has also been a member of the delegation for relations with Canada. She sits in the Parliament as a member of the European Liberal, Democrat and Reform Party, and has been selected to top the Scottish Lib Dem list for the 2004 elections.

IAN HUDGHTON (SNP) was born in 1951 in Forfar and educated at Forfar Academy and Kingsway Technical College, where he qualified with a City and Guilds Certificate in Building Science in 1973. He ran his own painting and decorating business until 1986. He was a councillor on Angus District from 1985-95 and served as housing convenor. He was then a member of Angus Council, of which he became leader in 1996. He was also a member of Tayside Regional Council from 1994-96, where he was property convenor. While a councillor, he became one of Scotland's members of Europe's Committee of the Regions. Hudghton was first elected to the European Parliament as the SNP member for North East Scotland at the by-election in November 1998 which followed the death of Allan Macartney, then the party's deputy leader, who had first won the seat in 1994 from Labour. This was a convincing win for the SNP, knocking a poorly-organised Labour campaign from first into third place, and significantly helping its momentum in the run-up to the 1999 Scottish Parliament election. Hudghton was re-elected to the European Parliament in 1999, at the top of a party list which came within 15,000 votes of outpolling Labour across Scotland. He sits in the Green-European Free Alliance Group in the Parliament, and informally divides Scotland with his fellow SNP MEP, Professor Sir Neil MacCormick:

Hudghton covers issues particularly affecting Central Scotland, North East Scotland, the Highlands and Islands (excluding Argyll), Mid-Scotland and Fife, plus Falkirk and Cumbernauld. He is a member of the committees on budgets and on fisheries, leading on a crucial issue for the SNP. He is a substitute member on agriculture and rural development and a member of the delegation to the European Economic Area Parliamentary Committee. He was easily re-selected to top the SNP's candidate list for the 2004 election.

PROFESSOR SIR NEIL MacCORMICK (SNP) was born in 1941, the son of John MacCormick, one of the founders of the National Party of Scotland and brother of Iain MacCormick, who was SNP MP for Argyll from February 1974-79. Neil MacCormick was educated at Glasgow High School, and the universities of Glasgow and Oxford, where he studied law. He was a lecturer in jurisprudence at St Andrews University from 1965-67, and from 1967-72 as a fellow and tutor at Balliol College, Oxford. From 1972, he was Regius Professor of Public Law and the Law of Nature and Nations at Edinburgh University, serving as dean of the law faculty from 1973-76 and from 1985-88. He was also provost of law and social sciences from 1993-97 and the university's vice-principal (international) from 1997-99. He has honorary doctorates from five universities. Through this distinguished academic career, he became one of Scotland's foremost constitutional lawyers, with an international reputation in jurisprudence and philosophy while a major intellectual asset to the SNP's thinking on its core constitutional policy. Though sometimes making him out of tune with the party's mainstream, he has been a consistent SNP pro-devolutionist. This has led him to edit and contribute to numerous books over the last 30 years, including editorship of *The Scottish Debate: Essays on Scottish Nationalism*, published in 1970, which included a typically ecumenical range of contributions including David Steel and Donald Dewar, both of whom were university friends. He was a member of the Constitutional Steering Committee under the chairmanship of Sir Robert Grieve which produced *A Claim Of Right For Scotland* in 1988, leading to the establishment of the cross-party Scottish Constitutional Convention – which, of course, his party then refused to join. He would also be out of kilter with party thinking on the honours system in 2002, when he accepted the offer of a knighthood in recognition of his academic achievements.

Within the party, he was a member of the national executive committee through the fiery days of 1978-91 and vice-president from 1999-2002. He unsuccessfully contested the Argyll and Bute constituency at the 1997 general election, and won a seat in the European Parliament two years later, as second on the SNP list. In the European Parliament he became a member of the committee of legal affairs and the internal market and also served as a substitute on the constitutional affairs committee. In his only term in the Parliament, he made his mark above all as a respected contributor to the thinking behind the EU Constitution as it was being drawn up by the Convention for the Future of Europe, chaired by Valerie Giscard d'Estaing. He was active in campaigning for a Scottish lecturer in Italy, fighting a long-running battle to have equal employment recognition to that afforded to locally hired Italian academics, while he also pushed for constraints on animal transportation within the EU. Like Ian Hudghton, MacCormick sits with the Greens-European Free Alliance, avoiding association with xenophobic nationalist parties from across the continent. The two SNP members informally divided their responsibilities, so that MacCormick looks after issues particularly affecting Lothian, Glasgow, South of Scotland, West of Scotland and Argyll and Bute. In September 2003, he announced he would not seek another term in office, partly through health concerns but also as an expression of his frustration with a party which was at that time reverting to fundamentalism during the challenge to John Swinney's leadership.

DAVID MARTIN (Labour) was born in Edinburgh in 1954 and elected a Labour MEP for the Lothians seat from 1984-99, and then as the first elected of the eight returned for the Scottish multi-member constituency in 1999. He was educated at Liberton High School and Heriot-Watt University, where he gained a BA (Hons) in economics. He later enrolled at Leicester University and gained an MA in European law and employment law in 1996. Martin worked as a stockbrocker's assistant and was the vice-president of mobile projects with the St Andrew Animal Fund, an animal rights agency. He was on Lothian Regional Council from 1982-84.

Once elected to the European Parliament, he became vice-chair of the Socialist Group from 1987-88, and has been vice-president of the European Parliament since 1989. He fought with the Socialist Group's support for the Parliament presidency in the second half of the 1999-2004 term, losing in January 2002 to Irishman Pat Cox, who had the backing of the Euro-Liberals. Remaining as senior vice-president, he has special responsibility for relations with national parliaments, struggling in the meantime to resolve the conflicting interests of devolved Parliaments within member states and their role in the EU constitution being drawn up by the Convention on the Future of Europe. He is a member of the committee on economic and monetary affairs while a substitute on the constitutional affairs committee. In the fifth term of the European Parliament, he was active in developing country relations, and a member of the delegation for relations with Canada. In his time as a MEP, he has been responsible for reports on traditional industrial regions, areas suffering from the decline in the coal industry, and on the Maastricht Treaty. He has also written pamphlets on the European Union, arguing for improved democratic accountability along with a federal approach to institutional reform, while criticising the Blair Government in London for its alliances with governments of the right in blocking social reform. He is also a guest lecturer in European Union politics at Glasgow University.

Martin expressed some frustration, even before running for the Parliament presidency, at the voting system splitting him from his Lothian constituency link, and he twice sought to win Parliamentary seats back in Britain. He made an unsuccessful bid for the Midlothian seat at Westminster when it was vacated ahead of the 2001 election by Eric Clarke. He then put his name in the ring for the Strathkelvin and Bearsden Scottish Parliament seat being vacated in 2001 by Sam Galbraith. But a power play by Chancellor Gordon Brown in Labour's National Executive Council is credited with blocking him. This was by using a party rule which bars elected representatives in one legislative body from standing for another. This was reported as stopping him from getting in the way of a Brown loyalist, Brian Fitzpatrick, who was favoured for the candidacy.

BILL MILLER (Labour) was born in 1954 in Gartocharn and elected Labour MEP for Glasgow from 1994-99 and for the Scotland constituency from 1999. He was educated at Kilmarnock Academy, Paisley Technical College and Kingston Polytechnic, studying land economics and town planning, and he worked as a surveyor for Glasgow District Council from 1978-94. From 1980-88, he was a lay official with NALGO local government trade union. He was also a councillor on Strathclyde Region from 1986-94, representing the formerly Tory Kings Park-Aikenhead ward, and serving as vice-chair and then chair of the economic development committee, from 1988-94. Elected to the European Parliament in 1994, he replaced Janey Buchan in the Glasgow constituency. In the 1999-2004 term, he has been vice-chairman of the committee on legal affairs and the internal market while a substitute member of the committee on regional policy, transport and tourism and a member of the EU-Latvia joint parliamentary committee. Among the reports on which he has worked were those on regulation of silicon breast implants (which got him more publicity than most MEPs achieve), machine safety, disability issues, alcohol, the bus and coach directive, and reform of the European Commission. He was also whip of the UK Labour group of MEPs, and responsible for liaison with the Scottish Executive and Scotland

Office. Married with two children, his main hobby is 'collecting vinyl records'. Going into the 2004 elections, he may find more time to spend with them, having been moved from second to third place in the Labour list, behind David Martin and Catherine Stihler, at a time when the reduced number of seats may mean Labour loses one of its three Scottish seats.

JOHN PURVIS (Conservative) was born in St Andrews in 1938 and has had his second period as a Conservative MEP since 1999. Educated at Glenalmond and St Andrews University, where he studied moral philosophy and political economy, he worked as a banker, first for Citibank in London, New York and Milan between 1962-69, as treasurer of investment bankers Noble Grossart in Edinburgh from 1969-73 and managing director of Gilmerton Management Services from 1973-86, offering financial consultancy focussing on international finance and business development in Europe. Since 1985, he has been managing partner of Purvis and Company, a business consultancy under which he has been on the boards of Belgrave Capital Management, of Legg Mason Investors European Utilities Investment Trust, as non-executive chairman of Kingdom FM radio station in Fife, and representing National Commercial Bank Services of Tennessee. Meanwhile, he has also run a farming business near St Andrews in Fife since 1969 and in Argyll from 1986-89. He was previously the MEP for Mid-Scotland and Fife from 1979-84, as group whip and spokesman on energy, research and technology for the European Democratic Group, to which the UK Conservatives then belonged. He was vice-chairman of the Gulf States Delegation from 1982-84. Subsequently, he held internal Scottish Conservative posts, including chairmanship of its economic affairs committee from 1986-97 and the vice-presidency of its voluntary wing from 1987-89. Within the fifth term of the European Parliament, he has been vice-chairman of the economic and monetary affairs committee, with involvement in the development of the European Central Bank and European Investment Bank, while also dealing with competition policy, financial services and taxation. He is a member of the committee on industry, external trade, research and energy, specialising in biotechnology research while Conservative spokesman on the subject. He is a substitute member on the EU-Bulgaria joint Parliamentary committee and a member of the delegation for relations with the Mashreq countries and the Gulf.

STRUAN STEVENSON (Conservative) was born in Ballantrae in 1948 and elected an MEP in 1999 from the top slot on the Scottish Conservative Party list. He was educated at Strathallan School, Perthshire, and the West of Scotland Agriculture College, and since 1968, he has been director of his family farming business, while also becoming involved in local government. He was a member of Girvan Council from 1970-74, then elected to Kyle and Carrick District Council from 1974-92, of which he was leader from 1986-88, while also Conservative leader on COSLA. He stood unsuccessfully for Westminster on three occasions: Carrick, Cumnock and Doon Valley in 1987, Edinburgh South in 1992 and the formerly safe seat of Dumfries in 1997, just as Labour gained it from the Conservatives in that year's landslide. This serial candidacy did at least qualify him to be chairman of the Scottish Conservative candidates association from 1992-97, while also his party's agriculture spokesman and chairing its arts and heritage committee.

He was the Conservative candidate at the North East Scotland European Parliamentary by-election in November 1998, helping knock Labour from first to third place while he came second to the SNP. Throughout this period, he was positioned on the more pro-devolution, 'wet' wing of the Conservatives, trying to move the party into the Scottish political mainstream rather than swimming against it. In 1979, he was one of those arguing for a 'yes' vote in the referendum, though by the 1997 referendum, his position had moved to a quirky 'no-yes' vote: 'no' to a Parliament, but 'yes' to it having taxation powers if there had to be one.

Before his election to the European Parliament, he was director of Saferworld, a foreign affairs defence think tank, from 1992-94. From 1994-99 he was a director of PS Communications, a PR and lobbying agency notable for recruiting politicians from across the Scottish party spectrum. In Brussels and Strasbourg, he has been chairman of the fisheries committee, giving him an opportunity to play a prominent role in the European issue which has had the highest profile in Scotland over recent years (the committee, after all, has the strongest Scottish representation, with all four parties having places on it). He is a substitute member of the committee on agriculture and rural development, and Tory spokesman on agriculture. With his PR background, he is better than the other MEPs at grabbing attention for his campaigns, including one against the farming of dogs for fashion fur. He also gained attention for the people of a part of Kazakhstan whose health and farmland has been devastated by Soviet nuclear testing, being rewarded for his efforts with the first honorary citizenship of the city of Semipalatinsk. He is on the delegation for relations with the People's Republic of China.

CATHERINE STIHLER (Labour) was born in 1973 in Bellshill – birthplace of many of the greatest talents to play for Celtic Football Club – and elected to the European Parliament in 1999 as Catherine Taylor. She was educated at Coltness High School, Wishaw and St Andrews University, where she studied geography and international relations followed by a masters in international security studies, and was president of the students association from 1994-95. She worked as a researcher for Aberdeen South MP Anne Begg from 1997-99. Aged only 20, she was elected to the Scottish Labour executive from 1993-95 and then 1997-99 and the UK NEC from 1995-97, marking her out as one of the coming ultra-Blairite talents in New Labour. Elected to the European Parliament aged 26, she secured a place on the fisheries committee, a subject on which she is Labour spokeswoman. She is a member of the committee on the environment, public health and consumer policy, serving as president of the public health working group in 2000, which in turn helped give her prominence in arguing for labelling and regulation of herbal remedies, and in pushing for more support to sub-Saharan Africa in combating AIDS. She is also a member of the delegation to the EU-Hungary joint Parliamentary committee, and served on the temporary MEP committee dealing with the 2001 foot and mouth outbreak. For the 2004 election, she has moved up Labour's ranking from number three to two with the help of 'gender zipping', displacing Bill Miller and making it likely she will return for a second term.

Westminster Successor Seats

As a result of the Scotland Act 1998, the number of Scottish seats at Westminster is being reduced from 72 to 59. This is to bring them into line with the average electorate of other seats throughout the UK. The Boundary Commission consulted through much of 2002 and 2003, finalising its proposed map in December 2003. The new seats are expected to apply at the next Westminster election. This change was due also to affect the Scottish Parliament, and the number of MSPs would be reduced to 108. However, following a Bill introduced to the UK Parliament in December 2003, the constituencies for which Members of the Scottish Parliament are elected will remain as they were. Most of the existing constituencies have obvious successors for Westminster, some are split several ways, and some disappear altogether.

Old Constituency	New Constituency	Current MP
Aberdeen North	Aberdeen North	Malcolm Savidge
Aberdeen Central	Disappearing seat	Frank Doran
Aberdeen South	Aberdeen South	Anne Begg
Aberdeenshire West and Kincardine	West Aberdeenshire and Kincardine	Robert Smith
Airdrie and Shotts	Airdrie and Shotts	Helen Liddell
Angus	Angus	Michael Weir
Argyll and Bute	Argyll and Bute	Alan Reid
Ayr	Ayr, Carrick and Cumnock	Sandra Osborne
Banff and Buchan	Banff and Buchan	Alex Salmond
Caithness, Sutherland and Easter Ross	Caithness, Sutherland and Easter Ross	John Thurso
Carrick, Cumnock and Doon Valley	Disappearing seat	George Foulkes (standing down)
Clydebank and Milngavie	Disappearing seat	Tony Worthington (standing down)
Clydesdale	Disappearing seat	Jimmy Hood
Coatbridge and Chryston	Coatbridge, Chryston and Bellshill	Tom Clarke
Cumbernauld and Kilsyth	Cumbernauld, Kilsyth and Kirkintilloch East	Rosemary McKenna
Cunninghame North	North Ayrshire and Arran	Brian Wilson
Cunninghame South	Central Ayrshire	Brian Donohoe
Dumbarton	West Dunbartonshire	John McFall
Dumfries	Dumfriesshire, Clydesdale and Tweeddale	Russell Brown
Dundee East	Dundee East	Iain Luke
Dundee West	Dundee West	Ernie Ross
Dunfermline East	Disappearing seat	Gordon Brown
Dunfermline West	Dunfermline and West Fife	Rachel Squire
East Kilbride	East Kilbride, Strathaven and Lesmahagow	Adam Ingram
East Lothian	East Lothian	Anne Picking
Eastwood	East Renfrewshire	Jim Murphy
Edinburgh Central	Disappearing seat	Alistair Darling

Edinburgh East and Musselburgh	Edinburgh East	Gavin Strang
Edinburgh North and Leith	Edinburgh North and Leith	Mark Lazarowicz
Edinburgh Pentlands	Edinburgh South West	Lynda Clark (standing down)
Edinburgh South	Edinburgh South	Nigel Griffiths
Edinburgh West	Edinburgh West	John Barrett
Falkirk East	Disappearing seat	Michael Connarty
Falkirk West	Falkirk	Eric Joyce
Fife Central	Glenrothes	John MacDougall
Fife North East	North East Fife	Sir Menzies Campbell
Galloway and Upper Nithsdale	Dumfries and Galloway	Peter Duncan
Glasgow Anniesland	Glasgow North West	John Robertson
Glasgow Baillieston	Glasgow East	Jimmy Wray
Glasgow Cathcart	Glasgow South	Tom Harris
Glasgow Govan	Disappearing seat	Mohammad Sarwar
Glasgow Kelvin	Disappearing seat	George Galloway
Glasgow Maryhill	Glasgow North	Ann McKechin
Glasgow Pollok	Glasgow South West	Ian Davidson
Glasgow Rutherglen	Rutherglen and Hamilton West	Tommy McAvoy
Glasgow Shettleston	Glasgow Central	David Marshall
Glasgow Springburn	Glasgow North East	Michael Martin
Gordon	Gordon	Malcolm Bruce
Greenock and Inverclyde	Inverclyde	David Cairns
Hamilton North and Bellshill	Disappearing seat	John Reid
Hamilton South	Lanark and Hamilton East	Bill Tynan
Inverness East,Nairn and Lochaber	Inverness, Nairn, Badenoch and Strathspey	David Stewart
Kilmarnock and Loudoun	Kilmarnock and Loudoun	Des Browne
Kirkcaldy	Kirkcaldy and Cowdenbeath	Lewis Moonie (standing down)
Linlithgow	Linlithgow and East Falkirk	Tam Dalyell (standing down)
Livingston	Livingston	Robin Cook
Midlothian	Midlothian	David Hamilton
Moray	Moray	Angus Robertson
Motherwell and Wishaw	Motherwell and Wishaw	Frank Roy
Ochil	Ochil and South Perthshire	Martin O'Neill (standing down)
Orkney and Shetland	Orkney and Shetland	Alistair Carmichael
Paisley North	Paisley and Renfrewshire North	Irene Adams
Paisley South	Paisley and Renfrewshire South	Douglas Alexander
Perth	Perth and North Perthshire	Annabelle Ewing
Renfrewshire West	Disappearing seat	James Sheridan
Ross, Skye and Inverness West	Ross, Skye and Lochaber	Charles Kennedy
Roxburgh and Berwickshire	Berwickshire, Roxburgh and Selkirk	Sir Archy Kirkwood
Stirling	Stirling	Anne McGuire
Strathkelvin and Bearsden	East Dunbartonshire	John Lyons
Tayside North	Disappearing seat	Peter Wishart
Tweeddale, Ettrick and Lauderdale	Disappearing seat	Michael Moore
Western Isles	Na h-Eileanan An Iar	Calum MacDonald

Notional 2001 UK General Election Results for New Constituencies

With new constituencies created for the next Westminster election, some number-crunching has been carried out to calculate how the parties might fare within the boundaries. Martin Baxter, a mathematician in the London financial sector with an interest in politics, has done such a reckoning. He based his figures on a combination of the 2001 Westminster election result, combined with the votes cast in the 2003 local council elections in those wards which are moving into new constituencies. His results agreed with those of Professor David Denver of Lancaster University, who carried out his own calculations along similar lines. Both men agreed that Labour is likely to have ten fewer seats than in 2001, down from 56 to 46 (counting Michael Martin, the Speaker, as if his seat were held by Labour), while the Conservatives, Liberal Democrats and Scottish National Party would each emerge with one fewer seat. One health warning on the figures is that not all council wards have a full range of party candidates from which voters can choose in council elections, the party share sometimes being skewed - particularly in rural areas - by the presence of independent candidates. It should be stressed that the following results are notional calculations of how the results for new constituencies might have looked under past voting patterns. The names against each seat are the best guesses, on the most recent information available, as to which MP might be expected to be returned for it. The findings appear here courtesy of Martin Baxter. More information can be found at his website: www.financialcalculus.co.uk/election

Aberdeen North

Electorate	69,622		Turnout	53.36%

	Votes		% Share
LAB	17,973		47.43
SNP	10,035		26.48
LIB DEM	4,809		12.69
CON	4,195		11.07
SSP	878		2.40
LAB MAJ.	7,938		21.37

MP Malcolm Savidge or Frank Doran (Lab)

Aberdeen South

Electorate 69,332   *Turnout* 61.45%

	Votes	% Share
LAB	16,661	39.25
LIB DEM	11,876	27.98
CON	8,215	19.35
SNP	5,103	12.02
SSP	593	1.36
LAB MAJ.	4,785	11.27

MP Anne Begg (Lab)

Airdrie and Shotts

Electorate 63,309   *Turnout* 50.56%

	Votes	% Share
LAB	20,083	62.46
SNP	5,869	18.25
LIB DEM	2,679	8.33
CON	2,030	6.31
SSP	1,304	4.08
OTH	186	0.58
LAB MAJ.	14,214	44.21

MP Helen Liddell (Lab)

Angus

Electorate 64,591   *Turnout* 55.72%

	Votes	% Share
SNP	12,281	34.01
CON	10,315	28.57
LAB	7,465	20.67
LIB DEM	5,192	14.38
SSP	752	2.09
OTH	104	0.29
SNP MAJ.	1,966	5.46

MP Michael Weir (SNP)

Argyll and Bute

| | Electorate | 69,571 | | | Turnout | 60.56% |

	Votes	% Share
LIB DEM	12,856	30.51
LAB	11,551	27.42
CON	8,871	21.05
SNP	7,435	17.65
SSP	1,420	3.37
LIB DEM MAJ.	1,305	3.10

MP Alan Reid   (Lib Dem)

Ayr, Carrick and Cumnock

| | Electorate | 74,159 | | | Turnout | 63.38% |

	Votes	% Share
LAB	23,888	47.84
CON	12,047	25.64
SNP	4,433	13.69
LIB DEM	3,152	6.71
SSP	1,141	2.48
OTH	328	0.70
LAB MAJ.	11,841	25.20

MP Sandra Osborne   (Lab)

Banff and Buchan

| | Electorate | 65,970 | | | Turnout | 52.87% |

	Votes	% Share
SNP	17,333	49.61
CON	7,144	20.45
LAB	4,893	14.03
LIB DEM	4,732	13.54
SSP	523	1.50
OTH	310	0.89
SNP MAJ.	10,189	29.16

MP Alex Salmond (expected to stand down)   (SNP)

Berwickshire, Roxburgh and Selkirk

Electorate 72,430   *Turnout* 59.56%

	Votes	*% Share*
LIB DEM	19,516	45.39
CON	9,278	21.58
LAB	7,919	18.42
SNP	4,805	11.17
SSP	847	1.97
OTH	635	1.47
LIB DEM MAJ.	10,238	23.81

MP Sir Archy Kirkwood   (Lib Dem)

Caithness, Sutherland and Easter Ross

Electorate 46,533   *Turnout* 60.64%

	Votes	*% Share*
LIB DEM	10,540	37.60
LAB	6,651	23.72
SNP	6,139	21.90
CON	3,753	13.39
SSP	624	2.26
OTH	322	1.14
LIB DEM MAJ.	3,889	13.78

MP John Thurso   (Lib Dem)

Central Ayrshire

Electorate 69,161   *Turnout* 61.45%

	Votes	*% Share*
LAB	21,300	51.12
CON	10,571	24.86
SNP	6,153	14.47
LIB DEM	2,773	6.52
SSP	1,391	3.28
OTH	327	0.77
LAB MAJ.	10,729	25.24

MP Brian Donohoe   (Lab)

Coatbridge, Chryston and Bellshill

Electorate 67,647   *Turnout* 58.27%

	Votes	*% Share*
LAB	25,938	62.76
SNP	5,835	14.97
LIB DEM	2,980	7.56
CON	2,715	6.88
SSP	1,913	4.85
OTH	61	0.15
LAB MAJ.	20,103	50.97

MP Tom Clarke (Lab)

Cumbernauld, Kilsyth and Kirkintilloch East

Electorate 67,802   *Turnout* 59.68%

	Votes	*% Share*
LAB	23,314	57.61
SNP	10,504	25.96
LIB DEM	2,446	6.04
CON	2,031	5.02
SSP	1,922	4.75
OTH	250	0.62
LAB MAJ.	12,810	31.66

MP Rosemary McKenna (Lab)

Dumfries and Galloway

Electorate 75,316   *Turnout* 64.93%

	Votes	*% Share*
LAB	15,851	32.31
CON	14,811	30.19
SNP	12,846	26.18
LIB DEM	4,677	9.53
SSP	879	1.79
LAB MAJ.	1,040	2.13

MP Russell Brown (Lab)

Dumfriesshire, Clydesdale and Tweeddale

Electorate	65,137	*Turnout* 69.80%

	Votes	*% Share*
LAB	16,741	37.02
CON	12,382	27.38
LIB DEM	9,068	20.05
SNP	6,194	13.70
SSP	733	1.63
OTH	98	0.22
LAB MAJ.	4,359	9.64

MP Jimmy Hood   (Lab)

Dundee East

Electorate	65,059	*Turnout* 60.78%

	Votes	*% Share*
LAB	14,608	37.25
SNP	13,968	35.62
CON	6,483	16.53
LIB DEM	3,345	8.53
SSP	813	2.07
LAB MAJ.	640	1.62

MP Iain Luke   (Lab)

Dundee West

Electorate	67,751	*Turnout* 54.92%

	Votes	*% Share*
LAB	18,461	49.19
SNP	10,683	28.46
CON	3,430	9.14
LIB DEM	3,423	9.20
SSP	1,534	4.09
LAB MAJ.	7,778	20.72

MP Ernie Ross   (Lab)

Dunfermline and West Fife

Electorate	70,373		Turnout	56.42%
		Votes		*% Share*
LAB		21,470		54.25
SNP		7,149		18.07
LIB DEM		5,608		14.17
CON		3,860		9.75
SSP		937		2.38
OTH		549		1.38
LAB MAJ.		14,321		36.19

MP Rachel Squire (Lab)

East Dunbartonshire

Electorate	66,724		Turnout	61.96%
		Votes		*% Share*
LAB		15,787		38.19
LIB DEM		10,385		25.12
CON		8,246		19.95
SNP		5,868		14.19
SSP		1,053		2.55
LAB MAJ.		5,402		13.07

MP John Lyons (Lab)

East Kilbride, Strathaven and Lesmahagow

Electorate	77,257		Turnout	61.92%
		Votes		*% Share*
LAB		25,256		52.88
SNP		11,314		23.69
LIB DEM		4,890		10.24
CON		4,636		9.71
SSP		1,669		3.49
LAB MAJ.		13,942		29.19

MP Adam Ingram (Lab)

East Lothian

Electorate	71,288		Turnout	63.38%
		Votes		% Share
LAB		22,190		48.99
LIB DEM		7,796		17.21
CON		7,137		15.75
SNP		6,961		15.37
SSP		842		1.86
OTH		376		0.83
LAB MAJ.		14,394		31.77

MP Anne Picking   (Lab)

East Renfrewshire

Electorate	69,249		Turnout	69.85%
		Votes		% Share
LAB		23,036		47.63
CON		13,895		28.73
LIB DEM		6,239		12.90
SNP		4,137		8.55
SSP		814		1.68
OTH		247		0.51
LAB MAJ.		9,141		18.90

MP Jim Murphy   (Lab)

Edinburgh East

Electorate	74,505		Turnout	51.78%
		Votes		% Share
LAB		18,966		49.33
LIB DEM		6,437		16.74
SNP		5,979		15.55
CON		4,724		12.29
SSP		1,751		4.55
OTH		591		1.53
LAB MAJ.		12,529		32.59

MP Gavin Strang   (Lab)

Edinburgh North and Leith

Electorate   74,762   Turnout   54.17%

	Votes	% Share
LAB	17,110	42.20
LIB DEM	8,388	20.69
CON	7,367	18.18
SNP	5,816	14.34
SSP	1,432	3.53
OTH	435	1.07
LAB MAJ.	8,722	21.51

MP Mark Lazarowicz   (Lab)

Edinburgh South

Electorate   68,884   Turnout   62.52%

	Votes	% Share
LAB	16,923	39.50
LIB DEM	10,690	24.95
CON	9,843	22.97
SNP	3,918	9.14
SSP	971	2.26
OTH	502	1.17
LAB MAJ.	6,233	14.55

MP Nigel Griffiths   (Lab)

Edinburgh South West

Electorate   75,787   Turnout   56.99%

	Votes	% Share
LAB	19,038	43.98
CON	11,352	26.22
SNP	5,910	13.65
LIB DEM	5,052	11.67
SSP	1,122	2.59
OTH	814	1.88
LAB MAJ.	7,686	17.76

MP Alistair Darling (Lab)

Edinburgh West

Electorate   70,604   Turnout   62.32%

	Votes	% Share
LIB DEM	17,032	38.63
LAB	11,668	26.46
CON	9,450	21.43
SNP	4,815	10.92
SSP	761	1.73
OTH	366	0.83
LIB DEM MAJ.	5,364	12.17

MP John Barrett   (Lib Dem)

Falkirk

Electorate   78,281   Turnout   58.46%

	Votes	% Share
LAB	24,148	52.70
SNP	10,699	23.35
CON	4,225	9.22
LIB DEM	3,473	7.58
OTH	2,305	5.03
SSP	975	2.13
LAB MAJ.	13,449	29.35

MP Eric Joyce   (Lab)

Glasgow Central

Electorate   70,378   Turnout   41.61%

	Votes	% Share
LAB	15,937	54.05
SNP	6,130	20.79
LIB DEM	2,918	9.90
CON	1,911	6.48
SSP	1,959	6.64
OTH	631	2.15
LAB MAJ.	9,807	33.26

MP David Marshall   (Lab)

Glasgow East

Electorate   70,167   *Turnout*   48.07%

	Votes	% Share
LAB	21,332	63.24
SNP	5,786	17.15
SSP	2,265	6.72
CON	2,129	6.31
LIB DEM	2,092	6.20
OTH	113	0.34
LAB MAJ.	15,546	46.11

MP Jimmy Wray   (Lab)

Glasgow North

Electorate   63,729   *Turnout*   44.00%

	Votes	% Share
LAB	13,752	49.15
LIB DEM	5,040	18.01
SNP	4,471	15.98
CON	2,247	8.03
SSP	2,006	7.17
OTH	461	1.64
LAB MAJ.	8,712	31.14

MP Ann McKechin   (Lab)

Glasgow North East

Electorate   70,899   *Turnout*   43.26%

	Votes	% Share
LAB	20,623	67.04
SNP	5,654	18.38
SSP	2,329	7.57
CON	1,638	5.32
LIB DEM	311	1.01
OTH	208	0.68
LAB MAJ.	14,969	48.66

MP Michael Martin   (The Speaker)

Glasgow North West

Electorate	67,087			Turnout	49.97%

	Votes	% Share
LAB	18,337	54.92
SNP	5,393	16.15
LIB DEM	3,865	11.57
CON	3,074	9.21
SSP	2,123	6.36
OTH	599	1.79
LAB MAJ.	12,944	38.76

MP John Robertson (Lab)

Glasgow South

Electorate	74,482			Turnout	50.46%

	Votes	% Share
LAB	19,277	51.30
SNP	6,364	16.93
CON	5,273	14.03
LIB DEM	4,347	11.64
SSP	2,234	5.94
OTH	58	0.15
LAB MAJ.	12,913	34.36

MP Tom Harris (Lab)

Glasgow South West

Electorate	66,335			Turnout	51.06%

	Votes	% Share
LAB	20,745	61.16
SNP	6,056	17.85
SSP	3,016	8.97
LIB DEM	2,156	6.36
CON	1,832	5.40
OTH	88	0.26
LAB MAJ.	14,689	43.30

MP Ian Davidson (Lab)

Glenrothes

Electorate 69,499   *Turnout* 55.41%

	Votes	*% Share*
LAB	22,800	59.02
SNP	9,063	23.46
LIB DEM	3,106	8.04
CON	2,623	6.79
SSP	999	2.59
OTH	43	0.11
LAB MAJ.	13,737	35.56

MP John MacDougall   (Lab)

Gordon

Electorate 69,631   *Turnout* 59.66%

	Votes	*% Share*
LIB DEM	15,822	38.78
LAB	8,878	21.68
CON	8,132	19.85
SNP	7,476	18.25
SSP	589	1.44
LIB DEM MAJ.	7,004	17.1

MP Malcolm Bruce   (Lib Dem)

Inverclyde

Electorate 65,485   *Turnout* 59.19%

	Votes	*% Share*
LAB	19,761	50.61
LIB DEM	8,131	20.82
SNP	5,452	13.96
CON	4,253	10.89
SSP	1,451	3.72
LAB MAJ.	11,630	29.78

MP David Cairns   (Lab)

Inverness, Nairn, Badenoch and Strathspey

Electorate   67,790   Turnout   62.86%

	Votes	% Share
LAB	14,422	33.69
LIB DEM	12,264	28.65
SNP	9,705	22.67
CON	5,227	12.21
SSP	784	1.83
OTH	401	0.94
LAB MAJ.	2,158	5.04

MP David Stewart   (Lab)

Kilmarnock and Loudoun

Electorate   72,922   Turnout   61.38%

	Votes	% Share
LAB	24,313	54.32
SNP	10,920	24.40
CON	4,547	10.16
LIB DEM	3,682	8.23
SSP	1,227	2.74
OTH	63	0.14
LAB MAJ.	13,393	29.93

MP Des Browne   (Lab)

Kirkcaldy and Cowdenbeath

Electorate   74,163   Turnout   55.77%

	Votes	% Share
LAB	23,838	57.69
SNP	7,754	18.76
CON	4,595	11.11
LIB DEM	3,796	9.19
SSP	1,175	2.84
OTH	165	0.40
LAB MAJ.	19,084	38.92

MP Gordon Brown   (Lab)

Lanark and Hamilton East

Electorate	76,173		Turnout	58.89%

	Votes			% Share
LAB	23,060			51.30
SNP	10,182			22.65
CON	5,699			12.63
LIB DEM	4,502			10.02
SSP	1,397			3.11
OTH	111			0.25
LAB MAJ.	12,878			28.65

MP Bill Tynan or John Reid (Lab)

Linlithgow and East Falkirk

Electorate	78,675		Turnout	55.90%

	Votes			% Share
LAB	23,126			52.85
SNP	11,334			25.9
CON	3,920			9.11
LIB DEM	3,984			8.96
SSP	1,044			2.31
OTH	382			0.87
LAB MAJ.	11,792			26.95

MP Michael Connarty (Lab)

Livingston

Electorate	76,299		Turnout	55.74%

	Votes			% Share
LAB	23,599			55.27
SNP	9,851			23.07
LIB DEM	4,335			10.15
CON	3,259			7.63
SSP	1,252			2.93
OTH	404			0.95
LAB MAJ.	13,748			32.20

MP Robin Cook (Lab)

Midlothian

Electorate	62,787		Turnout	61.43%
		Votes		% Share
LAB		18,664		48.23
LIB DEM		7,771		20.08
SNP		7,420		19.17
CON		3,586		9.27
SSP		977		2.52
OTH		280		0.72
LAB MAJ.		10,893		28.15

MP David Hamilton   (Lab)

Moray

Electorate	63,959		Turnout	57.12%
		Votes		% Share
SNP		10,979		30.10
LAB		8,898		24.40
CON		8,153		22.35
LIB DEM		6,468		17.73
OTH		1,093		3.00
SSP		883		2.42
SNP MAJ.		2,081		5.71

MP Angus Robertson   (SNP)

Motherwell and Wishaw

Electorate	67,499		Turnout	58.24%
		Votes		% Share
LAB		22,239		56.77
SNP		8,247		21.05
CON		3,703		9.45
LIB DEM		3,306		4.44
SSP		1,560		3.98
OTH		120		0.31
LAB MAJ.		13,992		35.72

MP Frank Roy   (Lab)

Na h-Eileanan An Iar (Western Isles)

Electorate	21,884		*Turnout*	60.13%
		Votes		*% Share*
LAB		5,924		45.02
SNP		4,850		36.86
CON		1,250		9.50
LIB DEM		849		6.45
SSP		286		2.17
LAB MAJ.		1,074		8.16

MP Calum MacDonald   (Lab)

North Ayrshire and Arran

Electorate	73,182		*Turnout*	59.99%
		Votes		*% Share*
LAB		21,395		48.73
SNP		9,332		21.26
CON		7,700		17.54
LIB DEM		3,745		8.53
SSP		1,215		2.77
OTH		514		1.17
LAB MAJ.		12,063		27.48

MP Brian Wilson   (Lab)

North East Fife

Electorate	64,813		*Turnout*	56.86%
		Votes		*% Share*
LIB DEM		18,153		49.21
CON		8,480		22.99
LAB		5,236		14.19
SNP		3,943		10.69
SSP		660		1.79
OTH		420		1.14
LIB DEM MAJ.		9,673		26.22

MP Sir Menzies Campbell   (Lib Dem)

Ochil and South Perthshire

	Electorate 71,738	Turnout 62.64%
	Votes	% Share
LAB	15,421	34.32
SNP	13,804	30.72
CON	9,541	21.23
LIB DEM	4,872	10.35
SSP	948	2.11
OTH	330	0.73
LAB MAJ.	1,617	3.60

MP vacant (Lab)

Orkney and Shetland

	Electorate 32,181	Turnout 52.00%
	Votes	% Share
LIB DEM	6,919	41.35
LAB	3,444	20.58
CON	3,121	18.65
SNP	2,473	14.78
SSP	776	4.64
LIB DEM MAJ.	3,475	20.77

MP Alistair Carmichael (Lib Dem)

Paisley and Renfrewshire North

	Electorate 68,642	Turnout 59.75%
	Votes	% Share
LAB	21,085	51.70
SNP	9,502	23.30
CON	5,533	13.57
LIB DEM	3,275	8.03
SSP	1,175	2.88
OTH	214	0.52
LAB MAJ.	11,583	28.40

MP Irene Adams (Lab)

Paisley and Renfrewshire South

Electorate   68,038   *Turnout*   58.54%

	Votes	% Share
LAB	22,691	57.05
SNP	8,096	20.36
LIB DEM	3,705	9.32
CON	3,441	8.64
SSP	1,319	3.32
OTH	521	1.31
LAB MAJ.	14,595	36.70

MP Douglas Alexander   (Lab)

Perth and North Perthshire

Electorate   70,718   *Turnout*   61.64%

	Votes	% Share
SNP	15,746	36.17
CON	11,840	27.20
LAB	9,720	22.33
LIB DEM	5,259	12.08
SSP	867	1.99
OTH	105	0.24
SNP MAJ.	3,906	8.97

MP Annabelle Ewing   (SNP)

Ross, Skye and Lochaber

Electorate   49,544   *Turnout*   63.20%

	Votes	%Share
LIB DEM	14,489	46.28
LAB	6,709	21.43
SNP	5,219	16.67
CON	3,282	10.48
OTH	896	2.86
SSP	713	2.28
LIB DEM MAJ.	7,780	24.85

MP Charles Kennedy   (Lib Dem)

Rutherglen and Hamilton West

Electorate	75,370	Turnout	54.22%

	Votes	% Share
LAB	24,246	59.46
SNP	6,039	14.81
LIB DEM	5,011	12.29
CON	3,455	8.47
SSP	1,924	4.72
OTH	103	0.25
LAB MAJ.	18,207	44.65

MP Tommy McAvoy   (Lab)

Stirling

Electorate	66,393	Turnout	64.63%

	Votes	% Share
LAB	18,462	43.07
CON	10,166	23.71
SNP	7,222	16.85
LIB DEM	5,005	11.68
SSP	1,171	2.73
OTH	843	1.96
LAB MAJ.	8,296	19.35

MP Anne McGuire   (Lab)

West Aberdeenshire and Kincardine

Electorate	62,214	Turnout	60.94%

	Votes	% Share
LIB DEM	16,507	43.54
CON	11,686	30.82
LAB	4,669	12.31
SNP	4,634	12.22
SSP	418	1.10
LIB DEM MAJ.	4,821	12.72

MP Robert Smith   (Lib Dem)

West Dunbartonshire

Electorate 71,710   *Turnout* 62.32%

	Votes	% Share
LAB	25,734	57.59
SNP	11,026	24.67
CON	3,545	7.93
LIB DEM	2,199	4.92
SSP	2,184	4.89
LAB MAJ.	14,708	32.91

MP John McFall (Lab)

Scottish Parliament Election Results 1999–2003

1 May 2003

Constituency Voting Figures

Electorate: 3,877,603   *Turnout*: 1,916,594 (49.43%)

Party	Votes	Votes%	FPTP MSPs
Labour	663,585	34.62	46
SNP	455,742	23.78	9
Conservative	318,279	16.61	3
Liberal Democrat	294,347	15.36	13
SSP	118,764	6.20	–
MP for Falkirk West	14,703	0.78	1
Stop Stobhill Hospital Closure	10,988	0.57	1
Independents	18,847	0.98	–
Local Health Campaigns	12,056	0.63	–
Scottish Senior Citizen's	1,597	0.08	–
Scottish People's Alliance	5,598	0.29	–
Others	2,088	0.11	–

Regional List Voting Figures

Electorate: 3,877,603   *Turnout*: 1,915,851 (49.41%)

Party	Votes	Votes%	List MSPs	Total MSPs
Labour	561,375	29.30	4	50
SNP	399,659	20.86	18	27
Conservative	296,929	15.50	15	18
Liberal Democrat	225,774	11.78	4	17
Scottish Green	132,138	6.90	7	7
SSP	128,026	6.68	6	6
Scottish Senior Citizen's	28,996	1.51	1	1
Margo MacDonald	27,143	1.42	1	1
Socialist Labour	21,657	1.13	–	–
Pensioner's Party	28,655	1.06	–	–
UK Independence Party	11,969	0.62	–	–
Scottish People's Alliance	7,718	0.40	–	–
Pro-Life Alliance	6,759	0.35	–	–

cont'd

Independent	6,620	0.25	-	-
Others	32,433	1.72	-	-
MP for Falkirk West	-	-	-	1
Stop Stobhill Hospital Closure	-	-	-	1

6 May 1999

Constituency Voting Figures

Electorate: 3,949,112   *Turnout*: 2,342,068 (58.16%)

Party	Votes	Votes%	FPTP MSPs
Labour	908,394	38.79	53
SNP	672,758	28.72	7
Conservative	364,225	15.55	-
Liberal Democrat	333,279	14.23	12
SSP	23,654	1.01	-
MP for Falkirk West	18,511	0.79	1
Socialist Labour	5,268	0.22	-
SWP	2,757	0.12	-
Independent	12,418	0.53	-
Others	804	0.03	-

Regional List Voting Figures

Electorate: 3,949,112   *Turnout*: 2,338,911 (58.07%)

Party	Votes	Votes%	List MSPs	Total MSPs
Labour	786,818	33.64	3	56
SNP	638,644	27.31	28	35
Conservative	359,109	15.35	18	18
Liberal Democrat	290,760	12.43	5	17
Scottish Green	84,024	3.59	1	1
Socialist Labour	55,232	2.36	-	-
SSP	46,635	1.99	1	1
MP for Falkirk West	27,700	1.18	-	1
Pro-Life	9,784	0.42	-	-
Independent	7,137	0.31	-	-
Others	33,068	1.41	-	-

UK Election Results in Scotland 1945–2001

5 July 1945

Electorate: 3,343,120   *Turnout*: 2,389,892 (71.49%)*

	Votes	%	MPs
Labour	1,144,310	47.88	37
Conservative	878,206	36.75	24
National Liberal	85,937	3.60	3
(*Total Conservative*	964,143	40.34	27)
Liberal	132,849	5.56	0
ILP	40,725	1.70	3
Communist	33,265	1.39	1
SNP	30,595	1.28	0
Common Wealth	4,231	0.18	0
Others	39,774	1.65	3

23 February 1950

Electorate: 3,370,190   *Turnout*: 2,726,684 (80.91%)

	Votes	%	MPs
Labour	1,259,410	46.19	37
Conservative	1,013,909	37.18	26
National Lib and Con	208,101	7.63	5
(*Total Conservative*	1,222,010	44.82	31)
Liberal	180,270	6.61	2
Communist	27,559	1.01	0
SNP	9,708	0.36	0
Others	27,727	1.02	1

25 October 1951

Electorate: 3,421,419   *Turnout*: 2,777,837 (81.19%)

	Votes	%	MPs
Labour	1,330,244	47.89	35
Conservative	1,108,321	39.90	29
National Lib and Con	240,977	8.67	6
(*Total Conservative*	1,349,298	48.57	35)
Liberal	76,291	2.75	1
Communist	10,947	0.39	0
SNP	7,299	0.26	0
Others	3,758	0.14	0

26 May 1955

Electorate: 3,387,536   *Turnout*: 2,543,254 (75.08%)

	Votes	%	MPs
Labour	1,188,058	46.71	34
Conservative	1,056,209	41.53	30
National Lib and Con	217,733	8.56	6
(*Total Conservative*	1,273,942	50.09	36)
Liberal	47,273	1.86	1
Communist	13,195	0.52	0
SNP	12,112	0.48	0
Others	8,674	0.34	0

8 October 1959

Electorate: 3,413,732   *Turnout*: 2,667,513 (78.14%)

	Votes	%	MPs
Labour	1,245,255	46.68	38
Conservative	1,060,609	39.76	25
National Lib and Con	199,678	7.49	6
(*Total Conservative*	1,260,287	47.25	31)
Liberal	108,963	4.08	1
SNP	21,738	0.81	0
Communist	12,150	0.46	0
Others	19,120	0.72	1

15 October 1964

Electorate: 3,393,421   *Turnout*: 2,634,539 (77.64%)

	Votes	%	MPs
Labour	1,283,667	48.72	43
Conservative	981,641	37.26	24
National Lib and Con	88,054	3.34	0
(*Total Conservative*	1,069,695	40.6	24)
Liberal	200,063	7.59	4
SNP	64,044	2.43	0
Communist	12,241	0.46	0
Others	4,829	0.18	0

31 March 1966

Electorate: 3,359,891   *Turnout*: 2,552,380 (75.97%)

	Votes	%	MPs
Labour	1,273,916	49.91	46
Conservative	960,675	37.64	20
Liberal	172,447	6.76	5
SNP	128,474	5.03	0
Communist	16,230	0.64	0
Others	638	0.02	0

18 June 1970

Electorate: 3,629,017   *Turnout*: 2,688,235 (74.08%)

	Votes	%	MPs
Labour	1,197,068	44.53	44
Conservative	1,020,674	37.97	23
Liberal	147,667	5.49	3
SNP	306,802	11.41	1
Communist	11,408	0.42	0
Others	4,616	0.17	0

28 February 1974

Electorate: 3,655,621   *Turnout*: 2,887,075 (78.98%)

	Votes	%	MPs
Labour	1,057,601	36.63	40
Conservative	950,668	32.93	21
Liberal	229,162	7.94	3
SNP	633,180	21.93	7
Communist	15,071	0.52	0
Others	1,393	0.05	0

10 October 1974

Electorate: 3,686,792   *Turnout*: 2,758,101 (74.81%)

	Votes	%	MPs
Labour	1,000,581	36.28	41
Conservative	681,327	24.70	16
Liberal	228,855	8.30	3
SNP	839,617	30.44	11
Communist	7,453	0.27	0
National Front	86	0.00	0
Others	182	0.01	0

3 May 1979

Electorate: 3,795,865   *Turnout*: 2,916,637 (76.84%)

	Votes	%	MPs
Labour	1,211,445	41.54	44
Conservative	916,155	31.41	22
Liberal	262,224	8.99	3
SNP	504,259	17.29	2
Communist	5,926	0.20	0
National Front	104	0.00	0
SLP	13,737	0.47	0
Others	2,787	0.10	0

9 June 1983

Electorate: 3,886,899   *Turnout*: 2,824,580 (72.67%)

	Votes	%	MPs
Labour	990,654	35.07	41
Conservative	801,487	28.38	21
Liberal-SDP Alliance	692,634	24.52	8
SNP	331,975	11.75	2
Communist	3,223	0.11	0
Others	4,607	0.16	0

11 June 1987

Electorate: 3,952,465   Turnout: 2,967,808 (75.09%)

	Votes	%	MPs
Labour	1,258,132	42.39	50
Conservative	713,081	24.03	10
Liberal-SDP Alliance	570,053	19.21	9
SNP	416,473	14.03	3
Communist	1,187	0.04	0
Others	8,882	0.30	0

9 April 1992

Electorate: 3,928,996   *Turnout*: 2,931,698 (74.62%)

	Votes	%	MPs
Labour	1,142,911	38.98	49
Conservative	751,950	25.65	11
Liberal Democrat	383,856	13.09	9
SNP	629,564	21.47	3
Others	23,417	0.80	0

1 May 1997

Electorate: 3,946,113   *Turnout*: 2,817,439 (71.40%)

	Votes	%	MPs
Labour	1,283,353	45.55	56
Conservative	493,059	17.50	0
Liberal Democrat	365,359	12.97	10
SNP	622,260	22.09	6
Others	53,408	1.90	0

7 June 2001

Electorate: 3,980,974   *Turnout*: 2,315,703 (58.17%)

	Votes	%	MPs
Labour	1,001,173	43.23	55
Conservative	360,658	15.57	1
Liberal Democrat	380,034	16.41	10
SNP	464,305	20.05	5
Scottish Socialist Party	72,279	3.12	0
The Speaker	16,053	0.69	1
Others	21,201	0.92	0

* Taking into account the two-member constituencies turnout in 1945 was 69.0 per cent.

The figures above are taken from F. W. S. Craig's *British Electoral Facts 1832-1987* for the elections from 1945-87, and from *The Times Guides to the House of Commons* cross-checked with House of Commons Research Papers for 1992-2001.

European Parliament Election Results 1979-1999

Share of Vote

	1979	1984	1989	1994	1999
Labour	33.0	40.7	41.9	42.5	28.7
SNP	19.4	17.8	25.6	32.6	27.2
Conservative	33.7	25.7	20.9	14.5	19.8
Liberal Democrat	14.0	15.6	4.3	7.2	9.8
Green	–	0.2	7.2	1.6	5.8
SSP	–	–	–	0.8	4.0
Other	–	–	–	1.7	4.9
Turnout	33.6	33.1	40.8	38.2	24.8

Number of Votes

	1979	1984	1989	1994	1999
Labour	421,968	526,056	666,263	635,955	283,490
SNP	247,926	230,590	406,686	487,237	268,528
Conservative	430,762	332,771	331,495	216,669	195,296
Liberal Democrat	178,433	201,822	68,086	107,811	96,971
Green	–	2,560	115,028	23,314	57,142
SSP	–	–	–	12,113	39,720
Other	–	–	–	12,798	31,163

Seats

	1979	1984	1989	1994	1999
Labour	2	5	7	6	3
SNP	1	1	1	2	2
Conservative	5	2	0	0	2
Liberal Democrat	0	0	0	0	1

1999: Those Elected from the Scotland-wide List in first election under single transferable vote system

Elspeth Attwooll	Liberal Democrat
Ian Hudghton	SNP
Neil MacCormick	SNP
David Martin	Labour
Bill Miller	Labour
John Purvis	Conservative
Struan Stevenson	Conservative
Catherine Stihler	Labour

Previous European Election Constituency Results 1979-94

(Elected by First-Past-The-Post in eight constituencies)

Glasgow

1994

Electorate: 463,364   *Turnout*: 159,666 (34.5%)

	Party	Votes	Votes%	Change%
B. Miller	Labour	83,953	52.6	-2.8
T. Chalmers	SNP	40,795	25.6	+0.6
T. Sheridan	Scot Militant Lab	12,113	7.6	-
R. Wilkinson	Conservative	10,888	6.8	-3.9
J. Money	Liberal Democrat	7,291	4.6	+2.6
P. O'Brien	Green	2,252	1.4	-4.9
J. Fleming	Socialist	1,125	0.7	-
M. Wilkinson	NLP	868	0.5	-
C. Marsden	ICP	381	0.2	-

1989

Electorate: 491,905   *Turnout*: 194, 638 (39.6%)

	Party	Votes	Votes%	Change%
J. Buchan	Labour	107,818	55.4	-3.8
A. Brophy	SNP	48,586	25.0	+14.3
A. Bates	Conservative	20,761	10.7	-5.8
D. Spaven	Green	12,229	6.3	-
J. Morrison	Liberal Democrat	3,887	2.0	-11.6
D. Chalmers	Communist	1,164	0.6	+0.6
J. Simons	Int Com	193	0.1	+0.1

1984

Electorate: 518,178   *Turnout*: 153,620 (29.6%)

	Party	Votes	Votes%	Change%
J. Buchan	Labour	91,015	59.2	+10.2
S. Chadd	Conservative	25,282	16.5	-10.8
C. Mason	Liberal–SDP	20,867	10.7	+6.3
N. MacLeod	SNP	16,456	13.6	-5.7

1979

Electorate: 534,414   *Turnout*: 151,139 (28.3%)

	Party	Votes	Votes%	Change%
J. Buchan	Labour	73,846	49.0	-9.2
B. Vaughan	Conservative	41,144	27.3	+1.4
G. Leslie	SNP	24,776	16.4	+4.9
E. Attwooll	Liberal	11,073	7.3	+3.3

Highlands and Islands

1994

Electorate: 328,104   *Turnout*: 128,272 (39.1%)

	Party	Votes	Votes%	Change%
W. Ewing	SNP	74,872	58.4	+6.8
M. Macmillan	Labour	19,956	15.6	+1.7
M. Tennant	Conservative	15,767	12.3	-4.5
H. Morrison	Liberal Democrat	12,919	10.1	+1.8
E. Scott	Green	3,140	2.5	- 7.0
M. Carr	Independent	1,096	0.9	-
M. Gimour	NLP	522	0.4	-

1989

Electorate: 317,129   *Turnout*: 128,590 (40.5%)

	Party	Votes	Votes%	Change%
W. Ewing	SNP	66,297	51.6	+9.7
A. McQuarrie	Conservative	21,602	16.8	+0.8
N. MacAskill	Labour	17,848	13.9	-0.2
M. Gregson	Green	12,199	9.5	-
N. Mitchison	Liberal Democrat	10, 644	8.3	-19.8

1984

Electorate: 307,265   *Turnout*: 118,034 (38.4%)

	Party	Votes	Votes%	Change%
W. Ewing	SNP	49,410	41.9	+7.9
R. Johnston	Liberal–SDP	33,133	28.1	-2.6
D. Webster	Conservative	18,847	16.0	-10.1
J. McArthur	Labour	16,644	14.1	-5.9

1979

Electorate: 298,802   *Turnout*: 118,214 (39.6%)

	Party	Votes	Votes%	Change%
W. Ewing	SNP	39,991	34.0	+4.7
R. Johnston	Liberal	36,601	30.7	+12.5
M. Joughlin	Conservative	30,776	26.1	-6.4
J. Watson	Labour	10,846	9.2	-10.8

Lothians

1994

Electorate: 522,363   *Turnout*: 200,413 (38.4%)

	Party	Votes	Votes%	Change%
D. Martin	Labour	90,531	44.9	+3.6
K. Brown	SNP	53,324	26.5	+6.1
P. McNally	Conservative	33,526	16.6	-7.0
H. Campbell	Liberal Democrat	17,883	8.9	+4.7
R. Harper	Green	5,149	2.6	-7.8

1989

Electorate: 527,785   *Turnout*: 219,994 (41.7%)

	Party	Votes	Votes%	Change%
D. Martin	Labour	90,840	41.3	+0.9
C. Blight	Conservative	52,014	23.6	-2.8
J. Smith	SNP	44,935	20.4	+8.4
R. Harper	Green	22,983	10.4	+9.0
K.Leadbetter	Liberal Democrat	9,222	4.2	-15.5

1984

Electorate: 526,068   *Turnout*: 185,581 (35.3%)

	Party	Votes	Votes%	Change%
D. W. Martin	Labour	74,989	40.4	+7.8
I. Henderson	Conservative	49,065	26.4	-9.2
J. D. Mabon	Liberal–SDP	36,636	19.7	+3.9
D. Stevenson	SNP	22,331	12.0	-4.0
L. Hendry	Ecology	2,560	1.4	–

1979

Electorate: 537,420   *Turnout*: 187,334 (34.9%)

	Party	Votes	Votes%	Change%
I. Dalziel	Conservative	66,761	35.6	+2.7
A. Mackie	Labour	61,180	32.6	-10.7
D. Stevenson	SNP	29,935	16.0	+2.2
R. Smith	Liberal	29,518	15.8	+6.2

North East Scotland

Euro by-election: 26 November 1998

Electorate: 584,061   *Turnout*: 119,605 (20.5%)

	Party	Votes	Votes%	Change%
I. Hudghton	SNP	57,445	48.0	+5.2
S. Stevenson	Conservative	23,744	19.9	+1.3
K. Walker-Shaw	Labour	22,086	18.5	-9.9
K. Raffan	Liberal Democrat	11,753	9.8	+1.5
H. Duke	SSA	2,510	2.1	–
R. Harper	Green	2,067	1.7	+0.5

1994

Electorate: 573,799   *Turnout*: 217,148 (37.8%)

	Party	Votes	Votes%	Change%
A. Macartney	SNP	92,890	42.8	+13.4
H. McCubbin	Labour	61,665	28.4	-2.3
R. Harris	Conservative	40,372	18.6	-8.1
S. Horner	Liberal Democrat	18,008	8.3	+2.3
K. Farnsworth	Green	2,569	1.2	-6.1
M. Ward	CPGB	689	0.3	–
L. Mair	NEEPS	584	0.3	–
D. Paterson	NLP	371	0.2	–

1989

Electorate: 559,275   *Turnout*: 213,206 (38.1%)

	Party	Votes	Votes%	Change%
H. McCubbin	Labour	65,348	30.7	+2.3
A. Macartney	SNP	62,735	29.4	+8.1
J. Provan	Conservative	56,835	26.7	-7.5
M. Hill	Green	15,584	7.3	-
S. Horner	Liberal Democrat	12,704	6.0	-10.2

1984

Electorate: 548,711   *Turnout*: 157,381 (28.7%)

	Party	Votes	Votes%	Change%
J. Provan	Conservative	53,809	34.2	+1.2
F. Doran	Labour	44,638	28.4	+4.2
D. Hood	SNP	33,444	21.3	+3.0
I. Philip	Liberal–SDP	25,490	16.2	-8.3

1979

Electorate: 481,680   *Turnout*: 157,471 (32.7%)

	Party	Votes	Votes%	Change%
J. Provan	Conservative	51,930	33.0	-1.7
Lord Mackie	Liberal	38,516	24.5	+15.3
D. Clyne	Labour	38,139	24.2	-6.9
C. Bell	SNP	28,886	18.3	-6.6

Mid-Scotland and Fife

1994

Electorate: 546,060   *Turnout*: 208,620 (38.2%)

	Party	Votes	Votes%	Change%
A. Falconer	Labour	95,667	45.8	- 0.3
D. Douglas	SNP	64,254	30.8	+8.2
P. Page	Conservative	28,192	13.5	-7.5
H. Lyall	Liberal Democrat	17,192	8.2	+4.2
M. Johnston	Green	3,015	1.4	-5.0

1989

Electorate: 539,276   *Turnout*: 221,862 (41.1%)

	Party	Votes	Votes%	Change%
A. Falconer	Labour	102,246	46.1	+3.4
K. MacAskill	SNP	50,089	22.6	+6.3
A. Christie	Conservative	46,505	21.0	-7.2
G. Morton	Green	14,165	6.4	–
M. Black	Liberal Democrat	8,857	4.0	-8.9

1984

Electorate: 528,529   *Turnout*: 187,641 (35.5%)

	Party	Votes	Votes%	Change%
A. Falconer	Labour	80,038	42.7	+11.5
J. Purvis	Conservative	52,872	28.2	-6.9
J. Jones	SNP	30,511	16.3	-7.8
A. Wedderburn	Liberal–SDP	24,220	12.9	+3.3

1979

Electorate: 538,483   *Turnout*: 188,561 (35.0%)

	Party	Votes	Votes%	Change%
J. Purvis	Conservative	66,255	35.1	+4.8
M. Panko	Labour	58,768	31.2	-8.5
R. McIntyre	SNP	45,426	24.1	+1.1
J. Calder	Liberal	18,112	9.6	+2.9

Scotland South

1994

Electorate: 500,643   *Turnout*: 200,957 (40.1%)

	Party	Votes	Votes%	Change%
A. Smith	Labour	90,750	45.2	+5.4
A. Hutton	Conservative	45,595	22.7	-9.5
C. Creech	SNP	45,032	22.4	+5.2
D. Millar	Liberal Democrat	13,363	6.7	+1.6
J. Hein	Liberal	3,249	1.6	–
L. Hendry	Green	2,429	1.2	-4.5
G. Gay	NLP	539	0.3	–

1989

Electorate: 497,108   *Turnout*: 204,220 (41.1%)

	Party	Votes	Votes%	Change%
A. Smith	Labour	81,366	39.8	+4.7
A. Hutton	Conservative	65,673	32.2	-4.8
M. Brown	SNP	35,155	17.2	+3.7
J. Button	Green	11,658	5.7	–
J. McKerchar	Liberal Democrat	10,368	5.1	-9.3

1984

Electorate: 484,760   *Turnout*: 164,389 (33.9%)

	Party	Votes	Votes%	Change%
A. Hutton	Conservative	60,843	37.0	-6.0
R. Stewart	Labour	57,706	35.1	+7.4
E. Buchanan	Liberal–SDP	23,598	14.4	+3.6
I. Goldie	SNP	22,242	13.5	-5.0

1979

Electorate: 450,761   *Turnout*: 155,480 (34.5%)

	Party	Votes	Votes%	Change%
A. Hutton	Conservative	66,816	43.0	+6.8
P. Foy	Labour	43,145	27.7	-8.5
I. MacGibbon	SNP	28,694	18.5	+5.7
J. Wallace	Liberal	16,825	10.8	-3.9

Strathclyde East

1994

Electorate: 492,618   *Turnout*: 183,571 (37.3%)

	Party	Votes	Votes%	Change%
K. Collins	Labour	106,476	58.0	+1.8
I. Hamilton	SNP	54,136	29.5	+4.4
B. Cooklin	Conservative	13,915	7.6	-3.8
B. Stewart	Liberal Democrat	6,383	3.5	+1.3
A. Whitelaw	Green	1,874	1.0	-4.0
D. Gilmour	NLP	787	0.4	–

1989

Electorate: 499,616   *Turnout*: 194,281 (38.9%)

	Party	Votes	Votes%	Change%
K. Collins	Labour	109,170	56.2	-2.4
G. Leslie	SNP	48,853	25.1	+7.5
M. Dutt	Conservative	22,233	11.4	-4.7
A. Whitelaw	Green	9,749	5.0	-
G. Lait	Liberal Democrat	4,276	2.2	-5.5

1984

Electorate: 498,458   *Turnout*: 154,832 (31.1%)

	Party	Votes	Votes%	Change%
K. Collins	Labour	90,792	58.6	+8.8
G. Leslie	SNP	27,330	17.6	+3.1
R. Leckie	Conservative	24,857	16.1	-12.5
P de Seume	Liberal–SDP	11,883	7.7	+0.6

1979

Electorate: 463,656   *Turnout*: 145,083 (31.3%)

	Party	Votes	Votes%	Change%
K. Collins	Labour	72,263	49.8	-5.3
M. Carse	Conservative	41,482	28.6	+1.0
G. Murray	SNP	21,013	14.5	+1.0
D. Watt	Liberal	10,325	7.1	+3.7

Strathclyde West

1994

Electorate: 489,129   *Turnout*: 195,881 (40.0%)

	Party	Votes	Votes%	Change%
H. McMahon	Labour	86,957	44.4	+1.7
C. Campbell	SNP	61,934	31.6	+7.8
J. Godfrey	Conservative	28,414	14.5	-7.3
D. Herbison	Lib Dem	14,772	7.5	+3.7
K. Allan	Green	2,886	1.5	-6.3
S. Gilmour	NLP	918	0.5	-

1989

Electorate: 500,935   *Turnout*: 210,094 (41.9%)

	Party	Votes	Votes%	Change%
H. McMahon	Labour	89,627	42.7	+1.9
C. Campbell	SNP	50,036	23.8	+6.2
S. Robin	Conservative	45,872	21.8	-5.6
G. Campbell	Green	16,461	7.8	-
D. Herbison	Liberal Democrat	8,098	3.8	-11.3

1984

Electorate: 499,162   *Turnout*: 172,291 (34.5%)

	Party	Votes	Votes%	Change%
H. McMahon	Labour	70,234	40.8	+4.7
J. Lair	Conservative	47,196	27.4	-9.8
J. Herriot	SNP	28,866	16.8	+0.3
D. Herbison	Liberal–SDP	25,995	15.1	+4.9

1979

Electorate: 495,799   *Turnout*: 176,459 (35.6%)

	Party	Votes	Votes%	Change%
A. Fergusson	Conservative	65,608	37.2	+5.3
V. Friel	Labour	63,781	36.1	-7.3
M. Slesser	SNP	29,115	16.5	+ 2.4
T. Fraser	Liberal	17,955	10.2	+ 0.1

Scottish Parliamentary By-Elections Since 1945

The following results are contrasted with the votes at the previous and subsequent general elections

1945

Scottish Universities

	Lab%	Con%	SNP%	Lib%	Others%	Turnout%
1935	–	30.4	14.2	27.8	–	51.2
		27.6		(Nat Lib)		
9-13.4.45	–	71.2	–	28.8	–	44.6
		(Ind)		(Nat Lib)		
1945	8.7	48.8	–	5.7	–	51.6
		(Nat)				
		32.6				
		(Ind)				
		4.2				

Three members elected under STV. By-election for one vacancy. Seat abolished before 1950.

Motherwell

	Lab%	Con%	SNP%	Lib%	Others%	Turnout%
1935	50.7	49.3	–	–	–	75.9
12.4.45	48.6	–	51.4	–	–	54.0
1945	52.7	20.6	26.7	–	–	72.8

Robert McIntyre becomes the first SNP MP due to no Conservative standing because of the wartime coalition truce; Labour win seat back at general election three months later.

1945-50

Edinburgh East

	Lab%	Con%	SNP%	Lib%	Others%	Turnout%
1945	56.4	37.3	6.3	–	–	69.4
3.10.45	61.6	38.4	–	–	–	51.0

See 27.1.47

South Ayrshire

	Lab%	Con%	SNP%	Lib%	Others%	Turnout%
1945	61.3	38.7	–	–	–	75.0
7.2.46	63.6	36.4	–	–	–	69.0
1950	60.2	39.8	–	–	–	85.4

Glasgow Cathcart

	Lab%	Con%	SNP%	Lib%	Others%	Turnout%
1945	41.2	58.8	–	–	–	67.6
12.2.46	37.1	52.5	10.4	–	–	55.6
1950	27.3	64.8	–	7.9	–	83.8

Glasgow Bridgeton

	Lab%	Con%	SNP%	Lib%	Others%	Turnout%
1945	–	33.6	–	–	66.4 ILP	58.2
29.8.46	28.0	21.6	13.9	–	34.3 ILP	53.3
					2.2 Ind	
1950	59.4	32.3	–	–	8.3	76.9

Wendy Wood stands as Independent Scottish Nationalist.

Scottish Universities

	Lab%	Con%	SNP%	Lib%	Others%	Turnout%
1945	8.7	48.8	–	5.7	–	51.6
		(Nat)				
		32.6				
		(Ind)				
		4.2				
22-27.11.46	11.5	68.2	–	8.0	12.3	50.7

Seat abolished prior to 1950 election.

Aberdeen South

	Lab%	Con%	SNP%	Lib%	Others%	Turnout%
1945	42.3	46.8	–	10.9	–	71.9
26.11.46	45.2	54.8	–	–	–	65.6
1950	35.5	53.7	–	10.8	–	84.9

Kilmarnock

	Lab%	Con%	SNP%	Lib%	Others%	Turnout%
1945	59.4	40.6	-	-	-	76.1
5.12.46	59.7	32.5	7.8	-	-	68.4
1950	56.6	35.8	-	5.4	2.2	86.2

Willie Ross enters the House of Commons.

Edinburgh East

	Lab%	Con%	SNP%	Lib%	Others%	Turnout%
1945	56.4	37.3	6.3	-	-	69.4
27.1.47	50.6	34.3	5.0	10.1	-	63.0
1950	53.2	38.8	-	8.0	-	83.2

Glasgow Camlachie

	Lab%	Con%	SNP%	Lib%	Others%	Turnout%
1945	-	42.3	-	-	57.7 ILP	65.0
28.1.48	42.1	43.7	-	1.2	6.4 ILP	56.8
					6.6 Others	
1950	51.5	48.5	-	-	-	80.7

Conservatives C. S. MacFarlane narrowly wins Camlachie, a Glasgow East End seat, from ILP due to both Labour and ILP standing; Labour win back at the following election.

Paisley

	Lab%	Con%	SNP%	Lib%	Others%	Turnout%
1945	55.6	32.7	-	10.0	1.7	73.9
18.2.48	56.8	-	-	43.2	-	76.0
1950	56.1	36.5	-	7.4	-	84.0

John MacCormick stands with the support of the Conservatives and Liberals on a pro-Home Rule ticket.

Glasgow Gorbals

	Lab%	Con%	SNP%	Lib%	Others%	Turnout%
1945	80.0	20.0	-	-	-	56.8
30.9.48	54.5	28.6	-	-	16.9 Com	50.0
1950	58.0	31.4	-	-	5.8 Com	77.3
					4.7 Others	

Best post-war performance by the Communists in a UK by-election.

Stirling and Falkirk

	Lab%	Con%	SNP%	Lib%	Others%	Turnout%
1945	56.1	43.9	–	–	–	71.5
7.10.48	49.0	42.8	8.2	–	–	72.9
1950	49.0	45.5	3.7	–	1.8	84.4

Glasgow Hillhead

	Lab%	Con%	SNP%	Lib%	Others%	Turnout%
1945	33.6	58.5	–	7.9	–	65.8
25.11.48	31.6	68.4	–	–	–	56.7
1950	33.8	60.8	–	5.4	–	82.2

1950-51

Dunbartonshire West

	Lab%	Con%	SNP%	Lib%	Others%	Turnout%
1950	49.3	47.8	–	–	2.9	85.5
25.4.50	50.4	49.6	–	–	–	83.4
1951	51.3	45.4	–	3.3	–	86.6

Glasgow Scotstoun

	Lab%	Con%	SNP%	Lib%	Others%	Turnout%
1950	46.0	46.5	–	4.9	2.6	84.6
25.10.50	47.3	50.8	–	–	1.9	73.7
1951	49.3	50.7	–	–	–	85.1

1951-55

Dundee East

	Lab%	Con%	SNP%	Lib%	Others%	Turnout%
1951	53.8	46.2	–	–	–	87.2
7.7.52	56.3	35.6	7.4	–	0.7	71.5
1955	54.3	45.7	–	–	–	82.3

Edinburgh East

	Lab%	Con%	SNP%	Lib%	Others%	Turnout%
1951	54.1	45.9	-	-	-	83.8
8.4.54	57.6	42.4	-	-	-	61.8
1955	52.5	47.5	-	-	-	75.4

Motherwell

	Lab%	Con%	SNP%	Lib%	Others%	Turnout%
1951	57.3	42.7	-	-	-	84.7
14.4.54	56.4	39.3	-	-	4.3 Com	70
1955	53.9	46.1	-	-	-	76.5

Inverness

	Lab%	Con%	SNP%	Lib%	Others%	Turnout%
1951	35.5	64.5	-	-	-	69.3
21.12.54	22.6	41.4	-	36.0	-	49.2
1955	19.9	41.4	-	38.7	-	67.6

Neil McLean narrowly holds the seat for the Conservatives in both the by-election and general election against a Liberal surge.

Edinburgh North

	Lab%	Con%	SNP%	Lib%	Others%	Turnout%
1951	41.2	58.8	-	-	-	80.0
27.1.55	40.6	59.4	-	-	-	46.4
1955	38.3	61.7	-	-	-	72.0

1955-59

Greenock

	Lab%	Con%	SNP%	Lib%	Others%	Turnout%
1955	51.4	48.6	-	-	-	77.9
8.12.55	53.7	46.3	-	-	-	75.3
1959	50.6	22.6	-	26.8	-	78.9

Edinburgh South

	Lab%	Con%	SNP%	Lib%	Others%	Turnout%
1955	32.5	67.5	-	-	-	77.2
29.5.57	30.9	45.6	-	23.5	-	65.8
1959	28.5	57.6	-	13.9	-	81.2

Glasgow Kelvingrove

	Lab%	Con%	SNP%	Lib%	Others%	Turnout%
1955	44.6	55.4	-	-	-	67.6
13.3.58	48.0	41.6	-	7.6	2.8 ILP	60.5
1959	46.2	50.8	-	-	3.0 ILP	70.9

Labour gain from Conservatives; Conservatives win back at the general election.

Argyll

	Lab%	Con%	SNP%	Lib%	Others%	Turnout%
1955	32.4	67.6	-	-	-	66.6
12.6.58	25.7	46.8	-	27.5	-	67.1
1959	25.9	58.4	-	15.7	-	71.0

Michael Noble holds Argyll for the Conservatives despite post-Torrington Liberal surge.

Aberdeenshire East

	Lab%	Con%	SNP%	Lib%	Others%	Turnout%
1955	31.5	68.5	-	-	-	59.8
20.11.58	27.1	48.6	-	24.3	-	65.9
1959	36.6	63.4	-	-	-	67.1

Galloway

	Lab%	Con%	SNP%	Lib%	Others%	Turnout%
1955	33.1	66.9	-	-	-	69.1
9.4.59	23.9	50.4	-	25.7	-	72.7
1959	20.4	56.2	-	23.4	-	75.6

1959-64

Edinburgh North

	Lab%	Con%	SNP%	Lib%	Others%	Turnout%
1959	36.0	64.0	–	–	–	73.9
19.5.60	30.3	54.2	–	15.5	–	53.8
1964	41.8	58.2	–	–	–	73.6

Paisley

	Lab%	Con%	SNP%	Lib%	Others%	Turnout%
1959	57.3	42.7	–	–	–	78.9
20.4.61	45.4	13.2	–	41.4	–	68.1
1964	52.9	13.2	–	33.9	–	79.8

Fife East

	Lab%	Con%	SNP%	Lib%	Others%	Turnout%
1959	30.1	69.9	–	–	–	75.2
8.11.61	26.4	47.5	–	26.1	–	67.3
1964	25.2	54.2	6.8	13.1	0.7	77.8

John Gilmour returned for the Conservatives. The Labour candidate was a young John Smith, supported by Donald Dewar and others from Glasgow University Labour Club.

Glasgow Bridgeton

	Lab%	Con%	SNP%	Lib%	Others%	Turnout%
1959	63.4	36.6	–	–	–	68.5
10.11.61	57.5	20.7	18.7	–	3.1 ILP	41.9
1964	71.6	28.4	–	–	–	63.6

Best result for the SNP so far in post-war times as their young, energetic candidate Ian McDonald wins plaudits and votes.

West Lothian

	Lab%	Con%	SNP%	Lib%	Others%	Turnout%
1959	60.3	39.7	–	–	–	77.9
14.6.62	50.9	11.4	23.3	10.8	3.6 Com	71.1
1964	50.3	18.0	30.5	–	1.2 Com	79.5

SNP advance continues under William Wolfe; Tam Dalyell returned to the House of Commons; this is the first of seven Dalyell-Wolfe contests in a seat the SNP never manage to win; Conservatives lose their deposit for the first time in post-war politics.

Glasgow Woodside

	Lab%	Con%	SNP%	Lib%	Others%	Turnout%
1959	43.1	49.2	–	7.7	–	75.2
22.11.62	36.1	30.1	11.1	21.7	1.0	54.7
1964	45.6	40.4	5.4	8.3	0.3	74.0

Neil Carmichael gains Woodside for Labour from the Conservatives due to increased Liberal vote.

Kinross and West Perthshire

	Lab%	Con%	SNP%	Lib%	Others%	Turnout%
1959	16.8	68.2	15.0	–	–	71.0
7.11.63	15.2	57.3	7.3	19.5	0.6	76.1
1964	18.8	66.6	14.1	–	0.5 Com	75.0

Election of Alec Douglas-Home as Prime Minister to the House of Commons, after George Younger had stood aside for him.

Dundee West

	Lab%	Con%	SNP%	Lib%	Others%	Turnout%
1959	49.6	48.3	–	–	2.1 Com	82.9
21.11.63	50.6	39.4	7.4	–	2.6 Com	71.6
1964	53.4	44.2	–	–	2.4 Com	81.5

Dumfriesshire

	Lab%	Con%	SNP%	Lib%	Others%	Turnout%
1959	41.6	58.4	–	–	–	77.4
12.12.63	38.5	40.9	9.7	10.9	–	71.6
1964	39.1	48.7	12.2	–	–	81.6

Rutherglen

	Lab%	Con%	SNP%	Lib%	Others%	Turnout%
1959	47.9	52.1	–	–	–	85.8
14.5.64	55.5	44.5	–	–	–	82.0
1964	52.6	42.8	4.6	–	–	86.0

1964–66

Roxburgh, Selkirk and Peebles

	Lab%	Con%	SNP%	Lib%	Others%	Turnout%
1964	15.8	42.8	2.5	38.9	–	82.2
24.3.65	11.3	38.6	–	49.2	0.9	82.2
1966	13.6	40.8	–	45.6	–	84.9

Election of David Steel to the House of Commons. The loss of a Conservative seat while in opposition causes the resignation of Alec Douglas-Home as party leader.

1966–70

Glasgow Pollok

	Lab%	Con%	SNP%	Lib%	Others%	Turnout%
1966	52.4	47.6	–	–	–	79.0
9.3.67	31.2	36.9	28.2	1.9	1.8 Com	75.7
1970	46.3	44.8	8.9	–	–	72.6

SNP surge allows the Conservatives to take the seat from Labour. Last Conservative by-election gain in Scotland for 33 years.

Hamilton

	Lab%	Con%	SNP%	Lib%	Others%	Turnout%
1966	71.2	28.8	–	–	–	73.3
2.11.67	41.5	12.5	46.0	–	–	73.7
1970	52.9	11.4	35.1	–	0.6	80.0

Winnie Ewing sensationally wins Hamilton, previously one of Labour's safest Scottish seats. Labour's Alex Wilson wins it back in 1970, but Scottish politics are never the same again.

Glasgow Gorbals

	Lab%	Con%	SNP%	Lib%	Others%	Turnout%
1966	73.1	22.8	–	–	4.1 Com	61.7
30.10.69	53.4	18.6	25.0	–	2.5 Com	58.5
					0.5 Others	
1970	69.3	20.8	7.4	–	2.5 Com	59.8

South Ayrshire

	Lab%	Con%	SNP%	Lib%	Others%	Turnout%
1966	67.2	32.8	–	–	–	75.1
19.3.70	54.0	25.6	20.4	–	–	76.3
1970	61.8	30.2	8.0	–	–	76.9

Jim Sillars enters the House of Commons for the first time standing on an anti-Nationalist Labour platform.

1970-74

Stirling and Falkirk

	Lab%	Con%	SNP%	Lib%	Others%	Turnout%
1970	50.7	34.8	14.5	–	–	73.1
16.9.71	46.5	18.9	34.6	–	–	60.0
1974 (Feb.)	41.9	23.6	34.5	–	–	81.2

Robert McIntyre standing as SNP candidate drastically reduces Labour's majority and indicates that even pre-'It's Scotland's Oil', the SNP is on the move again.

Dundee East

	Lab%	Con%	SNP%	Lib%	Others%	Turnout%
1970	48.3	42.4	8.9	–	0.4	76.1
1.3.73	32.7	25.2	30.2	8.3	3.6	70.0
1974 (Feb.)	33.7	26.4	39.5	–	0.4	81.1

Gordon Wilson standing for the SNP just misses winning Dundee East which he goes on to win in the subsequent February 1974 general election and hold until 1987.

Edinburgh North

	Lab%	Con%	SNP%	Lib%	Others%	Turnout%
1970	37.1	52.8	–	10.1	–	70.1
8.11.73	24.0	38.7	18.9	18.4	–	54.4
1974 (Feb.)	26.2	45.8	12.7	15.3	–	76.4

Glasgow Govan

	Lab%	Con%	SNP%	Lib%	Others%	Turnout%
1970	60.0	28.2	10.3	–	1.5 Com	63.3
8.11.73	38.2	11.7	41.9	8.2	–	51.7
1974 (Feb.)	43.2	12.7	40.9	3.2	–	74.9

Margo MacDonald wins Glasgow Govan briefly for the SNP, narrowly failing to hold the seat after boundary changes in the February 1974 election.

February–October 1974

No by-elections.

1974–79

Glasgow Garscadden

	Lab%	Con%	SNP%	Lib%	Others%	Turnout%
1974 Oct	50.9	12.9	31.2	5.0	–	70.8
13.4.78	45.4	18.5	32.9	–	3.2	69.1
1979	61.5	21.8	15.7	–	1.0	73.2

Donald Dewar holds Glasgow Garscadden against the SNP's Keith Bovey who comes under widespread criticism for his pro-abortion, pro-CND views, particularly from the Conservative candidate, Iain Lawson, who later defected to the SNP.

Hamilton

	Lab%	Con%	SNP%	Lib%	Others%	Turnout%
1974 Oct	47.5	9.5	39.0	4.0	–	77.2
31.5.78	51.0	13.0	33.4	2.6	–	72.1
1979	59.6	23.8	16.6	–	–	79.6

George Robertson holds Hamilton against the SNP's Margo MacDonald and puts the SNP 1970s bandwagon into reverse.

Berwick and East Lothian

	Lab%	Con%	SNP%	Lib%	Others%	Turnout%
1974 Oct	43.3	37.6	13.2	5.9	–	83.0
26.10.78	47.4	40.2	8.8	3.6	–	71.2
1979	43.5	40.2	6.5	9.8	–	82.9

1979–83

Glasgow Central

	Lab%	Con%	SNP%	Lib%	Others%	Turnout%
1979	72.5	16.4	11.1	–	–	59.5
9.4.80	60.4	8.8	26.3	–	4.1	42.8
1983	53.0	19.0	10.3	16.7	1.1	62.9

Glasgow Hillhead

	Lab%	Con%	SNP%	Lib%	Others%	Turnout%
1979	34.4	41.1	10.1	14.4	–	75.7
25.3.82	25.9	26.6	11.3	33.4	2.8	76.4
1983	33.3	23.6	5.4	36.2	2.1	71.9

Roy Jenkins returned to the House of Commons for the SDP; Conservatives lose their last parliamentary seat in Glasgow.

Coatbridge and Airdrie

	Lab%	Con%	SNP%	Lib%	Others%	Turnout%
1979	60.9	27.5	11.6	–	–	75.3
24.6.82	55.1	26.2	10.5	8.2	–	56.3

Seat abolished at 1983 general election due to boundary changes.

Glasgow Queen's Park

	Lab%	Con%	SNP%	Lib%	Others%	Turnout%
1979	64.4	24.0	9.4	–	–	68.4
2.12.82	56.0	12.0	20.0	9.4	–	47.0

Seat abolished at 1983 general election due to boundary changes.

1983–87

No by-elections

1987-92

Glasgow Govan

	Lab%	Con%	SNP%	Lib%	Others%	Turnout%
1987	64.8	11.9	10.4	12.3	0.6	73.4
10.11.88	37.0	7.3	48.8	4.1	2.8	60.4
1992	48.9	9.9	37.1	3.5	0.5	76.0

Jim Sillars' return to the House of Commons as he wins the previously safe Labour seat of Glasgow Govan; Labour's Ian Davidson wins back the seat in the 1992 general election.

Glasgow Central

	Lab%	Con%	SNP%	Lib%	Others%	Turnout%
1987	64.5	13.0	9.9	10.5	2.0	65.6
15.6.89	54.6	7.6	30.2	1.5	6.0	52.8
1992	57.2	13.9	20.8	6.3	1.8	63.1

Mike Watson wins Glasgow Central against the SNP's Alex Neil, stopping the SNP post-Govan surge.

Paisley North

	Lab%	Con%	SNP%	Lib%	Others%	Turnout%
1987	55.5	15.8	12.9	15.8	-	73.4
29.11.90	44.0	14.8	29.4	8.3	3.6	53.7
1992	50.7	16.4	23.3	8.2	1.4	73.4

Paisley South

	Lab%	Con%	SNP%	Lib%	Others%	Turnout%
1987	56.2	14.7	14.0	15.1	-	75.3
29.11.90	46.1	13.4	27.5	9.8	3.1	55.5
1992	50.7	15.9	24.1	9.1	0.3	75.0

Kincardine and Deeside

	Lab%	Con%	SNP%	Lib%	Others%	Turnout%
1987	15.9	40.6	6.4	36.3	0.6	75.3
7.11.91	7.7	30.6	11.1	49.0	1.6	67.0
1992	9.1	43.7	11.3	35.1	0.7	78.8

Alick Buchanan-Smith's death results in Conservative loss to Lib Dems, Nicol Stephen; Conservatives' George Kynoch wins back at the 1992 election.

1992-97

Monklands East

	Lab%	Con%	SNP%	Lib%	Others%	Turnout%
1992	61.3	16.0	18.0	4.6	0.1	75.0
30.6.94	49.8	2.3	44.9	2.6	0.4	70.0
1997	61.8	8.9	24.4	4.2	0.7	71.4

By-election caused by death of John Smith sees Labour's Helen Liddell hold on narrowly against the SNP's Kay Ullrich.

Perth and Kinross

	Lab%	Con%	SNP%	Lib%	Others%	Turnout%
1992	12.5	40.2	36.0	11.4	–	76.9
25.5.95	22.9	21.4	40.4	11.8	3.5	62.1
1997	24.8	29.3	36.4	8.0	1.5	73.9

Roseanna Cunningham wins Perth and Kinross from the Conservatives; she subsequently holds it at the general election: the first time the SNP had held onto a by-election gain.

1997-2001

Paisley South

	Lab%	Con%	SNP%	Lib%	Others%	Turnout%
1997	57.5	8.7	23.4	9.4	1.1	69.5
6.11.97	44.2	7.0	32.5	11.0	5.3	43.4
2001	58.4	7.5	19.4	10.4	2.7 SSP	57.2
					1.5 Others	

Hamilton South

	Lab%	Con%	SNP%	Lib%	Others%	Turnout%
1997	65.6	8.6	17.6	5.1	3.0	71.1
23.9.99	36.9	7.2	34.0	3.3	9.5 SSP	41.6
					9.1 Others	
2001	59.7	7.0	19.4	8.9	4.4 SSP	57.3
					0.6 Others	

Labour's Bill Tynan narrowly holds Hamilton South against the SNP's Annabelle Ewing.

Glasgow Anniesland

	Lab%	Con %	SNP%	Lib%	Others%	Turnout%
1997	61.8	11.5	17.1	7.2	2.4	64.0
23.11.00	52.1	10.8	20.8	8.1	7.1 SSP	38.4
					1.1 Others	
2001	56.5	9.9	15.2	12.1	5.6 SSP	50.1
					0.7 Others	

Falkirk West

	Lab%	Con%	SNP%	Lib%	Others%	Turnout%
1997	59.4	12.1	23.4	5.1	-	72.6
21.12.00	43.5	8.3	39.9	3.2	5.1 SSP	36.2
2001	51.9	7.5	24.2	7.1	4.7 Ind	57.6
					2.3 SSP	
					2.2 Others	

Labour narrowly hold Falkirk West after Dennis Canavan resigns his Westminster seat.

Scottish Parliament By-elections

Ayr

	Lab%	Con%	SNP%	Lib%	Other%s	Turnout%
1999	38.1	38.0	19.5	4.4	-	66.5
16.3.00	22.1	39.4	29.0	2.5	4.2 SSP	56.3
					2.8 Others	
2003	34.7	40.7	13.7	5.6	5.2 SSP	56.9

John Scott wins Ayr for the Conservatives from Labour - the first by-election gain for the Conservatives in Scotland since Glasgow Pollok in 1967.

Glasgow Anniesland

	Lab%	Con%	SNP%	Lib%	Others%	Turnout%
1999	58.8	10.7	20.2	6.3	3.5 SSP	52.4
					0.5 Others	
23.11.00	48.7	10.6	22.1	6.8	7.1 SSP	38.3
					4.7 Others	
2003	45.8	14.4	17.5	10.5	11.8 SSP	43.6

Labour hold on comfortably to Glasgow Anniesland seats in simultaneous by-elections for Westminster and Holyrood; the SNP performances in the two contests are its worst in a seat where it is the main challenger to Labour since Hamilton in 1978.

Banff and Buchan

	Lab%	Con%	SNP%	Lib%	Others%	Turnout%
1999	13.6	17.0	52.6	16.8	–	55.1
7.6.01	15.8	22.0	49.6	10.4	2.2	54.8
2003	11.0	20.9	52.9	8.5	3.5 Others 3.2 SSP	47.2

By-election caused by Alex Salmond's decision to concentrate on Westminster rather than the Scottish Parliament sees the SNP's Stewart Stevenson safely re-elected.

Strathkelvin and Bearsden

	Lab%	Con%	SNP%	Lib%	Others%	Turnout%
1999	50.7	16.4	22.1	9.8	1.0	67.2
7.6.01	37.0	12.1	15.5	17.2	18.2	66.2
2003	29.9	11.3	13.7	14.0	31.1	57.1

Labour's Brian Fitzpatrick is elected Labour MSP in the face of Jean Turner's Save Stobhill Hospital Campaign, who cuts his majority to 7,829. In the subsequent Scottish Parliament election two years later, Turner defeats Fitzpatrick by 438 votes.

Local Government Election Results 1974–2003

Scottish Local Election Results 1974–2003

	Lab		Con		SNP		Lib/LibDem		Independent	
	Votes%	Seats	Votes%	Seats	Votes%	Seats	Votes%	Seats	Votes%	Seats
Regional 1974	38.5	172	28.6	112	12.6	18	5.1	11	12.4	114
District 1974	38.4	428	26.8	241	12.4	62	5.0	17	14.1	345
District 1977	31.6	299	27.2	277	24.2	170	4.0	31	9.8	318
Regional 1978	39.6	177	30.3	136	20.9	18	2.3	6	4.9	89
District 1980	45.4	494	24.1	229	15.5	54	6.2	40	6.7	289
Regional 1982	37.6	186	25.1	119	13.4	23	18.1	25	5.1	87
District 1984	45.7	545	21.4	189	11.7	59	12.8	78	6.8	267
Regional 1986	43.9	223	16.9	65	18.2	36	15.1	40	4.8	79
District 1988	42.6	553	19.4	162	21.3	113	8.4	84	6.4	231
Regional 1990	42.7	233	19.6	52	21.8	42	8.7	40	4.5	73
District 1992	34.1	468	23.2	204	24.3	150	9.5	94	7.4	228
Regional 1994	41.8	220	13.7	31	26.8	73	12.0	60	4.2	65
Unitary 1995	43.6	613	11.5	82	26.1	181	9.8	121	7.6	154
Unitary 1999	36.6	545	13.7	108	28.9	201	13.6	148	6.5	135
Unitary 2003	32.6	509	15.1	122	24.1	176	14.5	174	10.1	240

Local Government Results by Council Area 2003

Aberdeen

	% Vote	Seats	Change in Seats
Lib Dem	35.4	20	+ 8
Labour	24.2	14	– 8
SNP	23.0	6	+ 3
Con	15.3	3	– 3
SSP	1.7	–	–
Ind	0.5	–	–
BNP	0.1	–	–

Population: 212,125

No overall control – Lib Dem-Conservative administration.

A formerly reliable source of Labour votes in the North East, the party's tally of councillors has fallen by more than half between 1995 and 2003, while the Conservatives have also lost ground and Lib Dems have doubled their representation from ten councillors in 1995. The pre-2003 Labour administration lost its grip and faced a run of bad publicity, losing control in the 2003 elections.

Chief Executive: Douglas Paterson
Council Leader: Councillor Katherine Dean
Civic Head: Councillor John Reynolds
Contact Details: Town House, Broad Street, Aberdeen AB10 1FY
Tel: 01224-522000
www.aberdeencity.gov.uk

Aberdeenshire

	% Vote	Seats	Change in Seats
Lib Dem	33.8	28	+ 1
SNP	27.9	15	- 4
Con	20.9	11	+ 3
Ind	13.9	14	=
Labour	3.3	-	-
SSP	0.2	-	-

Population: 226,871

No overall control – Lib Dem-Independent administration.

A Lib Dem heartland, with parliamentary representation by both Lib Dems and the SNP. Bigger towns include Stonehaven, Peterhead, Banff and to the west, Braemar. Farming, fishing, affluent oil industry workers and a commuter belt for Aberdeen, it has a rural, independent spirit.

Chief Executive: Alan Campbell
Council Leader: Councillor Audrey Findlay
Civic Head: Councillor Raymond Bisset OBE
Contact Details: Woodhill House, Westburn Road, Aberdeen AB16 5GB
Tel: 0845-6067000
www.aberdeenshire.gov.uk

Angus

	% Vote	Seats	Change in Seats
SNP	40.4	17	- 4
Ind	19.0	6	+ 3
Labour	14.6	1	=
Lib Dem	14.2	3	+ 1
Con	11.8	2	=

Population 108,400

SNP administration

The heartland of the SNP, where the party's roots go deep in couthy. traditional, small town and farming communities, and its control over the council is assured. It includes Montrose, Arbroath, Kirriemuir and Forfar, and skirts round Dundee.

Chief Executive: Sandy Watson
Council Leader: Councillor Rob J. Murray
Civic Head: Councillor Bill Middleton
Contact Details: 7 The Cross, Forfar DD8 1BX
Tel: 01307-461460
www.angus.gov.uk

Argyll and Bute

	% Vote	Seats	Change in Seats
Ind	51.1	23	+2
SNP	17.1	3	- 2
Lib Dem	14.7	8	+ 2
Con	13.2	2	- 1
Labour	2.7	-	- 1
SSP	1.2	-	-

Population: 91,306
Independent group administration.
Contiguous with the Lib Dem-held constituency, independents have long held sway in the council chamber. It has a slightly maverick approach to delivering widely dispersed services, covering Helensburgh, Dunoon, Campbeltown, Oban, Islay and Mull.

Chief Executive: James McLellan
Council Leader: Councillor Allan MacAskill
Civic Head: Councillor Billy Petrie
Contact Details: Kilmory, Lochgilphead PA31 8RT
Tel: 01546-602127
www.argyll-bute.gov.uk

Ayrshire, East

	% Vote	Seats	Change in Seats
Labour	49.3	23	+ 6
SNP	35.3	8	- 6
Con	12.5	1	=
Ind	1.6	-	-
SSP	1.2	-	-
BNP	0.2	-	-

Population: 120,235
Labour control, and with the SNP weakened by internal local wrangling, it went against the tide of Labour seat losses in 2003. Including Kilmarnock, Cumnock, former mining communities and farming, Labour's dominance is overwhelming.

Chief Executive: David Montgomery
Council Leader: Councillor Drew McIntyre
Civic Head: Councillor Jane Darnbrough
Address; Council Headquarters, London Road, Kilmarnock KA3 7BU
Tel: 01563-576002
www.east-ayrshire.gov.uk/

Ayrshire, North

	% Vote	Seats	Change in Seats
Labour	44.0	21	− 4
SNP	28.2	3	+ 1
Con	19.1	4	+ 2
Ind	5.5	2	+ 1
SSP	2.4	-	-
Lib Dem	0.4	-	-
Others	0.5	-	-

Population: 135,817
Labour control.
Based around Irvine, north to Largs and including Arran, Labour is strong in membership and voter loyalty, both for council and for parliamentary seats.

Chief Executive: Bernard Devine
Council Leader: Councillor David O'Neill
Civic Head: Councillor Drew Duncan
Contact Details: Cunninghame House, Irvine KA12 8EE
Tel: 01294-324100
www.north-ayrshire.gov.uk

Ayrshire, South

	% Vote	Seats	Change in Seats
Con	42.1	15	+ 2
Labour	36.7	15	- 2
SNP	17.3	-	-
Ind	2.6	-	-
SSP	1.1	-	-
Others	0.2	-	-

Population: 135,817
No overall control – Labour minority administration.
Labour had control of South Ayrshire by a large margin from 1995-99, but losses and defections saw it slide into minority control in 2001. It was a high hope for the Conservatives with considerable effort put in to gain their first unitary authority in 2003, but they just missed out, and Labour took control of the administration on a cut of the cards. It includes Ayr, Troon and Girvan, plus a substantial farming area.

Chief Executive: George Thorley
Council Leader: Councillor Andy Hill
Civic Head: Councillor Gordon McKenzie
Contact Details: County Buildings, Wellington Square, Ayr KA7 1DR
Tel: 01292-612000
www.south-ayrshire.gov.uk

Clackmannanshire

	% Vote	Seats	Change in Seats
Labour	44.3	10	+ 2
SNP	41.3	6	- 3
Ind	6.6	1	+ 1
Con	5.8	1	=
Lib Dem	2.0	-	-

Population: 48,077
Labour control.
The SNP had control of the Wee County before the 2003 election, but its administration was not without controversy, and while the Scottish Parliament seat of Ochil went from Labour to SNP, the council swung decisively the other way. Being so small, there is collaboration on services with Stirling.

Chief Executive: Keir Bloomer
Council Leader: Councillor Margaret Paterson
Civic Head: Councillor Derek Stewart
Contact Details: Greenfield, Alloa FK10 2AD
Tel: 01259-450000
www.clacks.gov.uk

Dumfries and Galloway

	% Vote	Seats	Change in Seats
Con	30.1	11	+ 3
Labour	24.1	14	+ 1
Ind	21.4	12	- 3
SNP	14.0	5	=
Lib Dem	9.7	5	- 1
SSP	0.7	-	-

Population: 147,765
NOC – Independent-Lib Dem-SNP administration.
The Conservatives had hoped to match their parliamentary gains in the South West with the prospect of becoming the council's largest group. However, their ambitions were thwarted and they were kept out of the administration by a three-way coalition.

Chief Executive: Philip Jones
Council Leader: Councillor Andrew R. Campbell OBE
Civic Head: Councillor Andrew R. Campbell OBE
Contact Details: Council Offices, English Street, Dumfries DG1 2DD
Tel: 01387-260000
www.dumgal.gov.uk

Dunbartonshire, East

	% Vote	Seats	Change in Seats
Lib Dem	34.3	12	+ 2
Labour	29.6	9	- 2
Con	19.7	3	=
SNP	11.3	-	-
Ind	2.6	-	-
SSP	2.5	-	-

Population: 108,243
NOC – Lib Dem minority administration.
Includes some of the leafier commuter areas around the north of Glasgow, such as Bearsden, Milngavie, Bishopbriggs and Kirkintilloch, where Labour and Lib Dems compete fiercely for the council with Labour losing ground in successive elections, and where hospital campaigner Jean Turner has one of the MSP seats.

Chief Executive: Vicki Nash
Council Leader: Councillor John Morrison
Civic Head: Councillor Patricia Steel
Contact Details: Tom Johnston House, Civic Way, Kirkintilloch G66 4TJ
Tel: 0141-5788000
www.eastdunbarton.gov.uk

Dunbartonshire, West

	% Vote	Seats	Change in Seats
Labour	46.5	17	+ 3
SNP	33.9	3	- 4
SSP	10.1	1	+ 1
Ind	6.5	1	=
Con	3.0	-	-

Population: 93,378
Labour control.
A scene of fractious Labour politics before the 2003 election, as rebels joined forces with Nationalists to form an administration, and Socialists hoped to build a base, but Labour decisively regained control in 2003 in a council area with some of the worst poverty-related problems in Scotland. It includes Clydebank, Dumbarton and Alexandria.

Chief Executive: Tim Huntingford
Council Leader: Councillor Andy White
Civic Head: Councillor Alistair Macdonald
Contact Details: Council Offices, Garshake Road, Dumbarton G82 3PU
Tel: 01389-737000
www.west-dunbarton.gov.uk/

City of Dundee

	% Vote	Seats	Change in Seats
SNP	34.1	11	+ 1
Labour	31.0	10	- 4
Con	15.9	5	+ 1
Lib Dem	11.5	2	+ 2
SSP	4.0	-	-
Ind	3.5	1	=

Population: 145,663
NOC – Labour-Lib Dem minority administration, with informal Conservative support.
Slumped from Labour control into a Labour minority administration before 2003, and the SNP had hopes of a breakthrough to take control of its first city council. The Nationalists did not manage to make enough headway at council level, and even though they emerged as the largest party, it failed to form an administration. Major issues include the limited tax base and predicted population decline over the next 20 years.

Chief Executive: Alex Stephen
Council Leader: Councillor Jill Shimi
Civic Head: Councillor John Letford
Contact Details: City Chambers, 21 City Square, Dundee DD1 3BY
Tel: 01382 434000
www.dundeecity.gov.uk

City of Edinburgh

	% Vote	Seats	Change in Seats
Labour	31.2	30	- 1
Lib Dem	25.5	15	+ 2
Con	23.4	13	=
SNP	14.7	-	- 1
SSP	3.9	-	-
Ind	1.1	-	-
Others	0.2	-	-

Population: 448,624
Labour control.

A quirk of the electoral system gives Labour a disproportionate share of the seats, and it struggled to hold its majority in 2003 by only one ward, on a day it lost two Scottish Parliament seats in the city. Congestion charging was the big election issue and remains a difficult one for the council. Labour-Lib Dem antagonism is a feature of the capital's politics, as is the poor performance of Nationalists.

Chief Executive: Tom Aitchison
Council Leader: Councillor Donald Anderson
Civic Head: Councillor Lesley Hinds
Contact Details: City Chambers, High Street, Edinburgh EH1 1YJ
Tel: 0131-2002000
www.edinburgh.gov.uk

Eilean Siar (Western Isles)

	% Vote	Seats	Change in Seats
Ind	71.1	24	+ 2
Labour	15.7	4	- 2
SNP	13.2	3	=

Population: 26,502
Independent group control.
Typically quirky politics have only brought party groups into the Stornoway council chambers in the past decade, but independents can be confident of controlling the administration. In 2003, 15 wards, nearly half, were uncontested.

Chief Executive: Bill Howat
Council Leader: Councillor Alex MacDonald
Civic Head: Councillor Alex MacDonald
Contact Details: Council Offices, Sandwick Road
Stornoway, Isle of Lewis HS1 2BW
Tel: 01851-703773
www.cne-siar.gov.uk

Falkirk

	% Vote	Seats	Change in Seats
Labour	41.0	14	- 1
SNP	33.9	9	=
Ind	14.6	7	+ 1
Con	7.0	2	=
Lib Dem	1.9	-	-
SSP	1.5	-	-

Population: 145,191
No overall control – SNP-Independent group administration.

The council covers Bonnybridge and Denny to Grangemouth and Bo'ness on the Forth. The SNP hold on Falkirk slipped in 2003, but it remains one of the few councils where the party takes the lead. As such, it is the only council outside COSLA.

Chief Executive: Mary Pitcaithly
Council Leader: Councillor David Alexander
Civic Head: Councillor James Johnston
Contact Details: Municipal Buildings, Falkirk FK1 5RS
Tel: 01324-506060
www.falkirk.gov.uk/

Fife

	% Vote	Seats	Change in Seats
Labour	33.4	36	– 7
Lib Dem	25.2	23	+ 2
SNP	20.8	11	+ 2
Con	10.3	2	+ 1
Ind	8.1	5	+ 3
SSP	1.5	-	-
Others	0.6	1	– 1

Population: 349,429
No overall control – Labour minority administration.
A one-time Labour stronghold with its solid former mining communities, and two former Communists on the council who stood in 2003 as independents. However, bad publicity for Fife Labour, including the fiasco surrounding the political demise of former council leader Henry McLeish, has seen the party's grip of Fife politics lose ground. North East Fife is the Lib Dems' strongest membership area in Scotland, so the Executive coalition parties are at odds in the Glenrothes council chamber.

Chief Executive: Douglas Sinclair CBE
Council Leader: Councillor Anne R. McGovern
Civic Head: Councillor John Simpson
Contact Details: Fife House, North Street, Glenrothes KY7 5LT
Tel: 01592-414141
www.fife.gov.uk

Glasgow

	% Vote	Seats	Change in Seats
Labour	47.6	71	– 3
SNP	20.5	3	+ 1
SSP	15.5	1	–
Con	7.6	1	–
Lib Dem	7.6	3	+ 2
Others	1.2	-	

Population: 577,869

Labour control.

It is hard to believe the Conservatives controlled Glasgow as recently as 1977–80. Since then, it has been solidly Labour, and neither the SNP nor the SSP has been able to break the electoral lock Labour maintains on all but a handful of wards. The Labour group is infamous for its factionalism, though that has subsided in recent years, and its leadership tends to want special status and treatment for Glasgow, demonstrated by pulling out of COSLA for two years up to 2003.

Chief Executive: George Black

Council Leader: Councillor Charles Gordon

Civic Head: Councillor Elizabeth A. Cameron

Contact Details: City Chambers, George Square, Glasgow G2 1DU

Tel: 0141-2872000

www.glasgow.gov.uk

Highland

	% Vote	Seats	Change in Seats
Ind	69.3	57	+ 7
Labour	11.6	8	– 2
SNP	10.2	6	– 2
Lib Dem	6.1	9	– 3
Con	1.2	–	–
SSP	1.1	–	–
Others	0.4	–	–

Population: 208,914

Independent group control.

A long-standing stronghold for independent councillors, even though three parties share its three large parliamentary seats. The blurred dividing line between party affiliation and independence is demonstrated by two former senior councillors now in the Scottish Parliament, Peter Peacock, an independent councillor who joined Labour, and John Farquhar Munro, a Lib Dem councillor who maintains his independence. Highland Council has a high status, acting sometimes as a sort of surrogate Highland parliament.

Chief Executive: Arthur McCourt

Council Leader: Councillor Alison L. Magee

Civic Head: Councillor Alison L. Magee

Contact Details: Council Headquarters, Glenurquhart Road, Inverness IV3 5NX

Tel: 01463-702838

www.highland.gov.uk

Inverclyde

	% Vote	Seats	Change in Seats
Lib Dem	42.6	13	+ 5
Labour	31.3	6	– 5
SNP	14.8	–	–
Con	6.1	–	– 1
Ind	3.5	1	+ 1
SSP	1.7	–	–

Population: 84,203

Lib Dem control.

The first council with Lib Dem majority control, in a long-standing oasis of strength for Liberals amid the industrial belt of the West of Scotland. Labour had long run the council, but was increasingly discredited, and the 2003 result saw a major turnover. Includes Port Glasgow, Greenock and Gourock, round the Clyde coast to Wemyss Bay.

Chief Executive: Robert N. M. Cleary

Council Leader: Councillor Alan Blair

Civic Head: Councillor Ciano Rebecchi

Contact Details: Municipal Buildings, Greenock PA15 1LY

Tel: 01475-717171

www.inverclyde.gov.uk

Lanarkshire, North

	% Vote	Seats	Change in Seats
Labour	55.6	54	– 2
SNP	32.6	11	+ 1
Ind	4.1	5	+ 1
Con	3.9	–	–
SSP	2.6	–	–
Lib Dem	1.1	–	–
Others	0.1	–	–

Population: 321,067

Labour control.

The strongest of Labour's heartlands, even though internal council factionalism and mismanagement has been a source of embarrassment to the party's reputation nationally. It stands a strong chance of retaining Labour control even after proportional representation is introduced in the face of Labour councillor opposition. Major centres are Cumbernauld, Coatbridge, Airdrie, Motherwell and Wishaw.

Chief Executive: Gavin Whitefield

Council Leader: Councillor James McCabe

Civic Head: Councillor Patrick Connelly

Contact Details: PO Box 14, Civic Centre, Motherwell ML1 1TW

Tel: 01698-302222

www.northlan.gov.uk

Lanarkshire, South

	% Vote	Seats	Change in Seats
Labour	48.8	51	– 3
SNP	27.3	9	– 1
Con	13.9	2	=
Lib Dem	4.8	2	+ 1
Ind	3.2	3	+ 3
SSP	2.1	–	–
Others	0.1	–	–

Population: 302,216

Labour control.

One of only three or four councils where Labour could hope to retain overall control after council voting reform introduces multi-member wards and single transferable voting. It has a reputation for being better run than some other councils where Labour dominates. Major urban areas are Rutherglen, East Kilbride and Hamilton, also covering more rural communities around Lanark and Biggar.

Chief Executive: Michael Docherty

Council Leader: Councillor Edward McAvoy

Civic Head: Councillor Mushtaq Ahmead

Contact Details: Almada Street, Hamilton ML3 0AA

Tel: 01698-454444

www.southlanarkshire.gov.uk

Lothian, East

	% Vote	Seats	Change in Seats
Labour	40.6	17	=
Con	23.1	4	– 1
SNP	19.3	1	=
Lib Dem	14.8	1	+ 1
SSP	1.6	–	–
Ind	0.6	–	–

Population: 90,088

Labour control.

Although much of the county is rural, the ex-mining communities close to Edinburgh dominate politically, so Labour returns big majorities without any major challenge.

Chief Executive: John Lindsay

Council Leader: Councillor Norman Murray

Civic Head: Councillor Patrick O'Brien

Contact Details: John Muir House, Haddington EH41 3HA

Tel: 01620-827827

www.eastlothian.gov.uk

Lothian, West

	% Vote	Seats	Change in Seats
Labour	43.0	18	− 2
SNP	36.0	12	+ 1
Con	9.2	1	=
Lib Dem	6.9	-	-
Ind	3.6	1	+ 1
SSP	1.4	-	-

Population: 158,714

Labour control.

One of the SNP's target council areas, the party did not make the headway it hoped in 2003, and Labour remains in control with a slightly reduced majority. This is the sort of council which will see its party politics transformed by the introduction of proportional representation for local government.

Chief Executive: Alex Linkston

Council Leader: Councillor Graeme Morrice

Civic Head: Councillor Joe Thomas

Contact Details: West Lothian House, Almondvale, Livingston EH54 6QG

Tel: 01506-777000

www.westlothian.gov.uk

Midlothian

	% Vote	Seats	Change in Seats
Labour	43.3	15	− 2
SNP	24.4	-	-
Lib Dem	17.2	2	+ 1
Con	11.0	-	-
Ind	2.0	1	+ 1
SSP	1.4	-	-
Others	0.9	-	-

Population: 80,941

Labour control.

With its mining communities, this used to be a virtual shutout of all Labour's opponents, with its councillors implacable opponents of voting reform. A small Lib Dem presence reflects the spread of affluent commuter housing beyond Edinburgh's green belt.

Chief Executive: Trevor Muir

Council Leader: Councillor Adam Montgomery

Civic Head: Councillor Sam Campbell

Contact Details: Midlothian House, Buccleuch Street, Dalkeith EH22 1DJ

Tel: 0131-2707500

www.midlothian.gov.uk

Moray

	% Vote	Seats	Change in Seats
Ind	49.3	16	+ 1
SNP	25.2	3	+ 1
Labour	12.7	5	- 1
Lib Dem	7.9	1	- 1
Con	4.3	1	=
SSP	0.6	-	-

Population: 86,941

Independent group control.

A messy, tempestuous and controversy-strewn recent political history has seen SNP, Labour and independents controlling the council, with Nationalist control of parliamentary seats lacking deep roots at local level.

Chief Executive: Alastair Keddie

Council Leader: Councillor Eddie Aldridge

Civic Head: Councillor Eddie Aldridge

Contact Details: Council Offices, High Street, Elgin IV30 1BX

Tel: 01343-543451

www.moray.gov.uk

Orkney

	% Vote	Seats	Change in Seats
Ind	100.0	21	=

Population: 19,245

The only all-independent council, where none of the parties put up any candidates and where eight wards were uncontested in 2003.

Chief Executive: Alistair Buchan

Council Leader: Councillor Stephen Hagan

Civic Head: Councillor Stephen Hagan

Contact Details: Council Offices, School Place, Kirkwall KW15 1NY

Tel: 01856-873535

www.orkney.gov.uk

Perth and Kinross

	% Vote	Seats	Change in Seats
SNP	35.6	15	- 1
Con	28.4	10	- 1
Lib Dem	22.2	9	+ 3
Labour	9.8	5	- 1
Ind	3.9	2	=

Population: 134,949

No overall control – Conservative-Lib Dem-Labour-Independent administration.

One of the hardest-fought councils between all four major parties. Opponents of the SNP formed an anti-Nationalist coalition before and after the 2003 election to run the council. It includes most of Perthshire up to the Highland line.

Chief Executive: Bernadette Malone
Council Leader: Councillor Jimmy Doig
Civic Head: Councillor Bob Scott
Contact Details: Council Buildings, 2 High Street, Perth PH1 5PH
Tel: 01738-475000
www.pkc.gov.uk

Renfrewshire

	% Vote	Seats	Change in Seats
SNP	39.3	15	=
Labour	36.8	21	=
Lib Dem	9.7	3	=
Con	8.9	1	=
SSP	4.7	–	–
Ind	0.6	–	–

Population: 172,867

Labour control.

The most notoriously stormy of councils, handily placed for the police station when debates get out of hand. The 1999-2003 period saw Labour's grip slip through defections, in an area where it has had notorious factional problems, but it did just enough to win back majority control with some slim ward majorities. A majority of two does not allow for any slippage over the next four years.

Chief Executive: Tom Scholes
Council Leader: Councillor Jim Harkins
Civic Head: Councillor Ronnie Burns
Contact Details: North Building, Room 1.2, Cotton Street, Paisley PA1 1BU
Tel: 0141-8403601
www.renfrewshire.gov.uk

Renfrewshire, East

	% Vote	Seats	Change in Seats
Labour	31.8	8	– 1
Con	30.9	7	– 1
Lib Dem	20.7	3	+ 1
Ind	8.5	2	+ 1
SNP	7.7	–	–
Others	0.5	–	–

Population: 89,311

No overall control – Labour minority administration.

A leafy suburban council area covering Eastwood, gerrymandered by the last Conservative Government to create its safest council. However, Labour has run the administration since the council was created, tacking carefully to middle class interests.

Chief Executive: Peter Daniels
Council Leader: Councillor Owen Taylor
Civic Head: Councillor Betty Cunningham
Contact Details: Council Offices, Eastwood Park, Rouken Glen Road, Giffnock G46 6UG
Tel: 0141-5773000
www.eastrenfrewshire.gov.uk

Scottish Borders

	% Vote	Seats	Change in Seats
Ind	30.4	15	+ 1
Con	28.6	10	+ 9
Lib Dem	26.3	8	– 6
SNP	11.5	1	– 3
SSP	1.9	–	–
Labour	1.3	–	– 1

Population: 106,764
No overall control – Independent group-Conservative administration.
An increasingly party politicised council. In 1995, there were 30 independents out of 34. Lib Dems and some independent councillors, including the former leader, were ousted in a major turnover in 2003, after budget mismanagement brought crisis to the council offices. That benefited the SNP in one parliamentary constituency yet they lost ground in the council, while Conservatives were the big beneficiaries.

Chief Executive: David Hume
Council Leader: Councillor David Parker
Civic Head: Councillor Alasdair Hutton
Contact Details: Council Headquarters, Newtown St Boswells, Melrose TD6 0SA
Tel: 01835-824000
www.scotborders.gov.uk

Shetland

	% Vote	Seats	Change in Seats
Ind	71.3	16	+ 3
Lib Dem	23.8	5	– 3
Ind Lib Dem	4.9	1	=

Population: 21,988
Independent group control.
Lib Dems, with parliamentary representation, are the only party with a presence to challenge the islands' independent group, or indeed to contest any of the seats, though they suffered a sharp setback in the 2003 election. Of the five seats Lib Dems retained,

four were uncontested. There can be a high turnover of independents at elections, with a major clearout of top figures in 1999.

Chief Executive: Morgan Goodlad
Council Leader: Councillor Alexander J. Cluness
Civic Head: Councillor Alexander J. Cluness
Contact Details: Town Hall, Lerwick ZE1 0HB
Tel: 01595-693535
www.shetland.gov.uk

Stirling

	% Vote	Seats	Change in Seats
Labour	36.4	12	+ 1
Con	27.8	10	+ 1
SNP	21.4	–	– 2
Lib Dem	12.7	–	–
Ind	1.6	–	–
SSP	0.2	–	–

Population: 86,212
Labour control.

For many elections, it has been the closest fought council between Labour and Conservative, with a cut of a pack of cards being used to choose which party controls the administration on more than one occasion. The 2003 vote created enough distance for Labour to run the council with a more comfortable margin.

Chief Executive: Keith Yates
Council Leader: Councillor Corrie McChord
Civic Head: Councillor Colin O'Brien
Contact Details: Council Offices, Viewforth, Stirling FK8 2ET
Tel: 01786-443322
www.stirling.gov.uk

Referendum Results 1975–2000

This section contains the results of three official referendums – two Scottish-wide – the 1979 and 1997 devolution ballots, and the Scottish figures of the 1975 UK-wide EEC referendum. Two other ballot results are also listed – both unofficial – the 1994 Strathclyde water privatisation vote and the 2000 Section 28 ballot, privately funded by campaigners against Executive policy on the homosexuality issue. The reason for their inclusion is that both ballots were influential in shaping Scottish political debates at the time, and have also been cited in international studies of referendums.

Official Referendums:

European Community Membership, 5 June 1975

	%	Votes
Yes	58.4	1,332,186
No	41.6	948,039
Yes Majority:	16.8	384,147

Turnout: 61.4%

Result By Region / Island

	Yes%	No%	Turnout
Borders	72.3	27.7	63.2
Central	59.7	40.3	64.1
Dumfries and Galloway	68.2	31.8	61.5
Fife	56.3	43.7	63.3
Grampian	58.2	41.8	57.4
Highland	54.6	45.4	58.7
Lothian	59.5	40.5	63.6
Strathclyde	57.7	42.3	61.7
Tayside	58.6	41.4	63.8
Orkney	61.8	38.2	48.2
Shetland	43.7	56.3	47.1
Western Isles	29.5	70.5	50.1
Total	58.4	41.6	61.4

Scottish Assembly, 1 March 1979

Do You Want the Provisions of the Scotland Act 1978 Put Into Effect?

	%	Votes
Yes	51.6	1,230,937
No	48.4	1,153,502
Yes Majority	3.2	77,435

cont'd

Turnout: 63.6%

Result By Region

	Yes %	Yes Votes	No %	No Votes	Turnout%
Borders	40.3	20,746	59.7	30,780	67.3
Central	54.7	71,296	45.3	59,105	66.7
Dumfries and Galloway	40.3	27,162	59.7	40,239	64.9
Fife	53.7	86,252	46.3	74,436	66.1
Grampian	48.3	94,944	51.7	101,485	57.9
Highland	51.0	44,973	49.0	43,274	65.4
Lothian	50.1	187,221	49.9	186,421	66.6
Strathclyde	54.0	596,519	46.0	508,599	63.2
Tayside	49.5	91,482	50.5	93,325	63.8
Orkney	27.9	2,104	72.1	5,439	54.8
Shetland	27.1	2,020	72.9	5,466	51.0
Western Isles	55.8	6,218	44.2	4,933	50.5
Total	51.6	1,230,937	48.4	1,153,502	63.6

Scottish Parliament, 11 September 1997

	Devolution		Tax powers	
	%	Votes	%	Votes
Yes	74.3	1,775,045	63.5	1,512,889
No	25.7	614,400	36.5	870,263
Turnout		60.1%		–

Results by Region/Island

	Devolution%	Tax Powers%
Borders	62.8	50.7
Central	76.1	65.6
Dumfries and Galloway	60.7	48.8
Fife	76.1	64.7
Grampian	67.6	55.1
Highland	72.6	62.1
Lothian	76.4	64.9
Strathclyde	75.7	65.0
Tayside	67.4	56.7
Orkney	57.3	47.4
Shetland	62.4	51.6
Western Isles	79.4	68.4
Total	74.3	63.5

By Local Authority: Scottish Parliament

	Yes %	Yes votes	No %	No votes
Aberdeen	71.8	65,035	28.2	25,580
Aberdeenshire	63.9	61,621	36.1	34,878
Angus	64.7	33,571	35.3	18,350

cont'd

Argyll and Bute	67.3	30,452	32.7	14,796
Clackmannanshire	80.0	18,790	20.0	4,706
Dumfries and Galloway	60.7	44,619	39.3	28,863
Dundee	76.0	49,252	24.0	15,553
East Ayrshire	81.1	49,131	18.9	11,426
East Dunbartonshire	69.8	40,917	30.2	17,725
East Lothian	74.2	33,525	25.8	11,665
East Renfrewshire	61.7	28,253	38.3	17,573
Edinburgh	71.9	155,900	28.1	60,832
Falkirk	80.0	55,642	20.0	13,953
Fife	76.1	125,668	23.9	39,517
Glasgow	83.6	204,269	16.4	40,106
Highland	72.6	72,551	27.4	27,431
Inverclyde	78.0	31,680	22.0	8,945
Midlothian	79.9	31,681	20.1	7,979
Moray	67.2	24,822	32.8	12,122
North Ayrshire	76.3	51,304	23.7	15,931
North Lanarkshire	82.6	123,063	17.4	26,010
Orkney	57.3	4,749	42.7	3,541
Perthshire and Kinross	61.7	40,344	38.3	24,998
Renfrewshire	79.0	68,711	21.0	18,213
Scottish Borders	62.8	33,855	37.2	20,060
Shetland	62.4	5,430	37.6	3,275
South Ayrshire	66.9	40,161	33.1	19,909
South Lanarkshire	77.8	114,908	22.2	32,762
Stirling	68.5	29,190	31.5	13,440
West Dunbartonshire	84.7	39,051	15.3	7,058
West Lothian	79.6	56,923	20.4	14,614
Western Isles	79.4	9,977	20.6	2,589
Scotland	74.3	1,775,045	25.7	614,400

By Local Authority: Tax-Varying Powers

	Yes %	Yes votes	No %	No votes
Aberdeen	60.3	54,320	39.7	35,709
Aberdeenshire	52.3	50,295	47.7	45,929
Angus	53.4	27,641	46.6	24,089
Argyll and Bute	57.0	25,746	43.0	19,429
Clackmannanshire	68.7	16,112	31.3	7,355
Dumfries and Galloway	48.8	35,737	51.2	37,499
Dundee	65.5	42,304	34.5	22,280
East Ayrshire	70.5	42,559	29.5	17,824
East Dunbartonshire	59.1	34,576	40.9	23,914
East Lothian	62.7	28,152	37.3	16,765
East Renfrewshire	51.6	23,580	48.4	22,153
Edinburgh	62.0	133,843	38.0	82,188
Falkirk	69.2	48,064	30.8	21,403

cont'd

Fife	64.7	108,021	35.3	58,987
Glasgow	75.0	182,589	25.0	60,842
Highland	62.1	61,359	37.9	37,525
Inverclyde	67.2	27,194	32.8	13,277
Midlothian	67.7	26,776	32.3	12,762
Moray	52.7	19,326	47.3	17,344
North Ayrshire	65.7	43,990	34.3	22,991
North Lanarkshire	72.2	107,288	27.8	41,372
Orkney	47.4	3,917	52.6	4,344
Perthshire and Kinross	51.3	33,398	48.7	31,709
Renfrewshire	63.6	55,075	36.4	31,537
Scottish Borders	50.7	27,284	49.3	26,497
Shetland	51.6	4,478	48.4	4,198
South Ayrshire	56.2	33,679	43.8	26,217
South Lanarkshire	67.6	99,587	32.4	47,708
Stirling	58.9	25,044	41.1	17,487
West Dunbartonshire	74.7	34,408	25.3	11,628
West Lothian	67.3	47,990	32.7	23,354
Western Isles	68.4	8,557	31.6	3,947
Scotland	63.5	1,512,889	36.5	870,263

Unofficial Referendums:

Strathclyde Region Water Privatisation Referendum, 22 March 1994

Electorate: 1,718,354   *Turnout*: 1,228,623 (71.50%)

	Vote	%
Against water privatisation	1,194,667	97.24
For water privatisation	35,956	2.76

Anti-Clause 28/Section 2A Referendum, 30 May 2000

Electorate: 3,970,712   *Turnout*: 1,260,846 (31.75%)
No. of ballots undelivered due to change of address or death: 318,110
Turnout claimed by organisers taking this into account: 1,260,846 (34.52%)

	Vote	%
For retention of Clause 28/Section 2A	1,094,440	86.80
For abolition of Clause 28/Section 2A	166,406	13.20
Invalid votes	11,356	
Envelopes returned empty	11,856	

Scottish Parliament Voting Intentions by Opinion Polls 1997-2003

System Three Scottish Parliament Opinion Polls:

	Con	Lab	SNP	LD	Other
November 1997	13	48	29	9	1
February 1998	9	44	33	13	1
March 1998	12	39	38	10	1
April 1998	8	40	40	10	1
May 1998	11	36	41	10	1

Scottish Parliament First and Second Vote Intentions

First Vote

	Con	Lab	SNP	LD	Other
June 1998	19	37	45	8	1
July 1998	10	40	41	9	1
August 1998	11	41	38	8	1
September 1998	12	40	39	9	1
October 1998	11	39	37	12	1
November 1998	11	38	37	12	1
Early January 1999	11	38	48	11	1
Late January 1999	10	41	39	9	1
February 1999	11	39	38	11	1
March 1999	10	45	32	12	2
Mid April 1999	11	46	26	13	4
Late April 1999	10	44	33	10	2

Second Vote

	Con	Lab	SNP	LD	Other
June 1998	11	32	43	12	2
July 1998	9	36	41	12	2
August 1998	10	39	40	10	1
Sept 1998	12	37	38	12	1
October 1998	12	37	35	14	2

cont'd

November 1998	12	35	35	16	2
Early Jan 1999	11	37	38	12	2
Late Jan 1999	10	38	38	13	1
Feb 1999	10	40	36	12	1
March 1999	11	40	32	15	2
Mid April 1999	12	40	27	14	7
Late April 1999	10	37	34	13	5

1999 First Vote

	Con	Lab	SNP	LD	Green	SSP	Other
Election 6 May	16	39	29	14	n/a	n/a	3
May	10	44	28	13	2	2	1
June	11	43	28	12	2	3	1
July	12	41	30	12	2	2	1
August	12	40	31	11	2	3	1
September	11	35	35	12	2	4	1
October	10	39	35	10	2	3	1
November	9	44	30	11	1	3	2

1999 Second Vote

	Con	Lab	SNP	LD	Green	SSP	Other
Election 6 May	15	34	27	12	4	2	5
May	10	36	30	17	3	3	2
June	10	34	31	13	5	3	3
July	10	34	31	14	3	5	3
August	11	29	29	17	5	5	3
September	8	32	32	15	5	4	3
October	9	36	31	13	4	4	3
November	10	33	30	14	5	5	3

2000 First Vote

	Con	Lab	SNP	LD	Green	SSP	Other
Early January	8	43	34	9	2	4	*
Late January	11	42	31	10	2	3	1
February	12	37	36	9	1	4	1
March	14	33	37	11	2	3	1
April	14	34	35	10	2	4	2
May	13	40	30	10	2	4	2
June	12	33	36	12	2	3	1
July	11	37	35	10	2	3	1
August	13	34	36	9	2	5	1
September	10	28	42	14	2	3	1
October	10	39	35	11	1	2	2
November	12	41	32	10	2	3	1

(* = less than 1% but not zero)

2000 Second Vote

	Con	Lab	SNP	LD	Green	SSP	Other
Early January	9	37	33	12	3	6	1
Late January	9	34	31	14	5	5	2
February	11	32	33	13	4	5	2
March	11	29	34	15	3	5	3
April	13	30	31	14	4	5	4
May	11	31	33	13	6	4	3
June	11	27	35	16	5	4	3
July	11	33	30	12	5	6	3
August	13	29	32	12	3	6	4
September	11	25	38	15	4	4	2
October	10	30	32	17	5	4	2
November	12	35	30	13	4	4	2

2001 First Vote

	Con	Lab	SNP	LD	Green	SSP	Other
Early January	11	37	35	10	2	2	2
Late January	10	39	35	9	2	3	1
February	12	36	38	9	2	3	1
March	10	44	34	8	2	2	1
April	12	39	34	8	2	3	1
May	10	39	35	11	1	3	*
June	10	40	31	14	1	3	*
July	11	38	28	15	1	5	1
August	11	43	28	11	1	4	1
September	11	43	29	11	1	4	1
October	8	45	30	12	1	3	1
November	11	40	32	11	1	3	1

(* = less than 1% but not zero)

2001 Second Vote

	Con	Lab	SNP	LD	Green	SSP	Other
Early January	11	34	33	11	4	5	3
Late January	9	33	33	13	4	6	2
February	12	29	36	13	3	5	2
March	9	36	32	11	5	6	1
April	12	32	31	12	5	5	3
May	11	30	34	15	3	5	1
June	8	31	32	18	4	4	2
July	12	33	28	16	3	6	2
August	11	36	32	14	3	5	1
September	9	36	29	15	2	7	2
October	7	37	29	15	4	6	2
November	11	35	31	13	3	6	2

2002 First Vote

	Con	Lab	SNP	LD	Green	SSP	Other
Early January	10	39	32	12	2	3	1
Late January	9	40	31	13	1	4	1
February	10	39	32	13	2	3	1
March	12	36	32	15	2	3	*
April	12	40	27	13	2	4	1
May	10	40	29	14	1	5	1
June	12	37	32	12	2	3	1
July	10	39	30	12	3	6	1
August	11	38	28	15	2	4	1
September	10	38	28	16	3	4	2
October	12	37	30	15	2	4	1
November	11	35	32	16	2	4	1

(* = less than 1% but not zero)

2002 Second Vote

	Con	Lab	SNP	LD	Green	SSP	Other
Early January	11	33	29	15	5	6	2
Late January	9	33	30	17	3	6	2
February	11	34	30	15	3	6	2
March	9	28	30	19	5	6	2
April	11	31	28	16	5	6	2
May	10	34	29	15	4	6	2
June	11	32	29	15	4	8	2
July	10	30	29	15	5	8	3
August	9	34	28	15	4	8	2
September	10	28	29	16	6	9	4
October	10	29	30	19	4	5	3
November	10	30	28	18	5	6	3

2003 First Vote

	Con	Lab	SNP	LD	Green	SSP	Other
Early January	10	40	30	13	2	4	1
Late January	11	32	31	16	3	5	2
February	10	34	32	14	2	6	1
March	11	31	31	16	3	6	2
Mid April	13	39	26	12	3	4	2
Late April	10	38	28	14	2	6	1
Election 1 May	*17*	*35*	*24*	*15*	*n/a*	*6*	*3*
May	11	38	26	14	3	6	2
June	13	33	25	16	3	6	3
July	13	31	31	15	2	5	2
August	10	33	31	16	3	4	2
September	12	33	31	15	3	5	1
October	11	35	29	17	1	5	2

cont'd

	Con	Lab	SNP	LD	Green	SSP	Other
November	15	35	34	13	2	4	1
Early January 2004	10	35	34	13	2	4	1

2003 Second Vote

	Con	Lab	SNP	LD	Green	SSP	Other
Early January	10	29	31	15	5	7	3
Late January	10	28	28	17	6	7	4
February	10	27	27	15	6	10	4
March	9	26	29	18	7	8	3
Mid April	11	30	27	14	7	6	4
Late April	9	28	28	13	7	10	5
Election 1 May	*16*	*29*	*21*	*12*	*7*	*7*	*9*
May	10	27	25	15	9	10	6
June	12	25	25	15	7	11	6
July	9	26	27	16	8	9	5
August	9	26	28	15	9	7	6
September	7	26	25	20	8	10	4
October	11	25	30	16	8	6	4
November	13	28	28	14	4	8	5
Early January 2004	11	28	29	13	7	7	3

Westminster Scottish Voting Intentions by Opinion Polls 1974–2003

System Three Westminster Voting Intentions:

1974-5

	Con	Lab	SNP	Lib	SLP
Election October 74	25	36	30	8	-
October	16	47	33	4	-
November	22	40	32	6	-
January 75	23	40	31	6	-
January	24	40	29	6	-
February	28	40	29	3	-
March	29	40	24	6	-
April	31	37	27	5	-
May	28	40	26	5	-
July	24	39	24	5	-
July	39	42	22	5	-
August	32	38	24	5	-
September	34	35	27	4	-
October	30	39	26	4	-
November	26	42	26	5	-

1976

	Con	Lab	SNP	Lib	SLP
January	28	30	36	5	-
January	27	33	36	3	-
February	28	24	33	6	8
March	28	34	29	4	5
April	28	31	30	5	5
May	32	35	25	4	3
June	32	34	27	4	3
July	31	33	27	5	3
August	30	30	30	4	4
September	30	30	28	9	1
October	31	31	31	3	3
November	35	24	32	7	2

1977

	Con	Lab	SNP	Lib	SLP
January	29	28	33	6	4
January	28	33	30	6	2
February	32	29	31	5	3
March	27	27	36	5	3
April	31	28	31	6	2
May	26	33	35	4	1
June	31	28	32	6	2
July	26	32	33	5	3
August	30	29	32	5	4
September	32	31	28	6	2
October	30	36	26	6	2
November	27	35	30	5	3

1978

	Con	Lab	SNP	Lib	SLP
January	28	34	29	6	3
January	28	38	27	5	2
March	30	35	27	5	2
March	29	38	27	4	2
April	24	47	24	3	2
May	27	47	20	4	1
June	26	47	22	4	1
July	30	48	18	4	-
August	24	52	18	3	3
September	27	48	19	4	1
October	23	53	21	3	2
November	25	48	21	4	2

1979

	Con	Lab	SNP	Lib	SLP
January	31	45	20	2	2
January	31	40	23	4	1
February	37	40	18	4	1
March	29	45	19	6	2
April	30	42	17	11	-
Election May 1979	*31*	*42*	*17*	*9*	*1*
June	21	53	17	7	2
July	29	47	12	8	3
August	23	54	16	6	1
September	25	51	13	9	1
October	31	42	17	9	1
November	22	53	15	8	2

1980

	Con	Lab	SNP	Lib	SLP
January	24	51	17	8	1
January	24	51	11	8	-
February	27	49	14	10	-
March	29	46	14	10	-
April	24	53	16	7	-
May	23	53	15	8	-
June	22	52	15	9	-
July	21	53	17	8	-
August	20	57	14	9	-
September	19	59	15	7	-
October	21	54	15	10	-
November	18	56	16	9	-

1981

	Con	Lab	SNP	Lib	SLP
January	19	47	18	13	-
February	16	54	17	9	-
March	17	46	22	10	-
April	15	51	19	11	-
May	18	51	18	11	-
June	15	55	18	9	-
July	18	51	18	9	-
August	17	51	19	9	-
September*	15	52	17	16	-
October	14	42	21	22	-
November	15	40	17	27	-

* formation of Liberal–SDP Alliance

1982

	Con	Lab	SNP	Alliance
January	18	38	19	25
January	20	40	14	25
February	17	46	18	18
March	19	39	19	23
April	23	42	15	20
May	25	46	15	14
June	27	43	14	16
July	22	44	16	17
August	24	42	18	16
September	20	48	14	18
October	26	46	16	12
November	28	45	11	14

1983

	Con	Lab	SNP	Alliance
January	30	45	15	11
January	30	47	12	11
February	22	47	13	18
March	25	49	13	14
April	25	48	10	15
May	32	44	12	12
May	32	40	12	16
June	26	40	11	23
Election June 1983	*28*	*35*	*12*	*25*
June	25	40	11	24
July	27	40	13	18
August	27	40	11	22
September	25	42	10	23
October	27	47	11	15
November	25	48	11	14

1984

	Con	Lab	SNP	Alliance
January	23	49	11	16
January	24	48	11	17
February	23	51	12	13
March	19	58	10	12
April	22	53	12	14
May	22	52	12	14
June	21	49	12	17
July	19	54	14	13
August	23	50	12	14
September	22	44	15	18
October	26	47	11	15
November	26	46	13	15

1985

	Con	Lab	SNP	Alliance
January	24	46	14	16
January	26	44	14	16
February	19	47	14	20
March	20	45	14	21
April	17	50	14	18
May	17	50	12	22
June	15	52	13	19
July	17	47	12	24
August	15	47	15	24
September	18	41	13	28
October	22	45	12	21
November	19	42	15	22

1986

	Con	Lab	SNP	Alliance
January	15	46	16	23
January	14	46	17	22
February	16	44	16	24
March	14	47	16	23
April	20	45	15	20
May	17	49	14	20
June	19	44	17	19
July	21	44	15	21
August	15	47	15	22
September	16	50	18	16
October	22	52	13	13
November	19	49	18	14

1987

	Con	Lab	SNP	Alliance
January	19	50	15	16
January	19	48	13	21
February	19	50	11	20
March	18	42	14	25
April	21	42	13	23
May	19	45	17	19
Election June 1987	*24*	*42*	*14*	*19*
June	21	49	15	15
July	19	53	14	14
August	24	48	12	15
September	23	50	14	12
October	22	50	12	15
November	23	45	16	16

1988

	Con	Lab	SNP	LD	SDP	Alliance
January	23	49	15	-	-	12
January	22	48	16	-	-	13
February	18	51	18	-	-	13
March	23	48	18	8	2	-
April	22	49	21	6	2	-
May	22	46	22	6	3	-
June	25	40	23	8	3	-
July	25	44	22	6	1	-
August	23	49	21	2	3	-
September	23	47	19	6	4	-
October	23	45	20	8	3	-
November	21	39	30	7	2	-

1989-90

	Con	Lab	SNP	SLD	SDP	Green
January	20	36	32	7	3	-
January	20	41	28	8	2	-
February	20	41	27	8	3	-
March	20	41	27	7	3	-
April	19	42	27	8	3	-
May	21	47	25	5	1	-
June	19	46	24	5	1	-
July	21	45	22	6	2	4
August	16	48	22	5	2	7
September	19	48	18	7	2	6
October	18	55	17	5	1	3
November	21	49	20	5	2	4

1990

	Con	Lab	SNP	SLD*	SDP	Green
January	16	50	21	6	1	5
January	21	48	18	6	2	3
February	21	52	17	5	1	3
March	15	54	20	7	-	4
April	19	49	20	8	1	3
May-	17	49	23	5	2	3
June	19	48	23	6		4
July	19	52	20	4		4
August	22	49	20	5		3
September	19	42	24	10		3
October	16	48	24	9		3
November	24	43	23	7		3

* in June 1990 the Social and Liberal Democrats became the Liberal Democrats

1991

	Con	Lab	SNP	LD	Green
January	21	45	23	9	2
January	30	44	18	7	2
February	23	46	22	6	3
March	23	42	22	10	2
April	27	42	18	11	2
May	23	44	20	11	2
June	25	46	16	9	3
July	24	46	20	8	2
August	25	45	19	8	2
September	24	43	23	9	1
October	23	41	24	10	2
November	18	44	23	13	2

1992

	Con	Lab	SNP	LD	Green
January	21	47	21	11	1
January	23	38	26	11	2
February	22	38	28	10	1
March	22	44	26	7	1
April	21	41	24	13	1
Election April 1992	*26*	*39*	*21*	*13*	*1*
May	27	36	25	12	1
June	26	39	23	10	2
July	24	44	22	8	1
August	25	44	22	8	1
September	23	46	20	10	1
October	20	42	27	10	1
November	20	47	23	9	1
December	18	48	22	10	1

1993

	Con	Lab	SNP	LD	Green
January	23	44	23	8	1
February	18	43	26	11	1
March	17	49	22	11	1
April	21	47	21	9	1
May	16	44	22	17	1
June	16	45	23	16	1
July	16	46	25	12	1
August	17	45	24	13	1
September	15	45	24	16	1
October	17	43	24	15	1
November	14	48	25	12	1
December	15	47	23	14	1

1994

	Con	Lab	SNP	LD	Green
January	15	47	23	14	1
February	16	47	22	14	1
March	13	47	25	14	1
April	13	46	26	14	1
May	14	44	27	14	1
June	10	53	24	12	1
July	12	46	30	11	1
August	12	51	27	9	1
September	12	55	24	8	-
October	11	51	29	9	3
November	13	47	27	10	-
December	12	55	25	8	1

1995

	Con	Lab	SNP	LD	Green
January	11	57	22	9	1
February	12	54	23	10	-
March	11	52	25	10	1
April	11	53	25	9	1
May	13	52	22	12	1
June	11	53	27	9	1
July	11	57	23	8	-
August	12	54	22	11	1
September	12	52	26	8	1
October	13	46	30	11	1
November	13	52	23	10	1
December	13	57	21	8	1

1996

	Con	Lab	SNP	LD	Green
January	11	53	23	11	1
February	12	52	23	10	1
March	12	53	23	9	-
April	13	54	23	10	1
May	13	53	23	9	1
June	12	54	24	8	-
July	15	51	25	9	1
August	15	51	23	10	1
September	15	48	29	7	1
October	13	49	24	12	1
November	11	55	23	8	1
December	12	53	24	10	1

1997

	Con	Lab	SNP	LD	Other
January	16	50	22	10	-
February	15	52	25	8	1
4-March	16	46	26	10	1
26-March	17	52	20	9	-
2-April	12	53	26	9	-
9-April	14	51	23	10	-
16-April	13	52	24	9	-
23-April	15	47	24	12	-
30-April	14	50	26	9	-
Election May 1997	*18*	*46*	*22*	*13*	*1*
May	9	57	23	10	1
June	12	54	23	10	1
July	10	54	24	9	1
August	14	50	25	11	1

cont'd

September	13	55	23	9	1
October	14	55	22	8	1
November	12	51	24	12	1
December	12	50	27	10	1

1998

	Con	Lab	SNP	LD	Other
January	11	50	25	12	1
February	14	46	28	11	2
March	12	48	28	9	2
April	14	44	30	11	1
May	14	46	29	10	1
June	14	43	33	9	1
July	13	48	28	8	2
August	13	46	31	8	1
September	13	45	31	10	1
October	14	43	29	12	1
November	13	42	31	13	2
December	13	46	28	11	2

1999

	Con	Lab	SNP	LD	Other
January	11	45	32	10	1
February	14	44	29	11	2
March	13	50	24	13	2
April	13	51	24	11	1
May	13	47	22	14	3
June	13	49	24	10	4
July	13	49	24	11	2
August	16	46	24	12	3
September	14	42	29	13	3
October	12	45	27	12	3
November	12	50	24	11	2

2000

	Con	Lab	SNP	LD	Other
Late January	14	49	24	11	2
February	15	45	27	11	3
March	16	40	29	11	3
April	17	44	26	9	3
May	14	48	24	10	4
June	17	39	31	11	3
July	15	46	26	9	4
August	15	45	28	9	3
September	15	33	33	17	2
October	13	48	27	10	2
November	16	48	24	9	3

2001

	Con	Lab	SNP	LD	SSP	Other
Early January	13	46	28	9	n/a	3
Late January	13	46	28	11	n/a	2
February	16	45	29	9	n/a	2
March	12	52	25	8	n/a	3
April	15	47	27	9	n/a	3
May	13	47	26	11	3	1
Election June 2001	*16*	*44*	*20*	*16*	*3*	*1*
June	11	50	24	12	2	1
July	13	44	21	15	4	2
August	13	49	21	12	3	1
September	13	52	20	11	3	1
October	9	54	23	10	2	1
November	14	47	25	10	2	1

2002

	Con	Lab	SNP	LD	SSP	Other
Early January	15	46	23	12	3	2
Late January	12	47	24	13	3	1
February	13	46	24	12	2	2
March	14	41	26	15	2	1
April	14	47	21	14	2	2
May	13	49	21	13	4	1
June	15	46	23	11	3	2
July	13	49	21	10	5	2
August	14	46	23	13	2	2
September	11	47	21	15	3	3
October	13	45	22	16	3	2
November	12	43	25	15	4	1

2003

	Con	Lab	SNP	LD	SSP	Other
January	12	45	24	14	3	3
February	14	42	25	15	1	2
March	12	42	25	15	4	2
April	13	38	25	17	4	4
May	13	45	22	13	4	3
June	13	41	22	15	5	3
July	14	40	20	17	6	3
August	15	40	24	14	4	3
September	13	41	24	14	4	4
October	12	39	24	18	4	2
November	13	43	22	18	3	2
December	17	42	24	12	4	1

Scottish Executive Ministers since 1999

As of April 2004, there have been four distinct Scottish Executive administrations, headed by three First Ministers, Donald Dewar, Henry McLeish and Jack McConnell. A total of 39 Scottish Executive ministers have been in office since May 1999, six of whom are no longer MSPs and ten of whom remain backbenchers. Of the total, 29 have been Labour MSPs, six have been Lib Dem MSPs, and there have been four law officers.

Scottish Executive Cabinet appointed 20 May 2003

First Minister: Jack McConnell
Deputy First Minister and Minister for Enterprise and Lifelong Learning: Jim Wallace
Minister for Justice: Cathy Jamieson
Minister for Health and Community Care: Malcolm Chisholm
Minister for Education and Young People: Peter Peacock
Minister for Finance and Public Services: Andy Kerr
Minister for Environment and Rural Development: Ross Finnie
Minister for Communities: Margaret Curran
Minister for Parliamentary Business: Patricia Ferguson
Minister for Tourism, Culture and Sport: Frank McAveety
Minister for Transport: Nicol Stephen

Deputy Ministers
Deputy Minister for Enterprise and Lifelong Learning: Lewis Macdonald
Deputy Justice Minister: Hugh Henry
Deputy Minister for Health and Community Care: Tom McCabe
Deputy minister for Education and Young People: Euan Robson
Deputy Minister for Environment and Rural Development: Allan Wilson
Deputy Minister for Communities: Mary Mulligan
Deputy Minister for Finance, Public Services and Parliamentary Business: Tavish Scott

Law Officers
Lord Advocate: Colin Boyd QC
Solicitor General: Elish Angiolini QC

Scottish Executive Cabinet appointed 27 November 2001

First Minister: Jack McConnell
Deputy First Minister and Minister for Justice: Jim Wallace

Minister for Education and Young People: Cathy Jamieson
Minister for Enterprise, Transport, and Lifelong Learning: Wendy Alexander (Iain Gray from May 2002)
Minister for Environment and Rural Development: Ross Finnie
Minister for Tourism, Culture, and Sport: Mike Watson
Minister for Social Justice: Iain Gray (Margaret Curran from May 2002)
Minister for Finance and Public Services: Andy Kerr
Minister for Health and Community Care: Malcolm Chisholm
Minister for Parliamentary Business: Patricia Ferguson

Deputy Ministers
Deputy Minister for Justice: Richard Simpson (from November 2002 Hugh Henry)
Deputy Minister for Education and Young People: Nicol Stephen
Deputy Minister for Enterprise, Transport, Lifelong Learning: Lewis Macdonald
Deputy Minister for Environment and Rural Development: Allan Wilson
Deputy Minister for Tourism, Culture, and Sport: Elaine Murray
Deputy Minister for Social Justice: Margaret Curran (from November 2002 Des McNulty)
Deputy Minister for Finance and Public Services: Peter Peacock
Deputy Ministers for Health and Community Care: Hugh Henry and Mary Mulligan (from November 2002 Mary Mulligan and Frank McAveety)
Deputy Minister for Parliamentary Business: Euan Robson

Law Officers
Lord Advocate: Colin Boyd QC
Solicitor General: Elish Angiolini QC

Scottish Executive Cabinet appointed 29 October 2000

First Minister: Henry McLeish
Deputy First Minister and Minister for Justice: Jim Wallace
Minister for Finance and Local Government: Angus MacKay
Minister for Health and Community Care: Susan Deacon
Minister for Social Justice: Jackie Baillie
Minister for Transport and Planning: Sarah Boyack
Minister for Enterprise and Life-long Learning: Wendy Alexander
Minister for Rural Affairs: Ross Finnie (including environment from March 2001)
Minister for Education, Europe and External Affairs: Jack McConnell
Minister for Parliament: Tom McCabe
Minister for the Environment, Sport and Culture: Sam Galbraith (until March 2001)

Deputy Ministers
Deputy Minister for Justice: Iain Gray
Deputy Minister for Health and Community Care: Malcolm Chisholm
Deputy Minister for Enterprise and Life-long Learning, and Gaelic: Alasdair Morrison
Deputy Minister for Social Justice: Margaret Curran

Deputy Minister for Rural Development: Rhona Brankin
Deputy Minister for Education, Europe and External Affairs: Nicol Stephen
Deputy Minister for Sport and Culture: Allan Wilson
Deputy Minister for Finance and Local Government: Peter Peacock
Deputy Minister for Parliament: Tavish Scott (from March 2001 Euan Robson)
Deputy Minister for Transport and Planning (from March 2001): Lewis Macdonald

Law Officers
Lord Advocate: Colin Boyd QC
Deputy to Lord Advocate: Neil Davidson QC

Scottish Executive: appointed 16 May 1999

First Minister: Donald Dewar
Deputy First Minister and Minister for Justice: Jim Wallace
Finance Minister: Jack McConnell
Minister for Health and Community Care: Susan Deacon
Minister for Communities (Local Government, Housing and Social Inclusion): Wendy Alexander
Minister for Transport and the Environment: Sarah Boyack
Minister for Enterprise and Life-long Learning: Henry McLeish
Minister for Rural Affairs: Ross Finnie
Minister for Children and Education (Culture, Arts and Sports): Sam Galbraith
Business Manager and Chief Whip: Tom McCabe

Deputy Ministers
Deputy Minister for Justice: Angus MacKay
Deputy Minister for Health and Community Care: Iain Gray
Deputy Minister for Enterprise and Life-long Learning: Nicol Stephen
Deputy Minister for Enterprise and Life-long Learning, the Highlands and Islands and Gaelic: Alasdair Morrison
Deputy Minister for Communities (Local Government): Frank McAveety
Deputy Minister for Communities (Social Inclusion, Equality and the Voluntary Sector): Jackie Baillie
Deputy Minister for Rural Affairs (Fisheries): John Home Robertson
Deputy Minister for Children and Education: Peter Peacock
Deputy Minister for Children and Education (Culture, Arts and Sports): Rhona Brankin
Deputy Business Manager: Iain Smith

Law Officers
Lord Advocate: Lord Hardie QC (from February 2000 Colin Boyd QC)
Solicitor General: Colin Boyd QC (from February 2000 Neil Davidson QC)

Secretaries of State for Scotland since 1885[*]

The Duke of Richmond and Gordon (Conservative)	1885
Sir George Trevelyan (Liberal)	1886
The Earl of Dalhousie (Liberal)	1886
Arthur Balfour (Conservative)	1886–7
The Marquess of Lothian (Conservative)	1887–92
Sir George Trevelyan (Liberal)	1892–5
Lord Balfour of Burleigh (Conservative)	1895–1903
Andrew Graham Murray (Conservative)	1903–5
The Marquess of Linlithgow (Conservative)	1905
John Sinclair (Liberal)	1905–12
Thomas MacKinnon Wood (Liberal)	1912–16
Harold John Tennant (Coalition)	1916
Robert Munro (Coalition)	1916–22
Viscount Novar (Conservative)	1922–4
William Adamson (Labour)	1924
Sir John Gilmour (Conservative)	1924–9
William Adamson (Labour)	1929–31
Sir Archibald Sinclair (National Government)	1931–2
Sir Godfrey Collins (National Government)	1932–6
Walter Elliot (National Government)	1936–8
John Colville (National Government)	1938–40
Ernest Brown (Coalition)	1940–1
Thomas Johnston (Coalition)	1941–5
Earl of Rosebery (Caretaker)	1945
Joseph Westwood (Labour)	1945–7
Arthur Woodburn (Labour)	1947–50
Hector McNeil (Labour)	1950–1
James Stuart (Conservative)	1951–7
John Maclay (Conservative)	1957–62
Michael Noble (Conservative)	1962–4
William Ross (Labour)	1964–70
Gordon Campbell (Conservative)	1970–4
William Ross (Labour)	1974–6
Bruce Millan (Labour)	1976–9
George Younger (Conservative)	1979–86
Malcolm Rifkind (Conservative)	1986–90
Ian Lang (Conservative)	1990–5
Michael Forsyth (Conservative)	1995–7
Donald Dewar (Labour)	1997–9
John Reid (Labour)	1999–2001
Helen Liddell (Labour)	2001–2003
Alistair Darling	2003–

[*]The post was known as the Scottish Secretary from 1885 to 1926, upon which it became known as the Secretary of State for Scotland.

Biographies of Prominent Scottish Politicians

No biographies of current Scottish politicians such as Gordon Brown, Alex Salmond or Charles Kennedy are carried in this section. For details of these and others, see listings under current constituencies. We have defined Scottish politicians in the broadest sense to include anyone who has contributed significantly to Scottish politics by standing for a Scottish constituency or representing one. Thus, we have included several non-Scottish politicians by birth, such as Winston Churchill and Roy Jenkins, who in long and successful careers, made a significant contribution either to Scottish politics or politics in Scotland.

Herbert Henry Asquith 1852–1928
Liberal MP for East Fife 1886–1918, Paisley 1920–24. Home Secretary 1892–95, Chancellor of the Exchequer 1905–08, Prime Minister 1908–16, Leader of the Liberal Party 1908–26. Prime Minister of radical Liberal Government which introduced Lloyd George's 'people's budget' and faced a constitutional crisis with the House of Lords.

Duchess of Atholl 1874-1960
Conservative MP for Kinross and West Perthshire 1923-38, the first woman Scottish MP and first ever Conservative woman minister serving as Parliamentary Secretary to the Board of Education 1924-29. She became known as 'the Red Duchess' for her opposition to German rearmament, support of the Spanish Republic and opposition to Tory appeasement. She was deselected for daring to oppose Chamberlain's dismemberment of Czechoslovakia at Munich, resigned her seat which forced a by-election which she narrowly lost to the official Tory candidate.

Andrew Bonar Law 1858–1923
Conservative MP for Glasgow Blackfriars 1900–06, Dulwich 1906–10, Bootle 1911–18, Glasgow Central 1918–23. Prime Minister 1922–23, Leader of the Conservative Party 1911–23. Born in New Brunswick, Canada, he came to Glasgow at the age of 11. Briefly Prime Minister, he was leader of the Conservatives for over a decade, in opposition and in government, supporting the Lloyd George coalition.

Robert Boothby 1900–1986
Conservative MP for Aberdeenshire and Kincardineshire Eastern 1924–50, Aberdeenshire East 1950–58. Briefly Minister for Food 1940. Critic of appeasement in the 1930s and ally of Churchill. Well known for the independence of his opinions including opposition to the Suez War and support for European unity and homosexual law reform.

John Buchan 1875–1940
Conservative MP for the Scottish Universities 1927–35. President of the Scottish History Society 1929–32, Governor-General of Canada 1935–40, Chancellor of Edinburgh University 1937. A celebrated writer, Buchan wrote over fifty books in his life, including the spy thrillers featuring Richard Hannay of which the most famous is *The Thirty-Nine Steps*.

Gordon Campbell 1921–
Conservative MP for Moray and Nairn 1959–February 1974. Secretary of State for Scotland in the Heath Government 1970–74. First post-war Secretary of State who was from the minority Scottish party. Defeated by Winnie Ewing in the February 1974 general election.

Henry Campbell-Bannerman 1839–1908
Liberal MP for Stirling Burghs 1868–1908. Prime Minister 1905–08, Leader of the Liberal Party in the Commons 1899–1908. Presided over the Liberal landslide of 1906. His government included such talents as Asquith, Churchill and Lloyd George. He died two weeks after resigning through ill-health.

Winston Churchill 1874–1965
Liberal MP for Dundee 1908–22. Also Conservative MP for Oldham 1900–04, Liberal MP for Oldham 1904–06, for Manchester North West 1906–08, Conservative for Epping 1924–45, for Woodford 1945–64. British Prime Minister 1940–45 and 1951–55, previously in Liberal Government as President of the Board of Trade, Home Secretary and First Lord of the Admiralty. As a Liberal, Churchill was defeated in Dundee by Edwin Scrymgeour, before rejoining the Conservatives and becoming a critic of appeasement in the 1930s.

Donald Dewar 1937–2000
Labour MP for Aberdeen South 1966–70, Glasgow Garscadden 1978–97, Glasgow Anniesland 1997–2000, MSP for Glasgow Anniesland 1999–2000. Shadow Secretary of State for Scotland 1983–92, Shadow Social Security Spokesman 1992–95, Shadow Chief Whip 1995–97, Secretary of State for Scotland 1997–99, First Minister 1999–2000. In office, post-1997, he oversaw the successful referendum campaign and the passing of the Scotland Act 1998. He subsequently became First Minister and formed a Labour-Lib Dem administration. He died in office in October 2000.

Walter Elliot 1888–1958
Conservative MP for Lanark 1918–23, Glasgow Kelvingrove 1924–45, Scottish Universities 1946–50, Glasgow Kelvingrove 1950–58. Leading Scottish Tory politician, Secretary of State for Scotland 1936–38 and author of *Toryism and the Twentieth Century* published in 1927. A moderate, thoughtful Conservative, he presided as Secretary of State over the development of administrative devolution and the shift of the Scottish Office to Edinburgh from London.

Winnie Ewing 1929–
SNP MP for Hamilton 1967-70, MEP for Highlands and Islands 1979-99, MSP for Highlands and Islands 1999-2003. Ewing's victory at Hamilton in 1967 gave birth to the modern SNP, while as a long-standing Europhile she became known as 'Madam Ecosse'. Elected to the Scottish Parliament in 1999, she enjoyed a defining moment when as its oldest member she opened it with the words, 'The Scottish Parliament, hereby adjourned on March 25th 1707, is hereby reconvened.'

Nicholas Fairbairn 1933–1995
Conservative MP, Kinross and West Perthshire, October 1974–83, Perth and Kinross 1983–95. Flamboyant Conservative MP and character. Solicitor General for Scotland 1979–82 who was forced to resign after making remarks on a Glasgow rape trial. The first volume of his autobiography called *A Life is Too Short* was published in 1987.

Michael Forsyth 1954–
Conservative MP for Stirling 1983–97 and Secretary of State for Scotland 1995–97. Tory right-winger and one time ally of Margaret Thatcher. Westminster City Councillor 1978–83, Chairman of the Scottish Tories 1989–90, (where he famously fell out with Malcolm Rifkind and had to be moved by Thatcher), Minister of State at the Scottish Office 1990–92, Employment Minister 1992–94, Home Office Minister 1994–95. A supporter of privatisation and the poll tax, he invented the term 'tartan tax' to describe Labour's plans for a Scottish Parliament with tax powers.

Willie Gallacher 1881–1965

Communist MP for West Fife 1935–50. Leader of 'Red Clydeside' shop stewards' movement during the First World War. Helped establish Communist Party of Great Britain and as MP for East Fife was the longest serving Communist MP in UK politics. President of the Communist Party from 1956–63. His book *Revolt on the Clyde*, first published in 1936, significantly contributed to the myth of 'Red Clydeside'.

Andrew Dewar Gibb 1888–1974

One of the founders of the Scottish Party in 1932, a right-wing pressure group which stressed that Scottish home rule could strengthen the Union and Empire. It combined with the National Party of Scotland to lead to the establishment of the SNP in 1934. An expert on Scots law and Professor at Glasgow University, he was Chairman of the SNP from 1936–40 and was subsequently heavily involved in the Scottish Convention. He was Chair of the Saltire Society from 1955–7.

Jo Grimond 1913–93

Liberal MP for Orkney and Shetland 1950–83. Leader of the Liberal Party 1956–67, Grimond saved the Liberal Party from near political extinction in the 1950s. He attempted to position the party as the non-socialist radical alternative to the Conservatives.

Keir Hardie 1856–1915

Independent Labour MP for West Ham South 1892–5, Labour for Merthyr Tydfil 1900–15. First Scottish Labour candidate who stood in the 1888 Mid-Lanark by-election, founder and Chair of the Independent Labour Party 1893–1900 and 1913–14. A supporter of independent Labour representation, he lost his seat due to his opposition to the Boer War. He was Chair of the International Socialist Bureau in 1914 when the idealism of socialist internationalism was broken by the power of nationalist patriotism; the events of 1914 clearly broke Hardie and he died the following year.

Margaret 'Peggy' Herbison 1907–96

Labour MP for Lanarkshire North 1945–79 and the first woman Scottish Office minister from 1950–51. She became Minister for Pensions in the 1964 Wilson Government and was a supporter of wage-related benefits and increasing family allowances who was blocked by the Treasury. She resigned in 1967 over government moves to means testing, but remained a staunch Labour loyalist, mentoring John Smith, who became the local MP in 1970, and later, Helen Liddell.

Alec Douglas Home 1903–1995

Conservative MP for Lanark 1931–45 and 1950–1, Kinross and West Perthshire 1963–October 1974. Minister of State at the Scottish Office 1951–55, Commonwealth Relations Secretary 1955–60, Leader of the House of Lords 1957–60, Foreign Secretary 1960–63. Made 14th Earl Home 1951, renounced peerage 1963, Prime Minister 1963–64, Leader of the Conservatives 1963–65, Foreign Secretary 1970–74. Started political career in the 1930s as Chamberlain's Private Parliamentary Secretary, succeeded Macmillan as Prime Minister and lost 1964 election to Wilson by the narrowest of margins.

Roy Jenkins 1918–2003

Social Democratic MP for Glasgow Hillhead 1982–7. Also Labour MP for Central Southwark 1948–50, Birmingham Stechford 1950–76. Minister in 1964–70 and 1974–6 Labour Governments, President of European Commission 1977–81, Leader of the Social Democratic Party 1982–3, leader of Liberal Democrat Peers 1987–97. A major figure of the centre-left in the 20th century, who attempted by creating the SDP to 'break the mould' of British politics, an objective he continued to pursue with his chairmanship of the Jenkins Commission on electoral reform in 1998.

Tom Johnston 1881–1965
Labour MP for Stirlingshire West 1922–24, 1929–31, 1935–45, Dundee 1924–29. Secretary of State for Scotland 1941–45 in Churchill's wartime coalition. He is noted for building economic and social consensus amongst the key institutions and players. He was a member of the Independent Labour Party and editor of Forward, the socialist journal from 1906–33. In 1945, he became Chair of the North of Scotland Hydro-Electric Board. His publications include *Our Scottish Noble Families*, published in 1909, which was a savage critique of the Scots aristocracy and nobility, *The History of the Working Classes in Scotland*, published in 1923, and his autobiography *Memories* which came out in 1952.

David Kirkwood 1872–1955
Labour MP for Dumbarton Burghs, 1922–50, East Dunbartonshire 1950–51. One of the leading 'Red Clydesiders', prominent in the Clyde Workers Committee in 1915–16, and elected to Glasgow Town Council and Westminster in 1922. He quickly moderated his views upon election to Westminster, became Baron Kirkwood in 1951 and his autobiography 'My Life of Revolt' published in 1935 contained an introduction by Winston Churchill.

Ian Lang 1940–
Conservative MP for Galloway 1979–83, Galloway and Upper Nithsdale 1983–97. Lloyds insurance underwriter before entering Parliament. Minister of State for Scotland 1987–90, Secretary of State for Scotland 1990–95, Trade Secretary 1995–97. Lang, a moderate Tory, was Secretary of State in John Major's administration and after the 1992 election attempted to introduce a more sensitive unionism to resist devolution.

Jennie Lee 1904–88
Labour MP for North Lanarkshire 1929–31, Cannock 1945–70. Minister for the Arts 1965–70. Well-known socialist and women's rights campaigner, she was married to Nye Bevan, leader of the Labour left in the 1940s and 1950s. As Arts Minister she presided over increased arts spending and the establishment of the Open University. She wrote her autobiography *My Life with Nye*, published in 1980.

John MacCormick 1904–61
One of the founders of the National Party of Scotland in 1928 which became the SNP in 1934. Party Secretary of the SNP 1934–42, Chairman of the Scottish Convention and National Assembly, which he left the SNP to establish. He stood in the Paisley by-election in 1948 on a pro-home rule ticket with National Liberal and Tory support, nearly defeating Labour and organised the Scottish Covenant in 1949. His autobiography on the home rule movement, *The Flag in the Wind* was published in 1955.

Ramsay MacDonald 1866–1937
Labour MP for Leicester 1906–18, Aberavon 1922–29, Seaham 1929–31, National Labour MP for Seaham 1931–35, Scottish Universities 1936–37. Born in Lossiemouth, Labour Prime Minister 1924 and 1929–31, head of the National Government 1931–35, Leader of the Labour Party 1922–31. MacDonald was the first Labour Prime Minister in 1924. In his second administration, he reacted to the financial crisis of 1931 by forming a National Government and leaving Labour. He was never forgiven for what was seen in many Labour circles as an act of treachery.

Robert McIntyre 1913–98
McIntyre became the first ever SNP MP when he won Motherwell in a by-election in April 1945 and held it for three months. One of the pivotal figures of the post-war SNP developing them organisationally and politically into a modern credible party. Chairman of the SNP 1948–56 when he wrote the party's new policy document in 1948, he was also President of the SNP 1956–80 and Provost of Stirling 1967–75.

John P. Mackintosh 1929–78
Labour MP for Berwick and Lothian 1966–February 1974, October 1974–8. Academic at Glasgow and Strathclyde Universities before election as an MP. Leading Labour right-wing thinker on social democracy, modernising government and devolution. Author of numerous books on British politics and government including *The British Cabinet* (1962), *The Devolution of Power* (1968) and the posthumous *Mackintosh on Scotland* (1982). His premature death in 1978 was a major loss to Scottish Labour.

John Maclean 1879–1923
A member of the British Socialist Party before the First World War, he became Soviet Consul on the Clyde after 1917. Refused to join the Communist Party and set up the Scottish Workers' Party which combined communism and nationalism. Contested Glasgow Gorbals in 1918 and 1922 unsuccessfully. He died in 1923 while campaigning on the hustings in the Gorbals.

Henry McLeish 1948-
Labour MP for Fife Central 1987-2001, MSP 1999-2003. Leader of Fife Regional Council 1982-87, Minister for State in the Scottish Office 1997-99, Minister for Enterprise and Lifelong Learning in the Scottish Executive 1999-2000, First Minister 2000-2001. McLeish became First Minister in October 2000, following Donald Dewar's death, and developed policies and a political style distinctive from Labour at Westminster, particularly on free care for the elderly. He was forced to resign one year into office over the 'Officegate' affair which centred on financial irregularities in his constituency office.

James Maxton 1885–1946
Labour MP for Glasgow Bridgeton 1922–32, Independent Labour, Glasgow Bridgeton 1932–46. One of the most inspiring leaders of the 'Red Clydesiders' and recognised across the political divide as one of the talents on Labour's benches. Churchill called him 'the greatest gentleman', he was Chair of the Independent Labour Party from 1926–31 and 1934–9, drew up the Cook/Maxton manifesto in 1928 to win Labour to radical policies and led the ILP split in 1932. Gordon Brown wrote his biography.

Bruce Millan 1927–
Labour MP for Glasgow Craigton 1959–83, Glasgow Govan 1983–8, Secretary of State for Scotland 1976–9 helped steer the Scotland Act 1978 onto the statute books. Appointed European Commissioner in 1988. After Willie Ross, he articulated a more sensitive and convincing devolution policy and was also Shadow Secretary of State for Scotland from 1979–83.

Jimmy Reid 1932–
AEU trade unionist who led the Upper Clyde Shipworkers work-in in 1971, Rector of Glasgow University 1971–4. Reid contested East Dunbartonshire for the Communists in the 1974 elections, and stood in Dundee East for Labour in the 1979 election losing to the SNP. He is now a celebrated journalist and sworn critic of everything to do with the New Labour project.

Malcolm Rifkind 1946–
Conservative MP for Edinburgh Pentlands February 1974–97. Opposition frontbench spokesman on Scotland who resigned with Alick Buchanan-Smith in 1976 over Thatcher's U-turn on devolution. Scottish Office minister 1979–82, Foreign Office minister 1982–6, Secretary of State for Scotland 1986–90, Secretary of State for Transport 1990–2, Secretary of State for Defence 1992–5, Foreign Secretary 1995–7. Rifkind, a Conservative moderate, presided over a dramatic decline in Tory electoral fortunes in 1987 and oversaw the implementation of the widely despised poll tax. He contested Pentland unsuccessfully in 2001 and was adopted as prospective candidate for Kensington and Chelsea in February 2004.

George Robertson 1947–
Labour MP for Hamilton 1978–97, Hamilton South 1997–9. Shadow Spokesman on Foreign Affairs 1981–93, Shadow Scottish Secretary 1993–7, Defence Secretary 1997–9, Secretary General of NATO 1999–2003. As Shadow Scottish Secretary he oversaw Blair's u-turn on a referendum on devolution and was shifted to defence upon Labour's return to power in 1997.

Willie Ross 1911–88
Labour MP for Kilmarnock 1946–79. Secretary of State for Scotland 1964–70 and 1974–6. Ross was a passionate anti-devolutionist and known as 'the hammer of the Nats'. In office, he presided over Labour's minimal conversion to devolution in the 1970s, and was responsible for setting up the Highlands and Islands Development Board and the Scottish Development Agency.

Edwin Scrymgeour 1866–1947
Independent MP for Dundee 1922–31. Prohibitionist and independent socialist, founder of Scottish Prohibition Party in 1904, elected Dundee Town Council 1905, defeated Winston Churchill in 1922 and was elected until 1931 without Labour support.

Manny Shinwell 1884–1986
Labour MP for Linlithgowshire 1922–4, 1928–31, Seaham 1935–50, Easington 1950–70. Minister of Mines 1924, Minister of Fuel and Power 1946–7, Secretary of State for War 1947–50, Minister for Defence 1950–1. A leading 'Red Clydesider' and Minister in the first Labour Government, he defeating Ramsay MacDonald in the 1935 election. He was Chair of Labour's Policy Committee which drafted the 1945 manifesto and wrote three volumes of autobiographies, the last of which was *Lead with the Left*, published in 1981.

Jim Sillars 1937–
Labour MP, South Ayrshire 1970–76, Scottish Labour Party MP, South Ayrshire 1976–9, SNP MP, Glasgow Govan 1988–92. Once widely thought of as a potential future of Scottish Labour, in 1976 Sillars broke away and formed his own Scottish Labour Party over Labour's lukewarm attitude to devolution. He lost his seat in 1979 and joined the SNP in 1980, shaping their 'independence in Europe' policy before sensationally winning Govan in 1988, which he lost in 1992.

John Smith 1938–94
Labour MP for North Lanarkshire 1970–83, Monklands East 1983–94. Leader of the Labour Party 1992–4. Energy Minister 1974–5, Minister of State for Energy 1975–6, Minister for the Privy Council Office 1976–8, Secretary of State for Trade 1978–9. Widely respected Labour leader who combined conviction and determination with a quiet, unassuming manner. A Labour right-winger, he remained in the party after the SDP split in 1981, and as Labour leader after the 1992 election, achieved a massive Labour lead over the Conservatives following 'Black Wednesday'. A passionate supporter of devolution, he once famously described it as 'unfinished business'.

David Steel 1938–
Liberal and then Liberal Democrat MP for Roxburgh, Selkirk and Peebles from 1965-83 and Tweeddale, Ettrick and Lauderdale 1983-97, and then MSP for Lothians 1999-2003. Leader of the Liberal Party 1976-88, originator of the Lib-Lab Pact 1977-78 which propped up Jim Callaghan's failing Labour Government, and creator with Roy Jenkins of the Liberal-SDP Alliance in 1981. Steel was subsequently Joint Chair of the Scottish Constitutional Convention from 1989-95, and elected Presiding Officer of the Scottish Parliament 1999-2003.

Donald Stewart 1920–92
SNP MP for the Western Isles 1970–87. The first SNP victory at a general election, Stewart was parliamentary leader of the SNP at their high point of 1974–79. He had the difficult task of holding together a disparate political group and in 1979 tabled the no confidence motion which brought down the Labour Government after the inconclusive devolution referendum result.

John Strachey 1901-63
Labour MP for Dundee 1945–50, Dundee West 1950–63, previously Birmingham Aston 1929–31. Minister for Food 1946–50, Minister for War 1950–1. Leading Labour thinker who was a radical, Marxist voice in the 1930s and author of such texts as *The Coming Struggle for Power* written in 1932. In the 1950s, he shifted dramatically and wrote *Contemporary Capitalism* in 1956, a book which influenced the Croslandite-Gaitskellite social democratic revisionism of the party leadership.

Teddy Taylor1937-
Conservative MP for Glasgow Cathcart 1964-79, Southend East 1980-97, Rochford and Southend East from 1997 onward. Taylor was that rare breed – a right-wing, working class Scottish Tory MP and also Thatcher's choice for Secretary of State for Scotland, who lost his seat to Labour in 1979. He won Southend East the following year, and became one of the select band of Eurosceptic Tory MPs who contributed to John Major's administration from 1992 being unmanageable. This was not surprising for Taylor as he had first resigned from Ted Heath's Government over Europe in 1971. He hass announced that 2001 will be his last election.

John Wheatley 1869–1930
Labour MP, Glasgow Shettleston 1922–30. Leading figure of the 'Red Clydesiders'. Health Minister in the first Labour Government and responsible for passing the Housing (Financial Provisions) Act 1924 which aided the building of council houses. When Labour was returned in 1929 as a minority government, he felt they should not take office and was not offered any post by MacDonald.

Gordon Wilson 1938–
SNP MP for Dundee East February 1974–87. National Secretary of the SNP 1963–71, National Convener of the SNP 1979–90. As Secretary, he spearheaded the organisational modernisation of the party in the 1960s, and was at the forefront of developing the 'It's Scotland's Oil' campaign in the early seventies. As Convener of the party from 1979, Wilson resisted the rise of the left-wing '79 Group and emphasised a more conservative nationalist perspective.

Arthur Woodburn 1890–1978
Labour MP, Clackmannanshire and East Stirlingshire 1959–70. Parliamentary Private Secretary to Tom Johnston 1941–5, Secretary of State for Scotland 1947–50, Shadow Secretary of State 1951–9. As Attlee's longest serving Secretary of State, Woodburn had to counter the rise of the home rule movement at a time when Labour was growing increasingly sceptical. His 1948 White Paper on Scottish Affairs proposed only minor tinkering in Scotland's government.

George Younger 1931–2003
Conservative MP for Ayr 1964–92. Chairman of the Scottish Conservatives 1964–5, Secretary of State for Scotland 1979–86, Defence Secretary 1986–9. Withdrew in 1963 Kinross and West Perthshire by-election as Tory candidate to allow Alec Douglas-Home to stand. As Mrs. Thatcher's first and longest Secretary of State, Younger had an unenviable task reconciling two opposites, but presided over the continuation of a distinctive Scottish policy tradition.

A Chronology of Scottish Politics since 1945

12 April 1945
Robert McIntyre wins Motherwell by-election for the SNP from Labour with 51.4 per cent to Labour's 48.6 per cent. He is the first SNP MP.

17 April 1945
House of Commons vote 273-199 that Robert McIntyre is not allowed to take his seat as he does not have any sponsors. The next day he obtains two sponsors.

June 1945
Labour manifesto makes no commitment on devolution, but it is mentioned in Speakers Notes and by most Scottish Labour candidates.

5 July 1945
At the UK General Election Labour is returned with a majority of 146. Scottish Labour wins 47.6 per cent of the vote and 37 seats, to the Conservatives 41.1 per cent and 27 seats.

October 1945
Scottish Labour conference passes a Scottish Executive statement calling for an examination of home rule.

20 January 1946
Scottish Council (Development and Industry) established.

October 1946
Scottish Labour conference shows concern at the failure of the Anderson Committee – appointed 1945 – to make progress on home rule.

22 March 1947
The Scottish National Assembly is created by Scottish Convention. The cross-party Assembly is addressed by Willie Gallacher and John Gollan of the Communists, David Gibson of the ILP and Thomas Scollan, Labour MP. A committee is elected to draw up a detailed home rule plan within one year.

29 January 1948
Labour publishes a White Paper on Scottish Affairs calling for non-controversial bills to be dealt with by the Standing Committee on Scottish Bills and the establishment of a Scottish Economic Conference.

18 February 1948
John MacCormick stands in Paisley as a National candidate with Conservative and Liberal support; Labour win 56.8 per cent to the National 43.2 per cent.

21 March 1948

The Scottish National Assembly endorses a Blue Print for Scotland calling for a Parliament.

October 1948

The Scottish Labour conference sees critical resolutions withdrawn, after it is agreed that an inquiry into devolution will be included in the next election manifesto.

29 October 1948

Scottish National Assembly launches the National Covenant – a mass petition calling for a Scottish Parliament.

October 1949

The Scottish Labour conference passes 'Forward Scotland' – a statement on the Government's record and Scottish policy. It welcomes the recent White Paper as 'the maximum amount of Scottish control, consistent with full membership of the British Parliament'.

3 November 1949

Scottish Unionists issue 'Scottish Control of Scottish Affairs' which criticises the Labour Government's centralisation and proposes a Royal Commission on Scotland.

14 February 1950

Winston Churchill with just over a week to voting declared in an Usher Hall speech in Edinburgh that he would 'never adopt the view that Scotland should be forced into the serfdom of socialism as a result of a vote in the House of Commons.' This is seen as the Conservatives playing 'the Scottish card' against Labour centralisation.

23 February 1950

A Labour Government is returned with a sharply reduced majority of 5. In Scotland, Labour win 46.2 per cent of the vote and 37 seats, to the Conservatives 44.8 per cent and 31 seats.

April 1950

STUC General Council statement 'The Future of Scotland' passed emphasising the territorial unity of the United Kingdom. An amendment from the NUM supporting a Scottish Parliament is defeated by 243 votes to 78.

25 December 1950

The removal of the Stone of Destiny from Westminster Abbey by Scottish nationalists.

October 1951

The Scottish Labour conference calls for a Royal Commission on Home Rule.

25 October 1951

Conservatives returned with an overall majority of 17 despite Labour across the UK winning more votes. In Scotland, the Conservatives win 48.6 per cent of the vote to Labour's 47.9 per cent with both returning 35 MPs.

23 July 1952

The Catto Report, on economic links between Scotland and the UK is published and suggests that Scotland obtains more expenditure than it contributes income.

24 July 1954

The Royal Commission on Scottish Affairs is published, which proposes extra powers for the Scottish Office, and committee changes on Scottish law reform.

26 May 1955

Conservatives returned with an overall majority of 60 under Anthony Eden. In Scotland, the Conservatives win 50.1 per cent – the only time in post-war Scottish politics a party would win a majority of the popular vote – to Labour's 46.7 per cent. The Conservatives win 36 seats to Labour's 34.

March 1956

Gaitskell tells the Scottish Labour conference that Labour no longer supports devolution, while a resolution is passed instructing the Executive to examine issues relating to setting up a Scottish Parliament.

26 July 1956

Nasser, the Egyptian leader, announces the nationalisation of the Suez Canal.

31 October 1956

The Royal Air Force and French Air Force bomb the Suez Canal two days after Israel has attacked Egypt. Hugh Gaitskell condemns the action as the United Kingdom and France face widespread international condemnation.

19 January 1957

The Scottish Labour Executive opposes home rule on 'compelling economic grounds'.

25 March 1957

The European Economic Community (EEC) or 'Common Market' is formed by the Treaty of Rome. Six nations become members: France, West Germany, Italy, Belgium, Netherlands and Luxembourg. The United Kingdom refuses to join.

13/14 September 1958

A Scottish Labour special conference is held. An Executive report 'Scottish Government' says that Scottish problems are only solvable by British-wide solutions.

8 October 1959

Conservatives under Harold Macmillan returned for a third successive term with a majority of 100. Scotland swings to Labour, as the Conservatives win 47.2 per cent of the vote to Labour's 46.7 per cent, while Labour finish ahead in seats by 38 to 31.

10 November 1961

Labour win Glasgow Bridgeton with 54.6 per cent, to the Conservatives 20.7 per cent and SNP's 18.6 per cent.

21 November 1961

Publication of Scottish Council (Development and Industry) Toothill report on the Scottish economy.

14 June 1962

Tam Dalyell wins West Lothian for Labour with 50.8 per cent, while the SNP's William Wolfe achieves 23.3 per cent.

7 November 1963

Alex Douglas-Home wins the Kinross and West Perthshire by-election with 57.2 per cent as sitting Prime Minister. The Liberals secure second place with 19.5 per cent.

15 October 1964

Harold Wilson is returned with an overall majority of 4. Labour win 48.7 per cent of the vote to the Conservatives 40.6 per cent, and 43 seats to 24.

1965

The Highlands and Islands Development Board set up.

9 December 1965

The National Plan for Scotland published.

31 March 1966

Wilson is returned with an overall majority of 97. Scottish Labour win 49.9 per cent of the vote, its highest ever vote, and return 46 MPs to the Conservatives 20.

9 March 1967

Conservatives win Glasgow Pollok from Labour due to the rise in the SNP vote – Conservatives 36.9 per cent, Labour 31.2 per cent, SNP 28.2 per cent.

2 November 1967

Winnie Ewing wins Hamilton for the SNP with 46.0 per cent of the vote to Labour's 41.5 per cent.

18 November 1967

Callaghan devalues the pound from $2.80 to $2.40. The next day in a TV broadcast Harold Wilson says 'this does not mean the pound in your pocket has been devalued' to general anger and ridicule.

April 1968

The STUC at its Annual Congress sees Mick McGahey of the NUM move a motion supporting a Scottish Parliament declaring: 'The best nationalists in Scotland are represented in the STUC and the Scottish Labour movement'. The motion is remitted, while an anti-devolution motion is heavily defeated. General Council agree a compromise of a committee of inquiry to report back the following year.

18 May 1968

Ted Heath's 'Declaration of Perth' at the Scottish Conservative conference when he announces the setting up a committee under Sir Alec Douglas Home to look at devolution.

April 15 1969

Wilson sets up the Crowther Royal Commission to examine devolution.

April 1969

The STUC at its Annual Congress supports an interim report which outlines the case for a Scottish Parliament with legislative powers.

30 October 1969

The Glasgow Gorbals by-election is held by Labour with 53.4 per cent to the SNP's 25.0 per cent and Conservatives 18.6 per cent.

March 1970

The Scottish Labour document 'Scottish Government (Mark II)' opposes 'Eire style separatism' and 'Northern Irish style home rule'.

19 March 1970

At the South Ayrshire by-election, Labour's Jim Sillars is returned with 54 per cent to the Conservatives 25.6 per cent and SNP's 20.4 per cent.

20 March 1970

The Conservatives Scottish Constitutional Committee chaired by Alec Douglas-Home publishes its report *Scotland's Government* which recommends a directly elected Scottish Convention of 125 members.

May 1970

Scottish Labour's submission to Kilbrandon restates its 1958 decision and opposition to a Scottish Parliament.

18 June 1970

Ted Heath returned in general election with a majority of 30. In Scotland, Labour win 44.5 per cent of the vote and 44 MPs to the Conservatives 38.0 per cent and 23 MPs. The SNP win 11.4 per cent of the vote, winning the Western Isles, but fail to hold Hamilton.

30 July 1971

Upper Clyde Shipworkers occupation and work-in begins led by the AEU shop stewards Jimmy Reid and Jimmy Airlie.

16 August 1971

STUC hold a Special Recall Congress in support of the Upper Clyde Shipworkers work-in.

16 September 1971
Robert McIntyre wins 34.6 per cent of the vote for the SNP in the Stirling and Falkirk by-election.

September 1972
Launch of SNP 'It's Scotland's Oil' campaign.

1 January 1973
The United Kingdom along with the Republic of Ireland and Denmark joins the European Economic Community (EEC).

1 March 1973
Labour hold Dundee East with 32.7 per cent to the SNP's 30.1 per cent. Gordon Wilson campaigns effectively on the SNP slogan 'It's Scotland's Oil' and subsequently wins the seat in February 1974.

6-24 October 1973
The Arab-Israeli war leads to a quadrupling of oil prices by the Organisation of Petroleum Exporting Countries (OPEC).

30 October 1973
The Scottish Council of the Labour Party publishes 'Scotland and the UK' which rejects devolution.

31 October 1973
The Kilbrandon Commission publishes its report outlining the case for devolution.

8 November 1973
Margo MacDonald wins Glasgow Govan for the SNP, with 41.9 per cent of the vote, compared to Labour's 38.2 per cent.

F28 ebruary 1974
At the General Election, a Labour minority government is returned. Labour in Scotland win 36.6 per cent of the vote and 40 MPs, the Conservatives 32.9 per cent and 21 MPs, and the SNP 21.9 per cent and 7 MPs.

12 March 1974
Labour Government's Queen's Speech declares: 'My ministers and I will initiate discussions in Scotland . . . and bring forward proposals for consideration'. Harold Wilson, in reply to a question from Winnie Ewing states, 'we will publish a White Paper and a Bill'.

3 June 1974
The Green Paper, 'Devolution within the UK: Some Alternatives for Discussion' is published, outlining five devolution proposals based on Kilbrandon.

22 June 1974
The Scottish Executive of the Labour Party votes against all the proposals in 'Devolution within the UK' by 6:5, and by the same majority that 'constitutional tinkering does not make a meaningful contribution towards achieving socialist goals'.

24 July 1974
Labour's NEC supports legislative devolution and the call for a special conference of Scottish Labour.

17 August 1974
The Scottish Labour special conferences supports devolution 'within the context of the political and economic unity of the UK'.

7 September 1974
A White Paper proposes directly elected assemblies for Scotland and Wales.

10 October 1974
At the General Election, the first-ever Scottish Labour manifesto, 'Powerhouse Scotland', is delivered to every home, outlining Scottish Labour's proposals for an Assembly. Labour returned with an overall majority of 3. In Scotland, Labour win 36.3 per cent of the vote and 41 MPs, the SNP 30.4 per cent and 11 MPs, and the Conservatives 24.7 per cent and 16 MPs.

11 February 1975
Margaret Thatcher is elected leader of the Conservative Party.

21 March 1975
The Scottish Labour conference votes 353,000 to 341,000 against substantial economic powers for an Assembly.

5 June 1975
The United Kingdom votes by 67.2 per cent to 32.8 per cent to remain a member of the European Economic Community. Scotland votes 'yes' by the narrower margin of 58.4 per cent to 41.6 per cent. Shetland and the Western Isles are the only areas of Scotland to vote 'no'. The SNP, along with large parts of a split Labour Party campaign for a 'no' vote.

8 July 1975
The Scottish Development Agency (SDA) is set up.

22 November 1975
A White Paper, 'Our Changing Democracy', proposes a legislative assembly for Scotland, and an executive assembly for Wales.

18 January 1976
The Scottish Labour Party is launched by Jim Sillars and John Robertson.

1 August 1976
'Devolution to Scotland and Wales: Supplementary Statement' published giving more powers to the Assembly.

28 November 1976
The Scotland and Wales Bill is published.

1 December 1976

Alick Buchanan-Smith, Shadow Secretary of State for Scotland and Malcolm Rifkind, Scottish spokesman resign over the Shadow Cabinet's decision to oppose Labour's devolution proposals.

16 December 1976

The Scotland and Wales Bill is given a second reading, by 292 to 247 votes, after the government concedes the principle of referendums.

19 February 1977

The Government is defeated on a guillotine motion on the devolution bill by 312 to 283, with 22 Labour MPs voting against and 15 abstaining. The Bill cannot become law due to lack of time.

23 March 1977

Labour survive a no confidence motion by 322 to 298, after agreeing the Lib–Lab pact.

May 1977

SNP make substantial gains in council elections across Scotland, winning 27 per cent of the vote. Labour is left controlling five district councils.

4 May 1977

The Scottish Conservative conference agrees to oppose a directly elected Scottish Assembly.

14 November 1977

The Scotland Bill is given a second reading by 307 votes to 263.

16 November 1977

A guillotine motion on separate Scotland and Wales Bills is carried by 313 to 287.

25 January 1978

The 40 per cent amendment – which became known as 'the Cunningham amendment' because its main advocate was George Cunningham, Labour MP for Islington South and Finsbury – is passed against the Government's wishes by 168 votes to 142; five Scottish Labour MPs vote for it – Cook, Dalyell, Doig, Hamilton and Hughes.

January 27 1978

Helen Liddell issues a Scottish Labour circular stating that Labour will not become involved in any umbrella devolution organisation. At a subsequent press conference, Liddell states: 'We will not be soiling our hands by joining any umbrella Yes group.'

January 1978

Labour Vote No formed.

22 February 1978

The Scotland Bill is given a third reading by 297 votes to 257.

13 April 1978

Donald Dewar wins the Glasgow Garscadden by-election, with 45.4 per cent of the vote, to the SNP's 32.9 per cent.

May 1978

The SNP do worse than expected in regional elections, with Labour winning 39.6 per cent, the Conservatives 30.3 per cent and SNP 20.9 per cent.

31 May 1978

George Robertson wins the Hamilton by-election with 51 per cent to the SNP's 33.4 per cent.

30 July 1978

John Mackintosh, the Labour MP and advocate of devolution, dies.

31 July 1978

The Scotland and Wales Bills are enacted.

26 October 1978

Labour hold Berwick and East Lothian with 47.7 per cent to the Conservatives 40.2 per cent and SNP's 8.8 per cent.

1 November 1978

James Callaghan announces that both the Scottish and Welsh referendums will be held on March 1 1979.

3 January 1979

The 'winter of discontent' begins. Lorry drivers begin a national strike starting a month of national strike action by ambulance drivers, water and sewage workers, dustmen and gravediggers against the Labour Government's pay policy.

February 1979

Labour Movement Yes formed.

13 February 1979

Lord Home states that a 'no' vote in the referendum is not necessarily a vote against devolution, but Labour's current proposals and the Conservatives will produce a more powerful Assembly.

1 March 1979

In the Scottish devolution referendum, Scotland votes 32.9 per cent yes, 30.8 per cent no, with 36.3 per cent not voting, thus, failing by a substantial margin the 40 per cent threshold of the electorate. A majority of those who voted supported the Labour Government's proposals: 51.6 per cent to 48.4 per cent. The SNP had campaigned energetically for the proposals, and post-referendum analysis shows that SNP voters were the most heavily pro-devolution. On the same day, the Welsh devolution proposals are defeated by a margin of four to one, with 11.9 per cent in favour, 46.9 per cent against and 41.2 per cent not voting.

3 March 1979

The Scottish Labour Executive reaffirms its commitment to devolution, but stops short of calling for implementation of the Scotland Act, asking that the Government 'in reaching the decisions on how to proceed would do so on the basis of a continuing commitment to devolution'.

11 March 1979

At the Scottish Labour conference all emergency resolutions on devolution are withdrawn, leaving the Executive statement that devolution 'will remain at the forefront of the programme', and urging implementation of the Scotland Act. The Chair, Janey Buchan, refuses to call any pro-devolution MPs in the debate.

22 March 1979

Callaghan declines to set a date for a vote in order to repeal the Scotland Act, and asks for all-party talks as a delaying tactic. A motion of no confidence is tabled by the SNP.

28 March 1979

The Government is defeated on a motion of no confidence, by 311 votes to 310.

3 May 1979

Conservatives returned with a majority of 44. Scotland votes 41.5 per cent Labour, 31.4 per cent Conservative, as the SNP is reduced to 17.3 per cent of the vote, with two MPs.

7 June 1979

The Euro-elections see the Scottish Conservatives win 33.7 per cent and five Euro-seats, Labour 33 per cent and two Euro-seats, and the SNP with 19.4 per cent and one seat, as Winnie Ewing is returned for the Highlands and Islands.

20 June 1979

The Repeal of the Scotland Act is passed by 301 to 206, with six Scottish Labour MPs abstaining – Cook, Craigen, Dalyell, Hart, McMahon and Miller.

18 August 1979

The SNP left-wing pressure group, the '79 Group is established with the aim of 'independence, socialism and a Scottish Republic'.

1 March 1980

The Campaign for a Scottish Assembly is set up, aiming to establish a cross-party Convention. It is chaired by Jack Brand, and supported by five Scottish Labour MPs. James Milne, STUC General Secretary, and George Bolton, Vice-President of the NUM, speak at its launch.

March 1980

The Scottish Labour conference supports calls for a Scottish Assembly 'with meaningful powers over the economy of Scotland'. The Labour Co-ordinating Committee is set up to win more left-wing influence in Scottish Labour, with one aim being a higher commitment to a Scottish Parliament.

9 April 1980
Labour hold Glasgow Central, with 60.8 per cent of the vote, to the SNP's 26.3 per cent.

September 1980
Labour Campaign for a Scottish Assembly is formed, with George Foulkes as Chair, and the support of 15 Scottish Labour MPs.

11 February 1981
Peugeot-Citreon announce the closure of the Linwood car plant. Two days later the STUC launches an unsuccessful campaign to keep the plant open involving politicians, local authorities and business.

28 May 1981
The SNP annual conference supports civil disobedience against the Conservative Government. Jim Sillars, a leading exponent of what becomes known as 'the Scottish Resistance' is elected Vice-chairman for policy.

16 October 1981
Jim Sillars and five other SNP members break into and occupy Royal High School in Edinburgh, the proposed site of the Scottish Assembly, to protest against unemployment and Tory rule of Scotland.

15 February 1982
Scottish Grand Committee meets in the Royal High School, Edinburgh for the first time.

25 March 1982
The Social Democrats win Glasgow Hillhead from the Conservatives – 33.4 per cent to the Social Democrats, 26.6 per cent to the Conservatives, 25.9 per cent to Labour and 11.3 per cent to the SNP.

2 April 1982
Argentinean armed forces seize the Falkland Islands. The House of Commons sitting the next day in emergency session agrees to send a naval task force.

3–5 June 1982
SNP annual conference. Campaign for Nationalism set up by Winnie Ewing and others to assert a more traditionalist nationalism and oppose the '79 Group. Gordon Wilson proposes the proscribing of all internal party groups in a leadership attempt to take on the '79 Group.

24 June 1982
Tom Clarke wins Coatbridge and Airdrie for Labour with 55.1 per cent to the Conservatives 26.2 per cent and SNP's 10.5 per cent.

26 August 1982
SNP national council votes to expel seven leading '79 Group members.

2 December 1982
Helen McElhone wins Glasgow Queen's Park for Labour with 56 per cent to the SNP's 20 per cent.

March 1983
Scottish Labour Conference proposes a Scottish Parliament with tax raising and economic powers as part of the Alternative Economic Strategy. Helen Liddell tells the party they cannot affiliate to the Campaign for a Scottish Assembly.

9 June 1983
Conservatives returned for a second term at a UK level. Scotland sees Labour win 35.1 per cent and 41 seats to the Conservatives 28.4 per cent and 21 seats.

February 1984
Scottish Labour Executive agrees to allow party organisations to affiliate to the Campaign for a Scottish Assembly.

14 June 1984
Euro-elections in Scotland see Labour win 40.7 per cent of the vote to the Conservatives 25.7 per cent and SNP's 17.8 per cent. Labour win five of Scotland's eight Euro seats, making three gains from the Tories.

11 June 1987
Conservative third term. Labour wins 42.4 per cent in Scotland and 50 MPs to the Conservatives 24 per cent and 10 MPs.

August 1987
Labour Co-ordinating Committee (Scotland) conference on post-election strategies and the need for cross-party co-operation.

13 September 1987
STUC Festival for Scottish Democracy boycotted by SNP and Liberals.

November 1987
Scottish Labour special conference. Labour Executive proposes parliamentary representation of Labour's White Paper on an Assembly.

November 1987
Jim Ross suggests the Campaign for a Scottish Assembly invite a Constitutional Steering Committee to report on establishing a Constitutional Convention.

February 1988
Scottish Labour Action launched.

March 1988
Labour launches Stop It campaign on poll tax of delaying registration.

March 1988
Scottish Labour conference sees Neil Kinnock address conference without mentioning devolution. Kinnock later comments he had not mentioned many issues including 'environmental conditions in the Himalayas'.

13 July 1988
Steering Committee present 'A Claim of Right for Scotland'.

August 1988
Scottish Labour Executive votes by just one vote to undertake an internal consultation exercise on 'A Claim of Right' and rejects non-payment of the poll tax.

17 September 1988
Labour special conference rejects poll tax non-payment.

September 1988
SNP annual conference agrees to support poll tax non-payment and unveils its new 'independence in Europe' policy.

10 November 1988
Jim Sillars wins Glasgow Govan for the SNP with 48.8 per cent to Labour's 37 per cent.

12 November 1988
Scottish Labour Executive receives 25 out of 27 responses supporting involvement in the Scottish Constitutional Convention.

27 January 1989
SNP refuse to join Scottish Constitutional Convention.

March 1989
Donald Dewar, just before the Scottish Labour conference, talks of devolution as 'independence in the UK'.

March 1989
Scottish Labour conference sees debates on Scottish Labour Action 'dual mandate' and greater autonomy for the Scottish party referred back.

30 March 1989
First meeting of Scottish Constitutional Convention. Scottish Labour and Liberal Democrat MPs sign A Claim of Right.

1 April 1989
Poll Tax introduced in Scotland one year ahead of England and Wales.

15 June 1989
Euro elections see Labour in Scotland win 41.9 per cent to the SNP's 25.6 per cent and Conservatives 20.9 per cent as Labour win seven of the eight Euro seats and the SNP one. Labour hold Glasgow Central with 54.6 per cent to the SNP's 34.6 per cent.

July 1989
Scottish Enterprise and Highlands and Islands Enterprise established.

10 March 1990
Scottish Labour conference agrees to support an alternative electoral system to first past the post for the Scottish Parliament.

22 September 1990
Alex Salmond elected National Convener of the SNP defeating Margaret Ewing with 486 votes to her 186 votes.

4 October 1990
Dick Douglas, MP for Dunfermline West, joins the SNP.

22 November 1990
Margaret Thatcher resigns as Prime Minister.

27 November 1990
John Major becomes leader of the Conservatives and Prime Minister.

29 November 1990
Labour win Paisley North and South. In North, Labour wins 44 per cent to the SNP's 29.4 per cent, in South, 50.7 per cent to 23.3 per cent.

30 November 1990
Scottish Constitutional Convention publishes 'Towards Scotland's Parliament'.

March 1991
Scottish Labour conference votes by nearly two to one against a Labour Campaign for Electoral Success motion defending First-Past-the-Post for the Scottish Parliament.

21 March 1991
Abolition of poll tax announced.

7 November 1991
Liberal Democrats win Kincardine and Deeside from the Conservatives with 49 per cent to their 30.6 per cent. Conservatives reduced to 9 MPs and third party status in Scottish parliamentary representation.

8 January 1992

British Steel announce the closure of the Ravenscraig steel plant.

29 January 1992

Poll in the *Scotsman* puts support for independence at historic high of 50 per cent.

9 April 1992

Conservatives returned for a fourth term. Labour in Scotland win 39 per cent and 49 MPs to the Conservatives 25.6 per cent and 11 MPs.

10/11 April 1992

Formation of Scotland United, a cross-party pressure group supporting a multi-option referendum.

16 September 1992

'Black Wednesday'. Britain is forced out of the Exchange Rate Mechanism after Norman Lamont pushes interest rates up to 15 per cent and spends billions propping up the pound.

12 December 1992

Democracy demonstration in Edinburgh at the same time as John Major hosts a European Union summit. Largest ever home rule rally.

March 9 1993

Ian Lang publishes *Scotland in the Union: A Partnership for Good*, a result of the 'taking stock' exercise.

1994

Scottish Council of the Labour Party changes its name to the Scottish Labour Party.

22 March 1994

Strathclyde Regional Council ballot on water privatisation announced with 97.2 percent against privatisation on a 71.5 per cent turnout.

12 May 1994

John Smith, leader of the Labour Party, dies.

9 June 1994

Euro-elections see Labour win 42.5 per cent to the SNP's 32.6 per cent with the SNP winning North East Scotland from Labour.

30 June 1994

Helen Liddell holds Monklands East against the SNP with 49.8 per cent to the SNP's 45 per cent.

21 July 1994

Tony Blair elected leader of the Labour Party and John Prescott, deputy leader.

25 May 1995

Roseanna Cunningham wins Perth and Kinross for the SNP from the Conservatives with 40.4 per cent to Labour's 22.9 per cent and the Conservatives 21.4 per cent.

October 1995

Labour and Liberal Democrats agree electoral system for Scottish Parliament of 129 seats based on a broadly proportional system.

30 November 1995

Scottish Constitutional Convention proposals, 'Scotland's Parliament, Scotland's Right' published. Michael Forsyth unveils proposals for Scottish Grand Committee.

26 June 1996

Tony Blair announces a two question referendum on Scottish devolution.

31 August 1996

The Scottish Labour Executive support two referendums on a Scottish Parliament as a compromise, the first, the original two vote question and a second ballot, before the tax powers are ever used.

6 September 1996

George Robertson, Shadow Scottish Secretary overrules the Scottish Labour's Executive's two referendum policy and returns party policy to a two question referendum.

7 March 1997

Five prominent Labour left-wingers defeated in elections to the Scottish Labour Executive by the Blairite 'Network'.

4 April 1997

Tony Blair on the day of the launch of the Scottish Labour manifesto, in an interview compares the Scottish Parliament's proposed tax-varying powers with that of an English 'parish council'. Asked about the West Lothian Question he comments: 'Sovereignty resides with me as an English MP, and that's the way it will stay'.

1 May 1997

Tony Blair returned as Prime Minister with an overall majority of 179. Scottish Labour win 45.6 per cent of the vote and 56 seats, the SNP 22.1 per cent and 6 seats and the Lib Dems 13 per cent and 10 seats. The Conservatives lose their last remaining ten seats in Scotland despite winning 17.5 per cent of the vote.

15 May 1997

Referendums (Scotland and Wales) Bill published.

24 July 1997

'Scotland's Parliament' White Paper published.

31 July 1997
Referendums (Scotland and Wales) Act receives Royal Assent.

11 September 1997
Scottish referendum gives emphatic endorsement of Labour's devolution proposals. A Scottish Parliament is supported by 74.3 per cent to 25.7 per cent and tax-varying powers by 63.5 per cent to 36.5 per cent on a 60.4 per cent turnout.

18 September 1997
Welsh referendum gives narrow majority to devolution proposals by 50.3 per cent to 49.7 per cent on a 50.1 per cent turnout.

6 November 1997
Paisley North by-election sees Labour's Douglas Alexander hold the seat with 44.1 per cent to the SNP's 32.5 per cent.

11 December 1997
Scotland Bill published.

13 January 1998
Consultative Steering Group set up.

22 May 1998
Good Friday Agreement endorsed in Northern Ireland referendum.

13 June 1998
Labour chooses its panel of 166 potential candidates for the Scottish Parliament. Three MPs, Dennis Canavan, Michael Connarty and Ian Davidson are excluded.

19 September 1998
Donald Dewar elected leader of the Scottish Labour Party with 99.8 per cent of the vote at a special conference.

22 October 1998
House of Lords votes 103 to 94 against the government to maintain 129 Scottish Parliament seats when the number of Scottish Westminster seats is cut.

11 November 1998
The House of Commons votes 303 to 173 to reverse the Lords vote.

19 November 1998
Scotland Act receives Royal Assent.

26 November 1998

SNP's Ian Hudghton wins the North East Scotland by-election with a 24,000 majority, with Labour a humiliating third behind the Conservatives.

15 January 1999

'Shaping Scotland's Parliament' Consultative Steering Group report published.

5 February 1999

Tony Blair unveils Labour's 'Divorce is an Expensive Business' campaign.

12 March 1999

SNP launch 'A Penny for Scotland' campaign after Gordon Brown's Budget proposes to cut income tax by one penny.

6 May 1999

First Scottish Parliament elections. Labour win 38.8 per cent of the first vote to the SNP's 28.7 per cent, Conservatives 15.5 per cent and Liberal Democrats 14.2 per cent. Labour gain 56 seats, to the SNP's 35, Conservatives 18, Liberal Democrats 17, Others 3.

12 May 1999

David Steel elected Presiding Officer.

13 May 1999

Donald Dewar elected First Minister with 71 votes to Alex Salmond's 35, David McLetchie's 18 and Dennis Canavan's 3.

14 May 1999

'Labour-Lib Dem Partnership' for Scotland signed.

17 May 1999

Labour-Lib Dem Executive announced of 11 ministers; 9 Labour, 2 Lib Dems. John Reid succeeds Donald Dewar as Secretary of State for Scotland.

18 May 1999

11 junior ministers announced.

10 June 1999

Euro elections on Scottish regional list system. Labour win 28.7 per cent, SNP 27.2 per cent, Conservatives 19.8 per cent and Liberal Democrats 9.8 per cent. Labour win three seats, the Conservatives and SNP two apiece and the Liberal Democrats one.

16 June 1999

Donald Dewar presents the government's first legislative programme of eight bills.

17 June 1999
Scottish Parliament approves Holyrood Building by 64–61 votes.

1 July 1999
Scottish Parliament officially opened by the Queen.

2 July 1999
Parliament votes to set up an Independent Committee on Tuition Fees by 70–48 votes.

23 September 1999
Labour's Bill Tynan holds Hamilton South in a Westminster by-election with 36.9 per cent to the SNP's 34 per cent. Labour's majority is cut from 15,878 to 556.

26 September 1999
'Lobbygate' publication in the *Observer* about Beattie Media, Kevin Reid, John Reid's sons and implicating Jack McConnell, Finance Minister.

29 October 1999
Wendy Alexander, Minister for Communities, announces the abolition of Section 28/Clause 2A which bans the 'promotion' of homosexuality in schools.

21 December 1999
Cubie Committee Report on Tuition Fees published.

27 January 2000
Scottish Executive proposals on abolishing tuition fees agreed 68–53.

16 March 2000
Conservative John Scott wins the first ever Scottish Parliament by-election from Labour. The Conservatives win 39.4 per cent, SNP 28.9 per cent and Labour 22.1 per cent, turning a Labour majority of 25 into a Conservative one of 3,344.

28 March 2000
Brian Souter, owner of Stagecoach, announces his intention to fund an unofficial referendum on the Scottish Executive's plans to abolish Section 28/Clause 2A.

5 April 2000
Parliament approves amended Holyrood Building plans costing £195 million by 67-58 votes.

27 April 2000
Tommy Sheridan's Abolition of Poindings and Warrant Sales Bill passed by 79 to 15 votes.

30 May 2000

Unofficial referendum on Section 28/Clause 2A produces 86.8 per cent opposition to repeal on a 34.5 per cent turnout.

21 June 2000

Scottish Parliament votes to abolish Section 28/Clause 2A, which had outlawed the 'promotion' of homosexuality in schools, by 99 votes to 17, with two abstentions.

17 July 2000

Alex Salmond announces his intention to stand down as National Convener of the SNP.

23 September 2000

John Swinney elected national convener of the SNP defeating Alex Neil, winning 547 votes to Neil's 268 votes. Roseanna Cunningham defeats Kenny MacAskill for the post of Deputy Convener.

11 October 2000

Death of Donald Dewar, First Minister.

21 October 2000

Henry McLeish elected 'interim' leader of the Scottish Labour Party defeating Jack McConnell by 44 to 36 votes in a mini-electoral college.

26 October 2000

Henry McLeish elected First Minister winning 68 votes to John Swinney's 33, David McLetchie's 19 and Dennis Canavan's 3.

29 October 2000

McLeish engages in the first Scottish Executive reshuffle bringing Jackie Baillie (Social Justice) and Angus MacKay (Finance) into the Cabinet and reducing the roles of Sarah Boyack and Sam Galbraith.

20 November 2000

Dennis Canavan withdraws his application to rejoin the Labour Party citing 'additional information' about his exclusion from the Scottish Parliament candidate panel and resigns his Westminster seat.

23 November 2000

Labour holds Glasgow Anniesland in Holyrood and Westminster by-elections. Bill Butler wins the Holyrood contest for Labour with 48.7 per cent to the SNP's 22.1 per cent, while John Robertson wins the Westminster seat with 52.1 per cent for Labour to the SNP's 20.8 per cent.

9 December 2000

Henry McLeish elected leader of the Labour Party and Cathy Jamieson, deputy leader with 99.2 per cent of a mini-electoral college.

21 December 2000
Labour's Eric Joyce narrowly holds Falkirk West in a Westminster by-election. Labour win 43.5 per cent of the vote to the SNP's 39.9 per cent as its majority is slashed from 13,783 to 705.

14 January 2001
Alex Salmond announces that he is standing again for the SNP in Banff and Buchan at the forthcoming Westminster election.

24 January 2001
John Reid becomes Secretary of State for Northern Ireland following Peter Mandelson's departure from the Government. Helen Liddell becomes Secretary of State for Scotland.

25 January 2001
Scottish Parliament agrees to support Sutherland Commission proposals for free care for the elderly after Liberal Democrat backbenchers indicate their unwillingness to support the Scottish Executive's position.

8 March 2001
Scottish Executive loses vote on an opposition motion on its fishing aid scheme after David Steel, Presiding Officer, uses his casting vote after a tied 55-55 vote. Tavish Scott resigns as Deputy Parliament Minister over the fishing vote and is replaced by Euan Robson.

20 March 2001
Sam Galbraith announces his resignation as Environment Minister and his intention to resign as a MSP.

7 June 2001
Labour win historic second UK term on a much reduced turnout. In Scotland, Labour win 43.2 per cent and 55 seats, while the SNP fall back to 20.1 per cent and five seats. Scottish Parliament by-elections in Banff and Buchan and Strathkelvin and Bearsden see Stewart Stevenson of the SNP and Brian Fitzpatrick of Labour respectively returned. In the latter, Labour's majority is slashed, as Dr. Jean Turner, standing on an anti-hospital closure ticket, wins 18.2 per cent of the vote.

23 October 2001
Henry McLeish issues a statement that he has paid £9,000 to the House of Commons Fees Office over financial irregularities on income from his constituency office in Glenrothes, Fife. Thus, 'Officegate' enters into the public domain.

6 November 2001
Henry McLeish submits a dossier of his constituency office income, which declares his total rental income since 1987 was £36,122, and offers to pay back a further £27,000. McLeish claims the whole affair is 'a muddle, not a fiddle'.

8 November 2001

Henry McLeish resigns as First Minister following his failure to include all the income he had earned in his statement of two days before. Jim Wallace becomes Acting First Minister for the third time.

9 November 2001

Jack McConnell announces his candidature for Scottish Labour leader.

11 November 2001

Wendy Alexander announces she is not standing for the post of Scottish Labour leader.

12 November 2001

Malcolm Chisholm announces his candidature, and withdraws the next day, claiming he is unable to obtain the required number of nominations – seven MSPs.

17 November 2001

Jack McConnell elected Scottish Labour leader with 97.3 per cent of the vote of the party's mini-electoral college.

22 November 2001

Jack McConnell is elected First Minister winning 70 votes to John Swinney's 34, while David McLetchie wins 19 and Dennis Canavan's 3.

27 November 2001

Jack McConnell's 'morning of the long knives'. Four Labour ministers are sacked: Jackie Baillie, Sarah Boyack, Susan Deacon, Angus MacKay and Tom MacCabe. Susan Deacon is demoted and leaves the Cabinet. Two junior ministers are also dismissed: Alasdair Morrison and Rhona Brankin. Prominent McConnell supporters are promoted: Andy Kerr (finance), Mike Watson (Tourism, Culture, Sport), Patricia Ferguson (Parliament) and Cathy Jamieson (Education), as well as Malcolm Chisholm (Health) and Iain Gray (Social Justice).

29 November 2001

Conservative Murray Tosh is elected Deputy Presiding Officer against Jack McConnell's nominee, Cathy Peattie, in a secret ballot by 68–45 votes.

21 March 2002

MSPs vote 89 to 15 with 15 abstentions for a 13.5 per cent pay increase.

3 May 2002

Wendy Alexander announces her resignation as Minister for Enterprise, Transport and Life Long Learning – 'minister for everything' as it was known. Iain Gray becomes Enterprise and Lifelong Learning Minister and Margaret Curran Social Justice Minister.

26 November 2002

Richard Simpson resigns as junior Justice Minister after saying striking firefighters were 'fascist bastards'.

9 January 2003

Scottish Executive loses vote on closing fire stations after a tied 56-56 vote with George Reid, Deputy Presiding Officer, using his casting vote with the opposition.

17 January 2003

Scottish Parliament votes 67-51 against Lib Dem and SNP motions against the impending war with Iraq.

17 March 2003

Robin Cook resigns from the Blair Government as Leader of the House of Commons in opposition to US-UK plans to attack Iraq without a new UN mandate. In his resignation speech, Cook states that neither international or UK opinion is 'persuaded that there is an urgent and compelling reason for this action in Iraq'.

1 May 2003

Second Scottish Parliament elections sees significant losses inflicted on Labour and the SNP, and the rise of the Greens and Scottish Socialists. Labour win 34.6 per cent of the first vote to the SNP's 24.4 per cent, while overall Labour win 50 seats, down six, the SNP, 27, down eight, the Conservatives and Lib Dems unchanged at 18 and 17. The Greens won 7 seats, SSP, 6, and others 4 seats.

7 May 2003

George Reid elected Presiding Officer with 113 votes to 7 against with 9 abstentions. Tricia Godman and Murray Tosh become Deputy Presiding Officers after winning 59 and 43 votes respectively in the first round, against Robin Harper's 23.

14 May 2003

Scottish Executive Partnership Agreement between the Labour and Lib Dem parties published with a commitment to voting reform for local government and to contentious legislation on anti-social behaviour.

15 May 2003

Jack McConnell elected First Minister with 67 votes in a contest with six other candidates. John Swinney wins 26 votes, David McLetchie 19, Robin Harper 6, Tommy Sheridan 6, Dennis Canavan 2 and Margo MacDonald 2.

20 May 2003

Jack McConnell's post-election reshuffle. Mike Watson is sacked, Jim Wallace goes to Enterprise and Lifelong Earning, Cathy Jamieson to Justice, while Frank McAveety and Nicol Stephen are given Cabinet seats on junior minister's salaries.

12 June 2003
Helen Liddell sacked as Secretary of State for Scotland. In a botched cabinet reshuffle, Alistair Darling, UK Transport Minister, becomes part-time Scottish Secretary as well.

27 September 2003
John Swinney wins the election for SNP National Convener against challenger and Glasgow activist Bill Wilson, winning by 577 votes to 111 – a margin of 84 per cent to 16 per cent.

23 October 2003
George Galloway, Labour MP for Glasgow Kelvin, expelled from the Labour Party for his remarks in opposition to the Iraq war, labelling Bush and Blair as 'wolves' and inciting British troops to disobey orders.

28 October 2003
The Fraser inquiry into the cost and management of the Scottish Parliament Building opens, headed up by Lord Fraser of Carmyllie.

29 October 2003
The Executive's flagship bill on anti-social behaviour is introduced to the Scottish Parliament.

17 November 2003
Introduction of the other controversial legislation of the second administration, providing for proportinal voting in council elections from 2007, the key coalition condition for Liberal Democrats.

10 February 2004
The Commons gives a second reading to a Government Bill de-coupling Westminster and Holyrood constituencies, by keeping the number ofMSPs at 129. A Commons select committee the previous week called for reform of the voting system, so that boundaries are kept co-terminous. Alastair Darling responds with a commission to look into the issue.

24 February 2004
The cost of the Holyrood building reaches £430 million, with a tight timetable to be ready for MSPs' use from September 2004.

25 February 2004
Jack McConnell unveils plans to attract 'fresh talent' to Scotland, in a bid to reverse population decline.

18 March 2004
MSPs vote by 60 to 59 to back a Scottish Executive decision to allow the commercial growing of GM crops in Scotland.

March 24 2004
Local Governance (Scotland) Bill Stage One introducing the Single Transferable Vote system for local government elections passed by 95 votes to 19 with 6 abstentions.